TRULY, M

John Dunning had
career, including ser...... US Navy and the
Shanghai Municipal Police. He spent four years in
a Japanese POW camp during the Second World
War and then worked in American intelligence.
He subsequently became a journalist, travelling to
China and Europe. He was the top selling author
of murder stories for *True Detective* magazines and
wrote over a thousand accounts of true crime.

He lived in Luxembourg as a full-time writer, until
his death in 1990.

Also in Arrow by John Dunning

CARNAL CRIMES
DEADLY DEVIATES
MADLY MURDEROUS
TRULY MURDEROUS
MINDLESS MURDERS
MURDEROUS WOMEN
STRANGE DEATHS

TRULY
MADLY
DEADLY

THE OMNIBUS

John Dunning

ARROW

This omnibus edition first published 1992

3 5 7 9 10 8 6 4 2

John Dunning has asserted his
right under the Copyright, Designs and Patents Act, 1988
to be identified as the author of this work

First published in 1992

Incorporating

TRULY MURDEROUS
First published in Great Britain
by Harwood-Smart 1977
Hamlyn Paperbacks edition 1979
Reprinted 1982, 1983, and 1984
Arrow edition 1986

© John Dunning 1977

MADLY MURDEROUS
First published in Great Britain
by Hamlyn Paperbacks 1985
Arrow edition 1988

© John Dunning 1985

DEADLY DEVIATES
First published in 1986
Reprinted 1987, 1989 and 1990

© John Dunning 1986

Random House, 20 Vauxhall Bridge Road, London SW1V 2SA

Random House Australia (Pty) Limited
20 Alfred Street, Milsons Point, Sydney,
New South Wales 2061, Australia

Random House New Zealand Limited
18 Poland Road, Glenfield
Auckland 10, New Zealand

Random House South Africa (Pty) Limited
PO Box 337, Bergvlei, South Africa

Random House UK Limited Reg. No. 954009

A CIP catalogue record for this book
is available from the British Library

ISBN 0 09 919321 3

Printed and bound in Great Britain by
Cox & Wyman Ltd, Reading, Berkshire

TRULY MURDEROUS

To My Mother, Mrs Crystal Belder

CONTENTS

Foreword by John Dunning   ix
Introduction by Colin Wilson   xi
 1 The Reek of Death   1
 2 The Fatal Orgy   25
 3 Repeat Performance   39
 4 The Future Belongs to Youth   57
 5 Frozen Stiff   72
 6 Mad Dog!   86
 7 A Family Affair   98
 8 Travels with a Killer   113
 9 Rough Justice   128
10 The Passionate Paramours of Portsmouth   143
11 To Love is to Kill   158
12 The Insatiable Wife   176
13 Ladykiller   192
14 Hatchet Work   206
15 Ghoulish Practices   220

FOREWORD
by
John Dunning

If the reader of a book of factual crime reports has the right to expect an accurate and literal presentation of the facts, so then does the writer of these accounts have the obligation to present them in this manner. Crime, and particularly murder, is by its nature secretive and more subject to deduction than to precise determination. Very often no one living knows exactly what took place, and equally often those who know are inclined to distort and conceal the true nature of events.

In this book I have made every effort to present a factual picture of the crimes concerned, but there are certain deliberate changes and omissions. I do not use the real names and titles of police officers because some Criminal Investigations Departments prefer that their investigators remain anonymous. Likewise, the names and descriptions of witnesses and other innocent persons are usually changed in order to prevent public identification and possible embarrassment.

Conversations and thoughts are, of course, reconstructed – and in such a manner as to render them intelligible to the English-speaking reader. Without wishing to offend those who believe in the homogeneity of the human race, the reactions and remarks of a French or German-speaking person confronted with a given situation are not identical to those of an English-speaking person.

The names, ages and descriptions of the victims and their murderers are as accurate as I can make them, as are the details of the events and the dates on which they took place.

If the presentation seems dramatic, it is because murder *is* dramatic. It is the ultimate experience. Once you have been murdered there is little else that can happen to you, other than in a metaphysical sense. The reader, snug in his armchair, may shudder as the knife enters the entrails, but the shudder is vicarious. Reading about murder is nothing at all like the experience itself.

During the past ten years I have written the accounts of some six hundred crimes, most of them murders, but the familiarity with horrifying events which this has inevitably brought has not dulled my awareness of the grim realities – I am always acutely conscious that murder is sordid, brutal and painful beyond belief.

INTRODUCTION
by
Colin Wilson

In the year 1910 there appeared in San Francisco a bulky volume entitled *Celebrated Criminal Cases of America* by Thomas S. Duke, a captain in the San Francisco police force. It was an epoch-making volume, for it was the first attempt at a comprehensive collection of the crimes of one particular period – in this case, the past eighty years; it was, if you like, a criminal history of America in the 19th century. And, as such, it still remains a work of singular fascination. For many years now, together with the more famous *Newgate Calendar*, it has been one of my favourite bedside books. And not solely because of its 'morbid' interest. It is the history of an epoch, and it gives you a better insight into the true nature of America in the 19th century than any number of history books about great statesmen and generals.

For we must face this fact: history, by its very nature, tells lies. History books deal with 'important events', the rise and fall of kings and nations. You could read all about the age of Shakespeare in the great historians; yet if some time machine could transport you back to London in the time of Queen Elizabeth, you would realize instantly that you didn't know the first thing about it. When Shakespeare got up in the morning, his mind was focussed on dozens of minor details, not on great events. What kind of a bed did he sleep in? What did an Elizabethan chamberpot look like? Did he use soap to wash his hands? Did he even bother to wash his hands when he got up? What did he eat for breakfast? Did he drink tea? How often did he wash his socks? How did he comb his hair? How did he trim his beard? (Did they have scissors then?) Unless we know the answer to hundreds of similar questions, we cannot even begin to formulate an accurate picture of the Elizabethan age.

But then, as you read Thomas Duke on American crime, you realize there is another kind of history which also gets left out of most of the history books. Of course, we know a little more about America in the 19th century than England in the 16th – to begin with, it is closer to our own age. It was visited by various English writers – like Charles Dickens, Fanny Trollope and Oscar Wilde – who left their impressions. It was a rough, turbulent and violent country, the land that paid scant attention to the genius of the author of *Moby Dick*, and that allowed Edgar Allan Poe to die as a result of some obscure bar room brawl. If you want to get a clear idea of what it was actually like to be Edgar Allan Poe, then you would do better to read Thomas Duke than even the most eminent historian. You can learn about the Vigilance Committees that were set up to do battle with squatters, about the Chinese Tongs that sprang up in the gold fields, about Alfred Packer, the cannibal who ate five fellow prospectors, about marauding Indians who murdered settlers, about the assassination of the Mormon leader Joseph Smith, about various bomb outrages committed by anarchists, as well as about such *causes célèbres* as the murder of Dr Parkman by Professor Webster, or of the architect Stanford White by Harry Thaw. This was the America that Poe and Melville really lived in, and saw around them every day. In some ways – perhaps in most – it was a better and more innocent America than the one that exists today. One of its stories describes 'The Murder of Norah Fuller by a Degenerate'. Norah was a fifteen-year-old San Francisco girl who was lured to a house by means of an advertisement, and there strangled, raped and mutilated. The murderer, a man named Charles Hadley, was never caught. A modern writer would simply call the chapter 'The Rape of Norah Fuller' and leave it at that. Duke obviously finds it a little difficult to understand such a crime; he is more at home chronicling various robberies, assassinations and poisonings. In his world, human beings needed a real *motive* for committing a crime, usually cash. And his reactions are always there, implicitly in the writing. The chapter on the Bender family, who killed travellers in their tavern, is entitled: 'The Hideous Murders Committed at Bender's Tavern in Kansas'. There is 'The Diabolical Plot Concocted by Dr Hyde of Kansas City', and 'Tom Blanck, the Desperado Killed near Seattle'. We are in a violent world, yet a world in which crime is never taken for granted. The underlying assumption seems to be that most of the population are law abiding, even virtuous, and that a few evildoers have backed out of their obligations to society.

In America, Duke's book was the beginning of a flood of anthologies of 'true crime stories'. In England, it had started rather earlier. The Elizabethans were fond of pamphlets describing the crimes and trials of notorious characters, and around the year 1700, various compilations of such cases began to appear under the title of *The Newgate Calendar* (although the most famous and comprehensive edition of that work appeared in 1774). This continued to appear, under various incarnations (such as *Chronicles of Crime)* until the late 19th century. In 1873, Luke Owen Pike produced a two volume *History of Crime in England*. In 1898, Major Arthur Griffiths published his popular two volume work *Mysteries of the Police and Crime*. But I suspect that it was the Crippen case of 1910 that suddenly aroused the interest of the British public in true tales of gore and mayhem. (This word – meaning committing violence upon the person – seems to be derived from the same source as maim.) Crippen – who dismembered his wife's body – was effectively condemned on the medical evidence given by Bernard Spilsbury. The case made Spilsbury's reputation; from then on, any case in which he gave evidence was newsworthy. And many of his later cases involved gruesome dismemberments – Voisin, Patrick Mahon, Norman Thorne. The reading public developed an appetite for horrors. It is also worth bearing in mind that a new reading public had come into being since the late 19th century; workmen were learning to read, and enterprising publishers deliberately catered for them with works of popular education. This was essentially the public of 'groundlings' for whom the Elizabethan playwrights produced 'shockers' like *The Spanish Tragedy* and *Arden of Feversham*. A few of them read Ruskin and Darwin; but the majority wanted their ha'penny newspapers with tales of violence and of scandal in high life. Since 1870, the 'best seller' among Victorian tabloids had been the *Illustrated Police News*, which specialized in sensational sketches of hangings, floggings and decapitations. After the turn of the century, there was suddenly a market for books with titles like *Cavalcade of Justice* or *The Fifty Most Amazing Crimes of the Last Hundred Years*. (It was a copy of this latter that was largely responsible for my own early interest in crime.) In America, Munsey invented the 'pulp magazine', and reached a new audience with its tales of incredible adventure. And then, some time in the 1920s (I have been unable to track down the date) an American magazine publisher hit on the idea of a magazine form of the old *Illustrated Police News*, with photographs taking the place of the drawings. 'True detective' magazines caught on quickly, and as the post-1918 crime rate soared, material was even more plentiful than in the Victorian era. 'Troodicks' (as John Dunning likes to call them) have never looked back.

And – perhaps unfortunately – there is no reason why they should. With the 20th century, we have entered a new age of murder. This is apparent even to the most casual student of crime. The Crippen murder is basically an 'old-fashioned' type of crime; it might have been dramatized by an Elizabethan playwright. It is essentially a drama of good against evil, of a fairly decent human being, under strain or temptation, giving way to 'diabolic' impulses – like Macbeth. The same element seems to enter all 'classic' murder cases – the Red Barn murder, Lizzie Borden, Professor Webster, Constance Kent. The Victorians found it necessary to apply the same explanation to the strange crimes of Jack the Ripper, who killed and disembowelled five prostitutes in 1888; the favourite theory was that he was some sort of religious maniac – perhaps also a surgeon – driven mad by brooding on sin. (It is perfectly clear to us that he was an ordinary sadist, probably with a morbid obsession about wombs.)

In 1918, New Orleans had its own series of 'Ripper' murders; an individual who became known as the 'Mad Axe Man' broke into houses at night, and attacked sleepers with a hatchet; in a few cases he also cut their throats. He was never caught; but, like the Ripper crimes, this series of murders suddenly ceased. There seemed to be no connection between the axeman's crimes – except that many of the victims were Italian grocers – and robbery was not the motive. The Axe Man crimes simply fail to fit the pattern of murder as it had been known up till then. He wasn't even a 'degenerate' – at least, there were apparently no sexual attacks on the victims. The new age of murder had begun.

And nowadays, we look back on the older type of crime with a certain nostalgia. The American Modern Library series, which specializes in reprints of 'classics', has included Edmund Pearson's *Studies in Murder*, with its long study of the Borden case. The Viking Portable Library – which has produced portable volumes of Shakespeare, Nietzsche and James Joyce – has also published a Portable Murder Book, consisting mainly of such classic mysteries as the murder of Julia Wallace and the crime of Constance Kent. We read such things as we read the Sherlock Holmes stories – as period pieces. We may deplore the violence, but we still read with a kind of fascinated detachment. But imagine an updated Murder Book that includes the Moors Murder case, the Manson murders, the mass homosexual killings by Dean Corll in Houston, and such recent cases as John Frazier, Ed Kemper and Herb Mullin. Could anyone – no matter how blasé – read such cases with detachment? They really belong in textbooks of pathology – like Magnus Hirschfeld's *Sexual Anomalies and Perversions*. We try *not* to think about what the Moors murderers did to their child victims, what Dean Corll did to teenage boys once he had tied them to his 'torture board'. This new type of murder seems to be motiveless because it is fundamentally 'psychological'.

What has caused this change in the pattern of murder? Where America is concerned, the answer is fairly obvious.

As Duke's compilation makes clear, America has always been a country with plenty of violence. But in the 19th century it was also a country with plenty of freedom – at least, in the purely physical sense. Life was hard for the underprivileged, but there were still inviting wide open spaces out west. By the 1920s, most of this feeling of freedom had vanished. Living standards were higher – industrialization had seen to that – but cities were bigger, and people felt trapped in them. A modern American is no longer in much danger of seeing his wife and children starve to death. But the children feel themselves regimented and controlled from the moment they are old enough to cross the street. The famous – the people who have 'made it' – exist up there in a kind of Olympus; you are 'down here', together with hundreds of millions of others, and nobody will ever see your name in a newspaper or see your face on TV. You are an immeasurably small fragment of an anonymous mass . . . But since a high proportion of that anonymous mass is at least as intelligent as the TV stars and politicians, they feel resentment at this unfair scheme of things. Everybody wants to be Somebody – or at least feel that the opportunity is there. Among the young, the natural reaction is to 'drop out'. The more idealistic talk about human rights and preservation of the environment. Others dream of violent revolution and destruction of the 'pigs' (i.e. the middle aged and successful). Others drift into the underworld of drugs. A youth like John Frazier becomes increasingly paranoid and finally murders the whole family of a successful Japanese optician – simply because he is obviously well-to-do. The 'Symbionese Liberation Army' kidnap an heiress and order her father to donate $2 million-worth of food to the poor, then brain-wash her into helping them commit robberies. A follower of Charles Manson writes letters to businessmen threatening them with death if they pollute the environment, then attempts to shoot the American President as a protest . . .

In other countries too, the pattern of crime is changing, although less drastically than in America. West Germany – the most prosperous country in Europe – has a flourishing

Urban Guerrilla movement, which robs, murders and kidnaps the 'capitalist oppressors'. In Italy, kidnapping becomes almost a national sport. In England, Ian Brady and Myra Hindley, the 'Moors Murderers', kidnap and murder children simply as an expression of Brady's contempt of society and his admiration for the philosophy of De Sade. In general, 'philosophy' – or a muddled idealism – seems to play an increasingly large part in crime. But while Urban Guerrillas and homicidal 'drop outs' continue to make the headlines, organized crime continues to spread and flourish – without publicity – in almost every country in the world.

For many years now, I have felt that these 'patterns of crime' deserved closer study. Criminologists are inclined to confine themselves to statistical analyses and studies of the criminal's behaviour in prison. But the most interesting criminals are often 'loners', and few of them are professionals. With the aid of Patricia Pitman, I compiled *An Encyclopedia of Murder* in 1961, and followed it with two further books on the changing patterns of crime in western society. In 1973 I drew up an outline scheme of a twenty-volume 'encyclopedia' of crime; this appeared under the title *Crimes and Punishment*, and although it makes many concessions to the taste of 'troodick' readers, it is still probably the most comprehensive general work on crime that has ever appeared.

There is one important respect in which I feel that *Crimes and Punishment* falls below the original conception. I had hoped to make it a work on *world* crime, with volumes on European crime, Australian crime, crime behind the Iron Curtain, crime in the Far East – even crime in Iceland and Greenland, if such a thing exists there. And the problem here was simply lack of information. Few nations in the world seem to have the interest in criminal history that characterizes the English and Americans. The French take a lively interest in *crime passionel*, but it was left to an Englishman, Rayner Heppenstall, to produce a comprehensive study – in four volumes – of French crime from the age of Vidocq down to modern times. When I wrote *An Encyclopedia of Murder*, information on German cases was kindly provided by a German editor, Frank Lynder, who sent me accounts of Denke, Seefeld, Grossmann, Pommerencke, Matushka and others. The editor of *Crimes and Punishment* – Angus Hall – established links with various police forces in many countries of the world, which was certainly useful. But what was really needed was a whole series of Frank Lynders – or perhaps of Edmund Pearsons: that is, of people who regarded crime with the eye of the novelist rather than of the policeman. A country's criminal history is basically a history of its most interesting cases, and these can only be chosen with an eye to psychological subtlety and dramatic effect. It would be marvellously convenient – a criminologist's daydream – if there was a Scandinavian version, a Japanese version, a Russian version, of *The Fifty Most Amazing Crimes of the Last Hundred Years*. But apparently there is not. In my own crime library of a thousand or so volumes, less than a dozen are devoted to crimes of other countries – apart from England and America – and many of these are anthologies with titles like *My Strangest Crime* by Police Chiefs of the World.

Oddly enough, it was this volume that led to my acquaintance with the author of the present volume, John Dunning. One of the cases contained in *My Strangest Crime* is written by Kriminal Hauptkommissar Mattias Eynck, and describes the curious series of murders allegedly committed between 1953 and 1956 by a psychopath named Werner Boost. According to his confederate – who confessed – Boost used to hold up courting couples in cars, and force them to take a drug that stupefied them. He then robbed the men and raped the women. One young couple were killed – the girl was given an injection of cyanide – and then their car was pushed into a haystack, which was set alight; another couple were knocked unconscious, then their car was driven into a deep pool, where they drowned. Boost was caught in 1956 when creeping up on another courting couple, and finally sentenced to life imprisonment.

In the early 1970s, an English 'troodick' magazine published an account of the case which differed in certain details from the account given by Hauptkommissar Eynck – most notably in the dates, which were all about ten years later. I had had occasion to find fault with 'true detective' magazines on a number of previous occasions, but their editors had never taken the trouble to reply to my letters. But on this occasion, the editor replied fairly promptly, saying that he had taken the matter up with the author, who would be writing to me himself. I checked up on the author's name – to which I had so far paid little attention – and realized that it was already fairly familiar to me. John Dunning specialized in articles on German crime, and his contributions were usually the most amusing and best-written in the magazine.

In due course, a letter *did* arrive from John Dunning – who lives in Luxembourg – explaining the discrepancies. It seems that he derives much of his material from an agency, which is, in turn, supplied by needy journalists. It had occurred to one of these suppliers that there is a readier market for recent cases than for those of older vintage. His solution was simply to update the older cases. Whether this stratagem actually improved his sales seems to me doubtful; editors of 'troodick' magazines are notoriously lax about dates. (They still have a nasty habit of leaving out all dates until the last line of a story, when they conclude: 'On June 7, 1954, so and so paid for his crimes in the electric chair at San Quentin . . .'.) At all events, it embarrassed Mr Dunning, who wrote to me on November 30, 1972, a letter that commenced breezily: 'View halloo and/or demi-yoicks! The fell scoundrel responsible for the outrage in the Boost bash has been run to earth and subjected to the merciless punishment he so richly deserved . . .'. Whereupon Mr Dunning proceeded to have the last laugh. It seemed that even Hauptkommissar Eynck was not free of sin in this matter of inaccuracy, and had allowed a number of mistakes to creep into his account of the case – which I had reproduced in my account in the *Encyclopedia of Murder*; he seems to have mixed up dates, given cases in the wrong order, and got several names wrong. Mr Dunning added the information that Boost was acquitted of all murders except that of a Dr Servé, for which he was sentenced to life imprisonment.

We continued to correspond, I continued to read his

contributions to *True Detective* avidly, and I suggested one day that his articles ought to be published in book form. The idea horrified him. To begin with, he said, he had some hundreds – possibly thousands – of articles. Secondly, they had been written at speed, for publication in a variety of 'troodick' magazines, and were not good enough for hard-cover publication. I was able to reassure him on this last point. Many journalists seem to have an inferiority complex about the writers of books, falsely assuming that it is an altogether more difficult and dangerous art. Writers of books know better; and writers who produce books *and* journalism – like G. K. Chesterton, H. G. Wells, Bernard Shaw, Arnold Bennett – probably know best of all. Shaw and Chesterton had themselves described in their passports as journalists. It *is* possible to write too casually and journalistically; it is also possible to write stodgily and pedantically, and this is the commoner – and more irritating – fault. I recall a journalist named Philip Guedalla, a contemporary of Wells and Chesterton, who produced some excellent volumes of occasional pieces; a few months ago I came across a book by him on the Second Empire, and prepared myself for a treat. It was unbelievably disappointing. Evidently he had decided that a writer of history should be on his best behaviour, and the result is dull and turgid.

But it is not simply because he writes well that I wanted John Dunning to venture into hard covers. German crime is one of those subjects on which it is frustratingly difficult to find information. Which is a pity since, from the criminologist's point of view, Germany is one of the most interesting countries in the world.

The German temperament is, in a way, peculiarly conducive to crime – far more so than the English or French temperament. The English are too easygoing to make good criminals; their 'genius for compromise' is against them. The typical English murder takes place in a domestic setting, and the motives are usually fairly trivial; a woman poisons her drunken husband with weed-killer; the husband strangles his nagging wife, then buries her in the back garden. The French allow their emotions to lead them into crime; a man murders his wife to marry his mistress, or plots with his mistress to murder her husband. But the German temperament is realistic and pedantic and grimly logical; as a result it can also be idealistic, exalted and romantic. Bach's Passions are typically German; so are Goethe's dramas, Wagner's operas and Thomas Mann's novels. But the German who sees murder as the solution of his problems approaches it with the same realism and thoroughness. Fritz Haarmann, the butcher of Hanover, not only killed young men for sexual purposes, but made a profit on the corpses by selling them as meat. Karl Denke, a landlord of Münsterberg, murdered tramps and journeymen and pickled their bodies in brine, apparently as a precaution against the famine that followed post-1918 inflation. Georg Grossmann, a pedlar, murdered innumerable women with whom he spent the night, and sold the bodies for meat. Peter Kürten, the Düsseldorf 'monster', easily surpassed Jack the Ripper; he killed men, women, children and animals, and was a necrophile as well as a sadist.

I have lost the documentation on one of my favourite German cases: a man who murdered his wife and children with extraordinary ingenuity. The family was found dead in a locked room, all hanged; apparently the mother had killed her children, then committed suicide. But the police inspector who examined the husband found in his room a novel with an ingenious method of murder. The fictional killer drilled a tiny hole through the door, inserted a long hair from a horse's tail, and used it to draw the bolt when the door was closed. After the murder, he bolted the door – from the outside – snapped off the horse's hair, then sealed the hole on the outside with brown wax. The police inspector examined the door of the murder room, and found a hole that had been filled in with wax. The murderer's sole mistake was to keep the novel that had given him the idea. Again, the story is somehow typically German; an Englishman, a Frenchman, an Italian, would not have the patience to plan a murder with this fiendish thoroughness. It was the same kind of thoroughness that produced Hitler's attempt at a final solution of the Jewish problem.

It can be seen why German murder cases fascinate all students of crime. It can also be seen why I was so anxious to persuade John Dunning to start collecting some of his more interesting cases into volumes. Fortunately, my persistence prevailed, and the present volume is the result – the first, I hope, of many.

The selection of cases is John Dunning's own. Anyone who knows any of my own books on murder – for example, *Order of Assassins* – will immediately see that there is a basic difference of approach. I have always been interested in 'extremists' – men and women who kill because they feel a fundamental alienation from the rest of the human community: Jack the Ripper, Carl Panzram, Peter Kürten, William Heirens, Peter Manuel. These are all characters who might have been invented by Dostoevsky, or observed by him in his Siberian prison, described in *The House of the Dead*. John Dunning has the journalist's eye for the gruesome, for human oddity, and for sheer dramatic tension. There are no Kürtens or Panzrams in this book, but nearly every story in it could be turned into a film or a TV drama. His quirky sense of humour emerges in the actual material as much as in the writing. What could be odder than the activities of the alcoholic Fritz Honka, who absentmindedly murdered four of his mistresses, stuffed their bodies in the attic, then forgot all about them, so that he was as puzzled by the smell of decay as his neighbours were? What could be more unintentionally funny than the activities of ex-policeman Ernst Karl, sentenced for the murder of two hoodlums, who appointed himself executioner of a rape-murderer in prison, and assured the audience in court: 'Have no fear, good citizens of Austria. Whether in prison or out, you can depend on me to continue and even intensify my battle against the criminals and law-breakers in our midst . . .'

But what really seems to fascinate John Dunning are those cases in which life seems to imitate art – or at least, the structure of the thriller. The police search frantically for the daughter of a murdered woman, convinced that she has also been murdered; in fact, she is quietly staying with a neighbour. The police in a small German town are convinced that a corpse lies somewhere beneath five hundred square miles of moorland; the chances of finding the body are minimal, but a cunning ruse persuades the killer to confess. A killer accuses his Turkish mistress of the crime and she confesses; but the police are convinced she is innocent, and work feverishly to find the vital piece of evidence . . . The story of the man who is frozen to death in the woods ends with a car chase that might have come straight out of Kojak. In all these tales we observe Dunning's unerring eye for the dramatic.

It is the final story in the volume that strikes me as most typical of Dunning's style and method. It is a horrifying and nauseating account of sexual perversion that will turn all but the strongest stomachs. The vampire seems to have walked straight out of the pages of *Dracula*. As the gruesome details pile up, you find yourself unconsciously creating a picture of a maniac with pointed teeth and fingers like claws. The actual description of the murderer, the shy little deaf-mute with his steel-rimmed National Health glasses, comes as an almost comic anticlimax. Yet the story takes on overtones of a different kind of menace when the police discover that Kuno Hofman was inspired by his collection of books on black magic, vampirism and satanism. He may have been mentally retarded, but he was intelligent enough to read and be influenced by what he read. Like Ian Brady, the child killer who admired the works of the Marquis de Sade, or Edward Paisnel, the rapist who terrorized Jersey for a decade, who owned a library of works on satanism and believed himself to be a reincarnation of the sadistic Gilles de Rais. These alienated 'outsiders' are perhaps the most typical, if not the most common, of modern criminals.

Equally typical – although perhaps less significant – is the bewildered Hans Appell, who murdered his brother-in-law Dieter when he discovered that he *and* his brother had sexual orgies with their sister in the marital bed . . . In this story, as in the tale of the home-made spear, Dunning reveals an ironic interest in the problem of the *crime passionel* in a permissive society.

No, altogether I can see no reason why John Dunning

should be modest about this book. He possesses qualities of intelligence, style and humour that raise him above the average; and he is entering a field in which there are dozens of hacks, but few outstanding talents. (My own short list would include William Bolitho, F. Tennyson Jesse, William Roughead, Alexander Woolcott, Edmund Pearson and Rayner Heppenstall.) And then, he has the additional advantage of having cornered an area of the market. There are many writers who have produced a whole shelf-full of books on assorted crime – Leonard Gribble and Edgar Lustgarten spring to mind – but they seldom venture across the channel; at least, beyond Paris. Mr Dunning probably knows the criminal history of Germany and Austria better than any man alive, and it is my fervent hope that he will now begin to make this systematically available to the English reader. (I would like to see a book on German mass murderers, from Haarmann and Grossmann to the recent autobahn killer.) If his own estimate is correct, he already possesses enough material for about fifty more volumes like this one. But even if he gives up after a dozen or so, he will have performed a real service for all those who – like myself – are fascinated by 'patterns of murder' in the 20th Century.

1

THE REEK OF DEATH

There was something very wrong with the old house at 74 Zeiss Street.

It stank.

Standing in her dark, narrow kitchen, Mrs Elsie Beier took a cautious breath. Yes, the smell was still there, but mingled now with something like pine needles. The contrast seemed to make it actually worse.

Hurriedly, she filled the kettle, stood it on the stove and retreated to the living room. There were traces of the smell in the air even here, but it was, at least, bearable.

'Either Heinz does something or I move,' muttered Mrs Beier in the flat, slurred German of her native Hamburg.

Heinz was the caretaker who looked after the building in return for the use of a small room at the back.

Of course, the place always had smelled. A building that old could be expected to smell, but that also helped to keep down the rent so that a widow on a small pension might be able to live there for twelve long years.

Mrs Beier had moved into 74 Zeiss Street in January of 1962 and now it was August of 1974. She had rather counted on spending the remainder of her days there, but she was beginning to fear that she would not have many days remaining if she was forced to live much longer amidst this stench. It was decidedly unhealthy.

She did not think that Heinz was going to do anything. It was nearly the end of August now and she had been complaining since the first week. Heinz had spoken to Fritz Honka, the night watchman who lived on the top floor above, and to Klaus Kienzle, the street sweeper who lived on the first floor below, about checking to see if their toilets were stopped up and Honka, at least, had apparently bought some deodorant tablets for she had seen him carrying them up the stairs. They were, no doubt, the source of the pine needle scent.

However, it was going to take more than deodorant tablets to kill that smell and, besides, it did not resemble any stopped toilet she had ever smelled. In fact, it did not resemble anything that she had ever smelled in her whole life.

On November 1, 1974, after almost daily complaints to anyone who would listen, Mrs Elsie Beier struck her colours and moved out. She moved completely across to the other side of Hamburg and although the rent was somewhat higher she paid it willingly. The stench in her kitchen was, by this time, beyond belief.

The apartment was promptly rented to forty-six-year-old John Fordal, a Norwegian seaman, who did not complain about the smell or even seem to notice it as he made a practice of passing his time ashore in such a profound state of alcoholic stupor that he could scarcely see or hear, let alone smell.

Seaman Fordal fitted well into 74 Zeiss Street. It was that sort of a building and Ottensen, better known to the local residents as Mottenberg or Moth Hill, was that sort of district.

Stretching along the fringe of St Pauli, the famous Hamburg entertainment quarter, with its great, main artery, the Reeperbahn, its thousands of prostitutes, its Eros Centre, its bars and strip joints and massage parlours and pimps and jack-rollers and the sailors of a hundred nations, Ottensen is neither glamorous nor respectable. It is a place where the old prostitutes, the crippled pimps, the alcoholic waiters and derelicts from all professions cling to a worthless life for lack of courage to end it.

It is not, of course, the bottom. The bottom is the great Bismarck monument at the Landungs Bridge where every night the grey alcohol-soaked hordes gather with their tattered blankets, stored during the day in the luggage lockers of the railway station, for another rest beneath the cold stars of North Germany.

Such a life is only possible to sustain under the numbing influence of substantial quantities of alcohol, and alcohol in St Pauli and Ottensen is more common than water.

Sex is also common, although not of very good quality, or perhaps it would be better to say of excellent quality due to the long experience of the practitioners, but aesthetically lacking because of the age and physical failings of those involved. It is, however, entered into with considerable enthusiasm by those still capable of it and it is cheap, a single beer or a packet of cigarettes sufficing for a night of intimacy, if not love.

The house at 74 Zeiss Street displayed almost all possible variations of the district's sex life with the family on the ground floor producing children in the orthodox manner and at intervals of nine months, Klaus Kienzle on the first floor being ready, willing, but totally unable and resigned to it, Seaman Fordal on the second floor often believing that he would like to, but then falling asleep so that his companion departed with everything movable in the apartment, and finally Fritz Honka, the dapper, thirty-nine-year-old night watchman with the little moustache, the cocked eye and the penchant for uniforms and peaked caps.

Divorced and the father of a grown son, Honka was, despite a staggering consumption of alcohol, apparently sexually active for he usually had one woman or another living with him in the attic apartment.

All of these women shared certain peculiarities. None of them was taller than five feet four inches, which happened to be Honka's height, and none of them had any teeth. Mr Honka, as he confided to his friends, had a great and perhaps not completely baseless fear of being bitten on the more sensitive parts of his anatomy.

Such women were, of course, not hard to find and Honka usually made his acquisitions in either the Golden Glove or the Elbschloss Keller, two terminal bars of the sort which employ a thumper.

The thumper is a person who goes from table to table at

3

intervals, beating the tops with a mallet to rouse the mostly unconscious customers sufficiently to order and pay for another drink. Not infrequently, no amount of thumping will arouse the customer and the police are then called to come and take the body away in the neat, white, metal trailer known officially as a corpse transporter.

Actually, the Hamburg Police have several corpse transporters as they have quite a number of corpses to transport. However, sometimes a sack is more suitable.

This was the case with the remains found on November 2, 1971 by, among others, two of the children of the Ernst Schmidt family living on the ground floor of 74 Zeiss Street. The scene of the discovery was the yard of an abandoned chocolate factory three blocks away and the object discovered was no more than an isolated human head. It had obviously been lying out in the yard for some time. Strangely, it had not decayed very much nor had it been seriously nibbled by rats of which Ottensen has a large contingent.

The police having been informed, a thorough search of the yard was carried out and two legs, two arms and two breasts were recovered. All of these were in remarkably good condition with the exception of the breasts which were little more than flaps of leathery skin with nipples.

Dr Ludwig Strauss, the cheerful, brisk medical expert attached to the Hamburg Department of Criminal Investigations, took these parts and placed them in a bath of glycerine and other chemicals where he swished them about gently at intervals for several months.

At the end of this time the head and the hands had regained so much of their shape that it was possible to make a photograph of the face and to take fingerprints from the fingers.

Although the photograph did not really do justice to the subject, the fingerprints permitted her identification as one Gertraude 'Susi' Braeuer, born near Dresden in 1929, a refugee from Communist East Germany in 1956 and since that date, aside from a few short intervals, a licensed prostitute.

Miss Braeuer's fingerprints had come into the police files

4

as a result of a charge of drunk-rolling in the Golden Glove on July 6, 1969, but she was currently wanted in connection with quite a different affair.

Late in 1969 Gertraude Braeuer had abandoned her profession and had gone to live with a thirty-four-year-old welldigger named Burkhard Stern. The couple had shared a garden house with Stern's eighty-year-old father in a suburb called Groot Osterfeld and plans were made for an early marriage.

Living next door was a two-hundred-pound porter named Winfried Schuldig, an ominous name as schuldig means guilty in German. On January 20, 1970 he invited Stern and his fiancée over for a drink.

It was presumably more than one drink for, according to Gertraude Braeuer's statement to the police, she had become drunk and had begun to engage in sexual intercourse with the host before the outraged eyes of her fiancé.

Stern had objected. There was a fight. In the morning, Stern was found lying in front of the door with his head smashed in. Schuldig pleaded self-defence. Braeuer, now sober, said that he had beaten Stern's brains out with a leg torn from the sofa.

While the case was awaiting trial, Gertraude stole the elder Stern's pension payment and disappeared. The police were unable to find any subsequent trace of her and Schuldig was acquitted, there being no witness to contradict his story of self-defence.

'Well, at least we know what happened to her,' said Inspector Frank Luders, the senior investigations officer of the Criminal Investigations Department. 'Better check out Schuldig. He had an obvious motive.'

'We checked him out at the time of the trial,' said his assistant, Detective-Sergeant Max Peters. 'There was no indication that he knew where Braeuer was any more than we did. It would help if Ludwig could give us a time of death.'

Dr Strauss was not, however, certain as to when Gertraude Braeuer had died.

'Near the end of nineteen seventy,' he said, 'but I could

be off by months. I could tell more if I had the torso. As it is, I can't even say how she was killed.'

Gertraude Braeuer's body remained missing. Had the police known where to look for it, the mystery of her murder would have been solved.

Eventually the sergeant was able to find witnesses who had seen the woman after September 7, 1970, the date of Winfried Schuldig's trial.

'Meaning,' said the sergeant, 'that Schuldig had no motive. His case was already dismissed before she was murdered.'

'Probably rough trade then,' said the inspector. 'You can send it to the Unsolved file.'

Rough trade is the prostitute's term for the perverts and psychopaths to whom so many fall victim.

Aside from the discovery of the head and limbs of Gertraude Braeuer, 1971 had been a comparatively quiet year for the residents of 74 Zeiss Street.

True, the police had been called in once, but that had been a minor incident such as might happen to any bachelor like Fritz Honka.

Fritz, or Fiete, the common nickname by which his friends called him, had been celebrating his thirty-fifth birthday on July 31st with the ruins of a prostitute named Erika Kynast whose fiftieth birthday fell on the same day. Miss Kynast was, of course, shorter than five feet four inches and had no more teeth than a chicken.

She was, however, remarkably agile and strong considering the amount of schnapps she had consumed and when Mr Honka's sexual advances became actually painful, she resisted.

Fritz Honka had responded by slinging her pantyhose around her neck and drawing them so tightly that her eyes nearly came out of her head. He had enormous hands, far larger than normal, and he was even stronger than she, although he had consumed as much or more schnapps.

Fortunately, Miss Kynast was able to get her fingers under the pantyhose in the last second so that she was not entirely deprived of breath and, taking advantage of Honka's preoccupation with his sexual needs, she kicked him solidly in the groin, fled naked down the stairs and shortly thereafter appeared at the local sub-station of the police, wearing the pantyhose around her neck and nothing else.

The police, who were used to such apparitions, went to 74 Zeiss Street and arrested Mr Honka who said that he was sorry, but that he had been carried away and that a woman who comes to a man's room and drinks the best part of two bottles of expensive schnapps should expect to do a little something in return for it.

He was charged with simple assault and released until such time as the hearing might take place. By Ottensen or St Pauli standards, it was not a serious matter.

During the remainder of the year, bachelor Honka made do with the casual acquaintances he picked up at the Golden Glove or the Elbschloss Keller. He was not a stingy man when it came to setting up the drinks which, of course, made him intensely popular in both places.

Although some of these friendships lasted for two or three nights, no suitable, permanent companion appeared until April of 1972 when forty-seven-year-old Irmgard Albrecht came to share the attic apartment at 74 Zeiss Street.

A widowed char woman, slightly taller than five feet and, of course, toothless, she was becoming tired of scrubbing floors and, moreover, found that it interfered with her drinking so that she was happy to take a vacation and enjoy the free food, shelter, drink and perhaps even the attentions of the gallant Mr Honka.

For, as she was later to state, Fritz Honka was a fiery, passionate lover, so jealous that whenever he went off to work or elsewhere he locked his beloved up in the living room so that she would not run off with some other man. It was also, perhaps, because he did not want her snooping about the apartment.

Mrs Albrecht found this flattering, but she was distressed by the fact that while locked in the living room she had no access to food or drink and, worse yet, none to the lavatory.

Fritz resolved these complaints by leaving her an ample

7

supply of food, a somewhat less generous amount of drink and a bucket.

Irmgard Albrecht was happy and content. The only criticism of her new home which she might have had was that it sometimes smelled.

When she mentioned this to Mr Honka, he replied that he too had noticed it and that he would get some cans of spray deodorant. He did as a matter of fact buy a whole case, but the spray was not strong enough to suppress the nauseating odour entirely. Miss Albrecht was not too disturbed. It was not the first stench to which she had been subjected in her life.

At this time Mrs Elsie Beier was still living downstairs and she had noticed nothing of any smell, nor would she for over a year and a half, but then her apartment was, of course, larger and lighter and had more windows than the attic rooms under the eaves.

This attic apartment was a stuffy, cramped and largely airless place. At the head of the narrow stairs coming up from the floor below was a short hall running parallel to the street outside and ending in a wall made of slats with a door in the middle. Behind the slats was storage space, theoretically for the use of all in the house, but in practice used for keeping coal briquettes and other junk belonging to Mr Honka. No one else in the house had anything to store there, but it was available to all.

To the right of the corridor next to the stairs was the kitchen with the lavatory beyond it and on the left was the entrance to the living room which had a door leading to the bedroom beyond the end of the corridor and adjoining the storage area.

Each of the rooms had one sloping wall formed by the roof and in this wall was set a small window. In the living room and bedroom, Mr Honka had decorated these sloping walls with magazine cuttings showing young ladies in poses varying from sweetly innocent to hard-core pornographic.

The remainder of the furniture had been assembled largely from the Sperrmüll, the junk which is placed out on the sidewalks once every few months for carting away by the

8

garbage disposal service. As is often the case with Sperrmüll, much of it was solid and of good quality, although not stylish.

During the spring and summer of 1972, the smell in the attic apartment of Fritz Honka grew even stronger, although it was still not apparent on the floor below. Miss Albrecht was of the opinion that the smell was strongest in the hall and in the bedroom, which she found puzzling. It had not occurred to her that the wall between the bedroom and the storage space was little more than a sheet of cardboard over a wooden frame.

By August, with the temperatures under the roof soaring into the nineties, the smell was becoming almost too much for her sturdy nostrils and in an effort to cheer things up Mr Honka suggested a small party.

Miss Albrecht loved parties so she set off immediately and soon returned with a guest, a forty-five-year-old prostitute named Ruth Dufner, whom she had found in a very convivial state in the Golden Glove.

While Fritz Honka sat watching in a chair with a bottle of schnapps resting in his lap, the ladies removed their clothing, clambered onto the bed and began to engage in simulated lesbian activities.

At least, they were simulated as far as Miss Dufner went for, when Miss Albrecht requested that she assuage the passions she had aroused, she refused.

This display of prudery so outraged Mr Honka that he fell upon the party guest and beat and strangled her so violently with his huge hands that she, fearing for her life, tore free and ran out of the room, down the stairs and into the street as naked as Erika Kynast had been.

Unlike Erika, she did not run to the police station but took refuge in the doorway of a courtyard where she was the subject of some ribaldry on the part of the neighbourhood children until the police arrived, wrapped her in a blanket and took her away.

Fritz Honka was once again arrested and charged with assault. The desk sergeant suggested that if he had any more

9

assaults in mind it might be well to commit them now so that he could be tried for all at the same time.

Honka made a few remarks about the ingratitude of party guests in this day and age and returned to his attic.

In May of 1973 Irmgard Albrecht severed her relationship with Fritz Honka and moved out of 74 Zeiss Street. There was no quarrel, not even a difference of opinion, but for some time Irmgard had not felt quite at ease. Something, she was not sure what, was troubling her. It was perhaps the smell, she thought.

Actually, the smell was not quite as strong as it had been, possibly because the weather was not as warm or possibly because there is simply a limit to the strength and endurance of any smell. Mr Honka was long since used to it.

Others, it seemed, found it less easy to accept and Fritz Honka's domestic arrangements were to remain troubled for the next two years when he would, once again, find a more permanent companion in the form of fifty-two-year-old Anni Wachtmeister, prostitute, under five feet four inches tall, toothless, etc.

It was also during this period and beginning with the first week in August 1974 that the Hamburg Police began to have problems with disappearing women.

Now disappearing women are not at all uncommon in Germany or any other Western European country. Many young girls leave their families to join communes or otherwise express their independence and not a few fall into the hands of the white-slave rings which furnish girls, and sometimes boys, to the brothels and harems of North Africa and the Middle East. Several thousand such girls disappear each year and, generally, they are never seen again.

They all, however, have a number of things in common. They are young. They are pretty. And they are stupid.

The woman who disappeared on or about August 3, 1974 was neither young nor pretty, although she was perhaps somewhat stupid. At least, her husband's account of her past life showed no evidence of any great intelligence.

Anna Hahn had been born in 1920 in Thüringen and had, consequently, been twenty-five years old when the American army marched in at the end of World War II. Not a woman to cling to lost causes, she had immediately acquired a friend and protector from the Americans and the title of Ami-Whore from her countrymen.

Some nine months later she presented her American friend with twin sons and, upon his return to the United States, agreed to his taking them with him. Anna herself could not go as she was still regarded as an enemy national and not qualified to espouse legally one of the conquerors.

It was, however, obvious that the twins would fare much better in the United States than as the sons of an Ami-Whore in Germany. Anna Hahn gave up her children and, a short time later, turned up in St Pauli where she acquired her first prostitute's licence, officially becoming a whore for all nationalities and not merely Amis.

From this point on, her career showed the typical decline from twenty-five dollar prostitute to ten dollar prostitute to five dollar prostitute and finally to all offers gratefully accepted. At the same time, her housing sank in quality from apartment, to studio, to furnished room and finally to the chilly airs of the Bismarck Monument.

This sad but fairly typical career of the St Pauli prostitute was all neatly recorded in the formal, official German of the Hamburg Vice Squad which, since they licence and inspect prostitutes, also keep track of them to a certain extent.

According to these records Anna Hahn was, by the end of 1968, at the end of her career and, presumably, not too far from the end of her life.

She was forty-nine years old and, whatever attractions she might once have had were no longer evident. She was suffering from a half dozen ailments and she was a confirmed alcoholic, never voluntarily doing anything other than falling down drunk. Her abode was the Bismarck Monument and a number of park benches. Her source of income was the performance of any sexual services desired at any place or time at any price and, generally, for a clientele too drunk to see clearly what they were getting.

It was obviously only a matter of time until disease, alcohol or mishap would put an end to her altogether.

Incredibly, none of this was necessary. Germany is a very social country and had Anna Hahn made application for assistance, she would have been placed in a comfortable home, well fed, her ailments treated and, if possible, taught a trade or profession less strenuous than that which she now pursued.

There was only one disadvantage. Not a drop of alcohol.

For Anna Hahn and for the thousands of others like her, this did not represent a choice. Better to die with your head on the table in the Golden Glove than to do without the only thing which made life bearable.

And, astonishingly enough, it was in the Golden Glove that the miracle took place.

Shortly before Christmas of 1970, Anna met in the Golden Glove a cook and waiter named Thomas Beuschel who also came from Thüringen in East Germany. For reasons best known to himself, Beuschel, who was only thirty-four years old, well-built and handsome, took Anna home with him where she gave him a demonstration of the arts which she had acquired in her long career and prepared him a duck in the Thüringen manner.

Beuschel must have been fond of duck for in April of 1971 they were married. Anna was fifty-one years old and a wreck, but she was saved.

Or was she?

Unfortunately, it is a matter of record that most prostitutes make at one time or another surprisingly good marriages and, just as surprisingly, often revert to their old habits.

Anna Beuschel was no exception. As Thomas Beuschel was to tell, rather sadly, the officer in charge of the Missing Persons Bureau, she had begun by costing him his job, to say nothing of her own.

Being a good waiter, Beuschel had quickly found employment with one of the better Hamburg restaurants and had arranged for his new wife to take over as ladies' room attendant.

Anna was, however, not very interested in ladies and no sooner had she got her hands on the tips than she converted them into the cheapest and most concentrated alcohol available.

Forgetting then that she was now a respectable married woman and that her prostitute's licence had actually expired, she decided to do a little advertising in the front entrance of the restaurant.

Anna believed in displaying the merchandize in the most crude and direct manner possible. Removing her underwear, she lay down on the floor and raised her skirts.

It was not a spectacle to stimulate any of the appetites of the amazed arriving diners and Beuschel and his wife were not only fired but thrown bodily off the premises.

After that, Thomas Beuschel did not make any further attempts to find work for his wife and did his waiting alone while Anna spent her days and most of her nights in the Golden Glove. Since her husband provided her with enough money to stay permanently drunk, this was probably one of the happiest periods of her life.

Inexplicable as Thomas Beuschel's attachment to his wife might be, there was no doubting his sincerity and he invariably dropped in at the Golden Glove when he came off work to see if she was there and conscious.

On the afternoon of August 3, 1974, she was there, but barely conscious.

'Go away!' she mumbled. 'Go away. Leave me alone.'

It was the last time he ever saw her alive.

The following day she was not there and, after a brief canvas of her second choice bars, he went to the police and reported her missing.

'Any idea of what might have happened to her, Mr Beuschel?' asked the Missing Persons duty officer who had just listened to a summary of Anna Beuschel's background. Her husband had found this necessary in order to explain why he had simply gone off and left his wife half-conscious in the Golden Glove.

Thomas Beuschel looked uneasy.

'The Elbe?' he murmured.

The Missing Persons officer thought that this was a very likely suggestion. The Elbe is the great river on the end of which Hamburg lies and quite a number of St Pauli prostitutes end up in its broad waters.

Generally, however, their bodies are fished out by the Water Police. The Elbe is a tidal river and things floating in it do not wash quickly out into the North Sea, but normally make several trips up and down as current alternates with tide.

However, the Water Police did not fish out Anna Beuschel nor did their colleagues on land find any trace of her. Eventually, the Missing Person report was forwarded to the Department of Criminal Investigations with a note that Mrs Beuschel had possibly been the victim of foul play.

'A strange conclusion,' remarked Inspector Luders, gazing morosely at the report. 'She had no money. She was old and unattractive. No one benefited from her death. Here, take this and see if you can turn up any kind of a lead.'

Two days later, the sergeant handed back the file.

'Not a thing,' he said. 'Missing Persons was thorough. There's no trace of the woman.'

On the same day that he suspended his investigation into the disappearance of Anna Beuschel, Mrs Elsie Beier was complaining bitterly to Heinz, the caretaker of 74 Zeiss Street.

'It's more than a body can stand!' she screeched. 'Just come in here and smell it for yourself!'

But Heinz would not. He did not like the smell any better than Mrs Beier did. It was a horrible smell, nauseating, foul, faintly and revoltingly sweetish.

It was an interesting point that, although both were old enough to remember the second world war, neither Heinz nor Mrs Beier had happened to be in one of the badly bombed cities where the corpses lay rotting in the ruins.

Anna Beuschel's case also came to the Unsolved files of the Criminal Police and, since her married name began with a 'b', found itself next to the Unsolved case of Gertraude Braeuer.

By one of those strange coincidences, so common in real life, but forbidden to fiction, the ladies themselves were filed in much the same manner.

14

On November 1, 1974 Mrs Beier gave up and moved out to be replaced by the less fastidious Mr Fordal, and on Christmas Eve of that same year a Miss Frieda 'Rita' Roblick disappeared after having been seen for the last time in the Golden Glove at approximately four in the afternoon.

The matter came rather quickly to the attention of the police as the fifty-seven-year-old Miss Roblick was, so to speak, an old customer of theirs. A confirmed alcoholic who had held a prostitute's licence in most of the larger cities in Germany, she was seldom able to resist the temptation to rob her clients before leaving them and had consequently acquired a police record of imposing thickness.

At the time of her disappearance she was actually on parole, and it was her parole officer who reported her missing.

The report on Frieda Roblick did not remain long in the Missing Persons office, but was sent to Inspector Luders with a sheet of paper noting the similarities between this and the Beuschel case only some four and a half months earlier.

Both women had been old, broken-down prostitutes. Both had been alcoholics. Both had been small women, only a little over five feet tall. Neither had had any teeth, a point important in cases requiring dental identification. And both had last been seen in the Golden Glove.

'Interesting,' said the inspector. 'I wonder if it means anything.'

The sergeant did not reply, but got up to go and look in the Unsolved file. After a few moments, he returned with another file in his hand.

'Except that she was somewhat younger,' he said, 'all those things also apply to the Braeuer case.'

The inspector took the file and leafed through it.

'She wasn't last seen in the Golden Glove,' he observed. 'Or, at least, we don't know that she was. Still . . .'

'Do you think it would be worth putting a stake-out in the Glove?' said the sergeant.

'Nobody from the force,' said the inspector. 'They'd end

up alcoholic. See if you can get one of the canaries who's already an alcoholic.'

A canary is a bird that sings. The German police usually have quite a number of such birds working for them on a part-time piece-work basis.

That same afternoon, a remarkably scruffy gentleman with a fine, red nose joined the revellers in the Golden Glove and began to alternate beer and spirits in the orthodox north German manner. Sometimes he put his head down on the table and appeared to lose consciousness, but this was a sham. There was probably not enough alcohol in all Hamburg to render the gentleman unconscious and, for this reason, he enjoyed the esteem of the police who were also paying for the drinks.

The gentleman with the red nose did not find out anything except that Frieda Roblick had mentioned to several persons shortly before her disappearance that she was onto 'something solid' and she would soon be enjoying greener pastures. It had been assumed by her listeners that she meant that she was about to take up residence with some man.

On January 10, 1975 the man with the red nose was still sitting in the Golden Glove listening and drinking, although not necessarily in that order of importance, when Ruth Schult disappeared.

Fifty-two years old, five feet three inches tall and with not a tooth to her name, Mrs Schult was a prominent fixture of the St Pauli scene. Beginning her career as a prostitute at an early age, she had in 1948 met and married a wealthy widower named Schult, but as a result of her immoderate consumption of alcoholic beverages and her commercial attitude toward chance acquaintances of the opposite or even same sex, had found herself divorced almost immediately thereafter.

She had then gone to practise her profession in Cologne, Dusseldorf and a number of other cities only to return to Hamburg and St Pauli as she became increasingly short of tooth and long of wind.

This being a fairly average career, it would not, in itself, have been enough to gain her fame.

16

What had done that was an anonymous telephone call to the Hamburg Police on the afternoon of March 9, 1974 in which it was reported that two naked men were raping a naked woman at the Bismarck Monument.

A police car had been dispatched and had found Ruth Schult and two male companions, all naked as described, but, far from being raped, she was cooperating enthusiastically and, it appeared, even directing the operation.

Hamburgers are not easily startled, but such an event in an open square and on a chilly March day had drawn something of a crowd including a number of newspapermen.

The following morning several newspapers carried headlines of 'Group-sex at Bismarck Monument!' and Ruth Schult's modest niche in history was assured.

Having served a short sentence for indecent exposure, she returned to her normal haunts, one of which was the Golden Glove.

It was, however, no one from the Golden Glove who reported her missing, but rather a waiter from a first class restaurant.

Not, of course, that Mrs Schult ate at first class restaurants or for that matter at any restaurants at all, but she was a woman of regular habits and invariably made her lunch of bread with a bit of sausage on a park bench facing the restaurant across the street.

Over the years, she had become a sort of fixture to the waiter gazing out the front windows of the restaurant and when on January 10, 1975 she did not appear, he was disquieted. He knew who the woman was and also that she was no longer young and he thought that she might be ill in her room, assuming that she had one at all.

He therefore reported the matter to the police who took rather more note of it than they might under normal circumstances. The fact was, Ruth Schult met all of the physical and moral qualifications for inclusion into the group of what was now beginning to become known as the Golden Glove Disappearances.

The investigations continued for a month and at the end of that time were dropped for lack of leads. There was little

17

question remaining in the inspector's mind; Mrs Ruth Schult had joined the club.

All this bothered him a great deal. He was used to superannuated prostitutes who died of alcohol and disease or who flung themselves from high buildings or bridges or who even got themselves murdered, but not of old prostitutes who simply disappeared.

'The fact is,' he told the sergeant rather sharply as if he were holding him personally responsible, 'it is not at all easy to dispose of a human body in a city like Hamburg. If these cases are all connected, and I am beginning to feel certain that they are, then someone is going to great trouble and I cannot see why.'

'Logically,' said the sergeant, 'the knowledge of the identity of the victims would lead to the identity of the murderer. However, that is not the case here because we know the identity of the victims and it hasn't helped us a bit.'

'Of course, we don't actually know that they are dead,' said the inspector, scowling ferociously at the top of the desk and tapping with his pencil. 'With the exception of Braeuer.'

'They certainly weren't shipped to North Africa or the Middle East,' said the sergeant. 'The sheiks would have crucified the white-slavers.'

'But,' continued the inspector, ignoring the remark, 'they have probably been killed because it would be even harder to make a living woman like that disappear than a corpse.'

The sergeant did not make any further comment. For months now, he had been racking his brain over the case of the missing prostitutes and the only result had been a monumental confusion.

Were the cases connected? Was there a pattern? And if so what in Heaven's name had become of the four hundred pounds or more of human flesh, dead or alive, which was presumably somewhere in Hamburg?

Astonishingly, there is some reason to believe that by March 16, 1975, when short, toothless, fifty-two-year-old Anni Wachtmeister moved into the attic apartment at 74

18

Zeiss Street with her new friend, Fritz Honka, there was no one who could have answered the sergeant's questions.

Miss Wachtmeister did not remain long at 74 Zeiss Street, moving out again on June 12th with the double complaint, made to anyone at the Golden Glove who was prepared to listen, that Fritz was too rough a lover for her liking and, secondly, that the place stank like the plague.

Before moving out, she had complained about the smell to Mr Honka who said that he was aware of it and that he was already buying deodorants by the case, something which was perfectly true.

He had also said that he had no idea what was causing it and it was to appear later that this was also perfectly true.

Unlike Irmgard Albrecht, who had left in a warm glow of mutual understanding, Anni Wachtmeister left rather precipitously and without bothering to put on all her clothes. She had often spoken of going back to fetch them, but had not done so a month later when, on the morning of June 17, 1975, the bells in the fire stations of Altona and St Pauli began to ring.

The fire which had been reported at 74 Zeiss Street at three-thirty-seven in the morning had begun in the second floor apartment of Seaman John Fordal and had been caused by his leaving a burning candle next to the bed as he fell asleep.

The bedding had caught fire and so had a considerable part of the furnishings before Fordal awoke, thought incorrectly that he was trapped, crawled out of the window and along the cornice to the stairwell window which he kicked in, and descended calmly, if unsteadily, to the street.

He was sitting on the kerb dabbing with his shirt tail at a nasty cut on his shin, which he had acquired kicking in the window, when the fire department arrived.

The fire in Mr Fordal's apartment was extinguished quickly but it had by then transferred itself to the storey above and was raging in the roof, a large part of which was destroyed before it was finally brought under control at approximately six-thirty.

In the meantime the house had, of course, been evacuated

and the door to Fritz Honka's attic apartment smashed in as the firemen did not know that he was a night watchman and would therefore be working.

They had, naturally, found no one in the apartment and at shortly before seven Walter Aust, a thirty-one-year-old, broad-shouldered, black-haired fireman, was digging through the smouldering rubble of the storage space adjoining Honka's bedroom.

Fireman Aust was unhappy because in addition to the smell of smoke and burned rags there was an underlying odour of something so foul that his nose refused to accept it.

Prodding in the darkness beneath the eaves, he caught hold of a length of charred timber with his gloved hand and drew it out.

There was a gold-coloured sandal on the end of the timber which he now saw was not timber at all. What fireman Aust was holding in his hand was a woman's leg and foot.

'Mein Gott, Erwin!' shouted Aust. 'Somebody was trapped up here! It looks like a woman.'

Fire Captain Erwin Schuen hurried over from the head of the stairs, followed by Fireman Wilfried Harz.

'We went through the apartment . . .,' he began and then broke off in mid-sentence as Harz shone his flashlight onto the object.

The leg was little more than a bone covered by brown, dry, leathery skin. It looked like the leg of a mummy and it gave off a horrifying odour.

For a second, the three firemen looked at each other in bewilderment.

'That's been here for a long time,' said Schuen finally.

He crouched and began to pull aside the pile of old rags from the corner under the eaves and as Harz shone his flashlight onto what lay beneath, a body appeared, the skin as dried and mummified as the leg had been.

That it was that of a woman there could be no doubt. Apart from a wine-red pullover, the body was naked and, although the face was a hideous mask of gaping eye sockets and rotting, toothless jaws, it was unquestionably a woman's face.

'Call the police, Walter,' said Fire Captain Schuen. 'This is out of our province.'

The police were immediately summoned, but before they had had time to arrive, Firemen Schuen and Aust had suffered another nauseating experience. Digging into a pile of coal briquettes, they had come upon a blue, plastic sack which had burst as they were dragging it out.

The wave of stinking gas which had shot from the sack had sent them reeling to the head of the stairs and had terminated the operations of the fire department in the attic until the air was cleared.

A short time later, the first officers from the Criminal Investigations Department arrived and, having learned that anyone in the house had access to the storage space in the attic and that the fire had been started by John Fordal, immediately placed him under arrest on the supposition that he had started the fire to conceal the evidence of murder.

However, Inspector Luders and Sergeant Peters then arrived and ordered a thorough search of the entire floor. By the time that Fritz Honka came home from his night watchman's job at a quarter to eight, the police knew that there was not only one body, but four, and that only Fritz Honka could be responsible for their being where they were.

Honka seemed only mildly astonished to find the house full of firemen and police officers.

'My goodness!' he exclaimed, gazing at the ruins of his apartment. 'What's going on here anyway?'

'There was a fire,' said Inspector Luders and then with deliberately startling abruptness, 'Criminal Police. What do you know about these two women?'

He thrust the personal identity cards of Irmgard Albrecht and Anni Wachtmeister under the night watchman's nose. They had been found in Honka's apartment and it was assumed that they represented two of the victims.

Honka glanced at the cards. 'They used to live with me,' he said, 'but they left and never came back to pick up their cards. If you want to get hold of them, you could try the Glove.'

The inspector was taken aback. Honka was not acting

like a trapped murderer at all and yet he almost certainly was.

The woman whose body had been found in the storage area by the firemen had definitely been murdered, although he still did not know how. The body found under the pile of rags had consisted of only the torso and the lower parts of the legs.

The arms, the thighs and the breasts had been in the blue plastic sack where they had rotted to an almost liquid consistency. It seemed improbable that the body could even be identified.

As a matter of fact, only one of the four bodies found in the attic appeared to be subject to identification and that was the torso lacking arms, legs, head, breasts and vagina found behind a low door leading off Honka's kitchen to the space under the eaves. This was believed to be the remainder of Gertraude Braeuer's corpse, the head and limbs of which had been found in the abandoned chocolate factory yard in November of 1971.

Lying on top of the torso of Gertraude Braeuer was the body of another woman which had not been mutilated in any way, but which had dried out and cured to resemble a side of bacon. This was later identified as the corpse of Frieda Roblick.

On the other side of the house, behind a trap door which had since been wallpapered over, in the wall of the living room, the dismembered parts of the corpse of Anna Beuschel lay heaped together.

All of these bodies were eventually identified by the police, but it was only through the confession of Fritz Honka at eleven-thirty that same night that it was learned that the dismembered corpse in the storage area was that of Ruth Schult.

The Missing Ladies of the Golden Glove had been found and the sergeant's question as to what could be done with four hundred pounds of flesh was answered.

It could not, however, have been answered before because the only person who knew all the details was forgetful. Fritz Honka could not even remember how many women he had

22

killed and carelessly shoved under the eaves of the attic, maintaining at first that it was only two and then three and finally four when the pictures of the victims were shown to him.

Nor, according to Dr Strauss, was he pretending. The women had been a bother to him, he had not known what to do with the bodies so he had simply shoved them out of sight and had forgotten about them.

Fritz Honka was telling the literal truth when he had said that he had no idea where the smell was coming from and he had not been alarmed by the presence of the police in his apartment because he did not remember that he was a murderer.

Abstinence from alcohol in the detention cells of the police headquarters, however, worked a considerable improvement in his memory and he was eventually able to recall most of the details of the murders, if not exactly to which woman they applied.

Mostly, he said, he had strangled the women because they had scoffed at his inability to have orthodox sexual relations. Honka, it seemed, preferred oral sex, although only with women who had no teeth, or, alternatively, anal sex. He also enjoyed necrophily, having on at least two occasions carried out sexual intercourse with the corpses of the women after he had strangled them.

Despite the mutilations of the breasts and sex organs of all the victims but one, Honka maintained that his purpose in cutting up the corpses was to dispose of them. However, with the exception of Gertraude Braeuer, he had always found the cutting up, carried out in the kitchen sink with the kitchen knife and a small hand saw, so exhausting that he had lacked the energy to remove the body from the building and had merely stuffed it into the most convenient corner under the eaves.

A strange murderer, Fritz Honka. With some women, he lived peacefully and even moderately happily for months on end. Others he strangled and stuffed into the corners around his apartment, forgetting that they were there and buying

23

deodorants by the case to combat the stench of their rotting bodies.

Was there a motive for these crimes?

If so, it is almost certain that Fritz Honka does not know what it was.

The crimes, however, took place. They were acknowledged. And Fritz Honka was sentenced to life imprisonment in punishment for them.

2

THE FATAL ORGY

Early in June of 1972 Kurt Rheiners made a spear. The thirty-six-year-old plumber was an above average handworker and it was a good spear.

The shaft of the spear was of hard maple, slightly over an inch in diameter and five feet long. Fixed firmly at the end was the blade, a slender dagger of high-grade steel, ten inches long and sharpened to a razor edge on both sides. The point was as sharp as a needle.

Having made the spear, Kurt did not quite know what to do with it. A few hundred years earlier a spear such as this might have been extremely useful in Hannover, West Germany where Kurt lived, but there was not much to be done with it in 1972.

Nor could he, for that matter, have explained why he had made the spear in the first place, except that he was slightly at loose ends with Julia and the boy, Thomas, off on vacation in the Tirol.

He had thought that it might be something a little different, a taste of freedom after eleven years of marriage so to speak, when he had let Julia and Thomas go off on vacation alone, but it had not turned out exactly that way.

The fact was, he was bored. Julia was only two years younger than himself, but she was a good deal younger at heart, and Thomas, already ten, made the difference between an empty, lonely house and one full of noise and excitement.

Kurt Rheiners sighed, stood the finished spear in the corner of the living room and went down to the Ant Tavern where he told Willi Jacobi how much he was enjoying his freedom, drank a good deal more beer than was good for his health, stood a good many more rounds than was good for his pocket and finally went home depressed and wondering what was the matter with him.

The newspapers and magazines were full of the adventures enjoyed by husbands while their families were away on vacation, but in real life this sort of thing appeared to happen much less frequently.

Not, of course, that there were not plenty of lovely young girls and, if the magazines could be believed, they should be approachable if not downright eager.

The trouble was, not many of them seemed to come into the Ant and Kurt felt himself a little too old to hang out in the discotheques where the noise hurt his ears and the lighting his eyes.

'Pity that Norbert doesn't bring that Petra Schumacher in with him a little more often,' murmured Kurt, drifting into beery sleep. 'I just wonder . . .?'

Actually, he had no need to wonder. Petra Schumacher was eighteen years old, pretty, and a modern German girl in every respect which meant that she was well versed in sexual matters – and not only from a purely theoretical standpoint.

She was, in the informal manner popular among younger Germans, engaged to Kurt's friend, Norbert Splett, the apprentice pastry cook.

Norbert was almost Kurt's best friend and probably would have been except for the considerable difference in ages, Norbert being only twenty.

Nonetheless, Kurt and Norbert had known each other for years and the relationship was warm, if sometimes slightly puzzling to outsiders who, until they knew otherwise, tended to suspect an overt or covert homosexual attachment.

In actual fact, there was none. Norbert was a somewhat sensitive soul and had broken off his apprenticeship as a butcher because he could not stand slaughtering the calves. Sexually his interests were directed toward the person of Petra Schumacher.

Sometimes, when they had had a good deal of beer together, Norbert would tell Kurt about how it was with Petra and the other girls of his age group. According to these accounts, it was just the way the magazines said it was.

26

Casual, carefree sex with no taboos and in all its forms, no more significant and no more difficult to arrange than a game of tennis. But, of course, a great deal more exciting. Norbert's accounts tended to make Kurt drool slightly.

The fact remained, however, that he was thirty-six years old and of the preceding generation. Yearn as he might, he simply could not bring himself to make a direct proposal to any of the young girls with whom he came into casual contact.

There was, of course, the alternative of the contact advertisements. Many German newspapers and magazines carry pages of sex contact advertisements and some magazines carry nothing else. There, under code numbers, are offers for homosex, heterosex, voyeur sex, bi-sex, group-sex and omnisex. In the magazines devoted to such advertising, the offers are usually illustrated by photographs of the advertiser or advertiseress in the costume and, frequently, in the poses in which they propose to entertain anyone answering the advertisement.

Some of these advertisements are commercially orientated, such as those reading, 'Beautiful girl (see photo). 18 years. Experienced. Wishes to be indulged by wealthy industrialist. Age not a consideration.'

The majority are, however, merely the Germans of the last generation trying to catch up with the sex revolution. Most of them are, like Kurt Rheiners, in their middle thirties.

Kurt had bought a good many such magazines and had studied them, making selections in various fields that sounded attractive, but he had never answered any. He simply did not have the nerve.

The thought of a total stranger or strangers turning up on his doorstep ready for a bout of group-sex or even perfectly ordinary one-to-one sex on the living room carpet was terrifying.

Kurt suspected that he would, under such circumstances, be disgracefully unable to perform and he was probably right. Germany's psychiatrists report that the most common complaint among younger men today is impotence brought on by an inability to match the standards set by the media.

Kurt Rheiners therefore did nothing and complained about it incessantly to the owner of the Ant. He did not mention his problems to Norbert Splett because he did not want Norbert to think of him as an old man or behind the times. He sometimes made up quite interesting stories of his experiences in connection with the contact advertisements which caused Norbert to think that it must be nice to be so active sexually at such an advanced age.

However, as time passed and the first two weeks of Julia's and Thomas's three week vacation were at an end, Kurt's complaints to Willi Jacobi began to take on a note of desperation and his consumption of beer and corn, the clear, potent, grain spirits so popular in North Germany, increased alarmingly.

Not, of course, that he got drunk. Like most Germans, Kurt had a hard head for alcohol and he and Norbert could, and frequently did, put away forty and more glasses of beer with, perhaps, half that number of shots of corn in a single evening without any very serious effect on the one or the other.

Petra Schumacher did not have a hard head for alcohol. Not because she was young. There are eighteen-year-old German girls who can drink a French vintner under the table. The reason that Petra Schumacher could not drink very much was simply that she seldom had anything much in her stomach.

The sad fact was that Petra had a slight tendency to overgenerous proportions and, although this rendered her extremely attractive to Kurt Rheiners and others of his generation, the modern trends were for something more gazelle-like.

On the evening of June 20, 1972 as Petra Schumacher entered the Ant Tavern with her fiancé, Norbert Splett, she had eaten during the preceding twelve hours precisely three very small potatoes and one small cup of yogurt. It was not the ideal condition in which to start a hard evening's drinking.

The time was more late afternoon than evening and, by midnight, the threesome of Kurt Rheiners, Norbert Splett and Petra Schumacher had disposed of a good many more than forty glasses of beer, to say nothing of the corn, and Petra was in a state where she was inclined to giggle wildly at anything or nothing and fling herself onto the nearest male neck available.

They left together and Willi Jacobi watched them go with approval and benevolence. Unless he was greatly mistaken, Kurt Rheiners was soon going to be relieved of an itch that had been bothering him for some time now.

Willi Jacobi would not see his friend and client, Kurt Rheiners, again, but another drinking partner named Hardy Bruggemann would, and under shocking circumstances.

The incident took place the following morning at approximately nine-thirty when Bruggemann dropped by the Rheiners' home to see how Kurt was getting on. Being an old friend, he did not hesitate when there was no answer to his knock, but simply opened the door and walked into the house.

Kurt Rheiners was in the living room, just in front of the door. He was completely naked and projecting from his back was the polished five-foot shaft of the spear which he had so carefully made. There was a wide trail of partially dried blood leading from the sofa to the body and a large pool surrounding it. The blade of the spear was driven completely into the body so that none of it could be seen at all.

Hardy Bruggemann was astounded and appalled. He did not know that Kurt Rheiners had made a spear and he did not recognize the shaft protruding from between his shoulder blades as a spear shaft.

To him it appeared that his friend had, in some inexplicable way, been impaled on a long, round piece of wood, presumably while lying naked on the sofa and had then dragged himself in the direction of the door before expiring.

How this could have happened he could not imagine.

However, as the surprise subsided slightly, his gaze took in other details of the room and he saw that Kurt was lying

29

amidst a welter of clothing, food, utensils and playing cards. The impression was that there had been a very lively party of some kind.

All of this transpired in less than an instant even while Bruggemann was running forward to drop on his knees beside the body of his friend. He had hoped to find some trace of breathing or a heart beat, but there was none and the body was already quite cold.

Bruggemann got sorrowfully to his feet and, for the first time, the realization struck him that Kurt Rheiners must have been murdered. There had been a wild party and one of the guests had rammed a wooden pole into his back with such force that it had killed him.

Having more than a scanty idea of his friend's extra-marital ambitions and having heard a number of his fictional stories concerning the contact advertising experiences, he immediately suspected the worst. Kurt had made a contact through the advertisements and it had turned out badly.

The thing to do now was to try and save as much of appearances as possible.

Picking up a pair of bloody trousers from the floor, he attempted to slip them over the dead man's legs, but found this much more difficult than he would have expected.

It was while he was struggling with the trousers that it occurred to him what he was going to have to do.

He was going to have to call the police.

Still holding the trousers in his hand, he went out to the hall and dialled the emergency number of the police from the small, printed card of emergency numbers taped to the wall over the telephone.

Up until this point, he had been acting in a state of shock, but there was now time to think while waiting for the police and, by the time that the first patrol car arrived, he was a very worried man indeed.

He had handled things in the living room, his fingerprints must be everywhere. It would be a wonder if he were not charged with murdering Kurt himself.

In fact, the two patrolmen from the car were much inclined to think just that. Both young and relatively inexperienced officers, they were nearly as dumbfounded as Bruggemann had been by the scene.

They did, however, recognize the spear for what it was and, after handcuffing the trembling Bruggemann to the radiator, one man went out to the patrol car to report while the other guarded the prisoner with drawn pistol.

This merely complicated matters still further for it was Sunday morning and the man on duty in the Criminal Investigations Department was a very junior detective third-class who could not leave the offices.

He had, of course, taken Hardy Bruggemann's original report as transferred to him from the communications centre, but he had not entirely believed it. Bruggemann in a state of shock had sounded not unlike a drunk.

Now, however, the patrolman from the patrol car was on the line and he not only maintained that there had been a homicide but that the victim had been speared to death.

It had been a very long time since anyone was speared to death in Hannover and the detective was not at all anxious to call out his superiors on a Sunday morning with such a report unless he was absolutely certain that it was true.

He, therefore, stalled in an agony of indecision and someone, presumably the dispatcher on the communications desk, called the emergency ambulance which rushed to the Rheiners' home carrying an intern with even less experience than the detective at police headquarters.

The intern, who had an exaggerated idea of the authority of the medical profession, insisted on taking the corpse to the hospital and was only restrained by threats of force from the patrolmen whose orders were to let no one approach the body.

This disagreement, however, finally produced constructive action as the intern calling police headquarters over the radio telephone in a great fury convinced the detective in the offices of the C.I.D. that, whatever the situation at the Rheiners' house, something was very radically wrong and would require the attention of the senior members of the department.

A half-hour later Detective-Sergeant Willi Froebes slid

31

out of his car and came loping up the front walk of the Rheiners' house looking very much like a Doberman pinscher and nearly as inclined to bite.

A dark, sleek, muscular man who did not suffer fools lightly, he disliked disorder of any kind and the scene at the Rheiners' house looked as if someone were shooting a low-budget, B-grade movie.

Hardy Bruggemann was still handcuffed to the radiator, the patrolmen and the intern were defying each other to the amusement of the hard-bitten ambulance driver and stretcher bearers, and a very considerable crowd had collected and was trying to peer through the windows of the house.

The sergeant straightened all this out as quickly and as ruthlessly as a sheepdog might have straightened out a herd of unruly sheep, sending the intern and his ambulance back to the hospital with burning ears and some valuable information on the penalties involved in interfering with a police officer in the performance of his duty, releasing the nearly hysterical Bruggemann from the radiator and sending the patrolmen into the crowd with instructions to collect any and all identity cards for future questioning.

He then turned his attention to the corpse.

'What do you know about this?' he asked Bruggemann.

'Nothing,' said Bruggemann. 'I just came to visit him and found him like this. I called the police.'

'You can go,' said the sergeant. 'Give me your identity card. You'll be called for questioning later.'

Hardy Bruggemann left gratefully and the sergeant went out to the patrol car, called headquarters and issued instructions that his superior, Inspector Karl Kreidemann, and the department's medical expert, Dr Manfred Hammerstein, be informed that a homicide had taken place.

He then lit a cigarette and settled down to wait. It being Sunday morning, Hammerstein, he knew, would be at the golf links. The inspector would, presumably, be at home, but he was not a man who was inclined to hurry, not even for a homicide.

Forty-five minutes later they arrived, the doctor still in his golfing clothes and shoes, and the inspector calm and

32

unruffled as ever. He was a tall man with long, aristocratic features and greying, bushy sideburns who looked far too distinguished to be a police officer.

The doctor did not look distinguished at all, being very young and having a deceptively timid manner of peering through his huge, horn-rimmed spectacles. He was, however, a very competent practitioner of forensic medicine and he promptly set about an examination of the corpse of Kurt Rheiners. While he was doing this, the sergeant went through the dead man's clothing and eventually came up with his identity card.

The inspector did nothing, but, having looked over the scene, withdrew to the police car where he lit a long, thin, black cigar and waited for the reports.

Presently, the doctor came out and sat down beside him.

'The man was speared to death,' he said without preamble. 'An extremely well-made weapon of high grade steel, not primitive workmanship at all. The blade entered his back just below the right shoulder blade, passed at an angle through the heart and left lung and emerged through the skin of the chest. He died approximately nine minutes later.'

'Not instantly?' said the inspector, frowning. 'Was the spear hand-held or thrown?'

'Hand-held, definitely,' said the doctor. 'It could not have entered at the angle it did, if it were thrown. He was lying down at the time.'

'Perhaps a fight?' suggested the sergeant, who had come out to stand beside the car and listen. 'He was knocked down and then stabbed as he lay on the floor.'

'Well no, not really,' said the doctor. 'As a matter of fact, he was lying on top of someone and it wasn't on the floor but on the sofa. There was no fight. He was just lying there having intercourse . . .'

'What?' said the inspector and the sergeant simultaneously.

'Yes, that was what he was doing,' said the doctor apologetically as if he were in some way responsible for this behaviour. 'He had nearly reached his climax, too, and the shock of the spear thrust was enough to finish the matter. It

33

must have been quite a shock for his partner as well. There's a possibility that the tip of the spear broke the skin of her chest or back, as the case may have been.'

'Are you quite sure of all this?' said the inspector, taking the cigar out of his mouth, looking at it reflectively and putting it back again.

'Yes,' said the doctor simply.

The sergeant looked exceedingly unbelieving, but said nothing.

'Time of death?' said the inspector.

'Between one-forty-two and one-fifty this morning,' said the doctor.

'All right, Willi,' said the inspector. 'Full lab squad out on the double. It will probably take half the day to locate them all. The body can be sent down to the morgue as soon as they're finished with it. I want the whole room gone over for prints. It looks to me as if there was some sort of a party there last night and there may even be witnesses to this. I'll be receiving reports at the office.'

The inspector thereupon drove back to police head-quarters. The first report he received when he arrived was from the charge room.

'There is a man down here,' said the officer on duty, 'who says that he speared someone to death last night. I thought you might be interested.'

'Send him up,' said the inspector.

A few moments later a tearful Norbert Splett was ushered into the inspector's office.

'I killed him!' he sobbed. 'I killed my best friend! He was raping my fiancée!'

'A grave provocation, certainly,' said the inspector. 'Sit down and tell me about it.'

The portable tape-recorder was brought in and the suspect was warned of his rights, following which Splett made a full confession to the murder of Kurt Rheiners.

'We left the Ant a little before midnight,' he said. 'Kurt, Petra and I. Petra was pretty drunk, but Kurt and I were all right.

'Kurt wanted us to go to his house. He said that he had

34

something to drink there and that we could cook some sausages and have a good time.'

'Did you have any idea of what he meant by "a good time"?' asked the inspector.

Norbert Splett looked slightly uneasy. 'Well, drinking and eating and so on, I guess,' he said.

'Continue,' said the inspector.

'When we got to the house,' resumed Splett, 'Kurt got out some wine and champagne and a bottle of cognac. We made some sausages and opened a tin of pusta salade.

'Then Kurt suggested we play cards.'

'For money?' said the inspector.

Norbert squirmed. 'For our clothes,' he said. 'Every time anybody got the jack or the ace of hearts, they had to take off one article of clothing. It wasn't very long before all of us were naked.'

'And then?' said the inspector. 'You still had no idea of the kind of good time Mr Rheiners had in mind?'

'I didn't feel good,' said Norbert Splett defensively. 'I can't drink cognac on top of beer. I had to go to the bathroom and bring it up.

'When I came back into the living room, Petra was lying on the sofa and Kurt was lying on top of her between her legs. They were both naked and she was fighting him.

'I thought he was raping her and I picked up the spear that was standing in the corner and stuck it in his back. I didn't think it would go in so easily, but it went all the way.

'Kurt made an awful noise and fell off Petra. I got her up and helped her into her clothes and dressed myself. Then we left and went to my place and went to bed. I got up just now.'

'And you made no effort to help Mr Rheiners?' said the inspector. 'You could have called a doctor.'

'He was dead,' said Splett. 'I knew he was dead. The spear went all the way through him.'

Norbert Splett was charged and taken to the detention cells while a team of detectives went to his apartment and arrested Petra Schumacher on charges of acting as an accessory after the fact.

In the meantime, the inspector drove back to the Rheiners' home where he informed the sergeant that the murder had been solved.

'Continue with the investigation as if it hadn't however,' he said. 'I'm not convinced that Mr Splett has told us the truth, the whole truth and nothing but the truth. I'll be interested in hearing Miss Schumacher's statement.'

Petra Schumacher's statement was identical to that of her fiancé.

'Which means,' said the inspector, 'that they cooked it up between them. It may be true, but it's not an independent statement. No two persons involved in such an incident would have completely identical versions of what happened unless they had discussed it and agreed upon it.'

It was Monday morning and the investigations at the Rheiners' house had been completed. The body was at the police morgue where Dr Hammerstein was carrying out the autopsy. Mrs Rheiners had been contacted and would be arriving with Thomas from the Tirol at noon.

'It isn't entirely the true version, in any case,' said Sergeant Froebes. 'I just stopped by the morgue and Hammerstein says that she wasn't fighting him. The girl's got nails like a cat, but the only marks are on Rheiner's back and they're not from fighting. He also says that she was sufficiently aroused that she left traces of her secretions on Rheiners' body.'

'Well, of course, Splett didn't say that Rheiners was raping her in his confession,' said the inspector. 'He said he thought he was raping her and it would be impossible to prove that he didn't think that. Give the lab a call and see if they're ready to report yet.'

The lab was not yet ready, but they were by noon, just shortly before the arrival of Mrs Rheiners.

'I think you'll be able to pin Splett on one point,' said the chief of the laboratory technical section. 'According to his statement, he just stuck the spear into Rheiners' back, but, in actual fact, it was wiped afterwards. There are no prints on it of any kind.

'Plenty of prints of all three participants everywhere else

in the room and there are sperm and female secretion traces on the carpet where they were sitting playing cards. The indications are that that was not all they were playing.

'It wasn't a real orgy or group sex, but everybody was getting pretty excited. There are also indications that somebody went through most of the house looking for something. There's no indication as to whether they found it.'

'Money perhaps,' said the inspector. 'We may be able to tell something when Mrs Rheiners gets here. She's due shortly. You didn't find any money or valuables in the house? Rheiners was comfortably well-off.'

'Valuables yes,' said the technician. 'Money no. There were a few coins in the drawers in the kitchen, but no real money.'

'The Ant, the tavern where Rheiners hung out, says that he was free with money and carried quite a sum of it on him most of the time,' said the inspector. 'The owner is pretty sure he had at least a couple of hundred marks on him when they left.'

'He didn't have it when we got there,' said the technician. 'Of course, half the population of Hannover had run through the place by then. The fellow who found him, this Brugge-mann, admitted that he'd picked up Rheiners' trousers, didn't he?'

'Yes,' said the inspector. 'But I doubt very much that he took anything out of them. We checked him out and there's no reason to suspect him of anything. Willi says he was on the verge of collapse when he got there.'

The technician looked at his notes. 'Let's see,' he said. 'That's about it. You wanted to know if there were traces of vomit in the lavatory. Negative. We took it apart. No vomit.'

'Is it possible that the flush would have cleaned it so thoroughly that you couldn't find traces?' said the inspector.

'Possible, but highly improbable,' said the technician. 'The fellow would have had to be a very tidy vomiter. Less than one per cent chance that anyone vomited in that lavatory within the past twenty-four hours.'

37

'All right,' said the inspector. 'Now, all we have left is Mrs Rheiners.'

A short time later Mrs Rheiners arrived alone, having dropped Thomas off with her mother.

The inspector immediately summoned Dr Hammerstein. He was going to have to tell Mrs Rheiners the circumstances of her husband's death and he was not at all sure how she would react.

As it turned out, her reaction was one of mixed sorrow and anger.

'It's all this stupid sex business,' she sobbed. 'Kurt was a good husband and I know he never cheated on me before. We were happy. But every time you pick up a newspaper or a magazine now, all you read is about the sex revolution and, if you go to the movies, all you see is sex films. Men like Kurt think they're missing out on something and they do foolish things. Did they rob him too?'

'That's what we're trying to determine, Mrs Rheiners,' said the inspector. 'Do you know if there would have been any substantial amount of money or valuables in the house?'

'There should have been around thirteen hundred marks,' said Mrs Rheiners. 'Kurt always drew a thousand marks out of the bank on Friday and he usually had three or four hundred left over from the week before. He might have spent a little more at the Ant because we were away, but he'd also have spent less on the groceries so it should have been about thirteen hundred marks.'

'There wasn't a penny in the house,' said the inspector.

Nor could the subsequent investigations turn up any place where Kurt Reiners might have spent the money which he had drawn out of the bank on the Friday preceding his death. It was quite simply missing.

On May 22, 1973, Norbert Splett was found guilty of unpremeditated murder with extenuating circumstances and sentenced to ten years imprisonment. The charges against Petra Schumacher were dropped and she was not brought to trial.

3

REPEAT PERFORMANCE

It was a golden autumn morning, on Tuesday October 23, 1973, in the great West German seaport of Hamburg and Inspector Frank Luders was standing at the window of his office nursing a cup of black coffee and gazing glumly down at the office workers scurrying past on their way to work.

Autumn is one of the better seasons in Hamburg, the spring tending to be raw and wet, the summer hot and sticky and the winter too cold for anyone but hardy north Germans.

The inspector's glumness was, therefore, not due to the weather, but rather to a profound conviction, well-based on personal experience, that the day was liable to bring some quite unpleasant surprises.

This is, of course, equally applicable to any other senior investigations officer attached to the Criminal Investigations Department of a large police force, but on this particular morning the inspector's forebodings were realized with distressing speed.

'Communications on the line, chief,' said Detective-Sergeant Max Peters, putting his tousled blond head in through the open door to the outer office. 'They think they may have a homicide. You want me to take it?'

'They think,' said the inspector without turning around. 'What do they mean by that? They have a corpse, but they don't know whether it was a natural death or an accident or murder?'

'No,' said the sergeant. 'They don't know whether they have a corpse.'

The inspector turned around and took a long pull at the coffee cup, looking reproachfully at his assistant over the edge.

39

'It's like this,' explained the sergeant hurriedly. 'A Dr Harold Gross came to the sub-station in Barmbek this morning early and asked for a patrolman to accompany him. He apparently owns a number of apartment houses and he couldn't locate the building superintendent in one of them. He had a locksmith with him and he was going to open the door and go in, but he wanted a police officer present.'

'Why?' said the inspector, putting the empty coffee cup down on the desk.

'I don't know,' said the sergeant. 'Maybe he thought something was wrong. Anyway, the station sent an officer with him and they're now at the apartment of the building superintendent. He's just called the sub-station to say that there's a big patch of blood on the wall and something that looks like a body wrapped up in a sheet in the utility room. The sub-station transferred the call to Communications and they've passed it on to us.'

'Tell Communications to send a car and then have them check whether there really is a body,' said the inspector. 'We've got enough things going without chasing off after any false alarms. Talk to the car yourself when they reach the scene.'

The sergeant nodded and disappeared. In something under ten minutes he was back.

'We've got a radio car at the scene,' he reported, 'and it's a body. I talked to the patrolcar officer myself. He says it's definitely homicide.'

'All right,' said the inspector, getting to his feet. 'Get Ludwig and meet me with the car at the front door.'

The sergeant looked mildly startled and made off down the corridor in the direction of the office of Dr Ludwig Strauss, the department's medical expert. He had not expected that the inspector would be going out personally on what seemed a more or less routine case.

There was, of course, no way that he could know that behind the dark, morose and haggard features of his superior, there lurked a spirit which could enjoy a fine autumn day as well as anyone else.

The police party was not long in arriving at the apartment

house at Buckelweg 4 which turned out to be a new, modern building five storeys high.

The building superintendent's quarters were on the ground floor next to the front entrance. Inside were Dr Gross, the locksmith, the patrolman from the Barmbek substation and the two officers from the patrolcar parked in front.

The inspector found this too much of a crowd and began by sending everyone with the exception of Dr Gross about his business.

'Once we've finished here, I'd like you to step down to the station with us and make a statement,' said the inspector. 'Do you know what happened here?'

'Not the faintest idea,' said Dr Gross. 'Kapfenberger didn't answer the door and there was this sign hanging on it so I got a locksmith and a policeman and came in. There was no one here and while we were looking through the apartment, the policeman found the blood on the wall. I didn't know. I thought it was ketchup.'

'Where?' said the inspector.

The apartment house owner silently led the way into the bedroom. A blanket had been nailed up to the plaster wall above the bed and one of the upper corners had been pulled loose so that it hung down, exposing an irregular, dark brown patch on the plaster.

'Blood all right,' commented the inspector who had seen enough of it to know.

He walked back out of the bedroom and across the kitchen to where a door opened into a small utility and laundry room. Dr Strauss and Sergeant Peters were engaged in trying to remove a blood-soaked sheet from what was obviously a corpse. They were having difficulty as the blood had dried, glueing the sheet to the body in many places.

'Why don't you cut it?' suggested the inspector. 'We can always put it back together again if it's necessary for the investigation.'

The doctor nodded briskly, got a scalpel out of his case and with a few deft cuts laid bare the body. It was that of a totally naked young woman with long black hair.

41

The sergeant stepped back out of the way and the doctor knelt beside the corpse and began his on-the-spot examination without which the corpse could not be moved to the morgue.

'Do you know this woman?' said Inspector Luders to Dr Gross who had turned very pale.

'Yes,' said Gross. 'It's my building superintendent's wife, Mrs Martha Kapfenberger.' He turned his head away from the corpse. 'Do you mind if I go in the other room? I'm not used to this.'

'Go into the living room,' said the inspector. 'I'll join you in a few minutes.'

He turned to the doctor who was going busily over the corpse.

'Well?' he said.

'Several blows over the head,' said the doctor. 'From the marks, a hammer. Minor skull fractures and a split scalp. That's where the blood came from. Cause of death was apparently manual strangulation while she was unconscious from the blows on the head.'

He bent the limbs, pressed his thumbs into the flesh of the thigh, lifted the corpse to check on the progression of the dark spots of blood which settle under the skin once circulation has ceased, turned back an eyelid and said, 'Seventy-two hours at least.'

'Uh-huh,' said the inspector. 'Anything else? Raped?'

'She seems to have engaged in intercourse shortly before death,' he said. 'No indication that it was forced.'

'All right,' said the inspector. 'Max, get on the radio and tell headquarters we want the corpse transporter and a squad from the lab. You take over here. I'm going to take Dr Gross back to the office and get his statement.'

'I'll come with you,' said Dr Strauss. 'There's nothing more I can do here and I've got some things I'll have to clear away before I can start the autopsy.'

All three men started out through the kitchen to the entrance hall, but came to a halt when Dr Gross suddenly rushed out of the living room.

'Oh my God!' he shouted. 'The poor child!'

'She wasn't a child,' snapped the inspector. 'She was a grown woman. Don't be so emotional.'

'Not her! Not her!' cried Gross in a state of great excitement. 'I just remembered the child. The Kapfenbergers have a little six-year-old daughter named Birgit. Where is she?'

The three investigators exchanged glances.

'All right,' said the inspector. 'Let's start looking.'

Fifteen minutes later they were all back in the entrance hall. The apartment was not large and there was no trace of a little girl in it.

The sergeant telephoned his instructions to headquarters from the police car and then went back to the apartment to wait while the inspector drove to headquarters with Dr Strauss and Dr Gross. Leaving the car standing in front of the building, he hustled the apartment house owner up the stairs to his office, sat him in the chair next to his desk, snapped on the tape recorder and said, 'Now, tell me what you know about this and quick. If the child's in the hands of a murderer, a few minutes could mean the difference between recovering her alive or dead.'

His manner was convincing and Gross began to speak so rapidly that he stumbled over his words.

'I have a number of apartment houses,' he said, 'and I have a building superintendent for each one. I only take men with families for the post and they must have good references because they collect the rents.'

'Whose references did you have for this one?' said the inspector.

'Mrs Inge Foerster,' said the doctor. 'She's a wealthy woman and prominent socially.'

'I know who Mrs Foerster is,' said the inspector. 'What is the man's name, age and so on?'

'Rudolf Kapfenberger,' said the doctor. 'Aged forty-five and an upholsterer by trade, if I remember rightly. The wife, the dead woman, was thirty-two I think. The little girl was six. I know that.'

He paused for an instant.

'I have the feeling that she wasn't Kapfenberger's child,' he said.

'You mean she was illegitimate?' said the inspector. 'How could you know that?'

'No, no, that wasn't what I meant,' said the doctor. 'I meant that I thought she may have been the child of a previous marriage. She didn't look very much like Mr Kapfenberger and she didn't seem that close to him, if you know what I mean.'

'I see,' said the inspector. 'You say that Kapfenberger collected the rents. When? On the first of the month?'

'That's right,' said the doctor. 'He was very conscientious about it and about everything else too for that matter.'

'When did you see him last?' said the inspector.

'On Sunday,' said Dr Gross. 'I was in South Africa for a month's vacation and I just came back on Saturday, so on Sunday I went around to all the apartment houses to see that everything was all right and to pick up the rents they'd collected on the first of October.'

'So you saw Kapfenberger on Sunday and picked up the rent,' said the inspector.

'No,' said Dr Gross. 'I saw Kapfenberger, but I didn't stop to pick up the rent money and go through the books because it was late and I was tired. I told him I'd be along the next day.'

'And?' said the inspector.

'I came the next morning and nobody answered the door and there was a sign hanging on it saying simply "Travelling" ', said the doctor. 'I didn't know what to make of it, but I thought maybe Kapfenberger had had a death in the family and had gone to the funeral. When he still wasn't there the next day, I got the locksmith and the policeman and went in.'

'Did you see Mrs Kapfenberger or the little girl on Sunday?' said the inspector.

'No,' said the doctor. 'I didn't go into the apartment. He invited me in, but I didn't go.'

'And you have no theory at all as to what may have happened?' said the inspector.

44

Dr Gross looked thoughtful.

'Well,' he said. 'There is a sort of precedent. Three years ago, one of my building superintendents in another building was hit over the head and robbed and it also happened while I was on vacation. The culprit was never caught.'

'What would your being on vacation have to do with it?' said the inspector.

'The superintendents have the money from the rents in their possession longer,' said the doctor. 'Normally, I would pick it up on the second or, at the latest, on the third of the month, but if I'm on vacation they may have to hold the money for several weeks. I suppose that someone might know about this and if they were successful the first time . . .'

'They might try it again,' said the inspector, completing his sentence. 'How much of your money would Kapfenberger have had on him?'

'One thousand, nine hundred and thirty-five marks,' said the doctor. 'I called the tenants yesterday. He hadn't collected from two and one was on vacation.'

'I thought you said he was very conscientious about the rent collecting,' said the inspector. 'Wouldn't it be better to handle all this through a bank?'

'Too many tricks,' said the doctor. 'The tenants claim they've transferred the money when they haven't or they send in incorrectly made-out cheques. Cash is better and if I have to employ a building superintendent anyway, he might as well collect. I can't imagine what went wrong with Kapfenberger. I've always had a very good impression of him. Charming person, really.'

'No doubt,' said the inspector dryly, 'but if the autopsy shows that Mrs Kapfenberger died before Sunday evening, then I'm afraid he's also a murderer. What time exactly was it that you saw him on Sunday?'

The doctor thought it over.

'Five-thirty,' he said finally. 'It was five-thirty or within a few minutes of it.'

'Close enough,' said the inspector. 'Our medical expert won't be able to fix the time much closer than an hour either way in any case.'

An hour either way, was, however, more than ample to establish Rudolf Kapfenberger as suspect number one in the murder of his wife, Martha.

Following the interview with Dr Gross, the inspector had called Dr Strauss at the morgue to advise him of the importance of determining the time of death and to ask for as speedy a report as possible.

The doctor called back at just before three in the afternoon.

'They only brought the body in a half hour ago,' he said apologetically. 'However, she was definitely not alive at five-thirty on Sunday.'

'I suspected that,' said the inspector. 'She was lying there dead in the apartment when Gross called. It could be that he's only alive because he found it too late to go in. Kapfenberger seems to be our man, but we've got a problem.'

'You don't know where he is,' said the doctor.

'Well, that too,' said the inspector, 'but the big problem is the child. Max has just come in from the apartment and the little girl's name is Polarek, not Kapfenberger. She's the daughter of the dead woman by a previous marriage. I'm afraid to put out a general alarm and pick-up order because I don't know what he might do to the child if he's pushed or cornered.'

'I see,' said the doctor. 'You're right, of course. The very fact that he took the girl with him would indicate that he intends to use her as a hostage or something like that. What are you going to do?'

'Sneak up on him quietly, if possible,' said the inspector. 'The only lead of any kind that we have is that Mrs Inge Foerster provided his references so maybe she'll know where he comes from or where he might be going. I've sent Max over to ask her.'

The inspector was still waiting in the office at six that evening when Sergeant Peters returned from his interview with Mrs Foerster.

The sergeant was wearing a very disgusted and discouraged expression on his normally cheerful face. Without a word, he went over to the coffee-making equipment behind the screen in the corner, made himself a large mug of strong, black coffee and returned to his desk.

'Well?' said the inspector impatiently.

'The little girl's probably dead,' said the sergeant.

'What makes you think so?' said the inspector.

'Aside from being Mrs Foerster's protegé, do you know who Mr Rudolf Kapfenberger is?' said the sergeant. He sounded bitter.

The inspector shook his head silently. It occurred to him that the sergeant was acting very strangely and he could not recall ever having seen him so emotionally involved in a case. He was aware, however, that the sergeant had a great many little brothers and sisters and that he was very fond of children.

'Mr Kapfenberger,' said the sergeant, 'is, or was, the lead tenor in the Celle church choir, the most promising pupil in his upholstery class, first violin in the Celle chamber music quartet and the godson of the District Attorney of Hannover.'

'Are you drunk, Max?' exclaimed the inspector in great astonishment. 'I know who the D.A. of Hannover is. He's younger than Kapfenberger. And besides, what the devil does this all have to do with the case?'

'I'm not drunk,' said the sergeant, 'but I'm going to be this evening. What famous institution is located at Celle?'

'The penetentiary,' said the inspector without hesitation. 'You mean . . .?'

The sergeant nodded. 'Life term for premeditated murder of his first wife,' he said. 'He was pardoned three years ago. While he was in prison, he was such a good boy that the D.A. offered to be his godfather when he got baptized for the first time and Mrs Foerster practically guaranteed his good behaviour to help get the pardon through. She is certain, she says, that he can become a useful member of society.'

'Useful in coping with the population explosion,' grunted the inspector. 'Did you tell her anything?'

47

'No,' said the sergeant. 'I said we wanted to give him the police medal for good behaviour. She believed it.'

'You know where he murdered his first wife?' said the inspector, reaching for the telephone.

'Hannover,' said the sergeant, 'on October 21, 1950.'

The inspector lifted the telephone and said into it, 'Communications? Luders. Get me the Hannover C.I.D. top priority. I want somebody with authority, even if you have to pull them away from their television set.'

'We could send somebody down to pick up his record,' said the sergeant as the inspector put down the telephone. 'Even if they mail it tonight, we won't get it until morning at best.'

'I'm not willing to wait that long,' said the inspector. 'I want them to read it to me over the telephone. Running around out there somewhere is a man who's killed two women and he's got a little girl with him. I want to know what offences he may have committed against children in the past and then I've got to make a decision. Either we come out in the open, order a nation-wide pick-up and alert, broadcast an appeal in the newspapers, radio and television and go after him with everything we've got or we lay low and try not to get him upset so that he'll harm the child.'

For nearly an hour the inspector and his assistant sat waiting in the office, drinking coffee and working on other cases in progress, of which there were quite a number. Finally, Communications called back. The officer in charge of the records at police headquarters in Hannover was on the line.

'You want me to read you this over the telephone?' he said incredulously. 'Have you got any idea of how long a record this bird has?'

'None,' said the inspector, 'but your District Attorney should. He's his godfather.'

'Ah well,' said the officer. 'He's a pretty progressive type. Does a lot of work on rehabilitation of criminals and so on. Wants to make useful members of society out of them.'

'This one needs a little more work,' said the inspector grimly. 'Start reading.'

Thereafter, he sat silently listening, the telephone propped up on one shoulder and his long, thin hand making small, precise notes on the block of lined paper in front of him. Occasionally, he said, 'Uh-uh' or gave a low whistle.

As the time continued to pass and the conversation showed no signs of ending, the sergeant laid down his own pencil and stared at the inspector in open astonishment.

It was a good twenty minutes before the inspector finally said, 'All right. Thanks a lot. Send us the works in the morning, will you?' and hung up. He had filled two pages of his pad with notes.

'Not a first offence, I take it?' said the sergeant cautiously.

'Well, no,' said the inspector. 'Not exactly. Here, I'll read you a short summary.' He read rapidly down the sheet of notes, ticking off certain items with his pencil as he went.

'Rudolf Kapfenberger, born October 20, 1929 in Chemnitz, now Karl-Marx-City in East Germany, illegitimate. Raised by his grandparents. According to the record, he could steal before he could walk. Stole from grandparents, aunts, uncles and, as he was able to get out and around more, anybody with whom he came in contact. He served three prison sentences before he was sixteen and, all told, has twenty-two convictions for theft, breaking and entering, burglary, robbery, armed robbery, assault and grievous bodily harm.'

'Dr Gross could hardly have picked a better man to collect his rents,' remarked the sergeant.

'Then,' continued the inspector, 'we have the little matter of the murder of the first Mrs Kapfenberger. According to the findings of the investigation, on October 21, 1950, Kapfenberger murdered Mrs Martha Kapfenberger, aged nineteen, by striking her over the head with a hammer and then strangling her to death.

'The naked body was found in the laundry room of their apartment and Kapfenberger had hung a "Gone travelling" sign on the door.

'Prior to his crime, he had embezzled the sum of one thousand four hundred and thirty-five marks from his

49

employers. However, this appeared to have nothing to do with the murder.'

'Well, what was the motive then?' said the sergeant. 'That case sounds almost identical to this one.'

'It is practically identical, assuming that Kapfenberger is the murderer,' said the inspector. 'Nobody knows what the motive was except the murderer because he never admitted to the crime, even after he was convicted.

'Mr Kapfenberger has another peculiarity. He never confesses or admits any knowledge of a crime even when he is arrested in the very act.'

'He sounds as crazy as a bat to me,' said the sergeant in bewilderment. 'He should never have been released.'

'That's what the court thought too when they sentenced him to life imprisonment,' said the inspector. 'It was with a recommendation that he be at no time in the future considered for parole or pardon. It was the opinion of the medical experts that he constituted a permanent danger to society.'

'Well then, why in the name of God did they pardon him?' demanded the sergeant in considerable indignation. 'And what about the little girl? Does he have a record of offences against children too?'

'God knows what offences he's guilty of,' said the inspector. 'The only ones known are where he was taken in the act or where the evidence was sufficient to convict him. In all his twenty-two convictions, he's never once admitted to committing so much as a misdemeanour. However, he's known to be a transvestite and he's been charged with molesting children although not convicted.'

'I just don't understand it,' said the sergeant. 'How could a man like that with twenty-two convictions, plus one for murder, have the district attorney for a godfather, enjoy the support of a prominent and wealthy woman, marry an attractive mother of a small child and obtain a well-paid position where he handled substantial amounts of other people's money?'

'It's in the record too,' said the inspector. 'According to Hannover, Kapfenberger has one of the most engaging personalities a man could have. He simply oozes goodness, decency and respectability. You know as well as I that criminals seldom look like the popular idea of a criminal. They're just ordinary people and sometimes they have attractive personalities. Being a criminal has nothing to do with it.

'Kapfenberger, it seems, has such a pleasant personality that he could have been a successful entertainer or a politician or in almost any profession that depends upon making a good impression with people. By chance, he's a born criminal, apparently lacking the ability to distinguish right from wrong.

'Or so says Hannover, at any rate. They knew that he was pardoned and they were expecting to hear from him again.'

'So what's your decision?' said the sergeant. 'Do we go all out after Kapfenberger or do we try to sneak up on him?'

The inspector leaned forward, rested his elbows on the top of the desk and cupped his forehead in his hands. For several minutes he sat quietly, his fingers pressing his temples.

Then he straightened up, leaned back in the chair and sighed.

'I can't decide,' he murmured. 'I hadn't expected anything like this. The man is completely unpredictable . . . if I'm wrong . . . Maybe I'm just tired. I don't want to have to make a decision that could cause a child's death.'

The sergeant fumbled with his papers.

'I wouldn't either,' he muttered. He got up and went over to the coffee pot. 'You want another cup of coffee?'

The inspector shook his head.

'Look at it this way,' said the sergeant, coming back to his desk with an empty coffee cup. 'He's had her since Sunday at least, so if he was going to do anything to her, he's probably done it by now. On the other hand, if he hasn't . . .'

'. . . we don't want to stir him up,' finished the inspector. 'Yes, that's probably the most logical approach. There's no possibility of moving in on him quickly. Hannover says he could be anywhere in Germany, that he's not particularly

51

attached to any one place. If we show our hand, he'll know we're after him and God knows what he'll do. Maybe he's crazy enough to believe that we don't suspect him.'

'Could we play on that?' said the sergeant. 'Plant a false story in the newspapers and the radio that we believe Kapfenberger and his daughter to have been kidnapped by robbers and that the kidnappers' identity was known?'

The inspector considered.

'It's a brilliant idea, Max,' he said finally. 'And I don't see what harm it could do, even if it doesn't work. However, there's not a great deal we could do with it yet tonight so let's sleep on it. We'll both have clearer heads in the morning.'

'Right, chief,' said the sergeant. 'Do you think I could borrow your notes there on Kapfenberger? I'd like to take a look at them before I go to sleep.'

The sergeant knew perfectly well that he was not going to sleep, or if he did, it would be poorly and not for long. In the Kapfenberger apartment that afternoon he had come across many pictures of little Birgit Polarek, a pretty little girl with big, dark eyes and a black fringe across her forehead.

The sergeant was, however, more tired than he realized and, lying down fully clothed on his bed after dinner, fell sound asleep and never awoke until half-past four in the morning.

He then got up, washed, shaved, changed his shirt and went back to the office where the inspector found him busily working when he came in at seven-thirty.

'You know,' said the sergeant, 'the coincidences and parallels in this thing are beyond belief. If Kapfenberger could have got the government to abolish the month of October, he could have been spared a lot of trouble and so would we.'

'Yes, I noticed that too,' said the inspector. 'Just about all the dates in his record are in October. I see you've been making up a chart.'

The sergeant nodded.

'Listen to this,' he said. 'Kapfenberger was born in

October 1929. He got his first conviction in October of 1942. He was married for the first time in October of 1949 and he killed his wife in October of the following year. One year later, again in October, he was sentenced to life imprisonment. In October of 1970 he was pardoned and in October 1971, he married the second Mrs Kapfenberger. Now it's October of 1973 and he's murdered her.'

The inspector dropped into the chair behind his desk.

'He must be aware of the significance of the month of October in his life,' he mused. 'There's a week yet to go in October. I wonder if that might mean that after the first of the month, the child would be safe?'

'I don't think so,' said the sergeant. 'He's had offences and convictions in other months too. It's just that October predominates.'

'Did you come to any other conclusions with the notes?' said the inspector. 'You weren't down here all night with them, were you?'

'No, no,' said the sergeant. 'I just came in a little early. The only other conclusion I reached was that the two murders were as identical as Kapfenberger could make them.

'Both women were knocked unconscious with a hammer while they were sleeping. Both were stripped naked and had had intercourse, presumably with him, shortly before their deaths. Both were strangled manually and wrapped in a sheet. Both were placed in the utility room and in both cases Kapfenberger hung a sign on the door saying "Gone travelling". Finally, in both cases, he had embezzled money just before the murders took place and, allowing for inflation, almost exactly the same amount. If I were to see this on television, I wouldn't believe it.'

'Nor would anyone else,' said the inspector. 'Well, I've made up my mind. We're going to try your plan first and, if that doesn't produce any results, we're going after him with everything. However, we're going to describe him precisely as the kidnap victim and maybe somebody will spot him and report.'

The plan was immediately put into effect and the first

newspaper and radio news reports carried descriptions of a robbery and kidnapping, during the course of which Mrs Kapfenberger had been murdered.

Whether Kapfenberger was taken in by the ruse or not could not be determined, for he simply ignored it. The descriptions, however, had an effect for two days later, but still in the month of October, Rudolf Kapfenberger was taken into custody by a patrolman in the Hamburg district of Wandbek, less than a half mile from the apartment house where he had murdered his wife.

Kapfenberger had been engaged in one of his favourite pursuits. He had been trying to steal a suitcase from a leather goods store and had been detected by the store owner who had called the patrolman on duty in the block.

Kapfenberger, who was alone at the time of his arrest, was recognized by the patrolman as the supposed kidnap victim and brought to police headquarters where he denied that he had attempted to steal the suitcase or that he knew anything about the murder of his wife.

'Impossible!' he protested. 'I saw her this morning and she was alive and well!'

The inspector had expected no more. Kapfenberger had never admitted to anything in his life and he was not going to now. It was not this which troubled him, but rather the fate of little Birgit Polarek. The mere fact that she had not been with Kapfenberger at the time of his arrest was ominous.

There was, however, still the slim hope she was merely sitting in a room somewhere. Kapfenberger had obviously been staying somewhere since leaving the apartment house at 4 Buckelweg. Perhaps the child was there.

Kapfenberger was, as might have been expected, not cooperative. In reply to the question as to where he had been for the past five days, he stated that he had been living with his wife, Martha, at 4 Buckelweg where he was the building superintendent.

He said this with such obvious sincerity and open honesty that even the inspector and the sergeant, who knew with certainty that this was not true, could hardly believe that he was deliberately lying.

'I wonder if he knows it himself,' said the inspector uncertainly. 'I've questioned thousands of suspects and i'd swear that this man is telling the truth.'

'But we know for a fact that he isn't,' said the sergeant. 'It's an indication of how he came to have such influential friends and how he came to be pardoned. He's the most convincing liar I've ever seen.'

'I'm going to ask him direct,' decided the inspector. 'The man can't be all bad. Maybe if I appeal to his better nature, he'll tell us where Birgit is.'

A few moments later, he straddled the chair in front of Rudolf Kapfenberger and, in as friendly a voice as he could manage, said, 'Mr Kapfenberger. I want you to answer me just one question and then, I promise you, you won't be questioned any more. In the name of all the many people who had so much faith in you and who thought that you were basically a good man, where is the little girl?'

Rudolf Kapfenberger gave him a warm, loving smile.

'What little girl?' he said.

The inspector got wearily up from the chair and without another word went back to the office where the sergeant was waiting.

'Better notify the Water Police and the Forestry Department,' he said. 'The body could be in the Elbe or maybe out in the woods somewhere. Tell the Park Service to keep an eye out too. A little corpse like that could be hidden anywhere.'

The sergeant nodded sadly.

'Right,' he said. 'By the way, Mrs Kapfenberger's sister, a Mrs Emma Fiedler, is coming in. She wants to talk to you about swearing out a charge against the person or persons responsible for Kapfenberger's release from prison. She says her sister knew nothing about his record.'

'She's wasting her time,' said the inspector, 'but I'll talk to her. When is she due?'

'Any time now,' said the sergeant. 'I'll go see if she's in the waiting room.'

55

He left the office and a moment later there came a sort of a mingled yell, yelp and shout from the direction of the waiting room.

The inspector recognized it as his assistant's voice and ran down the corridor, drawing his service pistol as he reached the waiting room door.

Inside, he was greeted by a strange spectacle.

A dark-haired woman was sitting on the bench staring at the sergeant, who was doing a sort of jig in the middle of the floor, with astonished, somewhat alarmed eyes. Sitting beside her was a little girl with a black fringe and big, black eyes. She was regarding the sergeant with obvious amusement.

'Wait, Max!' shouted the inspector, who had also seen pictures of Birgit Polarek. 'It could be her cousin.'

But it was not. The little girl was none other than Birgit Polarek.

'That Kapfenberger brought her over to me on Saturday morning,' said Mrs Fiedler. 'He said they were going on a little trip. If I'd only guessed what kind of a trip he was going to send poor Martha on . . . Well, anyway, I was so upset when I heard about her death that it didn't occur to me that anybody would be looking for Birgit. I thought you probably knew she was with me. I'm sorry if I caused any trouble, but I didn't read the newspaper accounts of the murder. I couldn't bear to.'

'It doesn't matter, Mrs Fiedler,' said the inspector. 'The main thing is, the child is safe. Kapfenberger apparently brought her to you before carrying out his murder so maybe in a backhanded sort of way he isn't all bad after all.'

The court disagreed. In their opinion, as in the opinion of the Hannover court twenty-three years earlier, Rudolf Kapfenberger was a menace to the general public. He was once again sentenced to life imprisonment with the recommendation that he not be considered for parole or pardon.

The date was, of course, October 21, 1974.

4

THE FUTURE BELONGS TO YOUTH

The waters of Shoreham habour are cold in winter and, if not particularly deep, quite deep enough for drowning even a tall young man.

Late at night on the last day of February 1973, they were also dark and covered with little wavelets running beneath the chill wind blowing in off the Channel.

The little waves slapped mischievously at the gasping mouth of the helpless boy as he bobbed desperately up and down, arching his body in a hopeless attempt to remain afloat.

But only magicians can swim when they are tied securely hand and foot and, perhaps, not even they with a great sack of stones and concrete blocks attached to their feet.

Relentlessly, the weight drew him down until the water closed over his head and still he fought, holding his breath in the hope of some miracle. Death at sixteen is not easy.

In the end, however, the air went out with a whoosh and the salt water rushed in, stinging, suffocating. Bright stars exploded in the dark water before his eyes. There was a great humming sound and all the lights went out.

Standing upright, its motorcycle booted feet pressed to the muddy bottom by the weight of the stones lashed to them, the corpse swayed gently and peacefully in the pull of the outgoing tide.

'Cor!' said the heavy-set young man standing on the pier. 'Did you see the way his eyes glared?'

'Didn't mind that so much as the bubbles,' said his companion with a shudder. 'If you ask me, you've gone too far.'

The corpse on the bottom of Shoreham Harbour did not

go far. It did not go any place at all, but remained where it was, held down by the rocks and nibbled by fish and crabs. Because of the cold water, it did not disintegrate or decompose rapidly and the features were still quite recognizable on April 20, over a month later.

Not of course that they would be recognized by any of the persons involved in the finding of the corpse, because they had never seen the young man while he was alive.

They were not very happy to see him after he was dead either.

'Bloody 'ell!' bawled the mate of the small coastal steamer. 'The flippin' screw's fouled on something!'

The observation, as might be expected from a professional seaman, was quite correct. The screw of the ship was fouled on something, a rope from the looks of it.

Being still in harbour, help was close at hand and presently a small boat rowed out and circled the stern of the ship and a frogman tumbled over the side to follow the rope tangled around the screw down into the depths.

A moment later he came arrowing back up, caught hold of the gunwale of the rowboat, spat out his mouthpiece and gasped, 'Jesus! There's a corpse down there! Call the police!'

The police were called and the body of the young man was brought up from the bottom of the harbour and laid out on the quay. He was a tall young man, a touch over six feet, and he had been rather handsome in the modern manner with long, thick, dark hair reaching to below his shoulders. He was dressed in blue jeans, a blue denim jacket and motorcycle boots.

He had been very firmly tied hand and foot with a length of three-quarter-inch manilla rope, and a plastic bag filled with stones and cement blocks was attached to his feet.

Detective Chief Superintendent James Marshall, Head of the Sussex Department of Criminal Investigations, had been notified and he soon arrived at the scene, bringing with him Police Pathologist Mr Hugh Malseworth Johnson who examined the body and stated that the cause of death appeared to be drowning, but that the body had been in the water for at least a month and it would be necessary to perform the autopsy before any other conclusions were reached.

Chief Superintendent Marshall had, however, already reached one conclusion and that was that this was a murder and a particularly savage and cold-blooded one. It was one thing to murder a man and toss his corpse into the sea, but it was quite another to weight a man down and throw him into the sea to drown. It was the sort of thing that people had once done to unwanted dogs and cats, but it wasn't even done to animals any more.

'I don't suppose you'd care to venture an opinion on whether he was conscious at the time?' he said.

Mr Johnson did not care to venture an opinion.

'I'll have more to say after the autopsy,' he said firmly. 'Only after the autopsy.'

Before having the body removed to the morgue for the autopsy, however, the superintendent had it photographed where it lay. It was not in very good shape and, being deprived of the refrigerating influence of the cold water, it appeared likely to break down rather rapidly. The photographs might well be the only hope of establishing its identity.

Identification was, of course, the first step in the investigation, for the identity of a murder victim often leads to the identification of the murderer. Few males are murdered by total strangers and a stranger would scarcely have gone to so much trouble to dispose of the corpse. Moreover, the cruel manner in which the young man had been killed tended to indicate a murderer with intense emotional motives rather than something impersonal such as robbery.

However, even with the photographs it was possible that identification would be difficult. The victim was young. His dress and hairstyle were trendy. Many such young men lived in a casual manner and without regular employment. What relatives they had might see them so infrequently that they would not even realize they were missing. The superintendent was not at all confident that he would find a corresponding Missing Person report in the files.

Nonetheless, there was one and it matched precisely the

description of the dead youth. It had been filed on March 2, 1973, by a Mrs Pauline Olive in the town of Hove, a scant four miles to the east along the coast.

The corpse was made as presentable as possible and Mrs Olive was brought to the morgue to view it. She immediately and tearfully identified it as the body of her son Clive Olive who had been sixteen years old at the time of his death.

According to her statement, Clive had left school at the age of fifteen and had attempted to enlist in the Navy. He had been refused because of a defect in his vision and had, for a time, done nothing in particular, spending his time hanging around the coffee bars in Brighton, Hove and Shoreham. The week before his disappearance on February 28 he had, however, obtained work in a bakery and had begun to talk about going back to school. This had pleased his mother, who described him as a good boy, but still not certain of what he wanted. She had last seen him on the afternoon of February 28 when he had left the house saying, 'Goodbye Mum. I'll see you later.'

Superintendent Marshall now sent his agents to check out the coffee bars in the three towns and also to check the bakery where Olive had worked.

The bakery provided no information as he had worked there for such a short time that he was hardly known and it was unlikely that anyone would have had such strong feelings about him as to murder him.

In the coffee bars, however, the officers began to pick up possible leads. A boy identified only as 'Ted' told the detectives that he had known Olive well, but had not seen him since the night of February 28 when he had been in a coffee bar in Church Road in Hove. He added that Olive, who was usually called Ollie, Clive or, inexplicably, Paul, had seemed worried and had muttered something about somebody who was going to beat him up.

Asked if he had any idea why someone would want to beat up Clive Olive, Ted replied that it might have been over a woman. Olive, he said, had not been able to keep quiet about any success he had with girls. If he had intercourse with a girl, he told everyone about it, naming

60

names, describing how the girl looked naked, how she had
made love and what she had said before, during and after.
He thought that this habit might have made Olive unpopular
in some quarters.

This appeared, to say the least, logical and the police
found confirmation of the theory when, as the investigation
continued, reports of such indiscretions on the part of Olive
in connection with a girl named Doris began to surface.

At the same time, so did other facts. Clive Olive had, it
seemed, not been quite as good a boy as his mother had
believed him to be. He had been a small-time drugs dealer
and, although apparently not addicted himself, had had the
reputation of being able to obtain virtually anything for a
price.

It also developed that he had been associated in one way
or another with an informal youth organization known as
the Hell's Angels Cougars or, alternatively, the Mad Dogs
of Sussex.

The exact nature of the association was not entirely clear,
but it was known that the Hell's Angels Cougars were
motorcycle enthusiasts and the clothing and boots worn by
Olive at the time of his death were similar to those favoured
by the members of such groups.

In addition, a tattoo of the letters H.A.C. had been found
on his right arm at the time of the autopsy and this was
thought to represent the initial letters of the club known as
the Hell's Angels Cougars.

Aside from the tattoo, the only important facts revealed
by the autopsy were that Olive had definitely died of
drowning, that the body had been in the water for over a
month, presumably since the date of his disappearance on
February 28, and that he had been savagely kicked and
beaten not only with bare fists but with something resembling a policeman's club as well. There were cuts on his
arms from the rope and Mr Johnson was of the opinion that
he had been alive and conscious when thrown into the water.

Attempts were made to trace the rope and the plastic sack
containing cement blocks and stones and it would eventually
be learned that these had been taken from a building site

and the demolition yard in Shoreham. In the meantime, however, they only tended to confirm the theory that Olive had been murdered by more than one person. In any case, it was almost certain that more than one person had taken part in disposing of the body as the weight would have been too much for even a very strong man.

The lead in connection with the girl named Doris proved more fruitful. A number of persons reported that Olive had boasted extensively of his sexual experiences with Doris and there had been gossip that a girl known as 'Butch' was angry over this as the girl in question was her brother's fiancée.

'Butch' was eventually traced and turned out to be eighteen-year-old Christine Dorn, born Christine Moore and married to twenty-seven-year-old Albert Edward Dorn. The brother who was supposedly engaged to Doris was twenty-one-year-old Brian Stephen Moore. Moore, his sister and Albert Dorn were all connected in one way or another to the Hell's Angels Cougars, but there was no evidence that any of them had known Clive Olive.

All of the leads were beginning to converge on the Hell's Angels Cougars and the police took into custody a number of the members of that group including Brian Moore and Christine and Albert Dorn.

Interrogation of the suspects produced the information that Moore had been on intimate terms with the girl known as Doris, but that at the time of the supposed affair with Olive, he had been absent picking fruit in Kent. Upon his return, he had gone around asking for information on Clive Olive and, in some cases, had paid for it.

There were reports that Moore had been extremely upset about what he termed the rape of his girl by Clive Olive and that he had threatened to 'get him'. This version of the affair was confirmed by Doris herself who stated that she had been a virgin up until the time that she was raped by Olive.

The motive for the murder was now established and the members of the Hell's Angels Cougars who had been taken into custody were released with the exception of Moore and the Dorns. Questioned individually, they eventually broke down and confessed to varying degrees of complicity in the murder.

Moore, in his statement, said that he had gone to Kent on a fruit-picking job and that, upon his return, he had asked his girl Doris if she still had her 'white wings'. This it seemed was a term meaning virginity.

Doris had replied that she had been raped, but, apparently, had not known the identity of the rapist and Moore had spent some forty pounds in an effort to learn who the man had been.

He could not, he said, forget the incident because it had given Doris complexes which interfered with their sex relations.

He accepted all responsibility for the murder and denied that his sister or Albert Dorn had had any part in it.

This agreed neither with the known facts nor with the statements of Mr and Mrs Dorn themselves and all three were brought to trial at Lewes Crown Court on November 27, 1973 with Mr Justice Thesiger presiding.

Mr Michael Eastham, acting as Prosecutor for the Crown, presented the case for the prosecution.

'The prosecution,' he said, 'will attempt to show that the defendant Moore was obsessed with the belief that his girl had been raped by the victim which is not to say that the defendant is a person of high moral character. Indeed, we propose to demonstrate quite the opposite.

'In his statement to the police he has said that he gave up his job to be with Doris and they had decided to become engaged, but he had felt that something was troubling her and he thought that this might be a former boyfriend of whom he had been told by a certain 'Dopey Joe'.

'He had, consequently, asked Doris directly if she had ever had intercourse with another man and she had replied that she had been raped.

'Having determined the identity of the alleged rapist, Moore resolved to "get" Olive or, at least, give him a beating.

'Still in his statement to the police, he said that on the day of the murder, February the twenty-eighth, nineteen hundred and seventy-three, he and the other two defendants took weights and a plastic sack from a construction site and a rope from a demolition yard. These objects were loaded into the Volkswagen van which belonged to Albert Dorn and they were later found by the police attached to the corpse of the victim.

'In his own words to the police, he said, "I thought I might lose my temper and kill Olive and I would then have to get rid of the body. The idea of attaching weights to it and throwing it in the sea came from the Mad Dogs who planned, at one time, to get rid of one of their leaders in this manner."

'He further stated that he punched Olive in the face and hit him with a truncheon which he had obtained while working as a guard. These actions took place in the back of the van driven by Albert Dorn with Mrs Dorn occupying the front seat next to him.

'Olive was crying and screaming and Dorn panicked, driving around Shoreham in an aimless manner, and Mrs Dorn became ill.

'Finally, Olive lost consciousness and Moore thought that he was dead. He tied him up with the rope, attached the sack of weights to his feet and Dorn drove to the waterfront.

'Moore took Olive's shoulders and Dorn carried the plastic sack of weights attached to his feet. When they reached the water, Dorn threw in the sack of weights and Moore simply let go of Olive's shoulders so that he was dragged in after it.

'Clive Olive was, however, still alive and conscious at this point for Moore says in his statement, "His eyes were open. Al said, 'Look, he's bobbing up and down.' It was the staring eyes that bothered me, but Al thought that the bubbles afterward were worse." '

The prosecutor was followed by Mr Johnson who testified concerning his examination of the corpse and outlined his reasons for believing that Olive had still been alive and conscious at the time he was thrown into the sea.

He was followed by Superintendent Marshall who

described the investigations which had led to the arrest and, subsequently, the confessions of the accused.

The defence, represented by Mr Felix Waley Q.C., then called as first witness the accused Brian Moore.

Questioned on his connections with the Mad Dogs of Sussex, Moore stated that he had joined the group in 1969, the same year that he had begun taking drugs. He had tried LSD, amphetamines, barbiturates, hashish and marijuana. He said that he had done this because he had broken off his relations with a girl and was feeling depressed.

Although this was not brought out during the trial, there were later published accounts that Moore had, at the time in question, attempted to commit suicide by entering a cage containing two leopards at a wild animal park where he was engaged as a trainer. The leopards had, apparently, not been hungry.

Asked if he were still taking drugs, Moore replied that he was not. He had, he said, met the girl named Doris and had found that he did not need drugs after that.

'Were you at any time separated from Doris?' asked the attorney for the defence.

'Yes,' said Moore. 'I went to Kent to pick fruit.'

'And what took place upon your return?' said Mr Waley.

'I went to see Doris and the first thing I asked her was if she still had her white wings,' said Moore. 'She said she had been raped.

'We talked about this a lot and I knew she was telling the truth. I was furious and I wanted to kill whoever had done it because I loved her with all my heart and whatever happens I always will.

'Later, I spent about forty pounds trying to find out who had raped my girl and I was finally given the name of Clive Olive.'

'How did Doris convince you that she had really been raped?' asked Mr Waley.

'We went to the hotel where it happened and took the same room,' said Moore. 'When we entered the room, she was able to convince me. I burned my Hell's Angels jacket and she burned the clothes she had been wearing.'

65

'What did you decide to do about Olive?' said Mr Waley.

'I decided to kill him.'

'How did you arrange that?'

'I met him on the night of February the twenty-seventh and we talked about drugs. I arranged to meet him on the following night.'

'Will you tell the court, in your own words, what happened that night of February twenty-eighth when you met Clive Olive?' said Mr Waley. 'Take as much time as you need.'

'My sister, Christine, and her husband, Albert Dorn, were with me,' said Moore. 'Al was driving the van and Christine was in the front seat with him.'

Moore paused and looked almost questioningly at the other two defendants. After a moment, he continued.

'Olive was in the back with me and I asked him if he knew a girl named Doris. He said no and I asked him again. He still said no and I said, "The one you raped, you bastard!" He still said he didn't know her and then he admitted that he had raped her.

'I was boiling with rage, furious. He struck out at me and I caught it on my left and hit him with my right. It slammed him up against the side of the van.

'We'd been parked, but when I hit him, Al got nervous and started to drive around. I was fighting with Olive in the back and I thought I'd killed him.'

'With your bare fists?' asked Mr Waley.

'I kicked him and hit him with a truncheon on the head, the hands, the body, any place. I was berserk. I thought I'd killed him.'

'Why did you think that?' asked Mr Waley.

'His eyes were staring and, when I took his pulse behind the knee like I'd been taught with animals, I couldn't find any.'

'You have heard the testimony of the pathologist that Clive Olive was alive and conscious at the time he entered the water,' said Mr Waley. 'What is your reaction?'

'I am shocked,' said Moore. 'I truly thought he was dead.'

'Continue with your account,' said Mr Waley. 'What happened then?'

'I told Al to drive to the harbour,' said Moore. 'I was angry because I hadn't found out what I wanted to know and the only person who could tell me was dead.

'I tied up his hands and feet and I fastened the sack of stones and blocks to his legs. Al backed the van up to the water and I dropped him in and kicked the sack of weights in after him.'

'Didn't you realize what you were doing was wrong?' said Mr Waley.

'I don't feel I have done anything wrong,' said Moore. 'I knew it was against the law, but what he did was against the law too. He raped my girl. Nobody else was going to do anything about that so I had to.'

The counsel for the defence terminated the questioning and moved that the charge be altered from murder to manslaughter on the grounds that the drugs taken by the accused had damaged his brain.

The cross examination was taken up by the prosecutor who wanted to know why he had felt it his duty to kill Olive.

Moore replied that it was so he would not rape any more girls.

The prosecutor then suggested that Moore had not committed the murder by himself, but had been assisted by his sister and brother-in-law.

Moore denied this, saying that Christine had had nothing to do with the murder and that Albert Dorn had only driven the van.

'You say,' said the prosecutor, 'that your motive for killing this boy was that he had sexual relations with your girl. Does this mean that you never had relations with her yourself?'

'No,' said Moore. 'It doesn't mean that. Doris and I made love but, because of what Olive had done, it was spoiled.'

Asked to explain, he said that, on one occasion, they had got into the same position in which Doris had been raped and that this had upset her very much so that everything was spoiled.

Questioned further about their relations, he said that they had taken no precautions as both he and Doris wanted a baby. He was opposed to the anti-baby pill as he had heard that it could produce deformities in the children later. Doris had taken the Pill in order to reassure her mother, but she had kept it under her tongue and had spit it out afterwards. She had, however, not become pregnant.

'Was Doris happy about what you had done to Olive?' said Mr Eastham.

'I don't know,' said Moore. 'We often talked about suicide. If the police got too close, we were going to jump off the cliffs at Peacehaven.'

'You have told this court that you have stopped using drugs,' said the prosecutor, 'but is it not true that you still use them?'

'You shut your mouth or I'll belt you one, mate!' shouted Moore and, seizing a water bottle which was standing on the witness stand, he swung it up over his head.

Two prison officers sitting in the dock rushed forward and, after a brief struggle, Moore was overpowered and disarmed. The trial then continued.

The next witness called by the defence was Dr Arthur Williams, a psychiatrist, who stated that he had spoken with Moore on the subject of his use of drugs and that he was satisfied that his statements concerning the use of LSD and other drugs were essentially correct.

Mr Waley asked if the use of such drugs could bring about abnormalities in the personality.

'My conclusions concerning Brian Moore,' said Dr Williams, 'were that he displayed an obsessional, paranoid and somewhat psychotic personality. It would appear that he suffers from certain mental abnormalities which would have an effect on his actions. This condition may have been aggravated by the use of LSD. I think that his concept of reality has been altered through use of the drug and he may experience difficulty in distinguishing between reality and fantasy.'

'Was he insane to the point where he did not realize that

what he was doing was wrong?' interposed Mr Justice Thesiger.

'In my opinion, he was sane,' said Dr Williams. 'He knew what he was doing was wrong, but he was unable to control himself. The impulse was irresistible. He could not overcome his grievance which became worse and worse until he reached a state where, I think, it was either kill Olive or commit suicide.'

The psychiatrist was then cross-examined by the prosecution who wanted to know if, in his opinion, Moore's conduct prior to the murder was such as to warrant his detention in a mental institution.

Dr Williams replied that, had Moore been his patient, he would have attempted to have him committed.

Dr Williams was followed by another psychiatrist, Dr Peter Noble, who testified concerning his interviews with Moore's parents. He had, he said, been a timid child and easily bullied.

'Moore does not seem to have been a very good Hell's Angel,' he concluded. 'He was always on the fringe. His character was made up of two opposing forces, the tough Hell's Angel on the one hand, and a man with a great love for animals on the other.'

Albert Dorn was then called to the witness stand and gave the following account of the events leading up to the death of Clive Olive.

'Brian was convinced that Olive had raped his girl,' he said. 'I was driving and they were in the back of the van. I could hear Brian say, "I'm going to give you a good hiding for what you did," and then he started hitting him.

'The boy was screaming and Christine started to cry. I didn't know what to do so I drove along the waterfront. I thought the traffic might make Brian stop.

'However, it didn't make any difference and, when I looked in the back, Brian had tied him up and fastened the sack of weights to his feet. He told me to drive to the harbour.

'I backed the van up and Brian carried him down and

threw him in. I thought he was dead. There were no screams or anything. Just a lot of bubbles.

'I told Brian, "I think you have gone too far." '

Mr Eastham took up the cross-examination of the defendant.

'Is it not correct,' he said, 'that your wife, Christine, was seated in the van during the time that all this was taking place?'

Dorn replied that she was, but, upon being asked if she knew what was happening, he replied that he did not know.

He was then asked if Mrs Dorn had seen the weights and rope being put into the van and replied in the affirmative. He also admitted that his wife had been the first person to speak to Olive on the night in question.

'I suggest,' said Mr Eastham, 'that your wife, the third defendant in this case, played an important part in the crime. I suggest that she was the bait with which the victim was lured to his death.'

'That is not true,' protested Dorn. 'She was only in the van because she did not want to be left alone.'

The summing up began on December 4, 1973 and the defence based its case on a supposed temporary or permanent drug-induced mental incompetence of the chief defendant, Brian Moore.

'The murder of this sixteen-year-old boy,' said Mr Waley, 'was performed in a manner displaying all the earmarks of a madman. It was a crime which arose from an insane obsession haunting a deranged mind and it was carried out with the ruthless cunning and remorseless cruelty of a maniac for a reason which could exist only in insanity.

'I ask you to find the defendant, Brian Moore, not guilty of murder by reason of diminished responsibility, but guilty of manslaughter instead.'

The plea was not successful. After six and a half hours of deliberations, the all-male jury found Brian Moore and Albert Dorn guilty of murder and Christine Dorn guilty of manslaughter.

While sentencing the two men to life imprisonment, Mr Justice Thesiger said that he was convinced that no one had minded in the least whether Clive Olive was alive or dead at the time that he was thrown into Shoreham harbour. The case was, he added, that of a most horrible murder.

He then turned his attention to Christine Dorn who had, four months previously, given birth to a child while in detention awaiting trial.

'I feel,' he said, 'that you are deeply implicated in this crime and that you were instrumental in luring the victim. I am certain that you exercised a comparatively strong influence on the other two defendants.

'I hereby sentence you to ten years' imprisonment.'

Christine Dorn responded by fainting dead away and it was some time before she could be revived and led back to the cells. As she left the court room, she turned and screamed, 'You bastard!' at the judge.

In order to avoid embarrassment to an innocent person, the name of Brian Moore's girlfriend has been altered.

5

FROZEN STIFF

It was three o'clock in the morning of New Year's Day, 1971 and Werner Schmidt was driving home to Bensburg with Mrs Schmidt sound asleep beside him in the front seat. Like all good Germans, the Schmidts had celebrated the New Year thoroughly and with enthusiasm.

It was for this reason that Werner was driving the big Mercedes rather cautiously over the snow-covered country road running from Hennef, where the celebrating had taken place, to Much, where another secondary road led off to the north-west and Bensburg.

The way was round about and the roads were not particularly good, but the fast, direct autobahn which led north from Siegburg to pass between Cologne and Bensburg might be dangerous, firstly because of the drunks who would be driving on it and secondly because of the traffic police.

Werner Schmidt suspected that he had taken on enough alcohol to cost him his driver's licence if he were to be picked up now.

His choice of route had, however, been fortunate. There had not been a single other car on the road since leaving Hennef.

The car rolled smoothly through the village of Neunkirchen in which not a light burned. The next village, he knew, would be Wohlfahrt and then, Much.

It was a dark night. There was no moon and the stars glittered like the tips of icicles against the blackness of the sky. A bitterly cold wind swept occasional eddies of snow across the macadam. The temperature was five degrees above zero. Inside the car, however, it was warm and cosy and Werner Schmidt was troubled by drowsiness.

He had just stretched out a hand to turn down the heating when the headlights picked up the figure beside the road. Schmidt's drowsiness vanished and was replaced by astonishment. For an instant, his foot lifted from the gas pedal and the Mercedes slowed.

Then, the foot descended again and the big car surged forward.

'Elsie!' called Schmidt, prodding his sleeping wife in the ribs with an elbow. 'Did you see that?'

'I don't see anything,' grumbled Mrs Schmidt, reluctantly half-opening a bleary eye.

'A man,' said Schmidt. 'A naked man. Standing beside the road and jumping up and down as if he was crazy.'

'Probably is too,' said Mrs Schmidt. 'Bunch of drunken kids. Keep your eyes on the road.' With which she promptly fell asleep again.

Behind the car in the flurry of fine snow thrown up by its passing, the strange figure stood motionless now, the high wail of its voice dying despairingly away. Tears were running from its eyes and freezing onto its cheeks.

The point was almost exactly half way between Neunkirchen and Wohlfahrt. There would not be another car until five in the morning.

The car which passed then was travelling south from Wohlfahrt in the direction of Siegburg where Hans-Dieter Mueller would be going to work on the early morning shift of a steel mill which cared nothing about New Year's Day or any other holiday.

The figure was not hopping now, but lay stretched in the snow beside the road.

Mueller saw it, but he did not stop. The place was lonely, it was still completely dark and he feared some kind of a trap. Such things are not unknown in Europe.

He did, however, do more than Werner Schmidt had done. He turned the car around and drove back to Wohlfahrt where he roused the local constable out of bed and reported the matter.

'Why the devil didn't you stop and help him?' demanded

Constable Gunther Weber. 'I could charge you with failing to assist a person in danger.'

'I didn't think it was safe,' said Mueller. 'I have to go to work.'

He left and Weber quickly dressed and set out in the police car for the place indicated. At five-thirty-four, as would be stated in his official report, he came upon the body of a young man lying beside the road.

The man was wearing only undershorts and his feet were bound together with baling wire. The body was cold and rigid and he was dead.

The discovery left Weber in something of a quandary. In Germany, village constables do not handle murder cases and this was, in his opinion, murder. He could think of no other explanation.

It was therefore essential that the Criminal Police in Cologne be advised immediately and equally essential that nothing at the scene of the crime be disturbed until they had arrived.

Although his car was equipped with a radio-telephone, there was no one in Wohlfahrt to answer it at this hour and he was not equipped to raise Cologne direct.

However, if he drove into Neunkirchen or Wohlfahrt to telephone, someone could very well come by and move the body in a well-intended attempt to help or by trampling around in the snow destroy important clues.

Someone, it seemed, had already been there for there were footprints in the snow leading from the edge of the road to the body. Mueller had, however, stated that he had not got out of his car.

He was standing pondering this problem when, to his astonishment, a police car appeared from the direction of Neunkirchen and came to a halt beside his own.

Three men in plain clothes got out and advanced on the constable.

'Inspector Karl Josef, Cologne Criminal Police,' said one of the men. 'We have a report of a possible homicide here.'

'Constable Weber, Wohlfahrt,' said the constable, slightly confused. 'Is your report from a Hans-Dieter Mueller?'

74

The inspector shook his head. 'An Adolf Meindorf,' he said. 'He's the bus driver on the Much–Hennef line. He and one of his passengers discovered the body and called us from Neunkirchen.'

'That explains the footprints,' said Weber. 'The driver who reported to me didn't get out of his car.'

While they had been speaking, the other two men from the Cologne police car had gone over to where the body lay and one of them had begun an examination of the corpse.

The inspector walked over to join them.

'Well, Armin?' he said.

Dr Armin Baumgartner, the department's medical expert, got a little heavily to his feet and began brushing the snow from his trousers.

'Homicide,' he said briefly. 'Murder by freezing. He's been beaten, but the cause of death is freezing. He's been dead for several hours now.'

The second man had been examining the marks in the snow.

'There's a trail here leading into the trees, chief,' he said, pointing to the open forest which began some ten yards from the road.

'See where it leads to, Franz,' said the inspector. 'If it goes on for a long way, come back and we'll get a party with dogs out here.'

The trail did not go very far.

'He was tied to a tree about two hundred yards from the road,' called the sergeant, coming back to the edge of the forest. 'Do you want to come and take a look?'

The inspector, the doctor and Constable Weber all went to look, walking carefully in the footprints left by Sergeant Moench.

'See?' said the sergeant. 'There's the tree he was tied to and there are some of the pieces of baling wire he was tied up with. He was apparently able to get loose from the tree and get the wire off his hands, but by then his hands were too cold to get the wire off his feet so he hopped to the road.'

'He was probably exposed here for some time before he could get free,' said the doctor, studying the hop marks in the snow. 'You can see how his strength was failing. The further he went the shorter the hops and there are several places here where he fell.'

'It's a wonder he even made it to the road,' said the sergeant. 'The temperature couldn't have been much above zero out here last night. And then he had the rotten luck that not a single car came along until it was too late. A strange sort of murder, isn't it chief?'

'A cruel murder,' said the inspector. 'The cruellest murder I have ever experienced or even heard of in all my time with the police. It should be easy to solve.'

The sergeant looked at him in astonishment. 'Why do you say that?' he asked.

'A man could not have more than one enemy who hated him so bitterly,' said the inspector simply. 'Once we have the identity of the victim, I think the identity of the murderer will be obvious.'

In this, however, he was gravely mistaken.

The identity of the victim was established easily enough. He was an electrician named Ulrich Nacken who had not come home on New Year's morning and had been promptly reported missing by his parents who feared an automobile accident.

Nacken, who came from Cologne, had just bought his first car in December. He was only eighteen years old.

'Well, so much for theories,' sighed the inspector. 'A boy of eighteen has hardly lived long enough to acquire such deadly enemies. I don't know what to think.'

'The murder was almost professional,' said the sergeant. 'We went over the whole area thoroughly, screened the snow around the tree. Not a thing. No trace of his clothing. No trace of the car.'

'You put out a description of the car to the highway patrol?' said the inspector.

The sergeant nodded. 'Nineteen sixty-six Ford, seventeen-M,' he said. 'Medium grey with a black rose painted on the trunk. The licence number is K-HM 943. Not a valuable car and Nacken didn't have much money on him either, according to the parents. He spent it all on the car.'

'A sad thing,' remarked the inspector. 'I talked to the parents and the picture I got was of a clean, serious, hard-working boy, not one to be mixed up with a tough crowd of any kind. Of course, that's the parents' version so it might be a little on the favourable side. I've got a list of his friends that I want you to check out. See if he was in any kind of trouble and also see if you can find out where he hung out normally. He could have left whatever place it was with his murderers.'

'There was more than one?' said the sergeant.

'Arnim says so,' said the inspector. 'He was hit in the face with two different size fists.'

'Did the autopsy show anything else?' said the sergeant.

'Well, he fixed the time of death at approximately four-thirty,' said the inspector, 'and the stomach contents showed a normal dinner and approximately two bottles of beer. Arnim thinks he was beaten up and tied to the tree shortly after midnight. It's important therefore that we find the last place he was seen.'

This did not turn out to be very difficult. Ulrich Nacken had had a large number of friends, young men and girls of his own age, and they agreed unanimously that his favourite spot when he was not working was the Toeff-Toeff Disco-theque in Cologne.

'Incidentally,' said the sergeant, reporting on this matter to the inspector, 'his friends agree with his parents' assess-ment of his character. He was a clean, serious, hard-working boy and nobody I spoke to could believe that he had any enemies.'

'I know the Toeff-Toeff,' said the inspector. 'It's a pretty harmless place. Did you check on whether he was there the night he was killed?'

'Yes,' said the sergeant. 'He was. A lot of people there know him. They say he left shortly before midnight and alone.'

'Then he must have been picked up almost immediately after he left the place,' said the inspector. 'Could have been some kind of a stick-up trap. Girl standing beside the road waving for help and when he stopped a couple of accomplices jumped out of the bushes. It's happened before.'

'It happens all the time,' said the sergeant, 'which is why people are reluctant to stop and help someone in distress now.

'On the other hand, why Nacken? His car wasn't new or worth much and anyone only had to look at him to see that he wasn't likely to be carrying much money.'

'True,' said the inspector, leaning his long, lean body back in the swivel chair. 'And then there's the savagery of the crime. Robbers might have killed him to avoid being identified later, but they wouldn't bother to strip him and tie him to a tree and all that business. I find it hard to believe that there wasn't a personal element in the killing.'

'So do I,' said the sergeant, 'but I don't know what it would be. Frankly, I don't know where we go from here.'

'I've assigned a stake-out for the spot where he was found,' said the inspector.

The sergeant looked startled. 'The murderers returning to the scene of the crime?' he said sceptically. 'That's only in detective stories.'

'Well, perhaps, but you must also consider that we've kept all news of this out of the papers. No one knows that Nacken is dead except the police, his parents and the persons you questioned. The murderers are almost surely not from any of these groups and I would think they must be growing curious. After all, someone could have come along, Nacken could have survived and the police could be in possession of a good description of the attempted murderers. If I were in their position, I'd want to know.'

The sergeant thought this over. 'It's logical,' he said finally, 'but I'm still more inclined to think that it was someone who knew Nacken well enough to check on whether he survived or not without going back there. For example, they could simply wait at his place of work and see if he turned up. Or they could call his home and ask for him.'

'You might check with the parents and see if anyone has called,' said the inspector. 'However, if your theory is correct then there would have been a motive. Any idea where to look for it?'

'Not really,' said the sergeant. 'All I can think of is the Toeff-Toeff. Whatever contacts he had, he had them there.'

'Go to it,' said the inspector. 'We have to follow any line of investigation that we can.'

The sergeant left the office and was not seen again until the following evening when he returned just as the inspector was preparing to leave for home.

'I think I have a possible motive in the Nacken case,' said the sergeant.

The inspector, who had been reaching for his overcoat, drew back his hand and returned to his desk.

'Yes?' he said.

'Nacken may have been mixed up in drugs,' said the sergeant. 'There are a couple of characters named Abie Frankenthal and Klaus Harker who sometimes hang out in the Toeff-Toeff. They're both pushers. Never been arrested, but Narcotics carries a file on them. They were drinking beer with Nacken the night he was murdered.'

The inspector considered. 'Pretty feeble,' he commented finally. 'Granted, the men are pushers. Granted, they were drinking beer with Nacken the night he was murdered. But, even so, that doesn't automatically implicate them as murderers. What would have been their motive? Professional criminals like that don't kill anyone unless they have to, and then they go about it more directly.'

'The only thing that's occurred to me is that Nacken may have been double-crossing them,' said the sergeant. 'I've been talking to Narcotics and they say that the reason that Frankenthal and Harker haven't been busted before is that they don't make the actual sales themselves. They supply a ring of teenage pushers who do the actual selling and take the risk. Could be that Nacken was one of them and didn't come across with the money so they decided to make an example of him.'

'It's possible,' admitted the inspector. 'And it would explain the cruelty of the murder, but wouldn't Nacken have had to be an addict in that case? Arnim didn't say

79

anything about indications of drug addiction in the autopsy and he would have if they were there.'

'Narcotics says most of the kids are addicts, but some of them are doing it just for the money,' said the sergeant. 'He needn't have had to be an addict. On the other hand, Narcotics also has sources of information on these kids and they say no one is spooked or even seems to know that Nacken is dead. Unless they did, it wouldn't be much of an example.'

'That could be explained by the fact that there's been no publicity on the murder yet,' said the inspector. 'Whoever the murderers are, they wouldn't be stupid enough to go around telling people that they'd cruelly murdered Nacken. They'd wait for it to come out in the newspapers.'

'I suppose so,' agreed the sergeant. 'You want me to bring in Frankenthal and Harker for questioning?'

'Why not?' said the inspector. 'Even if it doesn't do anything else, it may throw a scare into them about their drug pushing.'

The inspector and his assistant left the office and went home. It was past seven in the evening and already pitch dark. Twenty miles to the east, the day shift of the police stake-out in the forest between Wohlfahrt and Neunkirchen where Ulrich Nacken had died was just approaching the end of their duty.

Sitting inside the police car, parked just off the road and screened by a copse of young firs, were two very junior patrolmen named Arnold Klein and Leopold Brettweiler.

They were not very happy with their duty, and they were cold. The only way that it would have been possible to heat the car would have been to leave the motor running and this was not permitted.

'Fifty-six more minutes,' said Brettweiler, looking at his wrist watch. 'I wonder how many more years we're going to spend out here in the woods? I thought when I got off foot patrol, I'd have it made.'

'Cheer up,' said his partner, who was behind the wheel. 'Soon it will be spring and we can take sun baths and pick flowers. We can bring along some sausages and roast them over a camp fire and then, as autumn descends . . .'

'Oh shut up,' said Brettweiler. 'You say things like that, they could come true. Besides . . . Holy Moses!'

'Holy Moses?' said Klein.

'Look! Look!' whispered Brettweiler. 'There it is! The grey Ford!'

Out on the highway, a car was cruising slowly past.

'It's a Ford, all right,' said Klein, 'and it looks like a sixty-six. But I can't see the colour.'

He switched on the ignition.

'It's grey!' insisted Brettweiler. 'Watch for the licence plate when he gets past.'

The car was now abreast of them and as it moved slowly on past, both patrolmen could plainly see the lighted numbers, K-HM 943.

Klein let out the clutch and his thumb descended on the button of the siren. With a snarl like a starving tomcat, the police car lunged out into the highway, the siren rising in an urgent scream and the blue Martin's light on the roof revolving and flashing.

The driver of the grey Ford floored the gas pedal and pulled rapidly away from them. The police car with its cold engine sputtered and misfired as Klein nursed it through the gears.

'Get his tyres!' yelled Klein. 'He's going to run away from us altogether!'

Brettweiler drew his service pistol and leaning out of the window, emptied the magazine in the direction of the fleeing car.

With his first shot, the car's lights went out.

'You never touched him!' shouted Klein. 'Watch if he turns off. He's doused his lights and he's going to break into one of the side roads. If we miss him, he'll give us the slip.'

Off the highway were a number of smaller roads leading back into the forest. Some of these went on through and joined up with other roads and some were no more than logging tracks ending in a few thousand or even few hundred yards.

The Ford was now some considerable distance ahead and still gaining. It could, however, be seen as a black, fleeting shadow against the snow-covered shoulders of the road.

'There! There he goes!' shouted Brettweiler. 'He swung in to the right!'

'Are you sure?' yelled Klein, torn with the necessity of an instant decision. 'If you're wrong . . .'

'He went right!' insisted Brettweiler, snapping his reserve cartridge clip into the pistol.

The entrance to the forest road loomed up on the right, Klein slammed on the brakes, fought the wheel around and the police car plunged into it with screaming tyres. Gunning the motor, he shot the car down the double track and around a curve – and slammed on the brakes again just in time to avoid crashing into the back of the grey Ford, its nose buried in a snowdrift.

The driver of the Ford had made a bad mistake. The road he had chosen was a logging road and led nowhere.

He was now trying to struggle out of the driver's seat, a tall, dark and remarkably handsome man, but his overcoat had caught on the door handle and he could not free himself immediately.

'Stand where you are!' roared Brettweiler, piling out of the police car with the pistol in his hand. 'Hands over your head!'

The man sullenly complied.

'There must have been two of them,' said Klein, getting out of the car. 'The passenger side door is open and here are tracks.' He turned to the prisoner. 'Was there someone with you?' he demanded.

The prisoner did not answer.

'Never mind,' said Klein. 'He won't get far. And, just to make certain that you don't try anything, . . .' He produced his handcuffs and handcuffed the prisoner to the steering wheel of the Ford.

'Do you think we should try and follow the other one, Arnie?' said Brettweiler.

Klein shook his head. 'I'm going to get on the radio now and raise Cologne. They'll come out with a party and dogs and they'll have him in no time. If we go running around out there in the dark, there's no telling what might happen. See if our silent friend here has any kind of identification on him.'

Brettweiler went through the man's pockets and came up with an identity card.

'Yugoslav,' he said. 'Maybe that's why he doesn't answer. He can't speak German. The name's Slobodan Vucetic, aged twenty-seven, construction worker. And here's something else. A driver's licence in the name of Ulrich Nacken and the ownership papers to the car.'

At five minutes to eight that evening the inspector and Sergeant Moench were torn from their television sets by the news that the stake-out had made an arrest. At least one more man had fled and a search party with tracking dogs was being got together at the station. The dispatcher wanted to know if the inspector would be taking personal charge.

The inspector would. Ten minutes after the call, Sergeant Moench picked him up in his private car and the officers drove to the scene of the arrest.

Slobodan Vucetic was still handcuffed to the steering wheel of the Ford and the police search party had just set off into the woods, led by two tracking dogs on leash. The dogs were hardly necessary as the footprints could be easily followed with a flashlight.

'Well, is this our murderer?' said the inspector, walking up to Vucetic.

'He doesn't speak German, inspector,' said Klein.

Vucetic promptly made him a liar.

'Simic kill boy!' he said in broken German, speaking for the first time. 'I no hurt boy. Simic kill boy.'

'Is Simic the man who was with you?' said the inspector.

Vucetic nodded. 'He also Slobodan, Slobodan Simic. He kill boy. I no do nothing.'

'We'll see,' said the inspector. 'Take him down to headquarters and book him on suspicion of murder. We'll bring the other one in when the party gets back with him.'

The inspector was obviously not expecting a long wait and he did not have one. In less than an hour the search party returned with Slobodan Simic who the dogs had found hiding in a rack of hay, put out by the forestry department for feeding deer.

He corroborated Vucetic's statements completely with only a slight difference in detail.

Vucetic, he said, had killed Ulrich Nacken. He, personally, had done nothing.

Simic was only twenty-two years old and he was badly frightened. By the time he had reached the police station, he had already implicated still a third Yugoslav, twenty-nine-year-old Vjekoslav Potkonjac.

A team of detectives was dispatched to his address and soon brought him to headquarters where he added his voice to the mutual accusations and denials of personal guilt.

The confusion did not last long. The inspector was very skilled and very experienced in sorting out the true statements from the false and none of the Yugoslavs was particularly clever.

Long before midnight, Slobodan Vucetic and Slobodan Simic had confessed to the actual crime, exonerating Potkonjac who had been present, but who had not taken part.

Determining the guilt proved to be the simplest part, for the motive was so tenuous that the inspector feared a jury might not believe it. Strictly speaking, there had been no motive at all, not even the one of stealing Nacken's car. All of the Yugoslavs earned more money than Ulrich Nacken did and could easily have afforded better cars. Queried as to their reasons for murdering the young electrician, they seemed puzzled themselves. It was, they said, just something that happened.

'We were in Toeff-Toeff,' said Vucetic. 'We drink three, four beer. Not drunk. Little happy. After, we come out, there is boy. He is getting into car. Simic say, "I have girlfriend in Siegburg. We take car. Go Siegburg."'

'I put knife on boy's throat. Simic look in back of car and find wire. We tie up boy and put him in trunk. Then, we go Siegburg.'

After visiting Simic's girlfriend in Siegburg, the three Yugoslavs, for no reason that any of them could explain, had decided to get rid of Ulrich Nacken by leaving him in the woods and had driven to the point half-way between Wohlfahrt and Neunkirchen where they had tied him to the tree.

'We take clothes first,' said Vucetic. 'He didn't like so we hit him a little. Then, we tie to tree and go away.'

'You understood that he would die there within a short time, did you not?' said the inspector who was anxious to establish premeditation and deliberation in the crime.

'We know,' said Vucetic. 'Then, I look newspaper every day. No boy in woods. I think, "They still no find or he get away?" He get away, maybe more better go back Yugoslavia. Simic say, "We go look." '

'We go look. We get caught.'

The following morning the story, which had been suppressed up until now, appeared in all the newspapers and that afternoon Werner Schmidt called the newspaper in Cologne to say that he had apparently been the last person to see Nacken alive. He was prepared to grant an interview and, if they liked, they could take a picture of him at the scene.

The newspaper, which was more aware of the legal implications of this publicity, informed the police and immediately following his interview Schmidt was arrested and charged with failing to assist a person in danger, a serious offence under German law.

He was eventually tried, found guilty and sentenced to six months imprisonment and a fine of three thousand marks.

Slobodan Vucetic, Slobodan Simic and Vjekoslav Potkonjac were brought to trial on November 30, 1971, found guilty of premeditated murder without extenuating circumstances and sentenced to life imprisonment in all three cases.

6

MAD DOG!

Paris is a state of mind.

For the romantic, it is Montmartre, la Rive Gauche and the Boul Miche.

For the tourist, it is Notre Dame, the Tour Eiffel and the Champs-Elysées.

For the millions who each morning and evening pack the Metro on their way to and from the offices, shops and factories, it is more often than not the dreary, concrete forest of apartment houses rising in shoddy, concentric rings around the City of Light.

Paris grows. With every passing year, more of the charming little villages of the Ile de France are swallowed up by the irresistible concrete waves and one such village, some ten miles to the west of Paris, is Villennes on the Seine.

During the week, Villennes is practically deserted. The men and many of the women are at work and the children, except for the very small, are at school. Villennes is quiet, almost peaceful. Sunday is, however, something else. Everyone is home. The children play and yell in the streets. Adolescents race the motors of their motorcycles. Radios blare.

Whatever the good Lord may have intended, Sunday in Villennes is not a day of rest. And September 16, 1973 was a Sunday, an overcast, rainy Sunday where the normal possibilities of escape such as a walk in the surrounding country or an excursion to other less depressing places were lacking.

At approximately eleven o'clock in the morning the residents of the apartment house at 16, rue Clemenceau were startled by the sounds of pistol shots or, at least, what sounded like pistol shots.

A number of the less cautious tenants rushed out into the halls and within a matter of minutes the door to the ground floor apartment of forty-five-year-old René Maréchal and his forty-two-year-old wife, Nanette, was discovered to be standing open.

In the little entrance hall inside, the bodies of the Maréchals lay sprawled on the floor, René with a bullet through the right eye which had penetrated into his brain, killing him instantly, and Nanette, mortally wounded in the chest and abdomen.

She was still alive as the neighbours bent over her and she managed to gasp out, 'Grasso! He's mad! He rang the bell and started shooting. Help René. He's . . .'

The blood gushed from her nose and mouth and she died.

In the meantime, someone had already called the ambulance, and the emergency services of the Paris region being excellent as the result of much practice, it soon arrived.

A medical intern had come with it and he conducted a brief examination of the Maréchals and pronounced them dead.

'Has anyone called the police?' he asked. 'I'd advise you all to stay away from the bodies. The Criminal Investigations people don't like it when they've been disturbed. Were there any witnesses?'

There had been no witnesses apparently, but several of the neighbours had heard Mrs Maréchal gasp out the name of Grasso before she died and they said as much. They also indicated the door of the apartment next door, with the name Santo Grasso written with pencil on a scrap of paper and stuck beneath the bell with scotch tape. Then they all backed away, apparently believing that the intern would rush in and arrest the suspect.

The intern, of course, did no such thing, but lit a cigarette and went out to the ambulance to call the police. This action, or lack of it, apparently gave rise to some thought, for the people nearest the door to Grasso's apartment began to disperse and by the time the police arrived there was no one in the hall. Two of the neighbours who had heard Mrs Maréchal accuse Grasso of the murders were, however, waiting with the intern at the front door.

As in all big cities, the report of a homicide in Paris sets in motion a huge and complex machine of which the parts are patrol cars, radio-telephone dispatchers, technicians, finger-print and weapons experts, specialists in forensic medicine and criminal investigations officers.

The spearhead of this small army of men and women is, in almost all cases, the patrol car for the simple reason that there is usually one within a few blocks of the scene of the report. The patrol car's most important function is to determine that a crime has actually taken place.

This was easily ascertained by the two young patrolmen from the car which arrived at 16, rue Clemenceau and, upon being informed that the presumed murderer was in the apartment next door, one of the patrolmen drew his service pistol and took up station at the corner of the hall where he could cover the doorway to Grasso's apartment while the other went back to the patrol car to report to headquarters.

After a moment or two he returned, drew his gun and took up a position next to his partner.

'Charge room officer authorizes use of firearms if necessary,' he said. 'We're not to disturb him, but wait. Headquarters is sending out the specialists.'

The officers were calm, efficient and very wary. It is the only way to remain alive as a police officer in a city the size of Paris.

The specialists arrived promptly in a small, fast van containing six men and enough sophisticated weapons to overthrow the governments of a number of smaller states.

While three of the men took up positions covering the windows outside the house, the leader, a stocky, cat-faced man in his forties, went directly to the door of the Grasso apartment, the remaining two men fanning out to left and right with their automatic weapons at the ready.

The leader, whose name was Jules Lacat, was wearing complete body armour, a protective helmet and a face shield.

The full-automatic machine pistol lay easily along his right forearm, his finger resting lightly on the trigger.

Using his left hand, he pressed the doorbell, waited a moment and then called out in a loud voice, 'Criminal Police. Open the door and come out slowly with your hands over your head.'

There was no sound from the apartment.

Lucat tested the knob and finding the door locked, stepped back, jerking his head to the men on his left and right.

There was the deafening rattle of automatic weapons fire within the narrow confines of the hall and a torrent of lead ripped through the door, tearing out sections of the panels and smashing the lock to pieces.

The squad leader kicked the remains of the door back against the wall and went through, the machine pistol now held in both hands at waist height.

Behind him, his men moved in to either side of the door.

There was no sound within the apartment and, a few moments later, Lucat reappeared, working the slide of the machine pistol to throw the live round out of the chamber.

'Nobody home,' he said emotionlessly.

'Zut!' said a tall man with a spiky black moustache, who had been waiting just inside the front door. 'In you go, François. See if you can turn up a picture for the pick-up order.'

A slightly-built, young man with sandy-brown hair and sharp features, dashed into the apartment.

'Can I take the ambulance back now?' said the intern to the man with the moustache.

'Why not?' said Inspector Pierre Dupont, Senior Investigations Officer of the Paris Criminal Police. 'We will arrange for transport of the bodies to the morgue. Do you have any information on the case?'

'None,' said the intern and left.

Detective-Sergeant François Renard came out of the apartment with a number of photographs in his hands.

'This is him,' said the sergeant. 'One of these is his

Foreigners' Registration Card. Santo Grasso, aged thirty-eight and an Italian citizen. Comes from Sicily.'

The inspector sighed. 'They all do,' he said. 'Call head-quarters and give them the description. General pick-up order to all units. Detain and hold. Dangerous. Presumably armed. Use of firearms authorized.'

The sergeant went down the hall to the front door and the police car parked at the kerb outside.

'All right, the rest of you,' said the inspector to the little group of detectives awaiting orders. 'Go through the building and see if anyone here knows him or knows where he may have gone.'

The detectives made off silently. Forty minutes later, as the bodies of René and Nanette Maréchal were being loaded into the police ambulance for transport to the morgue, they returned.

No one in the building had known Santo Grasso. No one knew where he might have gone.

While they had been waiting, the inspector and his assistant had gone through the two apartments. They had found nothing to indicate that the Maréchals had known Santo Grasso any better than the other tenants and they had found nothing to indicate a motive.

'It was not robbery,' said the inspector. 'There are valuables and cash in the Maréchal apartment lying about openly and he didn't touch them.'

'He didn't even take his own money,' observed the sergeant. 'The impression I get is that he left without taking anything.'

Santo Grasso had, however, taken something. Two pistols, a rifle, a shotgun and close to a thousand rounds of ammunition.

It would have disturbed the inspector a great deal had he known this, but he was not going to find it out until nearly two hours later when twelve-year-old Patrick Gaumer and his ten-year-old brother, Marcel, returned home from a rather soggy game of touch-football in the park of the suburb of Ecqueville, less than five miles from Villennes.

Patrick and Marcel should actually have been home

90

considerably earlier, but they knew that their father, André Gaumer, had gone into Paris on some kind of business and there was no one in the apartment except their mother, Monique, and the seven-year-old youngest brother, Jacques. Monique, at thirty years of age and already the mother of three very exuberant boys, was too harassed to be a very severe disciplinarian.

In this case unpunctuality paid off, for had Patrick and Marcel come home when they were supposed to, it would undoubtedly have cost them their lives.

It would also have cost them their lives if they had been four inches taller, because when they arrived at the door of the fifth floor apartment and pressed the bell to be let in, three nine millimetre pistol slugs passed through the door, over their heads and into the wall of the corridor opposite.

Neither of the boys had the slightest inkling as to who might be doing the shooting, but they were both seasoned television viewers and knew gunfire when they heard it. Also, being big city French children, they were intensely practical. They therefore threw themselves flat on their stomachs, wormed their way to the stairs and descended the first flight headfirst. Following which, they took the elevator to the ground floor and ran to the nearest intersection where they found a traffic policeman on duty.

Sceptical, but ready for anything, the policeman followed them back to the apartment building and inspected the door with the three bullet holes from the safety of the head of the stairs.

Oddly enough, no one else in the building seemed to have heard the pistol shots for none of the other tenants had come out.

It would later be determined that the reason for this was that no one else on that floor was at home, but now the lack of onlookers made the policeman suspicious that the boys were pulling some kind of a trick.

He therefore walked quietly over to the door, drew his gun and standing to one side with his back to the wall, cautiously pressed the doorbell.

91

Three more nine millimetre slugs passed through the door.

The policeman quickly holstered his gun, laid down flat on the floor and wormed his way across to the stairwell, precisely as the boys had done.

Five minutes later, the communications centre at police headquarters in Paris knew that someone was shooting through a door in Ecqueville.

They, of course, had no reason to connect this with the murders of René and Nanette Maréchal in Villennes.

The report, however, set off very much the same reaction as had the killings in Villennes, and Specialist Lucat and his men soon arrived at the scene.

Once again, Lucat went to the door under cover of the automatic weapons of his squad, but this time there was a response. Two heavy rifle bullets smashed into his body armour with such force that he was knocked backward and received painful bruises which would remain black and blue for the following week.

This was not the first time that such a thing had happened to him and he got up, blew the door off its hinges with machine pistol fire and would have charged through had the hall beyond not been stacked to the ceiling with what was apparently all the furniture in the apartment.

While withdrawing, he was struck by a charge of buckshot from Santo Grasso's shotgun which, had it been at a little closer range and not partially deflected by the furniture barricade, could very well have broken his spine despite the body armour.

Limping slightly, the squad leader joined his men at the head of the stairs.

'Get the tear gas gun,' he ordered shortly. 'We'll have to smoke him out.'

He had not spoken in a particularly low voice and from the apartment across the corridor, there came a response.

'No tear gas,' said a man's voice. 'You shoot tear gas, the woman and boy die!'

The squad leader did not change his expression.

'Go get those two kids up here,' he said in a low voice to

one of his men and to another, 'See if Inspector Dupont's got here yet. He's on duty today.'

The two men went off down the stairs and returned in a few minutes bringing with them Patrick and Marcel Gaumer and the inspector and his assistant.

'Listen to this man's voice and see if it's your father,' said the specialist to the two boys and, raising his voice, he called out, 'You there in the apartment! What do you want?'

There was no reply.

'Okay. Hand me the tear gas gun,' said Lucat.

'No tear gas,' shouted the voice from the apartment. 'I kill the woman and the boy!'

'That's not dad,' said Patrick Gaumer. 'This man talks like a foreigner.'

There was a strange note of embarrassment in his voice which was not overlooked by the inspector.

'Whose voice is it, Patrick?' he said.

The boy looked unhappy and did not reply.

'It's mama's boy friend,' said Marcel. 'Old Santo Grasso.'

The police officers looked at each other.

'Your mother has a boy friend named Santo Grasso?' said the inspector. 'An Italian? From Sicily?'

'That's him,' said Patrick a little sulkily. 'He isn't her boy friend no more. That all happened two or three years ago. She doesn't have anything to do with him now.'

'You boys go downstairs and wait for your father,' said the inspector.

'Well, at least we know who we've got in there,' said Lucat, taking off his helmet to wipe the sweat from the bald patch on the top of his head. He felt for his sore ribs underneath the body armour. 'The boy means business.'

'Grasso,' called the inspector. 'This is the police. We know you're in there and we know that you killed René and Nanette Maréchal. Why did you do that, Grasso?'

There was a short silence and then Grasso answered.

'They make too much noise,' he said. 'I can't sleep. Is Sunday and I can't sleep.'

The inspector made a circle with his thumb and forefinger to indicate success. It was important in such cases to be able to engage in a dialogue with the hostage taker. At worst, while he was talking, he was not shooting and, at best, he could sometimes be persuaded to give himself up.

'Have you had trouble sleeping lately?' inquired the inspector sympathetically. 'I also had much trouble sleeping at one time. Perhaps, if you were to talk to my doctor . . .'

He continued to talk and, at the same time, slipped his notebook out of his pocket and wrote on the first page, 'Get some mikes on the apartment walls. I'm going to move up next to the door and see if I can get him to expose himself. Sharpshooters to try to cripple, but not kill. I want report on status woman and child inside as soon as mike's installed.'

'We don't have any body armour to fit you,' said Lucat dubiously, looking at the inspector who was a trifle over-weight.

The inspector waved a hand in dismissal. He was now chatting with the gunman about the delights of the climate in Sicily.

Flat on his stomach and with surprising agility for a man of his size and girth, he slowly crossed the corridor until he was lying flat up against the wall beside the door of the Gaumer apartment, keeping up the stream of talk all the time.

Grasso was not doing much talking, but he was at least occasionally responding to the inspector's remarks, which showed that he was listening.

At the head of the stairs, Specialist Lucat's sharpshooters rested the barrels of their rifles on the top step, searching for any sign of movement behind the tangled mass of furniture filling the apartment hall.

Sergeant Renard had gone into the apartment next door with a team of technicians and now he crept out and over to where the inspector lay.

'The bug men say there's three people breathing in there,' he whispered. 'No talk. Just breathing.'

The inspector nodded to show that he understood and then wrote on his pad, 'Tell Lucat to stand by. I'm going to try to bring him out now.'

The sergeant nodded in his turn and crossed the hall to

the head of the stairs. The sharpshooters aimed their weapons.

'Why don't you give this business up and come out, Grasso?' called the inspector. 'You can't get away and, if you had no other reason to kill the Maréchals than what you say, all that will happen to you is that you will go to the hospital. It is a very comfortable hospital and quiet. You will be able to sleep.'

Santo Grasso told the inspector what he could do with the hospital.

The inspector stopped talking and wormed his way back to the head of the stairs.

'He's becoming too excited,' he said. 'I don't like it. I'm afraid all we can do is try to wait him out.'

'We could make a double assault,' said Lucat. 'One party through the front door with fire axes to chop away the furniture and one down ropes from the balcony above.'

'He'd kill the woman and the boy,' said the inspector.

'He will anyway,' said Lucat bluntly. 'That's what he's there for. If he had any demands, he'd have made them by now. He doesn't expect to come out of there alive and he won't leave anyone else alive either, if he can manage it.'

The inspector did not reply. Lucat was a man who had had a great deal of experience with such cases.

As the afternoon and evening passed, Santo Grasso seemed to grow ever more excited and took to firing at cars and pedestrians through the windows of the apartment. Fortunately, no one was hit, but the area had to be cordoned off.

There was also an alarming number of shots being fired in the apartment itself, but the men manning the microphones attached to the dividing wall of the next apartment reported that they could still hear three persons breathing and Monique Gaumer attempting to calm and reason with her former lover.

She was obviously not having much success and at nine o'clock the following morning, the Sicilian, who had apparently not slept a wink throughout the night but was still filled with a frenetic energy, turned his mind to something else.

'No Santo!' screamed Monique Gaumer, her voice rising so that it could be plainly heard even without microphones. 'Don't do that! Not in front of the boy! Oh God! You are mad, Santo! Jacques! Turn your head! Don't look! Santo, you cannot . . .!'

Her voice died away and the microphone men could hear only a scuffling sound and the heavy breathing of the man.

'Set up your assault teams, Lucat,' said the inspector quietly. 'If he doesn't calm after this, we may have to risk it with tear gas. The man's lost all touch with reality.'

There had been a short period of silence following Monique Gaumer's outcry, but now the firing within the apartment resumed. Santo Grasso was apparently shooting with everything he had, the pistols, the rifle, the shotgun.

'He must have a truck load of ammunition in there,' remarked the inspector, 'but, if he . . .'

He was interrupted by the sergeant who came scuttling rapidly across from the apartment where the listening posts were installed.

'There's only one person breathing in there now!' he said.

'Go in and take him, Lucat,' said the inspector sadly.

Five minutes later, Specialist Jules Lucat and his men stormed the Gaumer apartment behind a barrage of tear gas. They met no opposition and the shooting within the apartment ceased abruptly as the first tear gas shell arced through the window.

As Lucat had predicted, Santo Grasso had left no one alive.

Sprawled on the living room floor, her half-naked body surrounded by the torn shreds of her clothing, Monique Gaumer lay dead with a nine millimetre bullet fired at close range through her brain.

At the other side of the room, seated at the table with his face obediently turned to the wall, was the corpse of little Jacques Gaumer. He had been killed with another nine millimetre pistol bullet fired into the back of his head at close range.

Santo Grasso was not in the living room. He lay in the front hall just behind his furniture barricade and, for his own execution, he had not made use of either of the pistols. Instead, he had placed the muzzle of the shotgun in his mouth and had stretched down to pull the trigger.

The charge of buckshot had blown his head off completely.

A FAMILY AFFAIR

It was January 7, 1974 and through the streets of Frankfurt am Main a Mercedes 250S was rolling slowly although the traffic was not heavy.

The man at the wheel was young, dark and had long, drooping moustaches in the style currently popular with younger Germans. His companion in the passenger seat beside him was older, heavier, clean-shaven and short-haired.

In a way, each of the men was a symbol of modern Germany in the seventies, the clean-shaven, ambitious striver after material success and the long-haired, liberal easy-rider of the new wave. Both spoke German, but there was scarcely more real communication between them than between an Eskimo and a Zulu. The worlds in which they lived were parallel and contiguous, but totally alien and incomprehensible the one to the other.

Perhaps in no other part of Germany is this division of society so marked as in Frankfurt where hippies and students share communes, fight pitched battles with the police and search for a new society in experiments with drugs and permissive sex while others work frenziedly to pile up still more millions, to buy more expensive cars, to hang still more jewellery on their expensive women.

The division is less by age than by philosophy.

On this particular evening a representative of still a third group was walking briskly along the sidewalk a hundred yards in front of the Mercedes.

Mrs Elly Bender was walking rapidly, not because she was in any hurry, but because she always did things rapidly.

By a coincidence, her age was exactly the total of those of the two men in the car.

Mrs Bender did not know this, nor would she have been interested if she had. A widow on a pension, she was on her way home and her thoughts were largely occupied with the possibilities of the evening's television programme.

As the Mercedes whispered past her, she did not even glance at it. There is nothing unusual about a Mercedes in Frankfurt.

Suddenly, however, there was a sharp explosion.

Looking up, Mrs Bender saw the Mercedes swerve slowly in towards the kerb and it occurred to her that it had blown a tyre.

Then, to her astonishment, she saw the door on the driver's side open and the driver half roll, half fall out into the street.

As he struggled to rise, the man in the passenger seat reached across and, lying half out of the open door of the car, fired two shots from a pistol at the young man with the moustache.

Mrs Bender clearly saw the man's body jerk as the bullets drove into his torso and then go limp.

Squinting through the smog of pollution which lies in a permanent blanket over the city, Mrs Bender could see a dark pool of blood beginning to form around the motionless figure.

In the meantime, the Mercedes rolled on and came to a noisy halt with its crushed fender flattened against the brickwork of a building foundation.

There was silence.

It was only when the tall, husky man who had fired the shots stepped out of the car and walked off a little unsteadily down the street that Mrs Bender realized that she had just been a witness to murder.

Being a responsible woman and conscious of her civic duty, she immediately made off in the direction of the nearest police station at a speed remarkable in view of her age and lack of athletic training.

She could have saved herself the trouble for there were

people living and working in the buildings along the street and they had informed the police by telephone very shortly after the incident took place.

By the time that Mrs Bender arrived back with a foot patrolman a sizeable crowd had gathered and two officers from a patrol car were at the scene and attempting to locate witnesses.

As it turned out, Mrs Bender was the only actual eye witness or, at least, the only one who would admit to it. Frankfurters are not any more inclined to become involved in criminal matters which do not concern them than the residents of any other big, violent city.

Mrs Bender was still in the process of making her statement to one of the patrol car officers when the Homicide Squad arrived from police headquarters. An advance team, it consisted only of Inspector Hardy Kastner and Detective-Sergeant Max Ochs.

Other patrol cars were also now arriving and, while the stolid sergeant took charge of operations, setting up a cordon of police around the area and blocking off the street, his chief went to inspect the body and then the stationary car, returning finally to listen to Mrs Bender's account.

'Get the tape recorder and take down this lady's statement,' said the inspector as the sergeant came up to where he and Mrs Bender were standing. 'And while you're at the car, check and see if the ambulance is on its way yet. We're going to need Adam.'

Adam was Dr Adam Zobeljaeger, the department's medical expert, who appeared with the police ambulance before the sergeant had had time to make the call over the car's radio-telephone.

'Well?' said the inspector who had followed him out to where he was kneeling beside the body.

'He's dead, if that's what you mean,' said the doctor. 'Three bullet wounds in the upper chest. One was very close range. Seven-sixty-five calibre, it looks like.'

'Gang killing perhaps,' remarked the inspector. 'We have a witness and she says it was a big man and very cool. Stepped out of the car and simply walked away.'

100

'This boy here wasn't any gangster,' said the doctor. 'He's got callouses and cuts all over his hands. Some kind of a hand worker, garage mechanic maybe.'

'See if there are any papers in his pockets,' said the inspector. 'I don't want to go through the car until the technicians have dusted it for prints.'

The doctor searched through the dead man's pockets. There were papers, money, a pocket comb and a picture of a very young girl.

'Dieter Poeschke,' said the inspector, reading from the personal identity card carried by most Germans. 'He was only just turned twenty-one. You were right. He was a garage mechanic. Lived in Frankfurt-Sachsenhausen. Says here he was married. My God! This couldn't be a picture of his wife, could it? She doesn't look a day over sixteen.'

But in this he was mistaken.

Sitting in her neat two-room apartment in Frankfurt-Sachsenhausen, a scant two miles distant from where her husband's body lay in a pool of blood in the street, the widow Silvia Poeschke was several days over sixteen, although not enough to make up six months, the length of time that she had been pregnant.

Silvia was feeling a trifle left out of things because she was sitting alone on her bed in the bedroom and listening to some remarkably strange sounds through the paper-thin partition between bedroom and living room.

She had been married only two weeks now and she was beginning to think that she had married into a very unusual family. Not, of course, that she was narrow-minded or anything like that, but the couple in the room next door were her brother-in-law and his sister and, unless she was greatly mistaken, they were engaged in sex.

Silvia was a very modern, very enlightened girl and she had taken it as completely natural that she and Dieter should have sex together and even that they should produce a child without benefit of clergy. It had been Dieter who had insisted on the marriage. She had not pressed him.

However, sex with one's own brother?

101

Silvia was not quite sure just how she felt about that. As it happened, she had no brothers, but still . . .

She was also feeling slightly embarrassed. It was the height of bad taste among modern young Germans to show sexual jealousy, but she was, she realized, jealous of Dieter and his sister.

All yesterday evening she had lain awake in the darkness, listening to the sounds which the two brothers and their sister were making beyond the wall, the giggles, the moans, the sound of flesh slapping naked flesh and Renate's whispered instructions.

'All right,' pouted Silvia, alone in her bedroom. 'If they're going to have group sex, they could at least count me in too.'

But, of course, she was six months pregnant and group sex might not be good for the baby. The widow Silvia was beginning to feel quite maternal.

Well, perhaps not completely maternal towards her brother-in-law. It was a strange sensation to have someone similar to Dieter in the same apartment and yet know that they were total strangers.

As a matter of fact, she might never have met Juergen Poeschke if it had not been for the amnesty.

Dieter had told her about his five year older brother who had been left behind in Communist East Germany with the grandmother when, sixteen years earlier, Mrs Anna Poeschke had fled with her son Dieter and her daughter Renate to the West. Juergen had been something of a legendary figure who had never accepted the restrictions of a Communist State. He had been jailed for escape attempts, beating up police officers and, on this last occasion, for assaulting a major of the Russian army on a visit to East Berlin.

The whole family had thought that Juergen was now lost forever and that, if he did not simply disappear entirely, he would surely spend the rest of his life in prison. But then there had been the amnesty two months earlier and Juergen had not only been released, but kicked out of the Worker's Paradise altogether. It was the perfect solution because it had pleased everyone: Juergen, his mother, brother and

102

sister in the West and, of course, above all, the East Germans.

If anyone had not been pleased, thought Silvia, it was Renate's husband, Hans Appel. He was thirty-four, ten years older than Renate, and as square as an ice cube. Silvia could not understand why Renate had married him, unless it was the money.

Hans had plenty of money. He had started out as a simple stone mason and, through sheer hard work and persistence, had become the owner of a good-sized construction company. He had loaded Renate with presents, jewellery, clothing, anything that she might want.

On the other hand, she did not see very much of her husband. He was practically always working and Renate was at home alone with the three children. Two of the children were her own. The six-year-old Claudia from her first marriage, and Tanja, the daughter which she had borne Hans a year ago. The third child was four-year-old Lydia, Hans' daughter by his first marriage.

'Three daughters,' mused Silvia. She was rather hoping for a boy, but then girls were nice too, of course.

In the room next door, Renate was making remarkable sounds. It was as if she was laughing and crying at the same time.

The laughing and crying was, however, all over and Renate and Juergen were sitting decorously listening to music on the record player when Sergeant Ochs knocked on the door.

The sergeant was always the one to notify the next of kin, not because his chief was inclined to push all of the unpleasant details onto his assistant, but because his appearance and personality were so reassuring that it tended to lessen the shock. The sergeant did not look very much like a police officer or even an official.

This time, the sergeant needed all his powers of reassurance and, having noted that the widow was in an advanced state of pregnancy, first took her sister-in-law into the kitchen to inquire whether the family doctor was immediately available before stating the purpose of his visit. The sergeant did not want to be responsible for bringing on a miscarriage.

As it turned out, there was a doctor in the same building and the sergeant proceeded to break his unpleasant news.

For a moment, the three survivors simply stared at him in disbelief and then, grasping that what he said was true and that Dieter had been murdered, burst into a simultaneous orgy of weeping, throwing themselves into each other's arms and sobbing uncontrollably.

There was no doubting the sincerity or depth of their grief and it was some time before the sergeant could calm any of them sufficiently to ask the questions which he had to ask.

Even then, the statements which he received threw no light at all on the identity of Dieter's murderer.

Dieter Poeschke, it seemed, had been a completely ordinary, reasonably hard-working garage mechanic, who, although he wore his hair and moustache long, was involved with neither drugs nor promiscuous sex and certainly not with any underworld activities.

He and Silvia had married only a month earlier, at Dieter's insistence, and his brother Juergen, who had arrived from East Germany two months earlier, had been staying with them for the past two weeks. There had been no trouble of any kind and, in so far as any of them knew, Dieter had had no enemies.

The sergeant posed his final question.

'Do any of you know a tall, husky, clean-shaven man among Mr Poeschke's acquaintances?' he asked. 'A man in his early forties or perhaps a little younger?'

It was the description of the murderer which Mrs Bender had given, but the sergeant did not mention this or even reveal that there had been a witness to the killing. It is the policy of the German police not to release any more information than necessary until a case has been solved.

Silvia's eyes opened very wide and she seemed on the point of saying something, but both Renate and Juergen said almost simultaneously, 'He had no friends like that.'

The sergeant looked at the widow who lowered her eyes and said nothing.

'I'm almost certain the girl knows who the murderer is,' the sergeant told the inspector upon his return to the office, 'but she's covering up.'

'You think she might have something to do with it?' suggested the inspector.

The sergeant shook his head. 'I can't believe it,' he said. 'No sixteen-year-old girl could simulate such shock and grief. None of those people were expecting to hear anything like that. They weren't even startled when I said I was from the police, just curious. And besides, what motive could she have? They've only been married a month and she's six months' pregnant.'

'The motive certainly isn't apparent,' agreed the inspector. 'However, we can worry about that when we have the murderer in custody. It shouldn't be too difficult to locate him. We've got a reasonably good description from the witness.'

'A description that could pass for a few thousand men in Frankfurt,' observed the sergeant.

'True,' said the inspector, 'but we can also deduce certain other things. For example, the murderer must have been known to the victim for they were riding together in the same car. What we have to do is check out every male between the ages of twenty-five and forty-five that Poeschke knew and the one who answers the description is our man.

'We then bring him in for a line-up and see if Mrs Bender can pick him out.'

'Sounds easy,' said the sergeant doubtfully, 'but what if it was somebody that he just met or simply a hitchhiker he gave a ride to?'

'If they didn't know him, why did they kill him then?' said the inspector. 'There wasn't any attempt at robbery and to shoot the driver of the car you're riding in seems to me to indicate a something more than casual intensity of feeling on the subject.'

'I suppose so,' said the sergeant, 'but I have the feeling myself that the investigation isn't going to be all that easy. For some reason or other, the widow and his brother and sister aren't co-operating.'

'Then try his mother,' said the inspector. 'She lives here in the city too and I've just turned up her address from Poeschke's papers.'

'Now?' said the sergeant. 'The others will undoubtedly already have told her that he's dead. She may not be in much shape for questioning.'

'Nonetheless, we have to do it,' said the inspector. 'Since there's no hint as to who the murderer is, for all we know he could be clearing out of the country right now. If there's any lead to be picked up, we want to pick it up immediately.'

The sergeant, who had not had any dinner and who had been coping with grief-stricken relatives for the past two hours, got rather unhappily to his feet and was heading for the door when Dr Zobeljaeger appeared.

'Hold it a minute, Max,' he said. 'I have a little information for you. The victim was shot three times with a seven-thirty-five calibre automatic. I got out two of the slugs and ballistics says it's Baretta ammunition. No record of the gun here and they're checking the central registry in Wiesbaden. Does that help?'

'Not in the least,' said the sergeant stolidly and continued towards the door.

Mrs Anna Poeschke proved to be no more helpful than had been her children and her daughter-in-law.

'There's just no one who could possibly have wanted to harm Dieter,' she sobbed. 'He was such a good boy and so loving to his wife and his brother and sister. Why would anybody kill him?'

'That's what we're trying to find out,' said the sergeant patiently.

Contrary to his expectations, Mrs Poeschke had not been informed of the death of her youngest son by the others and she took the news nearly as badly as they had.

'My children have always been so affectionate with each other,' she mourned. 'Dieter always used to say that he wanted to marry Renate when he grew up and so did Juergen for that matter.'

The sergeant cleared his throat. 'A lot of children get those ideas when they're little,' he said.

106

'Oh, they weren't so little,' said Mrs Poeschke. 'They knew what marriage was, but, of course, there are those silly laws here and even in Sweden where they do let the brothers and sisters marry now, they won't let a sister marry both brothers at the same time. It seems so foolish. After all, what business is it of the government?'

The sergeant did not answer. As an old and seasoned investigator with the criminal police in one of Germany's most violent cities, he had experienced some weird and wonderful things in his time and he regarded them all with his customary stolid, emotionless composure.

Now, for the first time in his career, he was literally struck dumb. There was no mistaking Mrs Poeschke's words. Her children were very attached to each other, so attached that, even in liberal Germany with its almost total lack of laws governing sexual behaviour, the attachment was illegal.

And with this realization, the conduct of the widow and the brother and sister whom he had interviewed previously took on new meaning. The question of the motive seemed to be answered.

'I understand your daughter is married to a Mr Hans Appel,' said the sergeant, making use of the information that he had received during the earlier interview. 'Is he a tall, husky, clean-shaven man in his forties?'

Mrs Poeschke caught on quickly.

'Hans is only thirty-four,' she said, 'but he wouldn't hurt Dieter. They were great friends.'

'But he is tall and husky and clean-shaven, isn't he?' said the sergeant.

Mrs Poeschke nodded grudgingly. 'But why would he kill poor Dieter?' she whispered. 'He didn't have a reason in the world.'

The sergeant did not attempt to explain to her what reason he had in mind, but thanked her for her co-operation and returned to the station where he found the inspector preparing to leave for home.

'Better stick around for a while,' said the sergeant. 'I think I know who killed Poeschke and I think I know why.

107

With your permission, I'm going over to Wiesbaden to make an arrest.'

The inspector listened to what he had to say and then decided to come with him. Forty-five minutes later Hans Appel ushered them into the living room of his comfortable apartment in Wiesbaden, twenty-five miles west of Frankfurt.

'I've been waiting for you,' he said. 'You took your time coming.'

'Did you murder your brother-in-law, Dieter Poeschke?' said the inspector who believed in coming directly to the point.

'Yes,' said Hans Appel flatly.

Appel was placed under arrest, cautioned as to his rights and taken to police headquarters in Frankfurt where he voluntarily made a full confession to the murder of his brother-in-law, Dieter Poeschke.

'I always liked Dieter and I got on with him well,' said Appel. 'Of course, we were different generations and he had different ideas to mine, but I didn't think that that really mattered so much. I thought it was all trendy stuff whipped up by the media and that underneath there wasn't all that much difference either.

'Dieter wasn't like a lot of the kids nowadays who lay around in the streets and kill themselves with drugs and things. He was a good worker and he made good money. I'd even thought of taking him into the company some day, if he wanted to.

'I liked the way he handled himself with Silvia too. A lot of young fellows his age would have just let things go, but Dieter said that now Silvia was pregnant they were going to get married, and they did.

'The trouble all started about a month before the wedding when Renate's older brother, Juergen, came over from the East Zone. I'd heard a lot about him from Renate and Dieter and I could understand that they were happy to see him. As I understood it, they'd been separated for over sixteen years.

'Dieter wasn't married yet at that time and he only had a single room and Mrs Poeschke only has a very small apartment too so Juergen moved in with us. I thought that was only natural. We had a big place and lots of room and it was going to be a little while before Juergen could get on his feet financially. As a matter of fact, I guess I was the one who suggested it.

'Well, everything was just fine. I got along well with Juergen and it was no trouble at all having him. As a matter of fact, I'm not home too much of the time. If you want to be successful in the contracting business today, you've got to look after everything yourself and some of our jobs are out of town.

'As I say, everything went well until about two weeks ago and then I came home late and Renate and Juergen had both gone to bed, Renate in our bedroom and Juergen in the guest room naturally.

'I went into the children's room to see if they were all right and Claudia was still awake.

'I started to tuck her in and she said, "If you won't tell anybody, I'll tell you a secret."

'I thought it was just some child's game so I said, "I won't tell. I promise." And then she said, "Mommy and Uncle Juergen were in bed all afternoon. They were all naked."

'I couldn't believe my ears. Claudia is a bright little girl and she doesn't make things up, but even if she did, I didn't see how she could think of something like that.

'I asked her if she was sure that she wasn't telling me a fib and she said no, that Mommy and Uncle Juergen took off all their clothes and got into bed and then they made a lot of funny noises and she thought they were tickling each other. They wouldn't let her into the bedroom.

'I was confused. I went out into the kitchen and I drank two or three brandies, something that I never do otherwise, and I thought about it.

'All I could think of was that Juergen really wasn't Renate's brother after all and that the whole thing was a conspiracy between her and Dieter and Mrs Poeschke so that she could bring a lover right into my house. I never dreamed that she and her brother were really having sexual

109

relations. It's just something that nobody does except sick people or maybe some place in Scandinavia.

'The next day I went down to the residents' registration office and asked to see Juergen's registration. He'd had to register as soon as he moved in with us, of course, and I made up a story about how he was sick and unconscious and I had to know the address of his relatives.

'Normally, they won't show you somebody else's registration, but they believed me and I got to see it.

'He really was Renate's brother.

'I didn't know what to think then. The information on the registry form had to be correct because they would have insisted on seeing his birth certificate and his other papers and I couldn't see how he could have forged a complete set of documents.

'What was more, I couldn't see why he would bother. If he was Renate's lover, he could just as easily have met her outside or even at the house. God knows, there was plenty of opportunity with me working so much of the time.

'I still didn't want to accept that Renate was actually sleeping with her brother, but I believe in having things out in the open so I went home and had it out with them.

'There was quite a row, mainly between Renate and me. Juergen didn't say too much. But the worst part was that neither of them actually denied it.

'Finally, I said that Juergen had to go. I didn't know what was going on and I didn't care what they said, but I wasn't going to have him in my house for another minute.

'Renate said, "All right, then I'll go with him," and they walked out of the apartment just like that. She didn't even take her clothes with her.

'I didn't know where they'd gone, but then I found out that they'd gone to stay with Dieter and Silvia so I went there a week later and tried to talk to Renate.

'I was convinced by now that there was nothing to my suspicions because I didn't believe that it would be possible for them to have sex relations when they were living with Dieter and Silvia. Silvia was always home and I thought that Dieter would be as shocked by such a thing as I was.

110

'I couldn't get anywhere with Renate. She wouldn't even talk to me, although I promised her a new fur coat and jewellery and just about anything she wanted if she'd come home.

'I still had the three children with me and I'd had to hire a woman to look after them. My business was going to pieces because I wasn't attending to it. And the only way I could communicate with Renate was through Dieter. I had to wait in the housemaster's apartment and Dieter would take my message up to Renate and come down with the answer, if there was any.

'About the only answer he ever came down with was that she wanted a divorce. I never mentioned the business with Juergen and neither did she.

'Then, finally, on January seventh I had the car in the garage and Dieter came over to Wiesbaden to pick me up. I'd been carrying my Baretta automatic on me ever since Renate had left and I had it that day. I don't know why. I certainly didn't intend to kill anybody.

'We drove to Frankfurt and had the same old business with Renate all over again and then Dieter started to drive me back to Wiesbaden.

'I was feeling pretty bad and I wanted to confide in somebody and I thought Dieter was the right person. After all, he was my brother-in-law and we'd always got on well together. I felt we sort of understood each other.

'So, as we were driving back to Wiesbaden, I told him what Claudia had said and about the row with Renate and Juergen because I was pretty sure that he didn't know anything about all that and I said I was sure that it was all just a misunderstanding.

'When I finished he looked at me sort of bewildered as if he didn't understand and said, "But Hans, both of us (at this point the late Mr Poeschke made use of the German equivalent of that fine, old Anglo-Saxon verb) Renate all the time."

'When he said that it was as if something inside my head snapped. I remember shooting him now, but I don't think I was actually aware of it at the time.

111

'Afterwards, I walked to the bus stop, took the bus to the railway station and came home. I thought you'd be waiting for me when I got here and I've been expecting you ever since.'

On July 29, 1974, the court in Frankfurt listened to and accepted Hans Appel's version of the events surrounding the murder of his brother-in-law and sentenced him to twenty-one months imprisonment. Even this sentence was not served as Appel was immediately released on bail pending a successful appeal to have the sentence set aside or suspended.

He is, however, a ruined man, his contracting company having fallen apart during his absence, and he apparently no longer feels any strong desire for material success.

Renate and Juergen are living together in a three-room apartment in Wiesbaden, the rent of which is paid by the Welfare Department.

Although police investigations of the charges of incest were initiated, they were subsequently dropped for lack of evidence. Incest is very difficult to prove if neither party is prepared to testify and both Renate Poeschke and her brother have steadfastly denied any relationship more intimate than that governed by brotherly love.

8

TRAVELS WITH A KILLER

Istvan Stefan Hollossy turned the cigar thoughtfully in his
fingers, bit off the end, spat it on the floor, lodged it in the
corner of his mouth and struck a match with his thumbnail.

'Are you telling me that our financial arrangement is
ended, Cornelia?' he asked in a calm, almost conversational
tone.

He gazed impassively at the pretty, dark-haired girl seated
on the sofa before him, his broad, flat face and slitted cat's
eyes making him look vaguely like one of the illustrations in
a child's book of lovable animals.

The girl made a nervous gesture with her hands.

'Janos and I want to get married, Stefan,' she said softly.
'We need the money.'

Sitting at the opposite side of the room, Janos Telek was
astounded to see a gun suddenly appear in Hollossy's hand.

There was the whiplash report of a 7.65 mm pistol being
fired within the confined space of the little attic room and
Cornelia Renz' pretty, dark head jerked backward.

A round, discoloured spot no bigger than the tip of a
man's finger had appeared, as if by magic, on the white skin
over her left eyebrow.

As Janos Telek watched, frozen with horror, the girl that
he had been planning to marry pitched forward onto the
carpet. Her left leg jerked twice in a reflex movement and
she lay still.

Twenty-two-year-old Cornelia Renz had been killed
instantly by a 7.65 mm pistol bullet fired at close range into
her brain.

The shock nearly deprived the twenty-six-year-old

113

Yugoslav of his reason and for several moments he lost all touch with reality.

How could Stefan Hollossy cold-bloodedly murder Cornelia? It had been Hollossy who had introduced him to her in the first place. And, although it all seemed long ago now, had only been some two months previous.

Janos Telek had come up to the German city of Luebeck on the Baltic Ocean where he had found work as a driver-salesman for a margarine company. Gifted for languages, he spoke fluent German as well as several of the Balkan languages.

It had been because of the languages that he had met Stefan Hollossy. The Hungarian had been drinking in the bar of the Blue Mouse, a popular Luebeck night spot, and Telek had addressed him in his mother tongue.

Hollossy had been so delighted that he had not let Telek pay for another drink all evening. He was, he said, the same age as Janos and a commercial artist by profession.

Commercial art seemed to pay very well, for Hollossy spent money as if he enjoyed an inexhaustible supply of it and, to an extent he did, as Janos found out two days later.

The inexhaustible source of money was named Cornelia Renz and she was sitting in the Kazoria, a Greek wine bar, when Hollossy and Telek came in.

'I need some money, Cornelia,' said Hollossy calmly, sitting down at the table and lighting one of his ever-present cigars. He smoked a comparatively expensive brand with the ominous name of Al Capone.

To Telek's astonishment, the girl had opened her purse and had given Hollossy several hundred marks. He was not only astonished, but also dismayed. Janos Telek had just experienced that remarkable phenomenon known as love at first sight and the transaction which had just taken place could only mean that Cornelia Renz was a prostitute and that Hollossy was her procurer.

Although it saddened him, the knowledge did not diminish his emotions and, when Hollossy went to the men's room, he quickly made a date with the charming Cornelia.

114

To his delight, she accepted immediately. The sentiments were, apparently, mutual.

On that first date Janos had learned all about Cornelia's relations with the Hungarian and the matter had not been nearly as bad as he had feared.

Cornelia was a prostitute, but not with her body and she did hand over a good part of her earnings to Hollossy, but he was not her procurer. Cornelia needed no procurer or protector as her clientele was very exclusive and so extensive that she could hardly take care of all of it.

The fact was, Cornelia was a masseuse and not just a self-taught one, but a trained, diplomaed, medically approved masseuse. She was employed at the Little Sea Castle, a luxury hotel catering to the elderly, located at Timmendorf Beach on the shores of Luebeck Bay a few miles to the north of the city.

There she massaged for an adequate, if not magnificent salary, the aching bones and muscles of hotel guests, none of whom would have dreamed of requesting that she massage anything else.

Now, Germany, Holland and the Scandinavian countries are teeming with masseuses, all self-taught and all highly specialized in parts of the body seldom requiring medical massage. Many of them are, however, far from attractive and, lacking Cornelia's formal training, they are inclined to go about matters in a rather heavy-handed manner.

A trained masseuse, such as Cornelia, literally has gold in her fingertips. Although she was fully aware of the potential, Cornelia had never made any effort to exploit her talents until she ran into Stefan Hollossy in the Nautic Bar, another Luebeck night spot.

Like all Hungarians, Hollossy was charming and, although he did not move in with her in the attic apartment in Timmendorf, they became lovers, an expensive arrangement for Cornelia as Stefan was a man with exclusive tastes and seldom or never the money with which to pay for them.

Cornelia's modest savings account was quickly exhausted with purchases such as a light green Fiat 124, so that Stefan could come to Timmendorf to see her without riding the

115

bus, and opulent weekends at the extremely luxurious Sea Horse Hotel.

It was a magnificent scale of living, but Cornelia's salary could not support it. At this point, the savings account being exhausted, Stefan pointed out that for a person of Cornelia's background and training, there were great opportunities of increasing the income. It would only be necessary to drop a few discreet hints in the right places . . .

Cornelia did not even hesitate. Although she retained her job at the Little Sea Castle, she began doing what is euphemistically termed 'special massage' on the side. Her clients were of both sexes and all were unanimously delighted. Cornelia was a very highly trained masseuse.

Why did Cornelia do this? She was a beautiful girl, professionally trained and above average in intelligence. She was not particularly infatuated with Hollossy, as witness the fact that she fell in love with Janos Telek immediately she met him. She was not even afraid of Hollossy whom she believed to be a commercial artist out of work.

There is a theory that victims are destined to the role by their own natures. Aggressor and victim do not play active and passive parts, but join together in a mutually complementary performance of a tragedy grasped by neither.

There was no reason for Cornelia Renz to prostitute her nimble fingers to pay for Stefan Hollossy's expensive cigars and nightclub bills, but she did it and, in so doing, effectively initiated her own death.

There had been, however, a brief period of happiness. Cornelia and Janos were in love. He had moved into the little attic apartment in Timmendorf, they had opened a new savings account into which he paid all of his salary and, on weekends, they had gone to Luebeck to eat dinner in cheap, Italian restaurants and enjoy themselves like two carefree children.

Stefan had not commented on the arrangement and it did not occur to either of them that he might have any objections. It had been a Thursday evening, April 3, 1975, when he had telephoned to say that he was in Luebeck and would like to

116

come out and see them. He said that he had an interesting proposition for Janos, but he would not say what it was.

Janos had told him to do so, they would all have a drink and a little something to eat together.

He had barely hung up when Hollossy appeared at the door. He had, it seemed, not been in Luebeck at all, but right there in Timmendorf.

The conversation which had followed had been short and to the point, so short in fact that Telek could scarcely grasp the fact that his sweetheart was dead.

One moment she had been sitting on the sofa, neat, pretty and speaking in her soft, gentle voice, and the next she had been lying on the carpet, the horrible little hole over her blank, staring eye and her open mouth gaping at the ceiling.

The whole affair had happened so quickly and unexpectedly that it was incomprehensible. Hollossy's appearance, the very short and matter-of-fact exchange of words, the sudden drawing of the pistol, the shot. From the time that the Hungarian had knocked on the door until Cornelia was dead was less than five minutes.

In a novel, Janos Telek would undoubtedly have sprung at the throat of the murderer and would either have revenged his dead sweetheart or died in the attempt.

However, this was real life and real death. Janos Telek was a margarine salesman, not a hero, and at that time he did not believe that he himself had more than another minute or two to live.

Surely, no one in his right mind would murder a young girl in the presence of a witness and then allow that witness to remain alive. He was positively astounded to see Hollossy replace the gun in the jacket pocket from which he had drawn it.

'Come on,' he said pleasantly to the paralyzed Telek, 'Grab hold of her feet and we'll toss her up onto the bed. God knows, this place is small enough as it is.'

Nearly insane with shock and fear, the Yugoslav did as he was told and together they placed the corpse on its back on the bed. There was scarcely any blood coming from the bullet hole, but the girl's eyes were wide open and stared

117

horribly, so that Telek became abruptly and violently ill, vomiting over his own shoes and trousers. Hollossy looked at him solicitously as he might have regarded someone being seasick and then took the corpse by the arm and rolled it over on its face.

Suddenly, he stiffened. 'Say!' he exclaimed. 'Isn't there an old woman lives next door here? If she heard the shot . . . Don't want any witnesses . . .'

The pistol appeared in his hand as if by magic and he slid out of the apartment door, as silent and deadly as a viper.

Janos Telek was as good a Communist as any other Yugoslav, but he fell to his knees and broke into fervent, if unorthodox, prayer. If Hollossy was prepared to kill an old woman simply because she might have heard the shot, what chance did he, an eye-witness, have?

Quite a bit apparently.

After a moment, Hollossy returned, the gun back in his pocket, with the observation that the lady was not at home.

'Get your stuff together and come with me,' he said. 'No tricks now. I mean business.'

Telek was utterly convinced that he meant business and the last thing in the world that he was contemplating was tricks. Gathering up his few personal belongings, he followed the Hungarian down to the courtyard where his own old Opel Rekord was parked.

'You drive,' said Hollossy, getting into the passenger seat in front. 'I'll tell you where to go.'

'I can't drive,' said Telek desperately. 'The cops took my licence last Saturday.'

It was perfectly true, but Stefan Hollossy apparently did not regard driving without a licence as a very serious offence.

'Don't worry about it,' he said jovially. 'If the cops stop us, it'll be a lot more than driving without a licence. You might not believe it, but I'm wanted in five countries and the least thing they want me for is bank robbery.'

Janos Telek did believe it and he had every reason to. As would later be revealed, Hollossy was wanted in Hungary, Austria, Switzerland, Germany and Sweden on armed robbery, assault with a deadly weapon and attempted murder charges. His most recent exploit before arriving in Luebeck had been a jail break in Sweden where he had been serving twenty years for armed robbery.

Oddly enough, up until the murder of Cornelia Renz, he had never actually killed anyone, although he had gravely wounded a number of people. Hollossy was not a killer in the sense that he enjoyed killing and did it for its own sake. Rather, he was a man who was determined to have whatever he set his mind to at all costs. During the course of his robberies, if no one offered resistance, no one was hurt. If anyone did, they were shot down instantly and ruthlessly.

Janos Telek, of course, knew nothing of all this and Hollossy did not go into details about the reasons for being wanted in five countries. However, he had seen what had happened to Cornelia and he was prepared to obey without question whatever orders his strange captor might choose to issue.

The only question that remained was: What did Hollossy want of him?

He was soon to find out. The Hungarian was gregarious and he had apparently become tired of playing the lone wolf. He liked Telek and so he had decided to make him his partner in crime.

'You must be practical in this life,' he explained reasonably. 'We need money for hotel bills, food, drink, women, clothes and travel, but we do not have any. Fortunately, there are people everywhere with money and it is only necessary to take it from them.

'Let us start with a simple example. We go into a store together, a small store where the owner is present. Such people always have money, sometimes quite a lot, sometimes not so much.

'Banks have more money, but they are more difficult. I cannot let you try a bank until you have had more experience. Have you ever killed anyone with a knife?'

Telek shook his head. He was utterly incapable of speech. Not only had he never killed anyone with a knife, he had never been in so much as a fist fight. He was horrified by even the thought of violence and was completely honest,

119

believing that the only happiness comes from money which you have earned yourself. Hollossy could hardly have picked a worse partner.

'Well, never mind,' continued Hollossy. 'Perhaps we can find a drunk for you to practise on.

'Now, listen carefully. We go into the store and I engage the owner in conversation. Then you come up behind him and slip the knife between his ribs.'

He paused and frowned, obviously thinking.

'It might be better if you were to split his head with a hatchet,' he said judiciously. 'If you did not do it properly with the knife, he might call for help or even fight with us. On the other hand, it would be harder for you to hide the hatchet in your coat. I will have to think about it.'

He fell silent and apparently did just that.

Telek was on the verge of fainting. He had grasped immediately why Hollossy wanted him to do all the knifing and splitting of heads.

Once he had killed or injured someone, he would be as much of a hunted criminal as the Hungarian. Whether he liked it or not, he would really be his partner in crime, at least until such time as he was captured and sent to prison for the rest of his life or shot down by the police.

They did not get very far with the Opel that evening for, on the outskirts of Ratzeburg, twenty miles south of Luebeck, they had a flat tyre and Hollossy decided to abandon the car.

He then marched his still shaking captive to the nearest tavern where he bought him three whiskeys, the same number for himself and a fresh supply of Al Capone cigars.

Hollossy seemed in the best of spirits and, after a brief flirtation with the barmaid, ordered a taxi and drove his new partner off to spend the night with what he described as friends.

Telek was astonished that such a man had any friends and he could not decide whether they were ordinary people or criminals like Hollossy. He spent a sleepless night, for every time he dozed off he was tortured by the vision of Cornelia's dead face with its sightless eyes staring at the ceiling.

The next morning Hollossy took him to the railway station where he bought two tickets for Hamburg. It was typical of the man that, as long as Telek was with him, he was never permitted to pay for anything. Stefan Hollossy was an extremely generous man with money, possibly because it was always someone else's.

Arriving at Hamburg at nine-thirty in the morning, Hollossy seemed at a loss as to what to do next and finally took his unwilling partner to see a showing of 'Archie, the Porno Butler', which was playing in a round-the-clock movie house.

This was followed by lunch, naturally at a first class restaurant, and the Hungarian then led the way to a department store where he stole a wig and a raincoat, 'For their work,' as he put it.

The afternoon was spent looking at jewellery stores which appeared to hold a great attraction for Hollossy. Telek made himself as accommodating as possible. He had no wish to die and Hollossy had shown him the three pistols which he carried at all times in his pockets.

'Always keep the pistol loaded and cocked,' he advised Telek earnestly. 'People will tell you that you can have an accident that way, but it is not as grave an accident as you can have if you need the gun in a hurry and it is not loaded.'

That evening, Hollossy rented a double room at the Union Hotel on Paulinus Square and, having locked the door from the inside, put the key in his pocket and fell instantly asleep.

Telek contemplated knocking him out with the table lamp, but was unable to find the nerve. The Hungarian had the reflexes of a cat and, if anything were to go wrong, the result would be fatal for Telek.

Shortly after two o'clock there was a demonstration of Hollossy's reflexes. A police car passing through the street below switched on its siren for a moment.

Instantly and in a single movement, Hollossy was off the bed and the muzzle of the 9 mm pistol, the big one, was pressed against Telek's right ear.

For a moment, they remained frozen, a tableau of a man and his murderer, and then the siren was switched off.

Hollossy relaxed, put the gun back in his pocket, went back to his bed and fell promptly asleep again.

Telek fainted.

The next day was spent in a further survey of the Hamburg jewellery stores, but Hollossy, who never slept twice in the same place if he could help it, did not return to the Union Hotel but took a room in a modest pension on the other side of town.

By this time Janos Telek was so exhausted from the nervous strain that he had no sooner laid down than he fell sound asleep. He was awakened at shortly after midnight by Hollossy shaking his shoulder.

'I've been thinking,' said the Hungarian. 'We're getting short of money. The old woman who runs this place may have some. Why don't you go down and kill her and see what you can find?'

The appalled Yugoslav, his tongue oiled by terror, sat up in the bed and offered one of the most passionate and convincing arguments of his life as to why it would not be advisable to kill and rob the owner of the pension.

'If we do that, the police will be looking for us and it will be impossible to rob the jewellery stores,' he concluded.

Hollossy found this reasonable.

'You are a good partner, Janos,' he said, turned over and went back to sleep.

Telek did not sleep another wink all night.

By morning he had come to the conclusion that he would make a break for it at the first opportunity. If he continued as he was, he was going to end up a hunted criminal or possibly dead in any case. He might as well be shot down by Hollossy as by the police.

The next day was Sunday and Hollossy was, apparently, an observer of the Sabbath for he did not leave the room, having all meals and the Sunday papers brought up by the same woman he had suggested killing and robbing the night before.

To Telek's amazement, although they now had very little money left, Hollossy tipped her generously.

The following morning Hollossy and Telek set off bright

and early to scout out the jewellery stores in Spitaler Street, a pedestrian mall.

Telek was still determined to escape or die in the attempt and, as Hollossy's attention was focused on a particularly tempting jewellery store window display, he edged slowly off until he was near a corner.

Expecting any moment the impact of a bullet in his back, he suddenly broke for the corner of the building, sprinted around it, cut through the nearest alley, doubled back into a department store and out the side door and halted the first taxi by the simple expedient of standing directly in front of it.

'Take me to the police station,' he gasped, throwing himself on the floor of the back seat. 'I've been a witness to a murder.'

Ten minutes later he was pouring out his tale to the not entirely convinced ears of Inspector Frank Luders of the Hamburg Criminal Police while the inspector's assistant, Detective-Sergeant Max Peters, talked to the police in Luebeck and Timmendorf over the telephone.

The fact was, Telek's experiences had so unsettled him that he gave the impression of being drugged, insane or both.

There was no report in Luebeck or in Timmendorf of the murder of Cornelia Renz, but a patrolman dispatched to her address as given by Telek, forced the door, which Hollossy had carefully locked, and found the corpse exactly as Telek had described it.

In the meantime, the records section had been busy with Hollossy's quoted statement that he was wanted in five countries and had found that he was not exaggerating. All of the entries in his voluminous file stated that he was extremely dangerous and to be approached only with the utmost caution.

Minutes after this information reached the inspector's desk, a top urgency red alert went out to all patrol cars and foot units. Road blocks were set up at the edge of the city and teams of officers were dispatched to the railway station and the inter-city bus depot.

The area around Spitaler Street was cordoned off and search parties went through every building. Stefan Hollossy was no longer there.

'Do you have any suggestion as to where he may have gone?' asked the inspector, fixing Telek with a dour eye.

'He's gone to rob a jewellery store,' said Telek. 'Whatever he takes into his head, he does regardless. He won't go back to the pension. He never goes back to the place once he's left it.'

However, Telek could not say which jewellery store Hollossy might have in mind. He did not know Hamburg and he and the Hungarian had looked at a great many jewellery stores since their arrival in the city.

'Get a list of the jewellery stores in the city centre,' said the inspector to Sergeant Peters, 'and try and get at least one man to each of them as quickly as possible. It's probably a wild goose chase. Hollossy must know we're looking for him by now and, regardless of what this Yugoslav says, I doubt that he'll try to pull off a robbery right under our noses.'

The inspector gravely underestimated Stefan Hollossy. At ten minutes to four that afternoon while police officers were being rushed to all jewellery stores in the downtown section of the city, Hollossy walked into the Hoellinger Jewellery Store located at 21 Alstertor Street on the edge of the suburbs. He was carrying the stolen raincoat over his right arm and in the hand beneath it was the cocked 9 mm automatic.

Inside the store were seventy-four-year-old Josef Hoellinger, his sixty-six-year-old wife, Maria, and thirty-eight-year-old Cristel Semmelhack who for twenty years had played the multiple role of salesclerk, manageress, friend and daughter to the childless Austrian couple.

'This,' said Stefan Hollossy, throwing back the raincoat to reveal the gun, 'is a hold-up.'

Like many older people, Hoellinger was a man of great courage. Without the slightest hesitation, he jerked open the cash drawer and brought out a tear gas cannister.

With equal lack of hesitation, Hollossy pulled the trigger.

The heavy slug smashed into Hoellinger's face, completely tearing away his lower jaw and knocking him to the floor.

Coolly and with incredible accuracy, the Hungarian fired two more shots, striking both Maria Hoellinger and Cristel Semmelhack in the head and killing them instantly.

He then pocketed his weapon and sauntered out of the store.

Behind him, Josef Hoellinger, in terrible agony and bleeding heavily from his shattered jaw, dragged himself across the floor and out the front door into the street. He was still conscious and, although unable to speak, made gestures to the passersby who came running that they were to help his wife and salesclerk inside. They were of course beyond help, but Josef Hoellinger was rushed to the hospital where he eventually recovered from his wound.

In the meantime, the dispatcher's voice at police headquarters was calling steadily over the police radio, 'Red alert! Red alert! All units. Istvan Stefan Hollossy believed in area of Alstertor Street. Unrestricted use of firearms authorized.'

In the courtyard at police headquarters, Captain Bernd Wilhelm mustered the Special Squad of which he was in charge. Only twenty-seven years old, most of his men were considerably younger. The Special Squad called for quick reflexes.

'Load,' said the captain.

The bolts of six machine pistols snicked back, throwing the first shell into the firing chamber of the rapid-fire weapons.

'Usual procedure,' said the captain. 'If we go in, I lead the first squad. Karl is back-up.'

The squad nodded in understanding. The captain was always the first man in.

No one would, however, be going in anywhere in the Alstertor Street. Once again, Stefan Hollossy had been too fast for the police cordon and he was now being driven across town by a very nervous cab driver named Werner Novak. Novak was nervous because Hollossy was holding the muzzle of the automatic against his ribs and, having heard the broadcast over the cab radio, he knew who his passenger was.

Roughly a half mile from Alstertor Street, Hollossy suddenly ordered the cab driver to stop and back the cab into a dark entry. Novak did so and, certain that he was now to be killed, leaped out of the cab and ran wildly down the street.

Hollossy ignored him and ran off in the opposite direction, plunging through the door of a machine shop at 84 Iffland Street where twenty-six-year-old Walter Klein was just on the point of going home.

In what seems to have been a purely reflex action, Hollossy raised the gun and shot him in the stomach. He then ran back out of the door.

In terrible pain, Klein staggered after him and was just in time to see him disappear into the basement of number 20 Grauman's Way.

Dragging himself to the telephone, he dialled the emergency police number and gasped out his information. In the meantime, Werner Novak had also called the police and, within minutes, the patrol cars began to pour into the area.

The building at number 20 Grauman's Way was surrounded, but no attempt was made to enter the basement. The rat was, presumably, in the trap, but he still had all his teeth and he had demonstrated that he knew very well how to use them. The job was one for the Special Squad.

Captain Wilhelm and his men rushed to the scene, but they did not make any immediate attempt to enter the cellar either. They were police officers and not desperados. Risks were taken only if they could not be avoided.

A loudspeaker was therefore set up in front of the cellar and, for over an hour, Inspector Luders tried to persuade Stefan Hollossy to throw down his guns and come out.

There was not the slightest sound from the cellar.

'Could he have given us the slip?' worried the inspector. 'Only Klein saw him go in there and he was badly wounded. He could have come back out again while Klein was on the telephone. If so, we're here besieging an empty cellar with half the force while he's clearing out of the city altogether.'

126

'A little tear gas?' suggested the sergeant.

'Try it,' said the inspector.

The tear gas was unsuccessful. The door to the basement entered into a corridor running parallel to the front of the building and there was no way of getting the tear gas shells back into the basement proper.

'Well, I suppose it's us then,' said Captain Wilhelm, settling his helmet onto his head and pulling down the face visor. 'We've got to know whether he's in there or not, I take it.'

'I'm afraid we do, Bernd,' said the inspector. 'Keep your head down.'

At ten minutes past five, Captain Wilhelm led the charge of his squad through the door and into the basement, his machine pistol at the ready.

Stefan Hollossy was also ready. His first shot ranged upward and struck the captain in the jaw beneath his face visor.

The captain continued to advance, firing his machine pistol on full automatic until the magazine was empty. He was then seized by his men and dragged outside while struggling to reload. Taken to the hospital, he eventually recovered and returned to duty.

The second charge of the Special Squad was led by the back-up man, Karl, and drew no fire.

The lights were turned on and Hollossy was found lying dead at the back of the basement. He had been struck twice by Captain Wilhelm's fire, once in the right shoulder and once in the left leg.

The bullet which had passed through his brain was not, however, from any police weapon. It was from a nine millimetre automatic pistol.

It was still gripped firmly in his very dead, very stubborn hand.

ROUGH JUSTICE

It was quiet in the charge room of the Meidling sub-station of the Vienna police. The midnight to eight duty had mustered an hour and a half ago and were now patrolling the streets of the Austrian capital in the gentle darkness of the spring night. The page of the calendar for April 4, 1968 had still not been torn off the block hanging on the charge room wall.

At one-thirty-nine there was a discreet buzz from the switchboard and a red light began to flash. The duty sergeant reached over and pressed the button.

'Charge room,' he said.

'Patrolman four-six-eight,' said a clear, rather high voice from the loudspeaker. 'I am at the Excelsior Garage, forty-seven Stein Street. I have intercepted two robbers.'

'Good,' said the duty sergeant. 'Do you require help to bring them in?'

'I require the corpse transporter,' replied the voice calmly. 'They are both dead.'

'What!' exclaimed the sergeant, startled out of his official manner. 'What happened?'

'They opened fire on me,' said Patrolman four-six-eight. 'I returned the fire.'

'Are you wounded?' said the sergeant.

'No,' said the patrolman.

'Then remain where you are,' ordered the sergeant. 'This will have to be reported to the C.I.D. They'll send someone out.'

He cut off the connection and dialled the number of the Criminal Investigations Department at police headquarters.

'Meidling,' he said when the telephone was picked up.

'We've had a shoot-out in the Excelsior Garage, forty-seven Stein Street. One of our patrolmen and two robbers. The robbers are dead. Do you want to check it out?'

'Right,' said the voice from headquarters. 'On the way, Meidling.'

The only witnesses to the conversation at the sub-station had been two sleepy patrolmen on standby duty, but at police headquarters two reporters covering the night crime beat followed the car from the C.I.D. out to Stein Street.

Next day two of the morning papers carried the headline, 'Heroic Rookie in Shoot-out With Gangsters!'

There was a large picture of Patrolman Ernst Karl, twenty-three years old and four months on duty with the force, and several shots of the two gangsters lying dead on the garage floor in pools of blood, their guns still gripped in their hands.

'Remarkable!' commented Inspector Franz-Josef Alte, the distinguished, grey moustached and side-whiskered senior investigations officer, laying the newspaper down on his desk and opening his silver cigarette case for one of the special, hand-rolled sobranie cigarettes which were the only things that he had ever smoked.

'How so?' said his assistant, picking up the newspaper and retreating to his own desk on the opposite side of the room.

'Are you familiar with the Excelsior Garage?' asked the inspector.

Detective-Sergeant Karl-Gustav Schuhmacher nodded silently, his square-jawed, handsome face bent over the newspaper. After a moment, he pushed it aside.

'Daytime parking garage,' he said. 'Used by the office people.'

'Can you imagine what would be in there at one-thirty in the morning so valuable that two desperate gangsters, armed to the teeth, would be prepared to shoot it out with a police officer to gain entrance?' said the inspector.

The sergeant looked startled.

'There wouldn't have been anything in there at night,' he

said. 'Not even a car. You're right. It's damned remarkable. Let me see who handled it last night.'

He left the office and came back a half hour later.

'The night trick man went out,' he said. 'Boy named Schelling. He's only in plainclothes for eight months. All he did was take the patrolman's statement and have the bodies sent down to the morgue. Their guns are in ballistics. No record on either weapon and neither one had been fired.'

'Let me talk to Igor,' said the inspector, picking up the telephone.

Dr Igor Schminke, the department's medical expert, had nothing to report other than that both men had been shot through the head and that he had recovered the bullets and sent them to ballistics.

'They say that they're pretty badly deformed,' he added, 'but that they're police ammunition.'

'Satisfied?' asked the sergeant as the inspector hung up the telephone.

'Even less so,' said the inspector. 'A four-months-old rookie, under fire for the first time, and he's so cool and accurate that he shoots two dangerous gangsters through the head before they can even fire their weapons. Call the training centre and ask them what kind of a score Karl had at weaponry training.'

The sergeant did as he was told.

'Good,' he said, putting down the telephone. 'Not the top of the class, but good. He's a very enthusiastic cop. Great law and order man.'

'Maybe too enthusiastic,' muttered the inspector. 'I've seen it before. Well, go get me a rundown on the victims now, will you? I want to know if they really were gangsters and, if so, what kind of gangsters.'

The task took the sergeant a little longer, but when he returned to the office, his information was concise and accurate. It was the only kind of information that he ever presented, which was one of the main reasons why he was the inspector's assistant.

'To begin with,' he said, 'the names given in the newspapers are incorrect. The two men were really Walter

130

Poettler, aged twenty-four and Johann Khisl, aged twenty-three.

'They both have records, but not exactly as gangsters. They're just petty crooks, drunk-rolling, small-time swindlers, blackmail and . . .'

'Ah-ha!' interrupted the inspector. 'Blackmail, you say?'

'You think they may have been blackmailing Karl?' said the sergeant. 'You couldn't get much from a patrolman's salary.'

'But you could get something out of a patrolman if you're a two-bit crook,' said the inspector. 'For example, a patrolman on night duty in the business district goes along trying doors. Every once in a while he finds one that the owner's forgotten to lock. So he calls the station and they contact the owner who comes down and locks it. Supposing he didn't call the station, but somebody else?'

'I see what you mean,' said the sergeant, 'but that doesn't fit in with the picture of Karl at all. His section sergeant says he's got an almost pathological hatred of crime and criminals.'

'Could be faking it as a cover up,' said the inspector. 'Or he could be doing something against his will because this couple were blackmailing him. You talked to the section sergeant? What did he have to say otherwise. What's this Karl like?'

'Tall, skinny kid,' said the sergeant. 'Strong as an ox and earnest as an owl. All spit and polish as if he was in the army rather than the police. Volunteers for everything and they have to knock him out to get him off duty.'

'The last statement is not literally intended, I take it,' remarked the inspector. 'However, I think you'll agree that, if Karl was being forced into some illegal activity, he'd be very liable to kill the blackmailers, given his nature and attitudes.'

'I suppose so,' said the sergeant. 'What do you want to do about it?'

'Exactly what we'd do if the man wasn't a police officer,' said the inspector. 'Murder is murder and I believe we have good reason to suspect that these two men were murdered.

That they may have deserved it, is of no consequence. If we're to permit the murder of everyone who deserves it, Vienna will decimated.'

'Full investigation then,' said the sergeant, getting to his feet. 'Well, it shouldn't be hard to crack if we can find out what it was that they had on him.'

It was, as the sergeant said, not difficult to break the case of the murdering police officer nor was it much more difficult to find out why Ernst Karl had lured his victims to the garage and shot them down in cold blood as they entered.

Ernst Karl, the very tough cop, was homosexual.

'They were blackmailing him,' said Sergeant Schuhmacher. 'He's made a full confession. They threatened to have him kicked out of the force so he's been paying them practically his entire salary plus anything he could borrow. Said he was afraid that it was only a matter of time before they'd force him into doing something crooked, so he killed them.'

'Sort of "I'd rather murder you than commit a crime" thing,' said the inspector. 'I suppose it didn't occur to him that murder was a crime.'

'His defence is that the men were criminals so they deserved to die anyway,' said the sergeant.

'We've been through that before,' said the inspector. 'I can't see the court accepting it.'

The court did not accept it, but the jury was somewhat understanding of Ernst Karl's predicament. The verdict was guilty, but with strong extenuating circumstances.

On December 19, 1968 Ernst Karl was sentenced to twenty years imprisonment and sent to the federal penitentiary at Stein to begin serving it.

In theory, this should have been the end of the career in law enforcement for ex-patrolmen Karl, but Karl did not see it that way. Scarcely arrived in prison, he began holding his own private court proceedings in the exercise yards and recreation rooms. Fellow prisoners whose sentences were, in Karl's opinion, insufficiently severe punishment for the crime concerned were summoned before the court by Police Officer Karl, prosecuted by Prosecuting Attorney Karl, sentenced by Judge Karl and, had the guards not promptly intervened on more than one occasion, executed by Executioner Karl.

There was no attorney for the defence, no jury and no acquittals. Executions were carried out, or would have been had there been no interference, by means of Karl's own two very powerful hands serving as a garotte.

Needless to say, Ernst Karl instantly became one of the most unpopular prisoners to ever grace a penal institution and the warden was constrained to hold him permanently in solitary confinement. It was either that or face a full scale prison revolt by the other prisoners.

Ernst Karl was a stubborn man and convinced of his principles. It was going to be some very considerable time before he would even be allowed in the exercise yard with the other prisoners, and any man in the prison would have committed suicide rather than share a cell with him. In a way, it amounted to very much the same thing.

In the meantime, hindered in the performance of what he construed to be his duty as an ex-patrolman, his former colleagues who had placed him in this position were involved in equal, if not identical difficulties.

These stemmed from a case which had arisen long after Karl had left the service.

On the morning of May 10, 1973 an employee of the Municipal Waste Disposal Service, otherwise known as a garbage man, had opened a trash can belonging to a shop near the centre of the city and had found himself looking into the face of a young woman.

The head to which the face belonged had been severed just below the chin and one of the young woman's breasts was resting on top of it, something like a macabre skull cap.

The expression of the face was not peaceful and the garbage man, although not normally inclined to fainting spells, lost consciousness. By the time that the police party arrived at the scene he had recovered, but was still largely incoherent.

Dr Schminke, who had come out in the car with the inspector and Sergeant Schuhmacher, gave the garbage man a tranquillizing injection as it was thought that he might know something about the head in the garbage can.

As it turned out, he did not, nor did he have any idea who the woman might be.

A squad of technicians from the police laboratories had now arrived and the garbage can was carefully emptied out onto a large plastic sheet. Eventually, most of the woman was found in the garbage can and in other garbage cans nearby.

The body was taken to the police morgue where Dr Schminke arranged it in its proper order and cleaned the face and hair. After pictures had been taken for the purpose of identification, he conducted a thorough autopsy.

While the body was being removed to the morgue, the technicians had made an exhaustive investigation of the area and had found nothing which could possibly be construed as connected with the dismembered corpse.

'I didn't think they'd find anything,' remarked the inspector as the sergeant returned to the office with his report. 'She obviously wasn't killed there. Someone merely brought the body along and dumped it in the cans. It's astonishing that it wasn't merely set on the hoist and dumped into the truck. If it had been, we'd only have found it at the dump, or possibly not at all. How did the garbage man come to open it?'

'He said,' said the sergeant, 'in so far as I can remember, "I had a strange, eerie feeling as if my spine had turned to ice. An inner voice commanded, 'Open the can, Hannibal!' and so I opened it".'

'My own feeling is that he sees too many old movies on late television, but apparently he did have some sort of hunch. The can was unusually heavy, of course.'

'His name is Hannibal?' said the inspector. 'Hannibal what?'

'Gronk,' said the sergeant. 'We're checking him out now, but I think it's very doubtful that he has anything to do with the murder.'

'We don't know that it was murder until Igor reports,' observed the inspector. 'Could have been an accidental death with someone trying to dispose of the body in a panic or something like that.'

It had, however, been murder.

'Karate chops,' said Dr Schminke, settling into the chair beside the inspector's desk and accepting a cup of coffee from the sergeant and a cigarette from the inspector.

Being a very conscientious young medical officer, he had worked most of the night on the body and his blue eyes were slightly bloodshot.

'Time of death,' he continued, 'was late day before yesterday afternoon or evening. The body was cut up with what appears to be an ordinary butcher's knife and a small handsaw by someone who had no idea of anatomy, but who had plenty of time. He simply continued to hack or saw until he got through whatever section he was working on. He may have used a hatchet or a cleaver in some places.'

'Any attempt to conceal the identity?' asked the inspector.

'None,' said the doctor. 'The fingerprints are intact and the face was not disfigured. She didn't look too happy because I think she had been raped just before she was killed. There are traces of sperm in the vagina.'

'A small girl, I take it,' said the inspector, 'since she was inside a garbage can?'

'Not unusually,' said the doctor. 'Five feet two inches. A hundred and two pounds. Don't forget not all of the body was in the one can and, secondly, it's easier to get into the can when it's cut up in comparatively small pieces.'

'Did you find anything else?'

'Nothing,' said the doctor. 'No trace of clothing and I think the pieces were brought to the can in plastic sacks because there are no fibres of any kind clinging to the cut surfaces and they are, of course, very sticky.'

'The laboratory was able to establish that everything else in the can was from the shop it belonged to,' said the sergeant. 'We're checking the owner and the personnel of course.'

'Hardly likely they'd put the corpse in their own garbage can,' said the inspector. 'Missing Persons?'

135

'I was waiting for Igor's description and the picture,' said the sergeant. 'How old would you say she was, Igor?'

'Between eighteen and twenty-two,' said the doctor.

There were a number of girls between the ages of eighteen and twenty-two missing in the city of Vienna, but none of them corresponded to the description of the girl found in the garbage can.

'I've put out circulars,' said the sergeant. 'If she's from Vienna, somebody should recognize her.'

Somebody eventually did, but not for some time.

'The girl in that circular,' said the voice on the telephone to the communications central of the Vienna Police without preamble, 'I think that might be our Miss Morscher.'

'Your name and address?' said the communications officer, pressing the button for the monitor to come on the line and begin the trace.

There were a great many circulars out in Vienna and some of them were for very serious offences. Calls such as this had to be traced in so far as possible should the caller be unwilling to identify him or herself.

This was not the case here for the caller immediately replied that his name was Martin Katz and that he was calling from the Albo Manufacturing Company's stock control office. He was, he said, the manager of the office and until the preceding week there had been a girl working there who looked very much like the picture on the circular.

Katz had assumed that the girl had merely quit without notice. She had been with the firm little more than two months and had had a routine clerical job. After noticing the circular at the railway station, he had called Personnel and had been told that Miss Ilse Morscher had neither given notice nor had she drawn what money she had on the books.

He had then called the police.

A team was sent to the Personnel Department of the company and learned that the girl had come originally from Graz, had been twenty-one years old, unmarried and living locally in a small studio apartment.

The apartment was searched and produced nothing except some pictures of the dead girl and her relatives in Graz.

136

There were no pictures of men to whom she was not related and her parents, upon being contacted by the Graz police, stated that she had not had any steady male friend.

'There's no evidence of anything happening at the apartment,' said Sergeant Schuhmacher, 'and her personal identification papers weren't there so the assumption would be that she was accosted on the street, presumably by a total stranger, who took her somewhere and killed her. The motive was undoubtedly sex.'

'It's going to be difficult,' said the inspector, frowning. 'Do you have any leads at all?'

'We're working on the office staff, the girls she worked with,' said the sergeant. 'Since she had only been three months in Vienna, it's probable that these were the only persons that she knew. What I'm trying to do is get some idea of her personal habits, where she hung out when she wasn't working, her interests and so on. From that we might be able to determine where she was when she was picked up by the murderer.'

The results of the interrogation of Ilse Morscher's fellow workers at the office produced largely negative results. Ilse Morscher, it seemed, had been a shy, strait-laced girl who had never mentioned any contacts with men and who, if she had any special interests, had not mentioned them to her colleagues.

'She was like a tourist,' said the sergeant. 'It was her first time in Vienna, and when she wasn't working she went around looking at the sights of the city.'

'That's not much help,' remarked the inspector. 'Is that all?'

'Almost,' said the sergeant. 'If Igor is correct about the time of death, she was killed on Friday evening. Two of the girls at the office think they remember her saying that she was going to visit the Prater that weekend. They thought she meant Saturday, but she might have gone that same evening after work.'

'And?' said the inspector.

'I've marked out the route between her apartment and the Prater,' said the sergeant, 'and, given the distance and the

137

current bus schedules, the most logical thing for her to have done is to have walked there. What I plan to do now is go over to the Prater myself and buy some samples of sausages and candy.'

The Prater is, of course, Vienna's huge amusement park, famous for the giant Ferris wheel which is often used as a symbol of the city.

'According to the analysis of the stomach contents in the autopsy report,' said the sergeant, 'sausages and candy were among the last things she ate. I want to know if it was sausages and candy from the Prater. If it was, she was either killed there or en route between there and her apartment.'

'Very sound reasoning, Karl,' said the inspector. 'I think you're on the right track and I suspect you'll find she was killed on the way home. There are usually too many people at the Prater for a girl to be picked up against her will, and the evidence seems to be that she was not a girl to allow herself to be picked up voluntarily.'

The lead, no thicker than a single thread, held true. The sausages and candy which Ilse Morscher had eaten on the last evening of her life did stem from the Prater and one of the sausage sellers was even able to identify the girl from her picture. She had been a pretty girl with a shy gentle manner who had seemed out of place amidst the boisterous surroundings of the amusement park.

'So now,' said the sergeant, 'we're conducting a door-to-door canvas along the route between her apartment and the Prater. I'm not really all that optimistic though. There are too many things that could have intervened. The girl may have met her murderer at the Prater and gone somewhere else with him or he could have picked her up along the route when there were no witnesses. It's mostly residential and we don't know with certainty how late it was when the contact was made.'

The sergeant could have afforded a little more optimism. Almost immediately, persons were found who had seen a girl resembling Ilse Morscher coming back from the Prater on the evening in question. It was not long before the search was narrowed down to an area of less than two blocks.

'Since he had to have some private place to rape her and cut her up,' said the sergeant, 'the assumption is that the murderer actually lives in this area. We're eliminating those families where such a thing would be impossible and searching the apartments of the rest. I think we're going to get him.'

And get him they did.

The search of the apartment of Johann Rogatsch, a forty-two-year-old house painter with a record of minor sex offences, contained traces of blood of the same group as that of the dead girl.

The plumbing in the bathroom was dismantled and tiny chips of bone and hair were recovered from the drains. Burned fragments of women's clothing were found in the furnace in the basement.

The police interrogators applied pressure, keeping up a relentless barrage of questions against the stubborn wall of the suspect's resistance.

The end was, of course, inevitable. Exhausted and conscious of the weight of the evidence against him, Rogatsch became entangled in contradictions and inconsistencies in his own statements, gave up and confessed.

He had, he said, wanted nothing more from the girl than a kiss, but she had resisted and he had given her a karate chop. He had only begun taking lessons in karate and he had chopped too hard. He was sorry. It had been an accident.

The court accepted that he was probably sorry, but not that it had been an accident or that all he had wanted was a kiss. On January 4, 1974 Johann Rogatsch was found guilty of first degree murder and rape and sentenced to life imprisonment.

It was the maximum sentence which the court could pronounce. There was, however, a higher instance and it was sitting in the penitentiary at Stein to which Johann Rogatsch was now sent.

It was now some considerable time since Judge Karl had tried any cases in Stein prison, and he was therefore sitting in the exercise yard and not in solitary confinement, the warden having come to the conclusion that he had revised his ideas about the administration of self justice.

The other prisoners were less confident and Karl sat alone.

Presently he was joined by the new prisoner, Johann Rogatsch, who had never heard of Ernst Karl or his feelings on the subject of law and order.

Rogatsch had not been in the prison long and he did not intend to stay there much longer if he could help it. He had already approached several of the other prisoners with suggestions for a break-out and had been rebuffed. Not being a professional criminal, he knew none of the other prisoners personally and was not highly regarded by them either.

Rapist-murderers are not, as a rule, popular even in prison. There were undoubtedly many in the prison who thought that Rogatsch should have been executed for his crime, and perhaps for this reason no one warned him that the man with whom he was sitting was a sterner judge than any he was likely to find in the conventional law courts.

Johann Rogatsch was, however, not interested in backgrounds or past history. He was interested in getting out and for that he needed a partner.

'Hostages is what does it,' said Rogatsch. 'Everybody's taking hostages now and the cops can't do a thing. Now, the way I see it, all we have to do is grab the warden's kids. He's got two little kids. And then, maybe, we take one of the guards and we tell them, either we get turned loose, with a car and a head start, or the kids get it. They won't have no choice. What do you think?'

'I think your whole suggestion is illegal,' said Ernst Karl flatly.

'You just ain't kidding,' chuckled Rogatsch who thought that Karl was trying to be funny. 'Now, I know where I can get a table knife and we can sharpen it up in the workshop. The only chance we'll have at the kids is when they come over to their dad's office, but they do that every once in a while. We'll have to wait for the right time and then play it by ear.'

140

'The court is in session,' said Ernst Karl, gathering his legs under him and flexing his very large hands. 'Prisoner! How do you plead?'

'Guilty to everything,' answered Johann Rogatsch, taking his companion's actions for a game and finding him a remarkably witty person. 'And what I ain't did yet, I'll do as soon as I get a chance.'

'Johann Rogatsch,' intoned Karl in the same flat, solemn, toneless voice, 'you have pleaded guilty to the charges of intent to take hostage minor children and an employee of the prison service with the purpose of illegally escaping from Stein penitentiary. Do you have anything to say in your defence?'

'Only that I can't think of no better way to get out,' said Rogatsch, vastly amused. He had not noticed that the other prisoners in the yard had gradually drifted away and that he and Karl were sitting almost completely alone beside the wall.

'Your defence is rejected,' said Ernst Karl, moving slightly closer to the unsuspecting man. 'In the name of the state of Austria, I hereby sentence you to death by execution and may the Lord have mercy upon your soul.'

'I'll appeal against the sentence,' gasped Rogatsch, laughing so hard that the tears ran down his face. 'By God, Karl! You sure know the language! Anybody would think you were a . . .'

His last sentence was abruptly cut off as Ernst Karl's powerful fingers closed about his throat.

'The sentence will be carried out at once,' said Executioner Karl with just a touch of satisfaction in his voice.

None of the guards was close enough to intervene in time, and naturally none of the prisoners could recall having seen anything, but it was not difficult to solve the mystery of the murder of Johann Rogatsch in the exercise yard of Stein Prison. Ernst Karl not only confessed, but was extremely proud of his act.

'A dangerous criminal,' he said. 'It is fortunate that he could be eliminated before he caused any more harm. One of my best cases.'

141

The court before which he was tried on charges of unpremeditated murder thought it one of his worst cases and on December 2, 1974 sentenced him to life imprisonment. Incredibly, the court-appointed psychologists had found him sane and responsible for his actions.

Ernst Karl is now back in Stein prison and the prisoners are more nervous than ever. All of them know by heart Ernst Karl's reply to the judge when he was asked if he had anything to say before he was sentenced.

Karl had turned his back on the judge and had addressed the spectators in the crowded court room.

'Have no fear, good citizens of Austria,' he had said. 'Whether in prison or out, you can depend upon me to continue and even intensify my battle against the criminals and law breakers in our midst. I shall not rest so long as a single criminal remains unpunished.'

The inmates of Stein prison, convicted criminals to a man, are utterly convinced of the sincerity of his words.

10

THE PASSIONATE PARAMOURS OF PORTSMOUTH

It was three-twenty in the morning of November 5, 1971 when Police Constable Paul O'Donovan peered through the window of the parked car and saw the dead man with the cylindrical, wooden handle of the knife sticking out of his chest.

Normally, Constable O'Donovan would have paid little attention to a car standing in the car park on the Purbrook Heath Road, but this car was different from all the others. The windows were not steamed.

People in cars parked in such places and at such times are usually engaged in rather strenuous physical activity accompanied by a good deal of heavy breathing. It steams the windows.

This car was cold and silent and the dew lay thick on the roof. Whatever physical activity there might have been, it was over now and forever.

The activity for the police had, however, just begun and, as Detective Superintendent Harry Pilbeam, the forty-four-year-old Crime Co-ordinator for South-East Hampshire, stood shivering and waiting for the reports of his men on that cold morning of Guy Fawkes Day 1971, there was no way that he could know that he was embarking on a case which would prove to be the longest and the most complicated in the history of the Hampshire Police.

For, at this time, the investigation did not promise to be too difficult, the identity of the corpse having been immediately established and there appearing to be a number of possible clues.

143

Chief among these was the murder weapon itself, a slender, sharp-pointed Japanese paper knife. Thirty-five-year-old Peter Richard Stanswood had been stabbed seven times with it and, of great importance to the investigations, some of the blood on its handle as well as on the steering wheel of his car was not his, but of a totally different blood group which the police laboratory would later establish as being APGM 21 AK1.

Stanswood, one of the owners of a pedalo business on the Isle of Wight, had lived at 28 Ninian Park Road, Copnor, in Portsmouth, the naval port on the south coast of England. He was survived by his lovely thirty-two-year-old, red-haired wife, born Heather Pridham, and the couple's two children, Tina and Charles.

Even before dawn had broken on that grey November day, detectives working under Superintendent Pilbeam had called at the Stanswood home to inform Mrs Stanswood of the death of her husband and to determine whether she might possibly shed any light on the identity and motives of the murderer.

Stunned and nearly incoherent with the shock of the sudden news, she could only say that her husband's business associate in the pedalo business was a Mr Ken Thompson, but that they had got on well to the best of her knowledge. She suggested with apparent reluctance that the murder might have something to do with her husband's mistresses.

After a little urging, she provided the stupefied detectives with a list of names of over two dozen women with whom her husband had allegedly been intimate, including two who had borne him illegitimate children and one who was now pregnant with his child. She thought he might have been spending the preceding night with this last-named mistress, a Miss Wendy Charlton, who lived at 17 Taswell Road in Southsea. He had, in any case, not been home at all that night. Her statements were confirmed by the couple's children.

Although it had seemed impossible to the detectives that a man could have as many mistresses as Mrs Stanswood had said her husband had and still have time to devote to

144

business, it turned out that she had actually been guilty of an understatement. Peter Stanswood had had far more mistresses than even his wife suspected and had still been a diligent worker who earned considerably more than an average income.

Mrs Stanswood's guess about her husband's whereabouts on the night of the murder was, however, accurate. Miss Charlton confirmed that he had been with her and had, during the course of the evening, telephoned a Miss Linda Reading, one of the mothers of his illegitimate children. When he left somewhat later, she had thought that he was going to Miss Reading or home.

With the exception of the murderer, Miss Charlton was, apparently, the last person to have seen Peter Stanswood alive, but the police were already beginning to realize that what had seemed a comparatively simple case was turning into a complex tangle of adulterous sex relations involving such numbers of people that it sometimes seemed half the population of Portsmouth had had reason to want to murder Peter Stanswood.

Before the case would end, more than 20,000 persons would be questioned and over 2640 statements taken, some of them several times when it became obvious that the previous statements were false.

And many were false, for, if Peter Stanswood had been astonishingly active in the pursuit of extra-marital adventures, his exploits had been largely dwarfed by a veritable army of housewives who enjoyed their lovers on what amounted to practically a production line basis.

There had been few complaints from their husbands. They were acting as lovers for the other housewives.

Under such circumstances, it was scarcely strange that many of the persons interviewed were, to say the least, something short of candid. In many cases the detectives, anxious to avoid domestic friction, were forced to interview the men separately at their place of work and their wives during their absence.

As in all cases where the murder victim is married, the widow had been considered the prime suspect although it was certain that she could not actually have been present at the murder. She could, however, be responsible with the actual killing carried out by one of her lovers.

For Heather Stanswood too had had lovers, some two dozen of them, according to her own statement to the police, and the most recent, and therefore most interesting to the police, was a thirty-nine-year-old gas conversion worker named Kenneth Joseph Fromant, married, the father of two daughters and resident at Hilary Drive, Crowthorne, in Berkshire.

Fromant had a police record, having been sentenced to five years' imprisonment in 1950 for shooting another man in the thigh. The incident had taken place during a confrontation between London street gangs and the victim had been attacking Fromant with a broken bottle at the time.

Although this prison record might indicate a tendency to violence on the part of Kenneth Fromant, it did not make him any better a suspect than Mrs Stanswood's other lovers or the husbands and lovers of Peter Stanswood's mistresses, and Fromant stated in his interview with the police that he had been in Berkshire on the night of the murder.

This could be neither proved nor disproved, but there was good reason to believe that Fromant had terminated his affair with Heather Stanswood at least two months before the murder. Moreover, neither he nor anyone else appeared to have taken the affairs very seriously.

Heather Stanswood had, it was true, once filed divorce proceedings against her husband when he became the father of his first illegitimate child in 1961, but there had been a reconciliation and the case had never come before the court. Since that time, he had had literally dozens of mistresses, many with Heather Stanswood's knowledge and some, apparently, with her approval.

One such case was represented by Elizabeth Thompson, the thirty-two-year-old wife of Stanswood's business partner and Heather Stanswood's oldest and best friend.

Mrs Thompson, at that time the mother of three children and living at Bell Crescent, Waterlooville, had formed a friendship with the then Heather Pridham at the age of sixteen when both girls were working as machine operators in a dress factory. The friendship had continued after Elizabeth Binning had married Ken Thompson in 1959. Heather had married Peter Stanswood one year later and the two men had also become friends, Thompson moving to the Isle of Wight in 1970 to join Stanswood in his pedalo boat business. The Thompsons had then gradually become estranged, but long before this, Peter Stanswood and Elizabeth Thompson had been engaged in sexual relations, certainly with the knowledge of Heather Stanswood and, possibly, with the knowledge of Ken Thompson who may have had sexual relations with Heather Stanswood as well.

It was in Elizabeth Thompson's statement to the police that the first mention of gas conversion workers other than Kenneth Fromant was made. She had, she said, entered into a relationship with one of the gas conversion men following a fire which had cost her her home and most of her possessions. She had also suffered a broken leg and the gas man had been helpful at a time when she sorely needed help. This was in 1970, not long after her husband had gone to the Isle of Wight.

Later that year, she had severed her connection with the gas conversion worker, whose name was not revealed to avoid domestic complications, and had taken up with another gas conversion worker named Arthur Gavin.

Mr Gavin was the brother-in-law of Kenneth Fromant who had been the lover of Heather Stanswood until September of 1971 when he left her for Elizabeth Thompson. There were no hard feelings and the two friends apparently exchanged confidences and lovers almost casually.

Such complicated histories involving adultery and illicit sexual relations between hundreds or, possibly, even thousands of persons in the Portsmouth area were the most striking characteristic of the case and also the most troublesome to the police in solving it. They were, however, of vital importance for, as the investigations progressed, it became increasingly certain that it was some facet of these

147

intertwining relationships which had led to the murder of Peter Stanswood.

And with this certainty came the suspicion that one or more of the gas conversion workers, of whom there had been at times as many as a hundred in the city, were involved. Out of the hundreds of women interviewed, an enormous percentage admitted to having had adulterous relations with gas conversion men.

Aside from this, progress was slow. The source of the murder weapon had proved impossible to trace, there being many thousands of such Japanese paper knives which had been imported into the country. No fingerprints had been found on either the knife or the door handles of the car.

The autopsy had not been particularly helpful and had, actually, provided something of an additional mystery for it reported that traces of pheno-barbitone were present in the liver of the corpse. This could indicate that Stanswood had been, in some way, connected with the drug scene, but no evidence of this could be found.

There was also still no known motive. Stanswood had had no very serious enemies even among the men whose wives had granted him their sexual favours. No one had benefited by his death. In an atmosphere where casual, promiscuous sex was accepted as the normal pattern of life, it seemed hardly likely that anyone would have been so involved emotionally as to commit murder out of jealousy. Most of the husbands and wives appeared to know of the partner's extra-marital adventures and most of them seemed not to have cared.

If they had not cared before, they did now for, with the death of Peter Stanswood and the resulting publicity, it was no longer possible to gloss over such flagrant sexual activity. The people involved were not, for the most part, among the very young, usually thought of as liberal in their activities toward sex, but persons in their thirties, forties and even older. Open knowledge of adultery could be very damaging to such persons and, as one of the detectives put it, there were probably upward of a thousand persons in Portsmouth who did not sleep well as long as the investigations were going on.

And they went on for a very long time despite what seemed for a time a break almost at the beginning of the case.

The supposed break came less than a week after the murder and began with an incident in the Castle Tavern, Somers Road, Southsea. The occasion was a darts match with a team from the Royal Exchange Pub.

Peter Stanswood was well known in the Castle Tavern, where he had been a prominent member of the darts team. During the course of the evening, there was a drawing of tickets and, to the horror of all present, the name called out as winner by the girl behind the bar was Peter Stanswood.

An instant later, the horror was compounded when Peter Stanswood stepped calmly forward and claimed his prize!

It was, of course, not the murdered Peter Stanswood, but a roofing engineer from Purbrook by the same name who was on the darts team of the Royal Exchange Pub. Incredibly, although somewhat older, he looked very much like the dead man and had even frequented one of the same public houses, the Monckton Pub in Copnor Road not far from where the murdered Peter Stanswood had lived. For months afterwards, his wife was troubled by condolence calls from persons thinking him dead, and he found the whole experience extremely nerve-wracking.

Not a little of this nervous tension was produced by one of the police theories, i.e. that the murder of the other Peter Stanswood had been a case of mistaken identity. The murderer had really wanted to kill the roofing engineer and not the pedalo operator.

The theory was based largely on the fact that in the weeks preceding the murder, a number of anonymous calls had been received by the Peter Stanswood in Purbrook. Usually, the caller, a man, had asked for Peter Stanswood and had then said nothing more, but had remained on the line as the sound of his breathing could be heard. On other occasions, the caller had said nothing at all.

The roofing engineer had no idea who might have wanted

149

to harm him, but he accepted the police idea that, if the murder had been a case of mistaken identity, the murderer might attempt to correct his mistake, and for weeks he carried the telephone number of the police station in his pocket whenever he went out. He was also discreetly accompanied at a distance by one of Superintendent Pilbeam's men.

There was no attempt on the life of the surviving Peter Stanswood, but one significant thing did take place.

From the day that Peter Stanswood of Ninian Park Road was murdered, no further anonymous telephone calls were received by Peter Stanswood in Purbrook. To be on the safe side, the Post Office provided him with an unlisted number and the mystery of the anonymous caller was never solved.

One thing was, however, certain and that was that Peter Stanswood of Purbrook, a respectable father of three teenage children, was in no way connected with Peter Stanswood of Ninian Park Road or with the vast circle of subscribers to the joys of permissive, liberal sex in Portsmouth.

The gas conversion workers were, it seemed, almost to a man, and the investigations now led to one of the meeting places for gas men and adventurously-minded housewives in the Mecca Ballroom, Arundel Street, Landport.

Here, among the hundreds of women interviewed, was found the lead to the Scots housewife who, without realizing it, would provide one of the vital keys to the solution of the case.

It was July of 1972 and nearly nine months had passed since the murder of Peter Stanswood. On that afternoon the Scots woman, who asked that her name should not be revealed as her husband would not like it, was being interviewed by Detective Inspector Ernie Woolf and Detective Constable Roger Hurst. During the course of the interview she revealed, almost casually, that she had been visited on the night of the murder by her lover at the time, a gas conversion worker named Ian Dance.

This caused the detectives' ears to prick up for Dance had been interviewed and had denied being in Portsmouth that night. He was immediately brought back to police headquarters and, being confronted with the statement of his Scots mistress, he changed his story and admitted that he had been in Portsmouth on the evening of the murder. He had driven there, he said, in the company of another gas conversion worker, Mr Kenneth Fromant.

This was of great interest to the police, for the name of Kenneth Fromant had been on the list of friends, lovers and acquaintances with which Heather Stanswood had provided Inspector Woolf some two weeks after the crime.

Fromant had been interviewed at this time, but had denied being in Portsmouth, saying that he had been at his home in Berkshire.

Now, according to the statement of Ian Dance, he had been in Portsmouth after all and, although there appeared to be no connection between Dance and Stanswood, Fromant had allegedly been the lover of both his and his partner's wives.

On July 17, 1972, Fromant was brought to police headquarters in Cosham and interrogated for the second time. Confronted with the statement made by Ian Dance, he admitted that he had been in the Portsmouth area and that he had lied about this in his first statement.

He had, he said, spent the night with Elizabeth Thompson.

This was denied by Elizabeth Thompson, who was being interviewed in another room, but she did change her story also to admit that she had had sexual relations with Fromant on a number of occasions. Previously, she had admitted only to having had sex with him once.

Both Fromant and Thompson denied any connection with the murder of Peter Stanswood, but a sample of Fromant's blood, sent to the police laboratories, returned with the information that it belonged to Group APGM 21 AK1, the identical group to the blood found on the steering wheel of Stanswood's car and on the handle of the murder weapon.

Blood is, however, not like fingerprints and more than one person can have the same blood group. However, among all the persons tested so far, only Kenneth Fromant had Group APGM 21 AK1.

The police were, therefore, inclined to think that Fromant might very well be their man although they were still not in any position to prove it.

Their suspicions were strengthened a short time later by what Superintendent Pilbeam was to describe as a 'godsend' and a 'colossal piece of luck'. In spite of all the time which had elapsed, the car in which Dance and Fromant had come to Portsmouth was found standing in the yard of a garage at Bitterne, Southampton. Incredibly, it had not been driven since the night of the murder. It had failed its road test.

Samples of soil taken from the treads of its tyres were brought to the police laboratories where it was possible to determine that the samples were identical to the soil found at the scene of the crime.

Even with this, the case was far from complete. There was still no plausible motive and there was not the slightest evidence that Kenneth Fromant had ever even met Peter Stanswood while he was alive. In addition, although Heather Stanswood had listed Fromant as one of her lovers, he denied this and said he did not even know the woman.

Four months later, he was once again brought to police headquarters in Cosham and, this time, he changed his story again and admitted not only that he had known Heather Stanswood, but that he had had sexual relations with her over a period of time. He added, however, that he had had sexual relations with a good many Portsmouth housewives and that none of their husbands had been murdered. Why should he have chosen Peter Stanswood for a victim when he had never met him and his affair with Heather Stanswood had been so fleeting that he could scarcely remember it?

The police had no answer to this question, but they did have three major points in evidence against Kenneth Fromant. The car in which he had come to Portsmouth on the night of the murder had been at the parking area in the Purbrook Heath Road as shown by the soil on the tyres. The blood on the handle of the murder weapon and on the steering wheel of the victim's car were of the identical blood group to his. And he had engaged some two months prior to the murder in sexual relations with the wife of the victim.

The greatest difficulty was lack of a motive. If Kenneth Fromant was guilty of the murder, then it would appear that he had stabbed to death a total stranger for no reason at all.

Or had the killing really been a case of mistaken identity? Did Fromant think that the man he was murdering was the Peter Stanswood of Purbrook, the roofing engineer who had received the mysterious telephone calls?

The possibility was investigated as carefully as all of the other possibilities in the case. There was not the slightest evidence that Fromant had ever met or heard of the Peter Stanswood from Purbrook.

There had, it seemed, been no mistake. Someone had wanted to murder the Peter Stanswood who had been murdered and the person with the most plausible motive was still Heather Stanswood, his wife. Fromant, who had actually carried out the murder, had had no motive of his own, but had merely been acting at the instigation of his former mistress.

Early in 1975, the Director of Public Prosecutions came to the conclusion that the case against Fromant and Mrs Stanswood was sufficiently established and issued orders to the police to proceed against them.

On May 19, 1975, Superintendent Pilbeam went to the office of the manager of the North Thames Gas Board in London where Fromant was currently working and took him into custody.

'You are being placed under arrest,' he said, 'for the murder of Peter Stanswood.'

'What is there to say?' said Fromant stoically.

Oddly, although he had met the superintendent on several previous occasions, he appeared not to remember or recognize him at all.

He was taken back to Cosham where he and Heather Stanswood, who had resumed her maiden name of Pridham and who had also been taken into custody that same day, were formally charged with the murder of Peter Stanswood. Neither made any statement and they did not look at or speak to each other.

153

The committal proceedings against Kenneth Fromant and Heather Pridham were due to take place on July 12, 1975, but on the ninth, Mrs Pridham suddenly called for her solicitor and her barrister and, in their presence, made a startling confession to something which she said she had kept secret for nearly two years.

Elizabeth Thompson, she said, had confessed to her that she and Kenneth Fromant had murdered Peter Stanswood and had described exactly what had taken place that evening.

According to this statement, Elizabeth Thompson had called Peter Stanswood on the day of the murder and had made an appointment to meet him at the Purbrook Heath Road car park, presumably for the purpose of engaging in sexual intercourse.

Stanswood had accepted and when he arrived, she and Kenneth Fromant, who was her current lover, were waiting in the car in which he and Ian Dance had come to Portsmouth. Dance was not present, having been dropped off at the house of the Scots housewife with whom he was having an affair.

Elizabeth Thompson and Kenneth Fromant had then joined Peter Stanswood in his car, there had been an altercation and Fromant had received a cut in the arm from the Japanese paper knife which he had brought with him. Regaining control of the knife, he had then stabbed Stanswood to death.

Following the murder, Mrs Thompson and Fromant had driven to Mrs Fromant's home at 10 Philip Road in Waterlooville, where they had changed clothes and Mrs Thompson had stitched up the cut in Fromant's arm.

The motive for all this appeared to be that Elizabeth Thompson was in love with her friend's husband and resented his affairs with other women. Fromant seemed to have been drawn into the matter without being too clear as to what he was doing.

Elizabeth Thompson had, in the meantime, divorced her husband in 1973 and had acquired a new lover, a Mr Peter Jackson, to whom she bore a child early in 1974.

Brought to Cosham Police Headquarters and confronted

with the statement by Heather Pridham, she burst into tears, declared it nothing more than a pack of lies and was permitted to leave.

On July 12, 1975, the committal proceedings against Kenneth Fromant and Heather Pridham took place before the stipendiary magistrate Sir Ivo Rigby at Havant Magistrates Court and ended in committal for Fromant. Heather Pridham was ordered to be released as she was found to have no case to answer.

Checking of her statement concerning the confession of Elizabeth Thompson continued and, on August 5, 1975, Sergeant Cox went to Waterlooville where he arrested Elizabeth Thompson and brought her back to Cosham. She was charged by Superintendent Pilbeam with the murder that same evening and, on September 12, 1975, was committed to stand trial with Kenneth Fromant for the murder of Peter Stanswood.

The trial began on October 21, 1975 at Winchester Crown Court with Mr Justice Talbot presiding. The seventeen days that it lasted were so filled with testimony concerning the illicit sexual activities of a large segment of Portsmouth society that even the judge was moved to remark that Portsmouth was a city in which sexual promiscuity and adultery were rife within some social groups.

Much of the testimony was anonymous with names being suppressed by the police in order to avoid domestic quarrels and protect marriages, as far as possible. A very clear picture emerged, however, of the almost legendary exploits of the gas conversion men with the housewives of Portsmouth. Following the trial, these statements were destroyed.

The matter of the motive for the killing was never entirely made clear, but the indications were that Mrs Thompson had been more jealous of Stanswood than his own wife had been.

There were also suggestions that Kenneth Fromant had murdered Stanswood out of jealousy over his success with women. This theory was particularly popular with the foreign press which built up a sort of hypothetical competition between the two men based on the number of women with whom they had managed to commit adultery. Fromant had not been able to rack up as high a score as his rival and had, in a fit of jealous rage, murdered him.

This was, however, contradicted by the fact that Fromant had apparently never before in his life laid eyes on Stanswood up until the night of November 4, 1971 and, if he did not even know the identity of the man he was murdering, he could hardly have been jealous of his exploits.

Kenneth Fromant did not give any reason, his only comment on the murder being, 'that it was all for nothing'.

Called to the witness box to testify on his own behalf, he provided the court with one last sensation in a trial which was quite sensational enough to begin with.

'Yes,' said Kenneth Fromant. 'I was at the scene of the murder. I lied in my original statement. I was there and I was cut in the arm as Mrs Heather Pridham stated. However, I could not reveal the truth before because I wished to protect the true guilty party, Mrs Elizabeth Thompson! It was she who wielded the knife and not I!'

This 'confession' to his mistress's part in the murder did not impress the jury very much and on November 14, 1975, they found Kenneth Joseph Fromant and Elizabeth Thompson guilty of the murder of Peter Richard Stanswood. Oddly enough, the jury apparently found more evidence of Mrs Thompson's guilt than of Fromant's, for the verdict in her case was unanimous while Fromant was convicted with only a majority decision of ten to two.

Both were sentenced to life imprisonment by Mr Justice Talbot, who remarked that he did not think that the court had even yet heard all of the truth concerning the case.

And well he might, for there were a number of questions which were never answered.

The motive was, of course, one of the most important, but there was also the matter of the murder weapon which could not be traced and the origin of which remained unknown. It had also not been possible to ascertain when and where Peter Stanswood had received his invitation to drive to the Purbrook Heath Road rendezvous.

There was the question of the knife wound which Kenneth

Fromant had admittedly received in the arm. Had it been in the course of a struggle with Stanswood and, if so, how had Fromant managed to regain control of the knife and kill his adversary with it?

Then, there were the traces of pheno-barbitone found in the liver of the corpse. Had Stanswood been connected with the drug scene? There was not the slightest evidence that he was.

Perhaps Elizabeth Thompson and Kenneth Fromant know the answers to these questions, but, if they do, they did not reveal them at the trial or after. Instead, they sat engrossed in their own affairs and not even looking at each other until the trial was over.

Fromant received his sentence impassively and without changing expression. Mrs Thompson showed scarcely more emotion, but appeared to be on the verge of tears as she was led away to begin serving her sentence.

11

TO LOVE IS TO KILL

On the northern edge of central Germany, where the strangely formed hedges of the ancient kingdom of Muenster give way to the moors and low-lying plains of the north, lies the historic Teutoburger Forest, swinging in a great curve from Rheine in the west, through Bielefeld to Paderborn in the south-east.

To the north-east of Bielefeld lies Herford and, beyond that, Rehme. Rehme is not a very large town, not nearly as large as Herford or Bielefeld, but in the spring of 1961 an event took place there which was to put fear into the hearts of women and girls for many miles around.

Not immediately, though. When Oscar Riedel, a middle-aged foreman in a shoe factory, walking to the Rehme railway station to go to work, came upon the corpse of the girl lying in the ditch, it was taken as an isolated incident. That is, the public took it as an isolated incident. The police were not so sure.

April 8, 1961 was a Saturday, but the shoe factory where Riedel was employed was working. The German economic wonder was in full swing and some plants were working straight through the week.

Oscar Riedel did not mind. He liked his work and he was making money. Moreover, the spring was not as rainy as it often is in central Europe and this particular Saturday was bright and sunny enough to be in June.

Half-way to the railway station, Riedel came upon a figure lying in the ditch beside the road, a figure which he could not see clearly because of the rank growth of grass and weeds along the edge. Assuming that some drunk had fallen into the ditch and had passed out or even injured himself there, Riedel started to clamber down with a view to offering help.

He had only progressed far enough to get a clear look at the figure when he froze. This was no drunk. It was a girl, a girl standing almost on her head, her skirts up over her face and her legs widespread to display obscenely the naked lower torso. There was blood on her white thighs and belly and what looked like the shreds of torn underwear lay around her.

The conclusion that the girl had been raped was inescapable and Riedel promptly tumbled down into the bottom of the ditch to offer help. However, the hand which he seized was cold and stiff and there was no pulse in the slender wrist.

The girl had not only been raped, she had been murdered!

Shaking with horror, Riedel scrabbled out of the ditch and ran wildly off in the direction of town. Five minutes later the local constable knew that Rehme had had its first murder case in at least two generations.

Not, of course, that the constable could do much about it. Rehme is too small to have its own Criminal Investigations Department and such matters are handled out of the city of Minden, six miles to the north-east.

The constable, therefore, came out to the scene of the discovery, verified Oscar Riedel's report and immediately called Minden. Forty minutes later Inspector Gerhard Heidel and his assistant, Detective-Sergeant Leopold Eisenbach, arrived bringing with them the department's medical expert, Dr Herbert Krause.

The doctor immediately proceeded to an on-the-spot examination of the corpse while the sergeant began staking off the area in one metre squares.

'Are we going to need the lab squad, Leo?' said the inspector.

'Doubt it,' said the sergeant. 'If there's anything, it's right around the body. I can take care of it.'

The doctor had by now turned the dead girl's skirts back from her face and the inspector asked the local police if they were able to identify her.

They were. She was a twenty-three-year-old local girl who lived with her parents and worked as a salesgirl in one of the shops. Her name was Ingrid Kanike. Being a small town, they also knew that she had been neither engaged nor going steady.

'She was a nice girl, but a little plump,' said the chief constable. 'Worried about her weight a lot.'

'We'll go over and talk to the parents,' said the inspector. 'They have to be notified and they may be able to give us some idea of where she was last night and what she was doing, assuming, of course, that this happened last night.'

'It did,' said the doctor, 'around midnight.'

The inspector and the constable left and when they returned an hour later, the sergeant and the doctor had both completed their work.

'Nothing,' said the sergeant. 'I found her handbag. It hadn't been opened. Usual stuff a woman carries around with her. Small amount of money. From the marks on the ground, he simply grabbed her, dragged her into the ditch, tore off her underwear and raped her. Whether he strangled her before or after, I don't know.'

'After,' said the doctor. 'Or at least death took place after. He was probably holding her throat while he was raping her, but he only shut off her breath after he had finished.'

'Fully consummated, I take it?' said the inspector.

The doctor nodded shortly. 'Fully,' he said. 'The girl was a virgin which is where the blood on the thighs and belly comes from.'

'You think he may have known her?' said the inspector.

'Doubtful,' said the doctor. 'This is an almost classic sex crime. The man is a sadist who can, very probably, only achieve sexual satisfaction by killing or at least severely injuring his partner.

'He has a compulsion and the first available female is the one taken. This girl merely had bad luck. She probably never set eyes on him before in her life.'

'Well, I didn't get very much from the parents either,' said the inspector. 'They didn't even know she was missing. She went to a movie in Minden last night and should have come back on the train which arrives here at seven minutes past twelve.'

'And the murderer jumped her as she was walking home,' said the doctor. 'A clear picture.'

'Not quite,' said the inspector. 'Her parents said she often went to the movies in Minden and that then she got back after they had gone to bed. On a Saturday morning like this, the parents still weren't up when she went off to work so they wouldn't normally see her until evening. That's why they didn't know she was missing. They thought she'd gone to work.'

'That doesn't alter anything,' said the sergeant.

'No,' said the inspector, 'but they also said that she never walked home from the railway station at night. She was afraid and she took a cab.'

'We'd better take a good, hard look at the cab drivers here,' said the sergeant.

'Exactly,' said the inspector. 'So, if you would like to start with that, I'll send for the ambulance and get the body moved down to the morgue. You're sure there aren't any further clues?'

'There aren't any clues at all,' said the sergeant.

There were no clues at the railway station either. Although nearly all of the some fifteen or twenty persons who had been on the 12.07 train from Minden to Rehme were located, none of them could remember seeing Ingrid Kanike.

'She may not even have been on the train,' said the sergeant, reporting on the results of the investigation. 'The fact is, the girl was rather retiring and not at all conspicuous. Add to that the late hour and the half empty train and it's quite possible that she escaped notice. But we can't be sure.'

'What about the cab drivers?' said the inspector.

'Six of them at the railway station stand,' said the sergeant. 'All local men. All middle-aged. All married. Not one of them has been driving a cab for less than eight years. Herb says they don't fit the pattern.'

'Herb also says that we haven't heard the last of this,' said the inspector quietly. 'He thinks there'll be more.'

'Not in our district, I hope,' said the sergeant. 'Because

I can tell you right now, I don't think we're going to solve this one.'

Nor did they.

There were no clues. No leads. Nothing to investigate. Pictures and identification data was assembled on all the persons who had been on the 12.07 train from Minden as well as the Rehme cab drivers, but there was no reason to suspect any of them. No explanation was ever found as to why Ingrid Kanike had chosen just on that one night not to take a cab, but to walk home and into the arms of her murderous lover.

The case eventually ended up in the unsolved section of the Minden police records and no similar cases were reported anywhere in the area. Dr Krause had, it seemed, been wrong. The rapist was not a deviate who could find satisfaction only in the death of his partner.

Or was it that he did not have a very active sex life?

Four years passed and then, once again, there was the murder of another woman under, to say the least, mysterious circumstances. This time, the crime took place indoors and there were almost too many clues.

The victim was a twenty-six-year-old secretary named Ursula Fritz. She had failed to report for work on May 17, 1965 and, when she had still not appeared by Friday of that week, the firm had simply sacked her and had sent her final cheque by mail to her home address. No one had bothered to check on her personally.

Eventually, on May 25th, her landlady had come to the conclusion that she had skipped without paying her final rent, due on May 20th. She therefore used her pass key to open the door and enter the woman's one-room apartment.

Ursula Fritz had not skipped and, no sooner was the door opened, than the unfortunate landlady was struck in the face by such an unbelievable stench that she fainted and fell on the floor, receiving a nasty cut over the left eye as her head struck the edge of the door.

Recovering her senses after some little time, she crawled, dizzy and covered with blood, down the stairs and telephoned the police. She still had no idea what had happened

162

in Ursula Fritz's room, but she was quite certain that anything that smelled that way must be illegal.

All this took place not in Rehme, but in the city of Herford, eight miles to the south-west, and Herford has its own department of criminal investigations. It was an Inspector Anton Jech, a Detective-Sergeant Dieter Schmidt and a Dr Juergen Schoenauer who eventually arrived at the scene. They found that Mrs Schroeder, the injured landlady, had been quite right. What had transpired in Ursula Fritz' apartment was definitely illegal.

'She's been dead for over a week and it was warm in here,' said the doctor. 'I don't think that any kind of an examination is possible until we get her down to the morgue.'

'Then let's do it,' said the inspector. 'This had better be a crime or I'll have those patrolcar cops walking a beat in the factory district until they go on retirement.'

The two patrol car officers who had answered Mrs Schroeder's summons had simply reported a woman murdered in her bed to the station. This had brought out the homicide squad, but there was no real reason to believe that Ursula Fritz had died from anything other than natural causes. Fortunately for the patrolmen, it was soon established that Miss Fritz had not died of natural causes. She had been raped and strangled in her own bed.

'You're quite sure of that, Juergen?' said the inspector, 'with the body in such a state of decomposition? When was she killed?'

'The evening of May fifteenth,' said the doctor. 'I wouldn't have put these things in the autopsy report if I wasn't certain.'

'How can you tell she was raped?' asked Sergeant Schmidt.

'He ejaculated inside her,' said the doctor simply. 'Maximum penetration. She wasn't co-operating. She was struggling so hard to keep her legs together that she strained several of the muscles in her upper thighs.'

'Cause of death?' grunted the inspector.

'Manual strangulation,' said the doctor. 'He crushed her throat. The larynx was fractured.'

'A nasty business,' said the inspector. 'Our investigations

163

show that the woman was something of an old maid, didn't have any male friends and certainly none who would have been visiting her in her room.'

'And yet someone was,' said the sergeant. 'And he didn't break in. There were two glasses. One with her fingerprints and one with a man's. There were seven cigarette butts in the ashtray and only four burned matches. There were fibres of grey serge of a type used in men's suiting on the bedclothes. There was a man there and she didn't expect him to do her any harm.'

'The trouble is,' said the inspector, 'we can't find any man she knew that well.'

'If I were you, I would concentrate on persons with a record of sex crimes,' said the doctor. 'This has all the signs of a compulsive sex crime, a sadist who can obtain satisfaction only through the suffering of his sex partner. I would be willing to bet that this is not the first time he's done this.'

'Well, if it isn't, he wasn't caught the other times or he'd be in jail now,' said the inspector. 'Send a circular to all stations, nation-wide, Dieter. Give the circumstances and ask if anybody has anything similar in the unsolveds.'

Minden, of course, did.

'The circumstances of your case in the circular are almost identical to the case of Ingrid Kanike in Rehme in April of nineteen sixty-one,' said Inspector Heidel speaking to Inspector Jech over the telephone. 'We investigated it, but we never solved it. Do you have any leads in your case?'

'Clues yes, leads no,' said the inspector in Herford. 'Would you send me down copies of everything you have in the file? With Rehme only eight miles from here, I think there's a good chance the cases are connected. Maybe between the two of us, we can do something.'

It was essential that something be done, for the newspapers had recalled the case of Ingrid Kanike in Rehme four years earlier and were billing the new killing as part of a series. Many women and girls in the district were refusing to go out unaccompanied after dark and there was some criticism of the police.

'Never mind the criticism,' said Inspector Jech. 'It's

worth it if it keeps the women off the streets at night. The newspapers may just be right.'

The file on the Kanike case proved to be of no value in the Fritz investigation and it appeared that that too would end up in the unsolveds. Once again, there was nothing to investigate.

And then, a month after the discovery of the body of Ursula Fritz in Herford, an arrest was made in Rehme. A thirty-four-year-old unemployed butcher named Gerd Simmon was arrested near the Rehme railway station as he attempted to rape a fourteen-year-old girl.

Simmon was not a local man and the residents of Rehme, assuming that he was the mysterious rapist-murderer of Ingrid Kanike and Ursula Fritz, quickly formed a crowd and would possibly have lynched him had not Sergeant Eisenbach come rushing down in response to the local constable's urgent call and whisked him off to Minden.

Inspector Jech in Herford was immediately notified and, upon his arrival, Simmon was subjected to severe interrogation by Inspector Jech and Inspector Heidel.

Simmon did not deny the attempted rape of the fourteen-year-old nor did he make any effort to conceal his police record. He had been charged four times with attempted rape and child molestation and convicted twice, serving one sentence of two years and six months and one of three and eight. But he denied that he had had anything to do with the death of Ingrid Kanike and stated that he had never been in Herford in his life.

A strange-looking man with a great deal of carroty-red hair on his head and his entire body as well, he had exceedingly long arms and huge hands.

He appeared also to be totally lacking in nerves.

Nothing that the two inspectors could say shook him in the slightest. He was, he calmly admitted, a sex criminal. He could not help himself. He had never killed anyone.

After a long session of questioning which was actually more tiring to the police than the suspect, Simmon was removed to the detention cells, charged with the attempted rape in Rehme and held for further questioning.

The police withdrew to Inspector Heidel's office for much needed cups of coffee.

'Any comment or suggestions?' said Inspector Heidel.

'I think we're wasting our time with the questioning,' said Inspector Jech. 'We could put Simmon through a sausage machine and the pieces would come out saying, I am a sex criminal, but I have not killed anybody.'

'I think we're wasting our time with Simmon altogether,' said Dr Krause quietly.

'I would agree with that,' said Dr Schoenauer. 'Simmon is a fumbler. He probably doesn't even want to rape the girls or maybe he's incapable. In any case, there's nothing in his record about his actually raping anyone. It's all attempted, but never with success.'

'Exactly,' said Dr Krause. 'And the murderer of Ingrid Kanike and Ursula Fritz was as deadly as a steel trap. Once he got his hands on the woman, it was maximum penetration and death. Simmon bears the same relationship to him that a grass snake does to a king cobra.'

'Well, you gentlemen are the medical experts,' said Inspector Heidel, 'so we have to accept your opinion. However, I think that we might go over the people who were in that train the night that Ingrid Kanike was killed, in so far as they can still be located and see if any of them can recognize a picture of Simmon. He's not a man you'd be likely to forget.'

'We could also try the cab drivers,' said Sergeant Eisenbach.

'And we'll show his picture to Ursula Fritz's landlady and the people she worked with,' said Inspector Jech. 'As you say, he's a man you'd remember.'

No one did. Not a soul in Rehme or in Herford could be found who could recall ever having seen anyone who looked like Gerd Simmon.

He was eventually brought to trial for the attempted rape and sentenced to two years imprisonment.

'Do we give up now?' said Sergeant Schmidt. 'There isn't anything left to investigate, is there?'

'Give the material the routine cross check and send it to

the unsolveds,' said the inspector shortly. 'We'll have to wait for his next one.'

The routine check, carried out before a case is finally sent to the unsolved files, did produce something of interest this time.

'When Minden interviewed those cab drivers at the Rehme railway station the second time, one of them told a different story to the one he did at the time of the Kanike murder,' said Sergeant Schmidt, handing the inspector two typed statements.

The inspector took the statements and compared them.

'You're right,' he said. 'Call Minden and tell them about this. Rehme's their responsibility, but I'd like to hear what this fellow has to say. Wouldn't hurt to put a little pressure on him.'

The cab driver's name was August Fennel, he was fifty-four years old, married, born and raised in Rehme and a cab driver for close to twenty years. Inspector Heidel put pressure on him.

'Whatever the case,' he said, 'we have positive evidence here that you issued a false statement to the police. One of these versions has to be false. Now, I can charge you on that or I can hold you on suspicion of the murder of Ingrid Kanike. What I would prefer is that you tell me instead what really happened on the night of April seventh, nineteen sixty-one. It may then not be necessary to charge you at all.'

Fennel shuffled his feet. He was a watery-eyed man with the shoulders of a bull and the stomach of a dedicated beer drinker. When he spoke, his voice was startlingly high.

'I didn't want to get mixed up,' he whined. 'I ain't never had no trouble and I didn't want to get mixed up. I was afraid I'd get blamed for it.'

'You will get blamed for it,' said the inspector, 'unless you tell me exactly what happened.'

'I was at the station when the 12.07 came in,' said Fennel. 'The Kanike girl got into my cab. I knew who she was. I'd drove her before and I knew her address. Didn't know her name until after she got murdered though.

'Any time I'd drove her before, she'd been alone but that

167

night she had a man with her. They got into the cab together.'

'What did he look like, this man?' interrupted the inspector. 'Did you know him? Have you ever seen him before or since?'

'No, I don't think so,' said Fennel. 'To tell the truth, I didn't get too good a look at him. He was a young fellow, thirty maybe. Nice looking. About my height, I guess. He wasn't from Rehme.'

'All right,' said the inspector. 'I'll want you to look at some pictures later on and see if you can identify this man again. So, what happened then? You drove the girl and this strange man to her home?'

'No,' said the cab driver, looking extremely apprehensive. 'When we got just to that spot where they found her body later, the man told me to stop the cab, that they'd walk the rest of the way. I stopped the cab, he paid me the full fare and they got out. And that's all I know about it.'

'Did the girl appear frightened?' said the inspector. 'Did she get out of the cab willingly?'

'As far as I could see, she did,' said the cab driver. 'They were talking together in the back and they seemed friendly enough. She didn't say "Du" to him though.'

'Du' is the intimate form of address in German, used with relatives, children, and close friends.

Fennel was not charged, but given a severe talking to and released.

'If he'd told us the truth at the time,' said Inspector Heidel bitterly, 'we might have solved the case and Ursula Fritz might still be alive. So much time has passed now though, that the testimony is close to worthless.'

'I take it he wasn't able to make a positive identification from any of the pictures you took at the time,' said Inspector Jech who had come up to Minden to learn the results of the questioning of Fennel.

Inspector Heidel shook his head. 'He might have at the time,' he said, 'but it's been over four years now and whatever impression he did have, has faded.'

'Still, the fact that she got into the cab with this man

168

would seem to indicate that he was not a total stranger to her,' said Jech thoughtfully. 'You've checked out her male acquaintances? People she came into contact with at work?'

'We've practically reconstructed her life,' said Heidel. 'It wasn't hard. She lived at home. She only worked at the one place. She had the same girl friends from the time she was in school. We could account for practically all her time for long periods. She wasn't having an affair of any kind, if that's what you're thinking.'

'Not exactly,' said Jech. 'I was thinking more of a casual acquaintance, someone whom she knew well enough to share a cab with, but not well enough to use the intimate form of address.'

'Rehme is a small place,' said Heidel. 'A cab driver like Fennel knows almost everyone in town, by sight at least. He didn't know this man and we have every reason to believe that Ingrid Kanike never knew any casual male acquaintances from out of town. Don't forget, if she did know him, even casually, she'd know that he wasn't from Rehme and why would he be getting off the train there at midnight then?'

'You think he was on the 12.07 from Minden then?' said Jech.

'My own theory is that she met him on the train,' said Heidel. 'She was a plump girl who hadn't had too much luck with the boys and she ran into a handsome, well-spoken man on the train. He probably told her that he came from Rehme, suggested they take a cab together and then, once away from the station, persuaded her to walk the rest of the way to her house with him. She, no doubt, thought it was her big romance, poor girl.'

'Sad,' agreed Jech. 'But Fennel couldn't identify any of the pictures of the men who were on the train?'

'There are only four who come in question,' said the inspector. 'The others were too old, too young or we were able to establish definite alibis so close to midnight that it would have been almost impossible for them to have done it.'

'Two of them, Otto Johanns and Emil Bach, are from

Rehme. One, Karl Mueller, is from Minden and the other is from Bielefeld. His name is Dieter Beck. Oddly enough, all of them work in Rehme, three of them in the machine tool plant over by the river.'

'You're thinking of Croiset, I presume?' said Jech.

Hiedel nodded. 'You can't convict people on the statements of a clairvoyant, of course,' he said, 'but still, it is remarkable the accuracy he's shown with such things.'

Croiset was the famous Dutch clairvoyant, Gerard Croiset, who had been successful in solving many criminal cases throughout Europe. He had been called in by the family of Ingrid Kanike after the murder and had stated that the murderer worked in a machine factory near Rehme. There were, however, several machine factories and they employed a large number of men.

'Well, I guess that's the end of that then,' said Jech getting to his feet. 'I wonder when he'll kill the next one?'

'Four years from now, if he runs true to form,' said Heidel. 'By the way, I'm sending my sergeant down to you. I'd like him to get the exact time and circumstances of the Fritz murder and then we'll see if we can establish an alibi for any of the four men on the train with Kanike. Maybe we could eliminate one or two of them.'

'If we knew that it was the same man in both cases,' said Jech. 'I'm afraid your sergeant is going to have a tough time with the alibis. Our medical man wasn't able to establish the time of death precisely. She'd been dead too long when we found her.'

Nonetheless, Sergeant Eisenbach was able to eliminate one of the four suspects. Otto Johanns had been in the hospital for the entire week in which Ursula was raped and murdered. At this point the investigations came, once again, to an end, there being nothing further to investigate.

'A very unusual pattern,' commented Dr Krause. 'As a rule, a sex criminal of this type strikes more often and the intervals between his attacks become increasingly shorter. The fellow must be obtaining sexual relief in some manner, but it seems impossible that it could be by non-violent means considering what we know of his previous activities.'

'Well, if he's been raping anyone, it hasn't been reported,' said the inspector. 'Granted that far more rapes go unreported than otherwise, the area is sufficiently aroused by now that I think any woman undergoing an attack of this sort would report. You still think it was the same man in the Kanike and Fritz cases?'

The doctor nodded. 'And so does Schoenauer down in Herford,' he said. 'However, we disagree on when he'll strike again. Schoenauer says this year yet. I say not for another four years, the same interval as the last time.'

As it turned out, both the medical experts were wrong. It was the night of February 28, 1968 when the murdering rapist claimed his next victim. The body was found on the morning of the twenty-ninth by a railway track walker named Leopold Beisel.

Beisel had set out from Bielefeld that morning on an inspection tour of the ten mile stretch of track between that city and the village of Werther in the Teutoburger Forest to the west. Although February is normally one of the coldest months of the central European winter, the day was sunny and the temperature above freezing. It was ten o'clock and he had covered approximately half the distance when he came upon the body of the girl lying beside the tracks.

Beisel's first thought was an accident. There were passenger trains running over the line and, in Europe, a surprising number of people either mistake the exit between coaches for the toilet door or lean carelessly against a not properly locked door and fall out. This despite the fact that the doors on all trains are carefully and conspicuously marked in several languages. Depending upon how fast the train is moving and the manner in which they fall, a person may very well survive this. Beisel therefore ran forward with the intention of offering first aid or whatever else could be done, but stopped dead in his tracks as he came close enough to get a clear view of the corpse.

For corpse it was. The face was black, the eyes protruded horribly from their sockets and the tongue, black and swollen, hung so far out of the mouth that Beisel did not realize what it was. There were other indications as well.

The girl's skirt had been pushed up around her waist, her torn underwear lay in shreds around her and there were blue bruises on the widespread thighs.

Leopold Beisel read the newspapers and he instantly thought of the murdering rapist who had killed Ingrid Kanike and Ursula Fritz. There was little doubt in his mind that this was the third victim.

There was also little doubt in his mind that the woman was dead, but he went forward, knelt and laid his fingers on the artery in the throat. There was no pulse and the flesh was cold and hard to the touch.

Although he was not a Catholic, for reasons about which he himself was not clear he made the sign of the cross over the body and muttered a short prayer. He then got rather heavily to his feet and set off at a trot down the tracks. The nearest telephone was nearly a mile distant.

This time it was the team of Inspector Ludwig Pfeiffer, Detective-Sergeant Max Kramer and Dr Hans Fuchs of the Bielefeld Department of Criminal Investigations who arrived at the scene.

Beissel had given them a very good indication of what to expect in his report over the telephone, and in Minden and Herford Inspectors Heidel and Jech, Sergeants Eisenbach and Schmidt and Drs Krause and Schoenauer were also heading south for what was eventually to be a general meeting of Criminal Investigations Department personnel at the scene of the latest rape and murder of the series. On the question of whether the Kanike, Fritz and the present case were all parts of a series carried out by the same man the medical opinion was unanimous. It was.

On what to do about it, there was less unanimity. Inspector Pfeiffer was of the opinion that every sex criminal with a police record in the entire area should be brought in and screened for alibis. Inspector Jech thought that there should be wide-spread appeals to the public for information. And there was no way of knowing what Inspector Heidel thought for he said nothing. His unsolved murder was, of course, the oldest.

In the meantime, a large number of technicians from the

police laboratory in Bielefeld had arrived and were going over the area literally by the square inch. All they were able to find was the girl's handbag. It had not been opened and contained, among other things, her personal identity card. From this it was learned that the girl's name was Anneliese Herschel, that she had been twenty-one years old, unmarried and a resident of Werther.

'The only prints on the bag are hers,' said the chief technician. 'Apart from the bag, there was only this in the side pocket of her coat.'

'This' was an ordinary book of paper matches with advertising printed on it. The advertising read: Igloo Bar, Kon Street 4, Bielefeld.

'Check it out, Max,' said Inspector Pfeiffer, handing the book of matches to the sergeant.

The investigations at the scene of the crime now being completed, the body was sent to the morgue and the police party returned to police headquarters in Bielefeld. It was only after they had arrived that Inspector Jech remembered Gert Simmon.

'Wasn't he sentenced to two years and wasn't that just about two years ago?' he demanded.

No one was sure of the dates, but the penitentiary was telephoned and they confirmed that Gerd Simmon had been released on February 16th, twelve days before the murder.

'That,' said Inspector Jech, 'is too much of a coincidence to be one.'

There was no disagreement on this score and within a matter of minutes the telephone and telex wires were humming as the police forces throughout north Germany were alerted to be on the look-out for Gerd Simmon, thought to be the rapist-murderer who had been sought for so long.

While this was going on, Sergeant Kramer returned to headquarters with the news that Anneliese Herschel had, indeed, been in the Igloo Bar the night of her death and that she had left with a man. He wanted pictures of all possible suspects to show to the witnesses of whom there were several.

Pictures of Simmon, Fennel and the three remaining

173

suspects who had been on the train to Rehme on the night that Ingrid Kanike was killed were rushed down and the sergeant returned to the Igloo Bar.

At four that afternoon there was a great cheer as the desk sergeant on duty in Minden called to report to Inspector Heidel that Gerd Simmon was in custody.

'Splendid!' exclaimed the inspector. 'Where did they pick him up?'

'Right here,' said the desk sergeant. 'He's been in the detention cells for the past four days. He celebrated his release from jail a little too enthusiastically and just about wrecked a bar over on the east side. You want to talk to him?'

'No,' said the inspector despondently and hung up the telephone.

The search for Gerd Simmon was called off and it was to a decidedly gloomy conference of criminal police officers that Sergeant Kramer returned at nearly six o'clock.

The sergeant was not gloomy.

'Well, it looks like we've finally got him,' he announced. 'I have a positive, independent identification from three different persons, including the bartender.'

'Identification of whom, Max?' said Inspector Pfeiffer. 'We've just learned that Simmon was in jail at the time of the crime.'

'Not Simmon, chief,' said Max. 'Beck. Dieter Beck. The boy from Bielefeld who was on the train the night Kanike was killed.'

And Dieter Beck it was. Picked up at his home in Bielefeld, he made no effort whatsoever to deny the Kanike, Fritz and Herschel murders.

'I knew that you'd get me sooner or later,' he said apathetically as the Criminal Investigations officers from three cities clustered around. 'I'm glad it's over. I didn't want to kill those girls. It's just something that comes over me and then I can't help myself. I'll confess to the murders, but I don't want to talk about it.'

Beck did eventually talk enough to establish with certainty that he was the murderer of Ingrid Kanike, Ursula Fritz

174

and Anneliese Herschel. He had, it seemed, chosen them quite deliberately because they were types who would not be very popular with men and who were thus very susceptible to the attentions of a handsome, well-spoken man which Beck definitely was.

Contrary to the medical opinion, Beck had been quite capable of normal sexual relations and had had a number of girl friends all of whom described him as a completely satisfactory lover. Several reported that he had had a habit of caressing their throats with his large, powerful hands while making love.

They had found it rather touching.

During the trial which lasted from June 22 to June 26, 1969 the court found Dieter Beck's conduct more dangerous and inexcusable than touching and handed down a verdict of premeditated murder on all three counts. He was sentenced to three terms of life imprisonment.

12

THE INSATIABLE WIFE

Tortuous and twisting as a dream in the mind of a murderer, the Ems river rises near the ancient city of Muenster and weaves its way northward through the heart of the great German moors.

Klein Hesper, Gross Hesper, Gross Fullen, Niederlang, Sustrum and Bourtang, the silent, lonely, water-logged plains of Emsland stretch out along the Dutch border to Emden and the chill, grey waters of the North Sea.

A strange place to live, beautiful at times, sinister at others, and yet men have lived among the moors since the dawn of time. There is security in a place where the single false step of the stranger may lead to the deadly quicksand traps along the unmarked path.

Roughly in the centre of this great expanse of moors lies the little town of Meppen, with 30,000 souls, little more than a village, but still the largest community in its district. With the exception of Lingen, seventeen miles to the south, none of the villages have as much as 10,000 inhabitants and many are too small to appear on any map. In some of these smaller villages all the inhabitants have the same surname.

There are not so many villages, in any case, and between them lie the swamps, the reeds, the low bush, the occasional bit of higher, forested ground and the black, sullen lakes and ponds, some of which have a discernible bottom and some of which do not.

On May 30, 1972, a small, somewhat scrawny and very tough man named Georg Richter disappeared. He was twenty-six years old, married and the father of four daughters, Anja, six, Kathi, four, Alexandra, two, and Petra, one. He was very attached to these daughters.

On Monday, June 6th, Mrs Ursula Richter came into Meppen from the little community of Emslage-Ruehlerfeld where the family lived to report this disappearance.

As is customary in such matters, she gave her name, age, address and number of dependent children, causing Detective-Sergeant Dieter Schwarz, who was taking down the report, to start slightly and drop his pencil.

Mrs Richter, it seemed, was the mother of a six-year-old daughter, but only twenty years old herself. What was more, she looked it, being dark-haired, dark-eyed, astonishingly built and very lovely – so lovely, in fact, that the sergeant found it hard to believe that any man in his right mind would have voluntarily left her.

Mrs Richter was, apparently, not totally unaware of her attractions. Her mini-skirt was scarcely wider than a respectable belt and the looks which she bestowed upon the bedazzled sergeant were of a temperature to nearly explode the ammunition in his service pistol.

'My God! What was that?' exclaimed his superior, Inspector Horst-Dieter Geiger, after Mrs Richter's delightful hips had swayed out through the office door.

'Eh . . . uh . . . a missing person report,' said the sergeant. 'Her husband's been gone for a week. Goerg Richter, aged twenty-six. Didn't mention what he does for a living. Not much, I guess.'

'I should think not,' said the inspector. 'Too busy otherwise.'

'Well . . . uh . . .,' said the sergeant, still bemused.

'Hold it!' cried the inspector. 'Richter. Richter. I have the feeling we have something pending on a Richter. Take a look in the current files, will you?'

The sergeant took a look.

'You're right,' he said. 'Georg Richter. Emslage-Ruehlerfeld. Two charges of burglary and one of theft. Released on own recognizance and awaiting trial on all-three.'

'Only he's not awaiting,' said the inspector. 'See how easy it is to solve cases? The lady has barely left the office and we have been able to determine that her husband has disappeared in order to avoid trial and, no doubt, a subsequent jail sentence.'

'Brilliant!' said the sergeant in near sincere admiration, '—but Mrs Richter didn't want to know why he left, she wanted to know where he went to.'

'And, I suppose, when he was coming back,' said the inspector, reaching for the next report in his In-tray. 'Tell her when the statute of limitations expires.'

'I can't file it without an investigation,' said the sergeant.

'Then investigate,' said the inspector.

The sergeant investigated.

This signified mainly that he went to Emslage-Ruehlerfeld and talked to the neighbours, following which he had a beer in the local tavern and spoke at some length with the bar tender, in this case the owner.

'I'm not quite so dazzled by your solution of the Richter case as I was,' he remarked upon his return to the office. 'The Richters have a boarder. Nice young man. Nineteen years old. Muscles of a draft horse. Quite handsome too. His name is Kurt Adomeit.'

'Oh?' said the inspector, putting down the file that he was working on and reaching for his cigarettes. 'That does put rather a different light on the matter, doesn't it?'

'I fear for Mr Richter's safety,' said the sergeant, peering gloomily into the office coffee pot which was cold and empty.

'I fear that they've been a little too sly for us,' said the inspector. 'Has he really been missing a week?'

The sergeant nodded. 'At least,' he said. 'The gossip is bad. They say that Mr Richter was a boxer and that he used Mrs Richter as a punching bag. They also say that Mr Adomeit put her to other uses.'

'Put or puts?' said the inspector.

'He's off driving his truck at the moment,' said the sergeant. 'It's what he does for a living. I assume that he will take up his boarder's duties again once he returns.'

'But he wasn't out driving his truck a week ago when Mr Richter disappeared, right?' said the inspector.

'No,' said the sergeant. 'He apparently doesn't drive it

very often. Any idea as to where we should look for the body?'

'Certainly,' said the inspector. 'In the moors. There are about five hundred square miles of them and Mrs Richter and Mr Adomeit have had a whole week in which to select the most ideal resting place for the late lamented Mr Georg Richter. If they actually have done him in, we'll never find the body. I'm not even a local man and I know six pools within a half mile of here that you could lose an elephant in.'

'So it goes in the unsolved murder file,' said the sergeant.

'Not on your life it doesn't,' said the inspector. 'It's not a murder case. It's a Missing Person report. You and I may have some nasty suspicions, but there's no evidence of any kind that Mr Richter didn't leave simply to avoid trial. In fact, I still think that's the most likely explanation. Was Richter insured?'

The sergeant shrugged. 'I'll find out,' he said.

Georg Richter, it turned out, was not insured and further samples of the gossip in Emslage-Ruehlerfeld brought out the widely held opinion that Mr Richter had not objected too strongly to Kurt Adomeit's alleged attentions to his wife.

'The situation seems to be that he was crazy about the children, but he wasn't really all that keen on Mrs Richter,' said the sergeant. 'He got her pregnant when she was only thirteen and I guess he had the choice of marrying her or going to jail so he married her, but the consensus of opinion in Emslage-Ruehlerfeld is that the lady is too much for any one man.

'It was Richter who brought Adomeit into the house and some say that he was looking for help.'

'Just what I said!' said the inspector. 'The heat was on here, so he cut out. Our boy is undoubtedly living happily somewhere in Holland by now with a new name and, probably, a new wife.'

Two days later, the inspector's theory was confirmed.

A telephone call was received from the village constable of Neuringe on the Dutch border. He reported that there was a car with a Meppen licence plate standing on the

179

bottom of a deep, but clear pool near his village. If Meppen was interested in having it, they could come and get it.

The sergeant noted down the licence number, which the constable had been able to read easily through the water, and did a little checking with the local automobile licensing office.

'Odd,' he said after he had put down the telephone. 'Mrs Richter didn't mention that Mr Richter took the family car with him. As a matter of fact, she didn't mention that he owned a car.'

'And he does?' said the inspector.

The sergeant nodded. 'It's sitting at the bottom of a pond over by Neuringe,' he said. 'They say, if we want it, we'll have to come and fish it out ourselves.'

'Well, tell Sam to take the tow truck,' said the inspector. 'You probably better go along too. For all we know, Richter may be in it.'

Georg Richter was not in his car nor was anything else.

'Stripped,' said the sergeant. 'There's not so much as a chewing gum wrapper in it and there are no prints either. I went over the thing by the square centimetre.'

'Why?' said the inspector. 'Do you still think that Mrs Richter and Adomeit murdered poor Georg?'

'More than ever,' said the sergeant. 'What does that car over there on the Dutch border in fourteen feet of crystal clear water do? It points like a neon sign to Holland. Somebody is supposed to believe that Richter went over the border and that somebody is us.'

The inspector looked thoughtful. 'Maybe he was just lazy,' he said. 'He drove the car to the border and then got rid of it in the most convenient manner. He couldn't take it with him into Holland because the foreign licence plate would have been easy to trace.

'Doesn't hold up,' said the sergeant. 'It wasn't convenient. He'd have had to walk a couple of miles from where he left the car to a border crossing point. It would have been a lot simpler to take the train out of Meppen.'

'You convince me,' said the inspector. 'All right. What happened then? Mrs Richter and Mr Adomeit murdered Mr

180

Richter and, having disposed of the body, drove the car to the pond near Neuringe knowing full well that somebody would spot it sooner or later and that the assumption then would be that Mr Richter had gone into Holland, never to return. Is that what you have in mind?'

'Something like that,' said the sergeant. 'If Richter had really wanted to get rid of the car, there are enough ponds around there where it would never have been seen again. This pond had a hard bottom.'

The inspector sighed and got up to go and stand in front of the window. It was a beautiful, warm, early summer day and a gentle breeze was blowing in from across the moors, laden with the scent of flowers and green, growing things.

The inspector sighed again, more heavily, and turned back to his desk.

'All right,' he said. 'Assuming that it was murder, what can we do? You know yourself that the examining judge would never issue an indictment on nothing but suspicion. Where are we to get the evidence that a crime has even been committed?'

'There could be something in the house,' said the sergeant.

'After all this time?' said the inspector. 'If they took the trouble to drive the car over to the Dutch border and push it into a pond, they took the trouble to clean up the house before she ever reported him missing.'

'What you're saying is that this is a perfect crime,' said the sergeant. 'We know a man was murdered, but we can't prove it.'

'Maybe you know it,' said the inspector, 'but I don't. I agree that it's possible, probable even, but I don't admit that it's a perfect crime either. Not that there aren't perfect crimes and even in this district, but they'll have to get away with it longer than a couple of weeks before I call it a perfect crime.'

Ursula Richter and Kurt Adorneit got away with it, if, indeed, they were getting away with anything, for a good deal longer than a couple of weeks.

In June of 1973, one year after the disappearance of Georg Richter and following receipt by the Meppen Police of a report from the Dutch authorities that no trace of the man had been found in Holland, Ursula Richter filed suit for divorce on the grounds of desertion. It was, of course, granted without delay.

'Very circumspect,' observed the inspector. 'She waited a whole year and, as I understand it, her conduct toward Mr Adomeit, at least in public, has been beyond reproach.'

'Makes it all the more suspicious,' grumbled the sergeant. 'He's still boarding there and the children have practically accepted him as their father, but he and Mrs Richter are the souls of propriety. There isn't even any gossip any more.'

'Well, if there is, it won't last much longer,' said the inspector. 'I imagine that our love birds will be getting married shortly, now that Mrs Richter is a free woman again.'

With which statement he demonstrated that even inspectors of police can be very badly mistaken at times. An entire year passed again and it was only on June 16, 1974 that Mr Kurt Adomeit led the former Mrs Ursula Richter to the altar. The bridesmaids were Anja, Kathi, Alexandra and Petra Richter, now nine, seven, five and four respectively.

'All right,' said the sergeant. 'I admit it. It was a perfect murder. We'll never find the body. There'll never be any evidence. We suspected it was murder from the start, but we couldn't do a thing about it. They pulled it off right under our noses.'

The inspector scowled unhappily. 'I wouldn't mind so much if we just knew for certain,' he said. 'Is Georg Richter living under an assumed name in Holland or some other country or is he rotting at the bottom of some quicksand on the moor?'

'We'll never know,' said the sergeant, thus democratically demonstrating that police sergeants can be just as wrong as inspectors.

It was going to be almost another year before anything new was learned in connection with the Georg Richter case and then it was not directly.

'Mrs Richter . . . er, that is, Mrs Adomeit seems to have an unfortunate effect on her husbands,' remarked the inspector as the sergeant came into the office one morning early in June of 1975. 'Here. Take a look at this.'

He shoved a sheet of form paper across the desk.

'Osnabrueck police?' said the sergeant. 'What do they want with Adomeit?'

'They're not too precise,' said the inspector. 'They want to talk to him in connection with some kind of swindle. I get the impression that they're not ready to bring a charge yet, but they want us to pick him up, presumably to throw a scare into him.'

'Should I go get him?' said the sergeant, dropping the form back onto the desk. 'Could be that he's not here. The last time I checked I was told that he spent a lot more time driving the truck than he used to.'

'You're insinuating something,' said the inspector.

'The gossip in Emslage-Ruehlerfeld is that Adomeit can't take care of his wife any more than her first husband could,' said the sergeant. 'I don't mean financially.'

'And I suppose knowing the fate of the first husband, he's reluctant to bring in help,' said the inspector. 'You've never completely given up on that business, have you?'

'I check out the gossip every once in a while,' admitted the sergeant. 'You never know. There could be some kind of a break. Richter's father doesn't believe that his son simply ran off. Says he'd never have left the children.

'As for Adomeit bringing in help, as you put it, he wouldn't think of it. He's jealous as hell. Punched a couple of the local boys in the nose for just talking to his wife in the tavern.'

'Should I go see if he's there now?'

'In a minute,' said the inspector, picking up the telephone. 'I'm going to call Osnabrueck and see just what they have in mind. Could be that we can take advantage of this in some way if they have enough to hold him for any length of time.'

The inspector was on the telephone for some time, during which the sergeant went off to check on the progress of several other matters. When he returned the inspector was just putting down the instrument.

'Good thing that you didn't go out to pick him up,' he

said. 'They don't want him picked up. They want him shadowed the next time he comes to Osnabrueck. They think he's peddling phony drugs down there. A nice racket. The buyers can't very well complain to the police.'

'Shadow him?' yelped the sergeant. 'How're we supposed to do that? That truck driver drives a BMW 2002 and it's eighty miles down to Osnabrueck. The fastest thing we've got is a Volkswagen. He'd be out of sight before we left the city limits.'

The inspector pushed the chair back from the desk, clasped his hands behind his neck and gazed thoughtfully at the somewhat dingy ceiling.

'I'd like to have him in custody,' he mused. 'I don't know what we could get out of him, but I have the feeling that this is a sort of break, if we know how to exploit it. Say the man's a murderer, being in the detention cells should make him a little nervous, particularly if we hint that he's being investigated for something other than drug trafficking.'

'If the drugs are phony, they can't get him on drug trafficking,' said the sergeant. 'All they could charge him with is obtaining money under false pretences. And then they'd have to get one of the users to swear out a complaint.'

'No problem,' said the inspector. 'They've got some users on the payroll down there, but they haven't been able to pick up his trail when he hits the city. That's why they want him shadowed down.'

He sat forward in the chair and began patting his pockets for his cigarettes.

'You're right, of course,' he said. 'The BMW's too fast for us. We'll have to think of something else.'

'Well, he almost surely comes down State Road seventy through Lingen to Rheine and then takes the E8 into Osnabrueck,' said the sergeant. 'If you think it's important enough, I could go down and sit on the edge of the city limits and pick him up as he goes past, but I might have to sit there a week. Why can't Osnabrueck do the same thing?'

'I'll ask them,' said the inspector.

Osnabrueck could, provided that the Meppen police furnished them with a picture of Adomeit and the licence number of his car. The only information which they had was his name and the fact that he lived somewhere near Meppen.

'We can take care of that,' said the inspector, speaking to his opposite number in Osnabrueck over the telephone, 'but I'd like a favour in return. Will you see if you can get anything out of him that we could use to hold him up here for a week or so?'

'Nobody's that innocent,' said the inspector in Osnabrueck. 'We'll get you something.'

What they eventually got, after Kurt Adomeit had been picked up at the city limits and trailed to the small hotel and, later, the park where he transacted his business, was an admission that he had pulled the same swindle in several other cities in the area. This meant that he could be taken to his place of residence for trial rather than be tried on separate charges in a half dozen towns and cities.

'None of the other places are anxious to take jurisdiction anyway,' said the inspector. 'As you say, the only charge possible is obtaining money under false pretences and it'll be a wonder if he gets more than a fine.'

'Thought for a minute that we might be able to sustain an attempted murder charge. Some of the people peddling phony drugs use stuff that will kill you. But he didn't. It was completely harmless stuff. An addict could shoot a wheelbarrow load and get nothing more than frustrated.'

The sergeant was sent down to bring back the prisoner, which he did with some enthusiasm. He too was becoming convinced that there was, at least, a chance of a break in what he had always considered to be the Richter murder.

He was to be disappointed. The Osnabrueck police had leaned rather heavily on Kurt Adomeit and he looked a bit shaken, but he was by no means broken or ready to admit to anything. He was perfectly aware that the affair with the drugs was a minor matter and that, as a first time offender, there was little likelihood of his receiving anything more serious than a fine. No sooner had he arrived in Meppen than he began to demand his release.

The inspector stalled.

'Why doesn't he yell for a lawyer?' said the sergeant. 'He'd have him out of here in five minutes.'

'Doesn't want to pay him,' said the inspector. 'He's so sure of himself that he thinks he can save the lawyer's fee. He will too, unless we think of something quick.'

'I don't know what we could think of,' said the sergeant. 'He admits everything on the phony drugs charges, but if you ask him anything about Richter, he simply says he doesn't know anything about it and that he understood that he ran off to Holland. We can't get through his guard with anything.'

The inspector paced rapidly up and down the office.

'This Adomeit isn't sharp,' he muttered. 'He's just stubborn. He knows we can't break his story and he sticks to it. If there was a murder, the woman was the brains behind it . . .'

He turned suddenly to the sergeant. 'What's she been doing while Adomeit was in custody down in Osnabrueck?' he demanded. 'It's been over a week since he was picked up.'

'How do I know?' said the sergeant. 'I don't check her out twice a day.'

'Then do it now,' said the inspector. 'Go over there immediately. Find out what the gossip is. Has she been faithful to Adomeit while he was in jail in Osnabrueck?'

The sergeant's face lit up in abrupt comprehension.

'I get it!' he explained. 'Adomeit is jealous as hell! If he were to learn that his wife was two-timing him while he was in detention, he might get mad enough to lose his head and say something indiscreet.'

'Right,' said the inspector. 'Adomeit's a pretty straight-forward character and he's got a bad temper. If he loses it, he could say anything. So pray that Mrs Richter hasn't been able to control her passionate nature.'

'Couldn't we fake it?' asked the sergeant.

'If we don't mind changing professions afterwards,' said the inspector. 'We tell her husband something like that and it isn't true, the lady could sue us down to our underwear.'

'But say that she has been playing around,' said the

186

sergeant, 'how are we going to tell Adomeit that? He wouldn't believe us.'

'I don't know,' said the inspector, 'but I'll think of something. In the meantime, go and find out what's happening with Mrs Adomeit's love life.'

Not entirely to the sergeant's surprise, a good deal was happening in the love life of Mrs Ursula Adomeit. She had not only been unable to control her passions, but she had not even made a serious attempt. The first night after she had learned that her husband had been arrested in Osnabrueck, she had shared her bed with a lover. Since then, she had had at least four others.

'No question about it,' said the sergeant. 'Emslage-Ruehlerfeld is so small that everybody knows when you sleep with your own wife, let alone somebody else's. Mrs Adomeit has been up to her old tricks. Have you figured out how we're to slip the news to Mr Adomeit?'

'The old loud-mouth drunk act, I suppose,' said the inspector. 'We'll have to be sure that we get somebody Adomeit doesn't know.'

'I've got a cousin with the force in Lingen,' said the sergeant. 'He doesn't actually drink, but he can put on the best act you ever saw. He even looks drunk when he's cold sober.'

'Get him,' said the inspector.

Two hours later Kurt Adomeit, until then alone in the detention cells, acquired company as a seedy-looking man reeking of alcohol was pushed into the neighbouring cell.

'Lemme out! Lemme out! I'm innoshent!' bawled the man, falling against the bars which separated his cell from Adomeit's and clutching them for support. 'Hi Jack! You in for shtealin' the mayor's watch or his wife?'

'I'm in for being drunk – the same as you,' said Adomeit. 'Where'd you take on the load at this time of day?'

'The Black Lamb,' said the drunk. 'An' I ain't drunk. You're drunk!'

'You don't mean the Black Lamb in Emslage-Ruehlerfeld?' said Adomeit.

'Thash the one!' slobbered the drunk.

'I know some people over that way,' said Adomeit. 'What's the news in Emslage-Ruehlerfeld?'

'They got the hottest woman in Europe over there,' said the fake drunk. 'She's finished off two husbands and now she's takin' on every man in the village. There ain't enough of them to handle it. They're callin' out the army! They're . . .'

Adomeit had gone suddenly tense and pale.

'What's her name?' he snapped.

'Urshula, Urshula somethin' or other,' mumbled the drunk and fell over backwards as Kurt Adomeit's arm came straight between the bars like a piston rod, the hooked finger tips just grazing his throat.

'I'll kill you! You bastard!' hissed Kurt Adomeit. 'And I'll kill that bitch!'

The fake drunk began to scream in terror.

'Help! Help! He's crazy! He's tryin' to kill me!'

The uniform sergeant in charge of the detention cells came down the corridor.

'What's going on here?' he demanded.

'I want out!' snarled Adomeit. 'You're holding me illegally! I want a lawyer.'

'You'll have to talk to the inspector,' said the sergeant, unlocking the cell door.

Adomeit was still livid and trembling with rage when he was ushered into the inspector's office. It was obvious that what he had heard from his neighbour in the cells was only something which he had already expected and feared.

The inspector was friendly but firm.

'No,' he said, 'I'm not going to let you out of here right now, even if you get fifty lawyers. Look at the state you're in! That drunken fool apparently told you something about your wife's activities over in Emslage-Ruehlerfeld and, if I let you out now, you're going over there to do her an injury of some kind. You'll get in all kinds of trouble. And maybe there's nothing to the stories anyway.'

'The hell there isn't!' snarled Adomeit. 'I know that bitch! She'd stop at nothing! How many times did she come over to me minutes after Georg had climbed off her! She couldn't get enough! And if anybody stood in her way, why then . . .'

He paused abruptly.

'She got rid of them,' finished the inspector. 'Didn't she, Kurt? And one day, she'll get rid of you too. Or can you take care of her? Is that why she's going with every able-bodied man in the village?'

Adomeit looked as if he were on the verge of apoplexy. His face was as white as marble, but there were angry red flecks around his eyes and at the corners of his jaws. He seemed to be struggling for breath and he opened his mouth, but no words came out.

'You can kid yourself, if you want to, Kurt,' said the inspector, 'but don't kid me. We know that you and Ursula got rid of Georg and sooner or later we're going to be able to prove it. Get it over with now and save yourself a lot of trouble.'

This was all nothing but the purest bluff. All that Adomeit needed to say was what he had been saying for the past three years, that he knew nothing of what had happened to Georg Richter, and the inspector would be forced to let him go. There was no evidence. There was no body. There was no plausible motive.

Perhaps Adomeit did not realize this or perhaps he was simply too angry and torn by jealousy to think clearly, or perhaps he was simply tired of trying to cope with a woman whose sexual appetites were so much stronger than his own or any man's, but suddenly he let his breath out in a great whoosh and slumped down in the chair.

'I'll show you where the body's buried,' he said in a low voice.

Behind the desk, the inspector had also slumped with the release of the almost unbearable tension. He was sweating profusely and he was as exhausted as if he had carried out a physical struggle with the prisoner.

'Very sensible,' he said. 'We'll go immediately.'

The body of Georg Richter was buried five feet deep in the Esterfeld Forest, a scant mile from the Meppen Police headquarters. Since it was now July 1, 1975 and he had lain there since May 30, 1972, nothing remained but a skeleton with the skull smashed in.

189

'I did that,' said Adomeit, almost modestly. 'We had to because the rat poison just wouldn't work.'

Later at police headquarters, Kurt Adomeit made a full confession to the murder of what must have been one of the toughest little men in North Germany. Georg Richter had been a hard man to kill.

'Ursula and I became intimate at the end of 1971,' said Adomeit. 'She was completely insatiable and I think that Georg would have been grateful if he'd known we were having an affair. Maybe he did know.

'He wasn't jealous, but he was bad-tempered and he used to beat her up pretty badly sometimes.

'Finally, she said to me that he was going to have to go and she bought a tube of sleeping tablets. They were supposed to be very strong and she put the whole tube in his tea. It didn't even make him sleepy.

'She got some more sleeping tablets and she tried it again. She tried it three or four times and it never had the slightest effect on Georg. He didn't notice a thing.

'After a while, she got discouraged with the sleeping tablets and she bought a can of rat poison. It was supposed to be deadly. She put it in almost everything Georg ate, spoonfuls at a time.

'It didn't even give him an upset stomach.

'Then she tried mouse poison, which was supposed to be even stronger. I think Georg liked the taste. He mentioned several times that he thought her cooking was improving.

'I didn't like it. I thought it was sort of weird and I said maybe it would be better if she just asked Georg for a divorce, but she said no, he'd just beat her up and he wouldn't give her a divorce because he'd have nobody to look after the children.

'On the evening of May 13, 1972, Georg went to bed around ten o'clock. The girls had already been put to bed at eight and there was just me and Ursula still awake.

'After a while, she came in with the hatchet we used for chopping kindling all wrapped up with adhesive tape. She gave it to me and said, "Now is the time to do it. He's asleep."

190

'I went into the bedroom and Georg was sleeping with his mouth open. I took the hatchet and hit him on the head with the blunt end as hard as I could. His head just sort of exploded and splashed blood and brains all over the wall.

'We cleaned everything up and took him over to the Esterfeld Forest and buried him. Then Ursula got all the bed clothes and put them in the washing machine to get the blood off while I drove the car over to the Dutch border. We figured that if it was found there, people would think he'd gone to Holland.

'By the time I got rid of it, it was past midnight and I had to wait until morning to catch a bus back to Meppen. When I got back Ursula had cleaned everything up so good that there wasn't a trace of what had happened to Georg. In a way, I'm sort of glad we got caught. It's been bothering me for a long time.'

Confronted with this statement, Ursula Adomeit at first denied all knowledge of the crime, but, under persistent questioning, changed her mind and confirmed it in nearly all details.

Both she and Adomeit pleaded extenuating circumstances and were able to produce evidence that the dead man had frequently beaten his wife and had otherwise neglected her. This apparently made an impression on the court for it ruled that they were to be tried under the more lenient juvenile code and on November 12, 1975 handed down the maximum sentences under that code of ten years imprisonment for each.

13

LADYKILLER

With the approach of spring in Germany, Germans are much given to repeating the folk saying, *'Der April weiss nicht was er will'*, meaning that April doesn't know what it wants to do with respect to the weather.

This is usually a fairly accurate observation, but on April 19, 1967, which happened to be a Wednesday, April knew very well what it wanted to do in the little town of Darmstadt, West Germany.

It wanted to pour down golden sunshine from a cloudless blue sky and it wanted to raise temperatures to where unsuspecting birds would think it May and burst into their spring mating songs, and it wanted to stimulate the trees to put out the first, tender green leaves which was, of course, a very dangerous thing to do as April in central Europe is quite capable of producing a hard, killing frost out of its sleeve, so to speak.

None of these considerations bothered Ingrid Riedel in the least. As far as she was concerned, it was spring, the weather was beautiful, she was sixteen, her mirror told her she was pretty and, most important of all, it was twelve-thirty, school was out and Mummy and Heidrun would have lunch ready at home.

Ingrid had an excellent appetite and, despite her new-found dignity as an almost grown-up young lady, she could not resist a few skips as she trotted up the front walk to the door of the really quite nice villa at 9, Leo-Tolstoy Street.

To her astonishment, the door was locked.

'The ninnies!' said Ingrid, pressing the doorbell.

There was no reply.

'How strange!' murmured Ingrid. 'They've gone off somewhere and left me without lunch.'

She could not imagine where her mother and sister might have gone that they would not be back by this time, but it was obvious that they were not. The thing to do then was to go in and get her lunch ready herself. There would be plenty of things in the refrigerator.

Getting in was no problem. The lock on the kitchen window at the back of the house was defective and if you jiggled it right you could push the window up and climb in. Ingrid had done it before and she did it now.

Once inside the kitchen she was assailed by a weird feeling of loneliness. The house in which she had been born and in which she had lived all her life suddenly seemed much too quiet. It was, she thought, as if something had stopped, something like the ticking of a clock to which one has become so accustomed that it is only noticed when it stops.

'Mummy!' called Ingrid in a little, hesitant voice. 'Heidrun?'

The only reply was the same silence of the stopped clock, only now it was stronger. Ingrid squared her shoulders. She was a girl of very considerable personal courage and she had been taught to face problems rather than avoid them.

'There is something wrong with this house,' she said aloud in a clear, firm voice. 'And I shall see what it is.'

The words seemed to echo in the empty hall where the stairs led to the second floor and she felt the little hairs on her forearms and the nape of her neck rise. Nonetheless, she went out of the kitchen and down the hall to the stairs. Before ascending them she stopped at the front door, unlocked it and opened it a crack. The sight of the spring sunlight outside was somehow reassuring.

Upstairs, her parents' bedroom was tidy and the beds were made, meaning that her mother and sister had finished the housework before going wherever they had gone. So too was her own room where she had half expected to find a note explaining the strange absence. There was none, and she turned back to the stairs and then stopped in front of her sister's room. The door was closed, but there was nothing unusual about that. The Riedels were a tidy family and doors were normally kept closed.

'Heidrun?' whispered Ingrid, resting her fingers on the panel of the door.

Suddenly, she snatched at the handle and, in a sort of panic, pushed the door wide open. Heidrun was lying in bed with the bed covers drawn up over her face!

An immense feeling of relief swept over her. It was a joke! A silly joke! Mummy and Heidrun had hidden in their beds just to scare her. Everything was all right.

In two bounds, she crossed the room, caught hold of the top of the bed cover and jerked it completely away.

'You silly . . .,' she began and then the words died in her throat. The bed cover still clenched in her fist, Ingrid Riedel put back her head and screamed and screamed and screamed.

Lying on the bed was the naked body of her sister Heidrun. She lay spreadeagled on her back and her long blonde hair was fanned like a halo about her head. Only it was no longer blonde. It was a dark sullen red, the red of fresh blood, and all around her the sheets were soaked with what seemed an absolutely incredible amount of the same substance. Her mouth had fallen slightly open and her large blue eyes stared sightlessly at the ceiling.

Later, Ingrid was to have no recollection of stumbling down the stairs or of calling the police, but she did so for there was a record of a call being received at the Darmstadt police headquarters and five minutes later a patrol car arrived with two officers in it.

Ingrid was lying on the front steps in the spring sunshine and she was only able to speak in a whisper because she had screamed her vocal cords raw. No one had come to help her. The Leo-Tolstoy Street district is expensive and the houses are not close together.

While one of the officers remained with Ingrid, the other drew his gun and went up to the second floor of the house. The gun was there because Ingrid was not entirely coherent and he was not sure what he was going to find inside.

A few moments later he came back down with the gun holstered and a shocked look on his face. Heidrun Riedel had been twenty years old and the officer was only two years older. It was the first time that he had had to verify death in a corpse.

'Homicide,' he said in a low voice, turning his face away from the crying girl. 'I'll call the station and tell them.'

'Ask them if we can take this girl to hospital,' said his partner. 'She ought to be under a doctor's care.'

The station said that it was all right to take the girl to the hospital, but that one officer should remain at the scene to see that nothing was tampered with until the squad from the Criminal Investigations Department arrived.

'You're certain the girl is dead?' said the dispatcher. 'I shouldn't send the ambulance?'

'There's no pulse or heart beat or signs of respiration,' said the officer. 'She's dead.'

'Multiple skull fractures,' said Dr Philipp Frenzl, the department's medical expert, looking at Inspector Ludwig Eberling through his horn-rimmed glasses. 'Something very heavy like a hammer or the back of a hatchet. She hasn't been dead more than two hours.'

'Sex crime?' asked the inspector.

The doctor probed delicately with rubber-gloved fingers.

'Sex motive perhaps,' he said. 'She wasn't raped. The girl is still a virgin.'

'Perhaps she slept naked,' suggested Detective Sergeant Guenther Weber who was down on his knees looking under the bed. 'Ah-ha! Here's something!'

'What?' said the inspector, lowering himself to one knee and trying unsuccessfully to bring his head lower than the bottom of the bed.

'A hammer,' said the sergeant, 'a heavy hammer. Looks like there's blood on it.'

'Leave it where it is,' said the inspector. 'We'll move the bed later and photograph it in place. Probably the murder weapon.'

'You want the complete lab crew out?' the sergeant asked.

The inspector nodded. 'Tell them on the double,' he said. 'The body's barely cold. If we can get any kind of a lead, we may be able to get him before he goes too far. In the meantime, I'll take a look around the house.'

The sergeant went out to the police car parked at the kerb and called the station. He had heard about Ingrid Riedel from the patrol car officer who had remained at the scene and, after having ordered the laboratory crew out, he called the hospital to ask if the girl was in a state to be questioned.

She was not, as the doctor at the hospital had immediately placed her under heavy sedation and put her to bed.

'She was in deep shock,' he said in response to the sergeant's question. 'You're going to have to be very careful about questioning even after she comes out of it. An experience like this could have permanent effects.'

'An experience like what?' said the sergeant who knew nothing of the circumstances and who thought that Ingrid might have been attacked as well.

'The patrolman said he thought she'd discovered her sister's murdered body,' said the doctor. 'She didn't say anything herself.'

'He saw both of them so he may have noted a family likeness,' said the sergeant. 'We don't know yet who the victim is.'

As the sergeant returned to the house, the inspector was just coming up the stairs.

'There's another one in the basement,' he rumbled. 'Tell Philipp and then give me a hand to go over this house. God knows how many more corpses there are in here.'

The one in the basement was in fact the only other corpse.

'The mother of the girl upstairs, I would judge,' said the doctor. 'The family resemblance is strong. The circumstances are almost identical.'

Forty-eight-year-old Erna Riedel lay flat on her back on the concrete floor of the basement with the plastic sheet which had covered her body beside her.

Like her daughter, she was completely naked and, like her, she had died of multiple skull fractures, the blood soaking her blonde hair and spreading in a shallow pool around her head. Her eyes and mouth were closed.

'No indication of rape here either,' said the doctor,

probing again. 'Of course, she's a mature woman who's had children and there could have been penetration without violence. However, I can't detect any ejaculate inside the vagina and she was not in a state of sexual excitement herself at the time she was killed.'

'Which was when?' said the inspector.

The doctor shrugged. 'Roughly the same time as the girl upstairs,' he said. 'I can't give you a closer estimate until I get them over to the morgue for the autopsy.'

'Would you say the same hammer?' said the inspector.

'I should think so,' said the doctor, parting the blood-soaked hair to examine the wounds.

'Then this woman was presumably killed first here in the basement and the murderer then went upstairs, killed the girl there and left the hammer lying under the bed,' muttered the inspector. 'But what was the girl doing lying naked in bed at ten o'clock in the morning and what was her mother doing down here in the basement naked. Could this have been a family of nudists?'

The laboratory technicians, who had by now arrived, were able to answer the question. The Riedels had not been nudists and neither mother nor daughter had been naked at the time of their deaths.

'In both cases,' said the technician in charge of the squad, the women's skulls were smashed with the hammer and they were stripped immediately thereafter. We know it was immediately because there is only a relatively small amount of blood on the clothing. Oddly, he seems to have tried to conceal it.'

'Oddly is right,' said the inspector. 'What did he do it for in the first place? The doctor says he didn't rape them.'

'Sex,' said the technician shortly. 'He masturbated over the bodies after he'd killed and stripped them. There are traces of semen on the floor and on the body of the older woman.'

'In short, a sex freak,' said the inspector. 'Would this be a normal pattern of behaviour for him?'

'Probably,' said the technician. 'Not, of course, that he's necessarily killed someone before. His thing may merely be masturbating over a naked woman and he wouldn't have too much trouble finding willing partners for that.'

Dr Frenzl did not agree.

'Considering the violence of the acts,' he said, 'I cannot believe that this was a simple matter of wanting to masturbate over a naked woman. The violence itself was a part of the pattern of sexual behaviour and it would not be surprising if he has a record of attacks on women. Not rape, mind you. He may well be incapable of conventional rape. But a violent assault on a woman and the removal of her clothing.'

It was seven o'clock in the evening of the day of the murders and the doctor had come to the inspector's office to report on the initial findings of the autopsy which was not entirely completed. It was far enough along, however, to determine that there would be no surprises. The Riedels, mother and daughter, had died within a half hour of each other and at approximately nine-thirty in the morning. There were no other indications.

'Well, maybe he's got a record,' said the inspector, 'but not with us. Guenther is still checking with records in Frankfurt and Mannheim, but I have the feeling he's not going to come up with anything.'

'What were the lab's conclusions on the hammer?' asked the doctor. 'They were over to take the fingerprints and some casts of the wounds for comparison.'

'Positive,' said the inspector. 'It was the murder weapon in both cases. The weird thing is that the only prints on it are Mrs Riedel's and they're on the head. The lab's conclusion was that the hammer belongs to the house and that Mrs Riedel handed it to her murderer. Possible, of course, if she didn't know that he was going to murder her.'

'What about the husband?' said the doctor. 'Has he been located?'

The inspector nodded. 'He was on a business trip in Austria,' he said. 'I talked to him on the telephone. He's coming back tonight, but he won't be able to help us. Didn't have any idea of who might have done it. Thought it must be a madman.'

'In a way it was, no doubt,' said the doctor thoughtfully.

'So there are no clues, no leads, nothing? What are you going to do?'

'There's a possible lead,' said the inspector. 'Mrs Riedel kept an address book and in it, among her friends and relatives, are the names of a number of hand workmen, gardeners, plumbers and so on. She noted beside each name what they did and where to get hold of them.

'Now, certain things we can deduce. There's no evidence of any kind of a struggle in the house so the murderer was admitted peacefully. He was someone they knew and someone who had some business there.

'Secondly, if Mrs Riedel actually handed the hammer to her murderer as the lab thinks, then it was not for him to kill her with, but for some kind of a job that he was supposed to do. *Ergo*, the man was presumably a hand workman of some kind and, possibly, one who had worked for her before.'

'Shrewd,' said the doctor. 'And what luck are you having?'

'I'll know in a few minutes,' said the inspector. 'Fritz is checking the list for possible criminal records and I've got four men trying to trace the whereabouts of the people this forenoon.'

'Then I'll wait,' said the doctor. 'You don't happen to have a cup of coffee around here anywhere I suppose?'

There was, of course, as in all self-respecting criminal investigations offices, a pot of hot coffee discreetly concealed behind a screen in one corner, but the doctor had barely had time to pour a cup and return to his chair when the reports began to come in.

'Mostly negative,' grunted the inspector sourly, checking off the names on the master list on his desk. 'They were practically all working this morning. There are only two left. One we can't locate and the other's out of the country.'

'I should think he'd be the top suspect,' observed the doctor. 'When did he leave?'

'Yesterday, according to his wife,' said the inspector. 'So, if she's not lying and if he really did leave the country yesterday, he's eliminated too.'

The telephone rang. 'Eberling,' growled the inspector,

picking it up. 'Yeah Fritz. Good boy. Nothing on the others? Okay. Bring it on over.'

He put the telephone back into the cradle and his thick, black cigar back into the corner of his mouth.

'One of the hand workmen has a record,' he said. 'Robbery. Breaking and entering. Fellow named Klaus Schmidt. Forty-two years old. Plumber by trade.'

'I thought they could all be accounted for this morning except two,' said the doctor. 'Is this one of the two?'

'This is the one we couldn't locate,' said the inspector. 'The other one's a thirty-three-year-old house painter named Hans Schuetz. He's the one that's married and told his wife he was going to France to look for work.'

'A married man would be a less likely suspect,' said the doctor, frowning, 'but this Schmidt doesn't sound so likely either. His record isn't over sex crimes. It's over robbery. This was a sex crime.'

'Or are we merely supposed to think that?' said the inspector.

'A faked sex crime?' said the doctor. 'Well, I suppose it could be . . . Was anything taken from the house?'

'Not insofar as we've been able to determine,' said the inspector. 'We'll only know for certain tonight when Riedel gets in from Austria. Personally, I doubt that anything was taken. There were plenty of objects of value in the house and even quite an amount of money.'

'But how so robbery then?' said the doctor in bewilderment.

The inspector shrugged like a water buffalo heaving out of a mud wallow. 'Who knows?' he said. 'Maybe the robbery went wrong. Maybe Mrs Riedel or the daughter caught him red-handed and he killed them. Then in order to avoid suspicion, he deliberately didn't take anything and rigged it to look like a sex crime. Don't forget, unless Guenther finds something with the other towns, we don't have any record of a sex criminal with a similar *modus operandi*. There's more reason to believe that the murderer is a hand worker rather than a sex criminal.'

As the inspector had anticipated, Sergeant Weber was

unable to find any record of any similar sex crime either in Darmstadt or in any of the neighbouring towns. Nor could any trace of Klaus Schmidt, the plumber-burglar, be found.

'He left his room without notice and without even using up all the rent he'd paid in advance,' said the sergeant. 'It would be almost an admission of guilt, but unfortunately he left before the crimes took place.'

'Could still be construed as an admission of guilt,' observed the inspector. 'He may not have planned on killing the women, but he may have planned on burglarizing the house and, since he knew he'd be a suspect, he was all set to cut out in any case.'

'Could be,' said the sergeant. 'That's much the manner in which he went about it in the case where he was convicted. Arranged to get work as a handyman in a big house and then filed the catches on the locks so that he could get in at night. Mrs Riedel may have caught him doing something like that. There was nothing wrong with the locks though. I checked them.'

'We'll find out, if I can get him into an interrogation room,' said the inspector grimly. 'All we need is to know where he is.'

And twenty-four hours later, he had his wish. Klaus Schmidt was, it seemed, right in Darmstadt. A police informer reported that he was seen on most evenings in the Tip-Top Bar.

'I'll take the stake-out myself,' said Sergeant Weber. 'That's a rough place and if we put more than one man in there, it's going to get around. By the same token, I wouldn't like to leave this to one of the junior men. If Schmidt's guilty, he'd have nothing to lose by adding a cop to his score.'

'Go ahead,' grunted the inspector. 'It's your funeral.'

It nearly was. Two evenings later, Klaus Schmidt walked into the Tip-Top Bar and was confronted by Sergeant Weber who had been drinking a beer at the bar.

'Criminal Police,' said the sergeant, flashing his credentials. 'You are to accompany me quietly.'

The squat, black-haired man took one look and, with

startling agility, leaped a good six feet sideways, landed running and was within a yard of the door leading to the toilets and the alley behind the building when Sergeant Weber snapped the slide of his service automatic, fired a warning shot into the wall over his head and called in a dangerously level voice, 'Don't move!'

Schmidt whirled, crouched and produced a gun of his own from the waistband of his trousers.

For a long minute there was stalemate.

'Drop the gun and put your hands up,' said the sergeant, moving forward and turning to present a smaller target.

Whether Schmidt would have dropped the gun or would have fired was a question which remained unanswered for, at that moment, a beer bottle sailed out of the crowd of customers, apparently aimed at the sergeant's head. The sergeant was moving and the aim was bad. Instead of striking him in the back of the head, it sailed past his ear and struck Schmidt squarely in the face, throwing him off balance.

An instant later, the sergeant's gun was rammed into his stomach and the wrist of the hand holding his gun was seized and twisted.

'I said, "Drop it!",' said the sergeant.

Schmidt dropped the gun and the sergeant, taking no chances, put handcuffs on him.

Leading his prisoner to the bar, he took a bill from his pocket and handed it to the bartender.

'A free beer for the boy who threw the bottle,' he said. 'The police appreciate your assistance.' And then led Schmidt out of the door to the accompaniment of some very picturesque cursing.

At police headquarters Klaus Schmidt was booked for resisting arrest and illegal possession of a deadly weapon, following which he was sent to the detention cells to ponder on the waiting interrogation room and the inspector in the morning.

Rather than ponder, however, he fell promptly and soundly asleep. Klaus Schmidt had excellent nerves and he was to prove it in the days to come. Nothing that the inspector could do or say would bring anything out of him other than the bare statement that he had not killed anyone and that he did not remember where he had been on the forenoon of the nineteenth, but he thought very probably that he had been sleeping somewhere.

The inspector was much irritated by this stubborn resistance, but he was also impressed.

'He's too confident,' he said. 'He knows he's got nothing to worry about. I don't think he's guilty.'

'Then the only other possibility we have is Schuetz,' said the sergeant. 'But he's not a possibility because his wife says he was in France at the time.'

'She says,' repeated the inspector. 'But was he? Get her down here and let's see how well she sticks to that statement. I'm going to let somebody else lean on Schmidt for a while. He's beginning to get on my nerves.'

Mrs Marta Schuetz was able to demonstrate the truth of her statements with written evidence.

'Here,' she said. 'This is the letter that Hans sent me the day he left. It's dated the seventeenth.'

The inspector examined the letter which was no more than a note.

'Please forgive me, Marta,' it read, 'but you will not be seeing me again until things get straightened out. I have taken fifty marks from our joint savings account.'

The letter was dated April 17, 1967 and signed Hans.

'Do you have the envelope in which this came?' asked the inspector.

Mrs Schuetz had thrown the envelope away.

'Satisfied?' said the sergeant, after the woman had left.

'Not by a long sight,' said the inspector. 'If we had the envelope, there'd be a postmark on it with the date. As it is, he could have written the letter last July . . . or on the afternoon of April Nineteenth.'

'The content was ambiguous to say the least,' said the sergeant. 'What did he mean, "please forgive me"? Forgive him for what? And, "until things get straightened out". What things?'

'You heard her,' said the inspector. 'She thought he meant

203

she was to forgive him for taking off like that and he wanted to get their financial affairs straightened out. They only got here from East Germany four months ago and I guess they've been having a hard time. Maybe he meant to forgive him for taking the fifty marks out of their . . .'

His voice trailed away and he sat staring at the sergeant with an expression of such fierce concentration that the sergeant involuntarily flinched.

'Get over to the Savings Bank!' he barked suddenly. 'If the withdrawal of that fifty marks took place on the seventeenth, we'll forget about Schuetz. If it was any other date, we'll call Interpol.'

The withdrawal slip was dated April 19, 1967.

'Aside from that slight slip, very clever, Mr Schuetz,' said the inspector. 'He knew that his wife wouldn't check the postmark on the envelope and he may have known that anything mailed at the main post office gets carried out locally the same day. She simply thought he mailed it on the seventeenth and she only got it two days later. In actual fact, he mailed at noon. What does Interpol say?'

'They're looking,' said the sergeant. 'They don't think they'll have too much trouble in locating him.'

Interpol is the European International Police Organization which attempts to co-ordinate police work between various countries. Their agents are rather good at finding people and, as they had predicted, they did not have very much trouble finding Hans Schuetz.

The house painter was living in Paris and working at his trade. As a foreigner he was, of course, registered with the police in his local *arrondissement*. It was merely a matter of finding out which one.

Schuetz was returned to Germany on a charge of suspicion of murder and, upon his arrival in Darmstadt, made a statement in which he neither confessed to nor denied the crime.

'I cannot recall having killed the Riedels,' said Schuetz.

During the months in detention which followed, however, the inspector was able to stimulate his memory to a remarkable extent.

A search of Schuetz's apartment turned up blood-stained work clothing which he had apparently hidden there while his wife was out shopping. Although he never admitted it, it seemed also probable that he had simply left the letter in the mail box at that time and had never mailed it at all.

Schuetz and his wife had not been on good terms and she had actually not seen him since the seventeenth, a fact of which he had taken advantage.

According to Schuetz, his troubles with his wife had also been one of the causes of the murders.

'We had not had sexual relations for a long time,' he said, 'and I could not afford to pay a prostitute. On the morning that it happened I had the feeling that Mrs Riedel had no objection to our becoming more intimately acquainted and, as I passed her in the cellar door, she brushed her hips against me. I think I must have lost my head then.'

It was practically the only confession that Schuetz ever made and he resolutely refused to discuss the details of the murders or his motives in carrying them out.

Despite the predictions of the laboratory technician and Dr Frenzl, Schuetz seemed to be fully normal sexually and had no record of sex offences or, indeed, any offences in either East or West Germany. His wife reported that they had led, up to the time of their estrangement, a normal sex life.

On October 13, 1968, a year and a half after the day when Ingrid Riedel had come so gaily home to find the greatest horror of her life awaiting her in blood-drenched silence, Hans Schuetz was brought to trial, pleaded guilty to two charges of unpremeditated homicide and was sentenced to life imprisonment. It was the maximum sentence which the court could impose.

14

HATCHET WORK

When Ingeburg Grunwald failed to return home from work on the evening of June 19, 1974, Mrs Elizabeth Hermann immediately called the police. Mrs Hermann was Ingeburg's mother and, although her daughter was twenty-two years old and a married woman, she was still inclined to be somewhat protective of her.

In Mrs Hermann's opinion, Ingeburg had not been very lucky, even though her problems were of her own making. The Hermanns had moved heaven and earth to prevent their then nineteen-year-old daughter from marrying the only one year older Wolfgang Grunwald, but it had all been in vain. Ingeburg had simply allowed herself to become pregnant and that, of course, was the end of the parental opposition to the marriage.

Looking back now, Mrs Hermann sometimes wondered if it would not have been preferable to have an illegitimate grandchild. After all, the marriage had lasted only two years until Ingeburg had come home with her baby and filed divorce proceedings against Wolfgang. Still, she thought, she could be thankful that there had been no unpleasantness. Wolfgang had not opposed the divorce. He had probably welcomed it. It was easier to project an image of a suave, sophisticated man-about-town without a wife and child.

But that did not alter the fact that Ingeburg was not home nor was she at the filling station where she worked. Mrs Hermann had called and the attendant had said that she had left at four o'clock, the usual time. It was now six and there was no reason in the world why she should not be home. Ingeburg was not the sort of girl to go off somewhere without telling her mother.

Mrs Hermann had an uneasy feeling that Wolfgang Grunwald might have something to do with this disappearance. Could it be possible that he was attempting a reconciliation? She did not mention this possibility to the Officer-in-Charge of the Missing Persons Section at police headquarters, but merely contented herself with the information that her daughter was missing and that she was estranged from her husband.

'We'll look into it and call you back,' promised the officer. 'If she does contact you in the meantime, please let us know. I'm sure everything will be all right.'

The last sentence was routine and did not in any way reflect the true opinion of the officer. Munich, one of Germany's largest cities, is as dangerous for pretty young girls as large cities are anywhere and Mrs Hermann had stressed that her daughter was very pretty indeed.

The Missing Person Section's files were full of reports of missing pretty young girls and it could safely be assumed that a certain number of them were now leading exciting, if not necessarily pleasant, lives in the harems and brothels of North Africa and the Middle East.

The officer therefore handed the F.I.R., as the First Information Report form is called, to a young plainclothesman lounging in a chair beside his desk and instructed him to see what Wolfgang Grunwald might have to say about the disappearance of his estranged wife.

The plainclothesman was back in less than an hour.

'Negative,' he said, dropping the F.I.R. onto the desk and himself back into the chair. 'The husband's watching television with the grounds for the estrangement: Turkish woman named Bahar Kandlbinder. Looks pretty rough. She's at least ten years older than he is.'

'Kandlbinder?' said the officer. 'That's a Turkish name? It's German as Schultz.'

'Maybe she's married,' said the plainclothesman. 'I didn't ask, but she's Turkish all right. I recognized the accent.'

'You check at the filling station?' said the officer.

'Yeah,' said the detective. 'Girl left at the usual time. Nobody noticed nothing.'

'Well, maybe she's gone to the movies,' said the officer optimistically. 'She'll probably turn up by herself.'

Mrs Hermann called at nine. Her daughter was still not home. She wanted to know what the police were doing.

She called again at eleven. She was very worried.

Then she called at one, at three, at four-thirty and at six. At the six o'clock call she was slightly hysterical which was hardly strange considering that she had not had a wink of sleep all night. There was not much that the night duty man could do for her. The F.I.R. had been checked and any further checking would have to be done by the Criminal Investigations Department. Missing Persons did not have the personnel.

She did achieve one thing. She created a strong desire in the Missing Persons Section to get rid of the case. At eight-thirty the following morning, Detective-Sergeant Sepp Meier found the F.I.R. in his In-tray.

The sergeant read it thoughtfully. When he had finished, he marked a question mark on it with blue pencil and dropped it into the In-tray of his superior at the desk opposite.

Inspector Josef Biedermann, ploughing into the day's work with his usual energy and sending up little puffs of smoke from the first of the day's short black cigars like a miniature steam engine, snatched it up, glared at it and gave a violent snort.

'What in hell do these question marks mean, Sepp?' he demanded. 'You're always putting question marks on things and dropping them in my box.'

'Means I want to know what you plan to do about it,' said the sergeant. 'You're the one who makes the decisions.'

The inspector scanned the report more carefully.

'Well,' he said. 'One thing is clear. Missing Persons wants to get rid of it and I can see why. Look at the calls here. Six, nine, eleven, one, three, four-thirty, six. The woman's driving them up the wall. What's your opinion?'

The sergeant shrugged. 'Not enough information to have one,' he said. 'I can pull Ferdy off the Bockwiller case for a while this afternoon if you want it checked out some more.'

The inspector tossed the F.I.R. back across the desk. 'Have him check it out,' he said and plunged back into the paperwork.

By that afternoon there was a break in the Bockwiller case and Ferdy could not be taken off it, so the sergeant left his paperwork and went out and checked it himself.

'Don't know what to make of this Grunwald business,' he remarked that evening as he and the inspector were preparing to leave the office.

'Grunwald?' said the inspector.

'The F.I.R. Missing Persons sent over this morning,' said the sergeant. 'Ferdy was busy. I took it.'

'And?' said the inspector.

'A little weird,' said the sergeant. 'The woman just left her place of work and disappeared. No reason. The husband didn't have any reason to do anything to her. He's all in favour of the divorce so that he can get married to his Turkish masseuse.'

'What in the devil is a Turkish masseuse?' said the inspector, stretching out a hand for the F.I.R. which the sergeant was holding.

'In this case, the daughter of a former Turkish military attaché,' said the sergeant. 'Name is Bahar Kandlbinder, age thirty, formerly married to a German named Kandlbinder, but now divorced, profession, masseuse specialized in only one part of the body. She's Grunwald's girl friend.'

'Specialized in only one part of the body?' said the inspector, getting red in the face. 'What the hell . . .?'

'Sex massage,' said the sergeant briefly. 'It's the in-thing.'

'Don't we have a vice squad?' said the inspector.

'Yes, but a liberal government,' said the sergeant. 'It's more or less legal.'

'God Almighty!' said the inspector. 'Well, it's not our department. What about the girl?'

'Not a trace,' said the sergeant. 'According to my information, she's not the type to run off and live in a commune so I suppose it's either the Middle East trade or maybe she ran into some kind of a nut.'

'Very possible,' said the inspector. 'Pick up a picture of

her and have some circulars distributed tomorrow. We'll have to see if anything turns up.'

Two days later something did.

A very broad man with one leg, who was a retired wrestler, was draining a lock on the River Isar which runs through Munich. At the bottom of the lock, Locktender Otto Bickel found a woman's handbag. The bag contained money and identification papers in the name of Ingeburg Grunwald and Bickel immediately brought it to the police.

'Bad,' said the sergeant, coming back into the office from the police laboratory where the technicians were examining the bag. 'It's been in the water since the day she disappeared and it doesn't seem to have been opened at all. Usual junk that a woman carries around with her and quite a bit of money.'

'Not slavers then,' said the inspector. 'They'd have kept both the money and the papers. I'm afraid all we can do now is wait for somebody to find the body. You're having the river dragged, of course?'

'Of course,' said the sergeant.

No body was found in the Isar and on Sunday, June 23rd, a young, rather noble-looking man with clear, blue eyes, wavy blond hair and a prominent chin, went off for a walk in the Hofoldinger Forest ten miles to the south of the city and solved the mystery of what had happened to Ingeburg Grunwald.

The body lay at the foot of a steep slope on its back, the limbs extended like a starfish, and the head was no more than a shattered mass of splintered bone, torn flesh, extruded brain and black, dried blood from which one dull, sightless and socketless eye glared hideously. There was a good deal of dried blood on the rest of the body as well and the girl's clothing was badly torn and disordered with the exception of her nylon stockings and black, high-heeled shoes which were, incongruously, in perfect order. Since the body had been lying there for four days, it had attracted a large number of insects and even some small animals.

Hans-Dieter Hofstein, the young walker, was violently

ill, wept, nearly fainted and then made off as fast as his legs could carry him, muttering, 'Oh God! Oh God! Oh God!'

It took him twenty minutes to reach the nearest telephone and, it being a Sunday, it took the station over an hour to collect the personnel and the vehicles and bring the entire police homicide party to where Hofstein was waiting.

The young man told them exactly where the body could be found, but refused to accompany them, stating quite simply that he would rather spend the rest of his life in jail than have to view the corpse again.

He was, of course, not taken to jail, but his identification papers were carefully checked. There have been cases where a murderer 'discovered' the body of his own victim.

That this particular victim was the missing Ingeburg Grunwald was quickly established, the sergeant having brought out a set of the girl's fingerprints taken from personal possessions in her home earlier. While the sergeant was rolling the prints for comparison off the dead fingertips, Dr Guenther Brockmuehle, the department's medical expert, was making a quick examination of the body as found.

The examination was quick because, although required by regulations, it was not very useful under such conditions where clouds of insects rose with every manipulation of the corpse.

'All right, all right,' said the doctor, getting back to his feet and looking around for the stretcher bearers. 'Let's get her into the box. Bring one of those towels and beat off the flies as well as you can. I'll deal with the rest when we get her down to the morgue.'

The stretcher bearers came forward with the metal coffin used for transporting corpses to the police morgue, Ingeburg Grunwald was loaded into it and the coffin was placed in the low, flat trailer known as a corpse transporter, which had been brought out behind the police car.

'Was she raped?' asked the inspector, standing to one side and emotionlessly puffing on his cigar. He was not a man without feeling, but this was his job. He had seen a great many corpses in his time and some had been in worse shape than this one.

'No,' said the doctor. 'Her underwear is in place and there's no laceration of the external genitals. Looking for a motive?'

The inspector nodded. 'Weapon? Time?' he said.

'Hatchet or small axe,' said the doctor. 'Her head was split like a pumpkin. Several blows. Probably from behind. There are no defence marks on the hands or forearms. Time, I can't tell you until I've done the autopsy. Three or four days at least.'

'She disappeared on the afternoon of the nineteenth,' said the inspector.

'Probably then,' said the doctor. 'Can I take her down to the morgue now? Even if I don't start the autopsy until tomorrow, I'm going to have to do something about the bugs immediately.'

'Go ahead,' said the inspector. 'I'm going to stay out here with Sepp for a while. I want to see what the lab boys turn up.'

The laboratory technicians who had come out with the party had staked off the area in one metre squares and had been going over it square by square, any finds being spotted and noted on a sheet of squared paper.

Although it was Sunday and overtime pay in the Criminal Investigations Department was no more than a fond dream, they worked methodically and rather slowly so that the inspector had to wait for some time.

Finally, the technician in charge of the group came over and said, 'Well, that's it. I don't believe that we'll find anything else. Want to hear it?'

'I'm not standing out here because I love nature,' said the inspector shortly.

'She wasn't killed where the body was lying,' said the technician. 'She was killed up above the slope there and the body was then thrown over.

'There's a logging trail up there and the marks of a car's tyres. We have casts. There are three sets of footprints leading away from the car tracks, one set of which are the dead woman's. We have casts of the other two. A man and a woman or a teenage boy. The small ones are sports shoes.

'Twenty-six yards from where the car was parked the woman was hit so hard over the head that her heels sank a half inch into the ground. It's fairly soft.

'Good bit of blood at that point and then carry and drag marks to the top of the slope here. They couldn't have been very strong. There were two of them and the woman wasn't that heavy, but they dragged her more than they carried her.'

'Here's the description of the clothing she was wearing when she disappeared,' said the inspector, handing him the F.I.R. 'Does it check?'

The technician checked the clothing against his own notes.

'Everything checks except this red velvet jacket on the F.I.R.,' he said. 'It wasn't on the corpse.'

'She must have left it in the car,' said the inspector. 'Tell me, would a woman in her right mind come out here for a walk in the woods with her estranged husband and his mistress?'

'How would I know?' said the technician. 'I only find and assess what's there. You boys are the deduction experts.'

'There's no sign of a struggle or that she was dragged out of the car?' asked Sergeant Meier, who had been listening silently to the report.

'Nope,' said the technician. 'Everyone was walking normally except for the little one. He or she seems to have been running over the stretch between the car and the scene of the murder.'

'Strange,' said the sergeant. 'The little one was running, but it was Grunwald who was murdered. What would that mean?'

'The only thing any of this means to me,' said the inspector, 'is that these three people must have all known each other and they must have had a reason for coming out here to the woods. With two of them the reason was, no doubt, murder, but that certainly wasn't the reason that Mrs Grunwald had. It might help us if we could determine what her reason was.'

'Logically, the other two persons would be Grunwald and

213

his Turkish girl friend,' said the sergeant. 'They could have made some kind of a pretext, discussing the divorce or something, to get her out here, but the problem is: Why? They were in agreement on the divorce and there was no question of a property settlement. None of them had anything, not even insurance.'

'Well, there was a motive,' said the inspector. 'This wasn't something done on the spur of the moment. It was planned. And if Grunwald and his friend did it, then they were goddamnably cold-blooded about it. The detective from Missing Persons checked them out at six-thirty and they could barely have finished killing the girl then.'

'Still, they didn't think of everything,' observed the sergeant. 'If these tyre tracks match the tyres on Grunwald's car and if these footprints match his and Kandlbinder's shoes, we've got them.'

Wolfgang Grunwald and Bahar Kandlbinder were taken into custody an hour later and brought to the headquarters of the Criminal Police where they were subjected to intense interrogation. Both denied all knowledge of the crime and stated that they had spent the entire afternoon and evening of the nineteenth together.

In the meantime, the laboratory technicians were busy with Grunwald's green Opel Kadet and the contents of the apartment which he shared with Bahar Kandlbinder. Casts of the car's tyres were taken and all of the shoes and clothing belonging to the couple were brought to the police laboratory. By eight o'clock that evening, the laboratory was ready with a report.

'The tyre tracks do not match,' said the chief of the laboratory section. 'The shoe prints are the right size for Grunwald and Kandlbinder, but they do not match any shoes found in the apartment. None of the clothing shows any signs of blood stains or places where blood stains were removed.

'We did not find any trace of a hatchet or small axe.'

'Perfect score,' remarked the inspector whose secretary had just brought him in some sandwiches from across the street and who was making his dinner at his desk. 'Go home,

Gerda. There was no reason for you to come in in the first place.'

The secretary left reluctantly. She was a large, blonde woman who did not think that the inspector could do anything without her and who, consequently, bribed the dispatchers to inform her when he was called in during off-duty periods.

'Shall I tell the Interrogation Room to turn them loose?' asked the sergeant, getting to his feet.

'No,' mumbled the inspector, his mouth full. 'They've had plenty of time to get rid of the shoes and the clothing and even to change the tyres on the car. They're not innocent. They're just smarter than we thought they were.'

'We can't hold them very long without material evidence,' said the sergeant. 'We aren't even able to suggest a motive.'

'You'll get the material evidence tomorrow,' said the inspector. 'We'll start by checking the dry cleaning shops to see if Grunwald or Kandlbinder turned in any bloody clothing on the afternoon of the nineteenth or the morning of the twentieth. Then we'll check the places that sell tyres and see if we can determine whether Grunwald bought a new set recently. And, finally, we'll check out the hardware stores and see if we can find a clerk who can recognize Grunwald or Kandlbinder as the purchaser of a hatchet during the week preceding the nineteenth. Also, you can have all the ashes pulled out of the furnace at the apartment house to see if there's any trace of that red velvet jacket. The heating's off now, but they could have burned it up in the furnace anyway. It's coal. If there's nothing in the firebox of the furnace, get an exact description of the jacket and put out circulars all over town. I want action on this case.'

'I gathered that,' said the sergeant dryly.

Action there was, and results too. First of all, the store where Wolfgang Grunwald had bought a heavy hatchet of the trademark 'Bear' on June 13th, less than a week before the murder, was located. Grunwald had been careless. The store was only four blocks from the apartment house where he lived and some of the clerks knew him by sight. Then, the tyre store where Grunwald had bought a new set of tyres

215

two days before the murder was found. Finally, the red velvet jacket which had belonged to Ingeburg Grunwald was found hidden under a bush on the Theresien Wiese, the meadow-like fairgrounds along the Isar. It had been drenched with blood.

Confronted with this evidence, Wolfgang Grunwald promptly broke down and confessed to a knowledge of the murder which he said had been committed by his mistress, Bahar Kandlbinder.

'Ingeburg was going to have her put into an insane asylum,' he said. 'So Bahar asked me to buy the hatchet and get her to come out to the woods with us to talk over the divorce. While I waited at the car, Bahar and Ingeburg went on into the woods and then I heard a sound like someone splitting open a hollow log. A minute later, Bahar came back and said that she'd killed Ingeburg and that I was to help her get rid of the body. We threw it down the slope and then went back to town where I took our shoes and the hatchet and threw them in the Isar. The following morning, I changed the tyres on the car. I was afraid of being caught because I knew that I should have reported Bahar to the police for killing my wife, but by then it was too late.'

Bahar Kandlbinder had a different version.

'Wolfgang hated Ingeburg because, after they had separated, she was angry and she told his company about a lot of things that he'd stolen there and money that he'd taken and he got into a lot of trouble.

'Then, in the first part of June, I told him I didn't want to continue with him any longer and he became very angry. He boxed my ears and then he took my head and hit it against the bed post. I started to scream for help and he wrapped me up very tightly in a blanket. His face was like a crazy man's and I stopped calling and stayed very quiet. Then he seemed to get over it and everything was all right. I didn't say anything more about leaving him.

'When we went out to the woods with Ingeburg I still didn't think he'd really do it and I stayed in the car with the hatchet while he and Ingeburg went into the woods. All at once, he yelled, "Bring it to me!" and I knew he meant the hatchet. I ran after them and Ingeburg was standing with her back to us. I don't think she suspected anything. I handed Wolfgang the hatchet and then I saw he really was going to do it and I turned around and put my hands over my face.

'There was a terrible sound as if something had chopped into a big cabbage or a water melon and then more chopping sounds. I can never forget those sounds as long as I live. I will confess to anything, but I don't want to talk any more about what happened there in the woods.'

'So who is telling the truth?' asked the sergeant as he and the inspector returned to their office following the interrogation of the two suspects.

'She is,' said the inspector, 'but we're going to have to be a little tricky. Only the two of them were present so it's his unsupported word against hers. He's German and she's a Turk and a sex masseuse to boot. I'm afraid if we leave it the way it is, the jury will convict the wrong person.'

'So what do we do?' said the sergeant.

'We charge Kandlbinder with the murder and Grunwald with being an accessory after the fact,' said the inspector. 'Announce that to the press.'

'But . . .?' said the sergeant.

'We want Grunwald to think he's in the clear,' said the inspector. 'He'll go right up to the trial thinking that the most he can get is two or three years as an accessory. Then we'll hit him with the murder charge and provide the prosecutor with everything we can to sustain it. It'll be close to a year before this comes to trial so we'll have plenty of time to work on it. What we want to show is that Grunwald not only carried out the murder, but also carefully planned it in advance.'

'Are you sure we can?' said the sergeant dubiously.

'Absolutely,' said the inspector. 'Because he did. The hatchet and the tyres were bought well in advance. He knew just what to do with the bloody clothing and the hatchet after it had been used. He realized that there would be shoe prints and tyre marks. The whole thing shows the effects of careful thought over a period of some time. Do you think that a Turkish sex masseuse is capable of that?'

The sergeant shook his head. 'No,' he said. 'She isn't and, as a matter of fact, I believe her when she says she wanted to break off with Grunwald. After all, he wasn't much of a catch. No money. Nothing in the way of prospects. And probably not even much of a lover by her standards. I agree with you that the woman is innocent of the actual murder, but are you going to tell her what you're trying to do?'

'No,' said the inspector. 'There are only two of us who know so, if it gets out, it was either you or me who leaked it. I'd hate to break in a new assistant, but . . .'

'You won't have to,' said the sergeant. 'But it's going to be a rough year for Mrs Kandlbinder.'

On the face of things, Bahar Kandlbinder did not appear to suffer as greatly under the murder charge as the sergeant had anticipated, but resigned herself with oriental patience to her apparent fate. She was, however, extremely reluctant to discuss the murder and, in what seemed to be an effort to avoid further questioning on the subject, made a full confession to having killed Ingeburg Grunwald herself!

'I'm sorry that I didn't confess before,' she said. 'It happened just the way Wolfgang said it did.'

She had in fact only been informed that Wolfgang Grunwald had accused her of the murder and not of any of the details of his account. Subsequent questioning showed that she had no idea of what he had told the police.

'Which,' said the inspector, 'merely confirms my opinion that the woman is innocent. She thinks that she's going to be railroaded by a German court for a murder she didn't commit so she's being as co-operative as possible. All she wants is to get it over with.'

In the meantime, things had been going well with the search for evidence of Wolfgang Grunwald's guilt. Tests carried out in the police laboratory showed that the first blow which had split Ingeburg Grunwald's head nearly in half could not have been delivered by a person as short as Bahar Kandlbinder unless she was standing on something.

Nothing had been found at the scene on which she could have stood nor was any mention made in either of the confessions of her standing on something to strike the first blow.

The report which Ingeburg had made to her husband's company concerning his thefts and embezzlements was verified and a number of witnesses were found who stated that Grunwald had said on several occasions that he would 'get even' with her for it.

Finally, the clue of the footprints found at the scene tended to support Bahar Kandlbinder's version of the events. The Grunwalds had walked ahead into the forest and she had come running after them with the hatchet when Grunwald called her.

One month before the trial was due to take place the indictments were altered and Wolfgang Grunwald was charged with the murder of his wife. However, the shock did not provoke him to a confession, as the inspector had hoped, and he clung stubbornly to his original statement that he had only been a helpless witness to the murder carried out by Bahar Kandlbinder.

The court did not think so. The police had done their homework too well and on May 22, 1975, less than a year after the murder of Ingeburg Grunwald, Wolfgang Grunwald was found guilty of premeditated murder with no extenuating circumstances and sentenced to life imprisonment.

Bahar Kandlbinder was found guilty of acting as an accessory after the fact to murder and was sentenced to two and a half years. Even though the verdicts were not appealed, Wolfgang Grunwald never acknowledged his guilt and steadfastly maintains that Bahar Kandlbinder and not he is the true murderer of his wife.

15

GHOULISH PRACTICES

Vampire. A reanimated corpse which sucks the blood of living victims.

Ghoul. An evil demon which feeds on the flesh of corpses.

Necrophile. One who seeks to engage in sexual relations with the dead.

Strange creatures, but not at all uncommon. They can be seen on television almost any night of the week and only very small children are frightened. Everyone else finds them amusing for they know that there are, of course, no such beings.

Well, perhaps not, but what was it then that was in the mortuary of the great cemetery of Hamburg-Ohlsdorf, West Germany, on the night of April 14, 1971?

Something was there and it left clear traces of why it had come and what it had sought. The only thing not clear was what it was.

Curiously, the night of April 14, 1971 was well suited to such terrible activities. The weather was cold and wet with black, low-hanging clouds driving across the face of a sickly pale, waning moon. As midnight drew near, the wind rose, wailing and sobbing among the tombstones and sending sharp, startling rattles of rain against the tall gothic windows of the darkened mortuary.

In the hall where the corpses lay, awaiting the final ceremony of their burial, there was neither light nor heat. The dead have no need of either. Nor was the hall locked or guarded. No one would ever escape from that hall and no one but a madman would ever seek to enter.

And yet, as midnight passed and the church tower bell boomed slowly out its solemn twelve strokes, there was movement in the chill darkness of the hall of corpses; quick, furtive movement where there should have been no movement at all.

There was the scrape of a match and the tiny, yellow leaf of a candle flame sprang into being. Crooked, grotesque shadows danced along the wall and there were the sounds of coffin covers being drawn back and the rustle of paper. The corpses were all clad in paper shrouds until it would be time for them to put on their finery for the funeral.

With some, of course, it would make little difference what they wore, for the coffin would not be opened during the ceremony. Such was the case with little Käthe Bauer who had died at the age of twelve when struck by a car as she crossed the street on her way home from school. Käthe had been a pretty little girl, but the rear wheel of the car had gone directly over her face. At the funeral on Sunday, the coffin would remain closed.

It was open now and Käthe, who had died a virgin, was taking part in a sort of wedding feast where she was not only the bride, but also the dinner!

In the morning, when Mortuary Attendant Gerd Fröhlich came in to work at a quarter past eight, she was still seated at the festive board, her naked little-girl's body leaning against her coffin, the bloody marks of the bridegroom's passionate kisses and caresses on her budding breasts and lightly haired genitals and a deep cut across the veins of her left wrist.

On either side of the coffin were the stumps of burned down candles from the mortuary's own supply and some of the other corpses had been raised in their coffins to serve as guests at the wedding.

For a wedding and a feast it had definitely been. The thick, semi-congealed blood of the corpse had been sucked out of the veins in places, there were bite marks in the white flesh of the thighs and throat and a determined attempt had been made to consummate the marriage, an attempt which had been foiled only by the stiffness of the corpse. Across the cut on the left wrist was the imprint of another wound, but this in the fresh, red blood of the living and not the gummy, brown ichor of the dead.

Had Gerd Fröhlich been a man with a weak stomach, he would not have chosen to work in a mortuary, but this was something considerably beyond anything that could be expected in the way of normal mortuary work. Fröhlich barely made it to the lavatory where he lost his breakfast and, as it seemed to him, everything that he had eaten for several years. He then wiped his mouth and staggered, still retching, to the office where he dialled the number of the police.

His description of what had happened was so vivid that Inspector Frank Luders of the Hamburg Department of Criminal Investigations came out personally to have a look.

He was accompanied by his assistant, Detective-Sergeant Max Peters, and the department's medical expert, Dr Ludwig Strauss, who carried out an immediate examination of the body of Käthe Bauer.

While the inspector, looking not unlike a funeral director himself, stood glumly watching the doctor at his work, the sergeant went out to the police car and returned with a finger print kit.

'A lot of prints here,' he remarked, dusting the edges of the open coffins. 'What do you think he had in mind? Grave robbing?'

The inspector did not reply, but the doctor said, 'Hardly. These people weren't laid out for their funerals yet. There's nothing to rob.'

'He may not have known that,' said the inspector.

'He wasn't interested,' said the doctor, stepping back and stripping off his rubber gloves. 'What we have here is a ghoul and a necrophile. He wanted food and sex from the corpse. From the looks of the cut on her wrist, I would judge that he also wanted to exchange blood with her. He seems to have succeeded in everything but the sex. She was not dead long enough or too long, however you look at it, for that.'

The inspector was, necessarily, a man with strong nerves, but there was almost a shrill edge to his voice now as he

222

snapped, 'That's nonsense, Ludwig! There's no such thing as a ghoul!'

'Very well then,' said the doctor. 'If you insist, it was a perfectly ordinary, well-balanced person who came in here last night, tried to have sex with this little girl's corpse and sucked quite a bit of blood out of her. He also bit off a few small pieces and apparently swallowed them as I don't see them here. By my definition this is a ghoul, but if you are convinced that it was just a casual visitor . . .'

'Point taken,' interrupted the inspector. 'I suppose you would agree that this is a dangerous psychopath?'

'Definitely,' said the doctor without hesitation.

'Then spare no efforts, Max,' said the inspector. 'I'd like to get him before he tries this on someone alive.'

No efforts were spared, but the police were unable to find the slightest clue as to the identity of the mortuary's strange visitor. The Hamburg police also circulated a description of the incident to all police stations in Germany, but the little village of Bisselmark, forty miles to the east of Hamburg, did not receive the circular for the simple reason that Bisselmark is too small to have a police force.

Had there been one, however, it would have been presented with the most incredible case on the morning of April 17, 1971 when the local undertaker entered his place of business to find his latest and, at the moment, only client sitting upright in her coffin with her knees hooked over the sides.

A woman in her forties who had died of cancer two days earlier: her eyes were propped open with match sticks and the crotch of her underwear had been cut away.

Standing in a circle around the coffin were a number of burned down candles and, since it had been raining the night before, the marks of muddy shoes in a strange pattern as if someone had been performing some sort of ritual dance.

The undertaker was shocked and frightened, but he hurriedly replaced the corpse in its coffin and cleaned up all traces of what had transpired the night before. As he feared that the family might hold him responsible for the desecra-

223

tion of the corpse, he said nothing to anyone and it was only much later that he reported the incident to the police.

Following the incident in Bisselmark, the ghoul moved west, so far west in fact, that he left the mainland altogether and landed on the North Sea island of Sylt.

Sylt enjoys an interesting reputation in Europe because it is the site of the largest concentrations of nudists in Germany and, possibly, in the world.

Every summer brings thousands of sun-worshipping Germans, Danes, Swedes and Norwegians to splash in naked ecstasy in the chill waters of the North Sea or to frolic along the white sand beaches in temperatures which bring visions of ear muffs and parkas to less hardy races.

However, even for the Nordics, May 4th is a trifle early in the year for nude bathing and there were therefore only token numbers of visitors in Westerland, the main town on Sylt, when Pastor Harold Segen entered the antechamber of his church at approximately eight o'clock in the morning to find the lid of the coffin which was there removed.

Inside the coffin was Mrs Gertraud Frankle, who had died two days previously of circulatory disorders at the age of fifty-two. She was still lying peacefully on her back with her eyes closed, but, to the pastor's astonishment, the hilt of what looked to be a hunting knife projected from her chest.

Pastor Segen immediately notified the police and the body was examined by the medical adviser attached to the Department of Criminal Investigations.

His findings were that the knife, an ordinary souvenir hunting dagger with a chrome plated blade sharp on one side only and an imitation stag horn handle in the form of a deer's head bearing the inscription 'Souvenir of Sylt', had been thrust with considerable force directly through the woman's heart and then given a single half-turn.

The police did not suspect a ghoul because they knew that there was no such thing. Rather, they suspected an enemy of the family, but although the investigation continued for some months, no clue as to the identity of the culprit was discovered. The attack on the corpse in the church in Westerland was an isolated incident and nothing further of such nature took place in the town or anywhere on the island.

If ghouls take vacations, this one had taken his early for by May 30, 1971 he was back at work on the mainland and in a city with even more erotic associations than the nudists of Sylt. The city was Flensburg on the German side of the border with Denmark and its claim to fame was merely that it was the headquarters of the world's largest mail-order sex shop, founded by the equally famous Beate Uhse.

'Merely' is perhaps not entirely the right term in this case. There are statistics to the effect that one German in every five is a Beate Uhse customer which could mean that the Germans are very active in sexual matters, or precisely the opposite as many of the Uhse products are intended to make possible that which no longer comes naturally.

The scene was, as usual, a cemetery. In this case, the Mühlen Cemetery and on the night of May 30th there was nearly a full moon. Not that this had anything to do with it, of course. The ghoul was as active during the dark of the moon as at any other time, but perhaps he had need of light for the special operation which he had in mind and it would hardly have done to bring along a lighted lantern or even a flashlight. There are houses quite near the cemetery.

It was fortunate that there were houses because it is hard to say what might have happened to Marion Steiger on the morning of May 31st if a housewife living in one of them had not looked out and seen her run wildly into the street and collapse in the middle of the pavement.

Being a level-headed woman, the housewife first called the police and the ambulance and then went to see if she could do anything to help the young woman who was now trying to sit up and seemed to be suffering from a severe shock.

This impression was confirmed by the intern who arrived with the emergency ambulance, but the police could make no sense of what she was saying and finally set off in the direction from which the housewife had seen her come.

Only the cemetery lay in this direction and just inside the gate to it lay a woman's purse. Inside the purse was the personal identity card of Marion Steiger and a number of other personal items.

A little further on, the patrolcar officers came upon first one shoe and then the other and finally a veritable trail of flowers from what had obviously been a large bouquet.

'Look for a tombstone with the name Steiger on it,' said the senior of the two officers. 'There must have been something wrong with the grave. Maybe an animal got at it.'

A few moments later they found the grave of Helga Steiger who was Marion's mother. The grave was in perfect condition. The two officers came to a halt, puzzled, and then both saw simultaneously the scattered earth in the next row of graves. It looked as if a demonic grave-digger had been at work.

'Grave-robbers!' exclaimed the senior man, running around the gravestones to the other path.

But it was not grave-robbers and the sight which met his eyes gave him such a start that he automatically and unthinkingly drew his service pistol. The coffin had been buried deep, nearly six feet deep as the regulations required, but it had been dug completely free. One end was smashed to kindling and the corpse had been dragged to a sitting position with the hands resting stiffly on top of the unbroken lower end.

It was a man for it was dressed in a man's suit, but where the head should have been there was nothing but a ragged stump of neck.

'No wonder she was in shock!' whispered the second patrolman. 'What in God's name has happened here?'

His partner was, of course, unable to answer the question, but Dr Theodore Fichtenbauer, the medical expert attached to the Flensburg Police Department of Criminal Investigations, thought that he could.

'Somebody needed a skull,' he said matter-of-factly, letting himself down into the grave to squat on the top of the splintered coffin. 'Could be satanists or somebody who thinks he's a witch, or even a medical student.'

He probed casually with naked fingers in the already somewhat putrid flesh of the mangled neck, causing Detec-

226

tive-Sergeant Lutz Iggel to turn faintly green and gag slightly.

'If he was a medical student, it was his first year,' he remarked. 'Simply hacked it off with a butcher's knife or something similar.'

Inspector Richard Brinkmann, who had taken charge of the affair, decided that it had probably been satanists. As in other parts of the world, the decline in influence of the established religions had brought with it a rise in satanism, witchcraft, various Eastern religions and a number of home-grown sects.

A very large, very patient and very stubborn man, he pursued his investigations of the supposed satanists for over a year and a half without finding the slightest trace that any such group had ever existed in Flensburg.

It did not occur to him that this might be the work of a ghoul or vampire for he knew that there were no such things.

Perhaps the inspector might not have continued with the search for so long had he not found evidence of what had happened to the missing head. Two days after the desecration of the grave in Mühlen Cemetery, a middle-aged veterinarian named Karl Konzemius had opened the door to the small garden house in the garden which he leased on the edge of the city, to find a human nose and two ears lying on the floor.

The bits of flesh had begun to decompose badly and had attracted a number of flies and other insects so that, even though a veterinarian and accustomed to unpleasant sights, Konzemius was nearly overcome by nausea. When he had recovered from this, he carefully closed the door of the garden house and went to notify the police.

The inspector, his assistant and Dr Fichtenbauer came out together and a search of the garden house produced quite a few more parts of the head.

'Ah yes,' said the unshakable doctor, holding up the corpse's tongue. 'Here is the tongue and these were the eyes. He dug them out with the point of a knife.'

At this point, Sergeant Iggel left the garden house and

refused to return. In addition to the ghastly sight, the parts were beginning to smell quite strongly.

'This is presumably the scalp,' remarked the inspector, who was made of somewhat stronger stuff. 'At least, it's got hair on it.'

'Cut off everything he could,' said the doctor. 'All he wanted was the skull. What's that bottle there?'

'According to the label, it was burning alcohol,' said the inspector. 'It's empty now.'

'That explains these spots on the floor,' said the doctor. 'After he'd cut off everything that he could, he poured the alcohol over it and set it on fire to burn off the rest of the flesh. Wouldn't work of course. He'd need a lot more alcohol and, in any case, he obviously didn't get the brain out. However, it will eventually rot away and run out if he keeps it long enough.'

The inspector did not leave the garden house, but he did not look very much at his ease either.

The nose, scalp, eyes and ears of the dead man were placed in a small jar and buried with him for the second time. The skull remained missing, although by now most of the police forces in Germany were looking for it.

Like the Hamburg police, Inspector Brinkmann had sent out a circular to all police stations in Germany and, since there had now been several more incidents, there had been a considerable response.

There was, to begin with, the violation of the corpse of Käthe Bauer in Hamburg. Then the Westerland police reported the stabbing of the corpse of Mrs Gertraud Frankle. And finally, even the undertaker in Bisselmark came forward to recount the strange happenings in his establishment. He had read of the other cases in the newspapers and asked that the identity of the Bisselmark corpse be kept secret in order to spare the feelings of the family.

Inspector Brinkmann was still convinced that the deeds were the work of a sect of devil worshippers and he thought that it must be an entire gang to be ranging over such widely separated places as Hamburg, Sylt and Flensburg.

His assistant did not agree. Although a rather stylish

young man who wore his black hair nearly down to his shoulders and who displayed a distressing tendency to tie-dyed jeans and brilliant shirts, he had had an excellent training at the police school and he was, perhaps, slightly more open-minded than the inspector.

'There isn't any common pattern,' he argued. 'Flensburg is the only place where any part of the body was actually taken away and the only place where it was a man. In Hamburg, it was a little girl and there were definite sexual indications. In Bisselmark, there were indications that he'd examined her genitals, but not that he'd tried to have intercourse. And in Westerland, he didn't even disturb the corpse. Either these incidents are not connected or we're dealing with someone who's not following a rational pattern. I think it's the latter.'

'I don't know what to think any more,' said the inspector. 'Hamburg refers to the fellow as a ghoul, but there aren't any ghouls.'

'There aren't any satanists either,' said the sergeant. 'Not serious enough ones to go around beheading corpses. We've been following up this satanist theory for so long now that I've picked up a good deal of information on it. All that are known here in Germany are harmless.'

'Harmless!' said the inspector, a regular churchgoer and comparatively devout man, in a shocked voice.

'Physically harmless,' said the sergeant, who never went to church at all. 'Theology aside, these are mostly sex clubs with costumes. They get together and celebrate the Black Mass with a naked girl for an altar. Then they all have a nice little orgy and go home feeling wonderfully wicked and sweat it out in the shop or the office until the next meeting of the coven. It's about on the level of a bowling club. If one of those people came across a severed head, they'd die of fear.'

'I can see that you've gone into the thing thoroughly,' said the inspector, looking thoughtfully at his assistant as if he were wondering whether his investigations might not have led him further than was suitable for a police officer.

'All right. Supposing that we accept that the fellow is a ghoul. Where does that leave us?'

'With not quite so urgent a problem,' said the sergeant. 'We've been operating on the assumption that this is a group of satanists who could very well transfer their interest to living persons: a baby for the purposes of sacrifice or a young girl for the Black Mass. Right?'

'Right,' said the inspector.

'Well, if the fellow really is a ghoul or, at least, thinks he is, he's no danger to a living person,' said the sergeant. 'He's only interested in corpses. Granted, it's not pleasant to have bodies dug up and mortuaries raided, but at least there's no danger to human life.'

'Not too much different to Theodore's theory,' observed the inspector. 'He says that the fellow is a necrophile, a lover of corpses. Says its a recognized mental aberration. I say, if he loves corpses so much, why does he stick knives in them and cut off their heads?'

'Still,' said the sergeant, 'if this is the same fellow in all cases, he's never been known to harm a living person.'

'I was waiting for you to say that,' said the inspector. He dug through the mass of papers in his 'in progress' box and brought out a double-page, typed circular. 'Listen to this.'

He cleared his throat, leaned back in his chair and began to read.

'On the afternoon of June 27, 1971 a group consisting of Anton Berbach, aged forty-seven, insurance inspector, Ingeborg Thomas, aged thirty-four, housewife, and Heinz-Martin Thomas, aged thirty-nine, office employee, all resident in Feucht, were walking in the forest approximately three point five kilometres south-west of that city. At approximately three-forty-seven o'clock, they . . .'

'Where's Feucht?' interrupted the sergeant.

'Five miles south-east of Nürnberg,' said the inspector, 'on the highway to Regensberg. This is a circular from the Nürnberg Police.'

'But that's clear in the south of Germany,' said the sergeant.

'Right,' said the inspector. 'Your ghoul has gone south.'

He rustled the paper and resumed, '. . . they came upon the body of a woman lying near the path in a small clearing. The woman, later identified as Martha Krüger, aged thirty-six, housewife and resident in Feucht, had died as the result of one twenty-two calibre, long-rifle bullet which entered the left temple and remained embedded in the brain.

'In addition, the body showed fourteen knife wounds of varying sizes and depths. Several of the knife wounds displayed tooth marks and the imprint of human lips in blood. The assumption is that the murderer bit and drank the blood of his victim.'

'But that's a vampire, not a ghoul!' exclaimed the sergeant. 'It couldn't be the same man!'

'Just a minute,' said the inspector. 'I'm not finished yet.'

'Lying on top of the corpse of her mother was Lydia Krüger, aged three. The child was crying bitterly and was covered with her mother's blood. She was uninjured. The child's statement, made to the Thomases and Anton Berbach and later to the investigating officer of the Nürnberg Department of Criminal Investigations, was: "Mummy fell over and the man came and hit her with a knife. Then, he tried to eat her up. I was scared." '

'A madman who thinks he's a vampire,' said the sergeant. 'Do they have any leads?'

'Not a thing,' said the inspector. 'But then, ghouls and vampires don't leave any traces. They merely crawl back into their graves or fly away or whatever. Nürnberg thinks that it was the same man who broke into the mortuary in Hamburg. They've asked for photographs of the teeth marks.'

'It's impossible,' said the sergeant. 'How could you have a combination of ghoul-vampire? Vampires suck blood. You can't suck the blood of a corpse.'

'Oh yes you can,' said the inspector. 'At least, if it hasn't been dead too long. Theodore says that it's gummy and sticky at first and then it turns to a yellowish, stinking liquid which might not seem very appetizing to you or me, but which can be drunk. On the other hand, it would . . .'

But at this point the conversation was terminated as the

231

sergeant clapped his hand over his mouth and ran wildly out of the office.

'He's going to need a stronger stomach than that, if this case continues,' said the inspector, shaking his head.

Whether the case continued or not was a moot question. It did not, in any case, continue in Flensburg where no further reports of ghoulish or vampirish activities were received by the police. But the inspector continued his dogged investigation of possible satanist organizations.

In Nürnberg things were more active and, for the first time, the ghoul, vampire, necrophile or simply madman seemed to have struck twice in the same place. On November 3, 1971 forty-year-old George Weichert was riding in a car with his fifteen-year-old daughter, Steffi, when the driver lost control of the vehicle. Leaving the road, the car turned over a half dozen times and ended up in a forest fifty yards from the road. The driver escaped with no more than cuts and bruises, but George Weichert was killed instantly and Steffi died in hospital the next day. She and her father were buried side by side in Nürnberg's south cemetery on November 6th.

Oddly enough in view of later developments, the accident had taken place at the crossroads to Feucht and less than a mile from the point where a vampire had sucked the blood of Martha Krüger before the terrified eyes of her little daughter.

On the morning of November 7, 1971 a young man named Horst Weber came to visit the grave of a relative at the South Cemetery and at approximately nine-fifteen, rounded a high hedge to come upon the most horrifying sight of his life.

Steffi Weichert had been dug up from her grave and removed from her coffin. Completely naked, she sat stiffly on a mound of earth beside the open grave, her forearms resting on her wide-spread knees. Her head was tipped backward and the dull, sightless eyes were wide open and seemed to be staring almost greedily at the petrified young man.

She had been a pretty girl when alive, but the accident had badly damaged the upper part of her face and head so that the eyes stared out of a hideous mass of swollen flesh which had turned blue, black, green, purple and yellow.

Against these more sombre colours, the red trickle of fresh blood which ran from between her lips, over her chin and down between her young breasts, made a bright contrast.

As Weber stood transfixed, a light breeze lifted the fine blonde hair of the dead girl, lending the terrible face a grisly semblance of life.

Horst Weber did not believe in vampires except for those appearing in the movies, but here, before his very eyes and less than ten feet away, was a vampire which had during the night clambered from its grave to feast on some unfortunate victim and had been caught by the rising sun before it could get back.

Not, of course, that the sun had actually risen. It was a typical November day, overcast and cold, and the vicious little wind which whined about the cypresses and shook the hedges, seemed filled with eerie, wailing voices.

As far as he knew, he was completely alone in the cemetery.

Horst Weber followed the rules for dealing with vampires. He turned and ran like hell. Being a man mindful of his responsibilities as a citizen, he did not only run, but ran directly for the nearest police station, some six blocks away.

As chance would have it, he had gone less than two blocks when he nearly collided with a patrolman coming from that same station whose duty it was to maintain law and order in the district.

'There is vamp . . .!' gasped Horst Weber, skidding to a stop. 'That is, there's something wrong in the cemetery.'

He had caught himself in the last instant before telling a police officer that there was a vampire sitting in the cemetery, a remark which he felt certain would have gained him a free interview with the police psychiatrist.

To his horror and astonishment, the police officer seemed to grasp very well what he had intended to say.

'My God!' he gulped. 'It's the vampire! Run to the station and tell them I need help. I'm going after him.'

233

Whereupon the officer drew his service pistol, snapped the slide to put a round in the chamber and ran off in the direction of the cemetery, leaving Weber with the impression that he had somehow wandered onto the set of a B grade movie.

No German would disregard an order from a person in authority and he resumed his dash to the police station where he told what he had seen and what the patrolman had said with considerable trepidation.

Once again, his word was accepted without question and a party immediately roared away in the squad car while the desk sergeant called headquarters to alert Inspector Julius Misner, the investigations officer who had been assigned to the Krüger case and who had left instructions that he was to be notified of anything of a similar nature.

It being Sunday, the inspector was at home and by the time he had been contacted and picked up by his assistant, Detective-Sergeant Hans Bohm, and the sergeant had stopped again to pick up the department's medical expert, Dr Jürgen Platt, it was past ten before the party arrived at the cemetery.

As it turned out, there was no great hurry in any case.

'This happened hours ago,' said the doctor. 'Sometime during the middle of the night. And this isn't a vampire. It's a young girl who's been in some kind of violent accident, motor car, I should think.'

'I can see that,' said the inspector. He was a quiet inconspicuous-appearing man with a very matter-of-fact manner of speaking. 'The person who found her was frightened and reported her as a vampire. You're familiar with the ghoul-vampire cases in northern Germany and you examined the body of Martha Krüger. What I want to know is whether this is the same type of case.'

The doctor nodded and began a careful examination of the corpse.

'The blood on the mouth isn't hers,' he observed. 'He kissed her when his own mouth was full of blood.'

'Whose blood?' said the inspector.

'His presumably,' said the doctor. 'It wasn't hers. There's

a cut here under the left breast and he was sucking and chewing on it, but the blood isn't fresh. She's been dead three or four days.'

'In the Hamburg case,' said the inspector. 'He cut himself and pressed the wound to a cut on the girl's wrist.'

'Same principle here,' said the doctor. 'And, as in the case in Hamburg, he's tried to have sexual intercourse with her. Unsuccessful of course. The body is much too stiff.'

'But you would say then that it resembles the Hamburg case?' interrupted the inspector. 'What about the Krüger murder?'

'Hamburg, yes, definitely,' said the doctor. 'It was almost certainly the same man. It's highly unlikely that there would be two persons suffering from the same fixation running around here in Germany at the same time. It's not at all a common disorder.'

'But not unheard of either?' said the inspector.

'No, not unheard of,' said the doctor, 'but we don't know with certainty what is troubling our friend. Is he merely a necrophile, a person who is enamoured of the dead? Or does he really believe that he is a ghoul or, as the case may be, a vampire?'

'Does it matter?' said the inspector.

'Oh definitely,' said the doctor. 'If he's a necrophile or if he thinks he's a ghoul, then he's going to bother no one but dead people. If he thinks he's a vampire, then you're going to get cases like Martha Krüger. He may only be trying to drink the blood of corpses because he doesn't have access to the blood of living persons.'

'You keep saying "Thinks he's a ghoul",' interjected the sergeant. 'As I understand it, a ghoul is a person who eats the flesh of corpses and this one certainly does just that. It would seem to me that he's about as well qualified to be a real ghoul as you can get.'

'There is no such thing as a ghoul,' said the inspector firmly, putting an end to the conversation.

For the remainder of the day the detection experts from the police laboratory went over not only the area immediately around the grave of Steffi Weichert, but the entire cemetery.

No effort was spared because, unlike the other cases in the north of Germany, there was a possibility here that the ghoul who had dug up and mutilated the corpse of Steffi Weichert was also the vampire who had murdered and sucked the blood of Mrs Martha Krüger.

'I'm not an expert in abnormal psychology,' said the inspector, 'but I have had a good deal of experience with sex criminals and in such cases the offender frequently starts out with relatively harmless acts, he exposes himself to women or he attempts sexual contacts with minors. A proportion of these people never go any further than that, but some enter into a sort of constant progression from bad to worse. They begin, let us say, by exposing themselves to children, go on to actually engaging in sexual play, finally end by raping a child and then, if they're not taken out of circulation, killing one. One step leads to another.'

'But do they go back down the scale?' said the sergeant. 'If your theory is correct, the ghoul began his activities in north Germany where he sucked the blood of corpses and attempted sexual intercourse with them. Eventually, he came down here to us, but he did not carry out any acts against dead bodies. Instead, he began immediately with a murder. Then he went back to desecrating corpses. Is that possible?'

'I don't know,' admitted the inspector. 'We're dealing with a madman here. I don't think anyone can predict his actions or decide what he is capable of.'

Madman or ghoul he might be, but he was either a very sly or a very lucky madman. Not a single clue as to his identity had ever been found at the scenes of his supposed crimes and it was to be no different in Nürnberg.

'He didn't leave a trace,' said the technician in charge of the group. 'At least, he didn't leave a trace that can be connected with the desecration of the corpse. There are foot prints here in the cemetery, hundreds of them, and one set may be those of the ghoul, but there's no way to tell which set.

'We've recovered enough of his blood from the corpse to

236

identify the blood group, but you can't identify a man by his blood group. You can only say who it wasn't.

'He apparently wore gloves when he was digging up the body. He used one of the cemetery's own spades, but there are no prints on it.

'The only thing we have is photographs of the bite marks on the corpse. However, they're not very clear and, although they seem about the same size and shape as those on Mrs Krüger's body and the ones sent down from Hamburg, it's not an identification that would stand up in court.

'In any case, it doesn't help us because the identity of the ghoul or vampire or whatever he is isn't known in those cases either.'

'You've overlooked one thing,' said the inspector.

The technician looked startled.

'The ghoul reads the newspapers,' said the inspector.

The technician looked even more startled.

'He didn't disturb any other grave,' said the inspector. 'He went directly to that one and only that one. He knew she had just been buried.'

The inspector's logic was impeccable, but it did not help in solving the case for, although the death notices were read every day and no funeral of a young girl took place without a plainclothes officer unobtrusively present, no suspect was arrested. The persons present at the funerals were always friends or relatives of the deceased.

If attending funerals of young girls was an undemanding, if mournful, duty for the detectives of the Criminal Investigations Department, the watch on the cemeteries was not. It was now winter and the winters in southern Germany are cold, overcast, dismal and depressing even for persons not lying hidden behind tombstones in a cemetery in the middle of the night.

Understandably, these night watches in the cemeteries were done almost exclusively by the most junior men on the force and, although there must have been many times when other professions appeared infinitely more attractive, it is a tribute to the morale of the Nürnberg police that not a single rookie turned in his badge or reported himself sick.

The job was, however, without risk. Although the watch was maintained throughout the winter, the ghoul made no further appearances.

'Probably gone back to north Germany,' remarked the inspector. 'Or maybe out of the country altogether. He seems to move around a good bit. I think we can suspend the cemetery watch.'

'It's not popular with the men,' said the sergeant in what may well have been the understatement of all time.

The watch at the cemeteries and at funerals of young women was consequently dropped, but the inspector was mistaken about the ghoul's departure. He was still right there in Nürnberg and he was still active.

He had merely become somewhat more careful about hiding the traces of his activity. But not careful enough.

'You know, Ellie,' said George Warmuth to his wife one morning early in May of 1972, 'I don't know how it's possible, but I have the feeling that somebody's been fooling around with the bodies.'

'My heavens!' exclaimed Ellie Warmuth. 'Who'd want to do a thing like that?'

George Warmuth was the Mortuary Attendant at Nürnberg's West Cemetery, but he had never heard anything about a ghoul nor about the desecration of the corpse of Steffi Weichert.

Very few people not attached to the police had, and this was because Inspector Misner had made every effort to keep the matter secret. The German police are as a rule reluctant to divulge anything concerning a case until at least some progress has been made toward solving it. The advantage of this is that a suspect under questioning cannot say that he read an account of the matter in the newspapers to explain how he came into information concerning the case.

Warmuth did not even know that his mortuary had been under surveillance for the past five months, as had all mortuaries in the city, and he would have been very surprised indeed to learn that he and all his fellow mortuary attendants had actually been considered prime suspects, by Sergeant Bohm at least.

238

As the sergeant had put it, 'They're used to them as customers. It would be only one more step to become friends.'

Whether the ghoul could be considered a friend of his victims was dubious, but in any case the suspicion proved without foundation, although the inspector had considered it possible because of the ease and familiarity with which the ghoul seemed to move about cemeteries, mortuaries and other places with which the ordinary person would scarcely be familiar.

This was exactly the same conclusion reached by George Warmuth.

'I think,' he told his wife, Ellie, 'that it has to be one of the employees. Grave-digger probably. Nobody likes the job and we always have a big turn-over.'

'But what could they possibly want of the dead people?' said Mrs Warmuth. 'I haven't noticed anything.'

Mrs Warmuth was as familiar with the corpse hall and the other rooms of the mortuary as her husband as she was responsible for the cleaning. She did not as a rule have any contact with the bodies themselves.

'Well, it's hard to say,' said Warmuth. 'Any jewellery they're going to wear isn't put on until just before the funeral. Could be he's after gold teeth or it might be some kind of a pervert that's fooling around with the women's sex organs. I'm going to start waiting for him in the office tonight and see if I can't catch him red-handed.'

Red-handed was an excellent description of the condition of a ghoul taken in the act, but George Warmuth did not know that there was a ghoul about in Nürnberg.

Nor would it probably have bothered him much. A husky six-footer who had fought in some of the hardest battles of the Second World War, he often said that there was nothing left that could surprise him and that he doubted there was anything that could kill him after what he had lived through.

He was to discover very shortly that he was wrong on both counts. That evening after dinner he renounced his favourite television programme and slipped quietly over to the office of the mortuary where he sat waiting patiently and quietly in the dark. It was May 5, 1972 and a pleasant early spring night outside.

The ghoul was punctual. At shortly before ten o'clock there came the faint sound of the door leading to the room where the bodies were displayed before the funeral opening and closing.

Warmuth got silently to his feet. He had recognized the sound instantly and he knew in exactly which direction the intruder would be heading: the vaulted corpse hall in the basement.

It was his plan to descend to the hall before the stranger and wait for him in one of the alcoves along the wall and he moved swiftly to the stairway which was closer to him than it was to the corpse display room.

Arriving at the foot of the stairs, he was astonished to see that the lights were on, and for a moment he thought that the other had in some mysterious fashion managed to arrive before him.

Then he remembered that his wife had been down there earlier that afternoon for cleaning materials which were kept in a closet at the far end. Any time that Mrs Warmuth came down for cleaning materials, the lights were left burning.

This was because the light switch was not on the stairs, but half way down the hall. Although she had been the wife of a mortuary attendant for a good many years now, Ellie Warmuth still did not like to turn out that light and walk half the length of the corpse hall in the dark to the stairs.

Warmuth did not mind and he quickly switched off the light and slipped into the nearest alcove. If it were burning, the corpse robber or whatever he was might be frightened away before Warmuth could lay his great hands on him.

Almost immediately there was the sound of footsteps on the stairs and along the hall as the stranger advanced confidently to the light switch and turned it on. He obviously knew his way around the mortuary, but when Warmuth peered around the corner of the alcove, he saw, to his astonishment, that the man was not an employee nor ever had been in the time that he had been there.

He would have been even more astonished had he known

that he was looking at the ghoul which had kept Nürnberg's police lying out in the freezing cemeteries throughout the winter.

The truth was, the man did not look like a ghoul. He was short, almost slightly built, with dark wavy hair and a blunt nose, and he wore steel-rimmed glasses of the type paid for by the national health insurance.

Despite this sorry appearance, he was a very real ghoul and he promptly proved it by moving matter-of-factly to the nearest coffin and pushing back the lid. Inside the coffin, Warmuth knew, was the body of a thirty-seven-year-old woman who had only arrived at the mortuary the day before.

Warmuth was expecting that the man would now probe the woman's mouth for gold teeth or draw up the paper shroud to examine the genitals, but instead he leaned over, placed his hands on the woman's cheeks and kissed the corpse square on the mouth!

The action was so unexpected and startling that Warmuth gave an involuntary jump and started out of the alcove. As he did, the cuff of his trouser leg caught on one of the trestles standing there and dragged it along the cement floor with a loud scraping sound.

'Damn!' exclaimed Warmuth, expecting to see the little man race off in the direction of the stairs.

Amazingly, he did no such thing but remained where he was with his lips pressed to the mouth of the corpse.

Recovering himself, Warmuth ran forward and seized the little man by his shoulder.

'Here!' he shouted. 'What do you think you're doing?'

The man turned from the coffin, drew a black automatic pistol from his inside jacket pocket and shot George Warmuth in the stomach.

As the big man fell to the floor, the ghoul calmly holstered his weapon and ran off up the stairs.

'All through the war without a scratch,' grunted the severely wounded mortuary attendant. 'I'll be damned if I'll be killed by a midget.'

He then crawled up the stairs to the office, knocked the telephone off the desk, dialled the number of the emergency

241

ambulance and said, 'Man with a bad gunshot wound in the stomach. West Cemetery Mortuary. Make it fast, will you?' Following which, he lost consciousness.

The ambulance made it fast and this was fortunate for the 7.65 mm slug had pierced his large intestine, his small intestine and his bladder and he was well on the way to bleeding to death.

He did not die and, forty-eight hours later, he was already feeling well enough to describe his strange visitor to Inspector Misner. The inspector was not surprised because he had no preconceptions of what a ghoul should look like and it could as well be a little man with glasses as anyone else.

Forty-eight hours after the shooting was, of course, May 6th and a Saturday. The inspector's interview with George Warmuth had taken place at the hospital immediately after lunch and, although he had not been surprised then, he was soon going to be.

He had barely regained his office where the police artist was waiting to attempt a composite drawing from Warmuth's description as taken down on the inspector's tape recorder, when there was a call from the village of Lindelburg, twelve miles to the east of Nürnberg. A government game warden named Werner Beranek was on the telephone.

Beranek was almost incoherent with excitement.

'Just kids!' he yammered. 'They're just kids and both dead! He must have shot them. I should have cut down on him with the shotgun, but I didn't know. He's riding a red motorbike, the man you want. A red motorbike!'

'Calm yourself,' said the inspector. The switchboard had transferred the call directly to him upon learning that it was a homicide report. 'Who do you think shot who?'

Beranek pulled himself together with an effort. He had just run nearly two miles to reach the telephone and he was still badly out of breath.

'It's a young couple,' he said. 'They're in a grey Mercedes parked about a hundred yards from the turn-off to Wolkersdorf. I was coming down the Lindelburg road about half an hour ago and I saw the car. The doors were open and there was a little man with glasses and a leather hat fussing

242

around it and doing something. As soon as he saw me, he ran and got onto a red motorbike and drove off down the Wolkersdorf road as fast as the machine would go.

'I thought then that there was something funny so I ran up to the car and there was a couple in it, the boy in the front seat and the girl in the back seat. They were both covered with car rugs and when I pulled them back, I saw they were both covered with blood and dead. I immediately fired three shots into the air as an alarm, but nobody heard me so I had to run into Lindelburg to reach a telephone.'

'Stay where you are,' said the inspector. 'We're on our way.'

He dropped the telephone into the cradle and turned to the sergeant. 'Get every car in the area out to Lindelburg. We'll be looking for a little man on a red motorbike and I think that we can use Warmuth's description. Unless I'm greatly mistaken, our ghoul has come out in the open.'

The inspector's suspicions were confirmed that same evening when Dr Platt recovered the bullets from the corpses of twenty-four-year-old Marcus Adler and eighteen-year-old Ruth Lissy. They matched exactly the bullet taken from the body of George Warmuth.

Adler, who owned a transport business in Bruchsal, fifty miles to the north-west of Nürnberg, had come down to visit Miss Lissy, to whom he was engaged. According to the reconstruction of the crime, they had driven that afternoon to the solitary country road and had there engaged in sexual intercourse in the car. They had then decided to take a nap and Adler had lain down in the front seat while Miss Lissy had lain in the back.

While they were asleep, the ghoul had crept up and had shot both of them through the head, killing them instantly. He had then shot the girl a second time under the left breast, presumably to provide a flow of blood for drinking.

That he had drunk of the fresh blood there was no doubt. His lip marks were on Adler's head wound and on the wound beneath the left breast of the girl.

He had only begun with an examination of the girl's sex organs when he was surprised by Beranek for, although the body was found with the underpants removed and the thighs wide-spread, it was possible to show that she had not been entered by any person other than her fiancé. She had also been wearing her underwear at the time that she was killed for it was soaked with urine from her relaxing bladder.

'A terribly dangerous man,' said the inspector. 'He must have merely been riding past, saw the car and, after parking the bike, circled back on foot. He couldn't have known that they were coming there. It was just a chance opportunity and if he gets another, he'll take that too.'

The policy of secrecy had now been totally abandoned, partially because the ghoul was no longer merely a threat to the dead, but to the living as well, and partially because it had become impossible to maintain.

One of the most massive police efforts in the history of the Nürnberg police had gone into operation with patrolcars and road blocks halting and taking into custody every person found riding a red motorbike, drawings of the ghoul made from the descriptions posted in every public place and appeals to the general public for assistance being broadcast over the radio and television stations at frequent intervals.

'If he's here, I think we'll flush him out,' said the inspector. 'Warmuth says that the drawings are a good likeness and so does Beranek. The only thing I'm afraid of is that he's cleared out altogether.'

Four days had passed since the distribution of the posters and the publicity in the newspapers and radio stations and there had been no reports from the public. However, unknown to the inspector or anyone else, a heavy-set, middle-aged transport company worker named Helmut Kostan had thought of reporting his suspicions a half dozen times during that period.

The reason that he had not was the very nature of the crimes which seemed to him so awful that he simply could not believe one of his fellow workers capable of them. He had read the newspaper accounts carefully and the descriptions corresponded on every count. Beranek had said that the murderer of Marcus Adler and Ruth Lissy wore a leather hat and rode a red motorbike.

244

Kuno Hofmann, the little man with dark, wavy hair, with a blunt nose, with steel-rimmed health insurance glasses, who worked beside him loading trucks, sometimes wore a leather hat and he rode a red motorbike to work.

George Warmuth had said that the ghoul in the mortuary was wearing a grey and brown striped jacket, a black or dark-blue V-neck sweater under it, brown, creaseless trousers and black shoes with bright, metal buckles.

Helmut Kostan had seen Kuno Hofmann wearing just such a costume less than a month earlier.

And finally, what seemed like proof positive, the ghoul had not been startled when Warmuth had accidentally made a noise nor had he said so much as a single word himself.

Kuno Hofmann was a deaf-mute.

And yet, Kostan hesitated. He was a simple man and a slow thinker, but he was certain of one thing, he did not want to get anyone in trouble with false accusations. Kuno Hofmann might be a deaf-mute, but he was a good worker and well-liked at the Demerag Transport Company, not least of all because of his habit of bringing pornographic films for showing during the lunch hour. No one had ever had an argument with him because he was the smallest man employed by the firm and, being a deaf-mute, he could not have had an argument in any case.

However, on the morning of May 10th an event took place which finally drove Kostan to action. Arriving at work, he saw Hofmann standing not in his overalls at the loading ramp, but in a neat, grey suit in the office.

'What's with Kuno?' asked Kostan of the foreman.

'He's quitting,' said the foreman. 'Guess he wants to go to Hamburg. He's got a piece of paper with that written on it.'

Helmut Kostan was finally convinced. Two minutes later, he was at the pay telephone in the café around the corner and talking to Sergeant Bohm at police headquarters.

'Maybe it ain't the fellow you're looking for,' he said apologetically, 'but he sure looks like him. You'd maybe better hurry. He's fixing to leave as soon as he gets his money.'

245

The sergeant did not even stop to replace the telephone in its cradle, but simply dropped it to the desk and ran out of the office. In less than two minutes, the ready car howled out of the station garage, and the sergeant and the three men on duty in the charge room piled into it. With flashing blue lights and screaming siren, the car tore through the early morning traffic and skidded into the courtyard of the Demerag Transport Company just as a little man wearing glasses stepped out of the office with his last pay envelope in his hand.

Kuno Hofmann was neither clever nor brave. He was exactly what he looked, a little, shy, mentally retarded man. He saw the police car and the detectives piling out of it with guns in their hands and he ran.

He did not run very far of course. The detectives were younger, stronger and much faster. After a very short chase, they returned, the limp ghoul dangling between two of them.

Patrolcars called in by the dispatcher at headquarters now began to arrive and Hofmann was taken in one of them to the offices of the Criminal Investigations Department while the sergeant and his party proceeded to his home address as listed in the files of the company.

Shortly after their arrival another party bearing a search warrant arrived from headquarters and the little house where Hofmann lived with an older brother and sister was searched thoroughly.

In Kuno Hofmann's room they found a Czech VZOR 7.65 mm automatic pistol which ballistics would later show to be the gun which had fired the bullets killing Marcus Adler and Ruth Lissy and wounding George Warmuth, and the now cleanly polished skull of the corpse which Hofmann had beheaded in Flensburg.

They also found an explanation of Hofmann's actions in the form of a collection of literature on witchcraft, vampirism and satanism. Sensational, paperback accounts intended for popular reading, Hofmann had apparently taken them quite literally.

At police headquarters, the forty-one-year-old Hofmann

offered very little resistance to questioning and admitted to most of the crimes with which he was charged, adding a number of which the police had known nothing. He appeared highly confused and was apparently unable to distinguish clearly between crimes actually committed and those merely thought about.

The son of a professional criminal with nineteen convictions, he and his brother had both been so savagely beaten by their father that they had become deaf-mutes and, on one occasion, both of Kuno's arms had been broken.

The beatings had also affected his mind so that his intelligence level was a low seventy, barely above that of a moron and he had had such severe sexual problems that his sister had, at one time, suggested that he buy one of the rubber dolls sold in German sex shops.

Nor was he a stranger to the police, having served a total of nine years in prison for a number of convictions on charges of theft.

Hofmann was, however, quite capable of making an adequate living and he did not lack company as he lived most of the time with his brother and sister and was always popular with the men with whom he worked.

Hofmann's problem was sex and he was not satisfied with his visits to the houses of prostitution. What he wanted was some more permanent relationship – a family, love.

The sole chance that he had had to marry a deaf-mute girl with whom he had fallen deeply in love was destroyed when the girl's parents learned of his jail record and it was not long after that when he came upon the first of the popular witchcraft books.

Kuno Hofmann had drunk the thick, gummy blood of corpses and had attempted to join his sex organs to their cold, clammy ones because he believed that this would make him big, strong and handsome, and big, strong, handsome men could marry and have loving wives and families.

Because it was his only hope, he wanted to believe this so badly that even his arrest did not shake his belief and he spent many hours in his cell writing earnest letters of appeal

247

to the authorities that they should furnish him with a few litres of fresh, warm blood, preferably from a virgin.

He had decided that corpse blood was ineffective because the people were dead and had then switched to living victims with the Adler-Lissy murders. Since that had not worked either, he now thought that it was because Ruth Lissy had not been a virgin.

Kuno Hofmann was never brought to trial as the medical opinion was unanimous that he was not responsible for his actions. He was sent to an institution for the criminally insane where he is expected to spend the remainder of his days.

And now, of course, there really are no vampires or ghouls in Germany because the only one there was is safely tucked away in an institution. There is just one small, slightly sinister point still unexplained.

Hofmann admitted to almost everything, but not to the murder of Martha Krüger. Nor is he known ever to have had access to the twenty-two calibre weapon with which she was killed. As a matter of fact, there is considerable reason to believe that Hofmann was with witnesses at the time of the murder.

If so, then who was it who killed the young mother and drank her blood before the very eyes of her little daughter?

It couldn't have been a vampire. There are no vampires.

MADLY
MURDEROUS

CONTENTS

Introduction 251
1 A Linguistic Misunderstanding? 257
2 Love Thy Neighbour 271
3 No Generation Gap in Germany 285
4 You'll Enjoy Meeting My Sister 301
5 Why Rape Strangers When You Have a Sister? 315
6 No Record, But a Good Try 331
7 The Devil in Mr Jones 346
8 Jailed Ten Years for Exceeding the Speed Limit! 360
9 Napoleon Came From Corsica and it Is Easy to See Why He Left 375
10 Reliable Domestic Help Is Becoming Impossible to Find 390
11 A Forty-pound Victim Eight Feet Long 406
12 Someone Could Be Waiting When You Come Home Tonight 421
13 The Butcher Shop Murders Were the Wurst 436
14 Nothing Half Baked About the Girls of Dolenja Vas 448
15 Yo-Ho-Ho and a Bottle of Schnaps 461
16 Homicides Performed, Quick Service, Reasonable Rates 476
17 Who Can I Get to Rape My Son? 491
18 Cold Buffet 503

INTRODUCTION

It may be that even those persons into whose hands the previous books in this series have fallen will be unaware of the commendable efforts of editors and agents to deter me from writing introductions. Unlike editors and agents, readers are not professionally required to read introductions and therefore, sensibly, do not as a general rule.

There are advantages to this state of affairs. As the introduction will be read only by the agent, the editor and very close relatives of the writer, it is possible to write almost anything, thus providing the writer with an outlet for his or her personal prejudices and, at the same time, sparing the reader their inclusion in the less tedious parts of the book.

Naturally, some limits must be observed. A reader may well mistake the introduction for the first chapter, and it will not do for him or her to be confronted with the opinion that he or she is probably as mad as the most psychotic of March hares.

The fact that this opinion can be statistically supported does not help matters in the least. Although the proportion of persons medically and legally insane within Western society is sufficiently large that some are certain to be included in the readership, the more choleric may take offence at being so distinguished and proceed to actions such as may be expected from disturbed spirits. The writer who wishes to avoid disembowelment or similar unpleasantness will, therefore, exercise restraint in composing the introduction.

Not so the body of the work. Here, defendants may be freely described as homicidal maniacs, psychopaths, mental incompetents, idiots, cretins, morons, feeble-minded, lunatics or anything else that will relieve them of the responsibility for their acts. Indeed, this is how they described themselves and how defence attorneys and experts describe them. Insanity is the most favoured excuse of the defendant whose guilt is proven and who does not want to be inconvenienced because of his act.

According to modern Western theories of crime there is no such thing as malice, every member of the human race is essentially good, and criminals do not exist. There are only misguided victims of the system who, with a little psychiatric counselling, can be converted into useful members of society.

Nearly all criminals are in wholehearted agreement with these theories, although they do little to support them. Despite a constant bombardment of statistics by the media to prove that psychology is invariably successful in the rehabilitation of violent offenders, I have been writing true crime stories for barely fifteen years and one valued collaborator has provided me with his third murder case, having been convicted, cured and released twice previously. I confidently await the fourth.

Others, less diligent or more agile in avoiding detection, can boast of two successive murders to their accounts, and the number of repeated lesser offences is legion.

Loathe as I am to criticize the findings of such an unimpeachable institution as the media, I humbly submit that there are quite a few persons who die painful deaths at the hands of these born-again useful members of society.

This does not mean that I would question the principle of non-responsibility by reason of insanity. A great many murders and other crimes are committed by persons who are, beyond all doubt, mentally incompetent. What is more dubious is the theory, more ideological than medical, that such persons can be cured to the point where it is safe for them to mingle with their potential victims.

Granted that some undoubtedly are, but, if even one cure in ten turns out to be imperfect, the risk to society in general and, particularly, children and others incapable of self-defence is, to my mind, unacceptable.

Unfortunately but predictably, the persons effecting the release of supposedly cured, violent criminals are required to accept no more responsibility for their acts than are the criminals.

There is, however, a difference. When a judge, social worker, penologist or psychologist effects the release of a convicted murderer who then proceeds to another murder, he or she does not plead not guilty to having made possible this second crime by reason of insanity, but merely observes that to err is human.

Perfectly true and, for this reason it might, perhaps, be advisable, in situations where error can result in the painful death of others, to be a trifle less arrogantly confident in making decisions.

It is hardly likely that the suggestion will be accepted. The release of criminals into society is normally carried out anonymously, or under such conditions as to make fixing of responsibility difficult or impossible.

Ergo, another suggestion. Might it not be well to arrange that no one has the authority to release a convicted felon?

Even less popular than the first! Modern trends are in precisely the opposite direction. Not only is it possible for persons who need take no responsibility for the act to effect the release of criminals, but in many countries sentencing is so light that the criminal scarcely requires such services. He has already served his sentence and departed before the ideologues have had time to arrange for his release.

Ideally, and ideologically, there should be no sentencing at all. If the accused is not a criminal, but merely a disturbed person, how can he or she be sent to jail? It is far better that he or she be sent to an institution for psychiatric observation and treatment.

This is, astoundingly, often successful. Psychiatrists do not maintain their reputations and clinics do not stay in business by reporting large numbers of failures.

Such treatment is, however, expensive and, as even the resources of the taxpayer have limits, the length of stay is usually brief. The patient is then released as cured of his or her antisocial tendencies and, should another offence occur, assured of success with an insanity plea on the basis of an official record of mental illness.

It helps, of course, if each succeeding offence is slightly more atrocious than the last, although in many cases such heights of atrocity have been reached that it is difficult to extend them, thus leading persons planning an insanity defence to make their crimes more appalling than they might personally have wished. It is popular among defence attorneys in some countries to plead that their mandate must be insane as the crime perpetrated was so dreadful that no sane person could have committed it.

Oddly enough, it appears to occur to no one that such dreadfully insane persons should not be lightly returned to the company of their potential victims because some one believes this ideologically desirable.

From the point of view of the crime writer, the situation is utopian. The choice of crimes, each more frightful than the last, is enormous and unending. There is never any shortage of material and, as even murder is a media event, the murderers compete for publicity by devising ever more ingenious and monstrous means of dispatching their victims.

But, although this has been challenged, crime writers are also human, and it is trying to spend the working hours writing about dangerous psychopaths who have been cured and have celebrated their recovery by torturing to death a child, after having read in the morning newspapers that the government is planning the release of vast numbers of rehabilitated prison inmates. Granted, the true reason may be simply lack of jail space, but this does not help the tortured child.

A crime writer thus finds himself in the position of one who sees numbers of persons being eaten by lions and can do nothing about it, while prominent, self-appointed authorities sit on the sidelines and shout, 'Lions are not dangerous!'

This can lead to frustration and a feeling of unreality. Media, courts, sociologists, psychologists, penologists and politicians all know that dangerous persons are being released into society and that they not infrequently commit new crimes. They do nothing about it and steadfastly maintain the opposite.

Actually, the very theory of law and law enforcement

appears to have undergone a change without the knowledge or consent of the members of society most concerned, namely the victims.

The whole concept of law, and the only one which makes any sense, is the protection of property and the weaker members of society. Without law, the protection of women (with apologies to the Women's Equality Movement) and children falls to the male head of the family in which they are included. If the male is weak, unwilling or dead, the protection is lacking and, even if he is strong and able, he cannot spend all of his time accompanying his wife to the market and his children to school. Within a community, the community itself must assume the task of providing security, or life in such a community is not possible.

This is the situation which is now developing on an international scale. None of the Western European democracies are safe places to live. There are substantial numbers of disturbed persons and, to use an unpopular term, criminals at large. Old persons, children and women are their most favoured victims, and their motives run from simple theft through forced sex to the satisfaction of sadistic perversion.

The number of such dangerous individuals increases steadily. Sentences are light and rarely served in full, and the criminal is so sympathetically treated in the press that there is scarcely any opprobrium attached to the profession. A systematic effort is made to depict criminals as victims of an unjust society, and it is continually repeated that the death penalty and heavy sentences are no deterrent to crime.

True, they may be no deterrent to crime, although this is not quite so indisputable as it is made to seem, but they are a powerful deterrent to the individual criminal, and the essential point which has been lost from sight is that society must offer security to its members whatever the cost. Concern for the rights of the accused is fine and just and humanitarian, but this concern must be superseded by the right of persons not to be murdered, tortured or raped. The accused may plead not guilty by reason of insanity but, if convicted of the act, must be put away permanently where they can do no further harm. Success in an insanity plea should be equivalent to life imprisonment.

Admittedly, this is no more than a stop-gap measure. If the proportion of mentally disturbed persons within society continues to grow at its present rate, the number of psychopaths will exceed the number of relatively sane . . .

What is to be done about this?

Nothing.

The number of persons with criminal tendencies is already so high that a return to more severe forms of law enforcement is probably impossible politically. Although polls in nearly every Western country show a substantial majority in favour of the death penalty, moves to reinstate it are voted down with monotonous regularity by the representatives of that same majority.

As in the traditional advice to rape victims (now offered seriously by many police departments), relax and enjoy it. Living in a society of the insane can be far from dull if reasonable precautions are taken . . .

In this book, you will find a number of such irrational persons and a few who were quite sane but, modern theory to the contrary, simply malicious. Compare them. I think you will find that the more insane they are, the more entertaining.

1

A LINGUISTIC
MISUNDERSTANDING?

One of the more vexing aspects of life is the difficulty in determining just how insane everybody else is. If they are only a little insane, they can be entertaining. If a trifle more so, they can be dangerous. For the denizens of our chrome, neon and plastic world, the trifle can be a matter of survival.

Obviously, the greater the number of persons with whom contact is made, the greater the number of those a trifle beyond the limit, and in the major cities it is probable that the average resident encounters someone dangerous nearly every day in the week.

This would be disturbing if it were obvious but, fortunately or unfortunately, these psychopaths often look no crazier than the nominally sane who, striving to cope with the pressures of big city life, are often not completely in possession of their faculties. There are days in a city like Paris when everyone looks as mad as a March hare in a marijuana patch.

But not, of course, in June. June is late spring or early summer, and there are few places in the world that are more romantic than Paris in the spring.

At least in theory. It is true that there have been some unfortunate experiments with architecture; that air, water and soil are hideously polluted; that the concentration of motor vehicles is such that it is impossible either to drive or to park; and that the fortunate are mugged by gangs of relatively small children while those less so are raped, robbed and murdered by the preceding generation, but still, it is Paris and there is nothing like it. Along the Champs Elysées the trees are in leaf. Flowers are blooming. The forests of the

257

Bois de Boulogne, filled with picnickers by day and whores by night, are green and, for those who have the time and money to afford it, there is a very pleasant restaurant, accessible only by boat, on the island in the Lac Inférieur which is not really inferior, but merely called that to distinguish it from the Lac Supérieur directly to the south of it.

At approximately seven-thirty in the evening of Saturday, 13 June 1981, a group of diners, seated on the terrace of this restaurant which commands a view of the lake shore some fifty yards away and the path running along it, were treated to a spectacle unusual even for Paris.

A slight Oriental, so small as to merit the appellation of dwarf, was struggling along the Chemin de Ceinture du Lac Inférieur bent nearly double beneath the weight of two large, cheap suitcases. Although the suitcases were equipped with the little wheeled frames used by tourists for dragging their luggage through Europe's porterless railway stations, the gravelled path rendered them largely useless.

The diners watched with the interest but detachment of the Parisian. The general opinion was that this was an Oriental tourist who had gone astray and was wandering about in the Bois de Boulogne looking for the railway station or, perhaps, the Tour Eiffel.

It was thought unusual. Not that there was anything remarkable about an Oriental or a dwarf or even a tourist lost in the Bois de Boulogne, but the combination of all three was not something seen every day and, besides, this was an uncommonly strange-looking tourist. As Orientals went, he had a rather large, fleshy nose, his face was long and hollow-cheeked and his hair was even longer and hung in dank, straight, scanty strands over his high, bulging forehead and around his prominent ears. Far from presenting the approved expression of the inscrutable Oriental, he appeared to be nearly out of his mind with nervousness and excitement and his eyes rolled wildly amidst the streams of sweat pouring down his face.

Beneath the bemused gaze of the diners, the strange figure passed down the path and slowly vanished from sight. The diners returned to their entrées.

By eight-thirty they had not yet arrived at dessert when, further to the north along the Chemin de Ceinture du Lac Inférieur and out of sight of the restaurant, strollers who had either already eaten or who could not afford to do so, came upon the same small Oriental, still struggling along with his suitcases. At the sight of them, he apparently came to the conclusion that the effort was not worth it and, abandoning his property, took to his heels and disappeared into the bushes and the darkness.

The most logical explanation for such behaviour was that the little man was a thief and that the suitcases were filled with booty, possibly even cash. The strollers, therefore, hurried forward to investigate.

At close range, however, they saw that, if this was a thief's booty, he had apparently robbed a butcher shop for thin trails of something red and sticky were running out of the suitcases on to the gravel of the path, and it did not take much imagination to identify this as relatively fresh blood.

Large city dwellers appreciate strong sensations so quite a number of the passers-by remained until the police had arrived in the hope that the suitcases would be opened and provide some spectacle of horror.

They were disappointed. The police did, indeed, open one suitcase and peer inside, but they did not open it enough for anyone else to see anything, and other police officers quickly arrived and sent the sightseers on about their business after having taken their names and addresses.

The suitcases were not, however, removed immediately, as the glimpse taken of the interior had determined that this was a matter for the Sureté, the Paris Criminal Investigations Department. What the officer peeping into the suitcase had seen was a human head; a head with no body and from which nose and lips had been cut away, but definitely a head. As the investigations would show, most of the rest of the body was in the suitcases as well.

But not all. Even the hardened investigators from the Sureté would have been startled had they known where those missing parts now were.

At the moment, they were more interested in knowing

259

where the little Oriental was. Large numbers of neatly dressed young men flooded the Bois de Boulogne, displayed their identification as agents of the Sureté and asked a great many questions. Vivid descriptions of the wanted man's appearance were received, and they corresponded much more closely with each other than is normally the case. Even in Paris, the suspect's appearance had been sufficiently odd to attract attention.

In a smaller community, such numerous and accurate descriptions might have resulted in a speedy arrest, but within the nine million inhabitants of the Paris agglomeration, even an Oriental dwarf was a single straw in a very large stack. Consequently, the police artist sat about preparing sketches based on witness descriptions which could be distributed to all police units, and a check of the consulates of the Oriental nations was undertaken.

At the same time, efforts were made to trace the suitcases, which were new, and these proved successful. They had been bought only the day before in a department store in the 16th arrondissement of Passy which runs along the edge of the Bois de Boulogne.

Clerks in department stores rarely remember their customers very clearly: there are too many of them. The clerk in this department store remembered the man who had bought the suitcases very well. He had been an Oriental, almost cadaverous looking, and he had been less than five feet tall.

This was of no help to the police. They already knew what the man looked like, and the fact that he had bought the cases in Passy could mean that he lived there or that he had wanted to use them in the Bois de Boulogne. It was still not known where the murder had taken place.

It was known that it was a murder. A single .22 calibre bullet had been recovered from the base of the skull. It had been fired into the nape of the neck at point-blank range and had resulted in instantaneous death.

This and a number of other strange and inexplicable results had been obtained by the autopsy, which had taken place immediately following the transfer of the two suitcases to the police morgue.

There opened, they had been found to contain the best part of a young, Caucasian female body cut up and wrapped in plastic rubbish sacks. Laid out on the marble slap of the autopsy table and reassembled like a jigsaw puzzle, it developed that there were a number of pieces missing. The nose was gone. The lips were gone. The breasts were missing, and so was the flesh of both thighs and both buttocks. They had been carefully cut away with something very sharp, probably a razor, and not by a person possessing any professional skill in anatomy, but merely someone who had taken his or her time and gone about the matter methodically and with common sense.

The sex of the murderer was tentatively established as male, for the sex organs of the corpse were recovered intact and contained traces of semen. Whether it had been deposited before or after death, there was no indication of forcible rape and no lesions of the inner walls of the vagina or the labia minor.

On the basis of this evidence, it seemed not improbable that the motive of the crime had been sex, but, as the expert in forensic medicine who had carried out the autopsy remarked, what was not there was more significant than what was. The nose and lips might be an attempt to avoid identification, although the fingerprints had been left intact. Breasts, thighs and buttocks were, however, all fleshy, tender parts which, in an animal, would have provided fine roasts and escalopes. In some ways, it looked as if the girl had been butchered for meat.

No one scoffed at this suggestion. It would not represent the first case of cannibalism in Paris.

The girl was soon identified. A careful check had been made of the reports of missing persons, not only those already received, but any new ones coming in, and on 15 June a group of students from the Université Censier turned in a description of a missing person which coincided with that which the police were seeking.

The victim was an unlikely person to have ended up mainly in two suitcases in the Bois de Boulogne as she was the serious, respectable daughter of a wealthy, retired industrialist in Holland. Aged twenty-five at the time of her death, Renée Hartewelt had completed her studies at the University of Leyden and had come to Paris four months earlier for postgraduate work in French literature and civilization with which she was fascinated. She spoke fluent French, equally fluent German and, of course, Dutch. A gentle, attractive girl with a pleasant personality, she had quickly made friends among the others students, and when she failed to appear for several days they reported her missing.

Although Renée had been well-to-do for a student and could easily have rented an apartment, she had not done so, but had followed the usual student practice of exchanging babysitting services for a maid's room, which was located at number 59 rue Bonaparte in the 6th arrondissement of Luxembourg on the Left Bank in an area infested with students.

In Paris, apartment owners seldom know much about what is going on in the maid's room, almost invariably tucked in under the eaves of the attic and the police hurried to the address in the hope that this might be the scene of the murder.

It was not. The room was in perfect order, and it was obvious that when Renée had gone out to meet her death, she had been expecting to return shortly. No clue whatsoever to the identity of her murderer was found.

This was disappointing. The investigators from the Sureté had hoped to find at least correspondence from or indications of the presence of some male. Female students arriving in Paris often made friends with persons about whom they knew very little. It was inevitable that a certain percentage of these should be mad and, as there was little doubt but that Renée's murderer was, at the least, seriously disturbed, it was possible that her death was the result of such a chance, casual acquaintanceship.

Apparently not, however, Not only was there nothing to indicate a more intimate-type friendship in the room, but her friends at the university reported that she had been little interested in such matters. Unlike many foreign students in France, Renée had really been interested in French culture.

Renée's belongings and, eventually, what remained of her body were sent to her parents and the investigation continued.

The investigation was now concentrating on the manner in which the Oriental dwarf had arrived at the Bois de Boulogne with his macabre baggage, and where he had been during the approximate hour which passed between him being seen by the diners at the restaurant on the island and when he had encountered the strollers and fled. It was assumed that he had wanted to dispose of the suitcases in the lake, and there was no explanation of why he had spent over an hour there and had not done so.

The matter was the more mysterious in that no sightings of the dwarf were reported during this hour. Had he murdered the girl in the forest, cut her up there and, after one unsuccessful sortie to dispose of the body, returned to his hiding place to recover from the emotions so evident in his appearance when seen by the diners before trying again?

It seemed extremely unlikely that an Oriental, even if born in France, would have such an intimate knowledge of the Bois de Boulogne, but there was little about this case that was not unlikely, and the police carried out a massive search of the forest, during which they discovered a large number of things, many of them illegal, but nothing connected with the murder or the strange little man.

Eventually, this question of the missing hour would be resolved, but only after the investigation had shifted from the Bois de Boulogne to the manner in which the little man had arrived there. At the moment, all that was known was that there was somewhere in Paris an Oriental dwarf who had apparently raped and murdered a Dutch girl and had cut away certain parts of her body. For what purpose was pure speculation.

The agents of the Sureté did not like this at all. It was bad enough when French girls were raped and murdered in Paris. Such things happening to foreigners could give the city a bad name.

On the other hand, there was, at least, a fair chance that the murderer did not have French nationality. A great many

Orientals, particularly Vietnamese, do, but Renée had been only four months in Paris at the time of her death and, given her studious nature, had probably not had contact with too many persons outside the university. It could, therefore, be hoped that she had been raped and murdered by one of her fellow foreign students. The instructors were, of course, mainly French.

The problem with this line of investigation was that there were a great many foreign students, and it was not a simple matter to trace everyone with whom Renée might have come into contact. The friends which had been interrogated all professed ignorance of any contacts she might have had to an Oriental dwarf.

None the less, the dwarf was a student and, had he not been identified first by other means, he would probably have been successfully traced through the university.

As it was, his identification was established through the testimony of a taxi driver who had been called to an apartment building at 10 rue Erlanger in the 16th arrondissement on the evening of 13 June.

There he had found waiting on the sidewalk in front of the building a very small Oriental man with two large, imitation leather, cardboard suitcases. He had got the suitcases into the trunk with great effort as they were very heavy, and the little Oriental had directed him to the Bois de Boulogne where he had got out not far from the Lac Inférieur and had set off down the path, half dragging, half carrying the suitcases.

Paris cab drivers are not easily impressed, but this fare was sufficiently odd that the driver remembered the incident very well.

So did two other cab drivers. One had picked up the little man and his suitcases in the Bois de Boulogne at a little after seven-thirty and had brought him and them back to the address at 10 rue Erlanger. The other had picked up man and suitcases for the second time at shortly after eight and brought them to the Lac Inférieur.

The mystery of the missing hour was now solved. The diminutive murderer had made two attempts to dispose of the remains of his victim. He had not been in the Bois de Boulogne, but riding to and from it in taxi cabs.

The police now knew that their suspect was a Japanese named Issei Sagawa, that he was a student at Université Censier, and they knew where he lived. They did not, however, rush straight in and arrest him.

France was, by now, a socialist country and this meant, among other things, that a great deal more attention would be given to the rights of the accused than to those of the public. It was, therefore, essential that the police present an absolutely watertight case if they hoped to obtain a conviction, something felt to be desirable as there was little doubt in anyone's mind that Sagawa was dangerously insane and, if acquitted or released on some pretext, could be counted upon to repeat his offence.

Everything which the police had at the moment was based upon the statements of witnesses who had seen Sagawa with the suitcases or, at least, some suitcases. No one could swear that the suitcases had contained the remains of Renée Hartewelt because no one had seen them open except the police, and they had not been in Sagawa's possession at that time. Moreover, there was the usual problem of identification of an Oriental by Westerners, many of whom would admit in court that all Orientals looked alike to them. Granted Sagawa's appearance was unusual, but a clever defence attorney could undoubtedly turn up a half-dozen Oriental dwarves in Paris and run them through the courtroom. In nine million people, there are a half-dozen of anything.

Although there was no explanation of what she had been doing there, it was practically certain that Renée had been murdered in Sagawa's studio apartment at 10 rue Erlanger, and it was possible that traces of the act would be found there. Sagawa had, however, had ample time to clean up and, if he had been as methodical in the other phases of the murder as he had been in the cutting up, he would have carried out the butchery in the bathtub and then cleaned the drains with lye, a common solution to the problem of bloodstains which occurs to a surprising number of murderers.

There were, therefore, a number of things which could

be investigated and which would improve the case before Sagawa was taken into custody.

The first of these remained without result. It would have been important to establish witness accounts of Renée and Sagawa being together, particularly on the day of the murder, but no such witnesses could be located.

The second line of investigation was also unsuccessful. Sagawa was thirty-three years old and it seemed unlikely that he should have turned violently insane only now. If he was crazy enough to rape, murder and cut up a girl, he had presumably been crazy for some time. A criminal record or a recond of extensive psychiatric treatment would be useful in establishing his guilt. He would presumably not be convicted as he would be declared incompetent to stand trial by reason of insanity, but, at least, the case would be solved.

This was something difficult to find out as Sagawa had arrived in France only in April of 1977, and any criminal or psychiatric records he might have would be in Japan, as it was quickly established that he had no record of any kind in France.

However, neither did he in Japan. Sagawa, the son of a wealthy Japanese industrialist, had taken his bachelor's and master's degrees at the University of Osaka where he had written his thesis on Shakespeare's *Macbeth*. He had come to Paris for postgraduate work in preparation for a degree of Doctor of Letters and was specializing in the study of the influence of contemporary Japanese writing on French literature. An inveterate academic, he was extremely well versed in English and also spoke some German and French.

Looking at this background report, it was difficult for the agents of the Sureté to believe that they had the right man. How would it be possible to convince a jury that an eighty-eight-pound, four-foot-eleven-inch Japanese academician and intellectual had suddenly decided, at the age of thirty-three, to rape, murder and butcher a twenty-five-year-old Dutch girl who towered over him by a head and outweighed him by thirty pounds?

Only through physical evidence or a confession, and the investigators were much relieved when it was determined that Sagawa had rented a machine for shampooing rugs on the day following the murder. Obviously, there had been, after all, bloodstains, and there was no machine made which would remove them so thoroughly that the technicians from the police laboratories could not find them again.

As it turned out, the police caution was unnecessary. Issei Sagawa had been methodical in his butchery, but he had not been at all careful about covering his tracks. Taken into custody he promptly confessed, and well he might for his studio was filled with evidence.

Neatly wrapped in its case, the .22 calibre rifle which had fired the bullet recovered from Renée's head was found standing in a plastic cupboard together with other of Issei's possessions. He had, he said, bought it immediately upon his arrival in Paris as he had been warned that the city was not safe.

This useful discovery soon paled into insignificance, however, with the examination of the contents of Sagawa's refrigerator. Wrapped in plastic and placed, partly in the freezing compartment for longer storage, and partly in the body of the refrigerator for immediate consumption, were one of Renée's thighs, one of her buttocks and both breasts. Nose, lips, the other thigh and buttock had, said Sagawa, all been eaten, mostly raw, although he had made the buttock into a sort of stew.

Speaking calmly, emotionlessly and almost detachedly, Issei Sagawa recited the details of his crime. It had begun, he said, when he found himself seated next to Renée at one of the lectures at the university. Both had been strongly interested in literature and they had quickly come into conversation. Renée, whose French was better than Issei's, had offered to help him with certain difficult translations and had come twice to his studio for that purpose. Her manner had been friendly, but impersonal. The idea of a romantic liaison between herself and the very small Japanese had apparently never crossed her mind.

It had crossed Sagawa's, and on the afternoon of 11 June after they had finished drinking tea and were seated opposite each other on cushions in Sagawa's studio, he had suddenly made a declaration of love followed by a blunt request for sexual relations.

Renée had shaken her head gently and had said, 'No, no. You must behave yourself.' She was aware that he was in love with her because he had previously told her so, although he had not asked for sex.

Sagawa had then put a Mozart tape on the tape recorder and had asked Renée to read aloud a poem by Schiller. While she was reading it, he had walked around behind her and, taking the rifle from the cupboard, had fired a single shot in the nape of her neck. She had fallen forward, killed instantly.

Sagawa had then removed the dead girl's clothing and had engaged in sexual intercourse with the corpse, following which, he had spread out sheets of plastic and newspapers to catch the blood and, going to fetch a knife, a razor and the scissors, he had begun to systematically butcher the corpse, placing the entrails and the severed parts in plastic rubbish sacks.

This had taken him a long time. He had no saw or hatchet with which to break the larger bones and had to work his way through the joints with the knife. He was, however, in no hurry, and stopped at intervals to take photographs of the work in various stages of progress.

These pictures were recovered by the police, and some two and a half years later a prominent editor would be sent to jail for having printed either them or other pictures made by the police at the time of the autopsy. In any case, they were pictures of the dismembered body of an intelligent, kindly, young woman whose only fault lay in a failure to grasp the extent of dangerously disturbed elements present in modern society. Had she still been alive, she might have been instructed by the behaviour of the editor in printing the pictures of her butchered body or by the reaction of the readers who undoubtedly enjoyed the spectacle very much and, perhaps, had idle daydreams of duplicating it.

That no one has probably represents a grudging acceptance of the fact that Sagawa's act is a hard one to follow. A Japanese dwarf murdering, raping and partially devouring a rather large, blond Dutch girl in Paris is such a spectacular media event that it may be impossible to improve on it.

For, once the details of the crime were known, it became, of course, a media matter and ceased to have any connection with reality. The editor jailed for printing the photographs was actually only doing his job and, if he was jailed, it was more for flouting authority than for any offence against morals or decency. After all, the job of an editor consists of giving the readers the type of material which they enjoy. If he does not do this, he soon ceases to be an editor.

Issei Sagawa was, of course, placed under psychiatric observation and, after a little more than a year, on 13 July 1982 predictably declared incompetent to stand trial by reason of insanity.

Sagawa was helpful in the psychologists' efforts to arrive at this conclusion. He told them in great detail precisely what he had done to Renée, and he insisted that he had known very well what he had been doing. He had even planned it in advance: it was not an impulsive act.

The doctors did not ask him why he had raped and murdered Renée. The question would have been fatuous. Throughout the world, girls, women and even children were being raped and murdered. There was nothing unusual about it at all. What the doctors wanted to know was why he had eaten part of the victim.

A lifelong ambition said Sagawa. He had always dreamed of eating a nice girl.

After this, there was no question in any of the experts' minds as to what would happen to Issei Sagawa. He would not stand trial, he would not be imprisoned, he would be sent to a relatively comfortable institution for the dangerously insane and that was exactly what happened.

There was a question in the mind of some non-experts. How long would he stay there? If past experience is any guide, not long. Modern ideology does not admit to the concept of the incurably insane any more than it admits to the incorrigibly evil. The human being is basically good and rational. If he is temporarily not, he can be made so through the wonders of psychology.

Issei Sagawa's fame was fleeting in France. The media cannot dwell too long on any subject as the attention span of their readers, bombarded with a thousand times the information they can absorb, is short and, anyway, these people were not French.

In Japan things went rather better. Sagawa's father resigned all of his directorships and retired to his, presumably, rather extensive estates. The prime minister issued a statement. There was endless talk of East-West symbolism, ritual murder and other chic theories. Many Japanese were said to be concerned over the reaction of the French to a brilliant Oriental scholar devouring young women in their capital.

This concern did not go unremarked, and one of the popular riders of the literary trend in Japan entered into correspondence with Sagawa and quickly brought out a book based on his letters and other sources.

The book, of course, immediately became a bestseller with over a million copies sold, and plans are now underway for a movie. The name of a famous producer, whose best-known film portrayed with remarkable realism the severing of a young man's genitals after close to two hours of almost uninterrupted sextual intercourse on the screen, has been suggested.

If the film is produced, and it would be amazing if it were not, it will undoubtedly be a smash hit and the murder, rape and butchery of Renée Hartewelt will be seen and savoured by millions.

As madmen go, Issei Sagawa is one of the more entertaining. He has provided recreation for millions, and has made and will make the publishing, movie and, perhaps, television industries enormous profits. He is even making a little money for me.

The only thing is: this was not so entertaining for Renée Hartewelt, was it?

2

LOVE THY NEIGHBOUR

Not all murders are as profitable or as entertaining to as many as that of the Japanese cannibal and the Dutch student in Paris. The vast majority pass with no more than a brief mention in the local press. They are the shabby, little, day-to-day homicides which take place under banal circumstances and in banal places.

Such as the apartment house where you live. Do you sometimes feel a little nervous about going down to the basement to empty the rubbish? It is very quiet down there, isn't it? People in the apartments upstairs would probably not hear you if you were to call out.

Or perhaps they could not hear you anyway. When was the last time you saw that attractive girl who lives down the hall? Has she moved out? Then why were there no movers? Or is she, perhaps, still in there? In what condition?

There is reason to believe that such thoughts occur to quite a few apartment dwellers, particularly in the larger cities and, in West Germany, Düsseldorf, with a population approaching three quarters of a million, is a fairly large city.

It is also a comparatively new city in so far as its buildings go. The visits of the British and American air forces during World War II left little standing.

By 1980, however, all had been replaced and much added, although the quality of the construction sometimes left something to be desired. Like many of its kind, the four storey apartment building at the corner of Tussmann and Derendorf streets on the northern edge of the city was built without soundproofing so that the tenants were frequently troubled with noise, transmitted, but distorted, by the concrete walls.

During early June of that year the sounds were particularly disturbing. There were muffled crashes, wails which could have been the wind, but perhaps were not, groans? screams? doors closing and opening, the sound of feet . . . Nothing really very different than what had been heard often enough before, but still . . .

The dustbins were in the basement and so were the laundry facilities, but it had been over a week now since Mrs Ilse Bauer had done the laundry, and the rubbish had been dropped off in the basement by her husband Walter every morning on his way to work.

Walter was aware, of course, that his young wife was becoming more and more nervous, but there was nothing that he could do and he assumed that she would eventually get over it. It was probably in part because she could not find a job. Like many younger German housewives she would have preferred to work, but jobs were scarce at the moment.

When he arrived home at approximately six-thirty in the evening of 12 June 1980, a Thursday, however, he found that Ilse's anxieties had developed a more specific focus, and where she had previously complained about there being too many noises, she was now concerned that there were not enough.

'There hasn't been a sound out of that apartment for two days now,' she said. 'I think that we should call the police.'

'Maybe they've moved out,' said Walter, heading for the bathroom. He was a heating systems installer and tended to get his hands dirty at work.

'Don't you think that I would have heard them if they were moving out?' said Ilse. 'I'm here all day and, if they were moving, the halls would have been full of furniture. I think something's happened. I was just reading in the newspaper yesterday about a family that was asphyxiated in their sleep when the gas stove sprang a leak.'

'They probably don't even cook with gas,' said Walter, scrubbing his face with the towel. 'All right, all right. I'll go across and ring the bell, but I'm going to feel like an idiot if they open up and ask me what I want.'

'You can save yourself the trouble,' said Ilse. 'I've been

272

over there to ring the bell four times this afternoon. Nobody answers and there's not a sound inside. They have two small children, you know.'

Walter stood looking uneasily at her for a moment or two, the towel still held in his hands.

'I guess you're right,' he said finally. 'We better call the police.'

The dispatcher at police headquarters sent a patrolcar. It was a routine report and a routine response. Many such calls were received every day in Düsseldorf and they were routinely checked out. Sometimes the police found a suicide, sometimes they found that the tenant had merely skipped out to avoid paying the rent, and occasionally they found a murder victim. More often than not they found nothing. The tenant of the apartment had merely gone off on vacation and had not bothered to tell anyone.

The locks on the apartment doors at number 12 Tussmann Street were not very sophisticated and, the patrolmen, having produced no response by knocking and ringing the doorbell, opened the door with the equipment which they carried for such cases and went in.

There was nothing in the entrance hall, and the doors leading off it were closed. The first door to the right opened into a bedroom, and there was no one in that either, but the second door led to the living room, and here the officers encountered a sight which stopped them dead in their tracks.

Lying sprawled on a fur rug in front of the sofa was the body of a young, blonde woman, naked, her face distorted in an expression of agony, the mouth open as if crying out for mercy, and her sightless eyes staring at the ceiling.

Beyond her, in front of an open door on the opposite side of the room, lay the body of a small boy wearing pyjamas.

The woman, the child, the fur rug and large areas of the floor were covered with dark, reddish-brown dried blood. The woman's body, in particular, was so enveloped in it that she looked as if she were wearing a tight-fitting, brown garment.

Although the patrolcar officers were both comparatively young men and had had no experience in homicide cases, they were well trained in the procedure to be applied and, while one officer remained in the hall outside the apartment, the other ran quickly down to the patrolcar and telephoned the dispatcher who immediately set in motion an operation which he had had all too much opportunity to practice.

Inspector Gerd Risch, the tall, blond, blue-eyed and pink-cheeked chief of the duty homicide squad was alerted and hurried with his assistant to the charge room. The duty medical officer came to join them from the police clinic, and a three-man squad of detection specialists carrying cases of equipment reported in from the police laboratory. Two unmarked cars from the Criminal Investigations Department pulled up in front of the entrance. The inspector, his assistant and the doctor climbed into one, the three men from the police laboratory got into the other, and less than forty minutes from the time that Walter Bauer had made his call to the switchboard at police headquarters, the homicide squad was at the scene.

The patrolmen were sent back to their beat and, while the inspector's assistant went across the hall to speak with the Bauers, the inspector and the doctor entered the apartment for a preliminary examination of the corpses, the laboratory specialists remaining waiting in the hall until it was completed.

Dr Georg Hofmann, a squat, broad-shouldered man with iron-grey hair and eyes and rimless, pince-nez glasses, had not completed his examination of the corpse of the woman when the inspector, who had gone into the room beyond the dead boy, came out to announce that there was a third corpse.

'Baby,' he said. 'It's lying in its crib. Must have been a total madman. He's wiped out the whole family.'

'Not the husband and father though, I see," said the doctor. 'Or was there one?'

It was a legitimate question. There are a great many divorced and single women bringing up children in Germany today.

'I don't know,' said the inspector. 'The baby seems to be the only other body. Maybe Juergen will be able to tell us when he comes back from the neighbours.'

Juergen was Detective-Sergeant Juergen Kettenmeyer, a quiet young man with medium-hair and egg-shaped eyes. Although he had not been long in criminal investigations, the inspector regarded him as a highly satisfactory assistant.

The sergeant, when he returned a few moments later, reported that there had, indeed, been a husband and father, a tall, handsome man who wore a beard and moustache. Aside from that the Bauers had known nothing about him.

'They say that there was the usual amount of bickering in a young family like that with children, but they never heard any really serious fights,' said the sergeant. 'Does it look like it was the husband?'

'Probably,' said the inspector. 'The wife and the kids are dead and he's missing. There are a lot of such cases nowadays. Stress in the family. The fellow cracks, butchers the wife and children and clears out. Tell the lab people to start hunting through here for identification. We'll want to get out a pick-up and hold order on the husband as quickly as possible.'

The laboratory men were summoned and began going through the apartment. Dr Hofmann concluded his examination of the woman's corpse and moved to the little boy lying in front of the door and, subsequently, to the baby in what had apparently been the children's bedroom.

'Well?' said the inspector.

'They were all killed at approximately the same time,' said the doctor. 'Two days ago, three days ago. I'll tell you more exactly when I do the autopsy. Murder weapon in all cases was a thin-bladed knife with a single sharp edge. Probably a switchblade. The woman was stabbed ten or fifteen times. The children, fewer. She put up a fight. There are defence cuts on her hands and forearms. She had intercourse very shortly before her death.'

'Raped?' said the inspector.

'Intercourse,' said the doctor. 'There's no evidence that it was rape.'

'Her husband may have come home and found her with her boyfriend,' said the inspector. 'She was a very pretty woman.'

It was true. Although almost every square inch of the body was smeared with blood, there were only a few smudges on the face of the corpse which, despite its expression of pain and horror, was young and pretty.

'I would think that the boyfriend would be here too,' said the doctor. 'If it was the husband, he must have been out of his mind with rage. Of course, he could have made good his escape while the husband was busy killing the wife and children.'

'Undoubtedly something like that,' said the inspector, 'but I'm wondering why the people next door didn't hear more of the final battle.'

'It may have taken place in the evening,' said the sergeant, coming over with two personal identification cards of the type carried by many Europeans. 'They told me that they were out some evenings. These look like the ID cards.'

'He didn't take his papers with him?' said the inspector. 'That's strange.'

He opened the cards and glanced through them. The dead woman was twenty-six-year-old Margaret Deck, married three years and eight months to twenty-eight-year-old Wilhelm Deck, master electrician, and the mother of two-year-old Thomas and baby Christian, whose entire life had amounted to only six weeks.

'Get out the pick-up order on Deck immediately,' said the inspector, handing the identification cards back to the sergeant. 'You can run a check with the residents registry to see where he comes from. People who commit a crime like that often run for wherever they grew up.'

The sergeant went off downstairs to the radio-telephone in the policecar and the inspector headed for the kitchen where the technician in charge of the squad from the police laboratory was making notes on the reports from his men.

'Anything of significance?' said the inspector. 'We're working on the tentative theory that it was the husband.'

'If it was, he was a cold-blooded rascal,' said the technician. 'After he'd finished murdering the victims, he went into the bathroom to wash up, and then to the bedroom where he changed his clothes. Neat habits. He hung the bloody clothing that he was wearing at the time of the murders up in the clothes closet. Then, it looks like he spent the night peacefully in bed and only left the next morning.'

'You have reason to believe that it happened in the evening?' said the inspector.

'They'd had lunch, but not dinner,' said the technician. 'The murderer had a snack after he got through with his work and he had breakfast. My guess would be that the murders took place shortly before dinnertime, or a little later. They may have been fighting around for some time before he actually got down to murdering them.'

'Maybe we'll get a more exact time for the murders after the autopsy,' said the inspector. 'The people next door apparently didn't hear anything, although it would seem to me that she would have yelled her head off.'

'What about the other neighbours?' said the technician. 'Maybe they heard something.'

'We'll check them out of course,' said the inspector, 'but there are only two apartments in this wing. The other two are in the wing on the Derendorf side, and I doubt that they would have heard anything.'

This turned out to be true. The tenants of the other two apartments on the third floor had not only been unable to hear anything from the Deck apartment, they had never even encountered any of the Decks other than once or twice when Wilhelm Deck or his wife had been emptying the family rubbish into the dustbins in the basement at a time when they were there for the same purpose.

However, those living in the building who had had contact with him at all described Deck as a pleasant-appearing man who had been somewhat reserved. His supervisors at the electrical installation firm where he had worked said that he was a good worker, highly competent technically, and that he had had a rather easy-going nature. He had had no trouble of any kind with any of his fellow workers and, in so far as anyone knew, his family life had been uneventful. He had, in any case, never mentioned any quarrels or differences to anyone at the firm.

The continuing investigation also turned up friends of the Deck family. They were all local people from the area around Tussmann Street which was the district in which both Wilhelm and Margaret Deck had grown up. Mrs Deck's parents had, however, died when she was sixteen years old and Wilhelm Deck's parents had been killed in a car accident three years earlier.

All of the friends of the Deck family insisted that the marriage had been a very happy one and that it was utterly impossible that Wilhelm could have murdered his wife and children. Even if he had been capable of such an action, something which no one who had known him believed, he had had not the slightest motive.

The inspector knew better. There had been a motive and he was tall, taller even that Wilhelm Deck, approximately the same age, had rather long, curly hair and a triangular-shaped face. He had been seen speaking with Margaret Deck in the basement on afternoons when her husband was at work by two of the other tenants, and the inspector thought it probable that he had been her lover. The case, in his opinion, thus became one of the very common murders for reasons of sexual jealousy.

While Wilhelm Deck was working and, presumably, tiring himself out too much to be very active in the matrimonial bed at night, his wife had been entertaining a lover in the apartment during the afternoons. It was not an uncommon thing to do and the German media tended to present such actions as modern, liberal and enlightened. Unfortunately, a good many Germans, even comparatively young ones, were not quite as liberal and as enlightened as the media and, if they came home unexpectedly and found their wives engaged in sexual activities with someone else, they tended to react violently.

The inspector thought that Wilhelm Deck had come home unexpectedly to find his wife in the act of having sex with her lover, for the body, when found, had been completely naked and Mrs Deck had taken off her clothing herself because it was not ripped or torn, but folded and hung neatly over the back of a chair in the living room.

Whether Deck had immediately thrown himself upon his wife and murdered her or whether there had been an extended quarrel first, it was not possible to say. In any case, while the Decks were occupied with each other, the lover had made good his escape. Deck had then murdered his family, had washed up and changed clothes, had had some refreshments, and had gone to bed for a good night's rest. In the morning he had got up, dressed and made off.

Where he had got to was not possible to say as yet, but it was apparently a long way from Düsseldorf, for every police officer in the centre of Germany was looking for him and he had not been spotted.

According to the autopsy report, Margaret Deck had been murdered at sometime between six-fifteen and seven o'clock on the afternoon of Tuesday, 10 June 1980. The children had been murdered at approximately the same time, Thomas by stab wounds like his mother and the baby Christian by having his throat cut.

This estimate of the time coincided with the statements made by the Bauers. Walter had worked late that day and had only come home at eight o'clock. Ilse, who had known that he would be working late, had taken advantage of the free afternoon to do a little shopping and to drop in to see an old schoolfriend. She had arrived home only fifteen minutes before her husband.

By this time, Margaret, Thomas and Christian were all dead and any cries for help that they might have made had gone unheard.

Otherwise, the autopsy report stated that Mrs Deck had had not only vaginal, but also oral intercourse with someone very shortly before she had been stabbed to death. In addition to the defence cuts on her hands and forearms where she had attempted to ward off the knife, there were seventeen stab wounds on the body, nearly all of them to the hilt of what had been a knife with a six-inch blade.

Thomas, being smaller, had been stabbed only six times, although one of the cuts was a slash wound so deep that it had nearly disembowled the little boy.

Christian had only a single stab wound high up on the left

side of the chest just under the collarbone, and his throat had been cut from ear to ear.

In Dr Hofmann's opinion, the mother had been killed first, and the sounds of the struggle had aroused the attention of Thomas who had come into the living room to see what was happening. He had been cut down in his turn, and the murderer had continued on into the bedroom to finish off the baby. The only plausible explanation for the murder of the children was madness, as they were too small to constitute any danger of identification of the murderer.

As it had been established with some certainty that the Decks had had no enemies and as nothing had been stolen, there seemed little question but that Deck was the murderer, and the only problem that remained was to locate him.

As this had, so far, proved to be impossible, the next best thing was to lay hands on Margaret Deck's lover. He was probably not anxious to become involved in the investigation, but he would have no reason to go to such lengths to avoid the police as the murderer himself.

The investigation, therefore, turned to the identification of the tall, young man with the curly hair and the triangular-shaped face who proved to be remarkably difficult to identify. Not many people had seen him and no one knew who he was, where he lived or what he did for a living. All of the times that he had been seen with or near Margaret Deck were within the past few weeks and, if he had indeed been her lover, then the affair had been going on for only a very short time.

It was while interrogating Mrs Deck's female friends that the police came across an unexpected lead. Twenty-five-year-old Ruth Frankenthal listened to the description of the supposed lover and then said that he sounded like a man from whom she had bought a deep freeze only two days before the murder. Margaret Deck, she said, had been with her at the time and had also been in contact with the man, but she was quite certain that he had not been her lover. In fact she did not think that Margaret Deck knew him any better than she did, which was not at all.

To the inspector's surprise, she said that the man lived in

the same building as the Decks, but on the second floor of the Derendorf wing. He had run into Margaret Deck in the basement when they were both emptying their rubbish and had told her he was moving out and wanted to sell some of his things. Would she be interested?

Margaret had gone to look at the furniture and appliances, but had found nothing that she could use. She had then gone to get her friend Ruth Frankenthal, and the two had returned together. Ruth had bought a deep freeze, and the man had helped the two women carry it downstairs and load it into Miss Frankenthal's station wagon. He had then accompanied the two women to Miss Frankenthal's apartment to help get the deep freeze upstairs.

Ruth described him as pleasant and well mannered, and she thought that he was quite taken by Margaret Deck, but she had not had the impression that he knew her at all well.

The inspector, the sergeant and the two detectives from the Criminal Investigations Department proceeded immediately to the apartment where Ruth Frankenthal had bought the deep freeze. A check with the owner of the building had already shown that it was rented to a Mr Robert Stuellgens, a butcher, who had moved in only at the end of March.

No one answered the doorbell at Stuellgen's apartment, so the police officers opened the door and went in.

The apartment was a shambles of broken furniture and scattered personal possessions, all of it smeared and streaked with dark brown traces of dried blood. Lying in it, in the middle of the living room, was the body of a bearded man who would later be identified as Wilhelm Deck. He had been dead since 10 June.

The autopsy which Dr Hofmann performed on the body showed that Deck had been murdered by eighteen stab wounds from the same knife that had killed his wife and children, and that his death had taken place at roughly the same time as theirs. He had put up a tremendous battle, but had apparently been weakened by loss of blood due to an initial stab wound in the back.

The inspector now felt that he had a clear picture of what

281

had taken place. Deck, correctly or incorrectly, had thought that his wife was having an affair with Stuellgens and, having murdered her and his children, had gone to finish off the lover as well. Stuellgens had, however, managed to get the knife away from him and had stabbed him to death.

This theory was retained for exactly as long as it took to run a check on Stuellgens through the central police registry.

Stuellgens had only been released from prison in January of that year after having served a six-and-a-half-year sentence for strangling and beating a young mother unconscious, raping her and attempting to rape her child.

It was not his first offence. Stuellgens, who came from the city of Essen less than forty miles to the northeast, was only thirty years old, but any time that he had not spent in prison had been devoted to sex offences, mainly dangerously brutal attacks on minor children. He had, of course, been cured of his antisocial tendencies many times.

The picture had, once again, become less than clear, but one thing was certain, Stuellgens had to be located and interrogated as quickly as possible.

This did not prove to be too difficult. As the inspector had remarked, a criminal often headed for home after his crime, and Stuellgen's mother still lived in the Essen suburb of Borbeck. He was arrested there by the Essen police a few days later, hiding in a garden house. He was still carrying the blood-smeared switchblade with which he had murdered the entire Deck family.

Brought back to Düsseldorf, Stuellgens made little effort to deny his guilt or to offer any rational excuse for his acts. Having had a good deal of experience with courts and the police, he was aware that he had little to fear and he, presumably, told the literal truth with respect to his motives.

He had, he said, encountered Mrs Deck in the basement of the apartment house when she was emptying her rubbish. He had thought that she was attractive and had come to the conclusion that he would have sexual intercourse with her.

He had, therefore, taken every opportunity to make contact with her and had made his intentions rather plain. Mrs Deck, an attractive woman who was, undoubtedly, familiar with propositions of this sort, had made equally plain that she was not interested.

Stuellgens final attempt at seduction had been when he made pretence of moving out in order to lure the object of his desires into his apartment to examine the furniture.

Margaret Deck had come to the apartment, but, when he urged her to sit down and have a drink, had abruptly left, returning later with Ruth Frankenthal. Stuellgens, who had had no intention of moving, had been constrained to sell her his deep freeze.

The incident had left him with the conviction that he was not going to be able to persuade Margaret Deck to cooperate by peaceful means and, as it did not occur to him to abandon his project, he had decided to rape her.

Unfortunately, Margaret Deck had a large and athletic husband and, while Stuellgens had little fear of women and children, he was not overly courageous where men were concerned. Deck, he concluded, would have to go.

He had, therefore, waited in the entrance for Deck on the evening of 10 June and, when the unsuspecting electrician had arrived home from work, had asked him to give him a hand in carrying down some furniture as he was moving out.

Deck had goodnaturedly agreed and, as he preceded Stuellgens into the apartment, had been stabbed in the back.

To Stuellgens's dismay, Deck had not been killed instantly, and there had been a savage struggle with Stuellgens hacking at his incredulous victim like the madman he was.

The match had been uneven for Deck was, of course, neither armed nor prepared for such an attack from a virtual stranger, and he was eventually killed.

Stuellgens, rejoicing that his hotly desired goal was now within reach, had walked through the halls of the apartment building with the bloody knife in his hand, had rung the Deck doorbell, and had informed the appalled Margaret Deck of her husband's fate. He had then forced her to strip at knifepoint and had raped her, following which he had demanded that she perform oral sex on him.

Although his objectives had now been achieved, Stuellgens decided that it would be unwise to leave Margaret alive and, after another struggle, ended by stabbing her to death as well.

The struggle had created a certain amount of noise and Thomas, who was in the bedroom, had come out to investigate.

Stuellgens had immediately stabbed him to death and, going into the bedroom to see who else might be there, he found the baby and, after stabbing it once, cut its throat.

In a state of exhilaration at the success of his plans and too excited to sleep, Stuellgens had decided that what he needed was recreation and, having washed and changed into fresh clothing and had a little something to eat from the Deck's refrigerator, went to get some change from Wilhelm Deck's pockets with which he spent an hour or two playing the pinball machines in a nearby café.

He then returned to the Deck apartment and spent the night in the Deck's bed, departing the following morning after breakfast for his mother's place in Essen.

This ingenuous recital earned Stuellgens what he presumably expected – a declaration by psychological experts that he was incompetent to stand trial as he could not distinguish right from wrong. It was said that he had had an unhappy childhood and this had had an unfortunate effect on his personality.

It might, perhaps, be possible for persons who are not experts in psychology to detect that Robert Wilhelm Stuellgens is unable to distinguish right from wrong, but there are probably few non-professional psychologists so optimistic as to believe that he ever will be.

However, the word 'incurable' is not psychologese. Stuellgens is now undergoing treatment which undoubtedly will prove successful, as it so often has in the past.

3

NO GENERATION GAP IN
GERMANY

If Robert Wilhelm Stuellgens was the victim of an unhappy childhood which interfered so seriously with the development of his personality that it led to less than satisfactory social contacts, he was not alone. To the careless reader of the popular press, it sometimes seems that all German childhoods are unhappy.

This does not mean that they are, necessarily, uneventful. Even in the most desolate, most isolated villages, there are fascinating pursuits for the youth who knows where to look for them. These pursuits are not dependent upon the weather.

And a very good thing too. Autumn comes early over the great German moors of the north, and with it comes the fog, thick, wet, greyish white, so that the scant traffic over the infrequent roads slows to a near standstill and the sparsely populated region seems more deserted than ever.

On the southern rim of this lonely region of trackless swamps lies the Teutoburger Forest, scene of ancient Germanic tribal battles and an eerie place to live even for local residents, secretive and sly with the race memory of a thousand massacres.

At the eastern end of the Teutoburger Forest, Bielefeld, with a population of some 200,000 persons, is the largest community and serves as district capital for the smaller towns and villages around it. One of these, ten miles to the east, as the crow flies, is the village of Lage and at 9.45 a.m. on 11 September 1969, a strongly built boy emerged from the mist and entered the single room of the Lage police station.

285

'There's a dead woman in the old house at Hoerste,' he announced impassively.

The two officers at the desks looked up in startled surprise. 'Dead from what?' said Sergeant Karl Drescher. 'Who are you?'

'Willi Boeke,' said the boy. 'I'm from Leopoldstal. My dad's the cabinetmaker there. I'm his apprentice. I don't know what she's dead from. She's just dead.'

'Go with him and take a look, Paul,' said the sergeant to Constable Paul Brebsen. 'And bring him back here with you.'

The constable got up, put on his heavy, waterroof cape and, followed by the boy, left the station to disappear into the fog.

As the sergeant knew, Hoerste was less than fifteen minutes walk away, an isolated little huddle of houses not even worthy of the name of hamlet, but he did not expect the constable to return in a half-hour. In such think fog progress was slow, as it was easy to go astray even if a man had lived all his life in the area.

He was, therefore, surprised and startled when Brebsen came running back to the station in just slightly over twenty-five minutes.

'She's dead all right!' exclaimed the constable, a little out of breath. 'And, unless I miss my guess, she's been murdered!'

The boy had followed Brebsen into the station and he went over and sat down in the chair near the coal-burning stove. He was wearing only a light jacket and no hat, and he appeared to be soaked through.

'You!' said the sergeant, addressing himself to the boy. 'What do you know about this?'

'Nothing,' said Boeke. 'I was just passing by the old Koetter house on the Brockmann place and I went in to get out of the wet. Nobody lives there. Then I saw the woman. I thought she was asleep or drunk, but when I saw she wasn't breathing, I figured she was dead so I came right over here.'

'What did you find, Paul?' said the sergeant. 'What makes you think she was murdered?'

back, nearly in the middle of the floor. She was a young, comparatively attractive woman with fashionable permanent-waved hair, and she was wearing a pale blue dress with a white flower pattern. The dress was pulled down modestly over her knees, but, although it was uncomfortably chilly, there was no sign of a coat or sweater. In the sharp white light of the torch, her features appeared calm and reposed as if she had merely gone to sleep.

'You two go back to the car,' ordered the sergeant. 'I don't want anyone tracking things up in here until we see what's happened. If this is a homicide, there may be clues we can make use of.'

The constable and the boy went back outside and the sergeant bent over the boy. A few minutes later, he too came out of the building and went straight to the policecar. 'Gross calling central,' he said into the radio, pushing down the transmitter switch. 'Reporting to Inspector Fleischer in Homicide.'

There was a crackling from the radio and then the inspector's voice. 'Fleischer here,' he said. 'What is it, Hary?'

'Looks like homicide, chief,' said the sergeant.

'She's dead and I think for some time. There seem to be some scratches and bruises on the body. Can't tell the cause of death. I think we'd better have the medical officer out and somebody from the laboratory.'

'Right,' said the inspector. 'I'll get things moving and come out myself. How far is it from Lage?'

'About three quarters of a mile,' said Gross. 'You'd better go to the station in Lage and have them bring you over here. It's very foggy.'

The inspector, however, appeared to have faith in his knowledge of the district and arrived, forty minutes later, direct from Bielefeld with the police medical officer, Dr Joachim Schreiber, in the front seat next to him and two young technicians from the police laboratory in the back.

The doctor and the technicians immediately followed the sergeant into the house, and the inspector walked over to the sergeant's Volkswagen. 'Is this the boy that found the body?' he asked.

'Well, how else would she come to be dead in that old house?' said Brebsen. 'It's the old stone cottage over on Fred Brockmann's place. Nobody's lived there for years. The woman's lying in the front room on her back. She's not an old woman either. Thirty maybe. I couldn't see enough to tell whether she had any marks on her, but she's been dead for a while. The body's stone cold.'

'If it doesn't seem to be a natural death it's out of our jurisdiction,' said the sergeant. 'I'll call Bielefeld and they can send somebody down from the criminal police.'

'He picked up the telephone and dialled the number of Inspector Gerd Fleischer, chief of the district homicide division in Bielefeld. 'Sergeant Drescher in Lage,' he said. 'I think we may have a case of homicide down here.'

The inspector listened to the details, motioning with one hand to his assistant to pick up the extension. 'All right,' he said finally. 'We'll have somebody down right away. Keep the boy at the station.'

He hung up the telephone and turned to Detective-Sergeant Harald Gross, a short, blunt-featured man with thick, stooping shoulders. 'Take it, will you, Hary?' he said.

The sergeant nodded and put down the extension. 'I'll call back over the radio and let you know what it is as soon as I find out,' he said. 'Maybe it's only a natural death after all.'

Forty-five minutes later, the green police Volkswagen came bumping slowly through the fog in the direction of Hoerste. Sergeant Gross was at the wheel, and Constable Brebsen and the boy sat in the back seat. 'There it is,' said the boy, leaning over the back of the front seat and pointing. 'There. To the left.'

The sergeant brought the car to a halt before an ancient, stone building with a tile roof and crumbling brick chimney. At the front of the house were two tiny windows and a low door which stood half open. Gross got out a powerful, electric torch from the luggage compartment of the Volkswagen and entered the building, followed by the constable and the boy.

There were only three rooms, all filled with dust and obviously unused for many years. In the largest room, to the right of the front entrance, the woman lay stretched on her

288

'Yes, sir,' said the constable, climbing out of the car and pulling the boy out after him. 'His name's Willi Boeke.'

'How old are you, Willi?' said the inspector. 'And how did you come to find the body?'

For the first time since appearing at the Lage police station, Willi Boeke showed signs of nervousness. Inspector Fleischer was no village constable, but a heavy-set, brisk sort of man with a broad, high forehead and an unmistakable air of authority.

'Fifteen,' said the boy, his voice breaking slightly. 'I just came in to get out of the wet.'

'Um-hum,' said the inspector. 'And what were you doing here in the first place? Do you live in Hoerste?'

'He lives in Leopoldstal,' said Constable Brebsen. 'His father's the cabinetmaker there.'

'I was on my way to Lage . . .' said Willi.

'Why?' said the inspector.

'Well, I – uh – I had something to do there,' said Willi, shifting from one foot to the other. 'I had to get something . . . I had to get some nails for dad.'

'Leopoldstal is closer to Bielefeld than it is to Lage,' observed the inspector. 'Why didn't you go there?'

'I – I don't know,' said the boy, beginning to stammer slightly. 'I guess I didn't know that. I thought it was closer to Lage.'

'Keep that boy in custody,' said the inspector. 'I'll be talking to him some more.' He went into the house and, after looking through the remainder of the rooms, went into the front room where the doctor was still examining the body.

'Any idea what killed her yet?' he asked.

'Hard to say,' said the doctor, standing up and wiping his hands on a piece of surgical gauze. 'The only signs of external violence are a few scratches and bruises. Nothing serious. There are some marks on the throat, but I can't see enough in here to tell whether she may have been strangled. I doubt it though. There aren't any signs of a struggle in the dust on the floor. At the moment, I'd be inclined to suspect something internal – poison or sleeping pills perhaps.'

'In other words, it could have been suicide,' said the

inspector. 'We may be able to confirm that if we can find out who she is. Are there any papers on the body?'

'No,' said the doctor, 'but Hary says he found a handbag in the corner when he got here. I expect he took it out to the car.'

The inspector went outside to where the sergeant, the constable and Willi Boeke were standing beside the cars. It had started to rain, a fine, cold drizzle, but the fog was as heavy as ever. The ambulance which had followed from Bielefeld had arrived, and was standing near the front of the house with the driver and the stretcher bearers crowded into the front seat.

Sergeant Gross had turned the handbag over to one of the detection men, who was in the process of extracting the contents with a pair of wooden tweezers to avoid obliterating possible fingerprints. 'Here's a personal identity card,' he said, holding the folded cardboard identification out to the inspector with his tweezers. 'You've seen the body. It's her picture.'

The inspector squinted at the little passport photo. 'Guldira Kressenzia Knapp,' he said, reading from the entries on the card. 'Maiden name: Busch. Twenty-nine years old. Eight years married.'

'Where is she from, chief?' said Sergeant Gross. 'Maybe I could go see if the family knows anything about this.'

'Springer Street, fourteen,' said the inspector. 'It's in Detmold. Yes, I think it would be a good idea if you went over and talked to the husband. The next of kin will have to be notified in any case and it's possible that it was suicide. See if she's left a farewell note anywhere.'

The sergeant got into his Volkswagen and drove away. Detmold, a somewhat larger town, was six miles further to the east, and south of Lage.

'Can we go back into the building now?' asked the young technician with the glasses. 'Is the doctor finished?'

'Ask him,' said the inspector. 'It's all right with me.'

'We need to know who's been in there,' said the other technician. 'Would everyone who's been in the building step on a sheet of paper here so that we can get a shoeprint?'

The police officers, the doctor and Willi Boeke came forward to leave their wet footprints on the sheets of white paper which the technician laid out on the stone slab in front of the building.

'Gross was in there too,' said the inspector, 'but you'll have to wait for his footprints until he gets back.'

The technician nodded and went on into the building, followed by his partner who was carrying a large box of equipment.

'The wonders of science,' said the inspector. 'Come here, Willi. You and I are going to sit in the back seat of the car and have a little talk. I have the feeling that you're not being entirely open with us.'

The boy came slowly over and climbed into the back seat of the inspector's Volkswagen with obvious reluctance. The inspector got in beside him and closed the door.

'Now,' he said. 'Let's get a few things straight, Willi. I've been a police officer for a very long time and I have talked to a great many people who had something to hide. Usually I can tell when a person like that is lying, and you're lying, Willi, or at least you're not telling us the whole truth. It's going to save both of us a lot of trouble if you come out now with whatever you know, and we're sure to find it out anyway so what about it?'

Willi Boeke remained stubbornly silent for several minutes. 'It was the way I told the constable,' he said finally, but his voice shook and he was obviously on the verge of tears.

'Sure it was, Willi,' said the inspector, 'but there's something more too. You didn't just happen to go into that house to get out of the wet. If you wanted to dry off, you could knock on any door around here and there'd have been a fire to dry out by. Besides, any boy who found a dead woman like that would have been scared out of his wits. He'd have run to the nearest house. That's Brockmann's. Instead, you went all the way into Lage to the police station. Now, why did you do that?'

Tears began to run down the boy's cheeks. He drew a long, shuddering breath that was half a sob. 'I was afraid somebody would think I killed her,' he said.

'Why?' said the inspector. 'Why would anyone think you killed Mrs Knapp?'

'Because we were doing it,' said the boy.

The inspector was not a man who was easily startled, but he jumped as if he had been shot. 'What did you say?' he demanded, turning in the seat to look directly at the boy who squirmed and turned pink. 'I thought you said you were fifteen years old.'

'I am,' said Willi Boeke, more calmly and with a touch of suppressed pride. 'Guldira was older than I am. She was twenty-nine. We've been doing it ever since I was eleven.'

'Listen boy,' said the inspector threateningly, 'if you're lying to me . . .'

'Ask my father,' said Willi Boeke. 'Ask Guldira's husband. They all know about it. They all tried to stop us.'

The inspector brought out a crumpled pack of cigarettes, shook one out and lit it, never taking his eyes from the boy in the seat beside him. He took a deep drag, blew out a long plume of smoke and said, 'All right, Willi, I believe you. So what happened? How did Mrs Knapp die, and what was she doing in that house?'

'It was last Sunday,' said Willi Boeke. 'I went to Detmold to spend the day with Guldira.'

'That would be the seventh of this month,' said the inspector. 'Today's Thursday.'

'That's right,' said Willi. 'It was Sunday the seventh. Heinrich – that's Guldira's husband – was gone, and he took the children with him.'

'Mrs Knapp has children?' said the inspector.

'Two,' said Willi. 'Uli's five and Sarah is six. They're just little kids. Anyway, Heinrich was coming back on Monday at noon so we left Monday morning as we didn't want to be bothered. Then I remembered the old stone house here in Hoerste. We got here Monday afternoon.'

'And then what?' said the inspector.

'We were feeling kind of bad,' said Willi Boeke. 'Everybody was picking on us and wouldn't leave us alone. We decided to put an end to everything.'

'You mean commit suicide?' said the inspector.

292

The boy nodded. 'We had two hundred sleeping pills. Guldira was going to take half and I was going to take the other half.'

'But you didn't take yours,' said the inspector.

'I took some of them,' said Willi Boeke. 'Then I fell asleep. That was Monday evening. When I woke up, it was Tuesday morning and Guldira was dead. I thought it was the sleeping pills at first, but then I saw she had some scratches and things and I figured that Heinrich had sneaked over when we were unconscious and killed her. I thought I'd probably get blamed for it and I didn't know what to do, so I stayed there until this morning. Then I went to the police in Lage.'

For several minutes the inspector sat smoking silently. Finally, he gave a deep sigh and tossed the cigarette butt out of the car window. 'Willi,' he said, 'in close to twenty-five years of investigation this is the most unlikely story that I have ever heard. It's so unlikely that I'm inclined to believe it. I don't think you could make such a thing up and I hope, for your sake, that you haven't, because if you have, we are going to find it out and then you'll really be in trouble.'

'That's just the way it was, sir,' said Willi Boeke stoutly.

The two technicians had come out of the house, so the inspector got out of the car and went over to them. 'Find anything?' he asked. 'Can the doctor take the body away now?'

'As far as we're concerned,' said the technician with the glasses, 'we didn't find out very much. Somebody's been staying in there for three or four days. The boy I expect as those seem to be his shoeprints. Not many shoeprints from the woman. There are a couple of blankets and some remains of food. No indication of any third party.'

'You can send the body to the morgue now, Joachim,' called the inspector to the doctor who was sitting in the back of the ambulance. 'Give me a complete autopsy report as soon as possible. Check the stomach. She's supposed to have taken sleeping pills.' He turned back to the technician. 'No trace of a third party, eh?' he said. 'What about shoeprints in the dust?'

'We can't be entirely certain,' said the technician. 'There

293

have been too many people in and out. There could be another set of prints that was obliterated.'

'See if you can raise Gross on the car radio,' said the inspector. 'Tell central that they're to keep calling until they get him. I want to talk to him.'

The technician went over to the inspector's car to carry out the instructions, and the men from the police ambulance went into the house with a stretcher and came out bearing the body of Guldira Knapp covered with a sheet. They put it into the ambulance and stood waiting.

'All clear, inspector?' asked the doctor.

The inspector nodded absently and the doctor climbed into the front seat next to the driver. The stretcher bearers got into the back with the body and the ambulance disappeared into the curtains of fog and rain, its headlights glowing yellow and its siren moaning softly.

'I've got Sergeant Gross on the radio,' announced the technician coming over from the car. 'He's in Detmold.'

The inspector walked to the car and picked up the transmitter. 'Hary?' he said. 'Have you seen Knapp?'

'Just left him,' said Gross's voice from the speaker. 'I'm parked in front of his house.'

'Bring him in,' said the inspector. 'There's some reason to believe that he may have killed his wife. God knows, he had a motive if what that boy says is true. I'll tell you about it when you get to Bielefeld. It's too complicated to explain over the radio.'

He hung up the radio-telephone and went back to the two technicians. 'Okay,' he said. 'If you're finished here for now secure the door and put the seals on it. We'll go back to Bielefeld. Hary is bringing in a suspect and I want to talk to the boy some more.'

The road from Detmold to Bielefeld is a main highway and, as a consequence, Sergeant Gross and Heinrich Knapp were already at the office of the criminal police when the inspector arrived with the two technicians and Willi Boeke.

While the inspector's secretary set about making coffee, the inspector got out of his waterproof, settled himself

294

behind his desk and began the interrogation of Heinrich Knapp, who was seated in front of it.

'To begin with,' he said, 'I have got a rather strange question to ask you. This boy here says he was your wife's lover. Is that true?'

Knapp shot a bitter glance at the boy, who looked away but did not change expression. He was a lean man in his middle thirties with the tanned face and roughened hands of a man who worked a great deal out of doors.

'Yes,' he said sourly. 'It's true.'

'And this has been going on for four years?' said the inspector incredulously. 'My God, man! Why didn't you do something about it?'

'What?' said Knapp. 'Old man Boeke did everything he could to keep the kid away from her. I did everything I could. What more could we do? All Guldira ever said was to go ahead and divorce her. She wanted to marry Willi anyway as soon as he got old enough.'

'Why didn't you?' said the inspector.

'We've got two kids, inspector,' said Knapp. 'I figured any mother is better than no mother at all.'

'Where have you been for the past few days?' said the inspector, changing the subject abruptly. He took a cup of coffee from the secretary and motioned that she should offer some to the two suspects.

'Where I always am,' said Knapp, taking the coffee gratefully. 'Working. Taking care of the kids. Looking after the house. Guldira hasn't been home since Sunday.'

'Do you always take care of the children when your wife isn't there?' said the inspector.

'My brother's wife helps out sometimes,' said Knapp. Suddenly he had become ill at ease and the words came slowly.

'Is she looking after them now?' said the inspector.

Knapp nodded without speaking.

'Good,' said the inspector, 'because I want you to stay here for a little while. I'd like to talk to you and Willi again after I've heard what the doctor has to say. I expect he'll be finished by this afternoon.'

The doctor was quicker than the inspector had anticipated. By three o'clock, a preliminary report lay on the inspector's desk and the doctor himself was seated in the chair that Knapp had recently occupied, prepared to answer any questions that had not been made clear in the report.

'So,' said the inspector, finishing the second and final page and laying the report on the desk, 'she died early Tuesday morning. She was full of sleeping pills, but the actual cause of death was strangulation while she was unconscious. Everything checks exactly with what young Boeke told me in the car.'

He paused, took out a cigarette and, having lit it, sat smoking and looking thoughtfully at the doctor. 'And yet,' he said after a time, 'somehow I don't believe it. I can't picture Knapp sneaking into that house and strangling his wife.'

'Doesn't strike me as reasonable either,' said the doctor. 'I've only talked to Knapp briefly, but, to begin with, he doesn't seem the type. More to the point though, if he was going to kill his wife, why didn't he do it any time within the past four years that this has been going on?'

'Exactly,' said the inspector. 'Hary is out in Detmold now trying to check Knapp's story about being home every evening and so on. I expect we'll find that that's just where he was.'

The inspector was, however, wrong. When Sergeant Gross returned from Detmold it was nearly eight o'clock in the evening, and the inspector had already gone home after releasing both Knapp and Willi Boeke. The sergeant's news was, however, so significant that he went directly to the inspector's house.

'It looks bad for Knapp, chief,' he said with a touch of regret in his voice. 'He was lying to you. He's been home taking care of the kids every night except one. Monday evening he left them with his brother's wife. He picked them up Tuesday afternoon, but I haven't been able to find any trace of where he was or what he was doing during that time. Was Joachim able to determine the time of death?'

'Early Tuesday morning,' said the inspector. 'Well, I'm

afraid you'll have to go pick him up again. I've already released him.'

'Tonight yet?' said Gross.

The inspector considered. 'No,' he said finally. 'Leave it until tomorrow morning. If he does make a run for it it will be practically an admission of guilt. I don't expect he would get very far and, I don't know why, but I don't think he'll clear out.'

This time the inspector was right. When he arrived at his office the following morning, Heinrich Knapp was already there and waiting for him.

'My sister-in-law told me you checked my story last night,' he said. 'I figured you'd want to talk to me again.'

The inspector lit a cigarette and held the pack out to Knapp. 'Tell me honestly, Mr Knapp,' he said. 'Did you kill your wife?'

Knapp shook his head slowly. 'No,' he said, 'I didn't kill her. I guess I may have thought of it sometimes, but I didn't do it. I know it looks bad for me especially after I said I was home on Monday evening, but I didn't do it. I'm innocent.'

'So why did you lie?' asked the inspector. 'Where were you really on Monday night?'

Knapp flushed brick-red. 'I was ashamed,' he said in a low voice. 'I was with a woman.'

'What's her name?' said the inspector.

'Inge,' said Knapp. 'That's all I know. She's a street girl. I picked her up in front of the Black Dog Bar in Detmold and I spent the night with her.' He was squirming with embarrassment and his eyes avoided the inspector's gaze. 'I'm not an old man,' he murmured. 'It's hard when you don't have a wife that's any use to you.'

'I dare say,' said the inspector. 'You understand I'm going to have to hold you this time until your story can be checked? I'm going to turn you over to one of my detectives and I want you to give him as exact a description of this Inge as you can, and any information you can think of as to where we can find her.'

Knapp was turned over to an investigator and the inspector

called in his secretary. 'Where's Sergeant Gross this morning?' he asked. 'Hasn't he come in yet?'

'He called in,' said the secretary, 'while you were talking with Mr Knapp. He said to tell you that he's had a call from the detail-checking-out people in Hoerste and that he'll contact you as soon as he knows what it is.'

The inspector was, however, too impatient to wait for the sergeant to call him, and he immediately instructed the radio central to try and make contact with the officers in Hoerste. Twenty minutes later, Gross came on the radio-telephone.

'I think we've got something significant here, chief,' he said. 'We have eight men out here checking with the local people to see if anyone saw Mr or Mrs Knapp or the Boeke boy, and they've located a woman who runs a little grocery store. I've just talked to her and she says that a boy came into the store on Monday evening and asked for a doctor. She told him that the nearest one was in Lage. He left then. From her description, I'd say that it was Willi Boeke.'

'That may be interesting,' said the inspector, 'but I don't see that it's very significant.'

'She says that the young man had blood on his hands, chief,' said the sergeant. 'As you remember, Mrs Knapp was scratched up a certain amount. Do you want me to pick the boy up and bring him in?'

'Definitely,' said the inspector. 'And bring the woman too. We'll see if she can pick him out of a line-up.'

The owner of the grocery store could. 'That's the boy,' she said. 'He's the one who came into the store.'

The inspector waited for only one more thing, the report from the detective who was trying to find Inge, the girl with whom Heinrich Knapp had allegedly spent Monday night. Shortly before noon he had his confirmation of Knapp's alibi. Inge had not been hard to find. She was a professional prostitute who had her beat in front of the Black Dog and who was well known in the district. She confirmed Knapp's statement.

'Bring the boy into the office,' said the inspector and, when Willi Boeke was seated in the chair before his desk, began immediately with a blunt accusation. 'Willi,' he said. 'You murdered Mrs Knapp. Now, let's not waste any more time. I want the truth.'

Willi Boeke was, however, not prepared to admit to the truth. For two hours he lied, denied and evaded the inspector's questions, but, in the end, he was no match for the experienced police officer. Defiant but flustered, he blurted out the truth.

'We were both supposed to take the pills,' he said, 'but I decided I didn't want to die so I threw mine away. Guldira didn't notice it in the dark. She took hers and sort of passed out. She didn't die though. After a while, I got tired of waiting and I thought I'd put an end to it. I had realized that I didn't want to marry her after all. She was too old for me and she already had two children.'

'And another on the way,' said the inspector. 'Did you know that?'

'Yes,' said Willi Boeke. 'It was mine and I figured I was too young to be a father. I tried to strangle her a little and she sort of came to and fought with me. That's when she got scratched and I got the blood on my hands. After it was over and she wasn't breathing any more, I got scared and I thought I'd better call a doctor. Then when I went to the store, I suddenly realized that I'd be blamed if she was dead, so I went back to the house and stayed there until Thursday morning when I went to Lage.'

'And you spent those nights sleeping beside the body of the woman you'd murdered,' said the inspector.

'Why not?' said Willi Boeke.

Willi Boeke was brought to trial before the juvenile court in Bielefeld on 4 November 1969 and, after having repeated his confession, was remanded to a home for juvenile delinquents where he will remain until his twenty-first birthday. Under German juvenile law it was the maximum sentence that he could receive.

Now, who was crazy here? Not Heinrich Knapp. He was merely trying to do his best for his children under trying circumstances. Guldira Knapp? Possibly. Any woman of twenty-five who falls passionately in love with an eleven-year-old boy is obviously suffering from more than the boredom of life in a small town, and Guldira was, demonstrably, sincere about wanting to commit suicide.

Willi Boeke was not. He did not take his pills but threw them away, and when Guldira's did not work promptly enough he took matters into his own hands. As he said, he wanted to get rid of her. Why? Was it because he feared the responsibilities of fatherhood? Or was it simply because the ecstasies of young love had already palled. The attention span of an adolescent, even regarding romance, is not long.

Nor was his sentence. It would be unfortunate if he were left with the impression that there is little personal risk attached to murder.

4

YOU'LL ENJOY MEETING
MY SISTER

Not that it is any justification for murder, but Willi Boeke's reluctance to found a family at the age of fifteen is shared by many Germans a good deal older. At about the time that Willi and Guldira began their tender romance, the German birth rate descended below the replacement level and has remained there ever since. It is estimated that by the year 2100 or so, there will not be enough Germans left to field a football team.

Many reasons have been advanced for this decline in fertility. Easily available birth-control drugs and devices. A materialistic attitude on the part of young Germans who prefer vacations and cars to kiddies. Fear of war. The large number of working women, etc.

One theory which has not been advanced but which, perhaps, deserves consideration is that the current generation of child-bearing age remembers all too well what kind of a time their parents had with them and are anxious not to be subjected to the same fate.

Ideologically and from the point of view of media-advertising revenues, youth liberation may be a wonderful thing, but it makes relations within the family difficult and not infrequently painful. When this new freedom for the immature is combined with the new sexual morality, the results can be positively lethal. Even in such a place as conservative and little influenced by international trends as France.

Of course, it depends a good deal upon where you are in France. Paris and the Mediterranean coast are mildly given to whatever excesses are internationally current, but less than a hundred miles to the north of Paris, in a city such as Lille, most of the population is extremely conservative.

Not, perhaps, by inclination. Rather, they are practically all out of work and not a few are wondering where their next meal is coming from. Under such conditions it is difficult to keep up with what is currently 'in'.

Even in Lille, however, family misunderstandings do arise, and on Saturday, 2 August 1980, when the ambulance arrived at the apartment house at number sixteen, rue Gosselin in the Lille suburb of Fives at a little after three in the afternoon, it was to find a large knife rammed to the hilt in the middle of thirty-seven-year-old Daniel Renaut's stomach.

The stocky, heavy-muscled truck driver set hunched forward on the sofa, his hands clamped around the handle of the knife and his thick moustache like a streak of charcoal across the deadly pallor of his face. He was sweating heavily, the glistening streams of perspiration running down his forehead, across his cheeks and into the open collar of the scotch-plaid shirt. Lower down, where the saw-edged blade of the knife was imbedded in his vitals, the blood was seeping slowly out to form a large, irregularly shaped dark patch over the pattern of the shirt.

His sister and her fiancé sat on either side of him, supporting him in their arms. As the paramedic and the stretcher bearers burst through the open door of the apartment into the living room, Renaut raised his head, opened his mouth as if he were trying to say something, and went limp as he lost consciousness.

The paramedic took one look at the protruding knife handle and motioned to the stretcher bearers. 'Into the ambulance with him!' he snapped. 'Quickly! We'll be lucky if we get him to the hospital alive.'

As the stretcher bearers eased the unconscious man swiftly and with the efficiency of much practice on to the stretcher and manoeuvred it through the narrow hall and down the stairs, the intern, following alongside, inserted the transfusion needle and lifted high the flask.

'Have you notified the police?' he called to the couple still sitting on the sofa.

The man and the girl shook their heads mutely.

302

'Notify them,' said the intern, and went off down the stairs.

A few moments later the communications centre at police headquarters in downtown Lille, the formerly great and grimy industrial city in the northwest corner of France, received a call over the radio-telephone from the driver of the ambulance speeding through the streets in the direction of the Lille Emergency Hospital. A man had been seriously wounded with a knife at 16 rue Gosselin in the suburb of Fives. The paramedic had not had the impression that the couple in the apartment were going to take his advice.

Although it was a weekend and the height of the vacation period, the Criminal Investigations Department of the Lille police was fully staffed. Even in the best of times the cities along the Belgian border in the industrial north of France tend to a comparatively high crime rate. Now, with massive unemployment and a plunging standard of living, violent crime was at such a level that nearly all sections needed to be manned around the clock.

On duty in the Criminal Investigations Department on this day was Inspector Bernard Gentry, a tall, handsome man with long, dark-brown sideburns and a permanently harassed expression, his assistant, Detective-Sergeant Pierre Dunoyer, a bear of a man, with a sizeable stomach and a rolling gait, and one of the department's three experts in forensic medicine, Dr Lucien Thibault who looked like an ageing choir boy. While the inspector and the sergeant set off for the rue Gosselin, the doctor headed for the emergency hospital to learn what he could concerning the condition of the victim, the nature of the wound and to make some estimate of what sort of implement had caused it. At the time, no one at police headquarters knew that the knife was still sticking in Daniel Renaut's body.

At the apartment in Fives, the police officers found twenty-five-year-old Martine Renaut, the sister of the injured man, and her fiancé, thirty-year-old Louis Devynck, still sitting side by side on the sofa, holding hands and looking stunned.

In response to the inspector's questions, both said that

they had no idea how Daniel had come to be stabbed, and that he had staggered into the apartment holding his hands over the handle of the knife. They had immediately called the emergency ambulance.

The inspector, who had heard a great many false statements in his life, immediately recognized this as one and instructed the sergeant to take Renaut and Devynck into custody and bring them to police headquarters. If they insisted on being charged, then they would be held on suspicion of wounding with a deadly weapon.

The sergeant led the two suspects down to the policecar, and the inspector took a quick look through the apartment. He found nothing of significance other than that someone, apparently a man, had been sleeping on top of the covers on the bed in one of the two bedrooms. The form of the body on the covers and the dent made by the head in the pillow were plainly visible.

At police headquarters, Martine Renaut and Louis Devynck were taken to separate interrogation rooms for questioning. In general their statements turned out to be identical. They were, however, going to have to repeat them many times, for the inspector had barely arrived back at the station when he received a call from the emergency hospital. It was Dr Thibault, who reported that Daniel Renaut had died while being carried to the operating room. The murder weapon, a bread knife, had been removed from the body, and he was bringing it back for possible identification and testing for fingerprints. The body was being sent to the police morgue for the autopsy.

The inspector did not pass the news of Daniel's death on to the two suspects, but simply resumed questioning. The longer of the two statements was that of Martine Renaut.

Like her brother and Louis Devynck, Martine had been born and raised in Fives, and had spent her entire life in the little apartment at 16 rue Gosselin. The apartment had originally belonged to her parents, Roger and Leontine Renaut, but Roger had died in 1965 and Leontine in 1973. Daniel, the only other child, had married that year and had moved to the little town of Mons-en-Baroeul.

The marriage had not turned out well and in 1977 he had obtained a divorce. Martine had not had much contact with him since he left home as his job as a long-distance truck driver kept him away a great deal of the time.

She had met Louis Devynck, a giant of a man with shoulder-length red hair, in September 1979 and, they having decided to marry in September 1980, he had moved into the apartment with her in January 1980. Devynck was employed as a mechanic in a garage in Lille.

Louis Devynck's statement agreed with that of Martine's in almost all details. His knowledge of her parents and her brother was, however, more sketchy. As he pointed out, all he knew of them was what she had told him. Although a native of Fives he had never met the elder Renauts before their death, and had only seen Daniel on one or two occasions. He had, he said, heard that Daniel drank rather more than was good for him and that he was known as a barroom brawler. He thought that it might be in some such brawl that Daniel had obtained his knife wound.

Although these were straightforward, reasonable and nearly identical statements, the inspector did not believe a word of them, but having insufficient evidence to bring any kind of a sustainable charge, he was left with no alternative other than to release both suspects with the warning that they were not to leave town or change their address without advising him.

Before the couple left police headquarters, the inspector informed Martine that her brother was dead and suggested that she make arrangements after completion of the autopsy for the transfer of the body from the police morgue to a funeral home for burial.

Martine had an unexpectedly violent reaction, broke down completely, became hysterical and had to be transferred to the police clinic for tranquillizing medication which was, however, so ineffective that she was forced to spend the remainder of the night there.

In the meantime, a contingent of plain-clothes investigators under the direction of Sergeant Dunoyer had gone to work in the Fives suburb. The case was now officially classed as homicide, and a correspondingly large assignment of manpower had been made for the purpose of the investigation.

Nothing unusual was discovered that evening other than that Devynck had been correct in his statement that Daniel Renaut drank more than was good for him and was given to brawling in bars. His divorce had apparently had a bad effect on him, for he had not worked regularly since and had spent his time mostly in taverns drinking or importuning casual acquaintances for small loans with which to finance further drinking.

In 1978 he had been a suspect in the robbery of a filling station, but had been released without charges for lack of evidence. It was not clearly determined how he had supported himself, but it was established that Martine and Louis had been lying when they said that they had seen little of Daniel. The neighbours reported that he had been constantly in and out of the apartment at 16 rue Gosselin.

A startling turn in the investigations took place on the following day when the sergeant appeared in the inspector's office with a large, ugly and brutal-looking man named Felix Martins. Mr Martins, said the sergeant, knew the Renauts and claimed that Martine was a prostitute and that her brother was her pimp. He was, he said, one of her customers.

This statement astonished the inspector very much for he thought he knew a prostitute when he saw one, and Martine Renaut did not look to him like a prostitute at all.

None the less, Martins stuck to his story.

'I met Daniel in a bar one night in June of 1978,' he said. 'We'd both been drinking and I was complaining that I didn't have much luck with the girls. He said if I wanted a nice girl he could fix me up with his sister. It would cost ten dollars and I might have to be a little rough with her because she was a masochist and liked to be slapped around. She'd play coy, but if I pushed her around a little, she'd come across.'

'Was Miss Renaut present in the bar when her brother told you this?' said the inspector incredulously. He had heard some remarkable things during the course of his career, but this was beginning to sound like something outstanding.

'No,' said Martins. 'She was home in her apartment at 16 rue Gosselin in Fives waiting for customers. All I had to do was go there, knock on the door and, when she opened up, push on in and say I'd come to get my money's worth. If she put up any objections I was to ignore them.'

'And did she put up any objections?' said the inspector.

'Fought like a tiger,' said Martins. 'She scratched me up pretty bad, but, for ten dollars, it was worth it. What can you get for ten dollars nowadays?'

'Not much for ten dollars, but you can get fifteen years for forcible rape,' said the inspector. 'She didn't bring charges against you?'

'Why should she?' said Martins. 'I told her I'd already given her brother the money and that if she wanted her cut she could ask him for it. After that, she sort of gave up.'

'That story is so weird that it has to be true,' said the inspector after Martins had left the office. 'My God! What was going on there with those people anyway?'

'Renaut appears to have been peddling his sister's hips without her knowledge or consent,' said the sergeant. 'I suspect that if we keep looking, we'll find others.'

He was not mistaken. Over the next few days, the police were able to turn up no less than four men in Lille who admitted to having paid Daniel Renaut for the privilege of having sex with his sister. The fee had been in all cases the same, ten dollars. So, too, had the sales pitch.

Said Jerome Cousty in his statement to the police, 'I was in this bar drinking and Renaut was standing next to me. I was telling him that I had a lot of trouble meeting girls and, when I did, I couldn't get anywhere with them. He said he knew where I could get a nice girl for not much money. She was a little fat, he said, but she was really good stuff and clean.

'I said, "How much?" and he said that ten dollars would be all right. I could give him the money.

'I said that I thought I would like to take a look at her before I paid because, although ten dollars really was a cheap price, I was living from unemployment compensation and I didn't have very much.

'He said that he didn't have her right there in his pocket, but that he could show me a picture. Then he pulled some pictures out of his pocket and gave them to me.

'I thought they would show her naked or something like that, but they were just ordinary photographs. One was in a living room, and the other one was outside at a picnic or something of that sort.

'Like he said, she was a little plump, but she wasn't bad looking and I figured that for ten dollars I couldn't go wrong.

'I lost my money though because she put up such a fight that I wasn't able to do it to her.'

'Didn't you ask for your money back from Daniel Renaut?' said the inspector.

Cousty, a thin, shabby sort of man with a week's growth of beard and very few teeth, nodded his head sadly.

'He said I wasn't forceful enough,' he said. 'Said she liked to be dominated by men. He said if I wasn't satisfied, I could have another go at her for free. It was pretty generous of him.'

'And did you?' said the inspector.

Cousty shook his head again. 'She hurt me pretty bad the first time,' he said. 'Scratched me all up and she hit me in the eye so that I couldn't see for a couple of days. I thought maybe I'd better not. It was better just to lose the ten dollars.'

Cousty said that Renaut had not told him that the girl was his sister, but the other two men, Gabriel Thonnes and Christian Desgagneaux, both claimed that he had.

As in the other cases they had encountered Daniel Renaut by chance in a bar, had spoken of their problems with women, and had been offered Martine's services for ten dollars. Both had been shown pictures of Daniel's sister and both had accepted the offer.

Desgagneaux, a stocky, powerful man, had overcome the girl's resistance by sheer force and, like Felix Martins, had literally raped her. Thonnes, actually the biggest and the strongest of the four, had been kneed so violently in the groin that he had had to beat a retreat, crawling away on hands and knees in great pain. As he was the last of Daniel's clients that the police were able to locate, it appeared that Martine had been becoming more efficient in defending herself.

'There are probably others, possibly a good many,' said the sergeant, 'whom we have not been able to locate or who are unwilling to admit that they were involved, and the only question that comes to my mind is why she didn't murder him before. She's obviously not a prostitute, and she was very definitely not in agreement with her brother's schemes for making money out of her.'

'Some of the clients must have realized it too,' said the inspector. 'That girl put up a savage resistance. Anyone with any brains at all would realize that she was not faking it for the sake of masochistic kicks. It's significant that all of the four who made statements are very simple men from the lowest class of society and nearly illiterate. Renaut could tell them something like that and they'd believe it.'

'Well, whatever the case, it's one of the most plausible motives for murder that I've ever heard,' said the sergeant. 'Do you want me to bring her in now and see what we can do about getting the confession?'

'Yes, I expect we have to,' said the inspector. 'I just hope that that red-haired boyfriend of hers doesn't try to provide her with an alibi.'

The inspector's hopes were in vain. Louis Devynck did provide his fiancée with an alibi, the best possible alibi.

He confessed to the murder.

'*Merde!*' swore the inspector. 'He's not guilty! He's protecting her!'

Louis Devynck continued calmly to dictate his confession. He had had the trouble with Daniel ever since he took up with Martine, he said. The man had continually hit him up for larger and smaller sums of money and, if he showed any disinclination to hand it over, had made coarse references to his paying the price for sleeping with Daniel's sister.

If insults did not work, then Daniel had come around and punched Martine in the head when Louis was absent working at his job. This had always produced results. Louis did not want Martine hurt and had paid.

On the afternoon of 2 August he had been at home in the apartment as it was Saturday and he was not working. Daniel had arrived at about three o'clock and had demanded twenty-five dollars, saying that he owed it to some men and that they were going to beat him up if he didn't pay.

Louis had refused saying that he had enough of paying,

and that if Daniel got beat up for not paying his debts it served him right.

Daniel had seized the mustard pot off the table and had made threatening motions with it as if he were going to attack the other man.

Devynck had responded by snatching up the bread knife which was also lying on the table.

Suddenly, Daniel had rushed at him with the mustard pot raised as if to strike a blow.

Devynck had no recollection of actually making a stabbing movement, but he must have been holding the knife out in front of him for, the next thing he knew, it was sticking in Renaut's stomach and the man was staggering backwards toward the sofa with his hands clasped over the handle.

Martine had not been in the room at the time, but Louis had called her, telling her that she should summon the emergency ambulance. She had immediately done so. He and she had then sat down on either side of the wounded man to support and comfort him until the ambulance arrived.

Although the inspector did not believe this confession, there were details in it that made it impossible to refute.

To begin with, the police already knew that the murder weapon came from the apartment in the rue Gosselin. The combination of food and grease traces on the handle matched precisely those found on other kitchen utensils in Martine Renaut's kitchen, and no other bread knife, basic for a French kitchen, had been found there.

Secondly, a broken mustard pot had been recovered from the garbage can and traces of mustard had been found on Renaut's clothing and hands, as well as similar traces on the living-room carpet and the sofa.

At the time the significance of the mustard stains was not clear and it was not known whether they were connected with the murder. Now, however, the confession by Louis Devynck brought out their importance and clearly demonstrated one thing. Whether guilty or not, Louis Devynck was in possession of precise knowledge of the details of the crime. It would be difficult to convince a jury that his confession was false and that he was not the murderer.

310

'And yet that is exactly what we are going to have to do unless we want to see an innocent man sent to prison,' said the inspector. 'I'm as certain that it was really Martine who was holding the knife as I have ever been of anything, but, if Devynck sticks to his confession, I don't see how we're going to prove it.'

'Well, maybe it was Devynck,' said the sergeant. 'After all, he had a strong motive too. Renaut was milking him for everything that he was worth and beating up his fiancée to boot. In either case, it was more manslaughter than murder. I don't think that either Devynck or Martine Renaut actually set out to murder Daniel. There was a quarrel, a brawl of some kind, Renaut grabbed up the mustard pot and made threatening gestures with it, and either Martine or Devynck picked up the kitchen knife to defend themselves. A jury isn't going to give either one of them very much for that.'

'They'd come down on him a good deal heavier than they would on her,' said the inspector. 'And he doesn't deserve it. He's merely being noble. The fact is, with his size and strength, he didn't need a knife to defend himself. He could have taken the mustard pot away from Renaut and stuffed it in his ear. The use of the knife was by someone smaller and weaker than Renaut trying to defend themselves, and that was Martine. She's guilty, and the thing that astounds me the most is why she doesn't admit it. I've told her myself that she's risking very little if she makes a confession, but she hasn't cooperated.'

'Yes, that is strange,' said the sergeant. 'She seems like a decent, respectable woman, and my impression is that she's genuinely attached to Devynck. I can't imagine why she would let him go to jail in her place, particularly when she'd get, at the most, a light sentence.'

The inspector could not imagine it either, but he was determined to avoid sending an innocent man to jail if he could help it, and he reluctantly decided on the use of harsher methods with the recalcitrant girl.

'Bring in Martine and bring in the four men who admit to having paid Daniel ten dollars for the privilege of having sexual relations with her,' said the inspector to the sergeant.

'We've got to shake her up a little. Get her off balance so that she'll make some kind of an admission rather than the denials that she's sticking with now.'

The sergeant did as he was told. Martine Renaut was brought to police headquarters where she was confronted with Jerome Cousty, Felix Martins, Gabriel Thonnes and Christian Desgagneaux.

She promptly went into a hysterical fit and was carried screaming and crying to the police clinic. She did not admit to anything.

'Pity that Louis Devynck isn't as emotional as Martine,' said the sergeant, returning to the inspector's office after having seen the girl to the clinic. 'If he got upset like that, he'd undoubtedly admit something, maybe the truth even.'

'Maybe we should try a confrontation between him and the four customers,' said the inspector, half jokingly. 'At this point, I'm about ready to try anything.'

There was a short, thoughtful silence in the office and then the sergeant said, 'Does he know about the customers and Daniel's money-making schemes? He didn't say a word about it in his confession. And yet you'd think that would be one of his strongest motives.'

'Maybe he doesn't want to embarrass her,' said the inspector. 'Maybe . . .'

'Maybe he doesn't know about them,' finished the sergeant. 'Maybe she never told him.'

'And she doesn't want him to know now,' said the inspector. 'If she were charged and tried . . .'

'. . . the story of her brother's activities on her behalf would become known,' said the sergeant. 'That's why she doesn't confess.'

'Yes,' said the inspector. 'That's why she doesn't confess.'

'But if Devynck already knew,' said the inspector, 'she wouldn't have any reason to hold back her confession any longer. How do we tell him?'

'Maybe we could let both of them listen to the tapes of the four customers' statements together,' suggested the sergeant. 'We could then separate them again for questioning. That way there wouldn't be any question but that everyone concerned was in possession of all the details.'

'All right, that sounds like a reasonable idea,' said the inspector, 'but I want complete security. There's no telling how either she or he will react to this and Devynck is a big man. I think it would be a good idea to have him handcuffed to something solid while he's listening to the tapes.'

The precaution was taken but proved unnecessary. Louis Devynck was a big and powerful man, but he was also gentle. His reaction to the taped statements of the four men to whom Daniel Renaut had sold his sister was not rage but sorrow.

Martine's reaction was almost one of relief.

'I was in a horrible position,' she said. 'If I didn't confess, Louis would have to go to jail in my place and, if I did, he would find out about all the dirty things that Daniel had done to me. I was afraid that he wouldn't want to have anything to do with me after that, and I didn't want to lose him.'

She need not have worried. Devynck was utterly convinced of her blamelessness in the matter, and even after she had confessed to the stabbing, continued to attempt to take the responsibility on to himself,

'He was not even present at the time,' said Martine. 'He had been working hard all week, and he was taking a nap in the bedroom at around three o'clock when Daniel appeared at the apartment. As usual he wanted money, and he said that three men were out to get him unless he could pay them the twenty-five dollars he owed them.

'I told him to keep quiet, that Louis was sleeping, and that he was not going to give him any more money. If he needed money, he should get a job and earn some.

'Daniel was furious and said a lot of filthy things about me and Louis. He started to shout that this was his home, that he had been born and raised here and that Louis was the intruder and should get out. He said he was moving in and that I could easily support both him and myself if I would be a little more reasonable with the friends he sent around.

'I lost my temper completely and started yelling at him too, but it only made him madder and he grabbed up a mustard pot from the table and started toward me.

'I picked up the bread knife and held it out in front of myself, but he kept on coming and he was sneering about how I thought I was going to defend myself with a bread knife.

'Louis had woken up and had come to the door of the bedroom, and I was not sure how much he had heard of what Daniel said.

'All of a sudden, he seemed to be right on top of me, and then I heard the mustard pot smash on the floor and he was reeling backwards holding his stomach. It was only when I looked at my hands and saw that I was not holding the knife any longer that I realized what had happened.

'I wasn't able to speak or do anything, but Louis immediately called the emergency ambulance.

'I'm sorry that I killed Daniel, but he was doing terrible things to me and I was afraid of him. Louis is completely innocent. He had nothing to do with it. He only came into the room a second or two before Daniel got stabbed.'

Martine Renaut was charged with unintentional homicide and ordered to be held for trial. Although she spent nearly nine months in pre-trial detention, it was the only time that she did serve, for, on 12 June 1981, she was found guilty of unintentional homicide with extremely extenuating circumstances and sentenced to four years' imprisonment suspended. She and Louis Devynck were married ten days after the conclusion of the trial.

It is difficult to say who was crazy in this case. However, for the sake of complete impartiality, it is probably best to include everybody.

Martine was certainly crazy to put up with her brother's exploitation of her admittedly plump but attractive body. Louis was crazy to keep paying off his future brother-in-law when a punch in the nose would have been more appropriate. Daniel was crazy to think that he could continue supporting himself by peddling his unwilling sister.

And the customers? Some were obviously none too bright, although there is a widespread belief within the male population that girls who get raped secretly enjoy it. They, perhaps, sincerely believed that Martine was having the time of her life.

Others were probably crazy like a fox. Considering inflation and the depreciation of the currency, ten dollars really was a very reasonable price.

5

WHY RAPE STRANGERS WHEN YOU HAVE A SISTER?

As there is no evidence that Daniel Renaut entered into retailing his sister before the death of their parents, it may be assumed that Martine had a reasonably happy childhood.

Even if she did not, she, at least, survived it. In the West German town of Menden, which is not one of the most attractive places in the world to live as it is on the edge of the great industrial and mining district of the Ruhr, Gabriele Goerke, more commonly known as Gaby, did not even make it through adolescence. At the time of her death she was just fifteen years old.

Nor had she been having it any too good for the year and a half preceding that Wednesday 8 July 1981 when she was sexually assaulted, strangled and buried in the forest not far from her home.

Gaby was, at the time, no longer living in her home, but in an orphans' asylum as were her thirteen- and eleven-year-old brothers, Georg and Peter, and her nine-year-old sister Petra. None of the children were, however, really orphans as both of their parents were still alive, but too preoccupied with the development of their own personalities to concern themselves with children.

Sigrid Goerke, a woman who took the counsels of the Women's Liberation promoters seriously, had just turned forty and, coming to the conclusion that her husband and five children did not constitute a meaningful relationship, liberated herself and went off to seek love, fame, fortune and anything else that was going.

Albert, her husband, took this badly. He was three years

older than his wife and had considered his domestic affairs more or less settled. Now, he suddenly found himself a single parent with a family of five. He could not even remarry immediately as Sigrid had not bothered to obtain a divorce and no one knew where she was.

There is a classic response to such situations and Albert made it. He started hitting the bottle. In no time at all, he was transformed from a hard-working, sober head of a family to a lolling drunk, and was promptly fired from his job.

The juvenile authorities stepped in and four of the Goerke children were sent to the orphanage. The oldest, Ralf, escaped by taking a drastic step. He married a seventeen-year-old girl the day after his eighteenth birthday, and having thus become responsible for her support could not be sent to the orphans' home. It was an arrangement satisfactory to all parties. Annette, the young bride, remained in school, and Ralf supported them both with his job as a heating plant installer.

Ralf was, therefore, in the clear and no longer concerned with the fortunes of the Goerke family, Sigrid was missing and Albert was drunk. This left Gaby, a pretty, affectionate teenager to hold what remained of the family together as well as she could. This she did conscientiously and, as the children were not separated in the orphanage, a sort of family life without parents began to emerge.

She was, therefore, greatly missed and, at her funeral on 12 July 1981, all of the Goerkes wept bitterly, and so did many of the nearly one hundred neighbours and well-wishers who attended. These non-family members who wept were women. The men did not weep, for their eyes, hot and bright with anger, were searching the crowd for strange faces. Lying in the trunks of several of the cars parked outside the cemetery gates were clubs and lengths of stout rope which they were hoping to be able to put to use.

If the man responsible for this funeral turned up and could be identified, there would be another funeral immediately.

The atmosphere was tense and Inspector Walter Fink of the Menden police Criminal Investigations Department was far from certain that his men, in plain clothes and scattered

316

throughout the crowd, would be able to control the situation if a likely suspect turned up. After all, this series of attacks on girls had been going on for over six months, and not a few were beginning to feel it was time to take matters into their own hands.

The inspector, a slight, neatly dressed man with a conservative haircut and the general appearance of a civil servant which was what he was, doubted that the killer would be rash enough to turn up at the funeral. If he was a local man he could hardly fail to know the temper and intentions of his fellow citizens, who had been growing increasingly restive ever since Friday, 30 January of the same year when seventeen-year-old Gerda Schaefer had acquired the dubious distinction of becoming the first-known victim in the worst series of sex crimes that the little town of fifty thousand had ever known.

Gerda also enjoyed a more desirable distinction. She was, in so far as was known, the only case in which the victim had escaped unscathed. It was thought that this was, perhaps, because it was the first attempt and the technique had not yet been perfected.

Gerda, a pretty, blonde girl who would have looked younger than her age had it not been for her rather startling physical development, had left school the preceding year and was employed as a salesgirl in one of the downtown shops.

The shop closed at six o'clock, and at approximately twenty minutes past six Gerda had been taking a short cut through a section of the forest park on the west side of the city.

She was within two hundred yards of her parents' home when something big and black loomed up out of the darkness behind her and a large, rough hand was slapped over the lower part of her face in what would become locally famous as the strangler's grip.

The strangler's grip was simple but effective. The last three fingers of the right hand were clasped tightly across the girl's mouth so that she could not open it or cry out, and the thumb and index finger grasped the nose, pressing the nostrils together and cutting off the victim's breath. At the

317

same time the elbow of the same arm pressed heavily against the girl's breast, holding her so tightly against her attacker's chest that she could scarcely move.

The prey thus immobilized, the rapist began with his left hand to unfasten Gerda's slacks and push them down over her hips. Her underpants followed and Gerda felt the cold air of the winter night on her naked thighs and belly.

But not on her buttocks. The man had dropped his own trousers and his hot flesh was pressing against her from behind.

He was, presumably, as later events would indicate, trying to enter her vaginally from the rear, but Gerda, who for a modern German girl of her age had had but little experience in such matters, thought that she was about to be raped anally, and this produced such a state of panic that, for a few moments, she was gifted with superhuman strength.

Wrenching herself out of the man's grip, she started to run, tripped on the slacks which had fallen down around her ankles and sprawled full length in the snow.

She would have been lost had not her attacker suffered the same fate. As would later be determined from the marks in the snow, he too had tripped over his pants and had fallen full length.

In the meantime, Gerda had scrambled to her feet and was running for home, holding up her slacks with both hands and screaming at the top of her voice.

The screams did it. By the time the people from the nearest houses came boiling out into the street, the would-be rapist had pulled up his trousers and was long since gone.

He had not lost his head either. He had run directly to the clean-swept, paved surface of the nearby road, and therefore it was impossible to tell which direction he had taken.

Gerda Schaefer was unharmed other than some damage to her nervous system and the Menden police, who were informed and carried out an immediate investigation, came to the conclusion that the attacker had been a transient. He could hardly be a local man for any local men with such tendencies were known and in the police files. Their whereabouts were checked for the time of the attack, and it was determined that none of them could have been reponsible for it.

In March the 13th fell on a Friday, an unlucky day for the police, but even more so for sixteen-year-old Ilse Diederich.

Unlike Gerda Schaefer, Ilse was still in school, but, like her, she was very pretty with long, brown hair reaching nearly to her waist and a figure which sometimes caused male observers to trip over their own feet. Being a modern, liberated girl, she was not a virgin.

Ilse was not passing through a stretch of forest but walking along a narrow, deserted street in the heart of town at approximately four-thirty in the afternoon on her way home from school.

The strangler had apparently been hiding in a small court-yard leading off the street and, as Ilse passed the entrance, he emerged, ran swiftly and silently up behind her, and applied his strangler's grip with such force that the girl briefly lost consciousness.

Although delightfully well built, Ilse was not a large girl and he lifted her easily, carried her into the courtyard, hoisted up her skirt, pulled down her panties and raped her, entering vaginally but from the rear.

As far as Ilse could estimate later, the whole process lasted only a few minutes, and she had scarcely had time to grasp what was happening when she found herself sitting on the cobbles of the courtyard with her pants down and the rapist gone.

As he had held her nose and mouth shut through the attack, it was a few minutes before she could regain her breath, but then she began to yell, not so much because she was frightened but because she was indignant. She had had a confused impression of her assailant and she thought that he was one of her classmates.

As it turned out, he was not. Every male pupil in Ilse's school was interrogated and their whereabouts for the time of the rape checked. By good fortune all of them could be cleared. Ilse had been mistaken.

Aside from a slightly sore nose and mouth, Ilse was not injured, but the rape had been fully consummated. An examination by her family physician produced evidence of forceable entry in the form of a number of minor haircuts on the labia major, and enough semen within the vagina to establish that the rapist belonged to blood group A.

The news of the rape went quickly through the little town and aroused great indignation, but less concern with the general public than it did with the police. The Schaefer case had not received much publicity, and few persons knew that the details of the attack were very similar to those concerning the rape of Ilse Diederich. The police did.

'I think it's obvious that what we have here is the beginning of a series,' said Inspector Fink, mulling over matters with his assistant, Detective-Sergeant Boris Schmidt, in the small office which they shared.

'Well, it shouldn't go on very long,' said the sergeant, who was big, bull-shouldered and had a rather ruddy complexion. 'A stranger in Menden stands out like a cow in a coffee shop.'

'I doubt now that it is a stranger,' said the inspector. 'A stranger wouldn't know the downtown area well enough to know about that courtyard, or to know that the buildings around it are used for warehouses and that there's normally hardly anyone there. One thing's certain though. We know he's young; so young that the Diederich girl took him for one of her classmates. We can run a check on whether anyone has an overgrown sixteen- or seventeen-year-old boy visiting them, but I suspect, in the end, we'll find that he's local himself. Assuming, of course, that we ever find him at all.'

'We certainly should,' said the sergeant. 'Menden isn't that big. Practically everybody here knows everybody else. Somebody will notice something suspicious and report in.'

'Then, I wish they'd do it quickly,' said the inspector, 'because he's got away with it twice now and he's sure to try again.'

The inspector was a good prophet. On the evening of Tuesday, 21 April, eighteen-year-old Liselotte Goebels went to the cinema. The film finished a little before eleven o'clock and Liselotte set off for home.

Menden is a town where there is not a great deal of night life and there were few persons on the street. Oddly, it was just while several persons were in sight, although not nearby, that the strangler stepped out of the shadows of a yard surrounding a private home and took her in his now famous grip.

Liselotte, who had heard all about the Menden strangler and who was anxious to resume breathing, offered no resistance.

Encouraged by this, the strangler pulled her behind a screen of bushes forming a hedge along one side of the house, shifted his grip rather awkwardly, and, having lifted her skirt, raped her from the front after Liselotte had pulled down her own pants. She was a practical-minded girl and, as she later told Inspector Fink, it was bad enough being raped without having your clothes ruined as well.

Although she reported the incident to the police, the rather matter-of-fact tone of the report caused the inspector to wonder how many other such cases there might have been that were not reported at all. Rape has become so common in many parts of the world today that, unless the victim is actually injured, it is often not reported.

Perhaps, just because she had retained such a cool head throughout the procedure, Liselotte provided the best description of the rapist to date. He was, she said, taller than average, above six feet or very close to it. Slim and athletically built, without beard or moustache, he wore the sort of soup-bowl, trimmed-mop haircut affected by some teenagers. He was, she thought, very young as he had been amazingly quick on the trigger, barely penetrating her before he arrived at his climax.

The description was largely an expansion and refinement of descriptions which had already been received from Gerda Schaefer and Ilse Diederich. There was no question but that it had been the same man in all three cases, although the police were scarcely better off than they had been before.

Menden is a small place, but it is not small enough for the police to arrest and check the alibis of every tall youth with a soup-bowl haircut.

'So we wait for the next one,' said Sergeant Schmidt. 'How many do you think he'll manage before he makes a slip?'

321

'Who knows?' said the inspector, shrugging his shoulders. 'There have been series like this that went on for years and, in some cases, the fellow was never caught. He died of old age or lost interest in sex or something, and the series just stopped of itself.'

'If you can rely on the descriptions,' said the sergeant, 'you and I will both be retired before this one dies of old age or loses interest in sex either. Well, at least he doesn't seem to have injured anyone very seriously so far.'

'He will,' said the inspector grimly. 'He will.'

Once again, the inspector proved to be a good prophet. On 15 May which, like the dates of two of the three preceding crimes, with a Friday, seventeen-year-old Maryse Lang was raped and strangled unconscious at approximately six-fifteen in the evening as she was walking home from work. Unlike the other victims in the series, she fought savagely with her assailant.

Miss Lang, a pretty, rather fragile-looking girl, was a member of a strict religious sect and she was not supposed to engage in sexual activity of any kind until after marriage, if then. In theory, death was to be preferred before dishonour.

It had come very close to being both. There was now no living soul in Menden who did not know that there was a dangerous rapist in their midst, and the police had repeatedly warned that victims were to offer no resistance, but to try to memorize whatever details they could of their attacker's appearance which might help in tracing his identity. The theory was that a victim was better off raped and alive than raped and dead.

Maryse Lang had disagreed, and she had nearly paid for it with her life. When she had begun to kick and struggle, and had actually managed to get her mouth open enough to bite one of the rapist's fingers, he had ceased his efforts to remove her underwear and had brought up his left forearm across her throat, holding it there with such force that the circulation of blood to the brain was cut off and she lost consciousness.

When she came to the rapist was gone, her underpants were around one ankle, and her throat was so bruised that she could speak in nothing louder than a sort of squeaky whisper.

There was no question but that she had been raped. Prior to the attack she had been a virgin, and her thighs and pubic area were covered with the blood from her burst hymen.

Maryse pulled on her pants, straightened her skirt and staggered off to the police station, a bare three hundred yards away, to file her charges in a painful whisper.

It was necessary for her to be hospitalized the following day, as she had received such a shock from her experience that she was developing suicidal tendencies.

Maryse Lang was unable to offer any description of her attacker at all. Whether this was because she had actually not seen him or because her frightened mind had pushed the details of the encounter down into her subconscious where it was no longer available could not be said, but her doctor suspected that it was the latter.

'Well, he's hurt one,' said Sergeant Schmidt. 'You've been one hundred per cent right so far. What's going to happen now?'

'He's going to kill somebody,' said the inspector.

And on Wednesday, 8 July 1981 he did.

It was suspected or, at least, feared that same evening when Gaby Goerke failed to return to the orphanage for dinner. The orphanage was not a closed institution and the children were allowed to go out alone if they were old enough, or in the company of other children if they were not.

Gaby had gone out at approximately five o'clock in the afternoon without mentioning where she was going to anyone, and it had been assumed by those who saw her go that she was going for a walk. The weather was warm, sunny, the height of the West German summer, and not only Gaby but a great many other people were taking walks in the woods which surround Menden.

When, however, Gaby failed to return to the home in time for dinner which was at seven o'clock, her brothers and sister became exceedingly anxious and asked permission to go and look for her.

The permission was granted and not only the Goerke children, but many of the other children and a number of the adult supervisors set off into the woods searching for some trace of the missing girl.

Gaby had been popular and she had not been the sort of girl who could be expected to run away from the orphanage, certainly not as long as her brothers and sister were there. When, by nine o'clock, no trace of her had been found, the director of the orphanage called the police.

Inspector Fink and Sergeant Schmidt were, of course, off duty at this hour, but they hurried to the orphanage from their homes and spoke to the children there. They were in hopes that Gaby might have given some hint that she was planning on spending the night with a boyfriend. The girls of her own age in the orphanage claimed that, from what she had told them confidentially, this would not have been impossible.

She had, however, mentioned no such thing, and had actually acted rather strangely and secretively, although she was normally a girl who confided freely in her friends.

The inspector thought that the reports of strange and secret behaviour were probably the result of the fact that she was now missing. Had she not been, the strangeness and secretiveness would not have occurred to anyone.

What frightened him, however, and what had brought him out of his home in the middle of the evening, was the knowledge that at least four other girls had been attacked in Menden during the past six months and, although Gaby was a year younger than the youngest-known victim so far, it was all too possible that she had become the fifth in the series. She was pretty, well built, and the strangler had never yet asked to see one of his victim's birth certificates.

Moreover, it was now known that he was capable of violence; dangerous violence which could end in the death of the victim. It would not have required much more pressure on Maryse Lang's throat to have sent her to the morgue rather than the hospital.

The only optimistic aspect was that it seemed hardly likely that Gaby would have resisted. She was almost certainly not a virgin, and she did not belong to any religious sect which had strong feelings about sexual intercourse. She knew about the

324

Menden strangler and she knew the advice of the police. She was a self-possessed girl who was not easily frightened. It was scarcely probable that she would have fought with the strangler and, in so far as anyone knew, he did not deliberately harm a victim who did not resist.

It was by now completely dark and the searchers had all returned to the orphanage. They had found no trace of Gaby, but some of the children said they had seen a strange, shaggy man running through the woods.

Had the inspector believed this story, he would have sent police parties out into the woods yet that night, but he did not. If Gaby Goerke had fallen a victim to the strangler, it had been hours before any of the search parties went out, and it was extremely improbable that the murderer would still have been running about out there.

In the past, his practice had been to leave the scene as rapidly as possible.

The inspector, therefore, suspended operations until first light the following morning which, it being summer, was at around six-thirty. At this time, parties of police and firemen plus members of civilian volunteers moved out into the woods and began systematically searching for the missing girl.

At eight-thirty, breakfast at the orphanage having been finished, the older children were given permission to join in the search and it was the children who, on the afternoon of Thursday, 9 July, found her.

Gaby lay buried beneath six inches of soft earth and leaf mould less than a hundred yards from her old home. One of the boys running back toward the orphanage had put his foot squarely into the soft earth of her grave and had gone head over heels. When he picked himself up and looked to see what had tripped him, he could see the material of the girl's dress through the dirt which he had kicked up.

The police were immediately notified and Inspector Fink and Sergeant Schmidt hurried to the scene. The supervisors from the orphanage had quickly herded the children away from the shallow grave and the body had not been uncovered.

So far, there was no certainty that it was Gaby in the grave, but it was a girl, and it would have been strange if it had been someone else.

It was Gaby Goerke as the Menden coroner, Doctor Martin Hofmann, quickly determined once he had brushed the dirt away from the child's face.

She lay on her back, her hands folded over her breasts, and her legs close together, but with her skirts raised so that she was naked from the navel down. She was wearing her knee-length stockings and shoes, but her underpants were missing. They were later found beneath the body when it was lifted out of the grave.

'The cause of death? The cause of death?' exclaimed the inspector in an untypical state of excitement. 'What was the cause of death?'

'Give me a minute,' said the coroner. He was an elderly man with a white moustache and little hair and, although he was very thorough, he was not very fast.

'All I want to know is was she strangled?' said the inspector. 'Was it the strangler?'

'It could be,' said the doctor cautiously. 'There's no blood or any wounds on the body that I can see. Of course, she may have received a blow over the head which is concealed by the hair or . . .'

'How soon can I have a preliminary autopsy report?' said the inspector.

'Not before you get the body over to the morgue,' said the coroner in mild reproof. 'I'll begin immediately you can let me have her.'

The inspector could, however, not let the body be sent to the morgue immediately as he was anxious that the technicians from the small police laboratory go over the area thoroughly before it was moved. He did not know what they might find, but, if there was anything, he wanted to be sure they found it.

His caution was rewarded. The technicians found a button. As it was buried beneath the earth with the corpse, and as it did not belong to any article of her clothing, it was possible that it belonged to the murderer. It was a shiny, black button, and the technicians thought that it might have come from a man's trousers; not the fly, but a button closing a hip pocket or something of that nature.

The button was slipped into a small plastic sack and taken to police headquarters where, to the surprise and delight of everyone concerned, it was found to have part of a fingerprint on it; or rather, said the technicians, a thumb print. The button had apparently been one to a hip pocket and the owner of the trousers had rested his thumb on it while unbuttoning the pocket. There was not enough of it to make possible a positive identification, but it could serve as a useful indication in the event of an arrest.

An arrest was made even before Doctor Hofmann had completed the autopsy. The children from the orphanage had been right. There had been a man running through the woods that afternoon. He *was* shaggy, and he had been seen and recognized by other witnesses.

His name was Ferdinand Sachs and he was considered by the Menden police to be Menden's most dangerous sex criminal, the Strangler not counted.

Sachs was twenty-four years old and had a record of a long string of offences against female children and very young girls. As a suspect he was far from ideal, for he was not known to have ever attacked a victim as old as Gaby Goerke to say nothing of the still older girls in the series.

On the other hand, Sachs was a trifle over six feet tall, wore his hair in a shaggy, uncombed mop reaching nearly to his shoulders, and he had been in the woods at the time that Gaby Goerke was murdered.

This time was, according to the coroner, a little after six in the evening of 8 July. The girl had not been strangled, but smothered, the nose and mouth having been held shut until she died of lack of air. It had been a rather slow, painful death, and it was precisely the sort of death which would result from a continued application of the strangler's grip.

On the subject of sexual molestation the coroner was less definite. There were, he said, certain indications that penetration might have taken place, and the fact that the body had been found with the genitals exposed tended to confirm that there had been some sort of sexual activity. There were, however, no traces of semen in the vagina.

Finally, the autopsy report concluded with the remark that there was no indication of a struggle, and Gaby had apparently not made the slightest effort to defend herself. The coroner found this strange.

So, too, did the inspector. He was wondering whether he was looking for one man or two. Was the murderer of Gaby Goerke the same man who had attacked Gerda Schaefer, Ilse Diederich, Liselotte Goebels and Maryse Lang? Or was it someone who had taken advantage of the publicity to fake a crime in the series?

Ferdinand Sachs swore by everything holy that he had had nothing to do with the murder of Gaby Goerke. He was, he said, incapable of sexual arousal by a girl who was already past puberty. The only thing that excited him was a female child under the age of ten and, even with her, he was capable of nothing more than masturbation.

The inspector would naturally have paid no attention to such a declaration had it not been for the fact that it was supported in the records by the statements of the psychologists and psychiatrists who had examined and treated Sachs at the various times of his arrests. According to what they had said, he was no more capable of sex with a fifteen-year-old girl than he would have been with a fifteen-year-old hippopotamus.

However, it appeared that the murderer of Gaby Goerke had not had sex with her and, if he had not, why had he killed her?

There seemed only one possible answer. If Gaby Goerke had been killed by the Menden strangler and had not been raped by him, the reason might be that she had known his identity. Perhaps she had surprised him attacking another girl in the forest and he had eliminated her because she was a witness who could identify him.

But in that case, what of the victim? Had he eliminated her too?

He could not have because there were no suitable females

328

missing for that date in Menden. If Gaby had known who he was, she had known it through some other means.

The inspector ordered a careful tracing of every male with whom Gaby was known to have come into contact. What he wanted was a list of all those who stood close to six feet tall, were young and sported a soup-bowl haircut. When the list was completed to the satisfaction of Sergeant Schmidt and handed in, there was only one name on it.

The inspector nearly threw the sergeant out of the office. The name was Ralf Goerke.

The sergeant was, however, quite serious. He had checked very carefully and there was no one else answering to that description whom Gaby had known.

Charging a hard-working young man who had only recently married with the sex murder of his own sister was not something that the inspector was prepared to undertake without material evidence, and discreet efforts were made to obtain a set of Goerke's fingerprints, not an easy matter as he had no criminal record.

This was, however, eventually accomplished, and the police identification experts said that the partial print on the button taken from Gaby's grave was identical to that of Ralf's right thumb.

It was not as much evidence as the inspector would have liked to have, but he suspected that it was all that he was likely to get, and two days after Gaby's funeral her brother Ralf was arrested and charged with the murder.

He began by denying it, but a search of his apartment produced a pair of trousers with a button from the hip pocket missing. Other buttons not missing matched the one in the possession of the police and, confronted with this evidence, Ralf confessed not only to the murder of his sister but to being the Menden Strangler as well.

He was not very clear as to why he had begun raping young girls when he had an equally young, attractive and affectionate wife at home, but he explained Gaby's murder by saying that she had recognized him from the descriptions given by the victims in the press and had tried to persuade him to stop. Fearful that she might expose him, he had strangled her to death. He denied any sexual motive to the crime, and even denied having removed his sister's underpants.

Held under observation for over a year Ralf Goerke was eventually found competent to stand trial, and in September of 1982 was sentenced to ten years' imprisonment. This might seem mild to some, but it was the maximum possible under German juvenile law. Ralf was, after all, only eighteen.

Inspector Fink is keeping his file handy. A juvenile sentenced to ten years in Germany rarely serves as much as half of that so Ralf can expect to be returned to society before he has achieved his twenty-fifth birthday. His wife, dismayed by his extra-marital activities, has divorced him and, after five or six years in prison, Ralf may feel that he is in need of sexual relief.

If so, he knows how to get it.

6

NO RECORD, BUT A GOOD TRY

As series criminals go, Ralf Goerke was not very impressive. Although he may well have attacked more girls than the number with which he was charged, his only real claim to originality lay in the murder and possible sexual molestation of his sister.

Of course, Ralf is still young and, as he will soon be out of prison, there is no telling what prodigies he may perform in the future.

One thing is certain. He forms a part of an old tradition extending back to the initiation of criminal record keeping in Germany. The Germans are a serious, extremely thorough people and some of the longest, most gruesome series of crimes have taken place and are still taking place there. Although the police are also serious, thorough people, not all of these crimes are solved.

In fact, it is not always known that a crime has been committed. Like any modern state, Germany loses track of a great many persons every year. Many of these are young people. The ties of the family having been loosened and the authority of the parents usurped by the civil servants of the state; even children of pre-pubertal age go off to live in communes, join the drug scene, take up prostitution or engage in other activities typical of liberated, unsupervised youth. As they may suspect that their parents will not approve of this concept of freedom, they not infrequently fail to tell them where they are.

Sometimes, they cannot. They are delighting unwillingly the customers of some Middle Eastern or North African brothel in return for room and board or they are dead.

In a society containing substantial numbers of disturbed

331

persons at liberty, girls and young women wandering about the streets alone are an easy prey and, with apologies to the believers in equality between the sexes, there are few females capable of withstanding the unexpected attack of an insane, adult male, possibly armed, and with every intention of obtaining sexual gratification by any means, murder included.

Even for a full-grown woman, there is little hope of escape or successful defence. How much less then for a child: a small delicately built, ten-year-old girl?

The four-pound hammer caught ten-year-old Ulrike Hellmann only a glancing blow on the back of the head, but the pretty little girl went sprawling, the blood from her split scalp welling into the thick, blonde hair with the cute fringe across the forehead.

Like a spider pouncing on a fly, the bearded man was upon her, rolling her on to her back, jerking her short skirt up around her waist and ripping away her panties. Kneeling, he fumbled with his own clothing.

It was 15 May 1981, a glorious, spring day, and Ulrike had been walking home from school along a little trafficked secondary road outside the city of Mainz, West Germany. The man in the red R4 Renault had passed her, slowed, stopped the car and, jumping out, had come bounding back toward her with the hammer in his hand.

Ulrike had turned and ran, but it had been too late. She had been overtaken and knocked down.

But not out. She was still conscious and she began to fight.

Like most young girls in West Germany, Ulrike had been taught not to resist a rapist. The theory was that it was better to be raped and alive than raped and dead. However, theories were one thing and practice was something else. Panic-stricken, convinced that the man was going to kill her, Ulrike Hellmann fought not so much for her virginity as for her life.

There were, at least, a dozen other girls and women who could have told her that she was quite right. The ones who were still alive, of course. Nine of them were not. Whether those who had died had resisted or not no one could say with certainty, but the three who had survived had. Ulrike was the unlucky thirteenth.

The series was believed to have begun on 17 April 1975, at a place less than thirty miles to the south of where Ulrike Hellmann was flopping like a hooked fish under the body of the rapist. The time had been approximately nine o'clock in the evening and Mrs Lilian Dresch, an attractive dark-haired housewife of twenty-eight, had been waiting at a deserted bus stop in Mannheim-Neckarau, a small, residential community.

A rather slight, unkempt-looking man with a full, black beard and moustache had parked his Volkswagen near the bus stop and got out.

Suspecting nothing, Mrs Dresch had not turned around as he walked behind her.

Suddenly an arm was thrown around her chest, a hand crushed her right breast and the man's other hand, coming over her right shoulder drove the blade of a long, sharp knife into her throat.

By some miracle, the point of the knife struck exactly the hard knot of the larynx and failed to penetrate.

Lilian Dresch let out a piercing scream, kicked backward and managed to tear herself loose. For a few seconds the bearded man and his screaming victim stood facing each other. Then, apparently deciding that the screams were going to attract attention, he turned and ran back to the Volkswagen. By the time that people from the neighbouring houses had arrived he was gone.

Lilian Dresch was taken to the hospital and treated for a minor throat wound. She had escaped, but it would be several years before she could bring herself to wait alone at a bus stop again.

The next victim in this series, although no one at that time knew that it was a series, was less fortunate.

On the evening of 9 June 1975, Monika Sorn, a pretty seventeen-year-old secondary-school student, failed to return to her parents' home in the village of Hemsbach, roughly a dozen miles from Mannheim-Neckarau. As the unexplained absence of a pretty, young girl with no tendency to run wild was logically cause for alarm, her parents immediately notified the police.

Search parties were organized, and Monika's body was

found shortly before midnight of the same day. It was lying in a field near one of the roads leading to the village, the skull crushed by a heavy, blood-smeared stone which lay nearby. Nearly all of her clothing had been torn away, and the autopsy would show that she had been raped but, presumably while unconscious or after death. The sperm recovered from her vagina showed that her rapist belonged to blood group AB, subgroup two. Otherwise, there were no clues as to his identity. The stone was too rough to retain fingerprints.

The usual check of known sex offenders in the area was made, but without results. There were plenty of sex offenders in the area because the courts normally permitted their release after short periods of psychiatric treatment which it was believed had cured them of their abnormal tendencies and converted them into useful members of society. In some cases, the cures had to be repeated and even repeated again, but the pertinent authorities did not become discouraged. With time, modern psychology would succeed even in the most stubborn cases.

As a result of this policy the police were forced to maintain files on a great many sex offenders and it was often fairly easy to determine who had raped whom by reference to the *modus operandi*. Sex psychopaths are creatures of habit and certain elements of their crimes tend to remain constant.

The only conclusion that the police could draw in the case of the murder of Monika Sorn was that, if this was a sex psychopath, it was a new one who was just starting out in the business. There was no recent record in the police files of a local murderer-rapist who beat in his victim's skull with a rock and then raped her while she was dying or already dead.

Although the next murder took place only a little more than three months later, it was not immediately connected to the murder of Monika Sorn because the scene was the village of Elmendingen near Bruchsal, which is approximately as far south of Mannheim as Mainz is to the north.

On 13 September 1975, eleven-year-old Liane Woessner, a vivacious, dark-haired girl, somewhat prematurely developed for her age, set off on her bicycle to visit her aunt in Bruchsal.

When her aunt, who was expecting her, became concerned by the fact that she had not arrived and called her parents over the telephone, it was discovered that she was missing and the police were notified.

The Bruchsal police found Liane Woessner rather quickly. She had only been dead for a few hours. Like Monika Sorn, she lay in a field near a secondary road leading from Elmendingen to Bruchsal and, like Monika Sorn, her skull had been smashed. Not with a stone this time, however, but with what the autopsy report described as a heavy, blunt object; probably a hammer or the back of a hatchet.

However prematurely developed she might have been, Liane had been a virgin and the rapist had had much difficulty in penetrating her, cutting himself in the process and leaving traces of his own blood on her thighs and sex organs. From this and from the semen recovered from her vagina, it was possible to determine that his blood group was AB, subgroup two. It was not an important clue. Many persons have this same blood group.

None the less, it was the only clue that the police recovered. Liane's bicycle was found in the ditch and her murderer had presumably thrown it there, but he had not left any fingerprints on it.

Perhaps because it was his first year, 1975 was an exceptionally busy time for the man who would eventually become known as the Hammer Murderer. His success rate was, however, only fifty per cent as he had not yet developed the deadly efficiency which would characterize his later activities.

The final crime by the Hammer Murderer for 1975 took place three days before Christmas in the charming little town of Weinheim, scarcely more than a village but boasting no less than three large and imposing castles in comparatively good repair, and less than ten miles from Mannheim with which it is connected by an electric inter-urban street-car service.

On the afternoon of the day, seventeen-year-old Susanne Bach, an attractive, dark-haired salesgirl in one of the local stores, was passing through a strip of city park when a man with a beard came up behind her and without warning struck her savagely twice on the head with a heavy hammer.

Susanne was knocked unconscious and fell forward on her face, but there were other pedestrians in the immediate vicinity and the Hammer Murderer ran off without doing anything else.

Susanne was taken to the hospital where she was treated for concussion. Her skull was, fortunately, not fractured, and she recovered with no ill effects other than a compulsive tendency to look over her shoulder whenever she was passing through a public park.

The Hammer Murderer had concluded his first year with two successful rapes and murders and two failures on both counts. It was not a bad beginning, but he may have been discouraged by the failures because it was not until autumn of the following year that another crime occurred which would eventually be attributed to him.

However, a considerable amount of time would pass before anyone realized that a murder had taken place.

Eighteen-year-old Monika Pfeifer was reported missing on 11 October 1976 by her parents, but the police in her hometown of Mainz did not suspect homicide. Rather, they thought her a possible victim of white slavers.

The white slave dealers are quite active in Central Europe and, particularly, West Germany which has a high percentage of attractive girls. Monika was more than attractive. She was beautiful with a stunning figure and long, naturally blonde hair which hung nearly to her waist, precisely the type that would fetch a top price in any North African or Middle Eastern harem or brothel.

The police, therefore, concentrated their investigation on the activities of white slavers in the area, and eventually apprehended several who were given short jail sentences and deported. Although they admitted to having traded mostly in blonde girls, none of them could recall the name Pfeifer, but this was not thought strange as they had not been interested in the girls' names in any case. Monika remained missing without trace.

Until 6 January 1977, at least. On the afternoon of that date, she was literally fished out of the River Rhine.

Although the famous Rhine now is and has been for some time little more than an open industrial sewer, optimistic Germans still attempt to fish its murky depths. One of these optimists sitting on the muddy banks of the river to the west of Mainz thought that he had hooked the biggest catfish in Europe, but it was Monika. The fish hooks had become tangled in her hair, which was about all there was to become tangled in as her body was completely naked.

Considering that she had spent the entire winter in the river, the body was in remarkably good condition and her parents had no difficulty in identifying her. The autopsy showed that her skull had been crushed with a heavy object, presumably a hammer, at about the same time that she had disappeared, and there was reason to believe that she had been raped. Although unusual for a beautiful, eighteen-year-old West German girl, Monika had been a virgin and her hymen had been ruptured either before or after death.

Coincidentally, while this autopsy was being carried out on 7 January, one day after the discovery of the body, a twenty-two-year old university student in Mainz was having a frightening experience.

It was approximately four o'clock on that afternoon and Barbara Kiel, dark, pretty and twenty-two years of age, had left the university, crossed the university parking lot and was walking down a narrow, deserted road with a stone wall along one side.

Presently, a Volkswagen came up behind her and deliberately attempted to crush her against the stone wall.

The man behind the windscreen and the sole occupant of the car had a full, black beard and moustache and looked, she thought, rather young. She did not, however, have much time to look at him as the bumper of the car broke both her legs and knocked her to the ground.

A girl with considerable presence of mind, Barbara Kiel huddled up to the base of the wall as close as she could. This prevented the driver from running over her and, after a few frustrated attempts, he gave up and drove away.

Barbara Kiel was eventually found by passers-by and taken to the hospital where she recovered from her injuries. Although she did not know it, she enjoyed an enviable distinction. She was the last-known victim that the Hammer Murderer failed to kill.

He did not fail on 28 March 1977, when he attacked one of Barbara's fellow students at the University of Mainz, twenty-three-year-old Sylvia Lauterbach, a lovely, dark-haired girl who had been walking along a path through the fields in the direction of the village of Bretzenheim where she planned to visit a friend.

Her corpse was found the following morning a dozen yards from the field path. She had been stripped naked with the exception of her stockings and shoes, raped, and her head had been crushed by multiple blows of what was believed to be a heavy hammer.

There was less questions this time that the murder weapon had been a hammer, for it had been driven far enough into the girl's head to leave a print of its shape. The police laboratory in Mainz estimated it to be a four-pound hammer of a type used in heavy metalwork and masonry. Four short dark hairs were found under Sylvia's fingernails, and the laboratory said that these came from a man's beard. Otherwise, they found nothing.

Like all of the preceding cases, the murder of Sylvia Lauterbach remained unsolved for lack of possible leads to investigate. Her circle of social and other contacts was routinely investigated, but produced no plausible suspect.

The police had not thought it would. Most murders are committed by persons known to the victim and so are most rapes, but, if the two are combined, it is more frequently a stranger who has chosen the victim because of personal attraction or convenience.

Moreover, when such a sexually motivated murder takes place it is rarely an isolated incident. The abnormality which led to one rape and murder will lead to others, and many elements of each succeeding case will remain identical as they are essential to the satisfaction of the murderer's emotional needs.

It was, therefore, the Mainz police Criminal Investigations

Department which first realized that a series was underway and took steps to assemble the files on unsolved sex murders or attempted murders in the southern half of Germany.

'Between the beginning of October last year and the end of March this year, we have had three cases of attacks on young women in the Mainz area,' said Inspector Walter Herschel, chief of the Mainz homicide squad, speaking to his plump, blond, and rather expressionless assistant, Detective-Sergeant Mark Schultz. 'The Kiel case is a little different than the other two, but it's the same sort of vicious attack. I think it's clear that what we have here is a series. Tell the records section I want a computer printout on all similar *modus operandi* in the south of the country for the past three years.'

A few years earlier, this would have represented a monumental task for the records section, but, for the computer, it was only a matter of hours before it came up with the files of Monika Sorn, Liane Woessner, Susanne Bach and, because of the Volkswagen and beard in the Barbara Kiel case, Lilian Dresch.

'Uh-huh. Just what I thought,' said the inspector, adjusting his thick, heavy body in the chair and squinting with small, sharp, deep-set eyes at the computer printout. 'It's a series. Is this all?'

'All the unsolveds,' said the sergeant. 'Records has the computer still searching for parallel cases where the identity of the murderer or attempted murderer is known. They needn't have all been unsolved.'

'Let's hope they haven't,' said the Inspector. 'Otherwise, all we can do is wait for him to kill the next one.'

It was not a long wait. The computer was unsuccessful in turning up a valid suspect and on 29 April 1977, twenty-one-year-old Marie-Therese Majer was raped and murdered. She had been walking along a country road near Schriesheim, a village outside the town of Heidelberg and almost equidistant from Weinheim and Mannheim. Like her fellow victims, she had been stripped naked, forcibly raped, and her skull had been smashed in with a heavy hammer, although not in that order.

It was the Hammer Murderer's invariable custom to begin by smashing in his victim's skull. Only when the girl was unconscious or dead did he proceed to removing her clothing and raping her. Whether his earlier attempts had shown that girls were more easily stripped and raped if they were unconscious or dead or whether he was incapable of sex with a living, conscious victim was not known.

The inspector pounced on the Marie-Therese Majer case, which he saw as an opportunity to end the bloody career of the Hammer Murderer before he claimed still more victims. A huge detachment of plain-clothes officers under the command of Sergeant Schultz was rushed to Schriesheim with orders to leave no stone unturned in the effort to uncover any possible clue to the identity of the murderer and reinforcements arrived from Heidelberg, Mannheim and Weinheim.

The operation was a total failure. As usual, the only traces of his presence which the Hammer Murderer had left behind were the marks of the deadly hammer on the head of the victim and his semen in her vagina. It showed that he had blood group AB, subgroup two, but the police already knew that.

Copies of all the records of the known or suspected cases, the autopsy reports where pertinent, statements of survivors, and the results of the investigations undertaken in each case had now been assembled in Inspector Herschel's office where they were being studied to see whether something which had failed to provide a clue in one case might not serve to provide a clue in another. So far, all that had been determined was that there was a near certainty that all of the cases were the work of one man, that he was young, wore a dark beard and moustache, was rather slightly built and drove a Volkswagen, either dark grey or blue. He never said a word or made a sound, but struck immediately and without warning.

Once again, the efforts of the investigators failed to provide a lead which could be followed up, and the inspector had no recourse but to sit back and wait for the next case. This time it was going to be a long wait.

On 21 April 1979, just eight days short of two years after the death of Marie-Therese Majer, fifteen-year-old Gudrun

Thomé, a secondary-school pupil who lived with her parents in the village of Rot near Heidelberg, disappeared without a trace. As Gudrun was very pretty and far from unapproachable, the local police suspected white slavers or an affair, possibly with an older man, but when the report of the disappearance arrived at the office of Inspector Herschel who now routinely received all reports of murdered or missing females, his first thought was of the dormant Hammer Murderer and he sent Sergeant Schultz down to Heidelberg to work in association with the Heidelberg criminal police.

A massive search of the area was undertaken with particular attention paid to the fields alongside the less heavily trafficked roads. Gudrun was found lying in one of them less than a mile from her home village.

The girl had fought hard for her life. There were traces of skin and beard hairs under her fingernails, and her left index finger was broken. She was badly bruised about the chest and shoulders and, for the first time, one of the Hammer Murderer's victims showed the typical black bruise marks on the insides of the thighs where she had clamped her legs over the rapist's hip bones in a vain attempt to prevent penetration. The Hammer Murderer could, it seemed, have sex with a living, conscious victim.

Gudrun had been alive and conscious when she was raped, a far from pleasant experience, because although she had not been a virgin, the rapist had been remarkably brutal. Her suffering had, however, apparently not lasted long as she had been quickly killed with blows to the head from the now hideously familiar hammer. As usual, the murderer had left no clue to his identity other than a few hairs from his beard and his semen in the vagina of the victim. It was that of a man with blood group AB, subgroup two.

Nine days later, a second, almost identical report landed on Inspector Herschel's desk. This time the victim was sixteen-year-old Ellen Abel, who came from the city of Saarbruecken nearly a hundred miles to the west of Mannheim.

Ellen had set out to hitchhike to a local discotheque on that evening and, as her parents had not expected her to come home very early, it was the following day before they became alarmed and called the police.

Like Gudrun, Ellen was found lying in a field near a secondary road, her clothing torn from her body, her legs still spread wide in the classic sprawl of the rape victim, and her head crushed with blows from the hammer. Unlike Gudrun, she had been dead at the time that she was raped. There were no bruise marks on the insides of the thighs.

The series had resumed with a vengeance and Inspector Herschel, frustrated and desperate over the continuing deluge of murders of girls and young women which he found himself powerless to prevent, braced for a bad year, but, following the murder of Ellen Abel, the attacks came to an abrupt halt. No new reports were received.

'Maybe he's dead,' said the inspector, having a quiet, semi-official lunch with his assistant on New Year's Day of 1980 in an inexpensive tavern not far from police headquarters. 'It's been eight months now. Maybe he's been run over by a truck.'

'It was a lot longer stretch between Majer and Thomé,' said the sergeant with callous disregard for his superior's feelings. 'I think he's just gone somewhere else. Saarbruecken was a good deal further away than any of the others. I think he's moved out of the area.'

'I hope he's moved out of this world,' said the inspector.

Neither the sergeant's theories nor the inspector's hopes were to be confirmed. By 4 June 1980 the Hammer Murderer was back, crushing the skull of twenty-year-old Marie-Elsa Scholte in a field near the town of Ludwigshafen on the west bank of the River Rhine across from Mannheim. After having crushed her skull with his hammer, he rather carefully removed her clothing and raped her. There were some indications at the autopsy that he had undertaken certain manipulations of the corpse, apparently for the purpose of stimulating himself.

'He's becoming jaded,' said the inspector. 'It's no longer enough for him to simply murder and rape the girl, he has to have additional stimulation. The next thing he'll begin torturing them before he kills them. My God! Where will he strike next?'

'Well, wherever it is, it won't be Ludwigshafen,' said the sergeant confidently. The Hammer Murderer had never struck twice consecutively at the same location.

On 23 February 1981, less than a year later, the Hammer Murderer killed sixteen-year-old Gabriella Bohn. In Ludwigshafen.

The girl had been, like so many of the other victims, a high-school student, pretty, dark-haired and a virgin. She had been raped after death and she had not put up any resistance, but she had suspected what was coming and had attempted to flee. The marks of her running feet and those of her deadly pursuer's were clear in the earth. They ended in a great splotch of blood where the back of the girl's head had split open under the impact of the hammer blow.

The murderer had then dragged her on another half-dozen yards before removing her clothing and satisfying his sexual needs.

The police learned something new about the hammer murderer. He wore size eight and a half, B-width shoes.

The inspector was surprised and grateful to learn even that much. Up to now the Hammer Murderer had been astonishingly lucky. Not once in the long series of his crimes had he suffered the misfortune of being interrupted by passersby: a truly remarkable circumstance in heavily populated West Germany where there is nearly always some traffic even on the most isolated roads.

'Sooner or later though, his luck has got to change,' said the inspector grimly. 'Sooner or later, someone is going to come by when he's actually attacking the girl.'

By sheer coincidence, on that day of 15 May 1981, and at almost the precise time that the inspector was voicing his opinion concerning the luck of the Hammer Murderer, less than three miles away little Ulrike Hellmann was fighting like a baby tiger for her life. Not a particularly large or strong girl, she would have already been dead had the Hammer Murderer not decided that raping her alive would prove more exciting.

343

He had, therefore, forced the struggling girl's legs apart, and was engaged in the difficult process of achieving penetration of such a young girl when thirty-four-year-old Karl Lenk came riding down the road on his bicycle. He saw the parked Renault R4 and the couple lying on the ground and, for a moment, he thought that they were simply making love.

Then Ulrike saw him and began to scream at the top of her voice. Startled, Lenk took a closer look, saw that the naked girl lying under the bearded man was no more than a child and leaped off his bicycle to run shouting in the direction of the rapist.

The Hammer Murderer scrambled to his feet, caught up the hammer which lay on the ground nearby and, running to the Renault, climbed in and roared away.

Lenk ran forward and knelt beside the shaking, naked, but uninjured girl. 'AL-204, AL-204,' whispered Ulrike with trembling lips.

'That's right,' said Karl Lenk who had also looked. 'That's his licence number. AL-204.'

The Hammer Murderer's luck had finally changed.

Not longer thereafter, Sergeant Schultz, flanked by two detectives with their machine pistols in their hands, walked past a red Renault R4 parked at the edge of a little meadow outside the town of Alzey, twenty miles to the south of Mainz, to where a young, bearded man was lying on the grass reading a book.

'Can I help you?' said the young man pleasantly, looking up from his book.

'I think so,' said Sergeant Schultz. 'I hereby arrest you on charges of the attempted rape and murder of Ulrike Hellman on 15 May 1981. You are cautioned that any statement you make will be taken down in writing and may be used against you. Do you have anything to say?'

Twenty-seven-year-old Bernd Bopp, a teacher at the secondary school in Alzey, had nothing to say, but a search of his car turned up the famous four-pound hammer in the trunk. The police laboratory would later find traces of at least four different blood groups on it.

Taken to police headquarters and formally identified by

both Ulrike Hellmann and Karl Lenk, Bopp became cooperative and confessed to the unsuccessful attacks on Lilian Dresch, Susanne Bach, Barbara Kiel and the murder of Sylvia Lauterbach. He did not deny the other murders, but said that, although he was certain that he had killed a large number of girls, he could not remember the precise places or circumstances of the crimes. He had, in any case, never known the names of any of his victims until they were published in the newspapers.

As is usual in such cases, Bopp was sent for psychiatric observation and evaluation while awaiting his trial. According to the psychologists, the motive for his crimes was unrequitted love. He had been hopelessly in love with Mechthild Karl, the twenty-three-year-old daughter of his German teacher at the time that he had been in school, but had never worked up the nerve to ask her to have sex with him. Instead, he had read German classical authors with her. Mechthild had found this boring and had transferred her interest to other, less literary-inclined suitors. Bopp had responded by beginning to rape and murder women and girls. Most of them had borne a certain resemblance to Mechthild.

At his trial, Bernd Bopp was unable to offer even as much explanation for his crimes as had the psychologists, but he did assure the court that, if he were released from prison, even after twenty years, he felt certain he would resume them. He had, he said, made certain preparations.

And indeed he had. During the course of the search of Bopp's apartment, a neat notebook entitled 'Diary of Death' had been found. It contained the names and addresses of 139 girls between the ages of eleven and twenty which Bopp had assembled, mainly from magazines carrying classified advertisements for friendship contacts and pen pals.

On 8 October 1981 Bernd Bopp was sentenced to life imprisonment.

The average time served on a life sentence in Germany is seven years.

The police do not like to think about what may happen if Bernd Bopp gets out of prison in seven years.

7

THE DEVIL IN MR JONES

Things have changed a good deal in Germany since the end of the war, and it would appear that they have in England too. Instead of the once popular 'muddling through', the British murderer now often goes in for careful planning, schedules, complex alibis and the confounding of police nostrils through the generous use of red herrings, where still commercially available.

However, England does not lack men who are capable and prepared to meet these challenges and, sometimes, when they do, the results are unexpected and spectacular.

They were certainly unexpected for thirty-four-year-old Mary Jones when, on the afternoon of 15 November 1978, a grey and chilly day, she found herself lying curled up in a large, wicker trunk, her hands bound tightly with stout cord, and her skirt pushed up to expose the bare thighs above her stocking tops and, actually, a good deal more as she had only a short time previously removed her underwear.

It was only when the heavy stones were being tucked into the corners of the trunk around her body that she began to have an inkling of what was in store for her.

By then it was too late to do anything more than appeal with her eyes. She could not move. She could not scream for the handkerchief bound over her mouth suppressed everything except smothered moans and mumbling and, in any case, there was no one to hear.

Even then, she still had not grasped the full horror of the situation. It was a silly joke. It had to be. They had just finished making love. You couldn't make love to someone and then drown them like a cat. It had been such wonderful love-making too. It was years since she had experienced so much pleasure from the sex act.

But she was agonizingly conscious of the nearby river and the strange, bearded face bending over her was without trace of mercy. A wave of pure terror swept through her mind with such force that she nearly fainted. She knew that she was going to die, and she knew what that death would be. It would be hideous. It would be soon.

The cold light of the November afternoon was abruptly blotted out as the wicker lid of the trunk clapped shut and the wooden pins which held it slid into place.

There was jolting and a sensation of movement as the trunk was lifted and dragged over the muddy gravel of the bank of the little river a few miles from the outskirts of the city of Manchester.

Although the top of the trunk was closed and fastened, it was not completely dark inside. Light was coming through a million tiny openings in the wickerwork. It was not only light which could pass through those little holes. So, too, would water.

She heard the man grunt as he gave a final effort and sent the trunk tumbling over the edge of the nearly perpendicular bank.

There was a terrible splash and the river water rushed in through all the little holes in the wickerwork. It was muddy and icy cold and not very deep. If she could have stood up, her head would have been above the surface of the water.

But she could not stand up because she was in the closed trunk, and she could not get out because her hands were tied and the weight of the stones had carried the trunk straight to the bottom.

Under the unreasoning impulse for self-preservation which refuses to cease hoping long after there is no hope, she extended her own suffering by holding her breath.

It could not, of course, last very long and, even as the current began bumping the trunk along the bottom downstream, her tortured lungs gave way and the cold, muddy water rushed into her mouth and nostrils, constricting her throat so that neither water nor air could enter. There was pain, fear, a feeling of suffocation and then nothingness.

That Wednesday evening, when Mary Jones did not return

to her cosy cottage on the outskirts of Liverpool, some thirty miles to the west of Manchester, her husband, a clean-shaven, handsome man who did not look his thirty-five years, spent the evening telephoning her friends and relatives. No one knew where she was and, on the following morning, Henry Jones called the Liverpool police. His wife, he said, was missing.

A detective from the Department of Missing Persons came out and took a statement from Jones. There was not very much to report. Mary and Henry had met at the end of 1968, shortly after Henry had been made office manager of the export-import firm for which he worked, and they had married in May of 1969. Prior to the marriage, Mary had been a secretary in another export-import firm, but she had stopped working once she was married.

The cottage in which they lived was actually Mary's, as she had inherited it from her first husband who had died a number of years earlier. According to Jones, the couple had neither financial nor domestic problems and he knew of no reason why his wife might have disappeared.

The detective, who did nothing else but work on such cases, asked rather bluntly whether Mrs Jones had had any male friends. Jones turned brick-red with irritation and embarrassment, replied stiffly that it was out of the question and then, after a moment's hesitation, said rather shamefacedly that in looking through his wife's address book for possible people to call concerning her whereabouts, he had come across the name of Tony Saunders. He did not believe for a moment that his wife had been engaged in an extra-marital affair, but he did not know any Tony Saunders and Mary had never mentioned the name to him.

The detective asked to see the address book and was given it. The name was written in long hand on the page reserved for names beginning with S, but there was neither address nor telephone number.

The detective inquired about Henry Jones's working hours and then took his departure. He did not, however, leave the area, but called on several of the neighbours. He was interested in learning if Mrs Jones had been, perhaps, receiving a male visitor in the afternoon while her husband was at work.

Almost by chance because he had no real reason to do so, he mentioned the name of Saunders and, to his surprise, one of the ladies immediately recognized the name.

A young man, she said, wearing a neatly trimmed beard and glasses had called at her house the preceding week. He had introduced himself as Tony Saunders from Brown & Company, and he had, obviously, wanted to sell her something. What it was she did not know, because she had said that she was not interested before finding out what it was and had closed the door in his face.

The detective went back to some of the other houses that he had already called on and found that Saunders had been at two of them. At one he had been turned away, but at the other he had received more of a welcome. He had not, however, made a sale as the housewife said that she could not make out very clearly what he was selling. She had found him quite personable and had given him a cup of tea.

The detective went back to headquarters and made up a report of the missing-person case of Mary Jones in which he said that there was some reason to believe that the woman had gone off with a door-to-door salesman named Tony Saunders.

Although Henry Jones had said that their married life was completely satisfactory, Mary might have had different ideas. They had been married for ten years, they had no children and women sometimes became more bored with their lives than their husbands realized.

Mr Jones called several times during the following days to ask what progress was being made in locating his wife and was assured that they were working on it. As a matter of fact, they were. One of the very junior officers in the Missing Persons Department had been sent around to check all of the firms named Brown & Company, of which there were several, to see whether any of them employed a salesman named Tony Saunders. The police could not, of course, bring Mrs Jones back to her husband against her will, but they could at least reassure him that she had come to no harm and was in good hands so to speak.

By the following Monday, 20 November, the detective was still going around to the companies with no success to report. However on that morning, a twenty-eight-year-old labourer, attached to the Department of Roads and Bridges, discovered the wicker trunk grounded on a gravel bar some four miles downstream from the point where it had entered the river.

The worker was wearing a raincoat and rubber boots because the weather had taken a turn for the worse and a mixture of rain and sleet had been falling since early that morning. He was, therefore, well equipped to wade into the stream and investigate what might be inside the trunk and he did so.

Not normally a very excitable young man, he was so startled by his discovery that he staggered backwards, stepped into a hole and was swept downstream himself for some distance.

Regaining his feet, he scrambled out of the river and ran as hard as he could go, dripping wet, to the nearest village where he telephoned the police.

A detachment was immediately sent out from Manchester, and the trunk was lifted out of the river and brought to the Manchester police morgue. There it was quickly determined that the dead woman inside was Mrs Mary Jones, the murderer having considerably dropped her handbag containing her driver's licence and other papers into the trunk with her. As her address was also on the driver's licence, it was only a matter of a few minutes before the Missing Persons Department in Liverpool knew that one of their cases had been solved.

Solved for the Missing Persons Department, at least, but not for the Liverpool homicide squad who were faced with the fact that Mary Jones had obviously been murdered; drowned like a cat in the wicker trunk with a number of heavy stones tossed in to weight it down. Her body was therefore transferred to the Liverpool police morgue, and after being positively identified by her husband, the investigation started.

Like many homicide investigations, it began with the autopsy. This carried out by an assistant medical examiner from

350

the Liverpool Coroner's Office, a comparatively young man with a round, serious face and neatly parted dark blond hair.

According to his report, the woman had been dead for approximately five days and in the water for the same length of time. The water being cold, the corpse was well preserved.

The immediate cause of death had been drowning, and Mrs Jones had known that she was going to drown and had been conscious at the time because she had ruptured a number of minor blood vessels in attempting to hold her breath.

There were no indications of violence on the body, although the cords binding the wrists had cut deeply into the flesh as a result of her struggles to free herself. There were a few minor scrapes on the knees, hips and buttocks, which were probably the result of her desperate movements within the trunk as she was drowning.

The examination of the genitals indicated that Mrs Jones had engaged in sexual intercourse, with a man whose blood group was O, very shortly before her death. Ejaculation had taken place at maximum penetration, and Mrs Jones's participation in the sex act had been enthusiastic for her vagina had been flooded with her own lubricating secretions.

The doctor noted that neither the bindings on the hands nor the gag had been applied in a deliberately painful manner, and that all of the cuts on the wrists appeared to be due to her own struggles and, from this, he concluded that Mrs Jones had submitted voluntarily to being bound and gagged. It had been, he suggested, a part of the sexual activities. The murderer had bound and gagged his victim in what she had believed was no more than a form of sex play, had engaged in intercourse with her, and had then drowned the helpless woman like some unwanted animal thrown into a pond in a sack with a stone in it.

The detective-inspector who had taken charge of the case immediately called for a search of the records. A man who would commit such a cruel and cold-blooded murder would, in his opinion, have to be as mad as a hatter, and compulsive killers of that type normally held to the same *modus operandi* in all of their crimes.

His assistant, a rather slight, sandy-haired, sergeant of

detectives, with the quick movements and something of the appearance of a fox, had the records checked and reported that there was no record of any such crime ever having taken place in England since the time that the police had begun keeping records.

This answer did not please the inspector at all. It presumably meant that some madman was only now just beginning his career. There was no telling how many other women he might murder before he was apprehended.

Although the medical experts agreed that the crime was probably the work of a seriously unbalanced person because it was hard to conceive of a man in his right mind callously drowning a young and attractive woman with whom he had just had intercourse, it was also possible that this was exactly what the murderer had wanted the police to think.

And because this possibility had to be considered, the inspector requested the Department of Missing Persons to send over a report on their investigations into the affair. He had spoken with Henry Jones personally at the time that the identification of the body was made, and he was aware that Jones had turned in a missing-person report on the day following his wife's disappearance.

The file was brought promptly to the inspector's office, and within a half-hour most of the Liverpool police were engaged in an active hunt for Tony Saunders.

The ones who were not were out canvassing the houses around the cottage where the Joneses lived to obtain as many witness sightings and descriptions of the mysterious salesman as they could assemble.

This operation was not particularly fruitful, and only one other house was found where Saunders had called. All of the descriptions, however, tallied closely. Saunders was a tall, well-built young man with a full beard and moustache and black, horn-rimmed glasses. He was neatly, but a little flashily dressed in a slightly loud checked suit with a regimental tie of some kind, and he was well spoken, although his voice was rather low and hoarse as if he had a sore throat.

Mrs Jones's address book had also been obtained from her husband and brought to police headquarters where it had been carefully studied. Significantly, the name Tony Saunders was the only one in the book which did not carry an address or a telephone number. It was possible that Mrs Jones had never known where her murderer lived.

It was also possible that she had not known his real name. It seemed scarcely probable that the man would have gone around from door-to-door, posing as a salesman, and giving his right name. Unless, of course, he really was a salesman, but that the inspector did not think. At none of the houses where he had called, not even the one where he had been invited in for a cup of tea, had he really tried seriously to make a sale or even revealed what he was selling. The salesman act was, in all probability, no more than a cover-up.

None the less, the inspector, a square-faced, square-bodied man with a somewhat florid complexion and a prominent jaw, was inclined to be optimistic. If the killer had been going from door to door in the area around the Jones's house, he had very probably been doing the same thing elsewhere and, if he had seen enough people, there was always a good chance that he had let slip something which would make it possible for the police to trace his identity.

An appeal was, therefore, run in the newspapers requesting housewives who had received calls from a door-to-door salesman named Tony Saunders to report to the police. The inspector was anticipating dozens of calls.

There was not a single one.

Puzzled, the inspector sent his men out to make spot checks in the various residential neighbourhoods. As it was possible that Saunders had used a different name in other places, they were equipped with what the witnesses said were excellent police sketches of the suspect made from the descriptions of the housewives on whom he had called.

One door-to-door salesman with a full beard and glasses was located. He was twenty-eight-year-old Thomas Henley and he had a police record, having served eight months of a fourteen-month sentence for assaulting a teenage girl in a park six years earlier. It had never been entirely clear what Henley had had in mind when he assaulted the girl and he, himself, was not very helpful, saying merely that the girl had laughed at him. He had ripped off most of her clothing, but had not made any actual attempt to rape her.

Taken into custody and placed under interrogation, he consistently denied any connection with the murder and insisted that he had never been in the Lodge Road area, the district where the Jones's house was located, in his life.

Placed in a line-up of men of similar appearance with beards and glasses, he was picked out by two of the housewives on whom the mysterious Tony Saunders had called, but the other witnesses failed to identify him and picked other men in the line-up who were, of course, innocent.

The results were inconclusive, but the interrogation of Thomas Henley continued and so, too, did the search for Tony Saunders. It was possible that Henley was Tony Saunders, but so far there was no real evidence of it.

In the meantime, other routine lines of investigation were being undertaken. Efforts were made to locate the point at which the body had entered the water in the trunk and Mrs Jones's relatives and close female friends were being questioned to see if she had ever mentioned involvement with a man other than her husband.

Actually, both of these not very promising leads produced more useful information than what had been considered the very solid clue of Tony Saunders's name in Mary Jones's address book and his calls on other housewives.

Tests made with the wicker trunk containing a sandbag of the same weight as Mrs Jones were so successful that the police were able to pinpoint within a half mile the point along the river where the trunk had entered the water, and a subsequent search soon located the scene of the crime. A few short pieces of the same cord with which Mrs Jones's hands had been tied were found, and there were marks in the mud and gravel where the trunk had been pushed and dragged to the bank of the river. In a clump of brush behind a large tree, a pair of knickers which Henry Jones identified as being similar to those owned by his wife, were found. They were not torn or stretched, but had been deliberately removed, possibly by Mrs Jones herself.

However, that was all. There were traces of tire marks

354

where a car had pulled off the road near the scene of the crime, but the rain had washed them out to the point where they were of little value for purposes of identification and, in any case, there was no evidence that they were connected with the murder.

The scene of the crime had been successfully located, but had not provided the investigators with anything valuable. Mrs Jones's conversations and confidences with her friends were to prove rather more useful.

Surprisingly, the information obtained here tended to lead the investigation off in a totally different direction. As early as 1975 Mrs Jones had begun to dye her hair, make more extensive use of cosmetics and dress more attractively. She had told her friends or, at least, some of them, that she was doing this because her husband was having an affair with a younger woman and she hoped to win him back. He had, it seemed, asked for a divorce, but she had refused.

To the relief of the police, this put the case in a more familiar frame. A man in his middle thirties, married ten years and probably a bit jaded with married life, becoming involved with a younger woman, asking for a divorce and being refused was classic. Such situations frequently ended in murder, particularly if the husband enjoyed a good position and could not afford a scandal.

If this information were true, then the inspector thought that his case was more or less solved. He knew who the murderer was. It was Henry Jones. However, whether he would be able to assemble sufficient evidence to bring him to justice was another matter. Jones had apparently gone about the murder in a vexingly devious manner. He had not done it himself, but had hired the mysterious Tony Saunders to do his dirty work for him.

The first thing, however, was to determine whether Jones had actually been having an affair or whether it was merely a figment of his wife's imagination. If what she said was true, then the affair would have begun when Jones came into contact with some young woman during the summer of 1975.

Although the investigations had to be carried out as discreetly as possible because there was no way of knowing whether innocent persons might be involved, it very quickly produced evidence that Henry Jones had, indeed, been having a very passionate affair and with, for him, an extremely important person.

Her name was Mildred Masters, and she was none other than the only child of the owner of the company for which Jones worked.

The implications were obvious. Jones was in a position to become, not an employee, but an owner of the company and to receive, thrown into the bargain, a lovely, twenty-two-year-old substitute for his now slightly faded wife of ten years. It would take a firm character to resist such temptation and Jones apparently did not have one.

He had asked for a divorce and had been refused. Mary Jones must have appeared to him as the sole, unreasonable obstacle to his happiness. From that conclusion it was only a step to the decision to get rid of her and he had done so, hiring the elusive Tony Saunders to seduce Mary and then murder her.

Certain as he was over what had happened, the inspector could not see how he was going to prove it. Saunders, whose name was almost certainly not Saunders, would have taken the payment for his deed and departed long since. He could well have left England by now, but it would not even have been necessary. Without knowing his name or any details concerning his person, there was no way in the world that he could be traced. There are a great many young men with beards and glasses in England.

The only possibility was if witnesses could be found who had seen Saunders and Jones together. There would have had to be some contact between the two men to arrange the details of the murder and hand over the money if nothing else.

Thomas Henley was still in custody and there was, of course, the possibility that he was Jones's hired killer. He continued, however, to deny all connection with the case and the questioning had not produced any flaws in his statements. Eventually the inspector would be forced to release him. There was no physical evidence to connect him with either Henry or Mary Jones.

356

It was decided, therefore, to concentrate the investigation on Jones's contacts and movements within the two or three months preceding the murder in the hope of coming across a young man with a beard who wore glasses and, possibly, sometimes called himself Tony Saunders.

While efforts in this direction were still proceeding, but without, as yet, any results, an investigator came up with the first piece of evidence tending to establish proof of Jones's guilt, although, perhaps, insufficient to obtain an indictment.

Going through Mary Jones's address book for the dozenth time, it occurred to him that the entry of the name Tony Saunders was not quite the same as the other long-hand entries. The lines of the script were not straight, smooth slashes of the pen, but slightly rough and irregular.

Taking the book to the police laboratory, he showed it to one of the handwriting experts and asked if the handwriting for the entry Tony Saunders was identical to that of the handwriting for the other entries.

The expert barely glanced at the book and immediately said that it was not the same. The name Tony Saunders had been written in imitation of the other entries in the book, but it was not identical.

It was not very difficult to obtain samples of Henry Jones's writing and, although the experts could not be completely certain, they were of the opinion that it was Jones who had written the name of Tony Saunders into his wife's address book.

There was now little question in anyone's mind but that Henry Jones was the murderer of his wife. There was also, however, little question in anyone's mind but that he was probably going to get away with it. His contacts with Tony Saunders had been so well covered that it was impossible to trace them.

The inspector, who had been holding back a number of details concerning the case from the press, gave up, suspended the operation, and made public what was known of the matter, including the actual scene of the crime which had never before been revealed.

The round-up story on the case appeared in the Manchester newspapers and almost immediately a sixty-eight-year-old man telephoned the police. He had, he said, information which he thought might be of interest to them.

It was indeed. The man had been passing near the scene of the crime on the afternoon of 15 November and had seen a small delivery truck parked near the river. He had not seen any persons, but he had thought that it was strange that a delivery truck for an export-import company should be parked in such a place and at such a time. He had remembered the name of the company printed on the side of the truck. It was the company for which Henry Jones worked!

The inspector did not know whether even this was going to be enough or not, but it certainly called for further action, and Henry Jones was taken into custody while a group of experts from the police laboratory, armed with a search warrant, went over his house in the hopes of finding something that might be connected to the crime.

They did not and they did not find any trace of the crime in the pick-up truck which Jones normally drove.

Making their report to the inspector in his office, the technicians said that the only thing that they had found that was in any way unusual was a number of theatrical costumes apparently belonging to Jones.

The inspector replied absently that they already knew that Jones was interested in amateur theatricals and had been taking parts in plays since he was a child. He apparently enjoyed running around with false whiskers and a wig.

Suddenly, the inspector stopped speaking and for several minutes there was a dead silence in the office.

Then, someone said something about it being impossible, but it was not impossible and it occurred to them all at one and the same time.

They had found Tony Saunders.

Jones began by denying that he had disguised himself with a beard, glasses and unusual clothing to go around and present himself to the neighbours as Tony Saunders from Brown & Company, thus setting up a fictitious murderer for his wife. In the end, however, he broke down and confessed.

He had, he said, been in an impossible position. He was in love with Mildred and his entire future depended upon being able to marry her. Mary would, however, not consider a divorce. There was no other solution; he had to get rid of her.

He had always been fond of amateur theatricals and dressing up so that the idea of establishing a false identity for murder came to him naturally. Early in October he had bought the glasses, a false beard and moustache and the suit without telling Mary anything about it. He had then come to ring his own doorbell and play the part of a door-to-door salesman. If Mary failed to recognize him, no one else would either, he thought.

Mary did not recognize him and was astonished when he pulled off his beard to reveal his true identity. Both he and she had found the situation stimulating and they had made love passionately.

Over the next month, further passionate love-making had taken place, always with Henry in disguise, and he had, without her knowledge, began making calls on the neighbours so as to establish the false identity. He had even told Mary to call him Tony Saunders and she had done so.

On the day of the murder he had slipped away from his work in the company van and had gone home after donning his disguise. Mary had been delighted to see her lover, Tony Saunders, and he had proposed making love in the open as an added element of excitement.

Mary had enthusiastically agreed, and they had driven to the river with the wicker trunk in the back of the van. Mary had not even noticed it.

Nor had she thought it strange that he bound and gagged her prior to intercourse. They had often practised bondage and simulated sadism in their previous relations.

Mary had found the location outdoors, the tying and gagging and the disguised appearance of her husband highly stimulating, and she had had multiple orgasms.

Then it was time to die.

On 26 October 1979 it was time for sentencing. Good actor but bad husband Henry Jones was sent to prison for life.

8

JAILED TEN YEARS FOR EXCEEDING THE SPEED LIMIT!

Henry Jones was, perhaps, unfortunate in being British. In some other countries justice would have been less stern. It would have been reasoned that Henry was in a position of stress, that he was not in complete possession of his faculties, possibly that he had had an unhappy childhood and that his siblings had received sweets from the mother when he had received none. In the end, he would have been given ten years and a scolding, meaning that he would be out and ready to remarry in five, a happy prospect for the true crime writer, if not necessarily for the future spouse and/or spouses.

However, this rigour in sentencing does not extend to all parts of the Commonwealth and less than a year following Henry Jones's lethal game of charades, another husband was to find a more understanding jury.

Of course, he was not a simple office manager. He was very wealthy.

As a general rule, very wealthy persons tend to occupy luxury mansions with extensive grounds and, as their wives can rarely be persuaded to do the cooking, the house work and take care of the garden single-handed, they employ large staffs of servants for these purposes.

This was the case with Mr Nigel Kearns, a thirty-four-year-old foreign-exchange dealer who had dealt so nimbly that he was generally conceded to be the richest man in all Adelaide, no mean distinction in a city now nearing a population of a million residents.

If Nigel Kearns was successful financially, he was even more so socially and matrimonially, being one of the brighter stars in the Adelaide social firmament and his wife none other than the dazzlingly beautiful Pamela who had been elected Miss Australia at the age of thirteen, had repeated the feat at age nineteen and had stupefied the competition with a third success at the ripe old age of twenty-one. After this, there was obviously no one she could marry in Adelaide other than Nigel, and there was no one in Australia that he could marry other than her.

The ceremony had, consequently, been carried out in the presence of every soul in Adelaide who was of the slightest social importance and the Kearns had withdrawn to their luxury mansion to live happily ever after.

As would, presumably, their many servants, one of whom was, on this morning of Sunday, 15 January 1980, struggling to get out of bed.

Actually, this should not have been very difficult. Miss Nellie Cooper, a housemaid by profession if not inclination, was just barely nineteen years old, pretty and rather athletic. Left to her own devices, she would have risen early that Sunday to go off to the beach for some swimming, but, as it happened, this was her duty Sunday and she would have to remain at the house. Hence the reluctance in rising.

Washing and getting into her clothes, Nellie reflected that, all in all, it could be a great deal worse. With three house-maids on the staff, you got, at least, two Sundays out of three free and you were better off than the two gardeners who had to work every other weekend. The cook, of course, took his one day off a week with no replacement at all, but cooks were hard to find. If a person had to make a living as a housemaid, then it was best as a housemaid for a rich family and this was the richest family around.

The servants' quarters were on the top floor of the three-storey building, and Nellie made her way down the backstair to the kitchen where she prepared herself a cup of coffee and some toast. There was no great hurry. It was unlikely that Mrs Kearns would ring for her much before ten o'clock. She was not an early riser and certainly not on a Sunday morning.

As for Mr Kearns, he was visiting his brother who was not poor either and who lived on a country estate sixty miles away. He would not be back before Monday or Tuesday at the latest.

Nellie Cooper drank her coffee and ate her toast. She then had a second cup of coffee, tidied up the kitchen a little, and eventually went out to wander through the magnificently furnished rooms of the great house. They represented for her an intimidating amount of work, but they were very splendid to look at.

By ten o'clock Mrs Kearns had still not rung for her breakfast and Nellie, bored and impatient for the day to pass, came to the conclusion that she would go up and see if Mrs Kearns was in her bedroom at all. Now that she thought of it, it was more than likely that she was not. Nellie knew a good deal about her mistress's sleeping arrangements, and that was not all that Nellie Cooper knew about Pamela Kearns. With so many servants in the house there was a good deal of gossip, and it was common knowledge that while Mr Kearns was exhausting himself in racking up still more millions to the point where he came home late in the evening and fell exhausted and limp into bed, Mrs Kearns was making the rounds of the beaches and the more expensive cafés where she acquired a large number of new friends, all young and all male. Very male.

Trudging up the stairs to the bedroom on the second floor, Nellie Cooper reflected that she need not have got out of bed so early at all. With Mr Kearns visiting his brother sixty miles away and not due to return until Monday or Tuesday evening, Mrs Kearns would almost certainly have taken the opportunity to spend an undisturbed night with one of those young, handsome and extremely virile chance acquaintances.

However, to be on the safe side, Nellie very quietly eased open the door of Mrs Kearns's bedroom and peeked inside, confidently expecting to see an empty, neatly made bed.

What she actually saw gave her such a start that she lost her balance and half fell through the door, bumping her forehead painfully against the door handle.

The bed was not neatly made, but a mess with sheets and

blankets thrown back over the foot and half on to the floor. Lying on it was a totally naked woman whom Nellie assumed was Mrs Kearns. She was lying on her back, but Nellie could not see her face because lying on top of her was an equally naked man. Nellie had no idea who he might be, but she was certain that it was not Mr Kearns. This man was heavier, less muscular, and his hair was almost black whereas Nigel Kearns's hair was medium brown.

Half falling into the room, Nellie had made considerable noise and she was astounded to see that the figures on the bed had failed to react in any way. Were they so exhausted by their activities that even such sounds would not wake them? And how could they sleep in that position in the first place.

Suddenly, Nellie Cooper felt very uneasy and even frightened. There was something wrong here, terribly wrong. She felt she had to do something, but she did not know what to do. How could she go up to the bed and rouse her mistress when there was a man sleeping on top of her? Something like that could cost her her job.

On the other hand, it did not seem right to simply go away and ignore the whole thing. The people couldn't be sleeping like that. They were sick or unconscious or drunk, or maybe they had taken drugs. In any case, she had to do something.

Tense and beginning to tremble a little, she approached the bed and stretched out a hesitant hand in the direction of Pamela Kearns's shoulder. From this angle she could see that it was Mrs Kearns, but her fingers never reached the bare shoulder because what she also saw was the small, brown hole, ringed by a bluish-black welt, in the flesh just above the right eyebrow. A narrow thread of blood had run from the hole, around the corner of the eye, and down over the cheek to form a dark spot on the white pillow case.

Pamela Kearns's lovely features were calm and composed and her eyes were shut, but Nellie Cooper was not deceived. Her employer was not sleeping. She was dead.

In the shock and confusion of the discovery, Nellie jumped to the conclusion that it was the man lying on top of her who had killed her and she stumbled backward and bolted out of the room. Frightened nearly out of her wits, she raced up the stairs to her own room, locked the door and began frenziedly pushing furniture against it. It was some little time before she had calmed sufficiently to realize the senselessness of her actions and began to think rationally.

Cautiously pulling the furniture away from the door, she quietly unlocked it. Although she had recovered from her initial reaction of hysterical panic and now realized that the man lying on top of Mrs Kearns must be dead as well, she was terrified that the murderer might still be in the house. She was assuming that he would be a burglar or thief of some kind. There was always the danger of this in such large, luxury mansions.

Creeping silently out of her room, she tiptoed down the corridor to the door of the room occupied by the gardener who should be on duty that weekend where, unwilling to knock or call out for fear of attracting the attention of the murderer, she tried the door handle and found that the door was unlocked.

The gardener was, however, not inside which was as it should be. At that hour of the morning he would be long since at work in the garden outside. She was going to have to go downstairs and through the big, empty house alone.

Removing her shoes so as to make no noise going down the stairs, she vacillated indecisively as to what she should do. Should she risk telephoning the police from one of the house telephones and, perhaps, be surprised by the murderer in the middle of the call? Or should she simply slip outside and run through the garden until she found the gardener?

This was obviously the safest choice, but what then? Patrick, which was the gardener's name, would, undoubtedly, rush inside to see what was wrong and the burglar might very well kill him too. The fact was, Nellie was rather favourably inclined toward this handsome, unmarried gardener, only three years older than herself, although there had been so far no declarations of intent by either party.

All in all, it might be better not to inform the gardener and, recalling that there was a telephone in the pantry used by the cook for ordering groceries and other household supplies and that the pantry had a stout door which could be locked, she went to it and locked herself in.

She was seized again by panic for an instant or two when it occurred to her that the burglar might have cut the telephone wires and that she would not be able to call out, but the reassuring dial tone came on immediately. Minutes later, Nellie Cooper was speaking with the duty officer on the communications desk at police headquarters in downtown Adelaide.

Speaking as clearly and calmly as she could manage, Nellie gave what she believed to be an accurate account of the circumstances. She was the housemaid at the home of Mr and Mrs Nigel Kearns. A burglar had broken into the house and had murdered Mrs Kearns and another person. She was locked in the pantry. Would the police please come as quickly as possible?

The communications officer replied that they would be there before she could hang up the telephone and, although this was not literally true, a patrolcar did arrive at the house within a matter of minutes. The two officers in it came first to the pantry to make certain that Nellie was all right, but they had to show her their badges through the keyhole before she would open the door. Nellie was a badly frightened girl, and she was not taking any chances now that deliverance was so close at hand.

The question of identification being solved, Nellie led the officers to the bedroom where her employer and the un-identified man lay. Their conclusion was the same as hers had been, namely that Mrs Kearns had been shot through the head. So too, it seemed, had the man. The murders had apparently taken place while the couple were actually engaged in intercourse.

As neither officer thought of asking Nellie who the man was, they assumed that he was Nigel Kearns and, although the theory of a burglar did not seem as likely to the police officers as it had to the housemaid, they agreed with her that the murderer might still be in the house.

There was a telephone in the bedroom and one of the officers immediately called police headquarters, confirming

Nellie's report of a double homicide and asking for a cordon around the house to prevent the escape of the murderer if he was still there. Minutes later, there was patrolcars racing in from every direction, but without sirens or warning lights. The cordon around the Kearns mansion went into place silently, efficiently and very quickly. The communications desk duty officer knew very well who Nigel Kearns was.

So too did the inspector of detectives who, with his assistant, a detective-sergeant, was on duty in the offices of the Criminal Investigations Department on that Sunday. Picking up the keys to one of the departments cars from the squad room, they raced to the scene with the siren wide open. Behind them, two specialists in heavy body armour, a squad of detection experts from the police laboratory and an expert in forensic medicine, were piling into a police van which would follow. If Nigel Kearns and his wife had been murdered under the circumstances as they had been described to police headquarters, this was one of the most important cases of homicide in Adelaide and no effort was being spared.

At the house the inspector, a short, brisk man with intimidatingly cold, grey-blue eyes and a sandy moustache running like a straight bar across his upper lip, found the police cordon so tight that not even a mouse could have squeezed through and the house itself full of police officers. They had just completed searching the building from attic to basement and had found no trace of the burglar.

No sooner had the inspector entered the bedroom than he began to suspect why. 'My God!' he said in a low voice, placing his lips as close to the sergeant's ear as he could manage, 'That's not Nigel Kearns.'

The sergeant, a very large, young man with a round, good-natured face and rather unruly, short, blond hair, had bent down to listen to what his chief was saying and he straightened up abruptly, walked to the edge of the bed and bent nearly double in order to get a look at the dead man's face.

'You're right,' he said. 'It's not Kearns. I've seen his

picture in the newspapers. That's Mrs Kearns though. There's nobody in Australia who wouldn't recognize her.'

'You realize what this means, of course?' said the inspector.

The sergeant nodded dumbly. Like the inspector, he had immediately grasped that the murderer of Pamela Kearns and this as yet unidentified man was very probably Nigel Kearns himself.

'We're going to have to go about this discreetly,' said the inspector. 'Kearns is an intelligent man and he'll have the best lawyers that money can buy. Unless I'm greatly mistaken, we're not going to find very many clues to the identity of the murderer here.'

The inspector was not mistaken. Someone had obviously entered the bedroom while the dead couple were engaged in intercourse and, having shot them, had left, closing the door behind him. There were no fingerprints on the door handle, but the laboratory technicians were able to observe certain smears on the polished brass which could have been made by someone wearing gloves. Aside from this, there was not the slightest indication of the murderer's presence in the bedroom at all.

Or, perhaps, there was. Nigel Kearns's fingerprints would eventually be recovered from many places in the room, but why should a man's fingerprints not be in his own wife's bedroom. It would have been strange had they not been there.

While the laboratory specialists began their examination of the room and the doctor began his examination of the bodies, the inspector and the sergeant took the statements of Nellie Cooper and the gardener, the only servants on duty who were known to have spent the night in the house.

Nellie's statement was very long as she went into excruciating detail concerning her discovery of the body. It was the most impressive event of her life up to now and she remembered practically every second of it.

Patrick's statement was very short. He had got up at the usual time and had gone to work in the garden as he was supposed to. He had not known that anyone had been murdered in the house. He was not, he added rather shortly, in the habit of looking into his mistress's bedroom before taking up his duties for the day.

Neither Nellie nor Patrick had heard the sounds of shots or anything else during the night, although both had been in their rooms on the top floor. However, test firing carried out by the detection experts showed that the sound of a .38 calibre pistol shot fired in the bedroom downstairs could barely be heard in the servants' quarters and was definitely not loud enough to awake anyone sleeping soundly.

It had been a .38 calibre pistol or so thought the doctor, although he said that final confirmation would have to wait until he had performed the autopsy and removed the slugs from the victims' brains where they were still lodged. A tall, thin, wiry man with a black moustache and a grave, rather ponderous manner of speaking, he reported that the man had died at almost the precise instant of arriving at his sexual climax. As it seemed unlikely that this would be a coincidence, he suggested that the murderer had been waiting outside the door, listening to and, perhaps observing the couple engaged in intercourse inside and had chosen the moment of orgasm for the murder, possibly because the victims' attention would then be concentrated on what they were doing and it would be possible to approach the bed unnoticed, even though the lights were on. Mrs Kearns, he said, appeared to have had several orgasms but whether the last had been at the moment of death or not, he could not say. Whatever the case, the couple had been at maximum penetration at the time.

Like the inspector, the doctor had immediately seen that the man was not Nigel Kearns and he asked if the inspector had any idea who he was.

The inspector knew exactly who he was. His driver's licence and other identification papers had been found in his wallet in the clothing hung neatly over a chair in the bedroom. He was twenty-nine-year-old Kenneth Craig, an unmarried middle-level management employee of an insurance company. One of the inspectors' men was now on his way to Craig's parents to report his death, arrange for the official identification at the police morgue and attempt to find out what they had known of Craig's relationship to Pamela Kearns, if anything.

Another three detectives were with the sergeant in a police car headed for the country estate of thirty-nine-year-old Ronald Kearns, Nigel Kearns's brother. Nellie Cooper had said that that was where her employer was spending the weekend and the sergeant had orders to take him into custody simply on the basis of the circumstances. There was sufficient evidence of motive and opportunity to bring charges of homicide against him.

Orders were orders and the sergeant did bring Nigel Kearns back to Adelaide with him, but he was careful to avoid informing him that he was under arrest and he was very polite and considerate in his manner.

The fact was both Ronald Kearns and his thirty-six-year-old wife Sheila had immediately confirmed that Nigel had spent Saturday night with them, and that it was not possible that he could have left during the night because the only car that was not locked up in the garages was one belonging to Sheila and it was parked directly under her bedroom window. It was a sports car which made a good deal of noise and it would have been impossible to start it without waking her.

This was bad enough, but there was worse to come.

Having completed the autopsies and having recovered two .38 calibre bullets which had been fired from a gun for which the ballistics department could find no record, the doctor reported that Kenneth Craig and Pamela Kearns had died almost simultaneously sometime between one-fifteen and one-thirty in the morning of Sunday, 15 January. Ronald and Sheila Kearns had said in separate statements that they and Nigel had only gone to bed at around midnight. For Nigel to have left the estate early enough to cover the distance to Adelaide and murder his wife and her lover by one-thirty in the morning, he would have had to drive extremely fast or leave while his brother and his sister-in-law were still awake. They were prepared to swear that he had not.

'Could they be protecting him?' said the sergeant.

369

'I doubt it,' said the inspector. 'They made their statements independently and they checked. If they were false, that would mean that they had worked the whole thing out in advance and I don't believe that they would do that. These are wealthy, highly respectable people and I doubt that they would condone murder even if the murderer was Kearns's brother. Besides, I've listened to enough statements in my life that I think I know when someone is telling the truth. Neither Kearns nor his wife think that Nigel did this. They probably think that he had good reason to and they're both relieved to know that he didn't.'

'That was the impression that I got too,' said the sergeant slowly. 'They were both relieved.'

In the meantime, the investigation into Pamela Kearns's more intimate social contacts had been pursued far enough by now to establish that, had Nigel Kearns been inclined to murder his wife for her sexual infidelities, he had had ample motive for close to five years.

Nigel and Pamela's marriage had been something of a fairy-tale romance. Chosen in free competition as the most beautiful woman in Australia, Pamela was at the height of her career when in March of 1970 she met Nigel Kearns who was already well on his way to his second million dollars and the eventual title of richest man in Adelaide through his dealings in foreign exchange.

In a way, they were an ideally matched pair. Pamela, who despite her appearance was a somewhat calculating maiden, had apparently had little contact with the opposite sex and had stated publicly on more than one occasion that she had no intention of becoming romantically involved with anyone other than a very wealthy man, and then only if officially engaged to be married. Nigel, no more given to impulsive emotions than his wife, had been busy making money and had little interest in such time-consuming and unprofitable activities as love and sex.

His interest in Pamela had been, it seemed, mainly because she was a celebrity and thus represented another trophy to be added to his successes. Characteristically, he had not wasted much time on courtship and preliminaries. Nigel and Pamela met in March; they were formally engaged in May; in July they were married. It was the most important social event of the year in Adelaide.

Following the wedding, there had been the obligatory world-tour honeymoon and, this taken care of, Nigel had bought the mansion in the most exclusive suburb of Adelaide, had staffed it with servants, had provided his wife with an unlimited supply of money and had gone back to making more of the same. He was, it was said, devoted to his beautiful wife, and there was nothing that she might desire which she could not have.

Except Nigel. Nigel liked Pamela, but he loved money, or rather, not the money itself, but the process of making it. The money actually did Nigel very little good. He never had any free time to spend it.

Nor did he have any time for romance. When he returned home after a long day of frenzied foreign-exchange dealings, he was so exhausted that he fell into bed immediately after dinner and slept straight through the night.

Pamela might have been cold in financial matters, but she was far from cold otherwise. Within five years, the magic had gone out of the marriage and she acquired what Inspector Barker thought was probably her first lover. In any case, he was unable to find anyone who reported contact with her at an earlier date.

This first lover was typical of all her subsequent adventures except the last. A handsome, blond beachboy, he had been twenty-five years old at the time. He had met Pamela at the beach where she spent a great deal of her time, and she had been in such a state of deprivation that they had actually had intercourse while in the water under something less than ideal conditions of privacy. He had not known then who she was, but finding out later, had been so impressed by his own conquest that he had never forgotten the incident.

Pamela had forgotten him quickly enough and had moved on to others. The inspector was able to find dozens of them, generally picked up at the beach or in the better-class cafés and bars. They were mostly young men of good families, some of whom worked and some of whom did not need to. If

371

they worked, it was in management positions. Pamela had not been fond of the unwashed masses.

Kenneth Craig appeared to not have differed much from his predecessors, although her affair with him had lasted slightly longer than the average. It was believed that she had met him sometime in August of the preceding year which would mean that they had been lovers for a little over four months.

Craig had seemingly taken the affair more seriously than most. He was, however, not the only one. Two of Pamela's previous lovers, twenty-eight-year-old Bill Rood and twenty-six-year-old Tom Drysdale, had nearly beaten each other to death over her. Both were rich, both had wanted her to divorce Kearns and marry them, and each had accused the other of alienating her affections.

Looked at from the objective point of view of the police investigators, it appeared that there had been little affection to alienate. The inspector's men were not even able to determine whether Rood had displaced Drysdale or vice versa, and there was some reason to believe that she had been carrying on affairs with both of them simultaneously. Pamela had been a girl with healthy appetites and the formidable staying power of the female.

Which was, perhaps, the explanation for her unusually long-term association with Kenneth Craig who was, in certain circles, mildly famous for his prowess in bed or any other convenient place.

The inspector did not, however, realize just how impressed Pamela had been by Craig until he interrogated thirty-year-old Martha Decker, Pamela's closest girlfriend and her only confidante.

Up to this point, the inspector had been inclined to regard either Bill Rood or Tom Drysdale as the most likely suspects. Both had been interrogated, but neither had been charged as there was no evidence against them. Their value as suspects was, moreover, considerably reduced by the fact that both had had an equal motive. This precluded charging either the one or the other, as the one charged could point out that there was no more reason to suspect him than the other lover. On

372

the other hand, the police could not bring charges against both because it was clear that the murders had been carried out by one man only.

As a result, the inspector had begun to think that he was not going to solve his case, but what Martha Decker had to say put a different complexion on things. According to her statement, Pamela had been, perhaps for the first time in her life, emotionally involved in her affair with Craig. She had wanted to marry him, but she was unwilling to relinquish Kearns's money. What she wanted was for Kearns to bring a divorce action against her so that she could obtain a generous settlement. She had, therefore, been almost flagrant in the affair with Craig and this explained why she had entertained him in her own home, something that she had never done with any of her other lovers. Nigel, said Martha Decker, had known about the affair since November of the preceding year.

This information put Nigel Kearns back at the head of the list of suspects, but it did not help the inspector solve his case. Kearns's alibi was absolutely watertight.

Up until Monday, 21 January 1980. On that date Mrs Sheila Kearns received a ticket for speeding. She had been photographed by a radar control doing close to eighty miles an hour in a thirty-mile-an-hour zone outside Adelaide.

Mrs Kearns was furious. Coming personally to the traffic department at police headquarters, she pounded on the desk and shouted that their radar equipment was defective. According to the charge, the offence had taken place at thirty-five minutes past midnight on 15 January. At that time she had been sound asleep in bed on the Kearns estate sixty miles away.

The equipment was not, however, defective and, if it did not show the driver, the camera had recorded very clearly the licence number of the speeding car. Sheila Kearns was going to have to pay her traffic ticket.

Bewildered, but unable to refute the evidence of the photograph, Sheila Kearns had no alternative but to pay and, had the murder of Pamela Kearns not been so recent and fresh in the minds of the police, the matter might have rested there. As it was, the officers of the traffic department found the incident strange and sent a report on it to the Criminal Investigations Department.

The inspector took one look at the report and knew that his case was solved. Somehow Nigel Kearns had managed to make use of his sister-in-law's car, had driven to Adelaide at breakneck speed, had murdered his wife and her lover, and had returned with what would have been a perfect alibi had it not been for the radar speed trap and the camera.

Confronted with the evidence, Kearns confessed and explained. He had known of his wife's infidelities and her plans to obtain a large settlement from him in return for a divorce. He had decided to murder her and her lover, and had deliberately arranged for the alibi by going to spend the weekend with his brother and sister-in-law. Immediately that they had gone to bed, he had crept out of the house, had taken the sports car out of gear and had pushed it without starting out into the road and to the top of a slope leading away from the house. He had only started it when he was safely out of earshot.

After a very fast trip, he had arrived in good time to stand listening outside the bedroom door while his wife and her lover approached their mutual climax. When he walked quietly into the room, they had been too occupied to notice him. He did not think that either had realized that a third party was present.

On the basis of his own confession, this was a coldly premeditated double homicide, but there were, of course, extenuating circumstances. Nigel Kearns was a wealthy and important man.

That, in itself, might not be regarded as an extenuating circumstance, although it sometimes has been, but the impressive list of men with whom his wife had deceived him was. As his attorney pointed out, it was bad enough that his wife was out picking up lovers while he was at work. Having to finance her future life with a new husband was too much.

The court was inclined to find some merit in this argument on 8 January 1982 sentenced him to the modest term of ten years' imprisonment.

9

NAPOLEON CAME FROM CORSICA AND IT IS EASY TO SEE WHY HE LEFT

With the exception of the carefully devised alibi, the case of the Pamela Kearns murder is classic; banal even. Money and sexual infidelity are at the base of a great many homicides, with sex enjoying a large lead over cash.

Although the media have been proclaiming sexual revolution and liberation for close to twenty years, a great many individuals have failed to get the message. Knowing full well that extra-marital activities of the spouse are nothing more than an expression of self essential to the satisfactory development of the personality, they still reach for knife, gun or blunt object when confronted with the spectacle of the companion, legal or otherwise, locked in passionate embrace with the dustman, the lady next door, the mayor, the au pair, etc., etc.

To the casual observer, it would seem that this sort of thing is handled rather straightforwardly in Anglo-Saxon countries or those predominantly so, but among the Latins, the situation can become confused to the point where it is difficult to keep the participants separated in the mind without a chart of relationships. In a place like Corsica, it sometimes seems that it is impossible to murder anyone without involving most of the population of the island.

This confusion exists only in the minds of non-Corsicans, of course. The local inhabitants know very well what is going on without any chart. They also know what to do about it.

The instant that the sound of the twelve-gauge shotgun

blast bounced off his eardrums, Postman Jacques Busquet half fell, half leapt off his bicycle and rolled into the ditch. A Corsican born and bred, he knew the sound of a shotgun when he heard it and he could estimate very exactly what a gunshot in that quiet residential section of the little town of Rutali known as Pantane meant. It was ten o'clock in the morning of Tuesday, 12 February 1980, and it was not the hunting season.

Normally a gunshot in Corsica, where some of the inhabitants are inclined to be excitable, is followed by answering gunshots, but, on this occasion, there were none. Postman Busquet cautiously lifted his head and peered over the edge of the ditch.

Thirty-eight-year-old Ange Casta at whose house he had delivered the mail less than five minutes before was thrashing around and groaning at the foot of the large chestnut tree which stood at the boundary separating his property from that of the Ettoris', the last house where Busquet had delivered the mail before hearing the gunshot.

Crouching in the ditch, he watched attentively but uncomprehendingly as thirty-six-year-old Angele Ettori emerged from her house and ran to where Casta was lying on the ground. Squatting down beside him, she attempted to lift his head.

She had hardly arrived, when Mathilde Casta, the forty-one-year-old wife of the wounded man, came rushing out of her house and fell upon Angele like an avenging fury. She had a small paring knife in her hand and she was apparently attempting to disembowel the other woman.

Angele fought back. They were both small, slender women, but wiry and astonishingly strong and almost evenly matched. Suddenly both began to scream at the top of their voices.

Postman Busquet climbed out of the ditch, hurriedly collected his mail sack and his bicycle and, mounting the latter, pedalled away as fast as he could go. The screams meant that large numbers of the Ettori and Casta clans would be arriving shortly and he did not want to be present when they got there.

He had not got a hundred yards down the road when the policecar from the gendarmerie station at Murato passed him heading in the direction of Pantane. It was doing close to ninety miles an hour, its sirens screaming like tortured tom cats and gendarmes hanging all over it. They were armed to the teeth. In Corsica, a major problem of the police when someone has been shot is to prevent the relatives of the family clans involved from killing each other.

They were none too quick. Corsica, the big French island in the Mediterranean off the coast of Italy and the birthplace of Napoleon, has a great deal of unemployment and many of the men of the Ettori and Casta clans were at home. They came boiling on to the scene, armed with knives, iron bars, shovels, axes or anything else that they had been able to scoop up. Their women came with them, more savage, more bloodthirsty, and deadlier than the males. In some respects, the Corsican woman is very thoroughly liberated.

Fortunately, there was a certain amount of confusion before the battle lines could be drawn and the policecar coming to a halt with a howl of brakes that drowned out the siren, the gendarmes peeled off it like grapes and waded in. Their tactics were simple: arrest everybody in sight.

In the meantime, the rest of the village was on the way. Rutali mayor Francis Maroselli arrived, wheezing like a walrus and bringing with him the local physician, Dr Lucien Monal, with whom he had happened to be speaking in the town hall less than a hundred yards away when the shot rang out. They were followed by the village priest, Father Giuliani, who came carrying the necessary for the last sacrament just in case.

Dr Monal, a very short, very stockily built man with blue-black hair and a small, black moustache, ran forward to where Casta was now lying motionless at the foot of the tree and knelt down beside him. Immediately he began signalling over his shoulder for the priest.

Father Giuliani hurried forward, knelt down and began to intone the rites of the last sacrament. Casta was lying on his back, his mouth and eyes wide open. Blood was gushing from between his lips and his breath came in long, rattling gasps.

Abruptly, the breathing ceased altogether and the powerful, longshoreman's body went as limp as a piece of string.

Father Giuliani crossed himself, concluded the ritual and got a little shakily to his feet. He, too, was a Corsican born and bred, but he was more appalled than attracted by violence.

The doctor automatically started to cross the arms of the dead man over his chest and then caught himself. The chest was a sea of torn flesh and ripped fabric from the shirt he had been wearing, and it was obvious that this was a matter for the investigators of the criminal police. They would want the body as undisturbed as possible.

The gendarmes had, by now, got the situation under control and had taken into custody a baker's dozen of Ettoris and a carefully balanced equal number of Castas, not counting the widow and Angele Ettori, who had been separated by four badly scratched gendarmes.

All the Castas were shouting that it was Angele who had murdered Ange and she and the Ettoris were not denying it, confiding their remarks to picturesque insults and abuse. It seemed, however, that there were no actual witnesses to the shooting.

Assured that open warfare had been averted, the captain in charge of the gendarmerie detachment came over and looked expressionlessly at the corpse for about a minute and then went off to the gendarmerie van to telephone the Criminal Investigations Department in the nearby city of Bastia over the police radio. Any homicide investigation in the northern half of the island would be carried out by the Bastia CID. The gendarmerie was not equipped for it.

Bastia is the largest city on the island, although, with a population of a little over fifty thousand, it barely surpasses in size its rival of Ajaccio on the west coast and further to the south. Despite its small population, its police have a large and efficient criminal investigations department as it has to handle the investigation work for all of the smaller communities surrounding it. There is always plenty to do. Whatever other unemployment there may be on the island of Corsica, there is none with the police.

The distance not being great and it being the middle of the morning of a week day in winter when all of the departments at police headquarters were at full strength, the corpse had scarcely ceased bleeding when Inspector Louis Sardinelli, senior investigator and homicide squad chief, arrived at the scene with his assistant, Detective-Sergeant Jean Ventura. They found most of the population of the village of Rutali present including the husband of Angele Ettori, thirty-eight-year-old Paul Ettori, who had been notified of the events at his job as a garage mechanic in the nearby village of Valrose and had promptly hurried home. He was a small man, brown-skinned and very heavily moustached.

Having taken a look at the corpse, the inspector asked a few questions and then went to the Ettori house where he found a twelve-gauge shotgun lying on the floor in front of the second-storey living-room window. From the window, there was a clear line of fire to the chestnut tree where Casta had been shot down.

The inspector, a compactly built man whose black hair was going a little thin on top, did not touch the gun or anything else, but went back outside and told the sergeant to call Bastia and have a squad from the police laboratory sent out.

'Is it necessary?' said the sergeant. He was a much younger man, round-faced, good-natured looking and disarmingly informal in his manner. 'The woman admits that she shot him.'

'She may change her mind,' said the inspector. 'In any case, the court will expect us to present whatever material evidence there is here. It's what we're paid for.'

The sergeant shrugged and went off to carry out his orders.

The inspector walked over to where Angele Ettori was standing with her husband, her fifteen-year-old son, her eleven-year-old daughter and two gendarmes.

'Did you shoot him?' he asked.

Mrs Ettori nodded silently, casting down her eyes.

'Why?' said the inspector.

'He was after me,' said Mrs Ettori, her voice an almost inaudible whisper. 'I was afraid.'

The inspector looked at the body lying under the chestnut

tree and up at the window of the house. The distance was approximately forty yards.

'You do not need to make a statement,' said the inspector. 'If you wish to speak to an attorney first, you may do so. However, if you want to make a statement, my assistant will take it down as soon as he returns. You understand that it can be used against you later?'

Mrs Ettori said nothing, but Paul Ettori began to yell that there was no need for an attorney or anything else. The man had been persecuting his wife. She had defended herself. It was her right.

At this, all of the Castas began shouting and cursing the entire Ettori family, Angele in particular, the most frequently used expression being 'putana', the local term for 'whore'.

The inspector looked questioningly at Mrs Ettori.

'They think I was having an affair with Ange,' she whispered, looking down at the ground and turning an attractive shade of dusky pink. 'It is not true.'

The inspector sighed. 'We shall see,' he said. 'Here is Sergeant Ventura now. He will take your statement and make a recording of it on this little tape recorder. You understand that you are under no obligation to make any statement at all unless you so wish?'

Angele Ettori did so wish and she made a rather short statement in which she said that Ange Casta had been pursuing her for some time. When she had gone to the post office or to do her shopping he was always there, and he had even come to the mayor's office where she worked as secretary to Mayor Maroselli and had attempted to kiss her against her will. She was a respectable woman and she had refused his advances, but he had become only more insistent. On that morning, he had been in his garden when she came out to collect her mail, and he had called out that he was coming over that afternoon and bringing a friend. They would deal with her, he had said menacingly.

Mrs Ettori said that she had been so frightened by this threat that she had gone to the garage and picked up her husband's shotgun which he had bought for hunting. The

380

shells were kept in the bathroom and she had chosen one at random and had fired out the window in the direction of Casta who was standing under the chestnut tree with the intention of frightening him. When she saw that he had been hit, she had immediately called the gendarmerie at Murato. She had thought that they would bring an ambulance.

It was obvious that, if this statement were to be accepted, the maximum charge would be unintentional homicide, and the inspector formally took Mrs Ettori into custody and sent her to Bastia to be detained until such time as the instructions judge would decide whether she should be released or held until the trial took place.

The names and addresses of all the persons in custody were then verified and they were ordered to disperse. This they did, but began almost immediately a pitched battle less than two hundred yards from the scene which was, however, quickly broken up by the gendarmes who had been anticipating just such a development.

A little later, a squad car with four technicians from the police laboratory in Bastia arrived, examined the gun, reported that there were latent fingerprints on it, and took it back with them. It was the only piece of evidence as there was, of course, nothing of significance to the investigation either near or on the corpse.

This too was taken away to the police morgue in Bastia where a routine autopsy was carried out on it for the purposes of the official report establishing cause and time of death. A small handful of buckshot was recovered from the body, but was of no value to the investigation as, unlike a rifle or pistol, it is not possible to determine from what gun the shot of a shotgun shell has been fired.

Long before these measures had been completed, the inspector had, of course, returned to his office in Bastia. There was nothing for him to do in Rutali. The statements from the very large number of persons there anxious to make them would be taken by the investigations officers from his department. He already knew that no actual witnesses to the shooting had been found and any statements made would be mainly useful in establishing the motive. As Angele Ettori

381

had already confessed, it was not her acts but her reasons for them that were of primary importance for the trial.

The inspector thought that it was murder and not unintentional at all. He knew a good deal about firearms and, in his opinion, it was an exceptional shot who could hit a man square in the chest from a distance of forty yards, even with a shotgun. To make the feat the more difficult, the charge had been buckshot, meaning that there had been a relatively small number of pellets. He, therefore, found Mrs Ettori's statement that this was the first time in her life she had ever fired a gun hard to accept.

So did the Castas. What with court dockets as crowded as they are, justice does not move very swiftly on the island and it was early summer of 1981 before Angele Ettori was finally brought to trial for the shooting of Ange Casta. She had spent less than a week in detention and, having performed a reenactment of the crime for the police, had been released to look after her family. It was not supposed that she would make an attempt to flee the country or take to the mountains. Indeed, she could hardly do so without admitting that she was guilty of murder and that the shooting of Casta had not been the act of self-defence which she maintained it was.

During this time, the village of Rutali and the surrounding district had been divided into what amounted to two warring camps. The Ettoris were very numerous and all of them swore to heaven that Ange Casta had been a lust-maddened satyr who had tracked Angele Ettori like a weasel hunting down a mouse and with much the same intentions. Had she not acted to defend herself, he would undoubtedly have raped her at the very least and his friends would probably have joined him.

To this, the Castas, who were equally if not more numerous than the Ettoris, replied that Angele was a notorious nymphomaniac. She had tried every trick in the book to lure him away from his legitimate wife, pitifully five years older than Angele and already a widow with two children when he had married her in 1964. It was only when, exhausted by her insatiable sexual demands, he had tried to free himself from her lascivious clutches, that she had confronted him with a choice between make love or die. The honest Ange, now repenting the practically forced infidelity to his faithful wife, had courageously chosen death and had been ruthlessly executed.

Neither of these versions was completely without flaws when compared dispassionately with the facts, but the emotions of the parties involved were so intense that the riot squad from the gendarmerie post at Murato had to make no less than five sorties to avoid the situation degenerating into actual armed conflict. There was, to say the least, a lively interest in the proceedings and outcome of the trial.

And not only among the Ettoris and the Castas. When the trial opened in the last week of June 1981, before the Superior Criminal Court in Bastia, the courtroom was packed with practically every able-bodied inhabitant of the Rutali area. Shops and businesses were closed as there were neither customers to buy nor employees to work in them. Even the mail did not get delivered as Postman Jacques Busquet had been summoned as a witness. He was neither for the prosecution nor the defence, but, as the closest thing to an eye witness to the shooting, was called upon to recount what he had seen and heard.

Also called as witnesses, but by the prosecution were Father Giuliani and Mayor Francis Maroselli. According to the pre-trial claims of the Castas, positive proof would be provided that Angele Ettori had practically raped the unwilling Ange Casta and had wilfully, feloniously and with malice aforethought murdered him when he refused to submit to further sexual persecution.

However, the first word in the trial went to the police, and Inspector Sardinelli gave his testimony in a terse, lucid and matter-of-fact manner. It was by no means the first time that he had been called upon to testify in such cases.

Referring to his notebook for dates and times, he outlined the steps taken by the investigation, starting with his arrival at the scene of the crime at seven minutes to eleven on the morning of 12 February 1980. He described the condition of the body and, using a chart, spotted its position in relation to the Ettori and Casta houses and the large chestnut tree on the boundary between them. The distance between the living-room window of the Ettori home where the shot had been fired and the point where Casta had fallen was one hundred and twenty-seven feet.

He passed on to the recovery of the murder weapon by the technicians from the police laboratory who had found the barrel of the gun still smelling of gun powder which indicated that it had been fired recently. It was a comparatively new gun which had been used but little, and Mrs Ettori's finger-prints were on it in the firing position, including one clear print of the right index finger on the trigger itself. The trigger was not cross-hatched as would have been the case in a more expensive weapon, but smooth and it had taken a fingerprint.

There had been an expended shell in the chamber of the gun when it was recovered by the technicians, and a part box of similar shells of the same make was found in the bathroom of the house. The charges in these shells ranged from number four to buckshot.

It had been determined that the expended shell in the breech of the shotgun had been charged with buckshot and a quantity of buckshot roughly equivalent to the charge had been recovered from the body during the course of the autopsy.

According to the findings of the autopsy report, Ange Casta had died of loss of blood occasioned by the puncturing of a large number of blood vessels in the chest and upper abdomen which had resulted in massive haemorrhaging quickly followed by death. It was an indication of his great physical strength and sturdy constitution that he had con-tinued to breath at all after having been shot, but it was thought unlikely that he had been conscious.

The inspector then ran the tape recording of Mrs Ettori's statement taken at the scene of the crime, commented that her subsequent statements had differed from it in no way, and concluded his testimony with the information that a number of pornographic magazines and photographs had been found under the mattress of the bed which Paul and Angele Ettori shared.

At this there were cries from the Casta side of the

courtroom of 'pictures of herself!', and from the Ettori faction of 'dirty swine!', and the judge had to threaten to clear the court in order to re-establish order.

Sergeant Ventura was then called to the stand and described a re-enactment of the shooting which Mrs Ettori had voluntarily carried out. He had been in charge of this operation as the inspector had been occupied elsewhere. Mrs Ettori, he said, had gone through the motions of loading the gun and firing a shot out the window, but without actually putting a shell into the chamber. In his opinion, the re-enactment reflected faithfully what had taken place on the day in question.

The police testimony had been necessarily short as, there being no question as to who had done the shooting and who had been shot, the investigation had been short. Angele Ettori had never denied shooting Ange Casta and she was not going to deny it now.

A small woman, dark and slender, she looked scarcely more than a child sitting demurely in the witness stand from which she was to tell her story and explain her action before returning to the pen reserved for the accused.

In response to the routine background questioning of the judge, she said she had been born in the tiny village of Cuttoli-Corticchiato in the extreme south of Corsica and had been the oldest in a family of eight children. Her father had been an employee of the highway department and the family had moved frequently.

She had met Paul Ettori toward the end of 1964 and had married him on 26 June 1965. Their first child had been born in 1966 and the second in 1970. She described the marriage as a happy one.

Following the birth of the second child, they had found the quarters in the house of her mother, with whom they had been living up until that time, too crowded and had bought the house at Pantane in Rutali into which they had moved in 1972.

In 1977, Ange and Mathilde Casta and one of the children from Mrs Casta's first marriage had moved into the neighbouring house of which the garden adjoined the garden of the

385

Ettori house. Mrs Casta's oldest daughter was no longer living with them as she was already married.

For the first two years there had been little contact between the Ettoris and the Castas, but in 1979 Ange Casta and Paul Ettori had become friends, playing cards together, lending each other tools and helping each other with the garden work. Very shortly thereafter, Casta had begun making improper advances toward her; advances which she had firmly rejected.

The testimony of the accused was interrupted by howls of rage from the Casta clan and the air turned blue with insults, curses and threats. The impression conveyed was that the Castas did not agree with the statements of the accused.

The presiding judge, accustomed to such scenes, calmly raised his voice to a shrill yell which penetrated the uproar and made clear that, unless there was total silence in the courtroom within ten seconds the bailiffs would begin clearing it.

There was total silence within ten seconds. No one wanted to miss out on the trial. Mrs Ettori continued.

Casta, she said, had begun with romantic suggestions. A mason turned longshoreman, he was on a different work schedule than Paul Ettori who was a garage mechanic and he was often home when Paul was not. On such occasions he would find some excuse to come to the Ettori house, and he had ended by telling her bluntly that she was the reason for his visits and that he would like to make love to her.

According to Mrs Ettori she had indignantly refused, but Casta had become more pressing. Wherever she went, shopping or on any other errands, he invariably turned up, and he had boldly come to the mayor's office where she worked and had attempted to fondle her. She had continued to resist his advances, but she was gradually becoming frightened.

'Why then, Mrs Ettori,' said the presiding judge, 'did you not tell your husband of these unwelcome attentions? As your husband, it was up to him to protect you from such advances by other men.'

'I was afraid that they would fight,' said Angele Ettori.

'Paul is a good man, but he is not very big. Mr Casta was very big, very powerful. He would have hurt Paul.'

The proceedings were once again interrupted by shrieks of rage, this time from the widow of the victim who leaped to her feet and delivered a passionate eulogy of her dead husband, described as more gentle than a mouse, with such speed that she had almost finished by the time the bailiff, in response to the judge's gesture, picked her up by the elbows and walked her out of the courtroom. She immediately stopped yelling and, as the proceedings resumed, crept quietly back in and recovered her place.

Angele Ettori said that matters had gone from bad to worse and that Casta had begun making obscene telephone calls to her both at work and at home in which he described in crude, physical detail precisely what he intended to do to her. She had been afraid to leave the house, and had asked her husband to drive her to her job in the mayor's office even though it was only a short distance away.

The judge then brought the focus of the questioning to the events of the morning of Tuesday, 12 February 1980, and Mrs Ettori repeated her statement of having been accosted by Casta when she went out to get her mail. He had called out, 'I'm coming over this afternoon with a friend and we'll take care of you.' This had frightened her so badly that she had got her husband's shotgun from the garage, had loaded it with a shell from the box in the bathroom and had fired a shot out the window in Casta's direction.

She had, she insisted, not intended to harm him, but merely to frighten him into leaving her alone. She had not deliberately chosen buckshot over the far less dangerous number four shot, but had merely caught up the first shell which came to hand. In any case, she said, she did not know one charge from another. She had never had a gun in her hands before.

It was becoming obvious that the witnesses for the prosecution and, particularly, the widow of the deceased were going to expire of apoplexy unless they came to make their statements very shortly, and the judge sent Angele Ettori back to the accused box and called Mrs Mathilda Casta.

Mrs Casta was also small, dark and very angry. She said that she knew with certainty that Angele Ettori had been having an affair with her husband because she had personally caught them in the very act of intercourse, once in a ditch at the foot of the garden, once in her own bathroom and once in a cellar. She had appealed to the mayor and to Father Giuliani to intervene and had pleaded with her husband to terminate the affair. He had said that he, too, would like to get out of it but that Angele was hard to shake off, and he had shown her a watch which Angele had given him for Christmas in 1979.

Several more Castas were called to the witness stand, including Mrs Casta's oldest daughter, and all confirmed her statements in detail. Father Giuliani and Mayor Maroselli were more cautious. Both confirmed that Mrs Casta had approached them concerning an affair between her husband and Angele Ettori, but they, themselves, had no personal knowledge of the affair other than Mrs Casta's statement. They had not spoken to Mr Casta nor to Mrs Ettori.

Brought back to the witness stand and questioned about the incident of the watch which she had allegedly given to Ange Casta for Christmas, Mrs Ettori said that she had not given him the watch; he had stolen it from her. She had bought the watch as a present for her husband and Casta had seen it lying on the table, had picked it up and put it in his pocket and had said that, unless she yielded to his wishes, he would tell everyone that she had given it to him.

At this point there was such an outcry on the part of the Castas and such a response from the Ettoris that the judge was forced to clear the courtroom, and it was over an hour before the trial could be resumed. In the meantime, a very large contingent of police strove, with only indifferent success, to prevent bloodshed in the street outside.

There was not much left to the trial in any case. Paul Ettori was called and asked about the pornography under the mattress of the bed of which his wife had already denied all knowledge.

Obviously embarrassed, he said it had been given him by a friend and, as he had no interest in it, he had hidden it under the mattress.

This statement produced some derisive and obscene remarks from the Castas which were followed by cheers as the prosecution called for the relatively harsh sentence of fifteen years.

The defence called for acquittal which produced yells of, 'Why not give her the Legion of Honour?'

In the end the court gave Angele Ettori neither fifteen years nor the Legion of Honour, but sentenced her to the modest term of five years' imprisonment.

The Castas rushed the police with intent to lynch, but were repulsed and the prisoner was led off.

'Be interesting to know what really did happen,' remarked the inspector, leaving the courtroom with his assistant. 'Wouldn't it?'

The sergeant nodded, but, privately, he was not in agreement. In Corsica, sometimes the less you know, the better off you are.

10

RELIABLE DOMESTIC HELP IS BECOMING IMPOSSIBLE TO FIND

Who was mad in the case of the murder of Ange Casta? A difficult question to answer, but for those not resident in Corsica, speculation is, at least, not dangerous.

Ange Casta was, in his pursuit of the housewife next door, not mad, but merely trying to relieve glandular pressure, a common enough ambition in men of his age and state of physical well-being.

On the other hand, the intensity of his pursuit would seem to fall within the range of a minor obsession if not a compulsive urge. Few would-be seducers go to the mayor's office to fondle housewives who are at work there.

And, indeed, if Mrs Casta was telling the truth, and there was considerable evidence that she was, then why would Casta need to fondle Mrs Ettori in the mayor's office? He could have done so with greater privacy in the ditch, the bathroom or the cellar where Mrs Casta was supposed to have surprised them doing more than fondle.

Unless all of the statements made at the trial were unvarnished lies, it would appear that Ange Casta was, at the least, eccentric.

No less so, Angele Ettori. Was she having an affair with Casta or not? Mrs Casta said she was. She said she wasn't. The witnesses testified according to family, but none claimed to have actual, first-hand knowledge.

Assuming that she was, what did she expect to gain by cutting down on her lover with her husband's twelve-gauge?

Assuming that she wasn't, ditto.

One thing is certain: she did not actually expect to kill him.

No evidence was found that she had ever had a gun in her hands before, and there was a blue-black bruise the size of a dinner plate on her right shoulder, indicating that she was not aware that a twelve-gauge has a noticeable recoil and that she had not held it properly or tight enough.

Probably the best reaction to the crime was that of Jacques Busquet. Jump into the ditch until the shooting is over.

Whatever the motives of all parties concerned, Angele Ettori was not particularly clever about her crime and she got sent to jail for it. Others were far more ingenious and ended up in the morgue. However, in the case of forty-five-year-old Petrus de Beer, it was stupidity and not madness which occasioned his downfall.

For a man holding such a high position in the civil service, if he had been determined to murder his wife, he should have been able to hit upon something better than strychnine which leaves such easily detectable traces in the body.

Nevertheless, strychnine was what he had used and, according to the analysis of the stomach contents, it had been administered in a cup of herb tea. There had been a generous quantity of it and forty-two-year-old Doreen de Beer had died quickly, although in great agony. Death by strychnine poisoning is not pleasant. The symptoms are a suffocating tightness in the chest, violent spasms and convulsions.

Petrus de Beer had telephoned his family physician on that evening of 15 April 1979 to say that his wife was not feeling well. Could the doctor come at once?

It was a massive understatement and, although the doctor had come immediately to the luxury villa in the exclusive residential section on the outskirts of Cape Town, the legislative capital of South Africa on the southern tip of the continent, by the time he arrived, Mrs de Beer was so obviously beyond help that he did not even call the ambulance.

As the doctor was unable to say with certainty what had caused Mrs de Beer's death, he refused to issue a death certificate and suggested that de Beer call the police immediately. There would have to be an investigation and probably an autopsy. He did not know what had killed

Mrs de Beer, but it did not look like a natural death to him.

De Beer had called the police and the duty homicide squad consisting of Inspector Jan Brinker, Detective-Sergeant Otto Shryker and a police expert in forensic medicine, Dr Martin Hampton, came out immediately.

Dr Hampton carried out a comparatively short examination of the corpse, following which he took the inspector aside and spoke to him in a low voice.

On the basis of his remarks, the inspector took de Beer into custody, cautioned him on his rights and asked if he would care to make a statement.

De Beer said that he would. It was that he was outraged by the behaviour of the police. He had just undergone the ordeal of losing his beloved wife of many years and, rather than receiving the sympathy and support to which he was entitled, he was being treated like a criminal.

The inspector said that he was being treated like a criminal because there was reason to believe that he was one. He then instructed the sergeant to call police headquarters and have a detachment sent out from the police laboratory. He wanted the villa searched from top to bottom.

As it turned out this was not necessary. The search lasted only a short time as the little bottle, still more than half filled with white crystals, was found in de Beer's desk drawer. It had fingerprints all over it and it did not take long to determine that they were de Beer's.

The corpse of the victim was transferred to the police morgue for the formal autopsy, and de Beer was taken to police headquarters and placed under interrogation.

The autopsy produced exactly the results that Dr Hampton had suggested that it would: death by reason of massive ingestion of strychnine. The interrogation produced nothing.

A huge, red-haired man six feet three inches tall, de Beer held a high administrative position in the civil service and he and his wife had been socially prominent. Despite the evidence of the bottle of strychnine with his fingerprints on it, he vigorously denied any responsibility for his wife's death. He had had, he said, no motive. Asked how he then accounted for Doreen's death, he suggested that she had committed suicide.

This theory did not strike the inspector as very probably as it did not explain what the poison was doing hidden in de Beer's desk or how his fingerprints came to be all over the bottle. There were no fingerprints on it belonging to Mrs de Beer or anyone else.

Nonetheless, de Beer's reaction puzzled the inspector. In the first place, as far as could be ascertained, he was telling the truth about having no motive. The death of his wife had brought him no advantage, financial or otherwise, and there were no reports of domestic friction between the couple.

Moreover, de Beer's refusal to confess to the crime in the face of the physical evidence against him was illogical. He was not a stupid man and he had to realize that he could easily be convicted without a confession on the basis of the evidence alone. Why continue to undergo the unpleasantness of interrogation when a confession would not harm his position and might actually improve it when he was brought to trial for the murder?

There was something else, too. De Beer was unmistakably astonished beyond all measure that the autopsy had been able to detect traces of strychnine in his wife's body. He had repeatedly asked if the doctor had been quite certain. Was the white powder really strychnine? Did strychnine really remain in the body?

The inspector assured him that it did and that the evidence was complete and confirmed. The only thing lacking in the case was the motive, but it would be quite possible to obtain a conviction without it. Why he had murdered his wife did not matter so much as the fact that he had, and this was a fact which the police were in a position to demonstrate conclusively.

As things now stood, the inspector pointed out, he would probably be hung for the crime. If, however, he made a confession and presumably was able to offer some extenuating circumstances or, at least, expressed repentance, he might save his neck.

De Beer thought this over and eventually came to the conclusion that there was much in what the inspector said. At his next session with the interrogators, he indicated that he was now prepared to make a statement on the murder and that he would like to make it directly to the inspector himself.

Taken to Inspector Brinker's office, he said that it was true, he had murdered his wife with a tablespoon of strychnine in the cup of herbal tea which she took every evening. The reason for doing this was that he wanted to marry their housemaid, a twenty-year-old, blonde girl who came from the village of Fort Beaufort and who had worked for the de Beer's since 12 October 1978.

The girl's name was Elsabe Loubser and de Beer said that they had been having an affair since 6 January 1979. Being a civil servant, he was extremely precise in his dates and details.

He had been attracted, he said, to the big, generously built, blonde girl from the moment that she came to work for them and had begun almost immediately to lay hands on her whenever the opportunity presented itself. She had raised no serious objections and, encouraged by this lack of resistance, he had progressed to greater intimacies until on the night of 6 January, he had gone to her room at approximately 11 o'clock in the evening after his wife had gone to sleep where he had found her lying naked on her bed. Cape Town being in the southern hemisphere, January is, of course, the middle of the summer and the weather was warm.

They had had intercourse and, to his surprise, Elsabe had turned out to be a virgin.

After that they had had sexual relations frequently, sometimes in Elsabe's room and sometimes with the girl bent over the kitchen table with her skirts raised.

By the middle of April 1979, he had fallen so deeply in love with the housemaid that he could not bear the thought of life without her and he had asked her to marry him. He would, he said, divorce his wife.

Elsabe had not refused to marry him, but she had pointed out that divorce was not a simple matter. South Africa is conservative and divorce is frowned upon. For a man in his position, a divorce, probably contested and followed by a marriage to a housemaid, could cost him his job and certainly his social position.

De Beer had realized the truth of this remark and, without being too clear as to what he had in mind, had muttered that there must be some other way. He insisted that he had not, at that time, been thinking of murdering his wife.

On the following day, however, Elsabe had taken advantage of a moment when they were alone together and had pressed into his hand the little bottle of white crystals. She did not say what it was for, but she did say that it was a deadly poison and that it left no traces in the body.

De Beer, ravished by what he believed to be a demonstration of reciprocal feeling by Elsabe regarding their relationship, had proceeded to poison his wife that same evening.

He now recognized the folly of his act and regretted bitterly what he had done. It had been a sort of temporary insanity brought upon by an infatuation with a woman twenty-five years younger than himself. He was not, he pointed out, the first to find himself in such a situation.

This was perfectly true and it not only explained the motive of the murder, but constituted a basis for establishing the extenuating circumstances which would, perhaps, save de Beer from the gallows.

Healthy, successful men who have passed forty are often highly vulnerable to very young women and the courts recognize that their actions under such circumstances are not always completely rational. There would be precedents enough for de Beer's attorneys to draw on.

At the same time, however, de Beer's confession made Elsabe Loubser an accessory before the fact to murder and, possibly, even an accomplice. If she had procured the poison and had given it to de Beer with the hint that this could safely solve his marital problems, then she was as much of an instigator as he.

She was promptly taken into custody and brought to police headquarters where she was confronted with de Beer's tape-recorded confession.

Having listened to it, she said that there was not a word of truth in what de Beer said. She had never been intimate with her employer. She had entertained a great respect and even affection for Mrs de Beer and she had neither given de Beer any poison nor even suspected that he was in possession of any. The only explanation that she could suggest for his statement was that he was trying to pass the responsibility for the crime off on to an innocent housemaid in order to save himself.

Inspector Brinker was not convinced. De Beer's confession had been too precise, too detailed to be a pure fabrication, and it was the only reasonable explanation of his motives. Thinking that the young housemaid might not stand up well under a direct confrontation with her former employer and alleged lover, the inspector arranged for one.

The results were disappointing. De Beer went all to pieces, pleading with Elsabe to tell the police the truth and admit that they had been lovers and that she had given him the poison.

Elsabe was demure. 'I don't know what you're talking about, Mr de Beer,' she said. 'I have always tried to give good service while I was working for you. I don't know why you should want to harm me with these lies.'

De Beer was taken back, raving slightly, to the detention cells and Elsabe Loubser was released. There was not the slightest evidence other than the unsupported word of Petrus de Beer which would permit her to be held.

She had not, however, convinced the inspector. He still thought that de Beer was telling the truth. Otherwise, there was no logic to his actions whatsoever, and he had already been examined by a psychologist who reported that he appeared to be sane. De Beer was not hallucinating; he was telling the truth.

Whether he was or not made little difference to the inspector's case. Although he personally believed that Elsabe Loubser was at least as guilty of the crime as was de Beer, there was nothing in the world that he could do about it.

For de Beer the difference was a matter of life and death. With the refusal of Elsabe to support his statement, his hope for clemency as a result of extenuating circumstances had vanished. South Africa has the death penalty and uses it. Barring miracles, his next stop would be the gallows.

The inspector, therefore, instructed the sergeant to assign a man to keep an eye on Elsabe Loubser to see whether anything suspicious might turn up in her behaviour. He was afraid nothing would and he was quite right. One of the de Beers being dead and the other in jail, she had, of course, lost her job, but it did not take her long to find another equally satisfactory one in a house only a few blocks away from where the de Beers had lived. Good housemaids are as hard to find in South Africa as anywhere else.

Elsabe Loubser, therefore, continued, rather placidly, her housemaid's career, although nearly everyone who had had anything to do with the case suspected that she was as guilty of the murder of Doreen de Beer as was Doreen's husband. The de Beers being prominent, the newspapers had printed an enormous amount on the case and had speculated concerning Elsabe's role in the matter as much as they dared without inviting a libel suit. Elsabe herself had not given any indications concerning possible libel suits and had cooperated enthusiastically with newspaper reporters wanting interviews, but the city was full of lawyers who knew exactly how much could be extracted for any such unfounded assertations.

In the meantime, Petrus de Beer remained in the detention cells at police headquarters and clung stubbornly to his story. He was no longer being subjected to interrogation, partially because he had confessed to the murder and no further evidence was needed, and partially because the inspector was inclined to believe his story.

Nothing whatsoever of interest or significance having taken place with Elsabe Loubser, her surveillance by the detective was terminated and Sergeant Shryker only made an occasional check to see whether she was still in Cape Town and still working in the same place. The inspector did not want to lose track of her altogether because he had been striving for the past six months to determine the source of the strychnine with which Doreen de Beer had been poisoned. If Petrus de Beer's story was to be believed and the inspector did believe it, then it was Elsabe Loubser who had obtained the strychnine and given it to him.

If the inspector could find evidence of this, it would prove Elsabe's complicity in the crime and tend to confirm de Beer's account. This, in turn, could have an effect on the severity of his sentence.

The inspector had thought that tracing the origin of the strychnine might not prove too difficult. Most commercial strychnine is in the form of rat poison, but that which had been administered to Doreen de Beer consisted of chemically pure crystals. These were not as easy to obtain as rat poison and, as a matter of fact, were less suitable for murder.

Pure strychnine is exceedingly bitter, so much so that the bitterness is perceptible in the proportion of one part strychnine to 700,000 parts of water. Had Doreen de Beer not been in the habit of drinking a herbal tea which was also very bitter, she would almost certainly have noticed the taste.

As a matter of fact, she probably had, but it had been too late. As little as one half to one grain of strychnine is enough to cause death, and de Beer had laced the drink very liberally with the poison. A single swallow had, probably, been more than adequate. Almost instantly the typical abnormal irritability of the reflexes would have set in. The body would have arced painfully backward, the limbs begun to tremble, the neck to stiffen unnaturally and the muscles of the face to contract into a hideous sort of grin. Doreen would, however, have remained conscious. It would be only the stiffening of the chest muscles which would terminate her breathing and result in death by asphyxiation.

As the contortion of the body and the grimace caused by the contracted facial muscles closely resemble the symptoms of tetanus poisoning, the family doctor had been unable to make a definite diagnosis. Dr Hampton, however, trained in forensic medicine, had immediately recognized the signs of strychnine poisoning.

The inspector's efforts were, in the end, doomed to failure. He was not able to show that Elsabe Loubser had bought or otherwise obtained crystalline strychnine and, as he was a thorough man who overlooked no possibilities, he was also unable to find any evidence that Petrus de Beer had either.

De Beer had still not been brought to trial although nearly a year had passed as his attorneys were delaying matters as much as possible in the hope that some substantiation of the extenuating circumstances that he claimed could be obtained. The public prosecutor, like Inspector Brinker, inclined to believe de Beer's statements even though he could not prove them and anxious to give the accused the benefit of the doubt, was not pressing very hard for an early trial either. The newspapers, having found other and more interesting things to entertain their readers, had practically forgotten Petrus de Beer and Elsabe Loubser.

The homicide squad had not and towards the end of January 1980 Sergeant Shryker came into the inspector's office with the news that love had come to the housemaid.

'At least, it looks that way,' he said. 'The fellow's been driving over from Port Elizabeth two and three times a week and that's close to seven hundred miles round trip. Miss Loubser must have something about her that is mighty attractive to some men.'

'She had something that was mighty attractive to Petrus de Beer,' said the inspector. 'Who's this one? Also an older man?'

'Young,' said the sergeant. 'One year older than she is. The name is Marthinus Rossouw. Big, blond, athletic, good looking. He works in the diamond business in Port Elizabeth. No information as to how he came into contact with Miss Loubser, but he's been coming over to see her regularly since about the middle of this month. When he's here, they spend the night at the Rochester Hotel.'

'Second-class hotel,' remarked the inspector. 'Maybe it isn't true love after all.'

'Think of the seven hundred miles round trip,' said the sergeant.

Neither of the officers attached any particular significance to Elsabe Loubser's new friend. She was a young, attractive woman and it would have been more strange for her not to have a boyfriend than to have one. The only fact of any interest which turned up was that she was apparently concerned about her reputation for, although Rossouw registered at the Rochester Hotel under his own name, she gave her name as Barbara Carrington.

'She's probably publicity shy,' said the inspector. 'She had the newspapers buzzing around her so much at the time of the de Beer murder that she doesn't want to have the whole business start all over again. She must have been aware at the time that practically everybody thought that she was implicated in the murder or even directly responsible for it.'

'Well, I'll continue to keep an eye on her from time to time,' said the sergeant. 'You never know what may turn up.'

This was a prophetic observation, but it was going to be seven months before it became evident. The date was August 1980, a Saturday, and the middle of the South African winter. Business at the Rochester Hotel was slow and desk clerk, twenty-eight-year-old Ian Fielding, was peacefully reading a magazine behind the admissions desk in the lobby when he was startled nearly out of his wits by a piercing scream coming from somewhere on the first floor.

A slight but physically courageous man, Fielding dropped his magazine and went running up the stairs. One of the chambermaids was standing in the long hall a dozen doors down from the staircase and yelling her head off. When she saw Fielding, she fainted.

Fielding ran forward to where she lay and, looking through the open door of the room just beyond her, was astounded and horrified to see the naked body of a young, blonde woman sprawled across the bed with her knees bent over the edge of it and her feet touching the floor. Because of the circumstances, the scream and fainting of the chambermaid, he immediately jumped to the conclusion that the woman had been the victim of a rapist.

Conscious of his responsibility for a guest at the hotel, he dashed into the room and attempted to revive the woman, but soon realized that she did not appear to be breathing at all.

Nor could he find any trace of a heart beat. Although he could see no marks of injuries on the body, the woman's face was badly distorted, the eyes starting from their sockets and the tongue protruding from the mouth, and he thought she might have suffered a heart attack.

Picking up the house telephone on the table beside the bed, he told the switchboard operator to call the emergency ambulance service and, after a moment's hesitation, added that she had better also notify the police. He was not certain that the woman was dead, but, if she was, then it did not look to him as if it had been from natural causes.

He was out in the hall trying to revive the chambermaid when the telephone in the room rang. Going over to pick it up, he found himself speaking with the duty officer in the Criminal Investigations Department at police headquarters. The officer wanted to know if there really was a dead woman in the hotel as the switchboard operator had impulsively reported.

Fielding said that there was the body of a woman in the room, but he was not certain whether she was dead or not. He was afraid she was and she certainly looked it. He had called the ambulance.

The officer told him he was to remain where he was and not to allow anyone to enter the room until the police arrived. He wanted to know whether Fielding could identify the body.

Fielding said that he could not without checking the register. He was excited and confused and the dead woman's features were so distorted that he could not recognize her.

The duty officer then asked him if he knew the name of Elsabe Loubser and Fielding replied that he did not. He could not recall ever having had a Elsabe Loubser registered at the hotel.

In the meantime, Inspector Brinker and Sergeant Shryker were driving at a normally illegal speed to the Rochester Hotel. Off duty on that Saturday, they had been alerted over the telephone by the duty officer at police headquarters that a man identifying himself as Marthinus Rossouw had surrendered to the police and had stated that that he had strangled to death a Miss Elsabe Loubser in the Rochester Hotel. Confirmation that a woman, either dead or unconscious, had been found in one of the hotel rooms had just been received from a hotel employee. As Miss Loubser had been involved in the de Beer murder case, Inspector Brinker and Sergeant Shryker were being called in.

Arriving at the hotel only shortly after the ambulance, they found that Elsabe Loubser was very definitely dead as the result of manual strangulation and that Fielding had not been able to recognize the name because he had known her only as Barbara Carrington. He had, by now, collected his wits and not only remembered the girl, but also her companion with whom she had been coming to the hotel for over a half year now.

As there was little that needed to be done, the body of Elsabe Loubser was immediately removed to the ambulance and taken to the police morgue. An autopsy, subsequently carried out by Dr Hampton, was able to determine only that Elsabe had been engaged in sexual intercourse very shortly before her death and that it was the result of manual strangulation by a very strong man who had used great force. The girl's larynx was completely crushed.

Having viewed the corpse at the hotel and having taken a statement from Ian Fielding and the chambermaid who had discovered the body, the inspector and Sergeant Shryker hurried to police headquarters where Marthinus Rossouw was waiting in the detention cells. So far his only statement had been to the effect that he had strangled Elsabe Loubser to death, and he had not yet been sent for interrogation.

Actually no interrogation was necessary. Rossouw willingly volunteered a detailed account of the crime and the events leading up to it.

He had met Elsabe Loubser, he said, in a dance hall in Grosvenor Street on 16 January 1980. They had been immediately attracted to each other and, on that same evening, had had intercourse in Rossouw's car.

They had made a date for the following weekend and from that time on had seen each other as often as Rossouw could manage to get over from Port Elizabeth.

He had, he said, fallen deeply in love with Elsabe and on 15 July he had asked her to marry him.

Elsabe had replied that there was nothing that she wanted more in the world, but she had seemed confused and nervous and she had not given him a definite reply. He had thought that she wanted time to think it over before committing herself.

By that Saturday, on 2 August, she had still not given him a reply to his marriage proposal, and he began to press her gently. They were in the room at the Rochester Hotel which they always occupied and they were both naked as they had just engaged in intercourse.

Elsabe had hesitated, appeared to be on the verge of tears and then seemed to come to a decision. There was, she said, something that he had to know. Her name was not really Barbara Carrington.

Rossouw had been surprised and puzzled. When he had met her she had told him that her name was Barbara Carrington and he had never had any reason to doubt it. What was her name then, he wanted to know?

Elsabe had said that her name was Elsabe Loubser and, when this produced no reaction, she had asked him if he remembered the de Beer murder case.

Marthinus Rossouw remembered the de Beer murder case very well. Like everyone else in South Africa, he had been practically smothered under the masses of copy churned out on the case by the newspapers. There were few people in the country who did not remember intimately the details of the de Beer murder.

The mention of de Beer immediately made the connection in his mind and he recalled that the housemaid had been named Elsabe Loubser. As far as he could remember, however, she had not been implicated in anything other than the unsupported charges by the murderer himself. Why had she seen fit to give him a false name in that case?

Elsabe looked embarrassed and said that, if they were to be married, she did not want to start off by having secrets from him. What de Beer had said was true. She had deliberately tricked him into murdering his wife with a poison that she knew could easily be detected in the body.

The thunderstruck Rossouw demanded to know why she had done such a thing, and Elsabe said that she had done it because she hated de Beer. She had been a virgin when she

403

came to work in the de Beer home and he had practically raped her. She had been unable to resist or complain because she was afraid of losing her job, and it was a very well paid one.

She had, therefore, put up with de Beer's sexual demands on her and had bided her time waiting for an opportunity to revenge herself.

The opportunity had come on 14 April 1979 when de Beer had asked her to marry him and, when she pointed out that divorce was impractical, had muttered that there must be some other way.

Elsabe, according to what she told Rossouw, knew a sort of faith healer and quack doctor from her own village of Fort Beaufort, and she had approached him asking him for a deadly poison which would leave clear traces in the body of a corpse. He had given her the little bottle of strychnine. She had not known that it was strychnine, only that it was deadly poison and that any competent doctor could easily detect it.

The following day she had given the bottle to de Beer with the assurance that it would leave no traces in the body of a corpse. De Beer, filled with love and blind trust in what he deemed to be his future wife, had said that he would take care of things and he had.

The final step in this diabolical plan which involved the cruel murder of a woman who had never shown her anything but kindness, was to deny the intimate connection between herself and de Beer; deny all knowledge of the poison; deny all knowledge of the murder and leave de Beer to hang for his crime without a trace of an extenuating circumstance.

It was the way she had planned it and it was the way it had worked, but, if she was now going to marry Rossouw, she could not do it without making a clean breast of the whole matter.

Having made her confession, she snuggled up to her lover, apparently expecting his approval.

She did not get it. Rossouw, it seemed, was anything but modern and progressive in his ideas on sex. Flying into a screaming, insane rage, he had grasped his proposed bride by the throat and had strangled her so violently and fatally that she had been dead before she hardly had time to realize what was happening to her.

The very memory of the event excited Rossouw so much that he began to yell even in the inspector's office. She had tricked him the same way that she had tricked de Beer, he roared! She was no decent, respectable girl. She had been sleeping with de Beer for months. He would never believe that she had not enjoyed it. What she had told him was all lies. She had thought herself that the poison would leave no traces in the body and that she could then marry the rich, socially prominent de Beer. It was only when the scheme had not worked that she had treacherously abandoned her lover. He did not regret killing her! She deserved to die!

Rossouw was taken off, more or less foaming at the mouth, to the detention cells to cool down. He left behind him, however, a statement which would save Petrus de Beer from the gallows. There had been extenuating circumstances in the murder of Doreen de Beer and the late Elsabe Loubser was, if anything, more responsible for the crime than he.

As neither de Beer nor Rossouw were completely responsible for their actions and as Elsabe definitely was for hers, neither murderer was hung, but received life and twenty-five-year jail sentences respectively.

It was reported, however, that Petrus de Beer nearly paid the supreme penalty upon hearing of Elsabe's death.

He almost died laughing.

Civil servants are not, however, noted for their sense of humour.

11

A FORTY-POUND VICTIM
EIGHT FEET LONG

The cases of the murders of Doreen De Beer and Elsabe Loubser represent what might be termed the garden variety of homicidal madness. De Beer was driven to madness by the belief, common among older men, that copulation with young females will result in a return of youth. Rossouw was reduced to insanity by sexual jealousy and deception in the character of his beloved. If the human race had evolved with only one sex instead of several, there would probably be close to ninety per cent fewer homicides. This would result in severe overpopulation.

Overpopulation means, among other things, that housing is going to be in short supply or, rather, in even shorter supply because in many places housing is in short supply without any overpopulation.

Belgium is not a particularly overpopulated country and yet housing is often something of a problem. It was, therefore, with considerable rejoicing that thirty-four-year-old Erik Aertbielen took possession of the cottage at 21 Wolstraat in the suburbs of the Belgian city of Antwerp on Monday, 16 August 1980. The previous tenant had moved out a week earlier and, as he had left the place exceptionally clean and tidy, there was little for Aertbielen to do other than to arrange his own affairs and make a survey of the house and garden.

This took him most of the week, but, by Saturday, 23 August, he had completed his arrangements inside the house and was preparing to lay out the garden.

It was, of course, too late in the year to do very much planting, but he could at least mark out some paths and spade up the flowerbeds and, on that sunny, warm afternoon with a cheery sea breeze blowing in from off the port, he set out to do so.

The first of the flowerbeds gave only cause for gratification. Although the preceding tenant did not appear to have put much effort into the garden, neither it nor the house were new and it had obviously been well cultivated over a long period of time in the past. The soil was rich, moist and comparatively loose.

Beginning with the second flowerbed at approximately a quarter past four in the afternoon, however, Aertbielen soon encountered a difficulty. He was spading deeply, the full length of the blade, and less than a foot beneath the surface of the earth something was preventing the spade from entering. It was not, however, hard like a stone, but something yielding.

Aertbielen, suspecting buried plastic sacks full of garbage, muttered a swearword and began to clear away the earth over the mysterious object.

An instant later, he dropped his spade and ran off a dozen yards. Whatever it was that lay buried there, it was sending up the most hideous stench that had ever invaded his nostrils.

Bitterly cursing the previous tenant whom he had, up until now, praised for having left the house in such good order, Aertbielen returned to the house, soaked a small towel in cologne, tied it around his mouth and nose and returned grimly to his task. Whatever this absolutely foul rubbish was, it had to be dug up and disposed of. Until it was the garden was unusable.

Aertbielen did not get very far with his project. The rubbish appeared to be wrapped in an old quilt, but as he got the spade under one edge and lifted it up, he dropped, for the second time, the tool he was using and ran off even further than before.

Looking up at him from the folds of the quilt was a hideously decayed human face. The cheeks had rotted through to expose the yellowed teeth. The nose was a small mound of putrefaction and the eyes swam like glazed marbles in the stinking liquid which filled the eye sockets. Despite its terrible condition, the face appeared astonishingly lifelike and he had had the impression that it was looking directly and sorrowfully at him. For an instant he was filled with a feeling of horror that it was about to climb out of the hole in the ground.

Although the sky was still cloudless, the August afternoon had suddenly gone a great deal less bright and it was obvious that there was going to be no more gardening that day. Afraid to turn his back on what lay in the hole in the earth, Aertbielen backed into his house, his nerves so shaken that he locked the door behind him, and went to telephone the police.

He was very impatient for them to come and do something about the corpse in his garden and, when the first patrolcar arrived, he was sitting on the curb in front of the house.

Although old and famous, Antwerp is not a terribly large city. Its population is only in the neighbourhood of 200,000 inhabitants. It does, however, have a sufficiently high crime rate that several homicide squads divide the duty around the clock. On this Saturday afternoon, it was the turn of Inspector Jean van Bulcke, chief of Homicide Three.

At that moment, the inspector was still sitting in his office waiting for confirmation from the patrolcar that the object in Erik Aertbielen's garden was actually a human corpse. As in any modern city, Antwerp has its share of psychopaths, alcoholics, drug addicts and practical jokers who account for a great many more homicide reports than there are homicides. If the squad was to go out on every report received, they would be almost continuously underway and mostly to no purpose.

In this case, however, confirmation was quickly received, the officers walking up to the hole while holding their breath and then making a hasty retreat to the patrolcar. It was, they reported over the radio-telephone a human body and a very dead one.

The inspector, sitting with the telephone receiver held to his ear, pointed his finger at his assistant, Detective-Sergeant Leopold Haan, who immediately jumped up and ran off down the corridor to summon the medical expert and the technicians from the police laboratory. Confirmation that there was a human corpse in the garden at number 21 Wolstraat was the stimulus which would touch off the homicide investigation.

Not much later, Inspector van Bulcke and Sergeant Haan arrived at the scene accompanied by Dr Jerome Beekman, the duty specialist in legal medicine. The detachment from the police laboratory was on the way, but had not yet arrived and, until it did, there was little the investigators could do except to go and peer into the hole while holding their noses.

Eventually it would be up to Dr Beekman to make an examination of the rotting corpse, but he could not do this until it had been brought up out of the shallow grave in which it lay, and that was a job for the laboratory technicians. They would not only have to extract the corpse, but also determine what potential clues might have been buried with it. These potential clues fell under two headings. One, they could be clues leading to the identification of the corpse. Two, they could be clues leading to the identification of whoever was responsible for the corpse being buried there. It could not yet be said that there would be clues leading to the identification of the murderer because there was, so far, no evidence that a murder had taken place. It was possible that death had occurred through natural causes and, until proved otherwise, no offence other than illegal burial of a corpse was a certainty.

However the question was not resolved by the doctor's examination of the body after it had been brought up, laid on a plastic sheet and the quilt surrounding it removed.

The quilt had not been tied, but merely wrapped around the body which, according to Dr Beekman, was that of a female, probably under the age of forty who had been dead and buried for close to six months. Decomposition was very advanced and the doctor was not at all confident that he would be able to establish the cause of death.

This preliminary examination having been completed, the corpse was enclosed in a plastic bag and lifted into a metal coffin for transport to the police morgue. There Dr Beekman would carry out the complete autopsy with the assistance of a team from the police laboratory who would search for clues to the woman's identity and attempt to recover identifiable fingerprints. Although the hands were very badly decayed, there was a possibility that enough skin remained on the fingertips to make an impression. The probability of other clues was remote. The corpse was entirely naked and bore no jewellery, except a small crucifix attached to a silver chain around the neck. The crucifix, also silver, carried no jeweller's mark and looked as if it might have been home-made.

In the meantime, the laboratory squad set about putting the earth at the bottom of the grave through a screen in the hope of recovering something that might be of value to the investigation.

The inspector, a bulky man with a rather oval figure and high complexion, stood watching them thoughtfully and silently. Presently, he was joined by the sergeant who had been taking a statement from Erik Aertbielen.

Aertbielen, said the sergeant, knew nothing about the matter. He had only moved into the cottage less than a week earlier and he did not know the name of the previous tenant although he understood that he had been a single man.

'I have the name of the real-estate agent that handled the rental of the house,' said the sergeant. 'He'll probably have the last tenant's name and, maybe, a forwarding address. You want me to go get it?'

'Yes,' said the inspector. 'Find out who the previous tenant was and if he was here for less than six months, find out who the one was before that. Beekman says she's been dead for six months or more, but I think we'd better extend that back for at least eight months. The condition the body is in, I don't think that Beekman can be too certain either.'

The sergeant nodded in silent acknowledgement and went away, a short, dark, rather slightly built man with a serious, busy sort of manner. He was conscientious and hard working, but, like all European police officers, he was basically a civil servant and he handled his work in the manner in which a civil servant would.

After a time, the technicians finished sieving the earth and came over to report that they had found a button, a throw-away-type cigarette lighter, some small pieces of wood and four cigarette butt filters. Whether any of these things had any connection with the corpse could not be said. They and the quilt in which the body had been wrapped were being taken to the police laboratory for further examination, evaluation and analysis. A report on the laboratory findings would be available on Monday morning.

The inspector nodded, went in to tell Erick Aertbielen that he could resume digging in his garden and returned to his office at police headquarters. There was nothing to do now other than to wait for the reports, one from the sergeant, one from Dr Beekman and one from the police laboratory.

He had hardly got settled in his office, however, when he received a frantic call from Erik Aertbielen. He had gone to get some earth from a sort of mound near the fence around the garden to fill in the hole where the woman's body had been buried and had come upon another corpse. This one smelled even worse than the first.

Aertbielen having established his credibility with the inspector, he did not wait for a confirmation, but notified the laboratory technicians and hurried back to 21 Wolstraat alone. Dr Beekman was still involved with the autopsy of the first corpse and the sergeant had not yet returned from his visit to the real-estate agent.

Aertbielen was quite right about the smell. It was worse than had been that of the dead woman, but he was mistaken in believing that there was only one corpse.

When the laboratory technicians had finally completed carefully opening up the mound of earth, they found not one body but seventeen – six boa constrictors and eleven rats. The rats were, of course, no more than skeletons.

'Boa constrictors?' said the inspector incredulously. 'Six boa constrictors and eleven rats? In Antwerp?'

'Well, they could be pythons,' said the technician in charge of the squad. 'Whatever the species, they're big snakes. The biggest one must have been about eight feet long when it was alive.'

'But what does it mean?' said the inspector. 'There must be some connection between the dead women and the dead snakes, but what . . .? And what about the rats?'

'They probably represent food for the snakes,' said the technicians. 'Offhand, it looks as if somebody has murdered a snake charmer and her act with her. Sounds crazy, I'll admit, but I suppose that snake charmers get murdered the same as anybody else.'

'Yes, I suppose so,' said the inspector. 'I just wish they wouldn't do it during my duty period. Snake charmers and that sort of thing are carnival people. They're continually travelling around to the little local fairs and they're the very devil to trace. They're an international lot, too. For all we know, the woman may not have even been Belgian.'

'The snakes definitely weren't,' said the technician.

Once again the laboratory specialists carefully sieved the earth in which the snakes and rats had been buried. Once again they recovered a number of miscellaneous objects which might or might not have some connection with the person who had buried them and, presumably, killed the snakes and rats.

It appeared that the snakes' heads had been cut off with something sharp and heavy, possibly an axe, and the rats seemed to have been crushed, for there were many broken bones in the skeletons. Whether this crushing had been carried out by the person who had killed the snakes or by the snakes themselves could not at the moment be said.

The killing of snakes, however large, not being classified as homicide or even a felony, the bodies were left in Aertbielen's garden and the technicians returned to police headquarters, taking with them only a few samples of the snakes' skin for the purpose of identifying the species.

The inspector too returned to his office and, although it was by now late in the evening, found his assistant waiting for him there. He had not been able to obtain very much information from the real-estate agent in charge of renting the cottage at 21 Wolstraat. The name of the previous tenant was Guy Baptist and he had moved into the cottage on 1 November 1979. The real-estate agent described him as an enormous man close to six feet six inches tall and extremely muscular. He had a long, black moustache, thick, black side whiskers and looked almost too fierce to be real. His manner

412

had, however, been gentle and soft-spoken, although he had a somewhat dramatic way of expressing himself.

'November, December, January,' said the inspector, counting on his fingers. 'Over eight months. He was occupying the house when the body was buried there. I suppose there's no forwarding address?'

'None,' said the sergeant. 'However Baptist was alone when he rented the house and he doesn't appear to have had any female visitors. I went back out to Wolstraat after I had talked to the real-estate agent and questioned the neighbours. They say that he was very quiet, had no contact with anyone in the street and was hardly ever home. No one reported ever having seen him with a woman or having seen a woman come to the house.'

'They didn't mention anything about boa constrictors, did they?' said the inspector. 'Or rats?'

'What?' said the sergeant, slapping the side of his head as if he thought there was something wrong with his ears. 'I thought you said . . .'

The inspector explained. 'Actually, there's a sort of connection there,' he said. 'The woman was apparently a snake charmer and, from your description, this Guy Baptist sounds like the sort of person you might find working around the carnivals and fairs. Could have been billed as a strong man or something like that. In any case, that's the direction we'll start looking. With an appearance like that, he shouldn't be too difficult to identify even among the carnival people.'

'It's definitely homicide then?' said the sergeant. 'Has Beekman already reported on the autopsy findings?'

The inspector shook his head. 'Not yet,' he said, 'and I don't expect him to before Monday morning. The condition the body was in, he'll have his work cut out for him. However, it's very difficult to imagine how a snake charmer, her snakes and rats all ended up buried in that garden if it wasn't homicide. Whatever Beekman reports, I think that we want to have a talk with Mr Baptist.'

'Maybe it would be easier to begin by trying to identify the snake charmer,' said the sergeant. 'I can't believe that there are all that many snake charmers in Belgium. After all, it's a small country. People like that must have booking agents for places other than just the fairs. If one suddenly turned up missing, it should be possible to trace her through the booking agents.'

'That's not a bad idea,' said the inspector. 'Go ahead and see what you can do about locating a snake act that failed to meet her bookings after November of last year.'

As the inspector had anticipated, there was no report from Dr Beekman until nearly noon on Monday and then it was inconclusive. As was customary, the doctor came to the inspector's office to make a preliminary verbal report on such findings of the autopsy as were of importance to the investigation. The official, written report, which would go into exhaustive detail, would follow later.

'Well, to begin with,' said the doctor, dropping into the chair beside the inspector's desk and accepting one of his cigarettes, 'there's no positive proof of homicide. I don't know what killed her. It wasn't anything that left a large wound in the torso or that broke the skull or any of the other bones. She could have been strangled, smothered, poisoned perhaps or she could have bled to death. On the other hand, she could have choked on a piece of toffee or suffered a burst appendix. The fact is, decomposition is too advanced to say anything with certainty. I can't even fix the time of death closer than within a month or so.'

'Any suggestions as to what she may have looked like when she was alive?' said the inspector.

'Five feet six inches tall,' said the doctor. 'Live weight would have been around one twenty or a little more. She was generously built. Black hair, not dyed. Black or dark brown eyes. Around thirty years old, give or take five years in either direction. You know that the identification section failed to recover any identifiable prints?'

The inspector nodded. 'I hardly thought they would,' he said. 'It doesn't matter. They would only have been useful if she had a police record, and there's no particular reason to believe that she did. You're not classing it as homicide then?'

The doctor shook his head. 'Cause of death for reasons unknown,' he said. 'Of course, considering the circumstances and where the body was found, I personally have no doubt but that it was a homicide. There's no evidence of it on the body though.'

The inspector had not expected anything more from the autopsy report, and he was not surprised when the laboratory also turned in a negative report later that day. None of the items recovered at the scene with the exception of the quilt in which the body had been wrapped could be shown to have any connection with the corpse. The only conclusion that they had been able to draw was that the woman and the snakes had apparently been buried at about the same time.

In the meantime, however, Sergeant Haan had been busy and had come up with a tentative identification of the victim. She was twenty-eight-year-old Monique Verstrepen, and she was not a snake charmer, but a striptease artist.

'She did erotic dances under the stage name of Nikki Lee,' said the sergeant. 'The snakes were part of the act. She came on to the stage with the snakes draped over her strategic areas and then, as she did her dance, the snakes crawled away one by one into a big basket and she ended up nude. Supposed to have been a great act. She was very much in demand and not just as a dancer.'

'What do you mean by that?' said the inspector.

'Part of her job was being friendly with the customers,' said the sergeant. 'It seems that she was very friendly. If the price was right, you could take her home and she'd spend the night. Must have happened pretty often. She was a very pretty girl. Here. I brought along a picture for you. It's one of her publicity shots.'

The inspector looked at the large, glossy photograph which the sergeant handed him. It was the picture of a beautiful, voluptuously built woman with long, black hair and dark eyes. She was dressed rather carelessly in one or two snakes which were not covering the strategic areas quite as conscientiously as they were supposed to.

'She matches Beekman's description from the corpse,' said the inspector, handing the photograph back. 'She's disappeared, I take it?'

'Not seen since November first of 1979,' said the sergeant.

415

'She had a dozen or more bookings and she didn't show for any of them. The booking agent said he couldn't understand it. Normally, she was extremely reliable. A real professional.'

'If it wasn't for the snakes,' said the inspector, 'I'd say that she simply went home one night with the wrong guy, but I can't imagine her taking her snakes along on a one-night stand like that. The things were heavy. It would have been a problem just transporting them around. I suspect that we're going to find that there was a more profound relationship between Miss Verstrepen and Guy Baptist than a simple pick-up in a nightclub. See what the booking agents have to say about Baptist. Have you checked to see if there was ever a missing person report on Verstrepen?'

The sergeant had not and the inspector picked up the telephone and asked for a check. The answer came back shortly. Monique Verstrepen had been reported missing by her sister in May of 1980. The missing woman's husband had been contacted where the couple lived at 21 Wolstraat, and he had said that his wife had gone on tour to England and was going from there to the United States. The sister had been satisfied with this explanation. Monique, it seemed, often went off on tour for extended periods, although she had never before gone overseas.

The inspector asked the husband's name and was not at all surprised to hear that it was Guy Baptist. He was, it seemed, fifteen years older than Monique and they had been married on 18 December 1976. There were no children. The missing person report gave no profession for Baptist, but the officer who had gone out to investigate the disappearance said that he had had the impression that Baptist was in some kind of theatrical business.

Equipped with this information, it did not take the sergeant very long to determine that Guy Baptist appeared at carnivals, fairs and in nightclubs, sometimes with his wife and sometimes alone, as Samurai Khan, a magician, juggler, fire-eater, sword-swallower and fakir who supported his huge bulk on the points of twelve sabres while a young and pretty assistant stood on his stomach.

Unlike his wife, Baptist had been appearing regularly at his

416

various commitments and was thought to be, at the moment, in Brussels, thirty miles south of Antwerp.

The Brussels police were immediately contacted with a request to locate Baptist and take him into custody. This, however, proved difficult as, like all of the carnival people, Baptist moved almost constantly and, having been in the business for a great many years, did not always make use of booking agents. Eventually, however, he was traced and taken into custody at the Railway Fair in Brussels.

Despite his size and appearance, Baptist offered no resistance and meekly accompanied the arresting officers to police headquarters where he was held until a slightly nervous Sergeant Haan and a detail of three detectives came down and brought him back to Antwerp.

As Baptist was not wanted by the Brussels police he had not been questioned there, but upon being asked by Inspector van Bulcke at police headquarters in Antwerp where his wife was, he replied that she had gone on tour to England and the United States.

The inspector then informed him that her corpse had been dug up from the garden of the house which they had occupied. He added that the bodies of her snakes had also been recovered.

Baptist sighed deeply and said that it was true, he had murdered his wife. He had not wanted to, but having done so, he had tried to conceal the fact as he did not want to spend his few remaining years in jail.

The inspector did not understand exactly what he meant by his few remaining years, but suggested that he begin at the beginning.

Baptist said that he and Monique had first met in 1971 when she had attended one of his performances. He was, at the time, divorced and had had an unfortunate experience with his first wife.

Although he had been trained as a pastry cook when a young man, he had not liked the profession and, following his compulsory military service, he found work as a truck driver. In 1958 he had had to deliver a carnival ride to a new owner, and had been propositioned by the ride operator to stay on and work with the carnival. He had done so and had taught himself all the various tricks of his act. The life suited him perfectly and he could not imagine working at any other profession.

Monique, too, had started out quite differently. She had been undergoing training as a dress designer, but she had been so impressed by Baptist's performance that she had come to see him after it was over and had asked if he would hire her as his assistant.

He had hired her and, very shortly thereafter, they had become lovers and had begun living together. Five years later they had married.

Their happiness, said Baptist, had lasted for two years and had then been destroyed by an act of infidelity. He did not know how much the inspector knew about carnival people, but their morals were, he said, very rigid. Marriage was for life and no extra-marital affairs were permitted.

The inspector, who knew that Monique had shared beds with a veritable army of customers from the nightclubs, raised his eyebrows involuntarily and Baptist, seeing and correctly interpreting the gesture, hastened to explain.

Monique's sexual activities with the customers, he said, were not infidelities. They were a part of the profession and a means of earning money. Monique was not emotionally involved.

It had not been Monique who had been unfaithful. It had been he. After Monique had worked out her routine with the snakes, she had become very popular in her own right and they had often booked separately. On one of these occasions when he was appearing in another town, he had had a brief affair with one of the other female performers. Unfortunately, another girl who knew Monique had also been part of the troupe and she had told Monique what her husband had done.

From that moment on, Baptist's life had been sheer hell. They were at that time living at number 14 Borsbeekstraat in the little town of Bergerhout halfway between Antwerp and Brussels, and they had usually managed to be home on those nights that they were not actually performing.

418

Monique, hot-tempered and insanely jealous, had been in an almost permanent frenzy of rage. She had smashed everything that they owned, had scratched and bitten her unresisting husband and had thrown wine, food and worse things into his face.

Guy, conscious of his guilt and unable to offer any defence, had accepted it all patiently up until the night of 1 November 1971. They had been due to move the following day to the cottage at 21 Wolstraat in Antwerp and all of their things were already packed.

Monique had been in a worse rage than ever and his patient acceptance of the abuse seemed only to goad her into greater excesses. Finally, she had seized one of the rats which she kept to feed her snakes which were, at this time in a large basket in the dining room, and had thrown it into his face. The terrified rat had bitten him on the cheek and this had been the final straw which snapped his patience.

He could not recall having seized her, but he was an enormously strong man and when he came to his senses again he was holding a dead body between his hands.

There being obviously no further employment for the snakes. He had chopped off their heads with one of his swords and had crushed the rats with his bare hands. When he moved the following day, his household effects had included eighteen corpses which he had then buried in the garden two days later.

'I'm sorry,' he said, clasping his huge hands between his knees. 'I didn't want to kill her. I loved her. But then, I didn't see any reason to go to jail for these last years. I wanted to die on the stage like any good trouper.'

The inspector still did not understand his reference to dying on the stage and his last few years, but following a physical examination and an interview with Baptist's doctor, the situation became clear.

As a professional fire-eater, Baptist suffered from a terrible occupational hazard. Every time he performed, the flame which he drew in and then blew out his mouth attacked his lungs and stomach. One lung was almost completely non-functional and the other was gravely affected. The condition of his stomach was such that an internal haemorrhage could carry him off at almost any moment. In the opinion of the doctor, he had, at the most, two years to live.

It turned out to be somewhat less.

Indicted for the murder of Monique Verstrepen in September of 1980, Guy Baptist or, as he preferred to be known, Samurai Khan died in the detention cells on 16 March 1982 without ever coming to trial.

12

SOMEONE COULD BE WAITING
WHEN YOU COME HOME
TONIGHT

Poor Samurai Khan was, perhaps, insane, but it was only temporary insanity and, had he ever come to trial, it would, no doubt, have been so recognized by the court. Having rats flung in your face is an experience to unhinge the reason of even the most stable-minded.

Monique was, if anything, crazier than her husband. Although a comparatively young woman, she had apparently never heard of the sexual revolution and did not realize that Samurai Khan's mistep was without significance. Her actions and end, once again, demonstrate clearly the dangers of conservatism and a refusal to accept the tenets of the New Morality.

Alas! Monique Verstrepen is not alone in her unreasonable attitude. There are others, many others, and their actions are sometimes even more violent than hers. Monique's reprisals were directed against her own husband, but there are persons who are so incensed by the New Freedom that they do not hesitate to take action against total strangers.

And, for the fullest blossoming of the New Moral Freedom, there is no place like the Spanish Balearic Islands. Not among the local Spaniards, of course, who still look upon Queen Victoria as a radical libertarian, but among the tourists who tend to confuse 'vacation' with 'non-stop orgy' and who greatly outnumber the local Spaniards in any case.

The largest number of tourists in the Balearic Islands and also the largest number of converts to the New Morality are the West Germans. Indefatigable tourists and well-heeled, they overrun the islands to the point where the uninformed might believe themselves in Hamburg or Frankfurt. Married or not, they come with the conviction that they are going to encounter an endless number of willing, able and not too hideous sex partners, and they do. This makes places like the island of Ibiza exciting.

Surprisingly enough, however, not for everyone or, at least, not in that way. Germany also has romantic souls for whom sex is not everything.

When Doris Erika Renate Heidemann came to the island of Ibiza in June of 1978, it was like the realization of a dream. A diplomaed hotel administration technician, the twenty-one-year-old girl from the German city of Düsseldorf had particularly wanted a job on one of the Spanish Balearic Islands and Ibiza was, without question, the most colourful of them all.

However, unlike the tourists, Doris thought Ibiza exciting for reasons that had nothing to do with sex, drugs, alcohol or the other standard forms of entertainment. It was warm. It was exotic. It was a place where she could practise her Spanish and gain experience in her profession.

An attractive but not pretty girl with a build that was more athletic than seductive, she was serious, hard-working, intelligent and highly efficient, all virtues formerly associated with the German character but now considered by some to be old-fashioned.

These old-fashioned characteristics were not, however, looked down upon at the Penta Club Bungalow Hotel in the resort city of San Antonio Abad where she was regarded as a most valuable employee who, by the beginning of August 1979 was already known to the often hard-pressed tour group leaders as a girl who could get things down when all else failed.

She would be sorely missed because Doris Heidemann would not be completing the season at the Penta Club Hotel this year.

Equally sorely missed would be Dr Don Luis German Perez de la Fuente, a thirty-two-year-old Spanish nobleman who was employed as a toxicologist at Guterrez Ortega Hospital in the city of Valdepenas.

Valdepenas is a very long way inland somewhere between Malaga and Madrid on the Spanish mainland. On the face of things, it seemed unlikely that Don Luis and Doris Heidemann would ever meet, and it was beyond the bounds of all probability that they would meet under the circumstances which they actually did.

However, even doctors and noblemen take vacations and, beginning 1 August 1979, Don Luis took his, setting off for the Balearic Islands of Majorca, Menorca and Ibiza, none of which he had visited before.

The highly educated and cultured descendant of an ancient family with a fondness for food and drink, he arrived in the city of Palma on the island of Majorca on that same day, 1 August and, finding it not to his liking, left the following day on the ferry for Ibiza. His vacation was for two weeks, but, as it was going to turn out, he would not be taking all of it.

On Ibiza, the doctor found accommodation at a first-class hotel in the largest town, also called Ibiza, and there he remained until the afternoon of 5 August when an unfortunate incident resulted in his departure.

In the meantime, in San Antonio Abad, on the western side of the island and less than eight miles from Ibiza with which it is connected by a modern highway, Doris Heidemann was having greater problems in finding accomodations for guests who had fallen victim to the common European practice of overbooking.

If this were not enough, there was also the social side of her job to consider and for the night of Saturday to Sunday, she was personally booked solid with dinner to be followed by a visit to one or more discotheques.

She was not looking forward to this very much. Like many Germans, she cared little what she ate as long as there was enough of it, and she regarded discotheques as a waste of time. However, her dinner companions were all important tour operators and travel-agency owners and the entertainment was of importance to the affairs of the hotel.

Before setting out for the evening, she performed one last service which might, under the circumstances, have been the most significant act of her life. A guest who through over-booking had no place to lay his head that night had appealed for her help. He was a fellow German and she was anxious to help him, but she knew with certainty that there was no bed free in San Antonio Abad that night and probably not in all Ibiza.

Except one. Her own.

Or rather two, for Doris had a small, spare bedroom in her ground-floor apartment at 12 Can Puig des Moli where she lived when she was home, seldom enough during the season. The rooms at the Penta Club Bungalow Hotel were too precious to be occupied by employees.

'Listen,' she said. 'I can't get you a room tonight, but you can sleep at my place. I don't know if I'll get home at all tonight, but, in any case, there's a spare bedroom. I'll leave the keys to the apartment at the desk.'

This last was necessary because Doris was on the point of leaving for dinner and the man had telephoned from the other side of town. She had no idea what he looked like even, but she wanted to make clear that all she was offering him was the bed.

The vacationer was grateful. He was coming immediately to pick up the keys.

Doris hung up the telephone, became involved in a half-dozen other matters simultaneously, got them more or less straightened out and left with her group for dinner and the discotheques.

She had forgotten to leave her keys at the desk. It was an oversight which proved fatal.

Monday morning is no more of a joyous occasion for the police in resort towns than in less exotic places, and Inspector Luis Hernandez of the Criminal Investigations Department of the San Antonio Abad police groaned slightly as he sank into the chair behind his desk and lit the first cigarette of the day.

In a normal town the size of San Antonio Abad, there would have been no criminal investigations department and few members of the uniformed branch, but San Antonio Abad was anything but normal in the summertime and their criminal investigations department was, if anything, seriously overworked.

As the inspector reached for the first file the telephone rang. A cultured voice speaking perfect, educated Spanish said, 'I have rid the island of the spirit of the Great Shark. You will find the vessel at twelve Can Puig des Moli.'

There was a sharp click as the conversation was terminated.

'Another hop-head on a bad trip, Pedro,' said the inspector, dropping the telephone back into the cradle. 'Twelve Can Puig des Moli. You want to take a look?'

On the opposite side of the office Detective-Sergeant Pedro Algernas raised his narrow dark face from the file he was processing and smiled. He was pleased to be getting out of the office, even if only for a short time.

'Any instructions?' he said. 'Should I bring him in? Or is it a her?'

'A him and a Spaniard,' said the inspector wearily. 'You'll have to play it by ear. He sounded completely crazy to me. Something about a great shark.'

The sergeant left the office and San Antonio Abad being a relatively small place, arriving in Can Puig des Moli within a matter of ten minutes on foot. It was, as might be expected in Ibiza at the height of the summer season, a gloriously sunny, warm day. The sea was blue. Flowers were everywhere. The streets were packed with vacationers. It was gay.

Doris Heidemann was not.

The sergeant, having rung the bell at number twelve and having received no answer, tried the door which he found unlocked and went in.

Doris was lying completely naked on the cold tiles of the living-room floor. She was sprawled on her back, her arms widespread and the sergeant's jaw dropped in horror as he saw that where her eyes should have been were only empty, bloody sockets. In a manner which he could not imagine, her eyes had been literally torn out of her head.

It was not all. The breasts were nearly ripped away and

were covered with enormous bite wounds, the marks of the teeth clearly visibile.

The genitals were a mass of dried blood and something was sticking out between the lips of the vagina.

The entire body was so covered with cuts, scratches and black bruises that, for a moment, the sergeant thought the woman was a negro.

Her race was, however, of minor importance. What mattered was that he was confronted here with what was unquestionably the worst homicide that he had ever seen or heard of.

Even though he realized that the woman must be dead, he knelt and automatically felt for a pulse or signs of respiration. There were none, of course, and he got to his feet relieved. It would have been even more horrible if this tortured mass of flesh were still alive.

Although there was a telephone standing on a side table not far from the body, he did not make use of it, but ran as fast as he could go back to headquarters where he reported the details of his discovery to a startled and apprehensive Inspector Hernandez.

The fact was this sounded like something that the inspector had long feared. With the ever-increasing number of drug addicts coming to the island each summer, he had often thought that it was only a matter of time before one of the grisly crimes common in such circles elsewhere took place.

Now it seemed that it had and, sending the sergeant to pick up the town's coroner and the entire staff of the small police laboratory, he hurried personally to the scene.

The sight which greeted his eyes was worse than the sergeant had described it, if anything, and the inspector, a short, stout, round-faced man who was perhaps a little too soft-hearted for criminal investigations work had to go outside and have another cigarette before he could begin the investigation.

In the meantime, the sergeant had arrived with Dr Felix Bastando, the tall, thin and slightly haggard-looking coroner, and the four members of the laboratory staff, and while the doctor proceeded to an examination of the corpse, the laboratory men set about attempting to identify the victim.

This presented no difficulty as Doris Heidemann's passport was in the drawer of a desk less than six feet from her body and, although the mutilated face on the floor bore little resemblance to the girl looking gravely out of the passport photograph, the height, weight and other general characteristics were enough to make reasonably certain the identification of the murder victim as the young German woman.

Also found in the desk was a rental contract for the apartment in Doris Heidemann's name, a number of letters from her family and friends in Düsseldorf and close to a thousand dollars in cash.

'Well, it was already obvious from the body that the motive was not robbery,' said the inspector. 'He must have been totally insane or drugged out of his mind. I wonder if this could be Angel Dust, that stuff we've been reading about?'

'According to her papers, she was working at the Penta Club Hotel,' said the sergeant. 'Do you think I should go over there and tell them?'

'Yes, do,' said the inspector, 'and question anybody you can find who knew her. Maybe they'll know who she was with last night.'

The hotel did, of course, know who Doris had been with the night before, and as the tour operators and travel-agency owners were all staying at the hotel the sergeant had no difficulty in contacting them.

They were not, however, of much help. They had parted from Doris at approximately three-thirty in the morning and had come back to the hotel in a group. It had been their understanding that she was going home.

By this time the news of the murder had spread through the hotel, and the desk clerk who had been on duty the previous evening came forward to report a curious and, as he thought, significant incident.

A man, he said, had come to the desk roughly a half-hour after Doris and the group of travel agents and tour operators had left and had asked if Miss Heidemann had left anything for him. On being told that she had not, he had looked at the desk clerk strangely and had asked for Doris Heidemann's private address.

The clerk had refused to give it to him and he had gone away looking angry.

He had been, said the clerk, a man with a frightening appearance, being very big and beefy with a heavily pock-marked face and slitted green eyes. He had been either totally bald or had had his head shaved. The clerk estimated his age to be around twenty-five.

To the sergeant, who knew nothing of Doris Heidemann's kind offer to let a vacationer whom she had never met sleep at her apartment, the matter was clear. The man had obtained the victim's address elsewhere, had gone to her apartment and had murdered her upon her return at approximately three-thirty in the morning.

As it was obviously important that the man be located and taken into custody before he had had time to leave the island, or kill someone else, the sergeant hurried back to the scene to tell the inspector of this development.

There he found that Dr Batando's estimate of the time of death agreed closely with this theory. Doris Heidemann had died at sometime between four and five o'clock that same morning or, as the doctor said, she would have been dying between four and five o'clock. Her murderer had taken his time about the business.

'As far as I can determine now,' said the doctor, 'she was trampled to death. He must have jumped up and down on her body until he broke practically every bone in it. All her ribs are broken, her collarbone is smashed, her breast bone is caved in, her internal organs are reduced to a pulp. Her eyes seem to have been gouged out with bare fingers, whether before she was dead or after, I can't say. One of them is lying on the floor there, but the other is missing. He may have taken it with him or even eaten it. The breasts . . .'

He was interrupted as one of the laboratory technicians turned pale green and made a rush for the door.

'There were bites taken out of the flesh of the breasts,' continued the doctor, looking as if he was inclined to join him, 'and I think the labia major of the vagina have been bitten through. The thing sticking out of it is a large, blood-smeared, ball-point pen of the kind sold for souvenirs.

There's another ordinary ball-point pen sticking between her ribs and I suspect he may have been trying to kill her by pushing it through her heart. If he was, he didn't succeed.'

'Is that all?' said the inspector, tight-lipped.

'Probably not,' said the doctor. 'There's what looks to me like semen spattered over the body, but I can't tell whether she was actually raped until I've done the autopsy.'

By now, every off-duty police officer, whether plainclothes or uniform branch, had been called in, and the inspector rushed men to the airport at La Canal and to the ferry dock at Ibiza with orders not to allow any male to leave the island until he had been positively identified and his destination recorded.

At the same time, patrolcars were put to cruising the streets of San Antonio Abad broadcasting over loudspeakers the description of the man who had called at the hotel desk the night before to ask for Doris Heidemann's address and appealing for help from the public.

There were, however, some puzzling aspects to the report which the sergeant had brought back. The anonymous telephone call reporting the crime that morning had been from a Spaniard, but the desk clerk stated that the man with the green eyes and the bald or shaven head was a foreigner; a German, he thought.

He was, of course, quite right and by eleven o'clock the broadcasting operation bore fruit when the big man with the green slitted eyes was spotted by local residents lying on the beach.

He was arrested and brought to police headquarters where he identified himself as a twenty-three-year-old tourist from Munich and said that he had never laid eyes on Doris Heidemann in his life.

He told the inspector of her offer to let him sleep in a room in her apartment and said that, when he had gone to the hotel to pick up the keys and had found none waiting, he had come to the conclusion that she had merely made the offer to get rid of him and had had no intention of letting him sleep in her apartment.

Desperate for a place to sleep, he had provided himself

inadvertently with a solid alibi. He had simply picked the oldest, ugliest and therefore, cheapest prostitute he could find and had made a deal with her to spend the night in her bed.

As he knew the address and the woman's first name, the police had no difficulty in corroborating his story and he was released.

By this time, news of the murder had spread over the entire island and a forty-seven-year-old cab driver named Juan Castro reported to police headquarters with an important clue.

He had, he said, taken a fare to Can Puig des Moli at six-thirty on Saturday night. The man had said that he was looking for a German girl named Sonya and his behaviour had been extremely odd.

According to the cab driver's description, so had his appearance. He was, he said, a huge man, round-faced and very fat but not old. He had spoken high-class Spanish with a mainland accent.

This detail rang a bell with the inspector. The anonymous telephone call reporting the murder had been made in just such a voice.

The entire staff of the Criminal Investigations Department descended upon the district in which the street Can Puig des Moli was located and, armed with the description of the suspect, soon found another person with whom he had spoken, an elderly gardener.

The gardener's description tallied precisely with that of the cab driver as did the manner of speaking and his request for information. The fat giant had been looking for a German girl named Sonya.

The gardener, knowing that there was only one German girl living in Can Puig des Moli and not knowing what her name was, had told him number twelve was the address he was seeking.

The man had thanked him and had gone off in the direction of Doris Heidemann's apartment where he had, it now seemed probable, remained, waiting for the girl to come home.

It had not been a boring wait. Ample evidence of what the man had been doing during this time had been found at the scene and had puzzled the investigators because it had not been realized that he had spent over six hours in the apartment.

He had spoken to the gardener at approximately seven o'clock and had, presumably, entered the apartment shortly afterward by the simple expedient of leaning against the door until the tongue of the lock tore through the wood of the door jamb. For a man of his weight, this would have been a practical means of entry as the apartment was not particularly solidly built.

Once inside, he had made himself very much at home and, the technicians thought, partially or entirely undressed. It was certain, at least, that he had not been wearing shoes at the time that he killed Doris Heidemann as the doctor reported that she had been trampled to death with bare feet.

Lying about the living-room floor were twelve empty beer bottles which represented all of the alcoholic refreshments in the apartment and a large book in English entitled *The Joys of Sex*. This, it seemed, had been the property of Doris Heidemann who, it was known, had spoken fluent English.

Whether the fat giant had spoken or been able to read English was not known, but the book was liberally sprinkled with traces of semen, the same, according to Dr Bastando, as they found on the body of the victim.

The course of events from the time that the suspect had arrived in Can Puig des Moli was now clear and, being in possession of a good physical description, the police set about trying to trace the identity of the suspect.

Juan Castro had reported that he had picked up his strange fare at a bar called Calle Sta Ines and questioning of the owner and an employee there produced further reports of abnormal behaviour and expressed interest in a German girl named Sonya.

He had entered the bar at around six o'clock and had said to the bartender, 'You are from Madrid.'

The bartender had politely replied that he was not from Madrid but from Grenada.

This response had made the fat man furious.

'I am a nobleman and a doctor!' he had screamed. 'If I say you are from Madrid, you are from Madrid, you scum!'

The owner of the bar had come over to calm the customer who had immediately changed the subject and begun to talk about a German girl named Sonya whom he had known in Madrid. He said that he had been informed that she was living in San Antonio Abad and that he had taken a cab over from Ibiza to visit her.

He had also said a great many other strange things concerning the influence of the Great Shark and how it was causing Ibiza to become a second Sodom of sex and nudity.

The owner had politically agreed with him, but had said that there was nothing that he could do about it and his main concern was his business. As far as he was concerned, the customers could drink as well naked as clothed.

He had added that there had been a German girl named Sonya living in the Can Puig des Moli some years earlier, but that he thought she no longer lived there.

The man had then asked to have a cab called and had left in it.

The bar owner had not thought that he was a doctor or a nobleman, although he spoke very refined Spanish, but some sort of a madman. He had never heard of Doris Heidemann and he did not know that there was a German girl living in Can Puig des Moli. He had only told his unwanted customer the story about the mythical Sonya to get rid of him.

'It's as if some mysterious power had doomed that girl to be murdered in the manner in which she was,' said the inspector. 'If she had left her keys at the desk or if the desk clerk had given the German tourist her address, he would have gone there and would have run into the fat madman. He might have been murdered, although he's big enough to have taken care of himself, but Miss Heidemann certainly wouldn't have been.

'Then, again, if the bar owner hadn't picked that street name out of thin air, the murderer would never have gone there.

'And finally, if he hadn't run into the gardener who

knew that there was a German girl living in the street but didn't know her name, he would not have gone to number twelve.

'There were an incredible number of coincidences that conspired to bring about that poor girl's horrible death.'

'It seems strange to me that a man as obviously insane as this one would be wandering around loose,' said the sergeant.

'Probably escaped from some institution,' said the inspector. 'These fantasies about being a nobleman and a doctor . . .'

He was soon to learn that they were no fantasies.

Continuing to follow the trail backward from the Calle Sta Ines bar, the investigators took up the remark made by the suspect that he had come over from Ibiza in a cab and, his appearance being unforgettable, soon found the driver.

Like all of the other persons with whom the man had been in contact, this cab driver had found him strange and had thought that he was probably on hard drugs of some kind.

He had said that he found the influence of the Great Shark very strong on the island and that he was going to San Antonio Abad to visit a German girl named Sonya whom he had met in Madrid.

The cab driver had not seen fit to comment, but he had heard things said at the Hotel Corso in Ibiza where he had picked up his fare that led him to believe that the man had been in some kind of trouble there.

Minutes later, the police were at the Hotel Corso where they received confirmation that the suspect had, indeed, been in trouble.

Although Ibiza is an informal sort of place, particularly during the tourist season, the manager of the hotel reported that his bizarre guest had gone too far, wandering up and down the hotel corridors stark naked and knocking on doors. When a person of the opposite sex opened, he made suggestions for sexual recreation and demonstrated physically that he was fully prepared.

A three-hundred-pound maniac not being everyone's idea of a suitable sex partner, there had been complaints and the manager had asked him to dress and leave. He had immediately done so.

Not long thereafter, a dumbfounded Inspector Hernandez stood looking at an entry in the hotel register. Written in a fine legible hand was: 'Dr Med. Don Luis German Perez Casanova de le Fuente. Toxicologist. Guterrez Ortega Hospital, Valdepenas, Spain.'

'He wrote this himself?' demanded the inspector. 'Did you check his identity?'

'He wrote it himself,' said the desk clerk. 'He insisted on writing it himself. He had a valid, Spanish identification card and it carried the same information.'

The inspector still could not believe it and he placed a long-distance call to the hospital in Valdepenas. Did they have a Dr Don Luis German Perez Casanova de le Fuente there? And, if so, where was he?

Yes, indeed, said the hospital. Dr de la Fuente was their toxicologist, a man from a noble family. At the moment he was on vacation in the Balearic Islands.

The telephone receptionist in Valdepenas wanted to know if something had happened to Dr de la Fuente, but the inspector was too stunned to reply and simply hung up the telephone.

With a precise description and the knowledge of the name and origin of the man who, it seemed, was the murderer of Doris Heidemann, the police had little difficulty in locating him in another hotel in Ibiza, particularly as he had made no effect at concealment and had simply registered in his own name again.

From the point of view of the mad physician, there was no reason why he should not have used his own name. He did not expect any trouble from the police and was sincerely amazed that they did not praise him for having, as he said, rid the island of the influence of the Great Shark.

'I could see that it was the Shark as soon as I arrived here and saw the girls showing their breasts and all the little short skirts with nothing under them . . . Then, I knew it was Sonya and that I must find her.

'She had hidden well, but I found her hiding place and I

434

waited. When she came, I was waiting naked as one must wait for Sonya and I said: "Sonya, I know that you are a man. I shall rid this island of the Great Shark."

'Then, I put the pen between her ribs, but she was, of course, abnormal and I could not find the heart. So, I took out her eyes with my thumb and finger. It is easy if you know how. And then, of course, I jumped on her . . .'

There was a great deal more to Dr de la Fuente's confession, or rather his proud recital of the manner in which he had dealt with the Great Shark, but actually no confession was necessary.

In the pocket of his shirt at the time of his arrest was a small tube which had contained sleeping tablets.

Inside the tube was Doris Heidemann's right eye.

There is no possibility that Dr de la Fuente will ever stand trial for the murder of Doris Heidemann. He is, in the opinion of the psychologists who have examined him, hopelessly and dangerously insane and it is believed that it will be necessary to keep him under close security for a very long time, probably the rest of his life.

What caused the doctor to go insane is not known. There was no reason to believe that he was mentally disturbed at the time that he left Valdepenas. Nor had anyone in his circle of friends, colleagues and relatives ever heard him refer to anyone named Sonya or to any German girl he had met in Madrid. It was, as a matter of fact, at least four years since he had been in Madrid himself.

The only clue to his behaviour is the fact that he was known to harbour conservative views on sexual morality and had often remarked that, although the German and other Nordic tourists brought money into Spain, the damage they were doing to traditional Spanish values exceeded the benefits.

13

THE BUTCHER SHOP MURDERS
WERE THE WURST

Dr Don Luis German Perez de la Fuente may have been mad, but he was, at least, morally motivated. Anxious to rescue his country from the malevolent influence of the mythical Great Shark and the equally imaginary Sonya, his mind apparently broke at the sight of the vast hordes of tourists overrunning the Balearic Islands and the result was the incredible butchery of a young woman whose conduct and morals the doctor would, in all probability, have found beyond reproach had he met her under different circumstances.

The entire case has the unreality of madness to it. The murderer thought he was killing someone who did not apparently exist. His motives were incomprehensible to the ordinary person. The *modus operandi* was horrible beyond belief. And he made no effort to conceal his act nor to escape the consequences of it, but was, in fact, obviously proud of it.

Others, more calculating, go to great lengths to conceal their guilt, kill as efficiently as any employee of a slaughterhouse, have all too understandable motives and pick on the most prosaic of victims. They are not mad because they are illogical. They are mad because they are too logical. They want money. Someone has money. They kill them and take it. A very direct way of thinking, but not as moral as the good doctor's confused thoughts.

On Friday, 4 January 1974, fifty-four-year-old Roman Rauch disappeared without trace in the city of Graz, Austria. Foul play was immediately suspected.

And with good reason. Rauch was a money postman.

In Austria, there are two kinds of postmen, one who comes around and drops mail in your box and another who brings you money. This money could be your pension, a win in the national lottery or simply a sum sent you by some individual or firm for any reason whatever. The money is paid out on your doorstep in cash. A money postman, therefore, carries very considerable sums of cash in small bills, and he carries them into every section of the city from the toughest to the most exclusive and this every working day of the week. In some ways it is rather remarkable that any of these men survive at all.

Roman Rauch had survived for a long time and he had never been robbed or attacked during his entire career as a money postman. He had been married and the father of two children, now grown up and away from home, and he had been fond of his job.

'I never see anything but happy faces,' he had often remarked to his colleagues and his wife. 'Everybody is happy to see the postman with the money coming to them.'

Now, however, Roman Rauch was missing and there was no telling what had happened to him. He should have concluded his route by eleven-thirty and returned to the post office. When he had not appeared by noon, the supervisor called the police. The post office is fully aware of how tempting targets its money postmen are.

So are the police. Within less than thirty minutes, the bluff, hearty, pipe-smoking chief of the investigations section, Inspector Arnold Kirschner, arrived at the post office with his assistant, Detective-Sergeant Joachim Bukovsky. The two men had been having lunch at a small restaurant near police headquarters. It was patronized almost exclusively by the members of the Criminal Investigations Department, and, although they had rushed away leaving the food standing and without stopping to pay, the patron had not been disturbed. He was quite accustomed to it.

Quick as the police reaction had been, the supervisor at the post office was ready for them and had already drawn up a route of the places that Rauch should have covered that

437

morning. He had then telephoned all those persons on the route having telephones and had narrowed the list to a half-dozen parties.

'They're all pensioners,' he said, 'and they don't have telephones. I've been able to trace Rauch up to this point. He paid out to a Mr Johann Fiedler at approximately ten o'clock and he should have paid out to Mrs Catherine Grobius here at around ten-forty-five, assuming that he wasn't held up. I've talked to her on the telephone and he hasn't been there. So, he disappeared somewhere between Fiedler and Grobius which covers six persons, but none of them have telephones so I can't pinpoint it any more exactly than that.'

'Any idea of how much he was carrying?' said the inspector.

The supervisor consulted the sheet of paper on his desk. 'A thousand six hundred and forty-two dollars and twelve cents after he left Fiedler,' he said. 'Minus anything he paid out after that.'

'Right,' said the inspector. 'All right, here's the location of the area, Boo. Bring out a half-dozen men from the station and have them check the addresses: the last place he visited and the first one he failed to visit. Then, throw everything we've got into the area and comb it.'

The sergeant nodded in comprehension and dashed out of the post office to telephone from the policecar parked in front of the building. He was an intense sort of young man, thin, harassed-looking with straight, rather long, blond hair and a very prominent nose. The inspector considered him to be one of the best assistants that had ever had.

An hour later, the police knew exactly where Roman Rauch had disappeared, but, despite the great number of officers thrown into the search, they could find no trace of him.

'It's a business district,' said Sergeant Bukovsky. 'Stores, shops and so on. He paid out a hundred and two dollars to Simon Landauer here in Buelow Street at approximately ten-twelve, and he should have paid out one hundred and six dollars and thirty-four cents to Leon Preis at roughly ten-twenty, but he didn't. So it was somewhere between those two places that he turned up missing. Assuming that he took the shortest route from one place to the other, he would have come right down Schoenau Street and that's practically all business. There's not even an alley where he could have been waylaid.'

'Any possibility that Landauer or Preis might have been a little greedy?' asked the inspector, chewing on the stem of his pipe.

'Greedy, maybe,' said the sergeant, 'but capable, not. Landauer is eighty-four, and Preis is seventy-six and nearly blind. Either one of them can just about make it to the front door. There's no possibility that they had anything to do with it.'

'Strange,' said the inspector. 'How in hell can a postman in uniform disappear in the middle of a busy shopping street like Schoenau? Have you found anybody who saw him there?'

The sergeant shook his head.

'And I don't think we will either,' he said. 'You know how it is with a postman or any other uniformed public servant. People just don't see them. They're an accepted part of the scenery, like lamp posts or dustbins. If we do find anybody, it will be some one who knew Rauch personally.'

'What about money deliveries in Schoenau Street itself?' said the inspector.

'Rare,' said the sergeant. 'It's mostly business places and they handle their transactions through the bank. The supervisor wasn't able to find any record of anything for the past six months.'

'Well, keep searching,' said the inspector. 'It's impossible that a hundred-and-seventy-pound postman in full uniform can vanish into thin air. He's somewhere in that area, dead or alive. All we've got to do is find him.'

But that the police could not do. The entire district was combed house by house, alley by alley and cellar by cellar. Not the slightest trace of the missing postman or the some fifteen-hundred-odd dollars that he had had on him when he disappeared was found. It was as if Roman Rauch, the balding, good-natured postman, who had liked his job and who had enjoyed bringing their pensions to the old people, had never existed.

Reluctantly, the post-office supervisor assigned a new man to the route. His name was Gerhart Rosenberger, he was twenty years old, and he had only very recently gone to work for the post office.

'I can't understand it,' said the sergeant irritably. 'If there'd have been a mouse hidden in Schoenau Street, we'd have found it. We've practically gone through the people's drawers. He's got to be there, but he isn't.'

'Desk drawers, I presume, you mean,' said the inspector. 'Well, we apparently have to accept that he isn't there and the only explanation that occurs to me is that he left voluntarily. Simply took the money and beat it. Doesn't often happen with a postman, but men of that age sometimes go all to pieces, get mixed up with a young girl or something like that. He may be sitting on the French Riviera at this moment.'

'With fifteen hundred dollars?' said the sergeant. 'He had over five thousand in his savings account and it's still there. He would have taken that too.'

'Yes, of course,' said the inspector wearily. 'So he didn't abscond and he's still in Graz which means that he must be dead. Somebody murdered him for that money.

'However, it's obvious that they must have got rid of the body immediately because we were in the district less than three hours after he was last seen alive. It's possible that it was a truck or a delivery van. The murderer persuaded him to get into it, killed him and simply drove away with the body.

'That, in turn, would mean that Rauch knew him personally and trusted him.'

'If that's true, it would make the case a lot easier,' said the sergeant, 'but what makes you think so?'

'He was an old, experienced money postman,' said the inspector. 'Do you think he would have got into a truck with a total stranger?'

'I wouldn't have thought he would get into one with his mother,' said Sergeant Bukovsky. 'You want to concentrate the investigations on the circle of his acquaintances then?'

The inspector nodded. 'Acquaintances, friends, colleagues, relatives even,' he said. 'It has to have been some-body he knew.'

But it seemed that it was not. Although the investigations continued on through January, February, March and into April, no likely, or even possible, suspect was uncovered and, after the first of April, there was an even greater mystery for, on that date, Gerhart Rosenberg, the young postman who had taken over Roman Rauch's old route, disappeared as suddenly and mysteriously as had his predecessor!

The post-office records showed that Rosenberg had had approximately seven thousand six hundred dollars on him at the time!

'Exactly the same thing!' said the inspector in astonish-ment. 'He paid out to Lindauer and not to Preis. In short, he disappeared at precisely the same point in his route as Rauch did. Somebody in that district has worked out a scheme for robbing and murdering the money postmen. We've got to solve this and quick. There are God knows how many thousands or even millions of people who depend upon the post office to bring them their pensions and other payments and, if this fellow gets away with this, it's going to spread all over Austria and the whole system of postal payments will be disrupted.'

'Someone in the district,' repeated Sergeant Bukovsky. 'You don't think any more that it was delivery truck or something like that?'

'I don't know what to think,' said the inspector. 'But we can check on the delivery-truck angle if we assume that the driver was known to the victims. It would be a person who was known to both Rauch and Rosenberger and, considering the difference in their ages and length of service with the post, that couldn't have been too many people.'

It was none at all. The investigations showed that Rauch and Rosenberger had not even known each other and that they had had no common acquaintances. Several of the other employees of the post office had known both men as col-leagues, but all of these could account for their time very exactly on the days of the disappearances. They had, as a matter of fact, all been working.

'Well, scratch that theory,' said the inspector. 'It wasn't a delivery van and it wasn't anybody who knew both Rauch and Rosenberger. It was somebody right there in the district.'

'Maybe it was,' said the sergeant. 'But I don't know who. All the pensioners who got their money through the post knew Rauch and Rosenberger by sight, of course, and so did some of the business people along his route, but we always come back to the same thing; he paid out to Lindauer and not to Preis so he disappeared in that relatively short stretch between sixteen Goethe Street and one-forty-four Chlodwitz, going almost certainly by way of Schoenau. I've walked over that stretch a hundred times. We've interviewed every person living there. We've searched the buildings and we searched the businesses on the day of the disappearances and afterwards. We haven't found the slightest trace of either man.'

'There probably isn't any to find,' said the inspector. 'Now, that it's happened twice, it's apparent that whoever is doing this is working to a carefully conceived plan and they're not going to leave any traces. None the less, we're going to have to continue the investigations whether there's anything to investigate or not. The post office is refusing to put money postmen on that route and the pensioners are having to come down to the post office to get their pensions. We're getting a lot of bad publicity over this. The papers have been running interviews with old, sick pensioners who have to crawl to the post office because the police can't provide security for the mailmen.'

'Couldn't we assign a man to accompany the postmen?' said the sergeant. 'The post office should be satisfied with that.'

'We could, of course,' agreed the inspector, 'but for how long and what happens if the fellow changes his area? We can't put a cop permanently with every money postman in the city.'

'I see,' said the sergeant. 'All right. What do we investigate when there's nothing to investigate?'

'Every person living or working along that stretch of street which Rauch and Rosenberger must have travelled in going from Simon Lindauer to Leon Preis,' said the inspector. 'And every person who had any reason to be anywhere along that route between the hours of ten and eleven on any day.'

'Already done,' said the sergeant promptly. 'Five times over, There are twenty or thirty people who could conceivably have killed the postmen and taken the money, but there's no evidence that anyone of them did or that any one of them had any particular reason to do so. If the motive was money, then that excludes no one because almost anybody can use money.'

'Some more than others,' said the inspector. 'You've got your lists of the people living along there. I want you to put people to checking on whether they've been making new purchases or paying off pressing debts or anything like that. Then I want you to make up a separate list of the houses where the housewife or some female was home alone at the time that Rauch and Rosenberger disappeared. Those two men weren't killed on the street. They were lured into a building and the female of the species is still the best lure going.'

The sergeant obediently took up these less than promising lines of investigation and pursued them with his customary vigour, but his daily reports remained monotonously void of interest.

'There were a few ladies who were home alone,' he said, 'both on the morning of January fourth and April first, but they're hardly the type to lure anybody, although a couple of them, at least, could have strangled both postmen to death with their bare hands and, maybe, simultaneously. None of them have shown any sudden affluence recently.'

'And the businesses?' said the inspector.

'There are nine,' said the sergeant. 'Schmitt's Grocery Store, Hold's Butcher Shop, the Sunshine Café, Ziegler's Second-Hand Book Store, Beisel's Stationery and News-stand, Hann's Real-Estate Office, Foerster's Bakery, Huber's Dry Goods and Brink's Café. All small, owner run businesses with the exception of the Sunshine Café which is part of a chain. As you know, business is nothing extra this year and Hold, Ziegler and Huber are all having trouble. However, none of them has paid off any debts and both Ziegler and Huber have some pressing ones.'

'And Hold?' said the inspector. 'How can a butcher be in trouble with meat the price it is?'

'Living too high apparently,' said the sergeant. 'He only took over the shop from his father two years ago, and he's now got a luxury apartment on Schiller Street and a luxury girlfriend to live in it with him. Name's Christa Pfeifer. Twenty years old and looks like she would be a pretty expensive girl to have around. Hold's twenty-six. He has a few debts with the tax people and the slaughterhouse.'

'But he hasn't paid them,' said the inspector. 'When did he get the luxury apartment? Before the postmen started disappearing or after?'

'A year and a half ago,' said the sergeant. 'Almost as soon as he took over the shop. However, we know for a fact that he's clear. There's no back entrance to the shop and we've got witnesses who can testify that Hold never left the shop at all on the mornings of January fourth and April first. The reason they know that is that he's all alone there. If he went out, he'd have to close the shop and he didn't.'

'And you searched the shop on the day of the disappearances?' said the inspector.

'That's right,' said the sergeant. 'It's a small place. Just the butcher shop itself and a very small sort of sitting room behind it. No back entrance. No back window. No basement. Large refrigerator, of course. It contained sausages and a tray of sausage sandwiches which he sells to the school children. Not bad. I tried one.'

'Well, if he didn't leave the shop and if there's no place there to hide a body, then Hold couldn't have done it unless he quickly chopped the postmen up and sold them as steaks and roasts to the customers,' said the inspector. 'Besides, what would a postman be doing in a butcher shop? One of the cafés, possibly, but not the butcher shop.'

'And now?' said the sergeant.

'Continue the investigations,' said the inspector grimly.

444

The sergeant continued, but he did not get anywhere.

Three days later both Roman Rauch and Gerhart Rosenberger were found; Rauch accidentally and Rosenberger because the police had been given an indication from the discovery of Rauch where to look.

Both men were dead and partially dismembered. Each was neatly packed in a large cardboard carton tied with twine and left standing, in the case of Rauch, on a public dump and, in the case of Rosenberger, at the edge of a flooded gravel pit which was often used as a dump. The weather having been cool at that time of the year, neither body was very badly decayed.

'Which is fortunate,' said Dr Peter Findel, the dark, hook-nosed police medical expert, peering at the inspector over the tops of his gold-rimmed glasses.

He had come to the inspector's office to report personally on the result of the autopsies as it would take time to have the official versions typed and the doctor had reason to believe that the investigators were, to say the least, impatient.

'Both men died as a result of a single hatchet blow to the back of the head, delivered with great force and, I suspect, some skill,' said the doctor. 'The bodies were also dismembered with skill. This was not the work of an amateur.'

'You think it was a doctor?' said the inspector in astonishment.

'No,' said the doctor. 'A butcher. Moreover, in both cases, the last food taken, and that very shortly before death, was a sausage sandwich. Does that tell you anything?'

'Hold!' said the inspector and the sergeant in one voice.

'Almost surely Hold,' said the doctor, who was fully informed on the results of the investigations up to the present. 'Although how you're going to prove it when you searched the shop and didn't find anybody, I don't know.'

'It's my fault!' exclaimed the sergeant. 'It must have been there all the time and I didn't find it. There's just one place those bodies could have been and that's in the deep freeze behind the counter. Hold was serving his customers out of it while we were there: steaks, chops, things like that. The bodies must have been there underneath the meat. How

445

could I have been so stupid! He made a fool of me twice in a row!'

'Well, don't let it bother you, Boo,' said the inspector. 'I doubt that there are very many persons who would have thought of such a thing either. One thing for certain, Hold is going to have some pretty upset customers if this ever gets out.'

'You mean it may not?' said the doctor in astonishment.

'I hope it will,' said the inspector, 'but you have to remember that, although Hold is undoubtedly our man, we have no evidence that would convince an examinations judge. We are not in a position to go for an indictment and, if we make our suspicions public without proof, it'll ruin Hold's business and he'll sue us. What we need is physical evidence.'

'You'll get it,' said the smarting sergeant grimly. 'Even if I have to spend the rest of my life finding it.'

As it turned out, the sergeant did not have to spend the rest of his life or even any very substantial amount of it in obtaining further evidence of the guilt of Karl Hold, the young, luxury-loving butcher.

The first break came with a sworn statement by a twenty-four-year-old employee of the real-estate company located opposite Hold's Butcher Shop. From her seat in front of the window, Gertrud Falschegger had an unobstructed view of the entrance to the butcher shop and she testified that she had seen Gerhart Rosenberger go into the shop, but not come out again. Although she could not remember anything about Roman Rauch, she had noticed the young and handsome Rosenberger on more than one occasion and was apparently in the habit of watching for him as he passed.

'Both Rosenberger and Rauch went into the butcher shop every morning,' said the sergeant. 'It's astonishing how things fall into place when you know what to look for. Now, in addition to the Falschegger statement, I've located a dry-cleaning place where Hold sends his things and on both January fifth and April second, that is, in both cases, one day after the disappearances, Hold sent the carpet of the little sitting room behind the shop in for dry-cleaning. The dry-cleaners no longer remember what it was in January, but in

April, there were bloodstains on it. They, of course, know that Hold is a butcher so they thought nothing of it. Finally I have located a customer of Hold's who says that the shop was closed briefly on the afternoon of April second. He was presumably cutting up the body of Rosenberger then and packing it in the carton. In the case of Rauch, he wouldn't have had to close because the day following was a Sunday. Do you think it's enough?'

The inspector thought so and, following his arrest and a few hours of interrogation, so did Karl Hold.

'It was the money,' he said. 'I needed money. Rauch had a habit of coming in to buy a sausage sandwich every morning when he was passing so on that morning I asked him if he would like a cup of coffee with it. I said I'd made some fresh coffee in the back room. He came in and while he was having his sandwich and cup of coffee, I hit him on the back of the head with the hatchet. He died instantly, of course. Then, I took him out and put him into the deep freeze behind the counter and covered him over with the meat. It wasn't too risky. Most of my customers are regulars and I know what time they come in. In any case, it's hard to see over the counter what's going on behind. Unfortunately, Roman didn't have much money on him so I had to give the new man the same treatment.'

The treatment which Karl Hold received from the court was more compassionate than that which he had accorded his victims. Although found guilty of premeditated homicide on two counts, he escaped the death sentence and, on 23 August 1974, was sentenced to life imprisonment. He will be eligible for release in about twelve years.

14

NOTHING HALF BAKED ABOUT THE GIRLS OF DOLENJA VAS

Although not only a citizen of a nominally capitalist country, but a businessman as well, Karl Hold did not make very efficient use of his victims. Granted, he cleaned them out of what money they were carrying, but, as a butcher, it should have occurred to him that he was in possession of a considerable quantity of fresh meat which, if not suitable for roasts or chops, could be turned into excellent sausage or hamburger.

It was a thought that had occurred to others in the past and will, no doubt occur to others in the future.

But not, of course, in Socialist countries such as Yugoslavia. If, as good Socialists must, you so love your fellow men that you are prepared to sacrifice your own interests for the good of society, you can scarcely be expected to turn them into sausage for private sale.

Unfortunately, however, even in the best of Socialist systems, incidents do take place and one of these was on 17 October 1977 when Vida Menas suddenly disappeared and was never seen again.

As she was eighteen years old and very pretty, this would not have been unusual in some parts of Europe, but Vida lived in Dolenja Vas, a very small village in the heart of Yugoslavia. Young girls did not normally disappear in Dolenja Vas. Vida was, in fact, the very first to have ever done so.

Her parents were, naturally, greatly puzzled and concerned and, after they and the rest of the adult population of Dolenja Vas had searched everywhere for her in vain, they

448

notified the police in Kocevje which was ten miles to the southeast and not a very large community either, but large enough to have a police force and even a criminal investigations department.

Inspector Marko Skolik, a heavy set, muscular man with a normally expressionless face, and his assistant, Detective-Sergeant Pyotr Brodnik, who was much younger, more handsome and less phlegmatic in his expression, came up to Dolenja Vas and investigated. The only thing that they could determine was that the girl had disappeared; something that the villagers already knew. She had not, as yet, had any steady boyfrjend among the local youths and she had last been seen by her own parents when she left the farmhouse at a little before two o'clock in the afternoon. No one could be found who had seen her after this time, and this was very strange because in such a small community as Dolenja Vas it is very difficult to avoid being seen no matter where you are going or what you are doing.

'She probably ran off to Ljubljana,' suggested the sergeant. 'They say that she was a pretty girl and there are more opportunities for pretty girls in Ljubljana than in Dolenja Vas.'

'It is forty miles to Ljubljana,' said the inspector, 'and there is only the one road. As she has no means of transportation, she must be walking. We shall, therefore, telephone the police in Ljubljana and ask them to look for her. She could not have arrived yet.'

Ljubljana is, of course, the capital of Yugoslavia and a comparatively large city. It is true that there were more opportunities for a pretty young girl in Ljubljana than in Dolenja Vas, but Vida, it seemed, had not gone there. Although a watch was kept, the girl never turned up and a policeman travelling over the road failed to spot her.

'Then she must have gone east to Karlovac, or west to Rijeka which is on the sea and would be an interesting place for a young girl, or even to Trieste which is, unjustly, not in Yugoslavia any longer,' said the inspector.

'Are you going to contact all of these places?' said the sergeant,

'Yes,' said the inspector and he did, but none of them ever reported finding any trace of Vida Menas.

This failure troubled the inspector quite a lot. He did not like having young girls disappear within his administrative district and he was, therefore, even more concerned when, on 4 May 1978, only slightly more than six months after the disappearance of Vida Menas, a second girl was reported missing.

This girl was nineteen, one year older than Vida, but also very pretty. She came from the village of Ribnica, less than two miles to the northeast along the road to Ljubljana from Dolenja Vas and even smaller than that community. Her name was Ljuba Smarovas.

The farmers in Ribnica knew, of course, of the disappearance of Vida Menas from the neighbouring village and, this time, the police in Kocevje were notified immediately.

A very large-scale search operation was organized, contingents of volunteers coming in from all the surrounding farming communities and a special tracking dog being brought down from the capital with its trainer.

The dog failed to pick up the girl's tracks, possibly because she had been, at one time or another, almost everywhere in the village and there was no clear trail for the animal to follow. As in the case of the disappearance of Vida Menas, the search parties found nothing.

The inspector returned to Kocevje a very worried man. Two girls had disappeared without trace in his administrative district and he should be investigating the disappearances. There was, however, nothing to investigate. The girls simply and suddenly disappeared. There were no witnesses, no clues, nothing which could be taken as a lead. There was not even any indication as to what had happened to Vida Menas and Ljuba Smarovas.

'The villagers say that a vampire is loose in the district,' said the sergeant. 'He is carrying off young girls to suck their blood.'

'This is a Socialist, progressive country,' said the inspector. 'We do not have any vampires and, besides, there is no such thing.'

450

'My grandfather says that when he was a young man a vampire came and carried off several girls from a village south of Karlovac. He said that they were later discovered working in a house of prostitution in Trieste. They had made a great deal of money.'

'Your grandfather is an old man,' said the inspector, checking himself just in time from saying 'idiot'. 'When he was a young man we did not have Socialism in Yugoslavia. As a matter of fact, there was no Yugoslavia even. The girls were carried off not by vampires, but by procurers who wanted to make money from them. Such things happen in capitalist societies.'

'Exactly!' said the sergeant in triumph. 'As this is a Socialist country and there are no prostitutes or procurers, then the girls must have been taken by a vampire. Who else would have a use for young girls?'

The inspector could not think of any answer to this, but he still did not believe that Vida Menas and Ljuba Smarovas had been carried off by any vampire and he ordered the sergeant not to believe it either.

'The only possibility,' he said, 'is that the girls left of their own volition. Vida Menas ran off somewhere and, Ljuba Smarovas hearing of her success, imitated her. It is not impossible that other girls will attempt to do the same.'

The inspector's words were prophetic for by 21 August of that same year yet a third girl was reported missing. Her name was Schipka Postalnyi, she was twenty years old and the prettiest girl in her home village of Prezid, less than fifteen miles to the southwest of Dolenja Vas as the crow flies, but a good fifty miles following the road.

It took the inspector and the sergeant over two hours to get to Prezid which lies on a parallel road to the one where Ribnica, Dolenja Vas and Kocevje are located. The road passes through the mountains and there are a great many curves and steep grades.

Prezid is even smaller than Dolenja Vas and Ribnica, and the people there had not heard of the disappearances of Vida Menas and Ljuba Smarovas, but they had been so startled and puzzled by the sudden disappearance of the

451

village's prettiest girl that they had immediately called the police.

This time there was a little more indication of the direction, at least, that the missing girl had taken. She had left her parent's home at approximately one o'clock in the afternoon to look for mushrooms in the forest to the east of the village. When she had not returned by five o'clock, her father had gone to look for her. He had been unable to find her and had eventually been joined by every other resident of the village, none of whom had been able to find her either.

Like the villagers further to the east, the people of Prezid thought that the girl had been carried off by a vampire and they wanted to know what the police were going to do about it.

There was not very much that Inspector Skolik could do. The villagers had already searched the area around Prezid and, as they knew it far better than anyone else, it was unlikely that bringing in a further contingent of police and volunteers would produce any greater results. In addition, he had already made the experience with the search for Vida Menas and Ljuba Smarovas. Neither had produced anything and he did not think that such a search would produce anything here.

He was, however, beginning to feel somewhat out of his depth and so he telephoned the National Gendarmerie Headquarters in Ljubljana to say that girls were disappearing in his administrative district, that he had been unable to discover the slightest trace of what was happening to them and that he did not feel that Kocevje could continue to accept the sole responsibility for the investigation. As the girls were, almost certainly, no longer in his district, they must be elsewhere in Yugoslavia and this made the cases a national rather than local affair.

The gendarmerie replied that they would arrange for a nationwide search and that he should send exact descriptions of the girls together with their photographs and, if possible, fingerprints to Gendarmerie headquarters where wanted circulars would be made up and distributed to all police units throughout the country. They thought that the girls had simply run away and would soon be found. Yugoslavia is not a place where it is easy to remain missing permanently.

Their estimate was going to turn out to be overly optimistic. Although Inspector Skolik and Sergeant Brodnik were able to obtain excellent photographs of the missing girls, precise descriptions and even, in the case of Vida Menas and Schipka Postalnyi, fingerprints, all of which were sent to Gendarmerie Headquarters in Ljubljana, no reports concerning the girls were received.

Or, at least, none had been received by 16 February 1979 when Lila Bratislav disappeared. Lila was twenty years old, very pretty and came from the village of Kocevska Reka, three or four miles to the southwest of Kocevje, cross country, but, again, much further by road.

The village people in Kocevska Reka knew all about the disappearances in Ribnica, Dolenja Vas and Prezid. By now everyone in the district did. Like the residents of the other communities, they thought that Lila had been taken by a vampire, and they thought that the vampire was living in Kocevje.

The inspector was inclined to agree with the second part of this theory, if not the first. All of the disappearances had taken place within the administrative district surrounding Kocevje and they had all been in villages so small that a stranger to the area would have been noticed. There had been no strangers reported at the times of the disappearances which meant that the murderer was someone who could be present in all of the little communities without attracting attention.

The inspector was, by now, of the opinion that it was murder and that the girls had not left of their own volition. One girl might have run away, either to some other part of the country or even outside it. Even two might have managed it. But not four.

If murder it was, then the motive was obvious. None of the girls had had any money or enemies. They had all been young and pretty. Some had, perhaps, been virgins, but they had probably not been obsessed with remaining in that condition.

453

A little force might have been necessary, but not murder. The killer would, therefore, be a sex psychopath.

This was a type of crime with which the inspector was totally unfamiliar. In the little farming communities of his district, there were, of course, occasionally crimes in which the motive was sex, but, so far, there had never been any homicidal sex deviates. As in most rural areas, there was a considerable amount of incest, ninety per cent of it unreported, some child molesting, also generally unreported, and a very occasional rape with violence.

The authors of such rapes were, however, nearly always normal farm boys who had taken by force what they had been unable to obtain through persuasion. Even so, he pulled out such records of sexual offences as he had and went through them carefully. There was no one in the records who could possibly be considered as a suspect in the disappearance of the four girls.

The National Gendarmerie, too, was becoming concerned over this startling series of disappearances from one small district, and a team of officers was sent down from Ljubljana to find out why nothing had been done about it. They reviewed everything that the inspector had done, talked to the people in the various villages from which the girls had disappeared and went back to Ljubljana no wiser than they had come. They were unable to suggest any new line of investigation to the local police.

Inspector Skolik was, therefore, doing nothing although he would have liked very much to do something. He would have liked to, at least, put out a warning to the people of his district that they should avoid leaving their daughters in the company of some specific person and that they should report the appearance of this specific person to the police. He had no doubt that there was such a person but, unfortunately, he had not the faintest idea of what he might look like or even where he came from, although he suspected Kocevje.

In the meantime, the villagers had more or less taken things into their own hands. Whether the person responsible for the disappearances of four young girls was a vampire or a sex psychopath made very little difference. The important consideration was that he be prevented from making off with any more girls and vigilante groups were spontaneously formed in all of the little villages throughout the district. Women went out of doors only in company with others, and at sunset the shutters of the houses were closed and the doors were barred. It would have been as much as a stranger's life was worth to knock on the door of one of the village houses at night anywhere in Kocevje district.

And yet, despite all of these precautions, on the afternoon of 5 December 1979, nineteen-year-old Mira Kosecki disappeared from the village of Stari Log less than five miles to the north of Kocevje.

Actually, Mira, who was, of course, very pretty, did not disappear from Stari Log itself, but from somewhere along the road connecting it with Kocevje. This was a perfectly straight, unencumbered stretch of secondary road with little traffic, and even Mira's parents had not objected to her walking into Kocevje in the middle of the afternoon. It seemed completely impossible that anything could happen to anyone on a public thoroughfare such as this.

Nonetheless, Mira, who had been planning to spend the night with her aunt in Kocevje, had been strictly instructed to telephone back to Stari Log immediately upon her arrival at her aunt's house. Her parents did not have a telephone in the farmhouse, but she could call the post office in Stari Log and the post master, who was her father's nephew, would come and tell them that she was all right.

When she did not call, her father, who could estimate very exactly how long it would take his daughter to walk to Kocevje, went to the post office and telephoned the aunt.

Mira had not arrived and her father set off down the road at a dead run, followed by most of the adult population of Stari Log, many of them carrying pitchforks, axes or clubs.

They ran all the way to Kocevje. They did not find any trace of Mira Kosecki. The fifth disappearance had taken place.

This was too much. The entire district was in an uproar, a contingent of soldiers from the Yugoslavian army was sent down to comb the forest and mountain valleys, and several persons travelling along the public roads were set upon and beaten by local villagers on the simple grounds that they did not know them.

Aside from a degree of excitement, all of this produced nothing. The girls were gone. There was no indication as to where, why or by what means.

Several men already having been beaten at various places in the district, the inspector was embarrassed but not surprised when a German tourist named Klaus Hochbauer appeared at police headquarters in Kocevje to report that he had been beaten badly by a strange man.

Hochbauer, who was forty-six years old and who had been touring Yugoslavia in his Volkswagen, had stopped to ask directions of a man walking along the road between Dolenja Vas and Kocevje. The man had not only failed to provide him with directions, but had, without any hesitation, dragged him out of the car and beaten his head so violently against a large stone lying beside the road that he had lost consciousness. When he had come to, the man was gone.

The inspector thought, at first, that this would probably have been one of the villagers from Dolenja Vas or some other local community who, not understanding German, had taken Hochbauer for the Vampire, as the person believed responsible for the disappearances of the five girls was commonly known throughout the district, and had thought to put an end to him. It was only when Hochbauer reported that he had also been robbed of all his money, a sum of a little over $600, that the theory became untenable.

The villagers of the Kocevje district were angry, frightened and dangerous. They were quite capable of violence to the person of such an obvious stranger as the German tourist. But, even if murderous, they were basically honest. None of them would have robbed him.

This meant that Klaus Hochbauer had been attacked, not by a suspicious and infuriated husband or relative, but by one of the few known criminal elements in the district. As they were so few as to make this practical, the inspector ordered

456

them all arrested. They were interrogated, their whereabouts at the time of the attack on Klaus Hochbauer determined and, within something less than a day, the inspector knew that none of them could have done it.

Moreover, Hochbauer's description of the man who had beaten and robbed him did not correspond to any of the potential suspects. He was, he said, not very tall, but strongly built and muscular. His age was estimated to be around thirty and he had black hair, black eyes and a two or three days' growth of black beard. Hochbauer had thought him to be exceptionally handsome.

In a more heavily populated area it would have been difficult or impossible to identify a person from such a vague description, but traffic along the roads in the Kocevje area is not heavy. The inspector thought that others might also have seen the man who had robbed Hochbauer and, if they had and if he was local, they would know him.

A criminal investigations department detachment under Sergeant Brodnik, moved out into the countryside and in a surprisingly short length of time a tentative identification of the robber was obtained.

He was, it seemed, thirty-two-year-old Metod Torinus, a bachelor who lived alone on a small farm just outside Dolenja Vas.

Torinus had no police record, had never attracted attention previously and was remarkable for nothing. He was merely one of the small farmers in the district among hundreds of others.

None the less, he answered to the description of the man who had attacked Klaus Hochbauer and he and no one else resembling him had been seen in the area at the time in question.

A police party, led personally by Inspector Skolik, proceeded to Torinus's farm where they took Torinus into custody, began to interrogate him and made an intensive search of the premises for the stolen money which had been mostly in German currency and was, therefore, easily identifiable.

Torinus denied the attack on the German tourist and said

that he knew nothing about the disappearances of the girls other than what everybody in the area knew. They had been carried off by a vampire. He appeared, however, to be highly nervous and, presently, the inspector noticed that he was most nervous when the searchers were near to the baking oven.

This was an old-fashioned construction, not inside, but outside the house, constructed of stone and mortar and with its own chimney. Such ovens were once standard for most of Europe, and many still remain in rural areas although they are no longer in use. They are large, massive blocks of masonry intended to hold heat sufficient for the baking after the fire which has been built in them has been drawn out and replaced with the bread.

'Look in the oven,' called the inspector. 'That is where he has hidden the money.'

'No, no!' cried Torinus. 'It is not true! I confess. I robbed the tourist, but the money is not in the oven. It is in a glass jar buried in the manure pile. Come. I will show you.'

The entire police party followed him to the manure pile behind the stable and the jar was dug up. It contained the money that had been stolen from Klaus Hochbauer.

'Excellent!' said the inspector. 'Take him back to Kocevje and charge him with highway robbery with violence. He will undoubtedly receive a long sentence for this.'

The sergeant moved to carry out his orders, but, as he was leading Torinus away, the inspector stopped him.

'Why do you have such a silly grin on your face?' he asked the prisoner. 'Are you so stupid that you do not realize the trouble you are in?'

Torinus remained silent and looked down at the ground, apparently attempting to adjust his features to a more suitable expression, but without much success.

'Wait!' said the inspector. 'Don't take him away yet. There is something funny here. When was it that he started looking so pleased?'

'When we went to dig up the glass jar with the money,' said the sergeant.

'My conscience was relieved because I had confessed my

458

crime,' said Torinus hurriedly. 'It was that which made me happy.'

'No,' said the inspector. 'It was something else . . . Let me see now, we were . . . the baking oven!'

Metod Torinus turned suddenly white as a sheet and began to tremble.

The reason became clear moments later when the inspector opened the great iron door of the baking oven and shined his flashlight inside.

'What is this?' he cried. 'What are these bones doing in a baking oven? Oh my God! That is a human skull!'

As a good communist the inspector did not, of course, believe in God, and it was some indication of the state of his emotions that he should call upon the deity. Under the circumstances, however, even a good communist was justified in such an exclamation for it is not often that an inspector of criminal investigations solves five homicides and a robbery within less than an hour.

Dr Josef Hartounian, a large, bald and jovial expert in forensic medicine, came down from Ljubljana and, having examined the bones in Metod Torinus's baking oven, pronounced them to be those of young females not older than twenty-four. Two of them could be positively identified as they had had dental work. They were Ljuba Smarovas from Ribnica and Lila Bratislav from Kocevska Reka. Mira Kosecki from Stari Log was tentatively identified from having suffered a broken collarbone as a child.

It did not matter, in any case, as Torinus had, by now, long since confessed to all five murders. Having nothing to lose, he also confessed to the five rapes that had preceded them.

Although sufficiently handsome that he would have had little difficulty in finding compliant female companions, Torinus suffered from an emotional abnormality which made sex with violence carried out on an unwilling partner necessary for the satisfaction of his desires.

According to his statement, all of the girls had accompanied him willingly and unsuspectingly to his farm, which was not doubted, although opinions varied as to why. Torinus said that they had gone there for sex. The girls' relatives said that they had been virgins and, if they had gone willingly to Torinus's farm, it had been for nothing more than cakes and coffee. It was pointed out that all of the victims had been killed during the time of the afternoon when they could be reasonably expected to have tea.

Whatever the case, upon their arrival at the farm, Torinus had leaped upon them, torn their clothing from their bodies, tied them hand and foot and, apparently, subjected them to sexual torture, this continuing, in some cases, so long that the girls' relatives were already searching for her before she was dead.

In the end, his sexual desires satisfied, Torinus had simply strangled the girls to death and had then cremated bodies and clothing in the baking oven.

He had, he said, been planning to clean the bones out of the oven and bury them somewhere else, but he had been busy and had not got around to it.

If he had, it is very probable that Inspector Skolik's case of the five missing girls would never have been solved and might very well have become the case of the ten missing girls or the fifteen missing girls or any given number.

Communist countries are not very liberal in their attitudes toward criminals and on 10 December 1980, after a relatively short trial, Metod Torinus was found guilty of multiple murder, sentenced to death and four days later executed.

15

YO-HO-HO AND
A BOTTLE OF SCHNAPS

The abrupt end of Metod Torinus, doubtedlessly quicker
and less painful than those of his victims, was, demonstrably,
a failure of Socialism. If he had been in an agricultural
commune, as he should have been, it would have been
possible to keep an eye on him and perhaps prevent this
wholesale destruction of useful workers and potential
mothers, to say nothing of the damage to the tourist industry.
Alas! Yugoslavian Socialism is not yet pure. Many farmers
still till the soil without proper supervision from public
servants and this is the result of it. A serious loss to the state
and a sordid, shameful business all the way around.

Not that things are handled a great deal better in the West,
but they are, at least, sometimes glamorous and filled with
the thrills and excitement of adventure and the always newsworthy escapades of the international jet set.

Of course, not everyone is as fascinated by the jet set as its
own members and those persons who make their living
writing about them. For the sailing crowd, jet-setters are
mindless milksops. What is 'in' is a yacht, the bigger the
better – transatlantic crossings, cruising in the Caribbean,
the South Seas or, for the timid, the Mediterranean.

Such a way of life builds hard men and courageous women,
a spirit of independence, the ability to rely upon one's self and
upon trusted shipmates, the keen eye in the bronzed face, a
slightly enhanced roll in the gait and a tolerance for startling
quantities of alcoholic beverages. It can also be dangerous.

On the morning of Saturday, 19 December 1981, when the
sailing yacht *Apollonia* out of Bremen, West Germany, made

461

landfall in the lovely harbour of the island of Barbados she was flying the signal flags for 'doctor needed on board' and the port physician hurried to the dock as she was being tied up.

The harbour master had come with him and they found only four persons aboard a sailing yawl which would normally carry a crew of six. One of these four was a young man lying in the cabin below decks and, having examined him, the doctor expressed amazement that he was still alive. He had been shot completely through the body from chest to back with a heavy calibre gun some considerable time earlier, but the bullet appeared to have missed all vital organs and blood vessels and had simply exited out his back near the spine.

He was, however, in an understandably serious condition and he was rushed by ambulance to the hospital for treatment.

In the meantime, the harbour master had summoned the police who began by establishing the identities of the four persons on board. They were forty-two-year-old Paul Termann, the navigator, his companion thirty-six-year-old Dorothea Permin, twenty-nine-year-old Dieter Giesen, an owner of a bar in Constance, a city in the south of Germany, and twenty-five-year-old Michael Wunsch, who was a student and the man who had been shot through. Wunsch also came from Constance and was a friend of Giesen's.

Speaking for all of the party, Termann, a strongly built man with a full, black beard, recounted a tragic story of death and madness on the high seas. Not only had Michael Wunsch been wounded, the captain and his mistress had both been lost overboard and it had to be presumed that they were dead.

The ill-fated voyage had begun nearly a month earlier in November when Termann and Dorothea Permin had made the acquaintance of thirty-five-year-old Herbert Klein in a bar in Las Palmas in the Canary Islands. Klein came from the city of Krefeld, West Germany, as did his twenty-five-year-old mistress, Gabriela Humpert. He had only recently bought the *Apollonia* which was registered in Bremen, and was looking for a crew to sail her to the Caribbean where he planned to charter the boat out for day trips.

Termann was an experienced navigator and, as he and Dorothea were interested in spending the winter months in the Caribbean, they had immediately signed on.

Unfortunately, while they were ashore celebrating the new association, someone had broken into the *Apollonia* where she lay in the harbour at Pasito Blanco and had stolen $3500 in cash and a number of valuable navigation instruments.

This had been a severe blow for Klein who, Termann thought, had been rather short on money, but Termann, who was not short on money at all, had offered to loan him $12,000, an offer which was promptly accepted.

Finances, captain, navigator and feminine company now being settled, there remained only the signing on of a couple of deck hands and these were quickly found in the persons of Dieter Giesen and Michael Wunsch who wanted to go to the Caribbean to practise skin-diving there.

On Saturday, 26 November 1981, the *Apollonia* had put to sea in excellent weather and with the crew in high spirits. Neither Klein nor Gabriela had had much experience in sailing, but the others had and things went smoothly.

Until Thursday, 3 December, when a vicious storm suddenly blew up out of nowhere and the crew of the *Apollonia* found themselves fighting for their lives and for the life of their ship. Fortunately, they had been sailing with reefed sails at the time but, even with a reef in, the boat was knocked down flat and, for a moment, it seemed doubtful that she would be able to right herself. Green water came pouring in over the lee railing, into the cockpit and down the companionway into the cabins. The storm had blown up so suddenly that nothing had been battened down.

For a short time, all was fear and confusion, but then the heavy, lead weight of the yawl's keel pulled her back upright. The wind dropped as suddenly as it had risen and the crew flopped down wherever they were and drew deep breaths of relief.

Only then was it noticed that Gabriela Humpert was missing.

For twelve hours they had sailed up and down, criss-crossing the area, hoping against hope that the girl had managed to keep herself afloat, but they had found no trace of her. She had been wearing heavy seaman's boots which had presumably filled with water and pulled her down like a stone.

Klein had gone wild. As the search continued and hope of finding the missing girl dwindled, he became more and more unhinged and finally began ordering the others about with a .357 Magnum revolver in his hand.

Michael Wunsch, the young student, had made the mistake of attempting to reason with him and Klein, losing all control of himself, had shot him at practically point-blank range. Wunsch had collapsed and the other members of the crew, fearing that Klein would kill them all, had rushed him.

Klein had fired two more shots, but had missed and, stepping back to escape the charge of the crew, had caught his foot on the low coping along the roof of the cabin and had fallen overboard.

Termann had thrown him a lifebuoy attached to a rope, but Klein had refused it and had swam away from the ship. The others were afraid to jump into the water after him because he was clearly mad and they feared that he might try to drown them. He had already shot Wunsch and had attempted to shoot the others so he was, obviously, capable of anything.

The ship was, therefore, brought around with the idea of coming up to him and fishing him out of the water with a boathook, but bringing a sailing ship around takes time and, by the time that the manoeuvre was completed, Klein had disappeared. The impression that the others had was that he had not wanted to live and had gone to join his drowned mistress voluntarily.

With Klein and Humpert lost, the most urgent matter was to get Wunsch to a doctor as quickly as possible. He was still alive, but obviously in a very serious condition and, as the radio had gone out of order several days earlier, they could

464

not call for help. They had, therefore, set sail for Barbados, their original destination, and had made landfall after six days.

This statement was made in the presence of the Barbados police, but repeated a second time before the German consul general. All of the persons involved were German citizens and they had requested that their consul be present.

As Herbert Klein could now be presumed dead, the *Apollonia* represented a part of his estate and was impounded by the authorities until such time as the question of his legal heirs could be cleared up. Paul Termann, Dorothea Permin and Dieter Giesen were all flown back to Germany by commercial airline and two weeks later Michael Wunsch followed them. The young man had had what the doctors describe as a truly miraculous escape. The heavy, .357 Magnum slug had passed between his lungs, touching neither of them, had come within a quarter of an inch of his heart, had struck no bones, had severed no major blood vessels and had passed out his back between the ribs a fraction of an inch from his spine. He had had a hole straight through him which, although exceedingly painful, was not really dangerous and, assuming that there was no infection, would heal itself.

By a second miracle, there had been no infection and Wunsch was already partially healed by the time that he had arrived at the hospital. Physically, that was. Mentally, he was a nervous wreck.

In the meantime, a copy of the statement made by Paul Termann, speaking for the crew of the *Apollonia*, in the presence of the Barbados police and the German consul general had been forwarded air mail to Bremen where it eventually landed on the desk of Inspector Johann Bauer of the Bremen Criminal Investigations Department. Bauer, a lean, muscular man with close-clipped, blond hair and very bright blue eyes, was chief of the squad assigned to investigating crimes along the Bremen waterfront. According to the statement a number of crimes had taken place aboard the *Apollonia* and, although eight hundred miles out in the Atlantic was something of an extension of the Bremen water-

465

front, it still fell within his jurisdiction for Bremen was registered as the ship's homeport.

The inspector began to process the case in a routine, matter of fact manner. It was, by no means, the first time that such things had landed on his desk and, in some cases, the actual events had taken place further away than the drama which had played itself out on the *Apollonia*, Bremen, with a population of six hundred thousand, is one of West Germany's large seaports and there are many vessels of all kinds registered there.

If the inspector's handling of the case was routine, it was also thorough and having read twice through the copy of Paul Termann's statement, a minor discrepancy caught like a burr in his mind.

'Take a look at this, Peter,' he said, tossing the statement over to his assistant, Detective-Sergeant Peter Bergmann, who sat at the desk facing his own. 'Fellow here says that the storm blew up so suddenly and unexpectedly out of a clear blue sky that they didn't even have time to batten down the hatches. Then, he says when the girl went over the side she was wearing sea boots which filled with water and dragged her down. If the weather was so good before the storm and it came up so suddenly, where did she have time to put on sea boots before getting washed overboard?'

The sergeant read silently through the report. He was a young man, blond like his chief, but round-faced, cheerful looking and pleasingly egg-shaped, being noticeably thicker in the middle than on either end.

'The same question applies to the reef in the sails,' he said, tossing the statement back. 'What do you intend to do?'

'Well, for starters, let's bring the lot of them up here and take separate statements,' said the inspector. 'This one was made by just one man speaking for all of them. Could be that the others will have different versions. In the meantime, I see that they've sent the log of the *Apollonia* along and you might check her location on 3 December and then ask the weather bureau just how bad that storm was out there in the Atlantic on that day.'

The sergeant nodded and went about carrying out his

instructions. Some forty minutes later he put down the telephone and said, 'There wasn't any storm within a thousand miles of that location on that date.'

'Huh?' said the inspector who was, by now, working on something else.

'The *Apollonia*,' said the sergeant. 'She wasn't hit by any storm on 3 December unless she managed somehow to get over into the Pacific. The weather bureau has satellite photos of the whole area for 3 December and there wasn't any storm.'

'Wrong date?' suggested the inspector. 'The second? The fourth?'

'I thought of that,' said the sergeant. 'Nothing for three days earlier and nothing for two days later. It couldn't have been more than two days later or they wouldn't have had time to reach Barbados when they did.'

The inspector sat silently and thoughtfully looking at his assistant for several minutes. 'I wonder what really did happen out there,' he said finally.

'Maybe I should take a run down to Krefeld and have a talk with the people there about Herbert Klein,' suggested the sergeant.

'I think you should,' said the inspector, 'and before we get the others up here for the reconstruction. This whole business is beginning to smell a little strong.'

The police had already arranged with the Winkler Shipyard on the River Weser to the north of Bremen for a reconstruction of the event on 3 December aboard the *Apollonia* on a ship of her approximate size and construction. Paul Termann, Dorothea Permin, Dieter Giesen and the now largely recovered Michael Wunsch had all been summoned to appear on 22 January to carry out this re-enactment of what had supposedly taken place, and the police had reserved hotel accommodation for them for that night.

The sergeant went down to Krefeld, a large, industrial city on the edge of the Ruhr district a few hundred miles to the south. When he returned, it was with the news that Herbert Klein had not been the wealthy, international yacthsman that he was supposed to be.

467

'He was the manager of a trucking firm,' said the sergeant, making his report to the inspector. 'Last year he went all to pieces, divorced his wife, sold everything he owned and bought the *Apollonia* for ninety thousand dollars cash. It must have taken every cent that he had. He then acquired the twenty-five-year-old mistress and set sail for the Canary Islands. His wife is thirty-three and still goes by the name of Birgit Klein. Her only comment was that she would have been better off if he had drowned himself before she met him. Fortunately, there were no children.'

'Another seeker of adventure in a world where any real adventures are either illegal or painful,' commented the inspector. 'Did he have insurance and, if so, who was the beneficiary?'

'I didn't think to check on that,' said the sergeant, embarrassed. 'You think maybe he isn't dead and that this is some kind of a deal to swindle the insurance company?'

'Could be,' said the inspector. 'There have been weirder schemes and Klein sounds like the type.'

'I'll check with his bank,' said the sergeant. 'They should know his financial situation.'

The bank knew more. They knew, for example, that Herbert Klein was alive and well and had been travelling extensively in Europe. He had cashed traveller's cheques in the south of France, in Italy, in Switzerland and in several places in Germany. The last had been cashed less than a week before in Hamburg.

'The man must be mentally retarded,' said the inspector. 'Doesn't he realize that, if he goes around cashing his cheques, they're going to come back to the bank and constitute positive proof that he's still alive. What in the devil is he trying to do and where's the girl?'

'In my opinion, an even greater question,' said the sergeant, 'is where is he getting the money to pay Termann, Permin, Giesen and Wunsch to keep their mouths shut. He has to be paying them because they're obviously lying and what other reason could there be for it?'

'What about the insurance?' said the inspector.

468

'He wasn't insured,' said the sergeant. 'He cashed in his insurance when he bought the boat.'

'Well, then what . . . ?' exclaimed the inspector. 'Get me Hamburg on the telephone immediately. We've got to get our hands on this Klein and the sooner the better. Let's just hope he stays in Hamburg long enough to cash another cheque.'

The inspector's wish was going to be granted. A physical description of Herbert Klein and a picture obtained from his parents were sent to the Hamburg police where they were made up into a wanted circular to be distributed to the tellers of all the banks in the city. If Klein turned up to cash one of his cheques, the teller was to signal one of his or her colleagues to summon the police and stall until they could arrive. This would normally not be very long. The Hamburg police are highly efficient and the city swarms with patrol-cars.

On Monday, 18 January 1982, the trap snapped shut. A man appeared at the teller's window of a downtown bank, handed in a traveller's cheque for $100 and presented his personal identification card. It was in the name of Herbert Klein and carried the Krefeld address.

The teller gave the appointed signal, knocked a tray of coins on to the floor and began picking them up while the customer waited impatiently.

He did not have long to wait. The officers from the patrolcar had been advised that Klein might be armed with a .357 Magnum revolver and they walked quietly up behind him on either side, pressed the muzzles of their service pistols into his ribs and advised him not to move.

A search produced no weapon but more traveller's cheques, and Klein was taken to police headquarters to explain what he was doing in Hamburg when he was supposed to be at the bottom of the Atlantic.

He promptly offered an excellent explanation. He was not Herbert Klein.

Perhaps forty-one-year-old Hans Kruger might have been less frank with the Hamburg police were it not for the fact that he had a police record and his fingerprints were, there-fore, on file. In any case, he would eventually have been brought back to Krefeld to explain what had happened to Gabriela Humpert if nothing else, and there he would certainly have come into contact with someone who had known the real Herbert Klein whom Hans Kruger resembled not at all. Klein had been tall and rather skinny with a good deal of hair and moustache and not much chin. Kruger was balding, broad-shouldered and had a jaw like the bow of a harbour tug.

In fact, he looked very much like a cartoonist's idea of a burglar and that was precisely what he was. Kruger was a thief, a burglar and a break-in artist. It was he who had broken into the *Apollonia* at Las Palmas, and it was this break-in which had netted him, in addition to the cash and the navigational instruments, the traveller's cheques and identification card of Herbert Klein. A man with considerable experience in such matters, he had had no difficulty in reproducing a reasonable facsimile of the yachtsman's signature.

Kruger had been arrested many times before and did not resent such actions on the part of the police. Transferred to Bremen to see if he knew anything about the mystery of the *Apollonia*, he assured Inspector Bauer that he did not, but volunteered the information that he had been able to take his time about plundering the *Apollonia* because he had received a tip that there would be no one on board.

The tip had come from an old friend, Paul Termann.

This was a valuable piece of information, although it did nothing toward solving the question of what had taken place aboard the *Apollonia* in mid-Atlantic, and the inspector put his assistant to checking yacht owners on the Bremen waterfront to see if any of them had any information about the black-bearded navigator.

And, indeed, several did and none of it was favourable. The most critical of all was his most recent employer but one, fifty-four-year-old Captain Guenther Lohse, owner of the sailing yacht *Orion X*. Captain Lohse had such strong feelings about Paul Termann that he sat down and wrote a seven-page statement in which he said, among other less flattering things, that Termann was a madman, a violent character and

470

a gun nut. Although too poor to afford more than a rowboat, he was obsessed with the ambition to own a yacht, and was prepared to do anything to get one. While serving on board the *Orion X* he had talked of nothing but drug- and gun-running which he believed would get him into the big money.

Termann had no sooner been shipped as navigator than he unilaterally declared himself captain, although Lohse both owned and captained the boat. This being pointed out to him, he compromised and appointed himself second captain, a position which does not exist on a ship. This led to such violent quarrels with the rest of the crew that Lohse had been forced to discharge him as everyone else on board had threatened to walk off if he remained.

Termann, concluded Captain Lohse, was also a bum navigator whose reckoning had the ship in the wrong ocean half the time.

'Call up the hotel and cancel the reservations for Termann and his girlfriend,' said the inspector to Sergeant Bergmann when he had finished reading this report. 'They'll be putting up in the detention cells here and they won't need them.'

'What about Giesen and Wunsch?' said the sergeant. 'Whatever happened, they had to be in on it. They signed the protocol of Termann's statement in Barbados.'

'It looks like it,' said the inspector, 'but, for the moment, I'm prepared to give them the benefit of the doubt. Constance reported that they were clean, didn't they?'

As the case had progressed and become more mysterious, the sergeant had contacted the police in Constance with a request that they check out the backgrounds of Dieter Giesen and Michael Wunsch. This had been done and the Constance police had reported that both men were exactly what they had said they were. Giesen was a respectable businessman and the owner of a high-class bar. Wunsch was a student and the son of a well-to-do Constance family. Both men were passionate fans of skin-diving and both belonged to a skin-diving club on Lake Constance, the large body of water which separates the southern end of Germany from Switzerland.

None of the parties involved had known, of course, that

they were being investigated and all appeared promptly on Friday, 22 January 1982, in Bremen for the re-enactment of the event. This re-enactment was, however, going to turn out a little different than anyone had anticipated.

To begin with, Paul Termann, Dorothea Permin, Dieter Giesen and Michael Wunsch never reached the hotel where they believed that rooms had been reserved for them, but were met at the railway station by an impressive contingent of criminal investigations department plain-clothes officers under the command of Sergeant Bergmann, were taken into custody and brought to the interrogation rooms at police headquarters. The inspector had, in the meantime, changed his mind and had cancelled the hotel reservations for Giesen and Wunsch also.

And it was Giesen and Wunsch on whom the questioning was concentrated. Both were apparently respectable, young men who were not known to have ever been involved in anything illegal and the inspector felt that they were the ones most likely to break down and reveal the truth.

His assumption was correct and, after little more than a few moments of interrogation and a warning that continued silence could result in charges of concealing a felony or acting as an accessory after the fact, both men made separate but identical statements of the events on board the *Apollonia*, not on 3 December but on the 13th, the only difference being a gap in Wunsch's account as he had been unconscious part of the time.

According to Giesen and Wunsch, the *Apollonia* had barely set sail from Las Palmas when Termann began to display the strange behaviour which had made him so unpopular on the *Orion X* and other vessels. Appointing himself captain, he had reversed any orders given by Klein and had begun commanding the others about like galley slaves. This included Dorothea Permin who not only supported him, but was so subservient to his will that she allowed him to accompany her to the toilet, apparently to make certain that she did not get into any mischief there.

Klein and his mistress, Gabriela Humpert, had attempted to resist, but they had been no match for the physically powerful and aggressive Termann. Giesen and Wunsch, unwilling to become involved, had tried to avoid taking sides and had contented themselves with hoping that the voyage to the Caribbean would be a swift one, and that they would soon be able to leave the most uncomfortable ship they had ever set sail in.

Both had thought that Termann was more than a little mad, but not actually dangerous up until that Sunday, 13 December, when he had produced the .357 Magnum and had advised Klein that he was not only taking over the command of the *Apollonia*, but the *Apollonia* herself. He, Termann, was now owner and captain and everyone was to obey his orders instantly and without question.

Foolishly, Klein had attempted to argue and Termann had gone into a hysterical rage, screaming that he would now kill both of them, meaning Klein and Gabriela.

There was no doubting his sincerity and the couple had thrown themselves on their knees and pleaded for their lives. Instead of killing them, Klein suggested, they could be set adrift in the ship's boat.

Termann would not hear of it, but he did not kill them immediately either. Instead, almost the entire day of 13 December was spent in a sort of macabre argument with Klein and Gabriela pleading and arguing for their lives and Termann sticking to his original plan of murdering them.

Finally, he had said that he would agree not to kill them, but only if they committed suicide themselves. Producing a second pistol, he had loaded it with two bullets and laid it on the seat in the cockpit. They could take turns in shooting themselves or one could shoot the other and them commit suicide. Termann then went below to the cabin to relax and wait at the foot of the companionway.

Another man might have picked up the pistol lying on the seat in the cockpit and shot Termann through the head as he sat there, but Herbert Klein, whatever his failings, was not a killer. Instead of murdering his enemy, he attempted to overpower him and, in so doing, lost his life and the life of his young mistress.

Klein had picked up the iron handle of the bilge pump

473

lying in the cockpit and, reaching down through the opening of the companionway, had swung it at Termann's head. He had hit him, but it was only a glancing blow and with not enough force to even throw Termann off balance.

The black-bearded killer who was holding the .357 Magnum in his hand had swung around and had fired instantly.

Unfortunately for Michael Wunsch, who was also sitting in the cockpit, he was no better a shot than a navigator and the bullet missed Klein and struck Wunsch in the chest. Wunsch fell to the floor of the cockpit unconscious and was not a witness to any of the acts which followed.

Giesen was, but he would have much preferred not to be. Following the failure with the pump handle and the shooting of Wunsch, Klein had run forward to hide himself in the bow compartment of the boat, but Termann had forced him out at gunpoint and brought him crawling back to the cockpit. There he was ordered to stand with his back to the railing and Termann fired a bullet at close range into his chest, the impact tipping him over the railing and into the sea.

Turning around from this accomplished murder, Paul Termann found himself staring into the fear-widened eyes of Gabriela Humpert. The second bullet passed directly between them.

Giesen had, of course, considered himself to be a dead man, but Termann also had his practical side. The *Apollonia* was too big to be sailed safely by himself and Dorothea Permin alone. Advising Giesen that he had connections in Germany and that, if he revealed so much as a word of what had happened upon their return, he would arrange for a killer to come down from Frankfurt and eliminate him, he wrote up the statement to be presented to the German consul and the police in Barbados and forced Giesen to sign it. When Michael Wunsch recovered consciousness, he was given the same warning and, overjoyed to learn that he was not to be executed immediately, had sworn silence and signed as well.

Giesen and Wunsch insisted that they had been simply too frightened of Termann to say so much as a word while they were still in Barbados. He was, they thought, quite capable of whipping out a pistol in the very presence of the German consul and shooting them down on the spot. The man was violently insane and even after their return to Germany they had been afraid to say anything before Michael's wound had healed enough that they could clear off if necessary.

The statements of Dieter Giesen and Michael Wunsch were flatly contradicted by Termann and Dorothea Permin who stuck to their original version and said that Giesen and Wunsch were trying to get them into trouble because they had quarrelled with them on the ship.

However, separation in the detention cells from Termann had a beneficial effect on Dorothea's character and, after a week of interrogation, she broke down and verified in all details the accounts given by Dieter Giesen and Michael Wunsch.

Paul Termann was indicted on two accounts of voluntary homicide and one count of piracy on the high seas, an unusual charge even for Bremen. Dorothea Permin was indicted on two counts of acting as an accessory after the fact to homicide and on one count of acting as an accessory after the fact to piracy in return for her cooperation with the police.

She was sentenced to only five years' imprisonment with three years suspended on 21 January 1983.

A month later, Paul Termann was given the maximum sentence of life imprisonment. Rather surprisingly, the psychologists who examined him expressed the opinion that he was sane.

16

HOMICIDES PERFORMED, QUICK SERVICE, REASONABLE RATES

The temptation arises to wonder who, if not Paul Termann, is insane. Or is it that, in a paranoically egalitarian society, even the logic of madmen is to be respected?

Termann was logical. He wanted a yacht. Klein had a yacht. Ergo, he killed Klein and took his yacht. A trifle simplistic, perhaps. After all, the yacht was registered in Klein's name and, without a bill of sale, Termann could scarcely hope to change the registration. However, it may be that he was planning to have a bill of sale made out and signed by his friend, Hans Kruger, who owed him a favour in any case. Perhaps, the psychologists were right. Paul Termann was sane, but rather more direct in his dealings than most of us.

Such directness crops up rather frequently in our modern societies, particularly in connection with the transfer of wealth. Those who do not have it feel that they are entitled to it and take steps accordingly. Homicide becomes a sort of social adjustment, and for those who are incapable by reason of lack of strength, resolution or technical training to carry out the sticky parts, there are skilled, reliable experts.

The acts committed by these experts fall into a curious category. They are homicides because someone is killed by the expert, but are they murder?

The hired assassin has no motive for his crime other than the fee he is paid. He does not dislike the victim; frequently has never before laid eyes on him or her. Had it been the victim who employed him, he would as cheerfully have executed his current employer. He is simply paid to kill.

So, too, are official executioners, soldiers, agents of the world's secret services and terrorists or freedom fighters. Granted, not all of these are paid in cash, but there is compensation of some sort, and terrorists who survive to bring about a successful change in the ruling group usually do rather well for themselves.

It would appear that, if the direct way of thinking of a Paul Termann is to be regarded as sane, then the direct homicides of the professional killers cannot be described as murder. There is a demand for the service. They fill it.

Such crimes are difficult for the police to solve as it is necessary to establish the motive of not the killer himself (or herself, in deference to woman's equality, although there are few female professional killers as yet), but of the person who hires him. This can be unclear. Murders are often committed for trifling motives.

But because a man makes lousy pizza?

For a time, it looked it, although pizza was about the last thing on the mind of thirty-year-old Walter Bronheim as he came riding his bicycle down Dolberger Street in the West German city of Hamm and entered the bicycle path leading through the small forest known as the Schafbusch.

Some two hundred yards to the west of the Schafbusch, the main highway running from Hanover to Cologne is intersected by a secondary road into which the bicycle path opens and, just before reaching this intersection, Bronheim came upon the body of a man lying on his back at the edge of the road.

The man was wearing dark blue trousers, black shoes, a black, cord jacket and a rose-coloured shirt with frills down the front and at the cuffs. The front of the shirt was no longer rose-coloured, but red with fresh blood.

Hurriedly dismounting from his bicycle, Bronheim ran forward and knelt down beside the man. He assumed that this was the victim of a hit-and-run driver and he was relieved, but also horrified to see that blood was still welling out of the man's chest which rose and fell with his laboured

477

breathing. His eyes were closed and he appeared to be unconscious.

Although Bronheim had had some experience in first aid, he grasped instantly that the man's injuries were too serious for anything that he might be able to do and he ran back to the bicycle and pedalled off in the direction of the village of Uentrop, the nearest community, to summon help.

As he rode he turned his left hand on the handlebars and looked at his wristwatch. The time was exactly ten minutes past nine.

It did not take Bronheim long to reach Uentrop nor to find a public telephone there, and he dialled the number of the emergency ambulance service in Hamm, reporting that there was a severly injured man lying in the road near the Schafbusch forest and saying that he would now return to where the victim lay and wait for the ambulance.

Hamm is a city of some 180,000 population and its emergency ambulance service has ample opportunity for practice because of the vast numbers of automobile accidents. Bronheim had had barely time to pedal back to where the man lay when the ambulance arrived.

The victim, a slender, dark-haired and olive-skinned man in his late thirties or early forties, was still alive but unconscious, and he was lifted quickly on to the stretcher, slid into the ambulance and taken away in the direction of Hamm.

The victim having been reported as still alive, the duty emergency doctor had come out with the ambulance and, as it raced through the streets with flashing, blue, warning lights and screaming siren, he began cutting away the blood-soaked shirt for the purpose of determining the nature of the injury and stopping the flow of blood.

The ambulance had covered less than half the distance to the hospital when he leaned over the partition, tapped the driver on the shoulder and said, 'Call the hospital. Tell them we have a gunshot wound. Multiple thorax. The police should be informed.'

The driver carried out his instructions over the radio-telephone and increased his speed, but, even as the stretcher with the wounded man was being carried through the emergency entrance, a long, violent shudder passed over the body and was followed by a cessation of all movement.

'Into the operating room!' snapped the doctor. 'There may still be a chance to . . .'

There was none. The man was dead and, as later examination would show, from four heavy-calibre bullets fired into the chest with such accuracy that a child's hand could cover the entry wounds. The damage that they had inflicted had been such that the victim had been doomed from the instant of impact and it was only remarkable that he had continued to live as long as he did.

This having been determined, the body was transferred to the police morgue for an autopsy to determine officially the cause and time of death. As there was little question but that the case was one of deliberate homicide, it would also be necessary to recover the bullets and any other indications which might be of value to the investigation which would follow.

This autopsy was carried out by Dr Oscar Wittauer, a relatively young assistant coroner with a long, sad face and a drooping blond moustache. Although the autopsy was routine, he took quite a time about it, causing Inspector Heinz Wagner of the Hamm police Criminal Investigations Department to fidgit irritably. A busy man with a near military haircut and a carefully clipped moustache which was beginning to go grey, he was anxious to get on with the investigation.

While he paced about the autopsy room, peering over the doctor's shoulder and generally getting in the way, his assistant, Detective-Sergeant Kurt Kettenmyer, went impassively through the dead man's pockets in search of identification. He was a young man who wore his wavy brown hair down to his collar and tended to scowl a great deal, not so much because he was bad-tempered but because he believed this to be a suitable expression for an investigations officer.

There were a good many things in the pockets and, as he removed them, he laid them out in a neat row on the edge of the table. First came a crumpled pack of cigarettes with four cigarettes of a popular brand in it, then an expensive-looking

479

cigarette lighter, followed by four keys on a souvenir keyring from the city of Berlin, the equivalent of $64.22 in small bills and coins, a collection of scraps of paper, mainly restaurant bills, a small penknife, a leather folder containing a personal identity card and a driver's licence and, finally, two photographs, one of a very pretty, young woman and the other of a little girl of about ten.

The inspector pounced on the case with the papers and was soon able to determine that the victim was forty-year-old Vincenzo Sapuppo, married, the father of one child, an Italian national from the city of Palermo, Sicily, and a pizza baker by profession. His local address was listed as 24 Brandenburg Street and the inspector sent the sergeant there immediately to notify the widow, arrange for the official identification by the next of kin and attempt to learn whether there were any obvious suspects in the murder.

In the meantime, the inspector having decided that nothing of any great significance was going to come out of the autopsy, he went off to view the scene of the discovery of the body and, presumably, the scene of the crime.

Two patrolcars had been sent by the dispatcher at police headquarters and they had blocked off a section of the road where traces of blood showed that the body had lain. Sitting in one of the cars was Walter Bronheim who was being held until someone took his statement.

The inspector did so and, having determined that he knew nothing of value to the investigation, sent him off about his business. The only information that he was able to provide was the exact time of the discovery, which the inspector thought might give some indication of the time of the shooting. Having seen the wounds, he did not believe that the man could have lived very long after receiving them.

Although it was obvious that nothing would be found at the scene, he was a thorough man and he called headquarters over the car's radio-telephone and arranged for a detachment from the police laboratory to come out and go over the area.

He did not wait for them, but returned to headquarters. It was unlikely that they would find anything at all, and the best he could hope for was an opinion as to whether the shooting had taken place there or elsewhere. The road was hard-surfaced so there would be no footprints or tire tracks to be connected with the shooting. The laboratory report was, however, necessary for the records.

The fact was, the inspector had already formed an opinion of his own, and that was that this was a gangster-type execution. He had thought so the moment he saw the bullet wounds, and his suspicions had received support with the knowledge that the victim was a Sicilian.

There were a great many Italian guest workers, as they were called, in the great industrial and mining complex of the Ruhr and they came mainly from southern Italy. Hamm was technically not in the Ruhr, but it was only twelve miles to the east of it and there were a great many Italians there, too.

Like ethnic groups everywhere, they had brought their traditional societies with them and one of these was the Mafia. There had been kidnappings, extortions, protection-racket violence and a gang killing or two.

Actually, the police had not concerned themselves very much with this local branch of an old organization as their activities had been confined largely to their own compatriots. The local Germans were seldom involved and, in any case, the crime rate in the Ruhr was at a level to make the efforts of the Mafia seem insignificant.

What the inspector thought the investigations would show, if they showed anything, was that Vincenzo Sapuppo might have started life as a pizzario, but that it had been a long time since that had been his primary source of income. Rather, he had been working in a small-time capacity as a leg man or collection agent for some group in the Underworld. He had, however, been more greedy than smart, had held out more than permitted and had been punished when his employers put out a contract on his ears.

The inspector would not have been surprised if Sapuppo had had a police record, but the records section said no, they had no Sapuppo in the files. As far as they were concerned he was clean.

Clean and remarkably lucky or unlucky, depending upon how you looked at it. According to the final autopsy report,

Sapuppo had been hit with four nine-millimetre slugs in the immediate vicinity of the heart and had been killed by none of them. Despite expert shooting, not a vital organ had been touched; not a major blood vessel severed. Had he been found in time he would have survived, but, according to Dr Wittauer, he had continued to live for as much as seven hours following the shooting without anyone coming to his aid. The only favourable aspect to the matter was that he had apparently been unconscious the entire time.

The four slugs had been recovered from Sapuppo's body and sent to the Ballistics Department which reported that they had been fired from a Beretta automatic and that there was no record of the gun.

This did not surprise the inspector in the least. A nine-millimetre Beretta was a killer's gun, and professional killers did not go around with guns that had a record with the police.

The inspector had already decided that the only possible direction which the investigation could take was to try and determine whom Sapuppo had worked for and then get them deported on some pretext as an example. There was obviously not going to be enough evidence to convict anybody of the murder.

Having thus cleared matters up in his own mind, the inspector was irritated when Sergeant Kettenmyer returned from his interview with the victim's widow bringing information which cast considerable doubt on his theories.

Mrs Sapuppo, said the sergeant, had been quite positive. Her husband had had no connections to the Underworld or, she had added, to anything that brought in money. He had been exactly what his identity card said, a pizzario and not even a very good one.

'She suggest that he was murdered by one of the customers?' said the inspector sarcastically.

'She said he's had trouble with his employers more than once,' said the sergeant, forgetting to scowl. 'She's a very unfortunate woman. Only twenty years old and . . .'

'Sapuppo was forty,' said the inspector. 'This must be his second marriage. That child in the picture couldn't be Mrs Sapuppo's if she's only twenty.'

482

'Maybe she said twenty-two,' said the sergeant. 'It's her daughter all right. She may have married very young. Do you want me to take a look at her background?'

'Definitely,' said the inspector. 'If Sapuppo didn't have any connections to the Underworld and he didn't have any money, then Mrs Sapuppo is about the only possible motive, short of something weird like a mistaken identity. That twenty-year difference in ages makes a love triangle of some sort a good bet.'

An excellent bet, actually. The Sapuppos being well known in the local Italian community, the sergeant had little difficulty in finding out nearly everything there was to know about Magdalena Sapuppo who, it seemed, had married in Sicily at the age of fourteen.

'Not her idea and not even his,' said the sergeant. 'The families arranged it. They apparently thought there was more money in making pizzas than there is.

'Mrs Sapuppo immediately got pregnant and produced her only child when she had just turned fifteen. Three years later, they came to Germany and they've been here ever since.

'Sapuppo's held a whole string of jobs as pizzario and Mrs Sapuppo was apparently telling the literal truth. He didn't have much talent for the profession, and he didn't make much money. No trace of any connection to the Under-world.'

'And the name of her lover?' said the inspector cynically.

'Luigi Mosca,' said the sergeant. 'Thirty. Married. Two kids. Heavy-equipment operator for a construction firm. He and Mrs Sapuppo have been at it for about two years, which is double the time any of the others lasted with her so it must be true love.'

'Had lots of them, did she?' said the inspector. 'Did Sapuppo know?'

'About the others and about this one, too,' said the sergeant. 'He spoke of his wife's lovers as casually as if they were part of the family. Could be she was too much for him what with that twenty-year age difference and all.'

'Fine,' said the inspector. 'But then, why bother to murder him? That cost money.'

'Brought it on himself apparently,' said the sergeant. 'He was planning to return to Sicily and take his family with him next month. Mrs Sapuppo couldn't stand the thought of separation from her loved ones.'

'Or vice versa,' said the inspector. 'Well, that should do it. Bring in Mrs Sapuppo and Mosca and we'll see what interrogation can do. Normally, a couple like that gets nervous about the other one selling out and they both end up blabbing their hearts out. True love holds up fine until it's a question of who's going to take the rap.'

Unfortunately, true love held up somewhat better in this case, possibly because it was obvious that no one was going to take the rap. The suspects' alibis were as solid as the Rock of Gibraltar. Hours before the shooting and long after it, Luigi Mosca and Magdalena Sapuppo had been in the constant presence of large numbers of disinterested witnesses. They were so obviously in the clear that the inspector could not even hold them for questioning.

'We should have guessed that,' said the inspector. 'The job was professional so they hired somebody to pull it off while they arranged their watertight alibis.'

'So they get away with it,' said the sergeant.

'Not at all,' said the inspector. 'What we do now is find the bird who pulled the trigger and offer him a deal if he testifies against his employers. People like that are practical. He'll cooperate.'

The inspector was, undoubtedly, right in expecting cooperation from the killer, and the only flaw in his plans was that it proved impossible to determine who he was. The sergeant spent a great deal of time and effort on this project, and he did learn many things other than the identity of the murderer.

He was able to determine where Sapuppo had apparently been not long before he was killed. The pizzario's car, missing since the time of the murder, was found parked near the Silvermoon discotheque in the town of Ahlen, twelve miles to the north of Ham. It was a yellow Peugeot 104 and the owner of the Silvermoon, an establishment patronized by a somewhat older clientele than was customary, said that he knew Sapuppo well and that he had been in the Silvermoon with another Italian until three in the morning of 15 September.

This would have been an important lead had it not been for the fact that the autopsy had established that Sapuppo was lying in the road with four bullets in his chest twenty miles away at the time.

There were other flaws in the discotheque owner's testimony. He was unable to describe Sapuppo, seemed to think that he was blond, an unusual hair colouration for a Sicilian although not unknown, and confused the details of his murder with those of another case.

Whereupon the sergeant took a look into his background, found that he had spent more of his life in institutions for persons suffering from nervous disorders than out, and came to the conclusion that the lead was worthless.

There remained, however, the fact that Sapuppo's car had been parked near the discotheque. By whom? Possibly the murderer. It was one of a number of questions that would never be answered.

The question as to the price of the killing was. It had cost precisely three thousand dollars, the amount which Mosca had borrowed on a personal loan from the Hamm Savings Bank two weeks before the murder took place.

Asked what he had done with this money, Mosca said he had lost the entire amount playing roulette. Asked why he had borrowed it, he replied, 'To play roulette.'

At this point the official investigation ended by reason of having nothing left to investigate. There had been little mention of it in the press. Mrs Sapuppo would have provided wonderful pictures and text, but, as she was not charged with anything, even an insinuation could have resulted in a lawsuit. As for the victim, the death of an incompetent pizza baker was not a story to grip the imagination of the German public.

Not the imagination of the public, perhaps, but certainly the imagination of Inspector Wagner who fumed and fretted and was profoundly annoyed that anyone, however lacking in professional skills, could be murdered practically under his nose and that he could do nothing about it. He was utterly convinced that Magdalena Sapuppo and Luigi Mosca were guilty of the murder, and he was very disappointed when a check of the records showed no entry for the heavy-equipment operator.

As a matter of fact, the only thing which the investigation of Mosca had shown was that he was a harassed man who was in over his head financially. Although he was a good, steady worker, he had a wife and two children to support plus, now, Magdalena whose husband had died without insurance. In addition, he had the payments on the three-thousand-dollar loan and the total was more than his salary would cover.

Persons in Luigi Mosca's position often do something foolish and on the afternoon of Tuesday, 10 February 1981, he did.

Although it was mid-winter, the day was dry and comparatively sunny if not exactly warm. On a country road outside Hamm, thirteen-year-old Dirk Reimann, son of a wealthy building contractor, was stolidly peddling his bicycle home from school as he did every weekday.

Presently, he was passed by a yellow Alfa-Romeo which cut in ahead of him, forcing him to stop.

Reimann, a stout youth with a deceptively sluggish appearance, got off the bicycle and stood staring phlegmatically at the three men in the car. Although two of them worked for his father, he had never seen them before and he did not know who they were or what they wanted.

The three Italians whose purpose it was to kidnap and hold for ransom the young contractor's son came boiling out of the car and all jumped on him simultaneously. According to their plan, he was to be quickly overpowered, dragged into the car and driven swiftly away to an abandoned farmhouse where he would be held until the ransom was paid.

This was a good plan, but it did not take into account the possibility that the victim might not be in agreement. Instead of meekly submitting to being overpowered, young Reimann began to take wild, roundhouse swings with his fists, kick with his feet and bellow like a bull with his tail on fire. One of the Italians was knocked sprawling with a punch in the nose.

Another doubled up and went hopping off with a savagely kicked shin. And the third, noting that the boy's roars were attracting attention and that passers-by were hurrying to the rescue, shovelled the casualties into the Alfa-Romeo and, taking the wheel, raced away at top speed.

But not fast enough. The indignant Dirk Reimann had noted the licence number and so had two of the approaching rescuers. A half-hour later, the police knew of the kidnapping attempt. Forty-five minutes later, they knew the identity of the owner of the yellow Alfa-Romeo. An hour after that, they had him in custody.

It was Luigi Mosca.

'Very good,' said the inspector, rubbing his hands together. 'Very good. Now, we have a bargaining position. Either he confesses to the Sapuppo murder, or we'll nail him with a short sentence for attempted kidnapping.'

The sergeant looked at him as if he would have liked to comment on his mental condition, but thought he had better not.

'You mean a long sentence, don't you?' he ventured.

'Short,' said the inspector. 'Followed, of course, by deportation to Sicily.'

'And that will cause him to confess to murder?' said the sergeant.

'Once I bring to his attention who will be waiting for him there,' said the inspector.

'The Italian police?' said the sergeant in obvious mystification.

'The Sapuppo family,' said the inspector.

The sergeant finally understood.

And so, too, did Luigi Mosca. After having given the matter only very little thought, he agreed with the inspector that he would be better off serving a sentence in Germany for murder than arriving a free man in Sicily to face the relatives of the man he had had murdered.

The actual murderer of Vincenzo Sapuppo, said Luigi Mosca, was thirty-five-year-old Vincenzo Madiri who lived in a village near Palermo and who killed persons on a contractual basis. Madiri, he added, was a cousin, but, even so, he had received no discount and had had to pay the full price including Madiri's round-trip air fare first class.

As the inspector had anticipated, Mosca concluded his statement with the assurance that the murder had been entirely Magdalena's idea and that he had opposed it from the start. She had, however, forced him by threatening to expose his infidelity with her to his wife.

This was not a very plausible excuse as Mosca had been living more or less openly with Mrs Sapuppo for close to two years and his wife not only knew about it, but so did everybody else in the Italian community in Hamm. It did, however, show that Mosca was still not thinking clearly.

Magdalena Sapuppo was. Taken into custody and advised of her lover's confession, she immediately branded it a lie from beginning to end. Luigi Mosca, she said, had had nothing to do with the murder. It was her husband, and it was she who had had him murdered. Mosca was merely trying to take credit so as to cheat her of the long jail sentence which she so richly deserved.

What had not occurred to Mosca had obviously occurred to her instantly. The first one out of jail would also be the first to arrive in Sicily.

Later, during the course of a confrontation between the two former lovers, the dispute reached near comic proportions.

'It was my husband. I alone am responsible,' said Magdalena.

'It was my cousin who killed him,' said Mosca. 'You had nothing to do with it.'

'You did not think of it,' said Magdalena. 'You did not have enough intelligence to even kidnap a thirteen-year-old boy. He drove the three of you before him like sheep. How could you plan a murder?'

'And who is still paying the payments on the loan from the bank?' howled Mosca in a frenzy of rage. 'It is my cousin. A top professional. All first class. It is my money. And who gets the long sentence? You? Hah! I demand justice!'

'I wouldn't be surprised but what he'll get it too,' remarked the sergeant after the confrontation was over. 'The thing that puzzles me is why nobody seems concerned about Madiri. He's the one who actually pulled the trigger. You'd think that he would be the one the Sapuppos would be after, but apparently not. He simply did the job and flew back to Sicily without a care in the world.'

'Maybe it's because he did it on a professional basis,' said the inspector. 'Nothing personal, so to speak. Or maybe it's because he is obviously not a good man to argue with. The Italian police may be able to tell us. I've asked for Madiri's arrest.'

The Italian police did not arrest Vincenzo Madiri, but they did send an officer around to take his statement, a copy of which was forwarded to Inspector Wagner in Hamm.

In it Madiri said that he did not know anything about the murder, had never heard the name of Sapuppo and had a great many cousins, one or more of whom might or might not be named Luigi Mosca. In any case, nobody had paid him to kill anybody and he had not. He was not in the killing business, but made his living doing small contracting jobs.

The police did not comment on the accuracy of the statement, but merely observed that the charges against Madiri appeared to be based on the unsupported statements of two confessed murderers. In any case, sovereign states do not extradite their own nationals and Mr Madiri had said that he was too busy to come to Germany voluntarily at the moment.

The inspector was not satisfied with this report and requested assistance from the German embassy in Palermo who sent one of the vice-consuls around to talk with Mr Madiri.

He found him up on the roof of his mother's house where he was carrying out certain necessary repairs to the tiles. There being no witnesses present, he confirmed that he was, indeed, a professional killer and that he had carried out the Sapuppo contract in Hamm. His understanding had been that he was being jointly employed by the widow and his cousin, but he was not prepared to put anything in writing. He was not worried about the Sapuppo family. They could hardly hold it against a man for practising his trade and, God knew, business was bad enough. Times were tough all over.

It was obvious from this that there was not very much that

489

could be done about Mr Vincenzo Madiri and Inspector
Wagner proceeded to bring charges of incitement to homi-
cide and acting as an accessory to the fact of homicide against
Magdalena Sapuppo and Luigi Mosca indiscriminately.

At their trial, both cooperated enthusiastically and were
rewarded, she with seven years' imprisonment and he with
nine. Sentencing was on 4 September 1981. Normally,
neither would serve much more than a third of these
sentences before being parolled and deported to Sicily.

It is considered probable that they will be met at the
airport.

17

WHO CAN I GET TO RAPE
MY SON?

Magdalena Sapuppo and Luigi Mosca do not really belong in this book. There was nothing mad about them. In a world with no generally accepted standards of morality, they acted practically and reasonably.

Vincenzo Sapuppo was threatening their happiness. It was, therefore, necessary to eliminate him, but neither Magdalena nor Luigi possessed the necessary skills. They were in need of the services of an expert and, as they did not have the cash to finance the job, they took a convenient bank loan.

The only thing that went wrong was that the payments were too high. Had they been stretched out over a longer period, it is possible that they could have lived happily ever after with no necessity of visiting lovely, but dangerous Sicily.

Unless, of course, Mrs Mosca began to stand in the way of their happiness in which case there would have had to be another bank loan and another tiring trip north for Mr Madiri who does not care for air travel and sometimes suffers from motion sickness.

He would, of course, be subject to other discomforts if Inspector Wagner knew that he was coming, but that would be unlikely. For the inspector the case is closed, and he has gone on to other, less trying matters. At least, he hopes they will be less trying. European investigations officers have enough problems without suspects clamouring for longer sentences while known murderers go uncharged. Such investigations can be emotionally exhausting.

But not for Inspector Richard Rademacher of the Criminal Investigations Department of the Salzburg police. Inspector Rademacher was never exhausted and on this Sunday, 18 February 1978, it was going to be a good thing too.

A small man, slightly built with the long, wavy, brown hair and pale sensitive face of a poet, the inspector was as neatly dressed and shaved as if he had just risen rather than having been pulled out of bed at one in the morning; and it was six in the evening now.

'In all my twenty-six years of investigation work,' said the inspector, 'and in everything that I have ever read on the subject of crime, I have as yet to encounter anything resembling this mess.'

His voice was, like his character, at variance with his appearance: high, clear, hard and emotionless. Known to his colleagues as a ruthless driver, he was even formidable physically.

'It would help if he would talk,' said his assistant. 'First he was hysterical, and now this thousand-dollar-an-hour lawyer telling him to shut up.'

Detective-Sergeant Pitt Krimzsky sounded a little hysterical himself. A tall, powerfully built man with tightly curled, blond hair and a jutting jaw, he had not stood up as well to the seventeen-odd hours on duty as had his chief, although he was close to twenty years younger.

'Call the hospital again and see if they'll let us talk to the girl now,' said the inspector. 'She wasn't badly hurt. There's no reason why we shouldn't be able to talk to her.'

The sergeant picked up the telephone on his desk which stood back to back with the inspector's and dialled. There was a short exchange of conversation in a not too friendly tone and the sergeant hung up.

'Tomorrow morning at the earliest,' he said. 'They say she's physically all right, but the shock of seeing her friend murdered made it necessary for them to put her to sleep until tomorrow. According to her papers, she's only twenty-two.'

'With forty years' experience,' said the inspector. 'The girl's a professional. That's obvious. What does the vice squad report?'

492

'Nothing, so far,' said the sergeant. 'I'll go down and shake them up.'

He stood up from the desk, stretched and left the office. He could as easily have telephoned the office of the vice squad, some of whose members had been called in to check on the identity of witness and victim, but he was secretly anxious to get away from his chief for a few minutes. It had been a long day since had been pulled out of bed in the early hours of that Sunday morning and the inspector's typical worrying and forcing of the case was beginning to get on his nerves.

The inspector, who was not unaware of this, let him go without comment and, alone in the office, got up from his desk to go and stare at the snow-covered scene outside the window. Darkness had fallen and the street lamps were on. So were some of the lights in the shop windows, but there were few pedestrians in the street and not much vehicle traffic. Salzburg, on the border between Germany and Austria, is a quietly beautiful, historic city and its residents incline to peacefully spent weekends once the tourist season is over.

Although he could not see it from the office, he could visualize the River Salzach winding northward from the city and forming the national boundary. In that same direction and less than three miles away was Anthering, the village from which Klaus Winkler had come to Salzburg five years earlier. He had been seventeen at the time, a slight, effeminate, only child of rich parents, and he had registered as a student at the Salzburg Academy of Beaux Arts.

At the moment, that was all that the inspector knew about Klaus Winkler, that and one other thing.

He was a murderer.

Why he had become a murderer the inspector could not guess. The neighbours who had summoned the police to the chic, expensive apartment building at twelve Mozart Street had been dumbfounded. The witness who had survived with only minor injuries could, perhaps, have explained, but she was in a state of shock and the doctors at the hospital would not let him talk to her. Like her murdered companion, she was a German national and not Austrian. Her name was

Renate Braun and the inspector was convinced that she was a professional prostitute and an expensive one. Einrich Winkler, forty-eight-year-old owner of the Winkler Metal Forming Company in Anthering, and his handsome forty-four-year-old wife Frieda had assured him that they knew nothing of the affair, although the inspector was not entirely convinced of that and, of course, big, beautiful, twenty-one-year-old Helga Schmidt could tell him nothing because she was dead, her dark, lovely head crushed by the violent blows of something heavy and irregularly shaped. It was thought that this would have been the blood-smeared, bronze statue of a naked man which had been found near her body and which the technicians in the police laboratory were now examining.

The person who could explain it all was Klaus Winkler and the inspector had thought that he would soon do so under interrogation, but so far he had not. It did not appear to be so much a question of a strong character resisting the interrogators. Winkler was anything but a strong character. Rather, he appeared to be in such a state of shock himself that he could not discuss what had taken place rationally. He was, it seemed, not only afraid of being taken for insane; he was afraid of actually being insane and thought he had lost touch with reality.

He had not lost touch with reality to the point where he was willing to confess to the murder, although he had not denied it either. The inspector thought that he might have by now had it not been for the extremely expensive attorney whom his parents had brought with them upon learning of his arrest. All three were now waiting in the outer office and the inspector could estimate what it cost to keep an attorney like that sitting all day Sunday in a police station.

The attorney had shut young Winkler up like a clam, but there was too much physical evidence for him to gain his release and the inspector felt confident that he would eventually be able to pry the clam open again. Unless he was greatly mistaken, the main cause of Winkler's silence was simply embarrassment. He was obviously a sensitive young man and this was a case that reeked sex.

Freak sex, too. In appearance, Winkler was almost a caricature of a homosexual and the things found in his apartment confirmed it.

So, what had he been doing with two beautiful, naked, sexy, young, German prostitutes?

The inspector could quite simply not imagine. Maybe Winkler was bisexual, but he certainly didn't look it.

The inspector sighed, called the switchboard to report where he could be located, and left the building to go to the police morgue where he suspected the autopsy would be practically completed.

It was completed and Dr Egon Harz, a painfully thin man with sunken cheeks, a long, sallow face and straight, long, black hair hanging in locks about his mournful eyes, was engaged in washing his hands. The corpse, with the terrible cross of the autopsy cut from collarbone to pubes still gaping wide, lay on the marble table.

The inspector inspected it dispassionately.

'Well?' he said.

'Identical to my report at the scene,' said the doctor. 'She was killed less than an hour before we arrived. Cause of death was multiple fractures of the skull. Probably the statue.'

'Sex?' said the inspector.

'She had been having a good time,' said the doctor. 'Lots of lubrication. A little semen in the vagina. Not much. Trace in the mouth. Saliva in the public hair and on the external genitals.'

'What the hell!' said the inspector. 'The man's a homosexual.'

The doctor shrugged and said nothing.

'All right!' said the inspector in an annoyed voice and left the autopsy room, closing the door a little more firmly than necessary.

The sergeant had returned from the vice squad when he arrived back at the office. He reported that the two girls had not been officially prostitutes. They had been too high class; too expensive for that. Erotic entertainers, said the sergeant. Very good. Very costly.

'Then, how did they get mixed up in a mess like this?'

snapped the inspector. He was not a man who liked loose ends or unexplained motives and in this case there was nothing else.

The sergeant did not reply. There was nothing he could say. The inspector already knew everything that he knew about the case and he was not prepared to do any speculating.

He had seen immediately that it was a mess from the moment they had been called out that morning. The dispatcher who had not even been present at the scene personally had said so over the telephone.

'A weirdo, Pitt,' he had said. 'We've had a homicide report from twelve Mozart and I've got a car there now. They say that there's a dead woman, another one hurt and a guy who's either high on drugs or in shock. Everybody's stark naked. The inspector's already on the way. He wants you to join him.'

The sergeant had immediately left for Mozart Street and, having less distance to travel, got there almost as soon as his chief.

The emergency ambulance, first to be called away, had been even quicker and the injured girl was being carried to it on a stretcher. Her only visible injury was a small cut on the left shoulder and the beginnings of a massive bruise around it.

The dead girl lay on the carpeted floor of the bedroom, halfway between the door and the bed. There was a certain amount of fresh blood on the carpet around her head, but no marks on the body and she looked as if she were merely sleeping. The intern with the ambulance crew had, however, checked for signs of life and there were none.

Klaus Winkler had been sitting in one of the easy chairs in the salon, leaning forward with his face buried in his hands. The officers from the patrolcar said that he had gone to the chair after letting them into the apartment and had been there ever since.

Otherwise, there were only the neighbours who had called the police. They had been awakened by what sounded like a battle royal and some piercing screams, apparently from the girl who had escaped. They had come to the door and

496

Winkler had let them in without a word. After seeing the girl lying on the bedroom floor and jumping to the conclusion that she was dead, they had left hurriedly and called the police. Winkler had apparently shut the door after them. The injured girl had neither said anything nor attempted to leave and the neighbours had thought that she and Winkler were related.

Renate Braun having been taken away to the hospital, the inspector approached Winkler and asked him to make a statement.

Winkler had looked at him in bewilderment and had said that his name was Klaus Winkler, but seemed confused over what had taken place. He gave his parent's address and asked that they be notified.

The inspector had then cautioned him on his rights and had ordered him taken to police headquarters. He also called for a detachment from the police laboratory to try and discover what had taken place in the apartment. No statements having been obtained, he did not know whether Winkler was a suspect or a victim, but he was not taking any chances.

Winkler became a suspect shortly after the arrival of the technicians who took his fingerprints, compared them to those on the bronze statue and noted the blood with which it was smeared. It looked, they said, as if there had been some kind of a sex orgy which had become violent.

The inspector had already come to the same conclusion. What had apparently been the clothing worn by the two girls had been hung up neatly on the backs of two chairs and two totally transparent and extremely sexy nightgowns had been laid out in the bedroom. There were also two expensive overnight cases stuffed with sex toys and pornography, all of it heterosexual. Pornography found in the apartment, however, was homosexual. Also in the cases were the girls' personal identification papers which was how the inspector learned their names and nationality.

Curiously, there were no signs of refreshments, no glasses or dirty plates, but there were two wet towels in the bathroom indicating that two persons had taken baths. A T-shirt and a pair of men's jeans lay on the floor of the living room, and a pair of men's shorts, expensive, silk and peach-coloured, had been flung over the shade of a lamp. This clothing apparently belonged to Klaus Winkler as it matched other items found in the closets.

Winkler's clothing was not all that was in the closets. There was other clothing in a larger size and there were two sets of toilet articles in the bathroom. The young man had not, it seemed, lived alone.

Faced with such contradictory evidence, the inspector had come to the conclusion that Winkler and his room-mate were bisexuals who had brought in a couple of expensive call girls for an evening's entertainment. A quarrel had, however, arisen and had degenerated into a physical battle with fatal results. As the other man was missing, the inspector assumed that he was the more promising suspect.

The laboratory technicians and Dr Harz were inclined to disagree. Everything in the apartment, they said, indicated a purely homosexual relationship. The male couple would no more have thought of inviting in a couple of females than they would of entertaining a pair of king cobras.

And there the matter had remained throughout the day while the inspector fumed and fretted and attempted to pry some kind of information out of somebody.

He had had just one success. Klaus Winkler's apartment mate had been identified. His name was Leopold Floer and he had been able to prove beyond a shadow of a doubt that he had not been in the apartment at the time of the murder and that he had nothing to do with it.

In fact, he was not even willing to believe what the inspector told him. He knew Klaus Winkler well, he said, intimately even, and it was utterly impossible for him to have been consorting with females, prostitutes or otherwise. Klaus did not like women. There was only one woman in the world that he would tolerate within a yard of himself and that was his mother.

The inspector had not been pleased at this confirmation of the doctor's and technicians' theories and the rejection of his own and, now that the autopsy was complete and there was still nothing concrete, he decided on an interview with Winkler's parents who were still waiting with the attorney in the outside office.

Taking them separately and beginning with Winkler, he chose to be blunt.

'I presume you are aware that your son is a homosexual?' he said.

Winkler flushed. 'I am aware of it,' he said shortly.

'Do you believe him capable of a relationship with a woman?' said the inspector.

'Not any more,' said Winkler, paused and then burst out in a torrent of angry words.

'It was Frieda! She ruined the boy! Always wanted a daughter and she made one out of him. My God! she was still putting him in dresses and giving him dollies to play with when he was ten. It's not his fault!'

'You could have done something, Mr Winkler,' said the inspector.

'I did,' said Winkler. 'When he was sixteen, I packed him off to boarding school. I thought they might still make a man out of him, but it was too late.'

'Have you tried psychiatric treatment?' said the inspector.

He did not know exactly where the interview was leading, but his years of experience in criminal investigations were telling him that there was something wrong with Einrich Winkler's statements although what it was he could not say.

'He wouldn't cooperate,' said Winkler. 'Finally, I had to give up. He wanted to come down to Salzburg, study at the academy and have his own apartment and I let him. What else could I do?'

'You knew he was living with a man named Leopold Floer?' said the inspector.

'I know none of his friends and I want to know none of them,' said Winkler.

The inspector's interview of Mrs Winkler was shorter, but it was enough to confirm that what Winkler had said was essentially true.

Assured that there was no hope of Klaus being released that night, the Winklers and their attorney went home and, a

499

little later, so did the inspector. He had finally accepted that he was not going to find out what had happened yet that evening.

This situation resulted in a near sleepless night for the inspector who was, in any case, a light and restless sleeper, but it had a more calming effect on Klaus Winkler in the detention cells and, on the following morning, he announced that he was prepared to make a statement.

The inspector was pleased, but less so once he had heard it for he did not believe a word of it. It was, in fact, the most improbable statement that he had ever heard, he told the sergeant, and the only explanation he could find for it was that Winkler's attorney had put him up to making it with the intent of offering an insanity plea.

'It was a little after eleven on Saturday evening,' said Klaus Winkler. 'Leo was not coming home that night and I was having a quiet time with some books.

'I was not expecting anyone so when the doorbell rang, I thought that Leo had changed his mind and was coming home. If I'd stopped to think, I'd have remembered that he had his own key and didn't have to ring the doorbell, but I didn't and I went and opened the door.

'There were two strange girls standing outside and, as I'd never seen either of them before in my life, I thought they must have got the wrong address.

'However, before I could say anything the biggest one, the one that got killed, said, 'Is Raymond Huncke here?'

'I said that I didn't know any Raymond Huncke and that they had the wrong address.

'She said, "Well, he used to live here and he gave us this address. Can we come in for a minute? We've come a long way and we're tired."

'I said, "Of course, Come in." and after they had come in, I offered them a drink.

'They laughed and said they didn't drink on the job and they were acting very funny, walking around the apartment and picking up things and looking at them.

'I didn't like that and I said, "You better go now. My friend is coming home any minute now and he is very

500

jealous." I wanted them to know I wasn't interested in girls.

'They just giggled and the little one went into the bathroom. I yelled, "Hey! What are you doing in my bathroom?" and she came to the door and started taking her clothes off. She said, "I'm taking a bath. That's what bathrooms are for."

'I thought that she was completely mad and when I turned around, the other one was taking off her clothes, too.

'I couldn't believe what was happening and I sort of lost my head and started screaming at them to get out and some other things, but they didn't pay any attention and when they'd finished with their showers, they came into the living room and started walking around naked in an obscene sort of way.

'I was just sitting in a chair and wondering if I had gone crazy or if somebody had put some kind of a drug into my food. I couldn't believe what was happening.

'All of a sudden they both sort of jumped on me, and one of them kissed me on the mouth! I almost lost my lunch! I was really sick! They were pulling my clothes off and rubbing themselves on me. I couldn't do anything. You wouldn't believe how strong they were.

'I was fighting and yelling, but they got my clothes off and they got me down on the floor and they began to touch me all over, but mostly my private parts. They were laughing like crazy and they were excited, too. I think they were touching each other. I couldn't bear to look.

'The worst part was that they were getting me excited, not the real me, of course, but my body and I had a sort of orgasm. I was so disgusted and frightened, too, that I made a terrible effort and I broke away from them and ran into the bedroom. I thought I could lock the door and call out the window for help.

'They were too fast for me though and they pushed me onto the bed and started playing with me again. One was squatting over my hips and I think she'd taken me right in her. The other was sitting across my face and trying to get me to kiss her. I was nearly smothered.

'I think I may have bitten her. I was desperate, and when I

501

got one hand free I was feeling around for something to defend myself, and I got hold of my little statue of Adam and I hit the big one with it. I don't know how many times I hit her. I was out of my mind with fear and disgust.

'Then, I saw the other one running and I threw the statue at her and hit her on the shoulder. I guess it was right after that that the neighbours came.'

'The attorney couldn't have made that up,' said the sergeant. 'And if he did, Winkler couldn't have memorized it. It has to be true.'

'It can't be,' said the inspector. 'This is a crazy world, but we're not at the point yet where beautiful, young prostitutes rape homosexuals in their own apartments for free.'

The inspector was, however, wrong in every respect but one. Two beautiful, young prostitutes had raped Klaus Winkler in his own apartment. The only thing was, it had not been for free.

Later that same day Renate Braun recovered sufficiently from her experience to make a statement, and she confirmed in every detail the story which Klaus Winkler had told the police.

With the addition of one detail which provided the explanation to what had otherwise been a totally inexplicable performance on the part of herself and her dead friend.

'We were hired,' she said. 'Two thousand five hundred dollars and expenses. If I'd have known how it would turn out, I'd have thrown the money in his face.'

'Whose face?' said the inspector, already knowing the answer.

'Einrich Winkler's face,' said Renate Braun.

'I thought it would make a man of him,' said Einrich Winkler.

On 26 June 1978, Klaus Winkler pleaded not guilty to homicide by reason of legitimate self-defence. The jury, although sympathetic, decided that the fate with which he had been threatened was not so terrible as to warrant quite such such a vigorous reaction, found him guilty of manslaughter and sentenced him to seven years' imprisonment.

He is serving his sentence in a men's prison, of course.

18

COLD BUFFET

There are superficial parallels in the Sapuppo and Winkler cases, mainly the use of qualified professionals to carry out the dirty work. Mrs Sapuppo did not feel up to murdering her husband. Mr Winkler could not rape his son. Outside help had to be called in.

Curiously, however, the principals of the Sapuppo drama, who were all from the underprivileged sector of society, were more conventional in their outlook and more sane in their actions than the participants in the Winkler tragedy, all of whom belonged to the favoured class. Girls included. No pizzario nor professional killer either ever earned two and a half thousand dollars plus expenses for three or four hour's work.

If there was anything crazy about Mrs Sapuppo and her lover, it was merely the failure to realize that Mr Sapuppo's relatives might react violently to his death and, even here, they probably believed that they could conceal their responsibility.

By contrast, the Winklers and everyone connected to them appear to have been suffering from serious delusions.

Mrs Winkler tried to make a little girl out of a little boy and nearly succeeded. Mr Winkler tried to make him back into a boy again and failed. The two prostitutes set out to rape a man whom they knew in advance to be a homosexual. Klaus, in the face of all anatomical evidence, believed himself to be a girl. The jury showed prejudice. Had Klaus really been a girl and the two prostitutes men, he would probably have been acquitted. Even the police were a little confused by the time the case was over. The official mind is not constructed for the contemplation of such extremes in human behaviour.

A good many official minds are not constructed for the contemplation of anything which does not fit current ideology with regard to crime and its prevention. For the past fifty years or so, the predominant theory on crime and criminals has been that there are none. What has been called crime is the justified actions of persons who are not criminals but under-privileged members of society. By correcting the injustices of society, crime and criminals will be eliminated.

This an excellent theory and its only fault is that it does not work. Violent crime has increased steadily and continues to increase despite all efforts at rehabilitation and reinsertion programmes. The human being is predisposed to the use of force and only force will restrain the dangerous tendencies of a substantial part of society.

Crimes against property have also increased, but at a slower pace, although it would seem exactly here that the underprivileged would exert their greatest efforts. There is, however, a reason for this.

Compare the sentences handed down and actually served for murder and for bank robbery and it will be seen that the murderer is substantially better off. It is rare for him or her to serve more than seven years for the crime. A bank robber can expect to spend twenty years or more behind bars and, if necessary, he will be hunted to the ends of the earth, particularly if he managed to make off with a sizeable amount of cash.

This may seem unjust, but it is economically understandable. Murderers are caught by civil servants on fixed salaries with modest tax-supported means at their disposal. Bank robbers and the like are tracked by private as well as public agencies and the means at their disposal are exceeded only by what the bank or insurance company hopes to recover plus the value of the deterrent effect.

In short, there is very little to be gained in catching and punishing murderers. There is a great deal to be gained in catching and punishing bank robbers.

This attitude is not confined to capitalist countries. In Socialist countries, economic crimes will get you executed as swiftly as will murder. The crime rate in socialist countries is low, either because there are no underprivileged or because everyone is underprivileged.

Or, just possibly, because of those swift and pitiless executions.

In the Western world, executions seem to exercise a peculiar effect on the emotions of legislators and other persons in positions of power. Although these, theoretically, are the representatives of the citizens who have elected them, and although polls in nearly every country show substantial majorities in favour of capital punishment, the rights of the convicted are given precedence in almost all cases. Very little consideration is given to the rights of children and older persons to live without fear of rape, torture and death. The protectors of human rights protect unevenly.

This state of affairs has given rise in recent years to the strange spectacle of criminals more civic-minded than their prosecutors. Violent criminals, recognizing the danger which they pose to society have literally pleaded with the courts to sentence them to death.

Sometimes, the courts have listened, more often not. When they have not, the results have occasionally been tragic. The judges or others whose decision led to the tragedy are never held responsible. They are described as great humanitarians in the press.

Sometimes, however, even a great humanitarian finds himself confronted with a situation where mercy seems out of place.

The lean, distinguished-looking man with the prominent, slightly hooked nose had risen to his feet and a sudden hush fell over the courtroom of the Superior Criminal Court in the city of Troyes, France. It was known that there would be an appeal for the death sentence.

'Your Honour,' began the man in a deep, low and oddly tranquil voice, 'ladies and gentlemen of the jury, members of the press and fellow citizens. It is not my intent to entertain you with long speeches. There is little to be said. The accused in this case has freely admitted his guilt. He has murdered wantonly and deliberately three times. He has assured the court that, given the opportunity, he will kill again. This man must never again be released into society and, as long as he is alive, there is such a possibility. It is, therefore, the duty of this court to eliminate the possibility in the only manner in which it can with certainty be eliminated, and that is by sentencing the accused to die on the guillotine.

'That is all I have to say. Condemn the accused to death and see that he passes under the guillotine surely and at the earliest possible date.

'I thank you and I count upon you to do your duty as human beings and as citizens of France.'

Thirty-nine-year-old Claude Buffet who had just demanded his own execution sat down and quietly folded his hands in his lap. He was, without question, the most controlled person in the courtroom.

A few feet away, Buffet's fellow accused, thirty-six-year-old Roger Bontems, was sweating copiously, his swarthy face turned pale with concern. He was no killer and he did not see how he could be sentenced to death, but even the mention of the guillotine made him nervous. Privately, as he had publically, he cursed the day that he had been assigned to share a cell with this homicidal madman.

The hush which had lasted while Buffet was speaking had ended and there were savage cries of 'Kill him! Chop off his head!' from the spectators, many of whom were friends and relatives of the victims.

Buffet gazed at them dispassionately with a sort of mild curiosity and rose to his feet once again.

For a second time, there was a dead silence.

'I do not apologize to the relatives of the persons I have murdered,' he said coldly. 'I accept no responsibility.' He raised his hand dramatically to point at the official picture of the president of France which hung in that as in all French courtrooms. 'There!' he cried, 'is the man responsible for the deaths of Nicole Compte and Guy Giradot! Take your complaints to him!'

There was something to what he said and every person in the courtroom was aware that, were it not for President Georges Pompidou, Claude Buffet would now be dead and Nicole Compte and Guy Giradot alive.

France had the death penalty, but the last time it had been invoked was on 11 March 1969. General Charles de Gaulle had been president then and he was not a man to have much sympathy with violent criminals.

Pompidou, who replaced him, was more of a progressive and he immediately began commuting all death sentences to life imprisonment, something which only the president had the power to do.

It was not a popular exercise of that power and not even a wise one. If something went wrong, then, exceptionally, the responsibility was all too clear.

Now something had gone very wrong indeed, and President Pompidou found himself faced with a decision which he would rather have avoided. He had already saved Claude Buffet from the guillotine once. Would he dare to save him again?

Basically, the whole business was due to a misfortune in timing. Had Buffet chosen to murder Francoise Besimensky a year earlier, General de Gaulle would still have been president when he was convicted and his head would have rolled.

However, Mrs Besimensky, a twenty-seven-year-old fashion model who was married to a prominent physician, was murdered on 18 January 1967 and justice in France being no more swift and certain than it is in most other places, it was October of 1970 before the trial took place.

By this time, General de Gaulle was out of office and Georges Pompidou was president. It was a fatal difference.

The case had begun prosaically enough for a Paris murder with the discovery of Mrs Besimensky's body lying among some bushes in the great park of the Bois de Boulogne on 19 January.

Mrs Besimensky had been killed by two bullet wounds in the upper part of the chest. The bullets, recovered at the time of the autopsy, proved to be nine millimetre, and they had been fired at extremely close range.

There were certain indications of a sexual motive. The woman's underwear had been removed and there had been apparently some tampering with the sex organs, although no traces of semen or of actual penetration were recovered. It was, therefore, possible that the sexual indications were false and represented an attempt by the murderer to mislead the police.

This theory was strengthened by the fact that no identification was found with or on the body which had, however, been left in comparatively conspicuous view guaranteeing its early discovery.

Efforts by the police to identify the victim were immediately successful as her husband had reported her missing when she failed to return home the preceding evening. Efforts to identify her murderer were less so.

The chief difficulty was the motive. If it had not been sexual, and there was good reason to believe that it had not, what then? According to her husband, Mrs Besimensky would not have been carrying a sufficiently large sum of money on her to be murdered for it and, in any case, there would have been no reason for a robber to murder her once he had his hands on the money.

Unless, of course, she knew him, but Mrs Besimensky did not move in social circles that could be expected to include robbers.

There remained a personal motive of some kind. Mrs Besimensky had been a beautiful woman. A lover perhaps . . . ?

Or Dr Besimensky. In the murder of a married person, the spouse is always and automatically the primary suspect until proven innocent.

Dr Besimensky was very quickly proven innocent and so, for that matter, in another sense, was his wife. Francoise Besimensky had not had any lovers.

This left the police with only the alternative which they liked least. The murderer of Francoise Besimensky was neither a robber nor a disappointed lover nor an outraged husband. He was simply a killer.

True killers are not uncommon in modern society and they have not been uncommon in the past. Jack the Ripper was one of the more conspicuous, but there have been many others and in all countries. In a dismaying number of cases, the true killers are not brought to justice and it is often not even known that a series of seemingly unrelated crimes is the work of a single individual. Motive is a very important factor in the solution of crimes, and the true killers have only their desire to kill, something which is not traceable.

This does not mean that the true killer has no motive at all. He does, but it is not one known to others. It is something inner, concealed and not apparent so that the killer appears a normal and, not infrequently, attractive member of society.

Confronted with what they suspect may be such a case, the police have little choice but to search the files for similar incidents, cling to any clues which may have been recovered at the scene and wait for the next murder.

Actually, they did not have long to wait, but what arrived was not a new murder but a lucky break, and it was provided by an attractive young mother of a five-year-old daughter.

Being rather careless in some respects, the attractive young mother was not married nor was she completely certain who the father of her little daughter was. This did not mean, however, that she was any less attached to her child, and when her current companion strangled the child unconscious while she was out shopping, she went to the police. She had, of course, severed relations with her violent friend, but she wanted to be certain that he did not return.

The police, to whom such reports were routine, ran a check of the files and found that the child-strangler was Claude Buffet, a man with a criminal record covering some sixty-odd offences, mostly theft or robbery.

Buffet, a man with an eventful if not, necessarily, distinguished career, had been born in the city of Reims on 19 May 1933, but, following the end of the war, the family had moved to Cognac where he had received his first sentence at age eighteen for the theft of a motorcycle.

The sentence had been suspended on the grounds of his youth and Buffet had gone off to join the French Foreign Legion where he had spent a good deal of time in the punishment cells for theft, fighting and similar offences. Sent to Vietnam, he had promptly deserted, but having no place to go, had turned himself in to the military police.

509

Having completed his service with the French Foreign Legion, Buffet had held a succession of jobs as a servant and waiter and was currently employed as a truck driver. He was not, however, popular with his colleagues who described him as arrogant, nor with his employers who said that he insisted on driving the truck while dressed in a starched, white shirt and deerskin gloves.

Such conduct was not criminal, but there were other indications that Buffet might have been involved in some of the numerous robberies of taxi cabs which take place continuously in Paris.

A little more effort was put into tracing his activities and, to the gratification of the investigators, it was possible to show that a nine-millimetre revolver which had been used in some of the cab robberies had been in Buffet's possession and presumably still was.

Up to this point, no one had thought of connecting Buffet with the Besimensky murder, but now a comparison of a bullet recovered from the upholstery of a taxi cab was made with all nine-millimetre bullets on record with the Ballistics Department and it developed that this bullet had been fired from the same gun that killed Francoise Besimensky.

The investigators were surprised. Buffet was an old customer, but they had always considered him to be rather small fry. Now, it seemed, he was one of their most sought murderers.

Taken into custody, Buffet, with his vast experience in such matters, promptly denied everything and claimed police harassment, but the nine-millimetre revolver was recovered from his apartment and so were some pieces of Mrs Besimensky's jewellery. After a valiant but unsuccessful attempt to place the blame for the killing on his current mistress, Buffet gave up and confessed to the murder of Mrs Besimensky whose name he had only learned from the newspapers.

According to Buffet's confession, he had not had anything against the victim nor had he even particularly wanted to rob her, although he had done so on the principle of 'waste not, want not'. The reason he had killed her was simply that he had been wondering for some time what it would feel like to kill somebody.

Now he was wondering what it would be like to be killed himself and, at his trial in October of 1970, he pleaded manfully for the death sentence, saying that he thought that the plunge of the heavy blade of the guillotine might prove to be quite exhilarating, even though for only a short time.

There was some speculation among the French, a cynical race in any case, that Buffet might be trying reverse psychology on the court in the hope of escaping the death sentence, but, if so, he was mistaken for the jury very promptly found him guilty as charged and sentenced him to die on the guillotine.

President Pompidou as quickly reversed the jury's decision and commuted the death sentence to life imprisonment.

Said Claude Buffet, 'You will be sorry.'

He knew what he was talking about.

Having been deprived of his exhilarating encounter with the guillotine, Buffet was taken off to the prison of Clairvaux in the east of France. It was a high-security prison with little chance of escape and early releases were not as common at that time as they are today.

There he was placed in a cell with one of the most luckless bank robbers in history, the thirty-six-year-old Roger Bontems, who was soon to provide the world with a crushing example of the dangers of keeping bad company.

Bontems was the more unfortunate in that he had little choice in the company he kept, but he and Claude Buffet got on well in any case. Both probably made an effort. Bontems was serving a twenty-year sentence for armed robbery and Buffet was in for life. They were obviously going to be together for some time.

Assuming that they did nothing about it, but on the morning of 21 September 1971 they made the fatal decision to attempt a unilateral reduction of their sentences and at a little before eleven o'clock the sirens throughout the prison began to wail. A break-out was underway.

It was something which did not happen very often, but the

prison personnel were prepared for it. Steel doors clanged shut. Guards along the walls slipped shells into the breeches of their riot guns and the machine-gunners in the corner turrets readied their weapons. It was not immediately known how many inmates were taking place in the escape attempt.

It was known that the attempt was taking place in the prison clinic and this sector was promptly blocked off from the rest of the prison. The situation, it appeared, was in hand.

Hurrying to the scene of the action, the warden found a group of armed guards under the direction of the chief guard in position before the closed doors of the clinic and one unarmed, badly shaken cell-block guard.

According to his statement, he had brought the cellmates Buffet and Bontems to the clinic because they had complained of having sore throats. With him had been another guard, twenty-five-year-old Guy Giradot, whose sympathies for the prisoners were well known and who was, consequently, popular with them.

The guards and the two prisoners had entered the clinic where they had been met by prison nurse Nicole Compte, an attractive, cheerful thirty-three-year-old mother of two little girls. She, too, was popular with both prisoners and prison employees.

Suddenly, Buffet and Bontems had whipped home-made but dangerous knives out of their clothing and, seizing Giradot and Mrs Compte, had put the edges to their throats.

The second guard, powerless to interfere without endangering the lives of the hostages, had run out the clinic door and had sounded the alarm.

In the opinion of the warden and the chief guard the situation was dangerous but not hopeless. It was true that the men were holding two hostages and Buffet, at least, had nothing to lose as he was already serving a life sentence. On the other hand, the clinic was deep inside the prison and, if Buffet and Bontems attempted to make their way out using the hostages as a shield, there would be opportunities for a sharpshooter to pick them off, even assuming that the many gates through which they would have to pass were opened for them. In addition, the prisoners could scarcely kill the

512

hostages as they would then have nothing left with which they could bargain. It was the common situation of a stalemate where neither side could take action.

The prison authorities had an advantage, however. There was little or nothing to eat in the clinic and, eventually, Buffet and Bontems would get hungry. Unfortunately, so would Giradot and Mrs Compte, but there was nothing to be done about that.

Approaching the door of the clinic the warden identified himself, pointed out that the prisoners' situation was hopeless, and called upon them to release their hostages and come out. If they did so promptly and the hostages had suffered no harm, there would be no disciplinary action taken. The incident would be forgotten.

It was the maximum that he could offer, but it was not enough for Buffet.

'We want two machine pistols, a thousand rounds of ammunition and a fast car,' he called. 'We'll release the hostages as soon as we're clear.'

'That is beyond my authority to grant and you know it, Buffet,' said the warden. 'You'll never get out of this prison.'

'Then,' said Claude Buffet, 'we'll cut their throats.'

'You'll be guillotined,' said the warden unsteadily. He knew death in a man's voice when he heard it.

'That was my original request, I believe,' said Claude Buffet.

The warden withdrew, the sweat running down his face.

'What are we going to do?' said the chief guard in a hoarse whisper.

'Notify the next of kin,' said the warden. 'Tell them to come at once.'

The guard's face was appalled. 'You think it's that bad?'

'Not quite,' said the warden. 'Bontems is no killer. Maybe if Mrs Giradot and Mr Compte make an appeal, he'll protect them from Buffet until we can break in. I don't know what else we can do.'

There was nothing else to be done and the appeals by the next of kin of the hostages had no effect other than to nearly break the hearts of everyone present for they were answered by the hostages themselves.

'I am still alive and unharmed,' called Nicole Compte. 'Kiss my children and tell them I love them.'

'Jeannette, my darling,' cried Guy Giradot, married less than a year. 'Go away. Do not remain here. Everything will be all right.'

But everything was not going to be all right and all of the men present felt it in their hearts. Buffet was a killer and he had nothing to lose. Bontems was, apparently, completely under his influence. The hostages could expect no help from him.

Buffet had convinced the warden of his sincerity and the advantage had now turned to him. Taking the offensive, he demanded that food and drink be sent in to the clinic.

The warden, his face contorted with the agony of a decision that no man should be required to make, refused. If he once gave in to the prisoners' demands on any point it would only lead to still further demands.

'If there is no food within a half-hour, we will kill one of the hostages and throw out the body,' said Buffet, speaking as calmly and emotionlessly as if he were planning to discard a pair of old shoes.

The warden believed him, but he could not comply even if he so wished. He had, by this time, been in contact with the Ministry of Justice in Paris and no concessions were to be made to Buffet and Bontems regardless of the circumstances.

'We'll have to rush them,' said the warden. 'There's no point in waiting any longer.'

At eleven o'clock in the evening, twelve hours after the escape attempt had begun, the guards smashed in the door of the prison clinic with a fire axe and took into custody Claude Buffet and Roger Bontems, both of whom stood rigid with hands held high over their heads so as to avoid any pretext by which so many avidly yearning trigger fingers could have sent the machine-pistol slugs ripping through their bodies.

The warden ran past them through the admissions room and into the ward of the clinic itself and the men following at his heels heard him give a deep, agonized groan.

514

Lying on the floor of the ward were the bodies of Nicole Compte and Guy Giradot. Their throats were cut from ear to ear.

Once again there was a trial, and once again Claude Buffet pleaded guilty to premeditated, deliberate murder and requested his own execution on the guillotine.

Roger Bontems, who had been separated from his cell-mate, did no such thing. He had, he admitted, wanted to escape from the prison, but he had not killed anybody and he had never had any intention of killing anybody. He did not request his own execution and said that he regretted not having killed Buffet the first time he laid eyes on him.

Once again, a raging jury granted Claude Buffet's request and sentenced him to death on the guillotine. They went, in fact, even further and sentenced Roger Bontems to the same punishment, although Buffet had assured them that Bontems had had nothing to do with the murders and had not even been in the room at the time.

All eyes turned to the president of France. Would he once again save Claude Buffet from the guillotine?

It was thought certain that he would commute Roger Bontems' sentence. The man had, after all, harmed no one and had apparently not even known that Giradot and Mrs Compte were being killed.

The president maintained a majestic silence. There was to be a general election on 4 March 1973 and the opinion polls had shown roughly one hundred per cent of the electorate in favour of the death penalty.

French executions used to take place early in the morning. At ten minutes past four of 28 November 1972, a limp Roger Bontems was marched to the grim machine, laid face down-ward as prescribed by law and, an instant later, his head dropped into the basket. One of the few persons in modern times to be executed for a lesser crime than murder, he was a victim of a political system where popularity overrides principle.

It had taken three minutes to cut off Roger Bontems' head, and it took another seven to hoist the blade back up and set another basket for the head in place.

At four-twenty of that morning, Claude Buffet strode to the guillotine, his manner brisk and eager. He had, he said, a last request. Could he be permitted to lie on his back so that he could see the blade descending?

Executioners are men with strong nerves.

'I regret, monsieur,' said executioner André Obrecht, 'the law requires that you lie face downward.'

Claude Buffet had, it seemed, been quite sincere in his wish to rid society of a dangerous element in the form of himself so was he really mad?

Yes, indeed. Although the psychologists who examined him pronounced him sane and responsible for his acts, no really sane person can cut the throats of harmless persons when there is not the slightest benefit to be gained from it. As for wishing to die, this is so common that it can scarcely be described as abnormal. Most persons with the death wish take care of matters themselves, however, and do not expect the state to kill them.

Was the president of France mad for commuting the sentences of a whole string of murderers and then sending to the guillotine a man who had murdered no one?

Not at all. The president won the elections handily.

Were the people who elected him mad?

Not really. The alternative was the socialists and their first act upon arriving in power was to abolish the death sentence altogether.

DEADLY DEVIATES

To our friends
Fernand and Andrée Hoffman

CONTENTS

Introduction		519
1	Good Night, Nurse	523
2	Romeo Wore Lipstick	540
3	Devilish Active, These German Kids!	555
4	Fit to be Tied	569
5	The Murder is the Motive	583
6	The Games Girls Play	597
7	Making a New Start	611
8	A Slightly Too Merry Widow	626
9	Treasures in Trash	639
10	Interesting Neighbours	653
11	Poor Natalie	669
12	Keeping It in the Family	684
13	Never Trust Anyone Over Seventy	697
14	An All-round Man	712
15	Youth! Liberty! Progress	728
16	A Hairy Tale	744
17	Artists and Models	757
18	Always Prepared	769
19	Getting to Know the Neighbours	783
20	The Zombies are Coming!	796

INTRODUCTION

Why should I kill thee? Let me count the motives. There are not really so very many.

Very often it is sexual jealousy. Husband takes girl friend or, in these sexually liberated days, boy friend and is butchered by outraged wife.

More frequently, it is the reverse. Or it can be that boy or girl friend decides to eliminate a disturbing element in an otherwise meaningful relationship.

The various persons involved need not, of course, be formally married either before God or Government.

Murders for gain are not as common as might be thought and, when they do occur, they are more often than not unintentional. Persons with money on their minds want to be out of jail to spend it.

As a matter of fact, most homicides are unintentional. The murderer was in a frenzy of rage, fear or lust, or was befuddled by alcohol or narcotics and, upon regaining his wits, found with astonishment and dismay that he had put an end to someone. This happens rather more often with men than with women, who are more deliberate and less hysterical in such matters.

Jealousy, money, overpowering emotions and, finally, the most terrifying motive of all because it can be neither understood nor predicted: deviation. When there is a dangerous malfunction in the mind of the individual.

Legal and penal authorities in many countries today believe that such malfunctions are subject to treatment and cure and, in some cases, they undoubtedly are.

The difficulty lies in that it is not always possible to determine which cases are cured or curable and errors fatal to innocent persons – tragically, many of them children – occur with monotonous regularity.

It is rare for anyone to be held responsible for these errors. Modern political and social systems are so constructed as to make the authors of decisions as anonymous as possible. Although there is great to-do about rights and privileges, little mention is made of responsibility.

It is a curious manifestation of our times that psychologists, penologists and social workers often have the power to reverse the findings of a court and release into society individuals who prove all too often to be not as harmless as was believed.

Capital punishment has been abolished in most countries, against the will of the majority, if the polls can be believed, and prison sentences become increasingly shorter with regard to actual time served. Real life sentences are reserved for persons who have robbed banks or swindled insurance companies. Murderers and rapists, even if their victims are children, are regarded as suffering from a minor illness which sympathy and a little treatment will cure.

The results of this policy are a brisk coming and going in the psychiatric institutions, with many regular customers, and a dismaying number of victims of rape and murder who would have escaped these fates had the penalties prescribed by law been carried out without interference.

The fact is, psychology is an inexact science and, until such time as it is possible to look inside the brain of the individual and determine precisely not only what he is thinking now, but what he will be thinking six months from now, no person should have the right to release a person convicted of acts of violence until the full sentence has been served or the case has been retried. There is little point in courts handing down heavy sentences if

520

they are to be set aside six months later by persons required to take no responsibility for their acts.

This does not mean that every person sentenced to life imprisonment should die in prison. It means that, if they are released, the decision should be made by persons whose responsibility can be clearly fixed and who will suffer penalties in case of error. Such responsibility might result in the application of more common sense and less ideological dogma.

Current ideology within those circles having to do with the detention of criminals appears to be that there is no such thing as a criminal. Men rape because their mothers were cruel to them. Men murder because of the inequalities of the social and economic systems. The criminal is the victim. The victim is, if anything, an inconvenience to be ignored and forgotten as quickly as possible. Anybody is a criminal. Nobody is a criminal.

In a sense, there is something to this idea. Anyone is a criminal to the extent that anyone is capable of killing. If the human had not been capable of killing in the interests of self or kin, the species could scarcely have survived. Killing has been a part of our biological heritage for a few million years and it is not about to be changed in one or two generations by ideology or anything else. The mills of evolutionary change grind slowly and, in a few hundred thousand years, we may expect to achieve the non-violent human. Assuming that non-violence is a survival factor.

This is, however, what might be termed normal killing, and what we are here concerned with is not murder committed in self-defence or the defence of others, but murders and other acts of violence committed because of a malfunctioning of the perpetrator's mind.

These show considerable variety and not all of them are cases where there is a danger to the general public. Homosexual murders, although the participants may be not entirely within the mainstream of sexual activity, are often not criminal deviations at all, but simple acts of jealousy. On the other hand, the rape or murder of a small child always is, and no person convicted of such an offence should ever be released into society. It is often overlooked today that the primary purpose of government is not redistribution of wealth or the reinsertion of felons into society, but the maintenance of public safety and the protection of the citizen from danger, internal or external.

In the cases dealt with here, there are some which are not truly deviate, which simply means something outside the generally accepted limits of the normal or average, and a good many which are. A few defy description.

This is about what might be expected from humans in general. We are complex beings, far from perfectly constructed, and a lot of things can go wrong.

As many of us have already noticed, when things can go wrong, they usually do.

I

GOOD NIGHT, NURSE

Standing in front of the door of the two-room apartment on the sixth floor of the building of which he was superintendent, Adrian Martens placed his finger on the button of the doorbell and left it there.

He was annoyed and impatient. He had other things to do and he did not feel that pulling nurses out of bed when they overslept was part of his job.

The apartment building was only four hundred metres from the hospital at 10 Avenue Monseigneur Weyenbergh and a large number of his tenants were nurses and other hospital personnel. Sometimes they overslept, and then the hospital would call – as they had this morning – and he would have to go up and ring the doorbell. They were always apologetic and grateful, but that did not compensate for lost time.

This one seemed to be a stubborn case. There was no response to the doorbell and none to his hammering on the door. Sighing, Martens went back down to the ground-floor office to fetch the pass key. It was beginning to look as if Miss Lutgarde Meeus had flown the coop.

Even hospital nurses sometimes cleared off without notice, but no sooner had he opened the door than he saw that this was something different. The apartment was a shambles, furniture knocked over, rugs kicked into a heap and, draped over the sofa, lay a pair of torn stockings, some ripped underwear and white strips of what looked like a nurse's uniform.

'Miss Meeus?' said Martens tentatively, his throat suddenly dry.

He took two steps into the living room and his gaze passed through the open bathroom door to fix on a fantastic sight.

What looked like the bottom half of a naked woman was leaning against the side of the tub. Her legs, slightly flexed and parted appeared to be broken for they were bent in the wrong direction.

'Miss Meeus!' yelled Martens, losing control of his voice and his nerves simultaneously. He was not a particularly nervous man, but the sight was shocking and totally unexpected.

Although he later had no recollection of it, he was crossing the room as he cried out and, arriving at the bathroom door, saw that what he had taken for a half woman was a whole one draped over the side of the bathtub, her head and shoulders submerged beneath the water with which it was filled. Horribly, the water was a deep red.

Under the shock of the discovery, Martens forgot about the indications of violence in the living room and jumped to the conclusion that Lutgarde Meeus had committed suicide.

Running out of the apartment, he tumbled down the stairs, too excited to think of the elevator, and telephoned the hospital. Their nurse, he gasped, had committed suicide in his building.

As he was extremely excited and out of breath from his run down the stairs, he was not very coherent. The switchboard operator at the hospital did, however, get the idea that something terrible had happened and, within minutes, nurses, interns and other hospital employees were sprinting for the apartment building. Pretty, twenty-eight-year-old Lutgarde had been popular with her colleagues.

'Had been' was the correct tense. It did not take medically trained persons to determine that Lutgarde was dead and had been dead for some time.

Even so, the duty doctor in the emergency room was summoned, but all that he could do was to confirm what they all knew; Lutgarde had been murdered.

In the meantime, Martens had recovered his wits sufficiently to call the police and a patrol car soon arrived.

The officers did nothing, however, other than to look at the corpse, chase the hospital personnel out of the apartment and contact headquarters over the car's radio telephone. The case was clearly homicide and the rest was up to the department of criminal investigations.

What next arrived was, therefore, the duty homicide squad of the Louvain police.

Louvain has a population of less than ninety thousand, but it is only ten miles to the east of Brussels and there is enough contagion from the Belgian capital to make more than one homicide squad necessary.

The one on duty this Wednesday morning of 29 September 1982 consisted of Inspector Karl Groot, a large, smooth-skinned, pink-and-white sort of man with somewhat scanty light brown hair; Sergeant of Detectives Jean Lutgens, who was tall, dark, sallow and rather lugubrious-looking; and a round-faced, cheerful little man who habitually wore his horn-rimmed glasses pushed up on his forehead because he could not see anything through them. This was Dr Bernard Rykers, an expert in forensic medicine and a very good one.

The corpse being in an excellent posture for carrying out a gynaecological examination, the doctor began with that, determining that Miss Meeus had been raped despite desperate resistance. There were lesions of the interior walls of the vagina, hair cuts on the external genitals and the typical black and blue bruise marks on the insides of the thighs caused by the victim clamping her legs over her assailant's hip bones in a vain effort to prevent penetration. The rapist had orgasmed and there was semen in the vaginal passage.

The time of death he estimated as at least twelve hours earlier, making it prior to ten o'clock of the preceding evening. A more precise time would be established during the course of the autopsy.

As for the cause of death, he was unable to say anything until the body had been removed from the bathtub. There was too much blood in the water for any injuries to the head to be seen.

The body could not, as yet, be removed from the bathtub, for the inspector wanted it photographed as it had been found and the laboratory technicians, now on their way, would prefer to carry out their search for potential clues before anything at the scene had been disturbed.

The precaution was routine, but, in this case, unnecessary. Despite an intensive examination of the apartment, nothing was found which could be positively identified as having any connection to either the murder or the murderer. Insofar as could be determined, he had been let into the apartment by Miss Meeus herself. There were no signs of a forced entry.

Nor were there any signs of entertainment: no dirty glasses or cups, no remains of food, no cigarette butts, and the bed in the bedroom had not been slept in.

The most probable course of events was that someone had rung the doorbell at around ten o'clock the preceding evening. Miss Meeus had opened the door and immediately been attacked and overpowered by the intruder before she had time to call for help.

He had presumably left immediately following the murder. There were no indications that he had been in any part of the apartment other than the living room and the bathroom. He had not looked for money or valuables, and Miss Meeus' handbag, lying in full view in the living room, had not been touched.

The inspector's conclusion was that he was dealing

with a compulsive sex criminal, a deviate whose only motive was rape and, possibly, murder. He did not think Lutgarde Meeus had been killed to prevent her from identifying her attacker. It was probable she had never laid eyes on him before in her life.

Not so he. The inspector knew a good deal about such sex deviates and he knew they often spent days or even weeks in stalking their proposed victims, following them discreetly in the streets, waiting outside their homes or places of work and searching patiently for a time and place suitable for the kill.

The autopsy showed this time to be earlier than Dr Rykers had thought. His estimate now was between six and six-thirty in the evening of 28 September.

According to other sources of information, this would have been very shortly after Lutgarde had returned home. She had gone off duty at the hospital at five and then done a little shopping for groceries in the neighbourhood stores where she was known. The last reported sighting was at approximately ten minutes to six. She had been wearing her nurse's uniform. This detail was noted, but its significance was not then realized.

It was this uniform which lay in shreds in the living rooms. It had been torn from her body with immense force – a point which Dr Rykers emphasized in the autopsy report.

The murderer, he wrote, was enormously strong and he had huge hands. They had literally crushed Lutgarde Meeus' throat, fracturing the hyoid bone and rupturing the larynx. It was blood from her throat and lungs which had coloured the water in the tub, but there had not been as much of it as appeared.

Otherwise, there were no injuries to the body other than bruises which had been incurred in Lutgarde's struggle with the rapist. She had apparently not managed to mark him for there were no traces of skin or hair beneath her fingernails.

Dr Rykers thought the struggle had been of short

duration and the strangulation was, perhaps, necessary for the deviate to achieve his sexual climax so that rape and murder had taken place almost simultaneously. He stated flatly in his report that the murderer was sexually abnormal and that it was unlikely that this was his first offence. There was, in all probability, a file on him in the police records, but, as no clues to his identity had been found at the scene, there was no way of knowing which one it was. Unfortunately, the killer had no marked idiosyncrasy, as did some sex criminals, which could serve as a sort of trademark.

Actually, the killer did; but at the time no one realized it.

Inspector Groot therefore proceeded with the customary routine of the investigation, checking out the backgrounds and, in so far as possible, the whereabouts on the evening of 28 September of every male with whom Lutgarde had had contact – and found nothing.

Granted that the murder was almost certainly a deviate sex crime, the question remained of why Lutgarde had let a stranger into her apartment. There was, of course, always the possibility of a simulated sex crime, although it was rare for one to be so cleverly imitated as this.

Postmen, dustmen, power, gas and telephone company personnel were traced, not only the bona fide service men, but also possible impostors. People who would never have dreamed of letting a stranger into their apartments freely opened their doors to men wearing the uniform of one of the public services.

Again, the results were negative. No public service men of any kind had been seen in the building on the day in question and the building superintendent, Martens, swore that none could have entered without his knowledge.

Just after taking Martens' statement concerning the service men, when Sergeant Lutgens was passing out through the main entrance hall in a not too cheerful mood – he had put in a great deal of effort on the case and, so far, had got nowhere – he saw ambling towards him a tall, strongly built man with a clean-cut, boyish face and a bashful expression. The young man was dressed in the white overalls and jacket of a house painter and was carrying a bucket of paint and some brushes.

The sergeant stopped him. 'Who,' he said, 'are you?'

The young man, who turned out to be not as young as he looked, said that his name was Michel Bellen and added, rather unnecessarily, that he was a house painter employed by a firm contracted to repaint some of the apartments in the building.

The sergeant looked thoughtfully at Bellen's hands, which were the size of banjos, identified himself as a police officer and asked to see his papers.

Bellen produced them. He was, it seemed, thirty-six years old, unmarried and had been born in Antwerp, thirty-five miles to the north. There was a restriction in the personal identity card to the effect that it was not valid for residence in Antwerp.

'Why?' demanded the sergeant, the hair on his neck beginning to rise. He knew of only one reason in Belgium why a man could not legally reside in the city of his birth.

'I was given the death sentence,' said Bellen in a low, embarrassed voice, looking at the floor.

That was the reason.

'For what?' said the sergeant, reaching for his hand-cuffs and his service pistol.

'Killing nurses,' said Michel Bellen shyly.

And that was the end of the case. Michel Bellen was none other than the notorious Killer of the Left Bank who, eighteen years earlier, had frightened the women of Antwerp nearly out of their wits, had raped three and killed two of them, had been described by the medical experts at his trial as a dangerous psychopath who could never be allowed to mingle with the public and had been condemned to death, a verdict which received the approval of nearly everyone, not excluding the defendant.

The whole process – murders, rapes, trial and sentencing – took place during less than thirteen months. It began four days before Sunday, 9 August 1964, when two elderly ladies taking a stroll on the Left Bank of the Schelde, the river which runs through Antwerp, a city of some 200,000 inhabitants, discovered the body of twenty-eight-year-old Lucienne Verhoeven, a professional nurse, lying among the bushes.

The young woman was a terrible sight for she had been strangled with such force that her eyes started from her head, her tongue protruded black and swollen from her mouth and the skin of her face turned slate blue.

She was totally naked, even her shoes having been removed, and the torn shreds of her nurse's uniform lay around her.

Even to two elderly ladies unaccustomed to such sights, it was obvious that she had been raped, for she lay as her murderer had risen from her, on her back, with sprawled thighs, her arms bent at the elbows in the last dying effort to tear the strangling hands from her throat.

It being August, there were many insects and, as the body had been lying there since the preceding Wednesday, it had been visited by birds and small animals.

One of the ladies immediately and understandably fainted and was nearly murdered herself by her companion who, terrified at being left alone with a corpse and an unconscious woman, shook her so violently that she later required medical attention.

The second lady being thus roused, both made off as fast as possible to report their discovery to the police. This took a little time as most of Antwerp is on the Right Bank and the Left Bank has few buildings and, consequently, few telephones.

Even when the police had finally been notified and

hurried to the scene, there was not a great deal that they could do other than identify the victim.

Miss Verhoeven had been reported missing on Thursday morning by her colleagues at the hospital, but there was no certainty of the exact time of her disappearance. Nor was there now any explanation as to what she had been doing on the Left Bank. The hospital was, of course, on the Right Bank, as was the apartment building in which she lived.

The case was assigned to a team of investigators headed by Inspector Jan Dykstra, a man who curiously resembled Inspector Groot in Louvain, who would be investigating a similar case eighteen years later. He was, of course, considerably older. When Lucienne Verhoeven was murdered, Inspector Groot was still a detective first class and only beginning his career. By the time of the Lutgarde Meeus murder, Inspector Dykstra was already retired.

Assisting Inspector Dykstra was a sergeant of detectives named Piet Haan, a very handsome young man who would later leave the police to make a successful career as an actor in television plays in which he almost invariably played the role of a clever crook.

These two, and a rather sinister-looking medical expert with a sharp, pointed moustache and a small, sharp beard, who was called Leopold Bulcke and was actually a very mild sort of person and a devoted family man, formed the nucleus of the detachment investigating what soon came to be known as the Murders of the Left Bank.

Having failed to discover anything of significance at the scene – other than the fact that it really was the scene of the murder and not merely the place where the killer had disposed of the body – the corpse was transferred to the police morgue, where Dr Bulcke carried out an autopsy of it.

In his report, the doctor stated that Miss Verhoeven

531

had been strangled by someone with enormously strong hands who had raped her simultaneously or nearly so.

The sexual frenzy of the rapist had been such that he had shown no more consideration for his own genitals than for those of his victim. He had cut himself rather badly for there was a quantity of blood of a different group than Miss Verhoeven's in her pubic hair. There was reason to believe that he had achieved orgasm, although any semen present had, by this time, broken down chemically.

There were no indications of resistance by Miss Verhoeven, who had, perhaps, hoped to save her life through cooperation.

She had lost it on the evening of 5 August some time after six in the evening and earlier than midnight. Due to the length of time before discovery of the body, he was unable to be more precise.

The doctor was of the opinion that the murderer was a compulsive sex psychopath who had no control whatsoever over his own actions and who, if he had not already committed such crimes in the past, could be counted upon to commit more of them in the future.

Although Inspector Dykstra did not care at all for this prophecy, it turned out to be accurate and, on 30 August, there was a repetition of the Verhoeven murder, as similar as the murderer could make it.

The similarity had a reason. The Killer of the Left Bank could obtain sexual satisfaction only through a specific combination of circumstances, those present at the rape and murder of Lucienne Verhoeven.

It was necessary that the victim be female, attractive, in her middle or late twenties and, above all, that she be wearing a nurse's uniform or something that looked like it.

Later, there would be reason to believe that the victim also had to possess a negative attribute. She could not be a mother.

Had the women of Antwerp known what was in

532

Michel Bellen's mind, they could have assured their safety simply by eschewing nurses' uniforms or laying claim, whether truthfully or otherwise, to motherhood.

But, of course, no one knew that Michel Bellen was the Killer of the Left Bank and, even when it was known, the psychologists were never in complete agreement as to what went on inside that physically attractive but dangerously aberrant head.

They did agree on one thing. Bellen was a menace to certain women and there was no reason to believe he would ever be otherwise. If he were not removed permanently from society, he would kill again.

Not, of course, that he wanted to. Michel Bellen was a gentle, shy and unassuming youth who would grow into a gentle, shy and unassuming man. He was kind, thoughtful and had a pleasant personality. There was not a thing wrong with him except that the greatest ecstasy of which he was capable was the rape and murder of a woman wearing a nurse's uniform.

It was the second murder, on the afternoon or evening of Sunday, 30 August, which gained Bellen his nickname of the Killer of the Left Bank and Inspector Dykstra a reputation within the department for perspicacity.

Twenty-seven-year-old Christiane Herreman was approximately the age of Lucienne Verhoeven. She was pretty. And she was a nurse. When she failed to report for work on Monday morning, some of her colleagues went to her apartment and, finding no trace of her there, called the police. They were still nervous over what had happened to Lucienne Verhoeven earlier that same month and they were aware that the murderer had not been identified.

The police were equally nervous and Inspector Dykstra ran a quick check of all the places that Miss Herreman might be and then ordered a search of the Left Bank. There were so many other parallels to the

Verhoeven case that he thought there might be another in the scene of the crime.

His reasoning was faultless. Christiane Herreman's body was discovered less than a hundred yards from the place where Lucienne Verhoeven had been murdered, and the only real differences in the two cases were the dates and the identities of the victims.

Miss Herreman had been stripped naked, strangled with terrifying force and brutally raped. Not as much time had elapsed before the discovery of the body as in the Verhoeven murder, so Dr Bulcke was able to establish the time of death as approximately six-thirty in the evening of 30 August within half an hour in either direction.

The information was of little use to the investigation, but the doctor was unable to provide anything else and the technicians from the police laboratory who went over the scene literally with magnifying glasses were no more successful. Bellen had completed another perfect murder under the noses of the police.

And, in fact, there is no telling how many such perfect crimes Michel Bellen might have committed had he stuck strictly to rape and murder. In these fields he was practically undetectable, aside from sheer bad luck such as someone stumbling on him while he was actually engaged in the crime.

That was, however, unlikely for Bellen did not take very long with his work. Rape and murder took place nearly simultaneously and he was always in such a state of excitement that penetration was followed by orgasm within seconds.

Neither did the murder last very long. The victim scarcely had time to realize that there was something wrong with this attractive but shy young man when their clothing was ripped away and the huge, deadly hands locked round their throats. The pressure was such that not only air to the lungs but the blood supply to the

534

brain was cut off instantly and unconsciousness followed within less than a minute.

It was later estimated that the attack took less than five minutes and, if Bellen were not disturbed during this short time, there was little hope of apprehending him. He never had any prior contact with his victims, other than having seen them wearing their nurse's uniforms, and he never left any traces of his identity at the scene, other than his semen and a little blood. His blood group was a valueless indication: it was the same as roughly a quarter of the population of Belgium.

The Killer of the Left Bank might have continued his career for some time, had he not been so discriminating in his choice of victims, but he could not, of course, help this any more than he could help raping and murdering nurses.

As a result, on 16 August, precisely two weeks before the murder of Christiane Herreman, he had already sown the seeds of his own destruction.

The direct cause of Michel Bellen's downfall was an attractive young woman named Josette Mauberge. At twenty-nine, she was one year older than the oldest of his other victims, but she looked, if anything, younger.

Although Bellen had no way of knowing this, she was not acceptable prey at all as she was not a nurse, but only a nurse's helper at the hospital. Deceptively, she wore a uniform which might easily be confused with that of a nurse.

Finally and, for Bellen, unfortunately, Josette Mauberge was not only a mother, but a fourfold one to boot. She did not, however, have a husband as she was divorced.

Not celibate and far less discriminating than Bellen, she was not at all reluctant to accept a ride on his motor scooter from this handsome, engagingly bashful young stranger. Nor did she raise any objection when, instead

535

of taking her home, he crossed the bridge spanning the Schelde to the secluded Left Bank.

As she later admitted, it had not been the most prudent thing in the world to do. Like everyone else in Antwerp, she had read of the murder of Lucienne Verhoeven, but it did not occur to her to associate it with this handsome stranger.

Arriving at a suitably private spot, the driver parked the scooter and seized Josette Mauberge in a grip of iron.

Josette took this for passion and, indeed, it was, but of a different kind than she could possibly imagine.

Holding her helpless with one hand, he tore away her clothing with the ease of a man plucking a chicken. He was so enormously strong that Josette, a healthy and far from feeble young woman, could do nothing other than protest that he was ruining her things and that, if he would wait a minute, she would take them off herself.

The man paid no attention to her, seemed not even to hear her. To Josette's alarm, he appeared to be having a sort of fit, his eyes glaring wildly and his mouth slightly open and drooling saliva. He did not look like the attractive stranger from whom she had accepted a ride less than twenty minutes earlier.

Flinging his naked victim violently to the ground, the Killer of the Left Bank parted her legs with his hands and entered her to the hilt, orgasming almost instantly.

This was not Josette's idea of romantic love-making, but she was no longer concerned with that. The penetration without preparation had been painful and she had now recalled Lucienne Verhoeven and what had happened to her on the Left Bank of the Schelde.

She did not have much time to think about it for, even as he penetrated her, the killer had laid his hands about her throat.

In that terrible instant when Josette Mauberge realized that her death was only seconds away, her maternal instincts overrode her own fear.

'I have four children!' she screamed.

The greatest magician in the world could not have pronounced a more efficacious formula. Bellen removed his hands from her throat, got to his feet, zipped up his trousers, shot her an embarrassed look, climbed on to his motor scooter and roared away without a word.

Mrs Mauberge lay on the ground trying to decide whether she was going to become hysterical or not. Her throat hurt a little and her private parts hurt a great deal, but she was basically unharmed.

After a time, she decided that she was not going to have hysterics, got up, managed to assemble enough of her clothing for decency and set off home at a brisk pace. It had occurred to her that the man might change his mind and come back. She had no way of knowing that her motherhood was more protection than a squad of armed bodyguards.

Mrs Mauberge did not go to the police to report her experience. If she had, she might have saved the life of Christiane Herreman, although not that of Lutgarde Meeus.

She did not go to the police for the same reason that many victims of rape do not. The ordeal of testifying before a court and a hostile defence counsel can seem as bad as the rape.

Moreover, her position was not strong. She would have to admit that she had let a total stranger drive her over to the bushes of the Left Bank and she could scarcely claim that it had been to pick wild flowers. Any self-respecting defence counsel would have little trouble convincing a court that she had practically invited rape, if not insisted upon it.

Josette did, however, have an uneasy feeling about the matter and she did realize that the man on the scooter might very well have been the murderer of Lucienne Verhoeven.

She turned the events over in her mind a good deal and, when Christiane Herreman's death was announced in the newspapers, she not only went to the police, but

537

she had a substantial amount of useful information to give them, including a remarkably exact description of the young man and his motor scooter.

The motor scooter proved to be more easily spotted than the man. Inspector Dykstra had posted plain-clothes officers at all of the city's hospitals on the theory that the Killer of the Left Bank was apparently obsessed with medical personnel, and Bellen was soon taken into custody.

Fortunately for the investigators and for the women of Antwerp, he proved to be cooperative. Although the police still had no evidence against him, other than a possible identification by Josette Mauberge which would have sustained nothing more than a charge of rape and probably not that, Bellen promptly confessed.

Yes, he said, he had killed two nurses and raped another. He did not know why. There was something about a nurse's uniform which excited him terribly so that he did not know what he was doing. He was very sorry. He hoped the authorities would do something to stop him.

The authorities would do something, but not enough. Bellen was examined by the country's leading psychologists and psychiatrists, who were unable to agree on anything other than that Bellen was dangerous.

The only thing unusual in his background was that he had suffered a head injury in his early teens and his personality had apparently changed following this. He had run away from home three or four times and had been caught stealing on several occasions. His parents, unable to control him, had asked that he be made a ward of the juvenile court and he had been under the court's control up to the age of eighteen. He had murdered Lucienne Verhoeven less than a year later.

It was not only the psychologists who maintained that Bellen was dangerous and that he would kill again, given the opportunity. So too did Bellen, and the court handed down the death penalty.

Belgium, however, was in the peculiar position of having the death penalty under law, but never carrying it out.

Bellen was sentenced to death on 24 September 1965. It was commuted to life imprisonment on 1 December of that same year.

Eighteen years later, on 3 May 1982, the penal authorities decided that Bellen had been in jail long enough and released him. He was carefully reinserted into society, found an apartment and a job, and supported financially until such time as he could support himself. Neither his employers nor anyone else in Louvain knew of his criminal record, not even the police.

On 27 September 1982, he saw Lutgarde Meeus in the apartment house where he was painting. She was wearing her uniform.

On 28 September, he killed her.

On 25 November 1983, Michel Bellen was sentenced to death for raping and murdering his third nurse.

Belgium still does not carry out the death penalty.

On 12 May 1984, Bellen's sentence was commuted to life imprisonment.

And?

2

ROMEO WORE LIPSTICK

The minute hand of the big clock on the charge room wall moved forward a click to midnight and, in that instant, the telephone on the duty sergeant's desk rang.

The sergeant, two hours into the night shift, put down his magazine and lifted the receiver. The caller was the dispatcher in the communications centre on the floor above.

'Reported shooting at the corner of Theresien and Luisen Strassen,' said the dispatcher. 'I've got two cars on the way. Give you a direct report as soon as they're at the scene.'

'Understood,' said the desk sergeant and broke the connection so that he could dial the number of the department of criminal investigations. If this was not a practical joke or an alcohol or drug-induced fantasy, somebody would have to go out.

Practical jokes and fantasies were both common enough on the night-shift in the Schwabing sub-station of the Munich police. The district had once been an artists' quarter and the people who now lived there thought that they were artists, which meant that they were high on something most of the time. And, consequently, they not infrequently assaulted or murdered each other.

The sergeant informed the young detective second class who answered the telephone that there was a shooting report awaiting confirmation and got out a first information report form, which he filled in with the date,

8 July 1976. Wednesday, the seventh, was obviously when the crime had taken place, if it had at all, but his first information had been received on the eighth.

Six minutes later, the telephone rang again. It was an officer from one of the patrol cars at the scene, reporting directly over the communications desk.

'Taxi,' said the officer laconically. 'Two women in front seat either unconscious or dead. Some blood. Looks like gunshot wounds. Instructions?'

'Remain at scene until arrival of CID,' said the sergeant automatically. 'Hold any persons present. Prevent unauthorized persons from approaching vehicle.'

He broke the connection and dialled the number of the criminal investigations department. 'Confirmed shooting at Theresien and Luisen,' he said. 'It's all yours. You can pick up the FIR on your way out.'

His part in the matter was now complete. The detectives assigned to the case would pick up the first information report and fill in the details. The dispatcher would already have sent an ambulance to the scene. A routine case for the night desk. The sergeant put his heels back up on the bottom drawer of the desk and resumed his reading of a detective magazine.

In the department of criminal investigations, Inspector Walter Schreiber, duty officer in charge of the shift, was preparing to answer the call personally under the sulky gaze of his assistant, Sergeant of Detectives Max Kaufmann.

The inspector looked smug. He was a man of faintly noble appearance, with a prominent chin and long, blond hair which looked as if it was artificially waved but was not.

The sergeant was sulky because it was not he who was going out. Like many plain-clothes officers, he did not like being cooped up in an office, particularly on a warm summer night, and he felt that the outside investigation work should be left to people who were not drawing an

541

inspector's salary to sit in offices and take charge of things.

However, the inspector was in charge, so if he wanted to go out, go out he did. He soon disappeared, leaving his grumbling subordinate in charge in his absence.

Fortunately for the sergeant's opinion of his chief and police organization in general, his confinement to the office did not last long. In something less than twenty minutes, the inspector called over the radio-telephone.

'I need you out here, Max,' he said. 'Put Willi in charge and come on out, but before you do, call headquarters and tell them we've got a double homicide and we need a car taken in to the garage for examination. They'll have to bring in some of the lab people to go over it. It's not clear what happened, but I think it was a bungled hold-up. I can't find the money bag, and this is a cab.'

'Did a call go out?' said the sergeant anxiously.

The question was one to make any police officer anxious. Munich, the biggest city in the south of West Germany, has a population of over a million and a half, which means that there is a good deal of violent crime and not a little of it involves taxi drivers or prostitutes.

The reason is the same in both cases. Both professions require picking up total strangers and taking them to often secluded places where money changes hands.

In the case of the taxi driver, at least, this means that he has to carry a substantial amount of change on him. Here he is at a disadvantage to the prostitute, who normally carries no change and immediately hands her earnings over to her pimp or seals them into a self-addressed envelope to be dropped into the nearest post box.

Prostitution is, therefore, slightly less risky than driving a cab, but neither is safe when some junkie, desperate for a fix, ponders the possibility of obtaining one through dynamic use of a switchblade.

Prostitutes respond to this threat by keeping pimps

542

handy, or large attack dogs, which are cheaper. Taxi drivers seek to defend themselves with a length of lead pipe under the seat or a pair of brass knuckles. A few carry guns, but not legally. In modern civilized countries such as West Germany, the government does not permit its citizens to protect themselves, whether it is capable of protecting them or not.

However, in compensation for the greater risk, taxi drivers have opportunity for dissuasion not available to prostitutes. Their cabs are equipped with radio-telephones and, in an emergency, the dispatchers at the various company offices can tie the entire fleet into a single network.

An attack on a taxi driver is regarded as an emergency and, as the circuit is almost always open, the dispatcher hears what is going on even if the driver has no time or breath to call for help.

What happens then is frightening. All over the city, cabs brake, swing around and go roaring in toward the location of the distress call. The effect is a little like a horror film of the future with robot cars gone mad and moving in for the kill.

And, as a matter of fact, that is precisely what the drivers have in mind. If they catch the culprit, they not infrequently beat him to death, particularly if the attack has ended fatally for the driver.

It was this possibility which alarmed Sergeant Kaufmann, not because he was personally averse to the lynching of murdering hopheads, but because such an operation invariably resulted in a messy case for the police, involving a great deal of work which could end with what he regarded as an unjust solution.

Dozens of uncooperative cab drivers would have to be interrogated, endless deliberately deceptive stories would have to be checked and, if the case was finally solved, some honest, hard-working cabbie would go to jail for having executed a killer who should long since have been executed by the government.

To the sergeant's relief, the inspector replied that apparently no call had gone out as there were no taxis at the scene other than the one in which the shooting had taken place.

The driver of this cab had been one of the two women shot, for it was her picture on the licence posted on the back of the seat.

It was a good picture of a good subject. Women taxi drivers were not unusual by any means, but it was not often that they were as attractive as this one. According to Inspector Schreiber, who had arrived just as the bodies were being loaded into the ambulance, she was maddeningly beautiful with long, silky blonde hair and a figure to bring tears to a man's eyes. She had been, he added, practically naked.

The sergeant did not believe this. He was a rather skinny, sallow young man with protruding front teeth and his hair falling over his eyes and he was very serious about nearly everything.

The inspector, who had been in criminal investigations too long to be serious about anything and risk his sanity, was inclined to torture him in various mild ways as he thought it good for the development of his character. This caused the sergeant to regard with suspicion such stories of having just missed seeing an improbably beautiful half-naked victim.

Who, it seemed, was perhaps not a victim at all or, at least, not a homicide victim. Despite the inspector's report concerning a double homicide, neither woman had been dead at the time that she had been loaded into the ambulance. It was merely that, to the inspector's experienced eye, their chances of survival did not appear good.

However the story about the woman driver being nearly naked was true. The other woman had been not far from it, either. What this meant, the inspector had no idea.

He had no idea what had happened at all, other than

that both driver and passenger had been in the front seat, the motor had been turned off at the time of the shooting and the money bag was missing.

According to the licence, the driver's name was Eleonore Bele and she was twenty-five years old. Her address was given as 28 Bahnhof Strasse in Unterfoehring, which was a suburb on the north-east edge of the city and not a particularly good one.

There was no indication as to the identity of the passenger, who had either not been carrying a bag or had had it stolen by the murderer.

After a time, a car appeared at the scene and two technicians from the police laboratory got out and went over the area around the cab. It was all clean-swept pavement and they soon came over to report that they had found nothing of any significance.

They then got back into the car and went home. It would be other technicians who would check out the cab once it had been towed to the police garage.

This operation was not something that required supervision by the inspector or the sergeant and they returned resignedly to the office. The sergeant telephoned the emergency hospital and was told that one of the women had been dead on arrival and the other was in critical condition. Both had been shot.

The sergeant then opened a homicide file, leaving the name blank as he had forgotten to ask the hospital which woman was dead. He did not know whether it was Eleonore Bele or the passenger.

The rest of the shift was quiet, with only a few drunken fights resulting in assault charges and one nonfatal knifing in a homosexual bar.

Although the inspector and the sergeant had only come off duty at six in the morning, they were back in the office by noon. They had been on duty at the time the case originated and the policy was to let a homicide team remain with a case they had started.

The first part of the investigation was to find out

whether it was single or double homicide. If the second
victim had not died, she might be able to solve the case
for them with little or no effort and, at the worst, she
could probably provide useful descriptions of the
murderer and the circumstances.

To the sergeant's relief, it appeared that the woman
who had been dead on arrival at the hospital was not
the lovely taxi driver, but the older and less attractive
passenger. Her body had already been transferred to the
police morgue and was now being autopsied. There was
still no clue as to her identity.

Eleonore Bele was alive, but unconscious and still
critical. She had been shot twice, once through each
breast. The doctors had removed one bullet. The other
was still in her, considered too dangerous to remove at
the moment.

The sergeant, still on the telephone, conveyed this
information to his chief.

'Where was the other woman shot?' asked the
inspector.

The sergeant inquired. 'In the crotch,' he said. 'Three
bullets.'

'That suggest anything to you?' said the inspector.

'Sex orientated?' said the sergeant. 'Breasts of one.
Genitals of the other.'

'Right,' said the inspector. 'Get hold of the records
section and see if they can locate a file on a woman
named Alster or Albers. There was a case a year or so
ago. Girl who specialized in holding up taxi drivers. Not
on drugs or anything. She just liked money. Could be
under juveniles. She was very young, as I recall.'

'Why her particularly?' said the sergeant, reaching for
the telephone again.

'She was a lesbian,' said the inspector.

It turned out that his memory was half good. The
name of the girl in question was not Alster or Albers,
but Altmeyer, Doris Altmeyer, and the case had not
taken place a year or so ago, but nearly four years earlier,

when Doris had been barely eighteen. It had, therefore, definitely been a case for the juvenile court.

In other respects, the inspector was more accurate. Doris was a self-acknowledged lesbian who wanted desperately to be a man and who had, more or less, convinced herself that she was one. She was also a specialist in knocking over taxi drivers and had been convicted on no less than five counts of armed robbery.

At the time, Doris had been using a Belgian Fabrique Nationale 7.65 mm automatic pistol and, according to the ballistics experts who examined the bullets extracted from Eleonore Bele and the corpse of the unidentified passenger, they were of the same calibre, although what gun they had been fired from could not be said. It was not Doris's original Belgian FN, for that had been confiscated by the police and was still in the police museum.

If the whereabouts of Doris Altmeyer's gun was known, Doris's were not. Being a juvenile, she had got off with a very light sentence and, as was usually the case, had served only a small fraction of that. She had been released at the beginning of 1975 and was supposed to have reported regularly to a parole officer, but he had not laid eyes on her so much as once.

If the police had thought about it at all, they would have assumed that Doris had gone back to holding up cabs. Most of the convicted felons released early for reintegration into society returned immediately to their original occupations.

The police had not thought about it, however. Nor had anyone else. In a city of a million and a half, Doris was merely a figure in a statistic and not a very important one either. After all, she had never actually murdered anyone.

But it was possible that she had now, and the inspector put the sergeant to hunting for her.

He himself took charge of a smaller detail engaged in trying to identify the passenger who had been killed.

All that Dr Wilfried Tesch, the police medical expert who had carried out the autopsy, was able to tell the inspector concerning the victim was that she had been healthy, in her forties, very well groomed, and possibly homosexual as her pubic area was shaved and she wore a small gold ring in her left labia major. She had never born a child or had a major operation. The immediate cause of death had been a severed femoral artery resulting in massive haemorrhaging. There was some dental work, and charts were provided for submission to dentists throughout the city.

The operation was begun, but proved unnecessary as the inspector's detectives, canvassing the homosexual bars and cafés with pictures of the dead woman, came up with a positive identification first.

As Dr Tesch had surmised, forty-four-year-old Inge Labe had been a lesbian and, as it turned out, a very well known one in some circles. She could not have been identified by her dental work, however, for she was not German. She was Austrian and came from Vienna, where the dental work had been done.

Being a foreign resident, Inge Labe was registered with the Foreign Registrations Office, where the records showed that she was a successful designer of women's clothing and that she lived in Schwabing at 144 Elisabeth Strasse.

A team from the police laboratory went through her apartment and found interesting although not particularly useful evidence of Miss Labe's preferred sexual activities. They also found so many fingerprints left by Eleonore Bele, still in serious condition at the hospital but now expected to recover, that they concluded she had been a very frequent visitor, if not a resident.

For Inspector Schreiber this changed the character of the case completely. He no longer considered money to have been the motive for the shootings and he did not think that Inge Labe had been a passenger in the cab at the time.

Rather than murder for robbery, the case was simply a love triangle, perhaps one in which the sexes of the participants were somewhat confused, but basically an emotional crime, the motive for which had been sexual jealousy.

This change in theory made Doris Altmeyer a less promising suspect, but it did not eliminate her altogether. Inge Labe had been killed and Eleonore Bele had been wounded, undoubtedly by a lesbian lover of one or the other. Doris was a lesbian and an attractive one. She could as well have been the jealous lover as anyone else.

She was not, however. This was learned with certainty only a short time later. Sergeant Kaufmann, who had been scouring Munich for her with no success, suddenly got the idea that Doris might have gone elsewhere to get in trouble and sent out a request for information over the police telex.

There was a reply within an hour. Doris had gone to Berlin, a mecca for German homosexuals, and resumed the only profession she knew, that of robbing taxi drivers, and was once again in jail. Questioned later about her views on the Labe murder, she expressed the opinion that the police were not right in the head. She would never, she said firmly, have held up a woman taxi driver. All her targets were men.

According to the police records, Doris was telling the truth concerning her professional practices and, probably, also concerning her opinion of the police. But if the police were not right in the head, it did not say much for her intelligence that they had now managed to send her to jail twice!

However, the inspector was not interested. A suspect had been eliminated and the investigation could move on to the next.

The next suspect was thirty-four-year-old Linda Schnitzler, who was small, dark, elfin, pretty and tough. Like

Eleonore Bele, she was a taxi driver and, like both victims, she was a lesbian.

Eleonore Bele, who had by now recovered sufficiently to be interrogated, said that she did not know her, but police contacts in local homosexual circles said that she not only knew her but had been living with her for years.

The sources also said that Linda had been insanely jealous of Eleonore and had beaten her up on occasion for real or fancied flirtations with other women. This was hard to imagine as Eleonore was half a head taller and twenty pounds heavier than her slight but wiry lover, but it was apparently true.

The police were soon to learn how firm a character Linda Schnitzler was. Having taken her into custody and charged her formally with the shootings, they attempted to interrogate a confession out of her and ran head-on into a small, grim stone wall.

Linda would not admit that she had ever heard the names of Eleonore Bele and Inge Labe. She would not admit that she was a lesbian. She would not even admit that she was a taxi driver, although the licence with her picture on it was in her cab. She would not admit to anything.

This was awkward for the police, but not insurmountable. A search of the apartment at 28 Bahnhof Strasse in Unterfoehring, where both Eleonore and Linda were registered, provided ample evidence that the couple had been living there for years. Both women's clothing was still present, as were all of their personal possessions and papers.

There was, therefore, proof positive that Linda and Eleonore had been living together for some considerable time as woman and wife, and there was evidence that Linda had been jealous. There was, however, no concrete evidence to connect her to the shootings.

No gun had been found in the apartment or in Linda's cab and the police were unable to locate any gunsmith's where a woman answering to Linda's description had purchased a gun. No witnesses had been found. Although it would have been possible to obtain an indictment at this point, without material evidence or a confession the chances of a conviction were slim.

Linda had, by now, convinced the inspector that he was not going to get any confession out of her, so he suspended the interrogation and turned his attention to Eleonore. He estimated Eleonore to be of less stern stuff, and she should know if it was Linda who had shot her.

Eleonore did, but she was reluctant to say. As she was not a suspect, but a victim, the inspector could not apply much pressure.

Instead, he resorted to sympathy, a tactic of which he could make convincing use as he was quite sincerely sympathetic to Eleonore's and Linda's problems. Having a good deal to do with homosexuals in his work, he was aware that their sexual peculiarity often caused them great unhappiness and was the source of much instability in their lives. Both Eleonore and Linda had been confirmed lesbians from early youth and neither had ever had any emotional contact whatsoever with men. Their relationship, sanctioned neither by society nor by any legal or religious bond, had been insecure and Linda, nine years older than her lover, had probably lived in a state of continual fear of losing her.

The sympathy worked to an extent. Eleonore admitted that she and Linda had been living together since May of 1969, when they met in a homosexual bar. It had been love at first sight and they moved in together immediately.

Eleonore also admitted that she was a little flighty and that she had sometimes indulged in flirtations with other women. Linda had beaten her up and she had deserved it. She insisted, however, that she had never actually been unfaithful.

Never, until Inge climbed into her cab on 21 May of that year. Eleonore remembered the date very well. She also remembered what had happened afterwards.

551

She drove Inge to her apartment in Elisabeth Strasse and was invited up for a drink. She accepted, and was so swept off her feet that she remained for the rest of the night. Inge, she said, was the most fantastic lover she had ever encountered. She was skilled beyond all belief.

Linda had beaten her up for this escapade, but she was unable to resist Inge and went back to the apartment repeatedly. In the end, however, they had to resort to making love in her cab as Linda learned Inge's address and often cruised by to see if Eleonore's cab was parked in the vicinity.

They had been making a little love on the night of 7 July in the cab, parked at the corner of Theresien and Luisen Strassen, when someone came up and shot them through the open window. She had no idea who it might have been.

The inspector replied that this was not true. She knew very well it had been Linda. There was no point in continuing to protect her. She was going to be indicted, tried and convicted.

Eleonore wept and said that she hoped not, but she still would not identify Linda as the murderess.

The inspector withdrew, temporarily defeated. Eleonore was not going to testify against her lover, even if she had shot her.

Even so, the police were now fairly confident of obtaining a conviction on the circumstantial evidence. Linda Schnitzler was brought before the examining magistrate formally indicted on one count of homicide and one count of wounding with a deadly weapon.

Two days later, the police received a frantic telephone call from a woman in Frankfurt who identified herself as Linda Schnitzler's mother. Her daughter, she said, was planning suicide. The police should stop her.

As it is German police policy not to give out any more information than necessary, the officer taking the call did not mention that Linda was in the detention cells awaiting trial and not, therefore, in a position to carry out her suicide plans, but merely transferred the call to Inspector Schreiber's office.

The inspector listened to what Mrs Schnitzler had to say and assured her that her daughter was alive and that he would take steps to prevent her from doing away with herself. He asked how she had come to know of the proposed suicide.

Mrs Schnitzler said that she had received a letter from Linda dated 6 July. She had been away visiting relatives for a few days and had only just returned to find the letter, which she now read to him.

It was short. '*Dear Mama,*' it read, '*Don't be angry. Eleonore has lied to me and deceived me. Bury me at home near you.*'

There was no mention of murder, but, if there were a conviction at the trial, this was evidence of premeditation. Careful not to alarm the woman, the inspector asked if she would send the letter down to him so that a psychologist could look at it. It might be useful in any treatment necessary. He did not mention that the treatment would be a judicial one.

The letter was received two days later. It did not impress either Linda or Eleonore, both of whom stuck to their original stories.

However, while waiting for the trial, which took place on 6 May 1977, Linda Schnitzler changed her mind and confessed to the shootings. She regretted what she had done, she said, but she had simply been unable to live without Eleonore and Inge was stealing her away.

Linda Schnitzler was found guilty on both charges but, despite the evidence of premeditation, was granted extenuating circumstances so that she was sentenced to a modest seven years' imprisonment.

Eleonore said that she would wait.

'What do I put in for the motive?' said Sergeant Kaufmann, filling out the closing case report. 'Deviate sex?'

The inspector looked at him thoughtfully.

553

'Was it?' he said.

'Was it what?' said the sergeant warily. He was never quite sure how serious the inspector was when he looked thoughtful.

'Deviate sex,' said the inspector. 'Of course, everybody involved in the case was sexually abnormal, but did that have anything to do with the shooting?'

The sergeant said nothing. He did not think that the inspector expected a reply.

'Wasn't Linda's jealousy as normal as that of any lover?' continued the inspector. 'Wasn't Inge's infatuation with Eleonore understandable in a person in her forties confronted with a lush and willing twenty-five-year-old? And wasn't Eleonore's refusal to incriminate the woman who shot her a pure example of the loyalty and devotion of one lover to another?'

He fixed the slightly open-mouthed sergeant with a grave and steady gaze.

'If the sexes had been orthodox, what would you have put down then?'

The sergeant closed his mouth. 'Romeo, Juliet and the Other Guy,' he said.

He typed in 'Deviate sex' and went on to the next entry.

3

DEVILISH ACTIVE, THESE GERMAN KIDS!

'*All those who read this book shall be damned for all eternity*,' read Detective Sergeant Peter Froebes in an emotionless official voice. '*May Our Lord Lucifer drag them down into the hottest fires of Hell.*'

He handed the little plastic-bound diary to Inspector Arnold Deutsch.

'Poorly educated person,' he remarked. 'There are half a dozen grammatical errors in every sentence.'

'Other interests than academic,' grunted the inspector, skipping through the pages, which were mostly filled with descriptions of black masses, witches' covens and magic sex orgies. A heavy man, broad-shouldered and thick in the middle, he had a blond close-cropped head which appeared to be connected to his body without benefit of neck. 'Girl, I should say, and young. Probably under twenty. Some of this may be imagination.'

'If it really is a young girl, I would hope that all of it is,' said the sergeant gravely. He was a handsome, unsmiling man with regular features and a near military bearing. He did not look in the least like a detective.

'Doesn't make any difference as far as we're concerned,' said the inspector. 'The question is, "Has it anything to do with this chap's death?" and I don't think it has. This was some kid he was making it with and she left her diary here. Probably so high on something or other she didn't know she had a diary or a place to leave it.'

'She could have been the reason he committed

555

suicide,' said the sergeant. 'I've seen this sort of thing before. These guest workers get in bed with some of the local talent who are out for sex and kicks or just trying to be "in" and they think it's true love. When they find out it's nothing, they crack up and kill themselves or somebody else.'

'Could be,' said the inspector. 'Well, all we can do is wait until Reichenauer tells us whether it was suicide or not. We'll see then.'

Reichenauer was Dr Otto Reichenauer, the greying, sad-faced medical expert attached to the criminal investigations department of the Duesseldorf police, who was now examining the body sitting on the sofa. He was not the only medical expert for the police, but he was the one who happened to be on duty at the time the report was received.

That had been at a little after six in the afternoon of Monday, 31 May 1982, a pleasant, sunny, late spring day in Duesseldorf, a city of close to three-quarters of a million inhabitants on the Rhine to the south of Bonn.

The person making the report was another guest worker, as the Germans call the cheap labour imported to keep down local wage levels, a thirty-year-old Spaniard named Manuel Hernandez.

Hernandez had said that he was a friend of the dead man, twenty-nine-year-old Jose Luis Mato Fernandez. Both came from Orense, a village not far from the Portuguese border, and both were employed on the same construction project in Duesseldorf.

Fernandez, known as Mato, had not turned up for work that Monday and Manuel went to his friend's apartment at 6 Metzger Strasse in the Derendorf area after he finished work to see what was wrong. The German economy was in a depression and an unexcused absence could easily cost a guest worker his job.

Mato did not need a job, however. He was sitting on the sofa in his living room, completely naked except for a shirt, which was open down the front. The handle of what looked to Manuel like a very large butcher's knife was sticking rigidly from his chest. Mato's right hand was resting on the handle of the knife and it was covered with blood. So too was the rest of Mato and most of the sofa.

The blood was not red, but dull brown and dry, so it was obvious that he had been stabbed some considerable time earlier.

Manuel, who had had experience in butchering pigs and other animals, did not doubt that his friend was dead and he did not approach the corpse, but quietly closed the door and went away to the Derendorf police sub-station.

The desk sergeant in the charge room had kept him there and sent a patrol car to investigate. When the report was confirmed, he alerted the department of criminal investigations at headquarters and the inspector, the sergeant and the doctor had come out.

The doctor concluded his on-the-spot examination and voiced the opinion that it was suicide. After all, the man's hand was still resting on the handle of the knife and the location of the wound was where it would be if he had wanted to stab himself through the heart.

Death had taken place some time early that morning, said the doctor, probably before ten o'clock. He would provide a more exact time in his report when he had completed the autopsy. The immediate cause of death was massive blood loss and he thought that the knife had probably gone through the heart itself.

'Okay,' said the inspector. 'You stay here, Peter, and I'll send out a team from the lab to go through all this stuff. There has to be an inventory for the final report and for the next of kin, if there is any. Probably be a question of who pays for the burial.'

Guest workers all had huge families while they were alive, but dead ones were often found to have no relatives at all.

The sergeant nodded and went out to the patrol car

to smoke a cigarette while he waited. The atmosphere within the apartment was not to his liking. The place was filthy and the kitchenette floor had apparently been used as a garbage bucket. There were old rags and junk lying all over and it smelled as if thirty or forty people had been holding a non-stop sex orgy for the past year or so.

The inspector and the doctor went back to head-quarters and, after an hour's wait, the technicians turned up. There is enough crime in Duesseldorf for the labora-tory to be manned round the clock, but they had had other matters to attend to.

And less disgusting, as they complained to the sergeant. Making an inventory of a place like that was more like cleaning cesspools than police work.

The sergeant pointed out that, if they did not like the work, they were free to seek employment elsewhere and suggested they got on with it. He did not like being there any more than they did and he could not leave until they had finished.

Thus encouraged, the technicians set to with a will and, by nine o'clock, the sergeant was able to report in to the inspector that operations at the scene had been terminated.

The corpse and the rooms of the apartment had been photographed as found. A scale diagram of the premises had been prepared. Everything that was not actual dirt or garbage had been sealed in plastic sacks and taken to the laboratory and the corpse had been transferred to the morgue. A neat, efficient job, carried out precisely according to the regulations, which was the way the sergeant did everything.

Having come on duty at two in the afternoon, the inspector and the sergeant went off duty at ten. The doctor, who kept different hours, had gone home immediately after completing his examination of the corpse.

He came in the following day at eight and began the

autopsy almost at once so that, by the time the inspector turned up in his office at two-thirty, he was nearly finished.

The sergeant, as was fitting, had arrived earlier than his chief and was engaged in going through the diary which had been found in the apartment the evening before.

'Hot stuff, eh, Peter?' said the inspector, lowering his two hundred plus pounds cautiously into his desk chair. 'Any indication of the identity of the author?'

The sergeant radiated unvoiced disapproval of the choice of language.

'Only that it was a girl,' he said. 'What she claims to have done at these devil-worshipping ceremonies wouldn't be physically possible for a man. We could probably trace her. She describes herself as the official high priestess of the Flingern devil-worshipping society.'

'If she's so popular in Flingern, what was she doing in Derendorf?' said the inspector, who did not regard the matter seriously.

Flingern was on the eastern edge of the city and Derendorf was to the north.

'Sleeping with guest workers,' said the sergeant matter-of-factly. 'She mentions this one by name.'

He turned the pages, cleared his throat and read: ' "*Lucifer, Lord of Darkness. Give me a sign. I believe in Thee. I want to belong to Thee. Come to me when Mato sleeps.*" '

'Any mention if he turned up?' said the inspector.

The sergeant closed the diary and put it in the drawer of the desk. 'I'll go and see whether Reichenauer is finished with the autopsy,' he said.

The doctor had not finished completely, but he had opened up the body and removed the knife from Fernandez's chest. It was an ordinary butcher's knife with a worn, much used blade some nine inches long.

'Terrible cut,' said the doctor. 'There's a hole here you can put your hand through. The third rib is completely

559

severed and the second part way. Went into the right chamber of the heart.'

'Hesitation cuts?' said the sergeant.

It was rare that the corpse of a suicide did not show shallow, tentative 'hesitation cuts' made while working up to the final act.

The doctor shook his head. 'This was a stab wound,' he said. 'It's more when they cut their wrists that you get hesitation cuts. Of course, he may have pricked himself on the chest a couple of times before he rammed it in, but those marks would be obliterated by the cut. On the other hand . . .'

'On the other hand what?' said the sergeant.

'I've never seen a man stab himself with such force before,' said the doctor. 'He must have been half out of his mind.'

'But it was him and not somebody else?' said the sergeant. 'You're certain?'

'Oh, I don't think there's much doubt of that,' said the doctor. 'I sent the knife over to Weapons Identification and they say it's his fingerprints on it.'

The sergeant inquired as to the time of death and was informed that it was at around nine on the morning of Monday. He then returned to his own office.

'Reichenauer thinks there's something funny with the case,' he said. 'He doesn't want to say so because he's already declared it suicide, but he's got doubts. I know him.'

'Well, if it wasn't suicide, then it was murder,' said the inspector. 'It sure as hell wasn't any accident. What else did Reichenauer say?'

'That the victim's last moments were happy,' said the sergeant. 'He was engaged in sex such a short time prior to his death that he hadn't washed yet.'

The inspector snorted. 'Reichenauer thinks there's something funny? I think there's something funny with Reichenauer. What kind of a suicide is this supposed to be anyway? A construction worker from some whistle-

560

stop in Spain gets it off with one of our young idealists and his sensitive nature is so wounded by something she said or did that he rams a knife into himself with enough force to butcher an ox – and that at nine in the morning of a Monday? If that was all it took, we wouldn't have a guest worker alive in Germany.'

'Maybe it was his first experience with one of our local girls,' said the sergeant. 'I take it you want to open an investigation?'

The inspector did, and one of the first things which the sergeant found out was that whoever Jose Luis Mato Fernandez had spent his last night on earth with, it had definitely not been his first experience with the local girls.

Fernandez was, in fact, mildly famous in certain circles and proudly bore the nickname of Five-a-Night, which referred to his ability to perform intercourse five times a night on a more or less regular basis.

The sergeant had no difficulty in locating great numbers of witnesses to this feat, all of whom claimed personal experience, and some of whom were of an age that would have got Fernandez a jail sentence had he been alive to serve it.

None of the ladies was, however, able to provide any suggestion as to who might have wanted to murder the gallant Spaniard. Indeed, many expressed the opinion that such a person would be out of his or her mind. Certainly, no woman would have done it.

'They're probably right,' said the sergeant, reporting to the inspector on his progress. 'I don't think any woman could have done it unless she was a weightlifter or something. Nine inches of blade straight through two ribs? That takes force.'

'What does Reichenauer say?' asked the inspector. 'Does he think a woman would have had the strength?'

'He says it's not pertinent,' said the sergeant. 'He's sticking to his original theory of suicide.'

The doctor was having more and more difficulty in

561

defending his theory now the investigation had begun; Fernandez was proving to be not a very likely candidate for suicide.

His life had been largely an open book and his friend Manuel Hernandez was able to tell the police almost anything they wanted to know about him.

He was not a complex character. An unskilled construction worker from a small, provincial town, he had come, like so many others, to Germany seeking the work and relatively high wages that were not to be had in Spain.

He had been in the country a little over eight years at the time of his death and had never been in any kind of trouble. Hernandez and his other friends described him as normal in every respect, a hard, conscientious worker who liked a glass or two in the café after work, but not a heavy drinker. He had an easy-going nature, had not got into fights and had many friends.

The only thing exceptional about him was that he had a reputation for unusual sexual staying-power. This had attracted numbers of young German girls who were, as they described it, gathering experience. Perhaps for this reason, Fernandez had not married.

Finally, there was one other aspect to the character of Mato Fernandez and it was one which the inspector did not like. A man of high principles, he had never knowingly become involved with married women or women who were formally engaged.

This was a set-back to the investigation. The inspector's theory of the murder – as it was now formally classified – was that Fernandez had met his end at the hands of an outraged husband or fiancé.

'Could also have been a father or a brother,' suggested the sergeant helpfully. 'Or, maybe, she was married and he didn't know it.'

The inspector did not think so. Practically all of the girls with whom Fernandez was known to have been intimate were so promiscuous that outraged fathers or brothers would have had to take up murdering full-time. And as for the lady being married without Fernandez' knowledge, why were there no married women among the legion that the sergeant had contacted?

'No,' said the inspector. 'It's something else. We're barking up the wrong tree or, maybe, Reichenauer is right after all.'

'I don't think so,' said the sergeant. 'The more I think about that knife wound, the less likely it seems to me that it would have been self-inflicted. I just can't imagine a man like Fernandez slamming a knife into his own chest with such force. If he had been some kind of a psycho, yes, but from everything we've learned about him, he was completely normal, apart from being a little over-sexed. I think we should try to trace the girl who left that diary in his apartment.'

'It wasn't any of his playmates you've talked to so far?' said the inspector.

The sergeant shook his head. 'None of them admitted to being devil-worshippers and the girl in the diary was into devil-worshipping in a big way. People like that are nuts to begin with. She could have killed him for some weird reason, like, say, the devil wanted it.'

'You may be reading too much cheap literature,' said the inspector, 'but go ahead. See if you can locate her. We don't have a great deal else to try anyway.'

It was true. Nearly all the possibilities in the investigation had been exhausted. There were no suspects and there was no indication of any motive for the murder of Mato Fernandez. He had had an active sex life and he had lived, off and on, with an almost endless series of enthusiastic German girls, but there was no reason in the world for any of them to want to kill him. A great many of his compatriots lived in a like manner, even if they were not capable of five performances a night.

The sergeant, although he had not mentioned it, had another reason for wanting to trace the owner of the diary. He suspected that she had been Fernandez' companion at the time of his death.

This could mean that she had lived at the apartment, possibly for lack of any other place to live, which, in turn, would have made her, in Mato's eyes, a dependent female and in need of supervision. For Mato, whose standards were those of his native village, had believed strongly that it was the duty of the male to enforce morality in the weaker sex.

This was obviously not a point of view which would have found much acceptance among the totally liberated, near insanely independent German teens with whom the Spaniard had shared his reeking bed.

The sergeant was wondering whether there might not have been a sort of cultural clash. A self-proclaimed queen of the devil-worshippers might not have been prepared to accept the authority of a Spanish peasant whose devotion to the double standard would have appeared outdated to her grandmother.

There was, of course, the trying question of why the young lady would have found it necessary to murder Fernandez. It would scarcely have been because she was emotionally involved. The sergeant knew what kind of a girl she was. Most such girls were emotionally burned out before they had passed their teens.

The motive would, therefore, be something weird, possibly incomprehensible to the ordinary person, and what more weird than devil-worship, black masses and witches' covens, all of which had featured prominently in the diary?

Although the owner of the diary was not identified by name, the entries were dated. The lady expressed a wish that Lucifer visit her while Mato was asleep on 30 April, exactly one month before Mato was stabbed.

Whether this had any significance, it did place her in Mato's apartment on that date. All that was necessary to identify her was to determine who Fernandez had been living with at the time.

This proved to be impossible. There had been heavy traffic in Mato's bedroom and it was not always clear who was resident and who was not. Probably Mato had not known himself. In any case, no one had had any particular reason to keep track and, after such a length of time, no one could remember.

Having encountered failure in this respect, the sergeant went back to the diary, wading through such unmaidenly appeals as, 'Lucifer, Lord of Darkness! I would sell my soul to Thee! I would help Thee bring ruin over the world. Give me a sign, Lord!' and some remarkably graphic descriptions of sex orgies, involving persons who were apparently multi-sexual, until he found the reference to the Flingern devil-worshippers.

He had hoped that there would be details to aid him in his search, but all there was were boasts of how no coven or black mass in Flingern was complete without the body of the high priestess serving as an altar.

The language left no doubt that the high priestess and the author of the diary were the same person.

It also left no doubt that, if there was anything sexual in the world which the high priestess and author had not personally experienced, it was because it was physically impossible or cost money.

The sergeant, therefore, took himself off to Flingern and began asking questions. As he was not known there and did not look like a police officer, he was soon able to learn that there was, indeed, an active and flourishing devil-worshipping society and was even able to obtain an application form for admission to it.

Devil-worshippers or not, the society remained German, and Germans liked things done in an orderly manner – which meant admission forms, membership cards, minutes of the meetings and, presumably, dues.

The sergeant did not sign up, partly because he would have been unable to justify the cost on his expense voucher and partly because he sincerely had no desire to belong to an organization for worshipping the devil.

Membership, moreover, was not necessary as the high priestess was publicity-conscious and her identity was easily learned.

High Priestess Sylvia Brakel was twenty-two years old, which was older than the sergeant had expected, but she did not look her age, having a pretty, round, baby face and a good deal of soft, long, blonde hair. Given a Girl Guide uniform and a book of raffle tickets to sell, she would not have looked out of character.

None the less, Sylvia was a genuine devil-worshipper, a witch, a past mistress in the art of the protracted sex orgy and the author of the diary found in Mato Fernandez' apartment.

The sergeant did not immediately take her into custody or even question her concerning her relationship to Fernandez, but began trying to identify her closer friends. He was able to turn up three of these, all nearly as weird as Sylvia herself.

The first and oldest was a twenty-four-year-old journeyman baker who rarely worked at his trade, but who was very active in devil-worshipping circles. His name was Christian Berger and he was proud to tell anyone who would listen that it was he who had introduced the high priestess to devil-worshipping before she had reached the age of eighteen.

Her other male confidant was twenty-nine-year-old Detlef Meister, a lorry driver. He did not drive lorries much more than Christian Berger baked bread. He too was a born-again devil-worshipper.

The third friend was technically female, but preferred not to think so. Nineteen-year-old Susi Boettcher had been a convinced lesbian from the time she was at school and referred to Sylvia as 'my wife'.

Having assembled this information on Sylvia Brakel and her friends, the sergeant presented it to the inspector and asked for instructions. There was no evidence against any of them, but Sylvia had been living with

Fernandez not long before he was murdered and he felt that they were all weird enough for anything.

So did the inspector, and he promptly ordered the sergeant to take all four into custody and grill them as hard as he dared. He was not very confident of the outcome. It was rare that an admission of anything could be extracted from such hard-bitten types.

Both the inspector and the sergeant had overlooked one thing, however. All of the suspects were devil-worshippers.

And devil-worshippers, of course, have reverse morals. You do not stick with your friends. You betray them.

Taken into custody, Christian Berger, Detlef Meister and Susi Boettcher all immediately denounced Sylvia Brakel as the murderess of Mato Fernandez. She had, they said, told them so herself.

Indeed, she had – and she was quite prepared to tell Sergeant Froebes too. She did not seem in the least concerned that this would lead to her being tried for murder. She did not seem concerned about anything.

Sylvia said she had murdered Mato because he objected to her sleeping with other men and women and taking part in sex orgies while she was living with him. It reflected, he had said, on his honour.

They had quarrelled over this previously, but Sunday night, 30 May was the final straw.

She came home at five in the morning after an exhausting black mass in which she had served not only as high priestess and altar, but also as object of the membership's most far-out fantasies, to find Mato waiting up for her.

There was another quarrel and she came to the conclusion that the best solution would be to kill him.

She waited until he fell asleep on the sofa, fetched the knife from the kitchen and, using both hands, drove it into his chest with a swing.

She aimed for the heart, she said, and added proudly that Mato never knew what hit him.

She then put his hand on the handle of the knife so that the police would think it was suicide, and went off to be comforted by Susi.

Sylvia's trial was very well attended and the audience was not disappointed.

She described how she and her grandfather had practised mutual masturbation when she was eight, how she had been gang-banged by a group of rockers when she was sixteen and how she had become the high priestess of the devil-worshippers through sheer sex power. She had, she admitted, a more than casual interest in sex, which was why she had been living with the famous Five-a-Night.

Sylvia expressed the opinion that her character had been warped by being sent to reform school for shoplifting while yet a child, but the court was not impressed. As she had been found, rather surprisingly, sane and competent to stand trial, they sentenced her to life imprisonment on 25 March 1983.

She greeted the verdict with the same indifference she had displayed toward everything else.

4

FIT TO BE TIED

As a general rule, whores tend to sympathize with other whores.

Although nominally competitors, they are all in much the same boat and it is not always the luxury liner that the uninitiated believe it to be.

The work is tiring and often unpleasant. Handsome, sexually normal young men do not need to frequent prostitutes. The service is available elsewhere free. The prostitute can be happy, therefore, if her clients are clean, young enough to get it over with quickly and not practising sadists.

Calculated on the basis of an hourly rate, the younger, more attractive practitioners are well-paid, but there is often little left of these high gross earnings. Maintaining a serious, conscientious pimp is expensive, and not many are prepared to run the risk of doing without one. For prostitution, as any insurance agent will tell you, is a dangerous profession. In terms of personal security, it is wiser to become a trapeze artist.

Karin Lewandowski had not had a pimp and so she was, of course, dead, her throat cut from ear to ear.

She had been a pretty woman, dark-haired, admirably curved, and she had not looked much more than half of her forty-one years.

Even so, business had been a little slack in recent years and one reason that Karin had not had a pimp was because she was too old to attract an acceptable one. It did not take a very bright pimp to estimate the number of years of top earning power left in that forty-year-old body, and why bother when the woods were full of enthusiastic eighteen-year-olds?

Karin had, therefore, run her business single-handed from apartment 846 of the towering Pharao House in the Oberfoehring sector of Munich. Had her throat not been cut, she might have been able to put aside a little something for her retirement from the savings on pimp fees.

As it was, although not retired in the conventional sense, she had definitely gone out of business – and she came close to taking her last customer with her.

He was a good customer, too, a regular who had a fixed appointment for every second Sunday at four-thirty in the afternoon.

However, the gentleman, who will here be known as Karl-Otto Schmidt, was slightly overweight and over-age, and when he pushed open the door of Karin's studio apartment to find her lying on the bed, bound, gagged and soaked in blood, he very nearly had a heart attack.

This would have been embarrassing as Karl-Otto was a respectable businessman and married. Unfortunately, his wife was not fond of sex or, at least, not with Karl-Otto. As a result, although he was spared the heart attack, he did end up with a bad headache from trying to decide what he should do.

Karin was dead, obviously murdered, and the logical thing to do was to telephone the police.

If he did that, however, he might be arrested, interrogated, required to appear as a witness and end up on the front pages of the newspapers. He could already see before his eyes a vision of his wife squinting in disbelief at his picture and the caption '*Local Businessman Discovers Dead Whore*', or something similar.

Well then, simply close the door and steal quietly away. Let someone else report the murder. After all, there was no hurry. Karin was not going anywhere.

But had she left something behind? A list of customers? He knew that she kept an appointment book.

She was rather forgetful. And his name was in it, he was certain. After all, he had been visiting her for over two years now. What would happen when the police traced the four-thirty appointment and found it was him? How could he explain having failed to report the crime?

He would be lucky if he was not charged with the murder himself.

Gritting his teeth and trying to calculate how much in the way of a property settlement his wife might get in the event of a divorce, he picked up Karin Lewandowski's telephone and dialled the emergency number of the police.

He was, he said, at the scene of a murder. Yes, he would wait for the police to arrive.

The officer in the communications centre at the huge police headquarters building kept him on the telephone for an unconscionable length of time, spelling out the address, confusing his name three or four times and giving him the impression that he was speaking to a mentally deficient police officer.

The point of all this was, of course, to keep Karl-Otto on the telephone until a patrol car could arrive and determine whether he was a madman, a drug addict on a bad trip, an alcoholic, a practical joker or whether there really had been a murder.

Following confirmation by the patrol car officers, the duty homicide squad was called away. This consisted of a remarkably bland-looking detective inspector named Ralf Dormann, a huge-limbed, red-haired and freckled sergeant of detectives named Sepp Heide and a medical expert named Leopold Langenauer, who habitually bore the slightly troubled look of a bank clerk who is wondering whether his accounts are really in order.

The inspector, a basically compassionate man, examined Karl-Otto's personal identification papers, listened to his explanation of how he came to discover the body and then assured him that his real name would never be revealed by the police and, as a matter of fact, it never was.

In the meantime, Sergeant Heide had been going through the small kitchen and bathroom to see if there were any indications of robbery. Prostitutes were generally killed by persons who mistakenly believed that they kept large sums of cash on the premises.

Although the sergeant did find signs of a search – and, apparently, a successful one, for there was not a cent in the apartment – Dr Langenauer did not favour robbery as a motive.

The victim, he pointed out, had been bound, gagged and, he thought, chloroformed. There was still a strong smell of chloroform around the bed.

She had obviously been entertaining a client, for she was wearing nothing other than black net stockings, a black suspender belt and a white blouse.

The blouse was now largely red, and so was the bed, the wall and part of the ceiling. Beneath the woman's chin gaped an enormous wound stretching across the neck from side to side. It had been made, said the doctor, with a straight razor or something equally sharp.

Karin's hands were bound behind her back and the end of the cord had been brought up and fastened around her neck in a slip noose. The bonds were drawn very tight and had cut into the skin.

Her feet were not bound and her legs were sprawled wide as if she had been making a deliberate effort to get them as far apart as possible.

Proceeding to the examination of the genitals, the doctor found out why.

'There's a double-edged razor blade inside the vagina,' he said. 'She didn't dare to move for fear of cutting herself.'

'Pervert then?' said the inspector.

'Definitely,' said the doctor. 'Bondage, sadism, what-have-you. There should be something on this boy in the files. It's unlikely that this is his first offence.'

'We'll see,' said the inspector. 'What do you find, Sepp?'

'Not much,' said the sergeant. 'I think he went through the place and took whatever money he could find. Nothing else obvious missing. I don't suppose she would have kept any real jewellery here in the shop.'

'Have to see whether she had a private residence,' said the inspector. 'Well, let's get the lab people out here and see what they turn up. When can I have the autopsy report, Leo?'

'Before noon tomorrow,' said the doctor. 'By the way, she's only been dead a couple of hours.'

'You'd better call out a detail to canvass the building and see if anybody noticed anything, Sepp,' said the inspector. 'Let me know what you turn up. I'll be in the office.'

The laboratory technicians did not find anything of apparent significance in Karin Lewandowski's apartment. There had been a great many persons there, presumably men, which was what might be expected in the business premises of a practising prostitute, but there was nothing to connect any of them to the murder. They agreed with the sergeant that the place had been searched for money, but there was no certainty as to whether any had been found.

After they had finished and the body had been photographed, it was taken to the police morgue to await the autopsy the following morning.

The technicians went home, but Sergeant Heide and his men remained until nearly midnight, questioning the tenants of the building and interfering seriously with business, as most of them were engaged in the same activity as Karin had been. They were not told at this time that she had been murdered.

The murder, but few details of the circumstances, was announced in the newspapers the following morning. Solidarity among prostitutes is never stronger than when one of them is murdered, so a number of telephone calls

573

were received at police headquarters from colleagues who had known Karin or who had recently had particularly weird clients.

Most of these were of no value to the investigation, but two were of possible significance.

Thirty-year-old Anna Brucker reported that she had had a client who wanted her to get into a white blouse and allow him to tie her up. She had refused to be tied as she was afraid of being left helpless, but she had put on a white blouse. The man had not been able to achieve orgasm and had become threatening. She had responded by taking the leash off her Dobermann and he had left. She described him as young, in his middle twenties, good-looking, less than average height, clean, well-groomed and well-dressed.

The other potential lead was from thirty-two-year-old Marta Siebrach who reported a similar, but more alarming experience. She had, unwisely, allowed the man to tie her and had been frightened nearly out of her wits when he inserted a double-edged razor blade into her vagina. He had said that it was so that she would hold still. He had also pulled the bonds much too tight before achieving his orgasm. Afterwards, he had been apologetic, had removed the razor blade and had untied her. He had given her some extra money, but she would have gladly renounced payment to get him out of the apartment. She thought he was crazy.

Marta Siebrach had also been asked to put on a white blouse, and this led the inspector to believe it was the same man as Anna Brucker's client and, possibly, the murderer of Karin Lewandowski.

Unfortunately, Anna and Marta could only provide descriptions. Neither had had any indication of the customer's identity and, although both spent the best part of a day going through the police mug books, they were unable to find any picture resembling the man in question.

Nothing useful had turned up in the autopsy report

either. Karin had died at approximately two o'clock in the afternoon and she had been unconscious from chloroform at the time. The murderer had made two slight cuts in her neck with the razor, before taking the full sweep which had opened her throat to the backbone. He had apparently failed to achieve orgasm as there was no semen in or on the body.

By this time, everyone known to have been in or near the Pharao House on Sunday had been contacted and interrogated and had their stories checked. There were no suspects.

There were also no witnesses who reported seeing anyone suspicious-looking in the building, but this was not significant. If the killer was the same man who had frightened Anna Brucker and Marta Siebrach, he did not look suspicious.

The identification section had collected a few hundred latent fingerprints from the apartment and some of them were of persons with police records. None had records of attacks on women, however, and, in any case, none of the fingerprints were so placed as to show a direct connection with the crime.

Karin's appointment book, which had so troubled Karl-Otto Schmidt, had been found, but it proved valueless. The only entries were those of first names, nicknames and terse descriptions, not all of them flattering. Karin had apparently been considerate in not wanting to compromise her customers in the event the book fell into the wrong hands.

The inspector was not too dismayed by this circumspection. He had not expected much from the appointment book anyway, as he assumed that it contained only the names of Karin's regular customers. The murderer had not been a regular.

Who he could have been was just about any male in Munich. Karin had not exactly had a walk-in business, but she had run permanent advertisements in the classified sections of two newspapers which, although they varied a little in text, left no doubt with the reader that the friendly services for reasonable fees that she was offering involved a degree of physical contact. She did not give the address, only the telephone number, and recommended that interested parties ring for an appointment.

'A little like Russian roulette,' remarked the sergeant. 'She never knew what she was going to get.'

'Neither do we,' said the inspector. 'And we're not as well-paid. Well, let's release a little more information to the press and see if that brings in anything. They should be happy to cooperate. After all, she was an advertiser.'

The little more information which the inspector had in mind was details of the kinky aspects of the case and, particularly, the white blouse, which was thought to have been furnished by the murderer as it was not Karin's size.

This could be significant, for in the case of Marta Siebrach, the client had provided a white blouse when she had said that she had none. Anna Brucker had had a white blouse, so it was not known whether her caller had brought one with him or not.

A rather lurid account of the circumstances of Karin's death appeared in the newspapers the following day and, the day after that, there was a response.

A forty-year-old woman named Helga Braun telephoned police headquarters to say she thought she might have some information concerning the Karin Lewandowski murder and who should she tell it to?

The switchboard officer said someone would come to take her statement and, in about five minutes, Sergeant Heide was there.

The haste was justified, for what Mrs Braun had was the first promising lead in the case.

Mrs Braun, who described herself as divorced, without friends and lonely, said that something had gone wrong with her telephone on 10 February and she had consequently called the repair service and asked for an engineer.

One had been sent round, an attractive young man in his mid-twenties, very neat, almost handsome, although a little smaller than average.

The young man had fixed her telephone and accepted a cup of coffee after he had finished. Just how it had happened she could not say, but the conversation had come around to sex and the young man, who never once mentioned his name, confessed that he had certain problems in achieving sexual satisfaction.

Mrs Braun had inquired as to what they might be and, after some embarrassed hemming and hawing around, he had replied that he was able to achieve orgasm only if his partner was wearing a white blouse and allowed him to tie her up.

The lonely divorcee had said that she had a white blouse and that she had no objections to being tied up as long as it was not too tight.

She had then removed her clothing and put on the white blouse. The man had also removed his clothing and tied her up with her bathrobe cord. They had engaged in intercourse and he had subsequently declared himself fully satisfied with the results.

So too was Mrs Braun, but, later on, she had begun to wonder whether she had not done something foolish. The man was a total stranger and while she was tied, she had been completely at his mercy. Pleasant as the encounter had been, it was not, she decided, something that she would risk again. Later, she had read the account of the Lewandowski murder in the newspaper and been so stuck by the similarity with her own experience that she decided to contact the police.

The police were duly grateful. Although the young man had not identified himself to Mrs Braun, his identity could easily be traced. Telephone service in Germany is provided by the postal service, and there would be an exact record of who had been sent to repair Mrs Braun's telephone.

Having taken Mrs Braun's statement and refused a cup of coffee, the sergeant went straight to the telephone service section of the post office.

When he returned to police headquarters, it was with the name and address of a man who liked to tie women up while they were wearing a white blouse and nothing else.

This telephone engineer was named Wolfgang Siegfried Grabatsch. He was twenty-five years old. He came from a good, middle-class family. He had never been in any kind of trouble. And he lived in the nearby village of Erding with his lovely nineteen-year-old wife, Brigitte.

To any ordinary person, Grabatsch would have appeared the most unlikely suspect in the world, but the officers of the homicide squad were well aware that criminals, even seriously disturbed psychopaths, do not have an appearance differing from the most law-abiding of citizens.

Juries are not, however, composed of police officers and appearance does count in the courtroom. If Grabatsch was the murderer of Karin Lewandowski, then the police were going to have to present solid evidence if they hoped to obtain an indictment, let alone a conviction.

The inspector knew, however, that there was no evidence to be obtained from the scene and that there would probably be no witnesses. If there was any proof at all, it would have to be obtained from Grabatsch himself.

He, therefore, approached the matter as carefully as if he were walking on soap bubbles. It was of utter importance that Grabatsch not be alarmed into destroying or disposing of any evidence there might be.

The first step was to find out just how good a suspect Grabatsch was.

He was, without question, the telephone engineer who

had taken care of Helga Braun's telephone and other problems, but he had not harmed her in any way. Bondage was a common enough perversion and, although the white blouse was unusual, clothing fetishes were not.

With Anna Brucker and, particularly, Marta Siebrach, the matter had been less harmless and more like the murder of Karin Lewandowski. The question was: Was this the same man?

There was only one way to find out and the inspector, with some assistance from telephone service supervisors, arranged for Anna Brucker and Marta Siebrach to obtain a look at Grabatsch without his knowledge.

Both immediately identified him as the man with a taste for bondage and white blouses.

This, the inspector felt, was enough or, rather, all he was going to get, and he immediately took Grabatsch into custody, brought his wife to police headquarters for questioning and searched his house and car very thoroughly.

The search did not need to be so thorough. Everything the police found was easily located for no effort had been made to conceal it.

In the trunk of the car was a tidy kit containing a bottle of chloroform, gauze compresses for applying it to the nose and mouth, adhesive tape, rubber gloves, a pair of tights and two white blouses.

In the house was one of the most impressive collections of pornography that the arresting officers had ever seen. It was heavily concentrated on bondage and included books, magazines, video tapes, films and photographs. Many of the photographs had been taken by Grabatsch himself for the subject was his wife, trussed like a turkey, wearing a white blouse and smiling into the camera. An obvious believer in the do-it-yourself principle, he had also composed a number of the typewritten pornographic manuscripts, featuring, of course, women tied up while wearing white blouses.

Significantly, there was no straight razor or any other weapon and, for a time, the inspector feared that his suspect was going to slip through his fingers.

The material found in Grabatsch's house was proof that he was profoundly interested in pornography and bondage, but so were a few thousand others in Munich.

The equipment in the trunk of the car was more incriminating for it included items such as had been used in the Lewandowski murder. There was, however, no proof that these items had been used in the murder or that it was Grabatsch who had used them.

If Grabatsch denied the crime and stuck to his story, there was little hope of indicting him and none at all of obtaining a conviction.

But Grabatsch did not deny the murder and, in fact, expressed relief that he had been apprehended. Had he not been, he said, there was no telling how many women he might have killed. He was, he added with rare under-statement, a man with serious mental problems.

Wolfgang Siegfried Grabatsch was not only an amateur author of bondage pornography, but an amateur psychologist as well. He was able to present the police with a thorough analysis of the personality problems which had caused him to become a murderer.

It had all started, he said, when he was only six years old. His grandmother, who was seventy at the time, had been taken to hospital. When he asked what was the matter with her, his mother regaled him with a remarkable story to tell a child of his age.

His seventy-four-year-old grandfather, she said, had insisted that Grandma dress up in an abbreviated costume of no more than a pair of high heels and black net stockings and had chased her through the house until she jumped out of a window in terror and broke her leg.

This event had made a profound impression on Wolfgang.

A few months later, he was playing indians with his eight-year-old cousin, Lilian Boos. Lilian persuaded him to take off his clothes, tied him up and took liberties with his private parts. At the time, she was wearing only a white blouse.

This had made an even stronger impression on him and he was never able to enjoy normal sexual relations, although he made several attempts.

Finally, in 1976, when he was twenty, he met a girl named Angelika Faber, two years his junior but not entirely inexperienced in sexual matters. He felt at ease with Angelika and managed to confess his secret fantasy of tying up a girl in a white blouse and making love to her.

Like Mrs Braun, Angelika had a white blouse and no objections to being tied up. They spent many happy hours, but there was an unfortunate tendency to tie the bonds tighter and tighter and Angelika eventually decided that she did not want to play that game any more. At the beginning of 1977, she dissolved their romance.

However, Wolfgang now knew what he wanted and how to get it. Making the acquaintance of Brigitte, who was only fifteen at the time, he had her bound, bloused and pregnant in a little over six weeks.

Far from being dismayed at the prospect of fatherhood, Grabatsch proposed to marry the girl, but, as this was violently opposed by her family and as she was still under the legal age, the marriage did not take place and Brigitte had an abortion instead.

Embittered, Wolfgang returned to Angelika, but, again, the bonds were too tight for her liking and on 12 September 1980, he and Brigitte were married. A remarkably understanding woman, she permitted him to keep the large collection of pornographic pictures which he had made of her predecessor.

Nor did she fail him now. Her husband might be a murderer and a sex psychopath, but, as far as she was concerned, he was a good husband and she was prepared to wait until he had served his sentence, whatever that might be.

It could have been a long wait, although no one really serves a life sentence in Germany today, but Wolfgang did not go to prison after all.

Having kept him under observation for some considerable time, the state psychologists agreed with his analysis that he had serious mental problems and recommended that he be sent not to prison, but to a psychiatric hospital where he would be recycled, reprogrammed and returned to the faithfully waiting Brigitte.

This is a common process and one that rarely takes very long.

Prostitution remains a dangerous profession.

In Munich, at least.

5

THE MURDER IS THE MOTIVE

During the summers of 1980, 1981 and 1982, someone was killing back-packers in France.

There was nothing very unusual about it. Someone was always killing back-packers in France and elsewhere. In the closing years of the twentieth century, all kinds of people were getting killed everywhere, so why not back-packers?

Formerly, it was hitch-hikers. Hitch-hikers were being decimated. And not surprisingly. If large numbers of nubile maidens chose to stand at roadsides and climb light-heartedly into the cars of total strangers, a certain percentage was going to get more than a free ride.

By the eighties, however, hitch-hikers were out and back-packers were in. Nobody was going to give a hitch-hiker a lift because they looked too much like hippies and everybody knew that hippies were all on drugs and would steal your car and murder you. Even girl hippies couldn't get lifts. Rapists too worry about venereal disease.

Back-packers were better, more sporting and wholesome. The idea was, the back-packer strode stoutly along, tent and gear strapped to his or her back, and with sturdy, but not necessarily unattractive legs roamed the Continent, healthily, ecologically and at modest cost.

In practice, the back-packer hitch-hiked. And, if the back-packer was female and pretty, she not infrequently got raped, killed, both or worse.

Contrary to popular belief, terminology does not change the world.

So what was so remarkable about those back-packers who died violent deaths in the first three years of the eighties?

To begin with, they were all men, young men, not particularly handsome, not particularly well-to-do and not homosexual.

But who, in heaven's name, would want to kill nonentities like these and for what reason?

Precisely.

Second, they were all killed by one or more bullets fired into their heads at point-blank range from a 7.65 mm pistol.

Third, they were all killed during the month of August.

And, finally, they were all asleep in their sleeping-bags at the time.

In short, the murderer killed young men quite deliberately while they were asleep and for neither sex nor money. No comprehensible motive. No prior contact between murderer and victim. No clues. And, apparently, no witnesses.

The French authorities could scarcely be blamed for failing to solve such crimes and, as a matter of fact, they were not.

Indeed, no one realized that there was a series of such crimes going on. The victims were not rich enough to attract sympathy and the scenes were scattered across France. Had there been more sex to the killings, even homosexual sex, the media might have shown greater interest, but who wanted to read about some young stranger getting himself shot while alone in a sleeping-bag?

Nobody, and so it is possible that the series actually began before 1980. There were a lot of points in the case that were never completely clear and the exact number of victims was one of them.

The first known victim was in Nice, the heart of the French Riviera and a place which attracts many persons in August, some of whom are back-packers.

This particular one was French. A twenty-two-year-old office employee named Claude Sevigny, he lived and worked in Paris. August was his vacation month, as it is for so many of the French.

The French economy being a near-permanent basket-case, Claude was grateful for having a job at all so he did not feel too badly about being underpaid. After all, he was young and unmarried. If he could not afford train fares and hotels on his holiday, he could back-pack and camp.

So he did. And came to Nice. During the night of Tuesday, 5 August 1980, at approximately eleven-forty-five, someone held the muzzle of a 7.65 mm pistol less than six inches from his head and pulled the trigger.

Claude died instantly and without waking up. Whatever hopes, ambitions or future he had had died with him. Sadly, the subsequent police investigation gave reason to believe that he had never even had a girl friend.

Nor many friends of any kind. His life had been uneventful. He was neither gifted nor stupid. He was neither rich nor terribly poor. He had passed his secondary school examination, but without distinction. He was not ugly, but he would never make it in the movies either. Like many young Frenchmen, he was somewhat shy.

Claude Sevigny was simply one of the ten or fifteen million members of his age group, a completely average young Frenchman.

So why would someone deliberately put a bullet through his head?

The sergeant of detectives assigned to finding out why had learned all these things about Claude Sevigny by the simple expedient of requesting a background report from the Paris police. They had responded promptly and thoroughly, but the answer had left the sergeant more puzzled than before. There was no reason for anyone to kill Claude.

Except madness, a totally irrational act committed for the sake of the act itself and having nothing to do with the victim's identity.

As the sergeant pointed out in the report with which he closed the case, insanity was practically the only plausible motive. The victim had only been two days in Nice and knew no one in the area. He had had no romantic associations and very little money, less than a hundred francs, which was not enough to even eat regularly. Nor could the murderer have believed that he had money. People who spend nights in a cheap sleeping-bag laid out in a waste lot are rarely thought to be wealthy. But, even if the murderer was so stupid, why did he not take the money which he had killed to get?

The only answer, wrote the sergeant, was madness. The murder was the motive.

On the basis of past experience, it was feared that it would be repeated in the future. It had, of course, occurred to the sergeant that it might not have been the first, but a search of the records turned up no similar case in the area within the past ten years.

The sergeant, therefore, kept an eye out for new cases, and when none were reported along the Mediterranean coast, he came to the conclusion that the murderer had also been on holiday and had now gone home.

Unfortunately, the murder of Claude Sevigny aroused not much more interest with the police than with the media. The sergeant of detectives in Nice had developed a certain empathy for Claude through delving into his background, but he was practically the only police officer who knew that he had ever existed.

If he had looked along the Atlantic coast, he might have had more luck. On Thursday, 14 August, nine days after the murder of Claude Sevigny, twenty-year-old Bernard Marechal was shot to death in his sleeping-bag on a deserted beach near St Malo, an old pirate city on the coast of Brittany.

The sergeant in Nice would have recognized the circumstances immediately.

Bernard, who came from the city of Metz in the east of France, had been on holiday from his job as an apprentice plumber. He was asleep at the time he was shot through the head, twice this time, with a 7.65 mm pistol at close range. He had had almost no money and what he had was not taken. Unlike Claude Sevigny, he had had a girl friend, but she was only sixteen and their relationship had been chaste. Had she gone on holiday with him, it might have saved his life. Or cost her hers.

St Malo being a smaller place than Nice, it was an inspector from the department of criminal investigations who investigated the Marechal murder. Despite his superior rank, he was no more successful than the sergeant in Nice had been in solving his case, and eventually came to the same conclusion. The murder could only be the work of a madman. There was no motive.

The Bernard Marechal unsolved homicide joined the Claude Sevigny unsolved homicide in the memory of the central records section computer of the National Gendarmerie, and the computer no doubt recognized that the cases were similar, if not identical. However, no one asked it and so, computerlike, it held its peace.

It did not matter, in any case. There were no more clues in the Marechal case than there were in the Sevigny case.

If there were any more such killings during 1980, the reports of them did not find their way into the computer memory of the central records section.

There probably were none. Later, when efforts were made to determine the total number of victims, the computer was consulted and never came up with any numbers greater than those the police already knew. Two each for August 1980, 1981 and 1982.

That the murders fell only in this month was significant. It was the month when the murderer was on holiday and had time and opportunity for killing. The rest of the year, he was apparently too busy at his job.

As a lead, the knowledge was worthless. It merely indicated that the murderer was employed and that he took his holiday in August. This was true of around twenty million people in France.

People, because there was no proof that the murderer was a man and, as a matter of fact, the sergeant in Nice had considered the possibility of a female killer, possibly some maiden who had been wronged by a back-packer.

It was as good a theory as any, but it had a slightly comical sound to it and the sergeant did not mention it to his superiors.

What he did mention took place the following August and it was not a murder along the Mediterranean coast, but one in Normandy, which is even further to the north than St Malo. It was also not on the coast at all, but close to eighty miles inland near the town of Mondicourt.

The reason that the sergeant learned of it was that the victim came from Menton, which is just up the coast from Nice and on the border to Italy. The police in Mondicourt had requested background information in order to establish some sort of motive for the murder of twenty-four-year-old Jean-Pierre Lacosta, who had been killed on 12 August 1981 by two 7.65 mm bullets fired through his head at close range while he was asleep in his sleeping-bag. Lacosta had been unemployed and had had barely the money to buy a pack of cigarettes on him at the time.

The Mondicourt police had logically come to the conclusion that Jean-Pierre had been on more intimate terms with some lady than was conducive to his health, and this lady could only be in his home town as he had not been in Normandy long enough to render anyone jealous.

The sergeant found all this remarkably familiar and, having received a copy of the Menton police report pointing to no known motive for the murder of Lacosta, he requested further details from Mondicourt concerning the circumstances of the case.

The circumstances were nearly identical to the Sevigny murder the year before and the sergeant immediately went to the commissioner who had had responsibility for the investigation of the case.

There was, he reported, evidence of what appeared to be a weird series. As it was taking place in widely separated regions of the country, he thought that it should be turned over to the department of criminal investigations of the National Gendarmerie.

The commissioner listened to the evidence and agreed.

Two days later, the Sevigny and Lacosta cases were formally turned over to Inspector Claude Descroix, a specialist in series murders, attached to the Homicide Division of the French National Gendarmerie.

Inspector Descroix and his assistant, Detective Sergeant Yves Saint, began their investigation by consulting the records and requesting information on any similar cases from police and gendarmerie units nationwide.

They immediately received the Marechal case from both the records section computer and the St Malo police.

They had barely had time to read through the file and note the nearly identical circumstances to the Sevigny and Lacosta murders when a fourth case was reported from the Atlantic coastal city of La Rochelle. An eighteen-year-old boy had been shot through the head while asleep in a sleeping-bag.

The inspector and the sergeant left immediately for La Rochelle. The murder had taken place on Sunday, 23 August 1981, and they had received notice of it on Monday morning. By Monday afternoon, they were at the scene.

This was the first opportunity that the gendarmerie investigators had had to observe the scene of one of the crimes committed by the Back-packer Murderer so soon after it had taken place. They were hoping for some indication that the La Rochelle police might have missed. Because of their specialized training and experience in the field, they were sometimes able to draw conclusions that local police investigators were not.

It was not to be the case here. Didier Vitry, who came from the city of Lyon on the opposite side of the country, had been a secondary school student. He had had almost no money. He had been back-packing and, on that Sunday evening, he had spread out his sleeping-bag and other equipment on a beach which, although near the city, was largely deserted because the pollution level of the water was too high to permit bathing. At approximately eleven o'clock, according to the autopsy report of the La Rochelle coroner, someone had held a 7.65 mm pistol within a few inches of his left temple and pulled the trigger. The bullet had gone straight through Vitry's head and exited on the right side, taking with it some fragments of bone and a fatal quantity of brain tissue. In so far as the investigators could determine, this was the closest that the murderer had come to the victim.

There was, however, one minor difference. Vitry's personal identification card was missing.

'Let's hope he didn't lose it,' said the inspector. 'If the killer took it, it's his first mistake and we may be able to make it his last.'

He was a short, plump, cheerful-looking man with rosy cheeks and twinkling blue eyes. With a white beard and white rather than brown hair, he could have passed for Santa Claus.

His assistant was a totally nondescript man with medium brown hair, medium brown eyes, medium build and the slightly concerned air of a not very successful insurance salesman.

'I'll get out a directive to all units to keep watch for it,' he said. 'He apparently moves around a good deal so one of the spot road checks might get him.'

The French police and gendarmerie make frequent road checks of vehicles. Mostly, they are looking for drugs or terrorists, but they could look for a stolen ID card as well.

The inspector and the sergeant returned to their base to wait for further reports. They were aware that the sergeant in Nice and some of the other investigators had come to the conclusion that the Back-packer Murderer killed only during August while he was on holiday, but this was no more than a theory and, in any case, August was not yet over.

It soon was, however, and the theory appeared to be correct for there were no more cases reported that year.

Nor the next year either, up until August. With the arrival of that fatal month, Inspector Descroix and Sergeant Saint began keeping an overnight bag packed. If there was any consistency in the murderer, he would soon strike again.

So far, it had been a frustrating case for the investigators. No trace of the missing ID card had turned up and there had been nothing else to investigate. All that they had been able to do with the case during the past eleven months had been to review what the local police had already done in the four murders in the hopes that something had been missed. Nothing had been.

It was a near certainty that, with the arrival of another August, yet more unsuspecting young men would be marked down for a pointless death and there was nothing that they could do about it. Warnings had, of course, been published in the newspapers and broadcast over the radio and television stations, but they had not noticeably reduced the number of back-packers on the roads.

'They're right, of course,' said the sergeant gloomily. 'The individual risk isn't high. Say there's fifty thousand back-packers stamping around the country during August and the murderer gets two of them. More than that will be run over crossing the street in less than a week.'

'True, no doubt,' said the inspector, 'but I would prefer not to cite the statistics in an unsolved report to the commissioner. They might not be regarded as an adequate explanation by the press.'

The media were by now in full cry and their comments on the police and gendarmerie efforts were not uniformly flattering.

'We've done everything we could,' said the sergeant resignedly. 'There's nothing now except to wait.'

Unfortunately for the nerves of the investigators, the wait was long. The first three weeks of August passed without a single report of any homicide which bore the trademark of the Back-packer Murderer. There were plenty of other murders and August was far from a holiday month for police and gendarmerie, but there were no pointless killings of young men in sleeping-bags.

'He's dead!' rejoiced the sergeant. 'Probably been run over by a lorry. There's only four days left to August. Back-packers are already getting scarce.'

It was true. With the nearing of the end of the holiday month, many of the back-packers and hitch-hikers had gone home to prepare for whatever awaited them there: school, a job or a search for one.

It was also true that the case might have ended in the death or crippling of the murderer. He was obviously moving around France a good deal in the summertime and his chances of being killed in a traffic accident were far higher than his victims' chances of being murdered.

The inspector was less optimistic. Normally, he was more so than the sergeant, but this time he was troubled by a sort of premonition that they had not heard the last of the Back-packer Murderer yet. It was the sort of feeling that he had had before and it had usually proved to be accurate.

It would prove to be this time too. The inspector and the sergeant had had their conversation on the afternoon of 27 August 1982. It was a Friday and they would soon be going off duty for the weekend. Circumstances permitting, they did not work on Saturdays or Sundays.

It seemed that circumstances would permit. Nothing of urgency came in during the rest of the afternoon and they went home still wary, but largely relieved. By Monday, there would be only two days left to August and the Back-packer Murderer would have to work over-time if he hoped to get in his usual quota for the month. Even the inspector did not think he could do it.

That evening, as the inspector and the sergeant were peacefully watching television in their respective living rooms, a nineteen-year-old youth named Charles Petit was dozing off happily in his sleeping-bag, spread out in a high meadow of the Jura Mountains near Beaufort on the eastern border of France. An unemployed carpenter's mate, he was back-packing slowly down the length of France to his parents' home in Nice.

He would get there, but not by back-packing. Charles Petit would come home in a sealed coffin by rail.

For, at a little before midnight, not long after the inspector and the sergeant had switched off their tele-vision sets and gone to bed, a dark form moved silently across the meadow lit only by the glory of a million stars, bent over the sleeper and, an instant later, the quiet of the summer night was split by the vicious crack of a 7.65 mm pistol, fired twice in quick succession.

The body of the dead boy jerked reflexively and lay still.

The Back-packer Murderer had claimed his fifth victim and, despite the optimism of the investigators, he was going to meet his August quota after all.

The inspector and the sergeant knew nothing of this, however, and spent their weekend tranquilly. The body was not discovered until Monday morning.

Later, it was possible to determine that, while the inspector and the sergeant had been crossing France from west to east to the scene of the Charles Petit murder, the murderer had been crossing France from east to west from the scene of the Charles Petit murder to the scene of his final performance near the city of Bordeaux on the Atlantic coast.

He barely made it under the wire. It was just short of midnight on 31 August 1982 when the killer bent over another sleeping-bag and fired four shots from his 7.65 mm pistol through the head of twenty-six-year-old Konrad Mayer, an electrical engineer who came from the village of Werlte near Oldenburg, Germany.

Perhaps it was because he was hurrying to get in his yearly quota of murders before the end of the month or, perhaps, the routine of repetition had made him careless, but the Mayer murder was not quite as flawless as the others. Once again, the Back-packer Murderer stole his victim's ID card, an extremely foolish thing to do as Mayer was not only not French, but looked German, being big, burly and blond.

He did not steal any money, although Mayer had a good deal more with him than the other victims had had. A seasoned hiker who regarded back-packing as a sport, he had set off three weeks earlier to back-pack through the north of Italy and the south of France, and from Bordeaux would have been going home. His death was particularly tragic as he was the third of four sons to die a violent death, although the other two had been accidental.

Mayer's body was discovered early in the morning of 1 September and Inspector Descroix and Sergeant Saint, who had found nothing of value at the scene of the Charles Petit killing, went racing back across the country on the same day, harassed and, to say the least, dismayed.

But not despairing. Informed over the gendarmerie radio of the short length of time between the murder and the discovery of the body and the fact that the victim's ID card appeared to be missing, the inspector ordered that road-blocks be immediately set up in the area around the city. The case had now taken on such importance that every means available was at his disposal.

Police cars from Bordeaux and communities nearby poured into the area. Inspector and sergeant were still on their way to the scene when an arrest was made.

It was something of an anticlimax. A patrol car watching for stolen vehicles had stopped an elderly Renault R-4 bearing one of the licence numbers they were looking for. It was driven by a frail, hollow-cheeked young man whom they had asked for his identification.

Incredibly, the man had offered them the ID card of Konrad Mayer!

'But this isn't your identification card!' exclaimed the patrolman, too astonished to comprehend that this was precisely what half France was looking for.

The young man's teeth began to chatter. He had turned pale and looked as if he were about to faint. 'I'm a murderer! I'm a murderer!' he whispered in a trembling, barely audible voice.

And so he was. A timid, frightened murderer. The dreaded Back-packer Murderer was a twenty-one-year-old commercial artist who looked like the 'before' illustration for a body-building course, and the deadly 7.65 mm pistol with which he had ruthlessly executed his victims was found in his car. Ballistics tests would show it to have been the murder weapon in all six cases.

What neither ballistics nor any other kind of tests could show was why Pascal Bertrand had pulled the trigger a total of twelve times.

Bertrand, who came from the town of Stiring-Wendel in Lorraine, said first that he had killed the six young men because they were trying to rob him.

When it was pointed out that they had all been asleep at the time and that a sleeping-bag was an unusual place to stage a robbery, he changed his story and said he had shot them in self-defence when they attacked him. He was unable to say why they had attacked him or how they had managed this while asleep in a sleeping-bag.

As a matter of fact, Pascal Bertrand's explanation of the murders was not very plausible or even rational. A better explanation was offered by persons in Stiring-Wendel who had known him. They said he was crazy.

Such oversimplification is not for professional psychologists, of course. Of the many who observed Pascal Bertrand, some said that he was suffering from an inferiority complex; some that he was suffering from a superiority complex; others that his parents had failed him; that he was homosexual and had no luck with the boys; that he was heterosexual and had no luck with the girls; that he was bisexual and had no luck with either; and, of course, that he was a victim of the rotten, capitalist society, although, with the exception of Konrad Mayer, he was more affluent than any of his victims.

In one respect they agreed. He was dangerous and, if he was returned to society, it was probable that he would once again begin reducing its numbers.

He was, therefore, put quietly away in an institution, where he provides fascinating subject-matter for any number of scholarly studies and experiments in applied psychology.

And there he will remain.

Until someone comes to the conclusion that he has been cured.

6

THE GAMES GIRLS PLAY

The man standing in the charge room of the small police headquarters building in Dierdorf does not look very dangerous.

He is a short man, stockily built and hard-muscled, and, although his clean-shaven face is drawn with stress, it still bears the innocent, slightly wondering expression of the near-eastern peasant in unfamiliar surroundings.

The surroundings are not really unfamiliar. Bekaddin Bagci has spent nearly a third of his thirty years in West Germany and most of that in Dierdorf.

Even so, he speaks very little German. He does not come from a background where language skills are emphasized. For his ancestors, scratching a living out of the hard soil of Anatolia was more important than attending school, even if there were one for poor peasants in that little farming village to the south of the Turkish capital of Ankara.

Now, however, this lack of German is causing him trouble for he is trying to tell the duty sergeant something, and the duty sergeant does not speak Turkish.

Finally, the frustrated guest worker smiles apologetically, reaches over the charge desk and takes the startled sergeant by the throat with both hands.

He does not squeeze hard, but his hands are rough with manual labour and very muscular.

The sergeant reaches for his service pistol.

'Great marvel he didn't shoot him,' said Sergeant of

Detectives Klaus Berger. 'For all he knew, the fellow was as crazy as a cuckoo clock.'

'Probably couldn't get the safety catch off his gun,' said Inspector Hans Krupp, the sergeant's superior. 'Not much practice with a gun in a place like Dierdorf.'

Neither the inspector nor the sergeant were attached to the Dierdorf police, which is a modest enough organization as the village has less than five thousand inhabitants.

It was possible that there was a touch of sour grapes in the inspector's remark. Dierdorf is a quiet and lovely community snuggled into the green forest of the Westerwald. Koblenz, fourteen miles to the south, where the inspector lived, is a busy, polluted town at the junction of the Rhine and Mosel rivers. It is not, however, large, the population being under a hundred and twenty thousand.

The inspector and the sergeant had been summoned to Dierdorf because a murder had taken place there and they were the permanent members of the rural homicide squad. Villages like Dierdorf had no homicide squad and, sometimes, no criminal investigations department. It was more practical to handle such matters from the larger city with its better facilities.

As a rule, the rural homicide squad did not have a great deal to do. The Palatinate district to the west of the Rhine is mainly agricultural and lacks the large urban centres which generate so much violent crime. When a murder did take place, it was usually easy to solve as the identity of the murderer was obvious, even if he or she had not immediately come to the police to confess. The main task of the homicide squad then consisted of establishing the circumstances so that the appropriate charge could be brought at the trial.

The charge was rarely murder. Almost exclusively concerned with the rights of the accused, the German judicial system imposes so many conditions for a murder charge that the accused would have to carry out his crime with the Criminal Code in one hand to make certain that he did not inadvertently provide the court with some excuse to reduce the charge to manslaughter.

The inspector was not anticipating any particular problem with this case. The chief of the Dierdorf police had telephoned to say that a Turkish guest worker had strangled his wife and come in to the station to report it. As he had been unable to make the duty sergeant understand what he wanted to report, he had demonstrated on the sergeant's neck and nearly got himself shot for his pains.

After the misunderstanding at the station had been cleared up, a team of officers went with the Turk to his third-floor apartment at 17 Ziegelei Strasse and reported back that the nude corpse of a young woman was lying on the floor of the living room. She had been dead for some time and, as her pubic area was depilated, they assumed that she was Turkish.

Nobody in the Dierdorf police spoke Turkish, but everybody knew that Turkish women removed their body hair.

One of the officers remained to guard the apartment and the other returned to police headquarters with the Turk, who was put in the detention cells.

This was clearly a matter for the rural homicide unit and the inspector and sergeant had set out immediately for Dierdorf, bringing with them the department's medical expert, Dr Leopold Finkbinder, a small, meticulous man with such a huge, curving moustache that he looked like a water buffalo about to charge.

The doctor was now examining the body and the inspector and sergeant were wandering aimlessly about the remarkably clean and tidy two-bedroom apartment, looking for nothing in particular and finding it. When the doctor had finished, they would pick up the Turk and take him to Koblenz, where an interpreter would be available for him to make his confession.

'Apparently liked loose clothing,' remarked the

sergeant, picking up an enormous pair of split-crotch lace panties from a chair near the living-room door. 'Either she imported them from Turkey or she had them tailor-made. You couldn't buy something this size in a shop.'

'And she couldn't have worn it either,' said the inspector. 'She'd have fallen through the thing. It wouldn't be a tight fit on a hippopotamus.'

'Well, then . . . ?' said the sergeant. He was a tousle-headed, dark-blond man in his late twenties with a wide mouth and a turned-up nose. He did not look very serious and the inspector privately thought him amusing.

'Then there was someone else here,' said the inspector. 'The fellow – what's his name? Baggy?'

'Bagci,' said the sergeant, consulting the first information report form which he had picked up at the Dierdorf station. 'Bekaddin Bagci.'

'Easier to pronounce than most,' said the inspector. 'Well, Bagci must have got himself a queen-size girl friend. German maybe. I doubt that the Turks grow them this big. Anyway, this here is his wife and she didn't like the idea so he strangled her.'

'Sounds logical,' said the sergeant. 'About the same as Germans. The only difference is we'll have to have the confession translated.'

The doctor had now completed his work at the scene and reported that the woman, presumed to be Mrs Bagci, had been strangled to death manually at around three or four o'clock of that same morning. She had been punched in the face several times, but not very hard. Otherwise, there were no injuries. She had apparently not attempted to defend herself, for he could find no traces of skin or hair under her fingernails.

'Her final moments were not entirely unhappy,' concluded the doctor. 'The indications are that she was in a state of intense sexual excitement at the time of her death.'

The sergeant looked questioningly at the inspector.

The victim being in a state of sexual excitement at the time of the murder did not tie in very well with the theory they had just been discussing.

The inspector looked thoughtful. He was a large, well-nourished man, carefully groomed and with a smooth, bland, rather expressionless face.

'Maybe this isn't Mrs Bagci after all,' he said finally.

But it was. Mrs Zuheylan Bagci, aged twenty-six and, since 8 July 1977, wife of Bekaddin Bagci, factory worker, resident in Dierdorf at 17 Ziegelei Strasse.

That was about all that Bekaddin Bagci was prepared to reveal in his confession, which had been duly made and translated. Other than that his wife was an angel and he was very, very sorry that he had killed her. He had, he said, lost his temper.

Over what, he would not say. Nor would he comment on the giant split-crotch panties in his living room. When questioned, he merely looked blank and did not reply.

In the meantime, the autopsy of the corpse of Zuheylan Bagci had been carried out and Dr Finkbinder confirmed his original impression that the victim had been engaged in sexual activities on a level which he thought near the limit of human endurance. In his opinion, Mrs Bagci had been suffering from an extreme case of nymphomania.

The inspector found himself faced with a very puzzling case, for the doctor had also stated in the autopsy report that he had recovered no trace of semen in or on the body, but a great many traces of saliva which stemmed from at least two persons.

The conclusion was obvious: Mrs Bagci had been engaged exclusively in oral sex prior to her death.

What was not obvious was with whom.

Presumably, with Mr Bagci and the owner of the tent-like panties, but who was this person and what had gone wrong with what now looked like a three-way sex party?

In modern, emancipated Germany, sex parties are not uncommon, even in a place like Dierdorf, and it is not uncommon either for them to end in homicide. Since the media proclaimed the sexual revolution a few years earlier, many middle-class and middle-aged Germans were giving group sex a try and discovering that, media to the contrary, sexual jealousy continued to exist.

'But these were not Germans,' said the inspector irritably. 'Did you ever hear of guest workers going in for this sort of thing? They're too conservative.'

'The Bagcis have been here a long time,' said the sergeant. 'Maybe they became integrated. You want to see the background report?'

The inspector did. It was actually a composite report made up from several sources, including interviews with relatives of Bekaddin Bagci and his late wife, from which the sergeant had extracted the salient facts.

Zuheylan, it seemed, was also a long-time resident of Dierdorf, having gone to work in a factory there at the age of sixteen.

She and Bekaddin, who worked in another factory, had actually met in Dierdorf, although they both came from the same village in Turkey.

The wedding had been celebrated in Turkey and Bekaddin had been the envy of the bachelors of the village, as Zuheylan was not only very pretty and magnificently built, but was considered to be intelligent and a good housekeeper.

This last could be confirmed by the police personally. They had examined the spic and span apartment, which building superintendent Oscar Hellmich said was kept permanently in that state. The Bagcis, he asserted in his statement to the police, had been excellent tenants, being quiet, clean and having few visitors. Asked about sex parties, he expressed great doubt that there had been any.

Had it not been for the evidence uncovered by the autopsy, the police would have been inclined to doubt it also. The Bagcis had known everybody in the Turkish community, of course, but they had had no close friends and, although Mrs Bagci had spoken reasonably good German, her husband's lack of the language practically eliminated any possibility of social contact with the local inhabitants, little inclined to mix with the guest workers in any case.

Following the wedding in Turkey, the couple had returned to Dierdorf and continued with their factory jobs. From that time until the morning following the murder on 17 December 1979, only two incidents appeared in the record.

On 4 March 1978, Zuheylan Bagci had been admitted to the Dierdorf hospital for treatment of bruises and scratches on her face, hands and breasts. They were not serious and, following treatment, she was sent home.

And, on 1 February 1979, Bekaddin Bagci had lost his job at the factory. Since that date, he had been taking unofficial odd jobs, but the bulk of the family income was being provided by Zuheylan, who was still working.

'There is obviously something missing here,' said the inspector, handing the background report back to the sergeant. 'If this is all there is, there was no reason for Bagci to kill his wife and she must, therefore, still be alive.'

He was a man given to carrying logic to illogical lengths.

'Maybe there was,' said the sergeant. 'You recall Finkbinder's report on Bagci's physical examination? The man must have been half-mad from sheer frustration.'

Bekaddin Bagci having been formally indicted for the murder of his wife, the police could carry out an examination of him with or without his consent. But he had, as a matter of fact, cooperated willingly – as, indeed, he did in all phases of the investigation that did not touch on his motives for the murder.

According to Dr Finkbinder, Bagci was a sexual bomb on the verge of exploding. A healthy, normal man in the prime of life, he had, said the doctor, not obtained any form of sexual relief in months.

The inspector had found this a little hard to swallow, but the doctor's statement had been confirmed by none other than Bagci himself. No, he had told the inspector, he had not had intercourse with his wife for nearly two months and he could not go to a prostitute because he was a married man.

'And this is the fellow who was supposed to have been holding sex orgies in his apartment?' said the inspector. 'The further we get into this case, the stranger it is. But you're right: Bagci must have been under tremendous pressure, living with a beautiful, oversexed wife with whom he could not, for some reason or other, have intercourse. Maybe it has something to do with the woman with the monstrous underwear.'

'I think so,' said the sergeant, 'and I've got every man available trying to identify her. It's almost certain that she isn't Turkish. I've checked the entire community in Dierdorf and there isn't a woman among them to fit those pants.'

'Shouldn't be many in the German community either, I would think,' said the inspector. 'If any detective ever had a fat lead to investigate, you do.'

The inspector's manner might be facetious, but it did not mean that he failed to regard the case seriously. He was a conscientious man and, for Bekaddin Bagci, a great deal depended upon the results of the investigation.

As things now stood, he would be tried on a charge of murder and, as he had confessed and showed no inclination to retract his confession, he would be convicted and given a heavy sentence, especially as there were no known extenuating circumstances.

Of course, if Bagci had ruthlessly murdered his wife over some triviality, he deserved a heavy sentence, but that was not the impression that the inspector had gained during the course of their interviews. Rather, he thought him a simple, sober sort of man with no tendency to violence who had been subjected to greater pressure than he could bear. There was no doubting his sincere sorrow over the death of his wife.

Although he could not convince Bagci of it, it was vitally important to determine what that pressure had been for the German Criminal Code stated:

> If the slayer through no fault of his or her own was incited to rage through mistreatment or grave insult to him or her self or a dependent person and, thereby, lost control of his or her faculties of judgement or if there were other mitigating circumstances, the charge shall be manslaughter and the sentence may range from six months' to a maximum of five years' imprisonment.

The difference was, therefore, between five years maximum and a possible life sentence, although a full life sentence is almost never served in Germany today, with the possible exception of persons convicted of crimes involving money.

There was no money in this case, but there was the very large clue remarked upon by the inspector, and the sergeant spared no effort to uncover the identity of its owner, whom, he thought, he could recognize on sight.

The first thing he was able to determine was that the panties had not been purchased in Dierdorf. No shop there carried such a size and some of the shop owners expressed disbelief that such a size existed.

It did, however, and the sergeant was eventually able to determine that such remarkable garments were sold mostly by mail-order houses specializing in sex toys, pornography and other modern forms of entertainment.

He was not able to locate the mail-order house which had sold this particular garment and it appeared probable that it had gone out of business. So many people had entered the field following the sexual revolution that the market was not sufficiently large to support all of them.

Having failed here, the sergeant set his men to

canvassing the neighbourhood of the Bagci apartment house. The woman had definitely been in the building, as she had left her pants there. Perhaps someone had seen her and knew who she was.

In one of the oversights which so often plague criminal investigations, the sergeant failed to question the building superintendent, Oscar Hellmich. Hellmich had already made a statement to the police and the sergeant assumed that, if he had not made any mention of fat women in the building at that time, it was because he had not known of any.

Fortunately, Hellmich learned of the police canvass and the object of it and came voluntarily to the Dierdorf police station to report that he knew of a fat woman who had often visited the building and could, for all he knew, have been visiting the Bagcis. He did not keep very careful track of who came and went as this was not included in his duties.

In any case, he said, the woman was not all that fat. She was a fine figure of a woman and no frail slip of a girl, but there were others fatter than she. Her name, he added almost casually, was Berta Schlupper and she could often be found at a local bar called the Pink Pussy.

The information astounded the sergeant, who had now spent enough time snooping around Dierdorf to know what the Pink Pussy Tavern was.

It was a purely homosexual hangout, and not just any homosexuals, but exclusively female ones, although not all of the patrons would have agreed to this definition of their gender.

'What in heaven's name does that mean?' said the sergeant. 'I've asked around and this Berta Schlupper is a notorious lesbian, but what were her pants doing in the Bagci apartment?'

'She sure as hell wasn't visiting Bagci,' said the inspector. 'Mrs Bagci must have been a lesbian and, if she was, that explains a lot of things.'

'Such as why Bagci was married to a beautiful, over-

'sexed wife and hadn't had sex for two months,' said the sergeant.

'And why Mrs Bagci was in a state of extreme sexual excitement at the time of her death, but without a trace of semen on her,' said the inspector.

'And even why Bagci won't discuss the motive for the murder,' said the sergeant. 'He's ashamed. Probably looks on female homosexuality as something perverted.'

'Well, it is,' said the inspector mildly. 'You can't maintain that it's normal. He probably came home unexpectedly and caught them red-handed. Berta took off, leaving her pants, and Bagci was so outraged and amazed that he punched his wife around a couple of times and then strangled her to death. Comes clearly under the manslaughter provisions of the code. He should get off with three or four years.'

'If we can prove it,' said the sergeant. 'I wouldn't think that Miss Schlupper would be anxious to testify in court that she was having an affair with Bagci's wife.'

But the sergeant was wrong. Thirty-eight-year-old Berta Schlupper was not in the least embarrassed at testifying to her homosexual relationship with Zuheylan Bagci, neither to the police nor later before the court. As she said, everyone she knew was aware that she was a lesbian, anyway.

Despite the impressive size of her underwear, Miss Schlupper was not an unattractive woman and she had been, she boasted, the Turkish woman's preferred partner.

Not, however, her only partner. According to Miss Schlupper and another lesbian, thirty-year-old Monika Fischbach, who also described herself as Zuheylan's preferred partner, the lovely Turk had been insatiable in her lust for love.

But only the love of women. Sex relations with men she found disgusting, and this included her husband.

This was only logical because Zuheylan considered herself to be a man and invariably took the male role

607

in her relations with Berta, Monika and a good many others.

Her sexual preferences had been established as a child as far back as she could remember. She had had female lovers before she even met Bekaddin.

She had liked him in a man-to-man sort of way as long as they were not married, but had vigorously discouraged his courtship.

Bekaddin, who had taken this for commendable maidenly reserve, had gone to ask for her hand from her father, who, having investigated Bekaddin's background and work record, had granted it and had quite simply ordered his daughter to marry him.

Zuheylan might be unconventional in her sexual preferences, but disobedience to her father was out of the question and she had married, reluctantly and with great misgivings.

The misgivings were fully justified. Bekaddin's torment had begun on his wedding night when his wife ate an apple and thumbed through a magazine while he was engaged in making love to her.

And this was only the beginning. The relationship between the couple had got steadily worse and Zuheylan was soon refusing her husband his marital rights for months on end.

She had continued with her homosexual activities, becoming increasingly more blatant as her feelings of friendship toward Bekaddin passed from indifference through dislike to hatred.

She had taken to bringing her lesbian lovers home with her and engaging in sex with them in the very presence of her husband. After he had lost his job and was partially dependent upon her financially, she sometimes forced him to sleep on a cot in the kitchen while she shared the bed with her lover.

Bekaddin had stormed and threatened, but to no avail. He did not understand what was wrong with his wife and held the German women responsible for seducing her. Hopelessly in love, he could not accept that Zuheylan actively preferred women partners to himself.

There had been terrible quarrels, but Bekaddin had never beaten Zuheylan. The time that she had been admitted to the hospital, her injuries were due to a scuffle among lesbians to determine who really was her preferred partner.

The matter had not been settled. Zuheylan could not be true to a single partner because the fire that burned in her was too strong for any single person, man or woman.

On the night of the murder, according to Berta Schlupper, Zuheylan promised her husband that she would come home by midnight and allow him his ration of sex. It had been six weeks since their last encounter.

Zuheylan, however, did not keep her promise and spent the night with two lesbians, leaving them both exhausted. She then sought out Berta and asked her to accompany her home as she was not yet sated and she could hope for no satisfaction from her husband.

Berta came. She knew Bekaddin and had actually lived for a time in the apartment with the Bagcis, until the quarrels had became too much for her.

Zuheylan assured her there would be no quarrel that night or, rather, that morning as it was by now nearly four o'clock.

They went to the apartment and found Bekaddin asleep in the bedroom, but he awakened when Zuheylan went in to take off her clothes and hang them up. She was a woman of tidy habits.

Berta remained in the living room and removed her underwear. She knew Zuheylan to be impetuous and she did not want it torn off.

Zuheylan returned to the living room, with Bekaddin following her. As Berta spoke no Turkish she did not know what they said, but Bekaddin was so vehement that she became nervous. He was, she thought, losing his mind and she had never before seen him in such a state.

Without stopping to pick up her pants, she ran out of the apartment and down the stairs. Even from the hall below, she could hear the voices of the raging Turks.

She had, she said, not been at all surprised when she learned that Bekaddin had murdered Zuheylan. It was something which everyone knew was sure to happen sooner or later.

Bekaddin Bagci confirmed generally the testimony of Berta Schlupper and the other lesbian lovers of his wife, but insisted that it was they who were entirely to blame. His wife, he wept, had been an innocent angel.

Whether she had been an angel previously, she was, presumably, one now, and the responsibility for her apotheosis lay with Bekaddin Bagci.

It was a responsibility which Bagci did not deny and one which the court could not ignore completely. Although sympathy for the tormented Turk was great, he was found guilty of manslaughter and, on 21 November 1980, sentenced to four and a half years' imprisonment.

The sentence was not appealed and he did not appear to regard it as too harsh.

Said Bekaddin Bagci, good Mohammedan, 'I fear God and I fear those women.'

7

MAKING A NEW START

Definitions are tiresome and often not very satisfactory, but it may be necessary to define what 'deviate' is.

The common understanding of the term is a person who is sexually abnormal, although it is becoming increasingly difficult to say precisely what abnormal is. There have been some outstanding experts in the field of psychology who maintain that nothing is sexually abnormal, which leads to the dubious proposition that a man who must disembowel his partner in order to achieve sexual satisfaction is behaving normally.

Many would think not, but what about bizarre actions which are not connected with sex? Is a person whose behaviour is so abnormal that few or none can understand it a deviate?

A difficult question and one which would no doubt give rise to controversy in some quarters.

It might be said that such persons were not deviates, but insane.

But there are persons who are not insane and know perfectly well what they are doing whose behaviour is still unintelligible to most or all of us.

Are they deviates?

The general definition is tedious, specific cases perhaps less so. So it may prove instructive to ponder the behaviour of the remarkable Mr Raupach, whose actions were rational and intelligible, but whose motives were not.

Or perhaps they were. No one knows what Mr

Raupach had in mind on that summer morning of 1983, apparently not even Mr Raupach.

It was a Friday, 8 July, and Heinz-Dietmar Raupach, a thirty-six-year-old employee of the Dresden Bank in the West German city of Frankfurt am Main, having pressed a husbandly kiss on his wife, said, 'Take care. See you this evening,' and departed in his beloved yellow Mercedes 280S for work. The time was shortly before eight.

As this was what Heinz-Dietmar said and did every morning of the week, Mrs Monika Raupach was not unduly impressed. An attractive, religious woman of thirty-three, she was the mother of two fine children, aged ten and eleven, and she worked half days at a local delicatessen. She and Heinz-Dietmar had been married since 5 April 1969 and she regarded her marriage as successful and happy. There were no financial problems. The total family income was fully adequate to provide for a comfortable scale of living.

There had, of course, been a little disturbance three years earlier when Heinz-Dietmar had confessed that he was having an affair with one of the neighbours, but he had vigorously rejected her offer of a divorce and she assumed that the matter had been laid to rest. She had not understood Heinz-Dietmar's misstep very well. She knew the neighbour and she was not only less attractive than herself, but fifteen years older to boot. Heinz-Dietmar, she thought, could have done better if he had set his mind to it.

None of these thoughts crossed the mind of Monika Raupach on that July morning. The matter had long since been settled and required no further thought. If Heinz-Dietmar sometimes showed a tendency to stray from the path of marital righteousness, well, the church did not approve, but, after all, they had been married for nearly fifteen years and, anyway, half the married men in Dietzenbach had a little something going on the side.

Monika Raupach, therefore, went cheerfully about her usual duties, working until noon at the delicatessen, preparing lunch for the children and then getting on with the afternoon's housework.

It was a little after three o'clock when she noticed that her husband's summer suits were not hanging in the wardrobe.

Monika found this strange, and she found it stranger still when she discovered that Heinz-Dietmar's suitcases, the ones which he always took on holiday, were also missing.

Troubled by a growing premonition, Monika checked the drawer in the living room where the family papers were kept.

Heinz-Dietmar's personal identity card and his passport were not there.

Monika Raupach laid down her duster and picked up the telephone. She dialled the number of her husband's office with a heart that was beginning to beat a little more rapidly than usual.

The news from the office did nothing to slow it. Mr Raupach was not there. He was gone for three weeks' holiday.

Monika Raupach's next call was to Pieta Schreiber. She did not, however, expect an answer. Mrs Schreiber was the forty-eight-year-old neighbour with whom Heinz-Dietmar had been diverting himself three years earlier.

To her astonishment, Pieta Schreiber was at home. No, she had not seen Heinz-Dietmar. No, she did not know where he was. And, what was more, she did not care. Click of broken connection.

Monika Raupach sat down weakly on the sofa. Something had happened with Heinz-Dietmar, but what? Had he left her? Was he with another woman? What was the matter with the man?

After a time it occurred to her that her husband had only gone on three weeks' vacation and that he would

613

have to return then or lose his job. In three weeks she would know. She was a patient woman. She could wait.

It was, however, five days short of a month before Monika next heard from Heinz-Dietmar, and it was not because he had returned from holiday, but because he had written her a letter.

There was no return address on it, but it was post-marked Innsbruck, Austria, and it had been mailed on 1 August.

It was not really a letter, but a sort of farewell note. In it, he said that Monika would never see him again. He was planning to commit suicide.

Monika did not know what to do. She did not think that planning to commit suicide was a violation of the law, so there was no point in going to the police. In the end, she went to the pastor of her church, who did not know what to do either, but comforted her with the assurance that things would be better in the next world.

Monika was not, however, going to get to the next world as quickly as her husband for, three days later, on the night of 6 August, a twenty-year-old motorcycle rider named Peter Funk came roaring up to the head-quarters of the Innsbruck gendarmerie to report that there was a car off the road near the village of Tulfes and it was burning like a torch.

A gendarmerie rescue squad set off immediately, although the time was two-thirty in the morning. During the months of July and August, the main road leading down from Germany through Innsbruck to the Brenner Pass is bumper to bumper with cars, and accidents take place round the clock.

The scene of this accident was not, however, the main road, but an isolated, very winding, secondary road which led from the small village of Hall to the smaller village of Tulfes. Five hundred yards from the point where the road entered Tulfes, there was a hairpin bend with a grassy slope below. A hundred and fifty yards down the slope stood a car which, even by the time that the gendarmerie party reached the scene, was still burning in a solid column of flame.

There was, of course, nothing that the gendarmes could do about it. Through the flames and smoke, they could see what appeared to be a human form behind the steering wheel, but anyone in the car would be long since dead. All that remained was to wait until the fire had burned itself out and then attempt to identify the victim.

That proved to be not too difficult. The car was a 1977 yellow Mercedes 280S with the German licence plate number OF-DR515 and, as German licence numbers indicate the locality in which the car is registered, a single telephone call was enough to determine that it had been the property of Heinz-Dietmar Raupach.

'Had been' because there was less remaining of Heinz-Dietmar than of the car. He was as thoroughly cooked as a barbecued pig, a blackened crust covering the medium to well-done flesh beneath. Nothing could be discerned, neither features, fingers nor anything that protruded from what looked more like a carbonized log than a human body.

None the less, enough for an identification had survived. A small patch of medium-brown hair where Raupach's scalp had pressed against the headrest remained. A wedding ring with the inscription 'Monika. 5.4.69' was on the stump of a finger. A key marked 'Dresden Bank' was recovered from the floor, together with a size nine and a half shoe. And on the ground near the front of the car was a German Army T-shirt, later identified by Monika Raupach as a rag which her husband had kept in the car to wipe condensation off the windscreen.

The identification was completed and the body was shipped back to Dietzenbach in a sealed coffin. The widow was not permitted to view the corpse and wept copiously at the funeral, as did the children and other relatives of the deceased.

Heinz-Dietmar Raupach had, it seemed, carried out

his suicide threat. When the local police asked his wife to make a statement concerning what Raupach had been doing in Austria for the Innsbruck gendarmerie file, she showed them the suicide note, which they photocopied and sent along with the report.

They assumed that the report would close the gendarmerie case, but, in fact, it opened it. The gendarmes had been looking upon Raupach's death as an accident, and with good reason, for the autopsy had shown that the victim's blood had contained enough alcohol to pickle a horse.

This, in turn, explained how Raupach had managed to go off the road at a point where in the history of the gendarmerie, there had never before been an accident.

Going off the road at this point was actually rather difficult. The hairpin bend forced a driver to slow to a near crawl and, even if the vehicle did wander off the paving and on to the grassy slope beside it, bringing it back on to the road was a simple matter. There were tyre marks in the grass showing that this had happened on several occasions in the past.

The yellow Mercedes had, however, continued in a straight line down the slope, come to a stop and burst into flames. As far as could be determined, it had not struck anything and it had not turned over.

'Then, why did it catch fire?' said Captain Aldo Mueller.

The question was directed at Gendarmerie Sergeant Franz Gustl, a very large young man with short blond hair and, at the moment, a rather hang-dog expression. The sergeant had conducted the investigation into the accident which had taken the life of Heinz-Dietmar Raupach.

'The assumption was,' said the sergeant, 'that he was drunk and smoking a cigarette. He passed out after rounding the hairpin bend and the car rolled off the road and down the slope. The cigarette fell on his clothes or something else inflammable and set the car on fire.'

616

'Whose assumption?' said the captain. He was a hard-muscled, hard-jawed, hard-driving officer who was known to his subordinates as fair, but not easy.

'Well – uh – mine,' said the sergeant. 'And Dr Sacher's, of course.'

Dr Albert Sacher was the gendarmerie medical officer who had performed the autopsy on the corpse of Heinz-Dietmar Raupach.

'Tell Sacher I want to talk to him,' said the captain. 'And come back. I want you in on this too.'

The sergeant did as he was told and, as the doctor's office was on the floor below, returned very promptly. He did not know what was bothering the captain, but he had an uneasy feeling that he was going to be held responsible for something.

The doctor was troubled with no such feelings. A dark and hairy little man with a snappish manner, he seated himself on the arm of the chair in front of the captain's desk, pointed out that he had a great deal to do at this particular time of year and asked what the captain wanted.

The captain silently handed him the statement which the Dietzenbach police had taken from Mrs Raupach.

The doctor read it. 'Well?' he said, handing it back.

'It wasn't an accident,' said the captain, passing the statement on to the sergeant.

'So?' said the doctor. 'Change the entry on the death certificate to suicide. You can do that on receipt of additional information.'

'But was it suicide?' said the captain.

'It wasn't old age,' said the doctor. 'The man burned to death.'

'And he was so determined that he simply sat there and burned to death without making any attempt to get out of the car?' said the captain. 'Quite a demonstration of will-power. Or was he so drunk that he didn't even feel it?'

The doctor looked suddenly thoughtful, got up, walked around the chair and sat down in it.

'No,' he said. 'He wasn't that drunk. He had close to three parts in a thousand alcohol content in the bloodstream, but the man was German. Unless he was a real freak, he'd have built up a tolerance from swilling beer. He'd have felt the fire.'

'Do you think he'd have the strength to sit there and burn consciously?' said the captain.

'No,' said the doctor.

'My conclusion also,' said the captain. 'Sergeant Gustl, I want you to reopen the investigation into this case, and let's not go about it quite so light-heartedly this time. Dismiss.'

'Dismiss' meant get out, and the sergeant got out. But, after a decent interval of time, he returned to ask if the captain had anything specific in mind as to what he was supposed to investigate. He could not see that it made a great deal of difference whether Raupach had died as the result of an accident or whether he had killed himself.

'You might begin by trying to determine if this *was* Raupach,' said the captain. 'Contact the German police and see what he had in the way of insurance.'

'Holy cats!' said the sergeant in an awe-struck voice. 'You think he murdered somebody for the insurance!'

'I think there's something very funny about this accident or suicide or whatever it is,' said the captain. 'What was Raupach doing here in the first place? The Dietzenbach police said he was on holiday. Since when do people go on holiday to commit suicide? If the man was here, he had some reason to be here. Find out what it was.'

The sergeant had no idea how he was to do this, but he did not dare ask. After thinking the matter over a little and sending off a request to the Dietzenbach police for information on the late Heinz-Dietmar's financial circumstances and the height of his insurance policy, if

618

any, he went out to the scene of the accident and walked around Tulfes, asking if anyone had seen a yellow Mercedes or if anyone there knew a German named Heinz-Dietmar Raupach.

To his surprise, a farmer named Walter Grumann said that he had seen a yellow Mercedes pass along the road at least twice within the past week. It was a rather conspicuous car.

Grumann seemed to be unusually observant and the sergeant took him into the local tavern, bought him a drink and questioned him about what else he might have noticed.

He had been doubtful as to whether he could safely include the drink on an expense voucher, but it turned out to be worth paying for himself.

Grumann said that he had not only seen the yellow Mercedes twice, but he had seen the driver of it in another car, a blue Volkswagen Rabbit with an Austrian licence plate. It had been moving slowly along the road to Hall, and on the evening of the accident he had seen it parked beyond the hairpin curve.

The sergeant was intrigued. Was he absolutely certain that it had been the same driver?

Absolutely, said Grumann. A big fellow, six feet or more, heavy built with brown hair. He had not looked like a local Austrian.

The sergeant did not ask what a local Austrian was supposed to look like, but hurried back to his office and sent off another request to the Dietzenbach police. He had seen Raupach only as a blackened stump. He wanted a picture of him as he had been alive.

The Dietzenbach police, somewhat puzzled by the Austrian gendarmerie's interest in a suicide victim, obtained a recent picture of Raupach from the widow and sent it down to Innsbruck.

Grumann recognized it immediately.

All of this took a little time, but, while waiting, the

sergeant had been busy and had identified the blue Volkswagen Rabbit.

He had guessed that it would be a rental car and it was. Raupach had rented it in Innsbruck on 4 August, using his own name, and had not yet returned it.

The sergeant did not inform the agency that the client was presumed dead and there was no telling what had happened to their car. Instead, he said that, if the client came to turn in the vehicle, they were to attempt to detain him and notify the gendarmerie at once.

The instructions to the agency were merely a precaution. The sergeant did not think that Raupach was liable to turn in the car. Wherever he had gone, he had taken it with him.

And, if there was no other reason to believe that Heinz-Dietmar Raupach was still alive, the missing Volkswagen was evidence enough.

It was, the sergeant thought, now fairly clear what had happened.

Raupach, probably with the collusion of his wife, had attempted an elaborate insurance swindle. Insured to the eyes, he had murdered someone resembling himself and had burned him up in the car. The blue Volkswagen had been the get-away vehicle to which he had transferred after torching the Mercedes. Back in Dietzenbach, the spurious widow was now happily collecting the insurance, and once things had quietened down a little, would be discreetly off to join her husband, risen, so to speak, from the dead.

Captain Mueller was impressed with this theory of the case and pointed out that it could also explain why Raupach's Army T-shirt had been found outside the car. Raupach had used it for a fuse after soaking the interior of the vehicle with petrol.

He immediately ordered a search of the missing-person reports for a six-foot-tall man with brown hair who had disappeared after 6 August with a view to identifying the victim, but the operation did not produce the anticipated results.

There was no missing-person report of a six-foot-tall man with brown hair for the period in question. Not in Austria. Not in Switzerland. Not in Italy. Not in Germany.

The police report from Dietzenbach did not improve matters.

Heinz-Dietmar had been insured for the trifling sum of three and a half thousand pounds. The car had not been insured at all and was not even completely paid for. There was still outstanding some three thousand pounds and, as Monika Raupach had co-signed for the credit, she was obliged to pay it.

That and another three thousand pounds in cheques which Heinz-Dietmar had written on their nearly empty joint account during the period 8 July to 6 August.

Monika Raupach was, without question, in dire financial straits and there was no way in which she or anyone else could have made a penny out of the death of her husband.

'It must have been Raupach after all,' said the captain. 'He didn't murder somebody. Somebody murdered him. That's why there's no missing-person report.'

'But it was Raupach who rented the Volkswagen,' said the sergeant. 'He had to show his ID card and licence.'

'No,' said the captain. 'It was somebody who looked like him. Raupach must already have been dead. The fellow was using his papers to cover the murder.'

'Sacher said the victim was burned to death in the car,' said the sergeant.

'Sacher must be wrong, or the murderer was maybe holding Raupach prisoner somewhere until he could complete his plans to burn him up,' said the captain.

'Why?' said the sergeant.

The captain opened his mouth, left it open for a moment and closed it again. 'You're right,' he said. 'There's no reason.'

There was more wrong with the case than a lack of motive. Where, for example, was the blue Volkswagen Rabbit now? Where had the murderer been holding Raupach until the time came to burn him up? How had he managed to keep him in the car and behind the wheel while he set fire to it? Dr Sacher was positive that the fire had been the cause of death and that there were no traces of any restraints on the victim's body.

Finally, what had Heinz-Dietmar had in mind when he ran off to Austria, wrote his wife a suicide note and issued three thousand pounds' worth of rubber cheques?

That, at least, could be investigated, for there was a record of where each cheque had been cashed. Whoever had cashed them would have been in contact with Raupach, for the bank in Dietzenbach was completely positive that the signatures on the cheques were his.

Raupach had moved around, it seemed. He had stayed in a sort of luxury tavern called the Bierwirt in the town of Amras, where he had been accompanied by an attractive young lady who could not now be located. He had stayed at the resort hotel Kupfer-Pfandl with a twenty-nine-year-old barmaid named Helena Kropski, who could be located, but who told the gendarmes that she had not even known her companion's first name. He had been a customer in the bar. He drove a yellow Mercedes with a German licence plate. He was generous and sexually not a freak. That was all.

Further cheques had been issued in Merano, Italy, and Athens, Greece. Heinz-Dietmar had had a weakness for luxury hotels and an aversion to sleeping alone in them.

'He certainly had a wonderful time before he got himself murdered,' remarked Captain Mueller, 'but he would have made things easier for us if he had kept a little of the money instead of spending all of it.'

Calculated on the basis of cheques cashed and sums spent, Heinz-Dietmar had had very little cash left at the time of his death, which fact effectively eliminated the captain's last hope of establishing any plausible motive.

Sergeant Gustl remained silent. Almost any theory that had been advanced or could be advanced had turned out to be full of holes, and he felt the less he said, the better.

'Nothing more we can do now,' continued the captain. 'We'll just have to wait until the Volkswagen turns up, if it ever does.'

The licence number of the rented Volkswagen had been turned over to Interpol, and, if it was found, it might be possible to pick up the trail from there.

Neither the captain nor the sergeant was very optimistic on this score. The driver would be heading south. He was, perhaps, by now in the Middle East or Africa.

But the gendarmes were mistaken. The blue Volkswagen was not heading south, but north, and on 29 September, Mrs Monika Raupach was summoned to the Dietzenbach police station.

'Mrs Raupach,' said the inspector who received her, 'I will be blunt. Your husband is alive.'

Monika Raupach stared at him with bulging eyes. 'I don't believe you!' she said weakly.

The inspector made a sign and a door leading to another office opened part way. Standing there was Heinz-Dietmar Raupach.

Monika staggered and clutched at the inspector for support.

'What does this mean, Heinz-Dietmar?' she blurted in a hoarse whisper. 'Are you coming back to us now?'

'Never,' said Heinz-Dietmar Raupach and closed the door.

Mrs Raupach fainted.

The inspector himself had nearly fainted when Raupach walked into the police station and calmly announced who he was. Having been kept abreast of the case by the Innsbruck gendarmerie, the Dietzenbach police believed Raupach to be dead.

That, it seemed, was what Raupach wanted everyone to believe and he had succeeded admirably. The plan for staging his own death had been perfect.

The only thing wrong with it was that it was pointless. Raupach gained nothing at all from his disappearance or from the murder.

For, as he admitted freely, it was murder. The body in the car was that of a casual drinking companion whom he picked up at the railway station bar in Innsbruck. He never knew his name or anything about him, but chose him simply because he was about his own size and appearance.

That the man had not been reported missing was not strange. European railway station bars are normally a social centre for lonely single men with neither family nor connections. If one disappears no one notices or cares.

Raupach said the murder had been committed in self-defence when the man attacked him. He gave him a karate chop and, seeing that it had killed him, became frightened and decided to fake an accident.

He was unable to explain how he had happened to rent the Volkswagen two days earlier and have it conveniently parked where he could leave with it after setting fire to the Mercedes.

In fact, Heinz-Dietmar was unable to explain any of his actions. He could not explain why he had so carefully plotted his disappearance. He could not explain why he had decided to return. He had simply been fed up with his life and had wanted a change, he said.

In that respect, he was successful. After a relatively short trial which left more questions unanswered than otherwise, Heinz-Dietmar was found guilty of the German judiciary's favourite charge of manslaughter. On 3 October 1984, he was sentenced to thirteen years in prison, where his life is totally different from what it was previously.

Monika Raupach obtained a divorce, returned the

insurance money and settled down to paying off her husband's debts, for which she was, of course, held legally responsible.

And nobody ever knew the name of the lonely man who had sought a little human warmth in the drab surroundings of a railway station bar and had been burned alive in Heinz-Dietmar's beloved Mercedes.

8

A SLIGHTLY TOO MERRY
WIDOW

It was a fine high-summer morning on 25 January 1983
when twenty-five-year-old Christopher Enderly appeared
at the central police station in Christchurch to report his
mother missing.

With a population of under two hundred thousand,
Christchurch is not a terribly large city, but it is the
biggest on New Zealand's South Island, which is
climatically cooler than North Island – the seasons and
geography of the southern hemisphere are reversed.

Christopher, an assistant accountant with one of the
city's commercial firms, was worried and he showed it.
A well-spoken young man with a somewhat scruffy beard
and rimless glasses, he said that his mother, fifty-one
year-old Sarah Enderly, had not appeared for breakfast
that morning and, when he went to look for her in her
bedroom, she was not there and the bed had not been
slept in. He was afraid that there might have been an
accident. It was very unlike his mother to stay away
from home overnight.

The duty sub-inspector asked a few details, assured
him that the matter would be looked into and, after
Enderly had departed for work, sent the first information
report over to the missing persons section.

Mrs Enderly, it seemed, was a widow, and Christopher
a half-orphan. His father, Gus Enderly, a merchant
seaman, had been lost in a shipwreck in 1977.

Although Sarah and Christopher were in reasonably
comfortable circumstances, the widow held a part-time

626

job as a waitress at the university restaurant from four in the afternoon until eleven in the evening.

As she had apparently not come home on the preceding evening, a detective from the missing persons section went to the university restaurant to see if she had been at work and whether anyone knew where she might have gone.

He returned with the information that Mrs Enderly had worked her normal hours and had left at the usual time of eleven.

The detective then drove out to the Enderlys' home, a sprawling, elderly villa at 7 Oakdene Road on the outskirts of the city, to see if Mrs Enderly had, in the meantime, returned.

She had not, and the detective spent the rest of the day checking out accident reports and admissions to the city's hospitals and clinics.

Mrs Enderly was not in any of them and the matter began to take on a more alarming aspect. A recent picture of the missing woman was obtained from her son and police requests for information were run in the local newspapers.

No one reported having seen her, which was ominous. Although not precisely beautiful, Sarah Enderly had a face that was not easily forgotten.

The picture, described by her son as flattering, showed a woman with a deeply lined face, a sagging double chin, pouches under the eyes and too much make-up, who looked all of her age and, perhaps, a bit more.

And because of Mrs Enderly's age and appearance, the missing persons section was inclined to take the matter more seriously. This was no teenage girl who had run off on a romantic adventure. There was scarcely any explanation for the disappearance other than a criminal act.

In the end, the missing persons section came to the conclusion that the case was beyond their competence and turned it over to the department of criminal investigations. There it was taken up by Inspector Harold Baker, a jovial fair-haired man with a fine, upswept moustache, who promptly assigned it to his second-in-command, Detective Sergeant Walter Cruikshank.

The sergeant, a darkly scowling man with thick black brows, a chin blue with close-shaven beard and an expression of total distrust in everything and everyone, read through the first information report, the report on the investigations by the missing persons section, gazed thoughtfully at Mrs Enderly's picture and assigned two of his detectives to prepare a background report on the missing woman, something which had not, as yet, been done.

Two days passed and there was no report from the detectives. The sergeant called them in and asked if they had any plans to stop drinking beer and carry out their assignment.

The detectives replied that they had had no time for beer and would report on their assignment when it was completed. So far, they had traced about twenty men who had been romantically involved with Sarah Enderly, but they were of the opinion that this represented no more than the tip of the iceberg.

The sergeant was fascinated and demanded an immediate interim report.

For at least four years, said the detectives, Sarah Enderly had been leading a love life to cause women thirty years her junior to pale with envy. She had not managed a different partner every night, but she had not missed often.

'Are you sure you've got the right woman?' said the sergeant, picking the photo portrait from the file and examining it with new interest.

The detectives were certain. Mrs Enderly had been reasonably discreet in her affairs, but the sheer volume had attracted attention. Known as the Sexy Widow of Oakdene Road, she was mildly famous in some circles.

For a woman with so many sex partners, she lived an

orderly life, taking care of her housework in the morning and in the afternoon going for walks in the park, where she selected her bed companion for that evening after she came off work.

There had never been any difficulty in making contacts. She was widely known as an enthusiastic sex partner and, as the encounters took place in darkness, her appearance was not a serious handicap. She was, moreover, not very particular and, as she never charged for the entertainment, her popularity among the types of men who spent much of their time in the park was assured.

Having listened with considerable astonishment to all this, the sergeant told the detectives to continue with their investigation, concentrating on the more recent encounters, and took the file in to Inspector Baker. Mrs Enderly, he reported, had probably been murdered by one of her lovers.

The inspector read through the reports, looked at Mrs Enderly's photograph and said, 'Why?'

'No reason at all, perhaps,' said the sergeant. 'Homicidal maniac. Deviate of some kind. Obviously, if you're going to switch partners seven nights a week, sooner or later, you're sure to run into somebody special. The odds just ran out on her.'

'Weird,' said the inspector, studying the picture. 'Well, all right. Open a homicide investigation on it. You'll have to try and pick up the trail from the university restaurant on Monday evening. Where did she take them? Cheap hotels?'

'Home,' said the sergeant. 'She always took them home.'

But not, apparently, on the evening of 24 January. According to the other waitresses at the university restaurant, Sarah Enderly had not been accompanied on that evening.

Normally, there would have been a man waiting for her to come off work, and her colleagues had found it entertaining to speculate on what Sarah had dredged up for that night's tender romance. Some of the lovers, they said, had been beyond belief.

Where then had Sarah gone on that warm summer evening? Had she headed for the park or, perhaps, some cheap tavern hoping desperately to scratch up something even at that late hour. Or had she simply gone home?

The sergeant did not know how Mrs Enderly had travelled from and to work and he had to ask her son.

He did not like this very much as he was afraid the son might ask about the progress of the investigation and he was not certain how much Christopher knew about his mother's private life.

A superficial check run on him had shown that he was a remarkably wholesome type, a Rover Scout, and not at all the sort of son who would approve of his mother frolicking between the sheets with every bum she could drag out of the public parks.

Enderly did not, however, ask any questions other than whether the police had found any trace of his mother yet. He replied to the sergeant's query that his mother had always travelled by bus as she had no other means of transport. It was convenient, as the stop was at the end of Oakdene Road and only some thirty yards from the house.

This was good news. If Mrs Enderly had taken the bus every day, then the bus driver should know her by sight, at least, and be able to say whether she had been on the bus the evening of 24 January.

The sergeant did not expect that she would have been. Obviously, she had not come home on the bus because she had gone off somewhere with her murderer to be killed.

'But she did,' said the bus driver, Ralph Daniels. 'The same as every night. Eleven-thirty's my last trip and there aren't usually many passengers. There were three that evening and she was the last to get down.'

Daniels said he had known Sarah Enderly well and

had sometimes chatted with her when she was alone, which was not often. She had been alone on that evening and they had exchanged a few words. He knew her reputation, but thought she was a pleasant woman and that her sex life was her own business.

The sergeant's reaction to this was to investigate Ralph Daniels. At eleven-thirty in the evening, Oakdene Road would have been practically deserted. It seemed impossible that anything could have happened to Sarah Enderly in the thirty yards from the bus stop to her home.

Daniels was not, however, a very good suspect. He was only twenty-three, younger than Sarah's son, and, although no Romeo, quite attractive enough to have no problems with girls of his own age.

What could he have wanted from fifty-one-year-old Sarah Enderly? Sex? She would have been delighted. Money? She would have had scarcely more than the bus fare on her, according to her son.

Still, Daniels was the last person known to have seen Sarah and, the trip being the last of the day, he could have taken twenty minutes or half an hour before returning without anyone being the wiser.

He was never questioned directly about his time, so it was not known whether he could have provided an alibi or not. As it turned out, it did not matter.

At the time, there was no such thing as an alibi for no one knew what had happened to Sarah Enderly or whether anything at all had happened to her. She was inexplicably missing, but she could simply have been unusually taken with one of her lovers and gone off somewhere with him.

If she had, however, it was after having returned home on the bus that evening and without her clothes or personal items, for Christopher reported that none of her things were missing.

'In that case,' said Inspector Baker, 'she has to be somewhere between the bus stop at the end of Oakdene Road and her own house. Check out the other residents.'

The residents of the other houses along Oakdene Road were investigated and questioned. None could be regarded even remotely as having been involved in whatever had happened to Sarah Enderly.

They all knew her, of course, and they all knew her reputation. Most of them found her activities highly amusing, but a few expressed sympathy for Christopher, who, they thought, would suffer a shock if he ever found out what his mother was doing with her leisure time. All agreed that he did not know yet, and some apparently thought him rather a simpleton.

'We've talked to everybody out there,' said the sergeant, reporting to Inspector Baker, 'and we've had a look at the houses. No search warrants required. They were all ready to cooperate. There's nothing.'

'What about number nineteen?' said the inspector, scanning the list of interviews. 'You've got no names down against it.'

'That's because nobody lives there,' said the sergeant. 'It's up for sale and has been for a year or so.'

'Actually,' said the inspector in mild reproof, 'that's the first place you should have looked.'

Sarah Enderly – or rather her lifeless body – was not, however, in the empty house, but in the garden behind it. She lay face down in a luxuriant growth of weeds and the flies had been busy. Had she not been discovered then, she would have become noticeable to passers-by within a few more days.

Inspector Baker came out personally to view the corpse.

'Head injuries?' he asked Dr Peter Ambrose, the department's young and earnest medical officer, who was examining the body.

'Hammer, I should think,' said the doctor. 'Seven very violent blows, all to the back of the head. The last three or four were probably delivered after she had fallen down. A bit too much time has passed to be certain, but I suspect the initial attack didn't take place here.'

632

The doctor's opinion was shared by the technicians from the police laboratory, who thought that Mrs Enderly would have been struck down from behind while walking along the road in the direction of her home.

She had then been dragged into the yard of the empty house and hit several times more over the head to make certain that she was dead.

Why this had been done was a total mystery. The victim had not been sexually molested and her handbag lay two feet away from the body. It contained more money than her son had thought she would have been carrying, but it had not been opened. The fingerprints on it were, however, not hers.

Her gold wristwatch was still on her wrist and had stopped at twenty minutes past three. As there was no way of knowing when she had last wound it, the position of the hands was of no value in determining the time of death. Dr Ambrose estimated, however, that it had been the same evening as her disappearance.

Mrs Enderly wore jewellery to a very considerable value, but none of it had been taken and it was obvious that robbery was not a motive.

'Neither money nor sex,' mused the inspector. 'It doesn't leave much except complete insanity, but, if there is a madman running around killing people with a hammer, how is it that we have only this one case?'

A survey of other recent unsolved cases was carried out immediately following the discovery of the body on the theory that this might be a part of a series, but nothing remotely resembling the Enderly murder was found.

'Hatred?' suggested the sergeant. 'Revenge for some real or fancied wrong?'

'Possible,' said the inspector, 'but I find it hard to imagine the circumstances that would lead to such hatred. Who could an elderly, widowed waitress in the university restaurant have wronged so terribly that they would be prepared to murder her?'

'She had an unusual hobby,' argued the sergeant. 'Maybe she took some woman's man away.'

'Yes, a woman with a good hammer and a strong arm could have done it,' said the inspector, 'but you know the kind of men she associated with. Do you think any sane woman would have committed murder for one of them?'

'No,' said the sergeant, 'but that leaves nothing except a homicidal maniac who killed once and once only. If that's the case, we might as well write it off as unsolved now.'

'We may have to,' said the inspector, 'but before we do, I want every man she was with identified and investigated. When was he with her last? Where was he on the night of the murder? Has he ever been under psychiatric treatment or charged with a crime of violence? Let me know when you've finished.'

The sergeant's eyes bulged. 'You're not asking much, are you?' he said reproachfully. 'The woman's been changing partners practically every night for four years and you expect me to . . .!'

'Oh, it couldn't be all that bad,' said the inspector soothingly. 'This is not a large city. She must have had a good deal of repeat business.'

The sergeant was not comforted and, as there are few things which sharpen the wits more than the prospect of a monumental amount of tedious detail work, rapidly came up with half a dozen new theories of the crime, none of which were tenable.

He had given up and resigned himself to his fate when he was suddenly rescued by new information from an unexpected source.

Unexpected and, up until that time, unsuspected. The name of Roger Ackworth meant nothing to the sergeant when he was informed by the duty officer in the charge room that a gentlemen of that name was there and wished to speak to whoever was in charge of the Enderly murder investigation.

Technically, it was the inspector who was in charge, but the sergeant said that he would see him and Ackworth was sent up.

A dignified, well-dressed, well-groomed man in his fifties, the sergeant could not conceive of him as one of Sarah Enderly's lovers and, indeed, he was not.

Rather, he was the father of a very attractive twenty-three-year-old girl named Melanie and Melanie, it seemed, was a Queen's Guide.

Mr Ackworth spoke gravely and slowly, carefully choosing his words, and the sergeant, becoming a little impatient, demanded to know what this had to do with the Enderly murder.

'Christopher Enderly was engaged to marry my daughter,' said Ackworth. 'He is also active in the scouting movement and they met at a scouting function last summer.

'Melanie was very taken with him and we agreed to receive him at our home on the day before Christmas. He impressed us as a respectable young man and we raised no objections to an engagement.

'We were, perhaps, hasty in this decision and, when we looked more carefully into Mr Enderly's background, we found that he was, unfortunately and through no fault of his own, totally unsuitable as a husband for our daughter.

'We therefore asked her to return his ring and sever her relationship with him and she did so on 18 January.'

'And?' said the sergeant, puzzled.

'She told us that he was exceedingly bitter,' said Ackworth, 'and that he made threats against his mother's life. Something to the effect that she would either stop or he would stop her.'

'Stop what?' said the sergeant, intrigued but uncomprehending.

'Mrs Enderly was the reason for terminating our

daughter's engagement to her son,' said Ackworth. 'Our investigations showed that she was leading an incredibly dissolute life. Christopher was blameless, but we could not allow our family to be associated with a family in which there was such scandalous behaviour.'

'Someone who hated her bitterly,' murmured the sergeant. 'Someone she had terribly wronged . . .'

'I beg your pardon?' said Roger Ackworth.

'Nothing,' said the sergeant. 'I've just found a person I've been looking for.'

'We should have thought of the boy before,' said the inspector. 'We knew his character was the direct opposite to that of his mother.'

'We thought he didn't know,' said the sergeant, 'but it seems he'd known for a long time before Melanie Ackworth told him. The scouts had warned him that he was going to have to give up his Rover Scout badge because of his mother's conduct.'

'Losing his girl must have been the final straw,' said the inspector. 'What does he say in the formal confession?'

Christopher Enderly had just finished confessing to the premeditated murder of his mother, and the sergeant had brought the typed and signed statement in to show the inspector, who had been tied up with other matters and unable to be present.

The sergeant handed it to him silently. It was not very long. Christopher Enderly did not go into details and he did not express repentance for his act. His only regret, he said, was that he had not murdered his mother over two years earlier, when he had first found out what she was doing.

He had been studying for his accounting examination at the time and was still working with his books when his mother came home from the waitress job which she had taken the preceding year.

As the house was big and their bedrooms were in

different wings, he had heard nothing other than the sound of the front door opening and closing and muffled footsteps in the hall.

Half an hour or so later, however, he had become thirsty. Going to the kitchen for a drink, he had heard moans from the wing where his mother's bedroom was located.

Fearing that she was sick, he had gone to her door and opened it a crack with the intention of asking her if there was anything he could do.

There was no light in the room, but there was a full moon shining through the window and, to his amazement, he saw that his mother was stark naked and engaged in wildly enthusiastic sexual intercourse with an equally naked strange man.

The couple had been far too occupied to notice him and he had quietly closed the door and gone to his room, where he had had a sort of nervous breakdown.

A great many things that had puzzled him had suddenly become crystal clear. The cryptic remarks which made everyone snigger except him. The strangely sympathetic manner of some people and the way in which he had been avoided by others. The talk which had abruptly died away when he joined some group.

Everyone in Christchurch knew what his mother was doing. Like the deceived husband, he had been the last to know.

He had not known what to do. Leave Christchurch? It was as if he were letting himself be driven out of the city for something that was not his fault.

Talk to his mother? Plead with her to abandon her promiscuous affairs?

He had not been able to do that, and to the moment of her death, Sarah Enderly probably never realized that her son knew of her incredibly sordid love life.

According to Christopher, she had not known that it was her son who killed her either. He had run silently up behind her and struck a single violent blow with the hammer. She had dropped instantly, either unconscious or dead, and he had dragged her into the neglected garden and struck again and again to ensure that the deed was complete.

Ironically, it was one of the few nights that Sarah came home alone that led to her death. Had she been accompanied, her son could not have struck her down in the presence of a witness.

There was much sympathy for Christopher with the general public, and the court will, undoubtedly, grant him extreme extenuating circumstances, but whether this will save him from a life sentence for the premeditated and unrepenting murder of his mother remains a question.

9

TREASURES IN TRASH

Time meant nothing. Time had meaning only if it were possible to measure its passage.

Here there were no clocks, no day, no night, only the endlessly burning bare electric bulb suspended from the ceiling.

Still, it must be October outside. It could not possibly be more than two weeks that she had been lying here in this dirty, dry, dusty room crowded with an incredible profusion of strange objects which she could not see clearly because her glasses had been taken away. Without them, she was nearly blind.

Blind, mute and helpless. Her jaws ached and the corners of her mouth were raw from the twisted rag with which she was gagged. It was little short of ecstasy when it was removed for her feeding.

She had to be fed. Her hands were never released, nor was the garrotte which circled her throat and led down to her ankles. It was not quite long enough for her to stretch her tall, blonde, once healthy body full-length, and she often had terrible cramps in her calves and thighs.

She could not decide which was worse, the careful, gentle feeding with a spoon as if she were a small child, or the hours when he lay beside her on the heap of musty cushions, gazing steadily and expressionlessly at her sex.

He did not touch her, did not touch himself. He only looked.

For what seemed hours on end.

The fear of rape which had flooded over her when he first drew down her violet training pants and panties had long since subsided. He had forced her with the garrotte to open her legs and she had not resisted, hoping that, once he had relieved himself, he would release her.

But it had not been that simple. The man was no rapist. He was something worse, far, far worse: a complete and utter madman. He would keep her here until she died of sheer longing to be free or until the electrical wire bonds cutting into her wrists produced a fatal infection.

The door was opening. It must be feeding time again. She could see the blurred figure approaching, the hands reaching out. In a moment, he would remove the gag. The joyous anticipation of being able to close her mouth filled her.

Hands fumbled about her face, seemed to caress her cheeks, slipped beneath her chin and, suddenly, the thumbs were pressing deep into her throat!

Air! Air! She could not breathe!

There was an unbearable sensation of suffocation. Panic poured adrenaline into her bloodstream and her feet drummed in reflex agony on floor.

Not for long. With a feeling of near relief that it was, at last, all over, darkness fell upon her blood-starved brain.

A pretty, twenty-five-year-old American student was responsible for this death. She would have been horrified had she known it, for Marguerite Herries Edwards was her best friend.

And because she was, Doris Gibbs had become anxious when the twenty-four-year-old law student suddenly and inexplicably disappeared.

Doris had gone to check her room, but she had apparently not been home for several days and none of the other students could recall seeing her.

It was, of course, possible that she had gone off on a trip somewhere. It was only 10 October and the 1982

640

winter semester at Montpellier University in the South of France had not yet begun.

But Doris did not think so. Marguerite, she knew, had had very little money. She had failed several of her examinations recently and her scholarship was in danger. Rather than going off on trips, she had been trying to scratch up some translation work to fill out her budget.

Marguerite had had an advantage over her fellow American students in that she came from cajun country in Louisiana and had spoken and read French fluently before coming to Montpellier University in 1980.

The ability had endeared her to her fellow students, who were often in need of help with the language, but, even had she spoken no French at all, she would have been popular for she was a warm, good-natured girl and, although not beautiful, physically attractive.

Doris had finally gone to the Montpellier police, who were polite and sympathetic. Doris was lovely and they found her American accent charming.

Unfortunately, there was nothing they could do. Marguerite was an adult, and an adult could only be reported missing by a member of the family.

Doris would not be put off. The last time she had seen Marguerite was on 7 October and she had been unable to find anyone who had seen her since.

Investing a little money in a transatlantic telephone call, she informed Marguerite's father in Louisiana of the situation.

He had been as alarmed as Doris. After all, Marguerite was only studying in France because of the frightening experience she had had with her former fiancé in Louisiana. He had suddenly lost control of himself one summer evening in 1978 while they were making love and had begun to strangle her.

Marguerite had managed to break free, but the engagement was, of course, terminated and the experience had been traumatic.

In seeking a complete change of environment, France

641

was a natural choice because of the language and, as she was an above-average student, it had not been difficult to obtain a scholarship.

The move had not been entirely successful. In the more relaxed atmosphere of a European university, her social activities had increased and her studies had suffered accordingly.

The year before, she had encountered a twenty-nine-year-old Iranian student in his last year of medicine and they had fallen in love. He had now completed his studies and was in Los Angeles trying to obtain permission to practise there. If he succeeded, they were planning to marry – which would have terminated Marguerite's studies and was, perhaps, a reason why she was no longer so interested in them.

Doris knew these things because she was Marguerite's best friend, and she told them all to the Montpellier police when the missing-person report had been formally filed by Marguerite's father.

It did not help. All that the police were able to determine was that the very last person to have seen Marguerite was, apparently, Doris herself, and that had been on the afternoon of 7 October at a little after three o'clock.

She had seen her only at a distance and they had not spoken, but they had both waved and Doris was certain that it had been Marguerite, wearing her violet training suit as if she had just come from jogging.

No progress had been made in locating the missing girl and it was no longer possible to exclude a criminal act, so the police printed and distributed an information-wanted circular bearing Marguerite's photograph.

It would later prove to have been Marguerite's death warrant.

The circular was posted on the university bulletin board at ten in the morning of 15 October and by that evening, the strangling hands had closed Marguerite's throat forever.

Marguerite would not remain missing much longer. Alive, she had served a strange, incomprehensible need. Dead, she was worthless trash.

As 17 October was a Sunday, forty-four-year-old Maurice Delacourt set off in the afternoon for his weekly walk. A pleasantly egg-shaped man, larger in the middle than at either end, he was attached to the gentle pleasures of the table and, being in comfortable financial circumstances, had a slight tendency to put on weight. The Sunday walks were intended to combat this tendency and perhaps they did.

At a little after four o'clock, Maurice found Marguerite.

She was lying amidst the low dry clumps of heather and broom covering a rise in the land known as the Mottes Redounes near the hamlet of Matelles, a good five miles from Montpellier.

Marguerite's bonds and gag had been removed, but she was still wearing her violet training suit, now very dirty, as she had worn it ever since her disappearance – with the pants and underpants pulled down so that her body was exposed from the navel to the knees.

Maurice Delacourt logically assumed that she had been raped and murdered, no uncommon occurrence in a civilized country such as France. Having tried in vain to detect any sign of life, he made off, as fast as his weight and physical condition would permit, to raise the alarm.

A police patrol car arrived quickly. The apparent fact of homicide was confirmed, although there was no identification of the victim as yet, and the Montpellier Gendarmerie was alerted.

At five o'clock, Inspector Jerome Orsini, Detective Sergeant Pierre-Louis Massenet and Dr Charles Sablon, all members of the gendarmerie department of criminal investigations, arrived at the scene.

While the inspector and the sergeant looked over the surrounding area, the doctor, a dark-haired, olive-skinned man with a neatly trimmed black moustache, began his examination of the body.

It did not take him very long. The woman, he said, had been dead for at least two days. The cause of death was manual strangulation. She did not appear to have been raped. And there were multiple marks and abrasions on the body which he was anxious to examine in the morgue. He therefore recommended that the body be taken there as quickly as possible.

The inspector was in agreement. There were no indications that the murder had been committed at this place and the body had presumably been brought there simply for disposal. There would be no clues to recover and there was no reason to hold the body until the technicians from the gendarmerie laboratory had concluded their investigations at the scene.

The body of Marguerite Herries Edwards, still anonymous, was, therefore, removed to the gendarmerie morgue in Montpellier, where it did not remain anonymous long.

The official identification was made by a sorrowfully weeping Doris Gibbs and other friends of the dead girl. They saw only the face as the body had already been opened for the autopsy.

The autopsy resulted in a highly interesting report. Dr Sablon was able to determine that the victim had been bound with something thin and smooth for nearly a week, had worn a garrotte around the neck, had been gagged continually, had slept on something hard, dusty and dirty, had been unable to wash herself or even clean herself following urination and bowel movement which, he suggested, had taken place in a rusty bucket as the mark of the rim was still present on her buttocks and the backs of her thighs.

She had not been molested sexually. There had been no penetration of the genitals and there were no traces of either semen or saliva in or on the body. The exposed condition in which she had been found, he suggested, had been a clumsy attempt to simulate a sex crime.

Cause of death had been manual strangulation by someone with rather small hands, and the time of death was the afternoon of 15 October between five-thirty and seven-thirty. She had made no attempt to defend herself, presumably because she was bound at the time.

'A remarkably mysterious case,' said Inspector Orsini. 'The girl must have been held prisoner somewhere from October seventh until the fifteenth, when she was killed because the wanted circulars panicked her captor.'

A short, squat man, broad in the chest and broad in the forehead, he had just finished reading the autopsy report and handed it to Sergeant Massenet.

The sergeant, equally short, equally broad, but twenty years younger, made a sort of grunting noise of assent.

'In a way, we killed her by looking for her,' he said. 'What do you think it was, a mental case?'

'Possibly,' said the inspector. 'There was no sexual motive and it certainly wasn't a question of ransom. About the only other possibility would be political.'

'Political?' said the sergeant. 'She was in politics?'

'Of course not,' said the inspector impatiently. 'But her boy friend was an Iranian. The different factions of Iranians here in France have been killing each other ever since the Shah left.'

'But she wasn't Iranian,' objected the sergeant.

'God damn it, Pierre-Louis,' said the inspector. 'Her fiancé was, and he's in the US. People like that are so crazy that, if they couldn't get at him directly, they might go indirectly through her. In any case, that's what we're going to start with. Check with the alien registration office and see how many Iranians there are here, and we'll see what we can do about turning up a potential suspect.'

'I think I'll start by finding out what kind of an Iranian the boy friend is, pro-Khomeini or anti,' said the

645

sergeant thoughtfully. 'That should eliminate half the suspects immediately.'

It was actually rather less than half of the suspects who were eliminated. Marguerite's fiancé turned out to be an anti-Khomeini Iranian and they were in a minority among the university students, which was what nearly all of the Iranians in Montpellier were.

'In my opinion, any of them would have been capable of it and worse,' said the sergeant, reporting on the Iranian lead to the inspector, 'but I doubt that any of them did because none of them have the facilities for holding a woman prisoner. They're practically all living in single furnished rooms and their landladies keep a sharp eye on them.'

'All right,' said the inspector, 'but keep a couple of men on the terrorist angle. It's in style now. Maybe some young terrorist trying to make a name for himself killed her because she was an American capitalist. We've had crazier motives.'

The sergeant assigned a team to continue investigating the possibilities of a political motive, although he privately thought it improbable, and altered the main thrust of the investigation to an intense survey of such social contacts as Marguerite had made during her stay in France.

It was almost certain that the murderer was someone resident in Montpellier or the surrounding communities. Who else would have had the facilities for holding a girl prisoner for over a week?

The inspector and the sergeant had both thought for a time that it might be Marguerite's former fiancé. They had learned of the strangling incident in Louisiana from Doris Gibbs and had seen a possible significance in the fact that Marguerite had died of strangulation in Montpellier.

The fiancé had had no known motive for the attempted murder and there was no known motive for the murder. If he had been insane enough to strangle her in Louisiana, he might be insane enough to follow her to France and finish the job.

Although the reasoning was flawless, the theory had come to nothing as an inquiry to the American police produced the information that the fiancé was in Louisiana and had not left there at any time during October.

There was no more success with the investigation into Marguerite's contacts. It failed to produce any plausible or even possible suspect. Nearly all of her friends had been students or university personnel and none of them were in a position to hold a woman prisoner, even if they had been strange enough to want to.

The investigators were running out of possibilities, but, fortunately, they were not alone.

Doris Gibbs was still running up and down, determined to do whatever she could to bring the murderer of her friend to justice, and on 5 November, she made an important discovery.

It was Marguerite's bicycle, a near-antique English model and the sole example of its kind in Montpellier, and it was leaning against the wall outside the Faculty of Science laboratory.

Doris did not touch it. She immediately notified Sergeant Massenet, who hurried to the scene and found the bicycle secured with a chain and padlock, the normal precaution taken by people who did not want their bicycles stolen.

He did not touch it either, but summoned the technicians from the laboratory and the identification section. They examined the bicycle and reported that it was covered with Marguerite's fingerprints, but no one else's, and had been standing against the wall for close to a month or, in short, from the presumed date of Marguerite's disappearance.

The conclusion which the inspector and the sergeant drew from this was that Marguerite had disappeared somewhere in the university itself, and they now recalled that the last known sighting of the girl had been at the university by Doris Gibbs.

Doris did not need to be summoned to testify. She was already waiting outside the inspector's office.

She too recalled that it had been at the university and outside the laboratory building of the Faculty of Science that she had last seen Marguerite, and she recalled something else.

Marguerite had not been alone. She had been standing and speaking to one of the university maintenance technicians, a small, largely bald man with a bad limp who was popular among the students as he liked to talk and was handy at fixing things. His name was Leon Deshayes.

And Doris remembered still more. On 15 October, the day that Marguerite had been murdered, she had run into Deshayes, who had asked her if she had seen Marguerite. He had, he said, found some translation work for her.

Doris had thought it strange that he did not know Marguerite was missing. Normally, he knew everything that was going on at the university, and Marguerite's friends had been searching for her for several days already.

'Well, he's a better suspect than no suspect at all,' said the inspector doubtfully, after Doris had left. 'But check him out. Maybe he owns a villa where he keeps girls prisoner.'

'One room would do, if it was private,' said the sergeant. 'I think he's our man.'

And because he thought so, he assigned a squad of his best men to investigate Deshayes' background and circumstances, which turned out to be more remarkable than even the sergeant had expected them to be.

Unfortunately, the circumstances were not such as to make Deshayes a better suspect. Quite the contrary. Given his situation, it was difficult to see how he could have found the privacy to murder anybody, let alone hold a large young woman prisoner for days on end.

'This Deshayes,' said the sergeant, making an interim report on the investigation, 'is one of the great weirdos of all time, but, compared to his wife, he's super-normal. You want to hear it from the beginning?'

The inspector did.

'Deshayes is fifty-three years old,' said the sergeant. 'He was originally an unskilled labourer, but in 1958 he had an on-the-job accident which left him lame. He was, consequently, given a training of sorts and placed with the university as a maintenance technician, which means janitor. He cleans things, scrubs the floors and so on. Salary is six thousand francs a month.'

'Not bad,' said the inspector. 'So what's weird about that?'

'Wait,' said the sergeant. 'On 11 January 1962, he married a school teacher named Andrea Picard, three years younger than himself. She was and still is completely bonkers and she turned Deshayes bonkers too.'

'Not the first such mental casualty to marriage,' said the inspector, 'but go on.'

'Mrs Deshayes was active in collecting old clothes and other junk for the benefit of Third World charity organizations while she was still a teacher,' said the sergeant. 'Whether because of this or coincidentally, she became depressive, mixed up and obsessed with collecting junk of any kind. The only thing was, she didn't pass it on to the Third World. She kept it herself.'

'Where?' said the inspector curiously.

'Wait,' said the sergeant. 'After a time, Mrs Deshayes became too nutty even to be a teacher and she was given early retirement. Pension: four thousand francs a month.'

'That's ten thousand a month between them,' observed the inspector. 'They could afford a villa.'

'They own,' said the sergeant, reading from a list, 'five

apartments, of which one is in the new luxury residence Palavas des Flots. In addition, they rent two other apartments and two cellars. They own two Renault R16s, a Renault R20TS and a Volkswagen bus. Guess where they sleep.'

'In the Salvation Army shelter?' said the inspector.

'In the Renault R20,' said the sergeant. 'You know why?'

'They're motor sport fans,' said the inspector.

'Because the seven apartments, the two cellars, the two R16s and the Volkswagen bus are full to the rafters with trash and garbage,' said the sergeant. 'That's all they do when he's not working, sift through dustbins and carry off the things that take their fancy. Everything takes their fancy. One more couple like that and Montpellier would be the only city in France not to have a rubbish disposal problem.'

'But a health one,' said the inspector, 'or do they take only dry trash, not real garbage?'

'Garbage too,' said the sergeant. 'It's what they eat. He collects the left-overs off the plates in the university restaurant and she digs around behind the greengrocer's shops and markets for discarded vegetables and fruit.'

'Good,' said the inspector. 'You've convinced me. Deshayes and his wife are as crazy as cockroaches in a cocaine factory. Why does this make them suspects in the Edwards murder? They couldn't have kept her prisoner in one of their apartments if they can't even get in to sleep there themselves.'

'Edwards was killed by a crazy person,' said the sergeant, ticking off the points on his fingers, 'because there was no motive. She was last seen talking to Deshayes. Her bicycle was found outside the Faculty of Science laboratory, which is one of the buildings Deshayes cleans and has keys to. There were very few people around the university at that time because the courses hadn't started then. The laboratory has samples of the dirt from the room she was kept in. I think they'll

650

match one of the unused store rooms or basements in the university.'

'And, by God, I think so too,' said the inspector.

They were both right. Locating the room in which Marguerite had been held prisoner was not difficult. All that was required was to determine from the maintenance department of the university what keys were in Deshayes possession. Only two were to store rooms that were seldom visited and the investigators hit on it first.

Although the laboratory would later match samples of the dirt from the floor of the room with samples taken from Marguerite's body and clothing, it was not really necessary. The discarded bonds and gag were lying there, stained with her blood. The rusty bucket provided as a toilet had not been emptied. The pile of musty cushions still lay near where marks in the dust on the floor indicated the outline of a human body. And, perhaps most poignant souvenir of all, Marguerite's glasses lay on a shelf, together with the retorts, test tubes and other pieces of equipment for which the laboratory no longer had use.

Arrested and charged with sequestration and homicide. Leon Deshayes denied all knowledge of the crime and claimed that he had not seen Marguerite since the end of August, when she had asked him to help her find some translation work.

Doris Gibbs, however, swore that she had seen Deshayes with Marguerite on 7 October and, when he was taken to the store room and confronted with the evidence of his crime, he broke down and confessed.

It was true that Marguerite had asked him to help her find translation work in the university and he had made an appointment for her to come and talk the matter over at three-thirty in the afternoon of 7 October.

Marguerite had come and they had talked while he was cleaning the laboratory. He admitted that he had already been planning to take her prisoner at this time, but she had suspected nothing and, as it was getting on for dinner time, had accepted his offer to fetch some food from the university restaurant, Le Boutonnet.

By the time they had eaten, it was already quite late and he had told her that the university gates were closed and that she would not be able to get out until morning.

She had been alarmed, but he had calmed her, saying that he knew of a place in the building where she could sleep.

She had followed him unsuspectingly to the store room and, as she passed through the door, he had snatched off her glasses and pushed her to the floor.

Marguerite had screamed and fought, but there were only maintenance personnel at the university and they had gone home. Handicapped by the loss of her glasses, she had been overpowered, and Deshayes had tied her hands with electrical wire and gagged her.

The description of what he had done was logical and intelligible. What was not were his reasons for it. Despite all his best efforts, he could think of none.

He had had no illusions about raping Marguerite. He had been sexually impotent for over five years at the time. He had also had no illusions about the possibility of ever releasing his captive. Had it not been for the wanted circular which had frightened him, he would have kept Marguerite prisoner for as long as she lived.

Leon Deshayes' confession was made on 26 January 1983 after forty hours of interrogation, and it will be a long time before the psychologists and psychiatrists can decide whether he is sane enough to be held responsible for his actions.

His wife was completely exonerated of all guilt or knowledge of the crime and took the matter calmly.

'I have to get busy now and round up a lot of bottles for the deposits,' she said. 'So that we can pay for Leon's legal expenses.'

10

INTERESTING NEIGHBOURS

'Bones in the breasts?' said Peter Gross. 'I don't believe it. The breastbone, sure, but . . .'

'Those aren't bones,' said Karin Peters, his plump but athletic companion. 'They're plastic breast implants. A friend of mine just last year . . .'

'Well, whatever they are, this is a human skeleton,' interrupted Peter, 'and we have to report it immediately. Where do you think the nearest telephone would be?'

Tall, thin and not very athletic, Peter was not familiar with the low, wooded mountains of the Eifel, a region to the west of the Rhine in West Germany.

A native of Hamburg, he had come down to the city of Duesseldorf, thirty miles to the north of where he was now standing, to work in an advertising agency.

Karin had been working in the same agency and their relationship had quickly progressed beyond the purely professional. On this Wednesday, 18 July 1979, they were embarking on their first camping trip together and had arrived in the Eifel only that morning.

It was now nearly noon and, after hiking for what seemed to Peter several hundred miles, they had begun looking for a place to set up their small tent.

He had just started across a tiny meadow in the open mixed forest of beeches and conifers when something under his boots went crack.

Intrigued, he had given the ground a kick and uncovered the top of a skull.

Never having had anything to do with skulls before,

he had not immediately realized what it was and continued to kick the earth and sod away until it became clear that here lay the remains of a human being.

Or was it? The skull was equipped with not only one, but two jaw-bones, and one of them was filled with a startling array of long, sharp teeth!

Even though the skeleton was only partly uncovered, it was obvious that there were too many and the wrong kind of bones, and lying among them were two hairy, leathery, sharp-pointed ears.

The round white disks which Peter had taken for breast bones, but which Karin had recognized as plastic breast implants, lay on top of the rib-cage on either side.

Although it was not far from the point where the skeleton was buried to Lake Rur, where there was a campsite and several hotels, they did not know this, and Peter trotted the mile and a quarter back to the village of Nideggen, which they had passed on the way out.

His companion remained behind with the skeleton. They were afraid that they would not be able to find it again otherwise.

Karin later confessed that she had become quite frightened while waiting for Peter to return with the police. She possessed a solid set of nerves and she was used to camping in the woods of the Eifel, but the idea of a monster lying buried there worked upon her imagination.

It was as if the woods had suddenly become lonely, isolated, much too quiet. Although it was a bright, sunny midsummer day, she had had the impression that it was growing dark.

When she thought that she saw the bones in the shallow grave move, she turned and walked quickly away until she could no longer see them.

Nideggen is a charming village of seven thousand three hundred permanent residents and, although it has a surprising number of hotels and taverns, it has very few policemen.

They are not needed. Nothing illegal ever happens in Nideggen and, if something did, it would be taken care of by the police in Dueren, a larger community ten miles to the north.

The main contribution of the constable who returned with Peter was, therefore, a precise knowledge of the district, which enabled him to reach the scene with a police car by making use of the forestry logging trails.

Having taken an unbelieving look at the skeleton, he left Peter with Karin, to her considerable relief, and drove to Lake Rur, where he telephoned a confirmation of Peter's report to the station in Nideggen.

There was, he said, the skeleton of a strange monster lying in the forest approximately a quarter of a mile to the north-east of Lake Rur. It looked to him like the remains of a circus freak.

'Nonsense,' said Dr Ulrich Bauer, squatting down to poke among the bones, which had now been laid bare. 'It's a perfectly normal female skeleton and she's been buried with her dog under her head. A little disarrangement, probably by small animals. Hard to say how long she's been here. A few years, at least. I'll be able to obtain a more exact date when I get her into the laboratory.'

The laboratory was in Wiesbaden, close to a hundred miles to the south-east, and the doctor had been summoned by the Dueren police because he was one of the country's leading experts on human bones.

A stocky, irritable man with glasses and a salt-and-pepper beard, he was kept travelling almost continuously. An astonishing number of human skeletons turn up in Germany, considering that it is a small country, and, while some date from the Second World War, others are more recent.

The Dueren department of criminal investigations had called in the doctor when their efforts to identify the victim failed. She apparently had been buried stark naked.

Unlike Peter and Karin and the Nideggen constable, they had not taken the bones for those of a monster. But they had not known exactly what they were either, and the Dueren coroner had declared any further investigation beyond his competence.

Such investigations were Dr Bauer's speciality and, having completed his examination of the bones at the scene, he had them transferred to Wiesbaden, where he arrived at an impressive number of conclusions with regard to the person of whom they had once formed a part.

She had, he said, been a woman in her mid-thirties, five feet two inches tall and weighing a hundred and ten pounds. She had died about two years previously of strangulation, suffocation, drowning, loss of blood or natural causes. The second finger of her left hand had been broken shortly before or at the time of her death.

She had never had a broken bone previously, but there was considerable dental work and she had had plastic implants in both breasts to increase the size and improve the shape. As such surgery was not cheap, it was possible that she had belonged to one of the performing arts where the size and shape of the breasts were professionally important.

The dog buried with her was a wire-haired terrier. It had died on the same date as the woman as the result of a smashed skull, the implement used having been, perhaps, an ordinary carpenter's hammer.

Diagrams and photographs of the dental work and the breast implants were included with Dr Bauer's report and copies were sent to police units throughout Germany and, because Nideggen is less than ten miles from the border, Belgium.

Normally, it would have been the dental work which provided the identification, but, in this case, it proved to be the breast implants.

A doctor in Duesseldorf who specialized in cosmetic surgery recognized them as a special pair which he had implanted in a thirty-four-year-old photographic model called Magdalena Blum eight years earlier, when gravity had begun to exercise an unfortunate effect on her professional equipment.

Armed with the knowledge of her name and profession, the police soon located Miss Blum's dentist, who completed the identification by confirming that the dental work was his.

As Magdalena Blum had been a free-lance model and not employed by any one studio, she had not been reported missing by the people with whom she worked, but had only been roundly cursed when she failed to show up for her appointments.

She had, however, been reported missing by her mother, but only after she had been dead for more than a month. As she had been resident in the town of Neuss am Rhein at the time, the missing-person report had been filed there, and it was now the Neuss department of criminal investigations which took over the case.

There was no certainty that Magdalena Blum had been murdered in Neuss or even murdered at all, but the crushed skull of the dog was an indication of violence and the burial in the forest without identification constituted sufficient reason to suspect a criminal act. Therefore, the case was immediately classed as homicide.

Miss Blum's next of kin, her mother, confirmed that her daughter had owned a wire-haired terrier named Schnuppi. It was partly because Schnuppi had disappeared at the same time that she had not reported her missing earlier. She had thought that, if Magdalena had taken the dog with her, it meant that she had gone off voluntarily.

Mrs Blum did not live in Neuss herself and, although she was on good terms with her daughter, she did not see her very often.

Magdalena, she said, had worried about her age and

657

had been anxious to marry and give up her career. However, despite her oustandingly good looks, she had not seemed able to find the right man for a husband.

A number of candidates had not worked out, but her mother did not know whether she had had anyone at the time of her death and, if so, who he was.

At the time of the disappearance, she had thought that Magdalena had finally found someone suitable and had impulsively gone off with him on what passed for a honeymoon in modern society.

Magdalena's landlord had called at the middle of June to say that the rent had not been paid and he had been unable to contact Magdalena. He knew her mother's address because she had signed the lease as a guarantor, and he expected her to make up the rent.

Mrs Blum had come down to Neuss. Neither she nor the landlord had a key to the apartment, which was on the third floor of a new building at 12 Schiller Strasse, so she summoned the police and a locksmith to open the door. As it was not her apartment, the police had to be present.

Somewhat to her relief, she found that Magdalena's personal identity papers, her toilet articles and some of her clothing were missing. So was Schnuppi, and Mrs Blum came to the conclusion that her daughter had simply gone off and stuck her with the unpaid rent.

It was because she was annoyed with Magdalena for going off like that without saying anything that she had reported her missing, rather than because she thought something had happened to her.

For the police, it had been an unfortunate conclusion. More than two years had now elapsed, making it extremely difficult to trace Magdalena Blum's romantic interests at the time of her death.

There were, however, hardly any other conceivable suspects with a plausible motive. Magdalena had been a successful model, but she had not been rich and, even if she had been killed in the course of an attempted robbery, the robber would scarcely have gone to the trouble of carrying her body out to the woods thirty miles away and burying it with her dog.

The only possible explanation for this careful disposal of the corpse was that there was a connection between Magdalena and her murderer which could be traced and, as it was not professional, it could only be personal.

'As for the dog,' said Inspector Walter Metzler, the short, balding chief of the Neuss homicide squad, speaking around the thick stump of his cigar, 'it probably died trying to defend its mistress.'

'Probably,' agreed his assistant, a dedicated-looking, young detective sergeant with blond side whiskers and round blue eyes whose name was Maximilian Friedmann. 'Could be too that he was afraid to leave it in her apartment because it would bark and call attention to her disappearance. Couldn't have taken it with him. It would have been a dead give-away.'

'What makes you think it happened in her apartment?' asked the inspector curiously.

'Where else?' said the sergeant. 'It wasn't there in the woods.'

'You're right for the wrong reason,' said the inspector. 'The reason that it presumably happened in her apartment is that her papers and clothes were missing and the murderer probably took them, though God knows why.'

'Probably,' agreed the sergeant. 'Of course, he could have taken her keys to let himself in after he murdered her. Could be that he was looking for something in the apartment and didn't find it – or maybe he did, after all, because her papers are missing, aren't they?'

'Humph-mumph,' grunted the inspector, chewing on the cigar. He sometimes felt that his assistant thought of rather too many possibilities. 'The actual scene of the crime doesn't matter much now anyway. After this length of time there probably isn't much hope of finding anything useful.'

659

'Probably not,' assented the sergeant. 'The lab chief says they can recover hair and textile fragments as much as five years old.'

'But not when there have been other people living in the apartment for the past two years,' said the inspector, becoming a little impatient.

'Probably not . . .' began the sergeant and, catching his chief's eye, came to a halt.

There was a short silence in the office.

'That's better,' grunted the inspector with some satisfaction, and returned to the file he had been studying.

The sergeant was young and dedicated, but the inspector was experienced and it was, therefore, the inspector who was right. There was little hope of solving a murder two years old of which none of the circumstances were known, including whether it was a murder or not.

A painstaking investigation of the persons with whom Magdalena had associated at the time was carried out, but the results were largely negative. Many were found who could not have murdered Magdalena. None were found who had had any reason to.

Worse yet, the investigators could not be certain that they had identified all of Magdalena's contacts. Significantly, perhaps, they had found no evidence that she had had any close male friend in the period immediately preceding her disappearance.

The situation was, however, not as hopeless as it seemed. Another and larger police department was also working on the Magdalena Blum case, although the Neuss investigators did not know it.

Nor, for that matter, did the other police department's investigators know it either.

What the Duesseldorf police were officially investigating was not homicide, but a modern version of the old badger game in which a husband and wife team attempt to lure a well-to-do victim into a sexually compromising situation and milk him dry.

At one time, a lucrative field for enterprising men with attractive young wives, the sex revolution had nearly ruined the business.

Respectable businessmen who would once have been terrified by the threat of exposure of sexual dalliance with a married lady the age of their granddaughter were now more inclined to boast. Compromising photographs were no longer purchased at fabulous prices, but were copied and shown to the victim's friends and, if the sexual liberation was very thorough, his wife.

As runaway inflation ruins pickpockets, the media's sex revolution had ruined the practitioners of the badger game.

The human mind is, however, ingenious and inventive, particularly where money is concerned, and new forms of the profession had arisen.

Generally, they involved violence. If the victim did not mind being exposed as a lecher, he often had deep-seated objections to having his genitals kicked off by a supposedly outraged husband. As the socialist-dominated courts had come to the conclusion that there was no such thing as a bad, young and poor person, the young and poor had little to fear for wreaking their just rage on the more wealthy members of an unfair society.

Thus reasoned thirty-two-year-old Peter Okrent, who, during the relatively short intervals when he was establishing a fresh claim to unemployment compensation, was an electrician, a profession which did not appeal to him as it involved work.

Unemployment compensation was not satisfactory either as there was not enough of it. Peter had an expensive hobby. He was a pornography fan and the material to which he was attracted was not cheap.

That Peter was in need of pornography at all might seem surprising for he was married to an eighteen-year-old Spanish girl named Theresa, who was very lovely, possessed of an exceedingly warm nature and troubled by few inhibitions.

Peter appreciated this, but it also eventually occurred to him that Theresa could be put to other and more lucrative uses. Investing some of his unemployment compensation in a large and dangerous-looking pistol, he and Theresa began to comb the better-class bars in search of a mark.

They soon found one and inveigled him with little difficulty into a tender encounter of the dangerous kind with Theresa. Peter came bounding in with his pistol to offer a choice between payment and a painful treatment of the offending parts of the victim's anatomy.

The victim, whose intelligence level was roughly double that of both young entrepreneurs combined, promptly agreed to everything, but said that he had no cash. Would Peter accept a cheque?

Peter would and was, of course, arrested immediately when he tried to cash it.

This was on 1 July 1977 and, to Peter's indignation, he was charged not only with blackmail, but threats with a deadly weapon, possession of an unauthorized firearm and procuring.

He was to have further reason for indignation for, having been brought to trial, he was found guilty and, on 8 September 1978, sentenced to eight years' imprisonment.

Theresa had supported Peter in all his work, but she appeared to be sincerely doubtful as to whether what they had done was ethical. She was also very young and pretty and the jury was all male.

Even so, there had been such a change of heart in the judiciary that Theresa was given three and a half years and the sentences were not even suspended.

The officers of the Duesseldorf department of criminal investigations were, therefore, well pleased with the results of their labours and considered the case closed.

And so it would have been had Peter Okrent not

sought to bring about a reduction in the length of his sentence. Aware that there were many programmes available for making useful members of society out of convicted felons, he saw no reason why he should not take advantage of one of them to gain his freedom.

Actually, there was a very good reason why he would have been better off to leave sleeping dogs lie.

It did not, however, occur to him and, as a result, a junior detective attached to the Duesseldorf department of criminal investigations was instructed to dig out Okrent's file so that a parole board could search through it for excuses to release him.

And, very unfortunately for Peter Okrent, this junior detective happened to have an excellent memory, so that when he read Okrent's address in Neuss am Rhein, which was where he and Theresa had been living at the time of their arrest, he was struck with the certainty that he had seen this address somewhere before.

It could not have been in connection with Okrent's case, however, for he had not worked on it and had actually never heard of it until being sent to dig out the file.

Finally, after racking his brains for over an hour, he came to the conclusion that he had seen the address in one of the information-requested circulars which were sent round to all police units in the area from time to time.

These were on file and, hunting back through the circulars, he soon came upon one from the Neuss department of criminal investigations. It concerned the unsolved maybe-homicide of Magdalena Blum.

The detective, who knew the fearful consequences of not going through channels, did not contact Neuss. Instead, he brought the matter to the attention of his immediate superior, who turned it over to the Duesseldorf homicide squad. They informed Inspector Metzler in Neuss that they had a potential suspect in his murder case in jail.

Inspector Metzler and Sergeant Friedberg both came immediately to Duesseldorf. There was no evidence that Peter Okrent had had anything to do with whatever had befallen Magdalena Blum, but he had been her next-door neighbour at the time of her disappearance, he was a convicted felon and, above all, he was the only potential suspect in the case ever to have turned up.

The inspector and the sergeant did not, however, see Okrent immediately. Having spoken with the officers who had handled the Duesseldorf case, it was obvious that interrogating him would merely have the effect of putting him on his guard.

Peter Okrent was not a man to lose his head and make self-incriminating admissions, nor was he likely to be overcome by qualms of conscience.

This made the inspector unhappy for, the more that he studied Okrent's file, the more he became convinced that he was a very good suspect indeed.

The sergeant did not think so. 'He doesn't have any previous criminal record,' he argued. 'The man has a profession. He's married. Head of a family. Probably had a tough time making ends meet. His wife was probably hounding him for things he couldn't afford to give her. The whole thing was probably her idea.'

'Then I suppose you would say that *she* probably murdered Magdalena Blum?' said the inspector, cocking a sardonic eye in the direction of his assistant and shifting the cigar to the other corner of his mouth.

'Probably,' acquiesced the sergeant automatically, 'but . . . I didn't say that! Why should she anyway?'

The inspector shrugged. 'Jealousy,' he said. 'Okrent has the morals of a mink in a marijuana patch. Blum was beautiful, a model, lived right next door. She was hard-up, wanted to get married. They were making it and Theresa caught them. Hot-headed. Spanish blood, you know . . .'

The sergeant was becoming bewildered. 'But Mrs

Okrent is a small woman,' he said. 'Blum wasn't big, but she was solid. I don't see how . . .?'

'You don't know the southerners,' said the inspector. 'She probably strangled her with her bare hands and . . .'

Probably concurred the sergeant without really knowing what he was saying. 'But she couldn't have carried her all the way . . .'

'Damn it! You're right!' said the inspector in mock fury. 'That kills the theory. He'd have had to help get rid of the body and we know he wouldn't do something illegal like that, don't we?'

'You didn't mean any of it,' said the sergeant reproachfully.

'I didn't when I started,' said the inspector, 'but I'm beginning to wonder now.'

'Whether Mrs Okrent actually did it?' said the sergeant.

'No,' said the inspector. 'Whether we could persuade her to tell us who did.'

What had occurred to Inspector Metzler while taking the mickey out of his assistant was that, in the police and court records which he had just been reading, Theresa Okrent had appeared to be sincerely repentant.

If the repentance was real and not simply feigned in order to influence the court, she might want to clear her conscience by confessing to whatever she knew about the murder of Magdalena Blum.

The inspector thought it over for the rest of the day, discussed the matter with Sergeant Friedmann and asked the opinion of the investigations officers who had handled Okrent's badger-game case.

In the end, all were in agreement, even the sergeant. There was no other lead to follow, no other potential suspect. It was Theresa Okrent or no one. The inspector had nothing to lose.

Theresa Okrent was brought to police headquarters in Neuss, where Inspector Metzler carried out the interrogation personally. He could be very persuasive when necessary, but, as it turned out, no great powers of persuasion were needed. Theresa Okrent's repentance was sincere indeed. She talked, and at length.

When she finished talking, she had achieved something unusual for a woman of her age: she had shocked a seasoned criminal investigations officer.

The murder, said Theresa, had taken place on the evening of Wednesday, 1 June 1977.

She and Peter had been sitting in the living room of their apartment. He had been thumbing through his collection of pornographic magazines in search of a little stimulus. Theresa, who needed none, was waiting patiently for what would happen once Peter had been stimulated.

It was the way they spent most of their evenings, she said, but this evening had been different. Suddenly laying down his magazine, Peter said, 'Why don't we ask the neighbour over for a drink? It would be friendly and the sex would be more fun with three of us.'

Theresa found nothing strange in this suggestion and went over to knock on Magdalena Blum's door. Neither she nor Peter knew her other than to speak to in the hall.

Magdalena unsuspectingly accepted the offer of a drink. There was no reason for her to be suspicious. The Okrents were an attractive young couple and she, undoubtedly, felt there could be no danger when both husband and wife were present.

Poor, lonely Magdalena did not even receive the promised drink. Instead, no sooner had she passed through the door of the Okrent apartment than she found herself looking into the barrel of the pistol which Peter had bought as an investment in the badger game.

Theresa was ordered to put handcuffs on the guest and, being a good, obedient wife, promptly did so.

Magdalena was then stripped to the skin, gagged and

666

given a thorough whipping with a leather whip which Peter had bought from a sex toy mail-order house.

Following the whipping, Theresa was told to bring out her sewing box and Peter tortured the guest by thrusting needles and pins into her sex organs and breasts.

This stimulated him sufficiently. He not only raped Magdalena, but engaged in sex with his wife as well.

He then removed Magdalena's gag, and she made a fatal error.

Had she said nothing. or pretended that she had enjoyed the hospitality of her hosts, Peter might have been stupid enough to let her go. But Magdalena was hurting in a great many places and outraged beyond all measure.

The instant that the gag was removed, she made many uncomplimentary remarks concerning Peter, Theresa and Peter's mother, whom she accused of unnatural, illegal and probably impossible sexual acts in becoming pregnant with him. She ended with the assurance that she was going straight to the police and they would then see.

Under the circumstances, these were suicidal utterances and Magdalena had obviously been insane with rage and humiliation to make them.

Made they were, however, and Peter promptly took the necessary action, looping a silk scarf around her neck and pulling it tight with the intention of strangling her.

In a desperate attempt to ward off her death, Magdalena raised her handcuffed hands and managed to get her fingers under the scarf.

Peter yelled at Theresa to pull her hands away and she obeyed. It was, it seemed, this act more than anything else which bothered her and moved her to confess.

After Theresa had pulled Magdalena's hands away from the scarf, Peter continued to draw it tighter until the victim lost consciousness and eventually died.

It took, said Theresa, a long time.

The body was then carried down to the car, wrapped in a carpet, and left in the trunk until the next day. Then they drove to the Eifel and buried it, together with Magdalena's dog, Schnuppi.

Peter had remarked after they took Magdalena's corpse down to the car that they would also have to get rid of the dog or it would betray them. She did not know whether he thought the dog would be able to communicate with someone over the murder or whether he meant that he would bark when no one came to feed him. In any case, he had gone to the apartment amd killed the dog with a hammer.

The day following, after they had disposed of the bodies in the forest, they returned to Magdalena's apartment and took away all of her private papers, which they burned, and such of her possessions as they thought they could use.

Peter had never mentioned the matter again and she thought he had forgotten it. It had, however, preyed on Theresa's mind.

Considering that without her help the case would probably never have been solved, the court was not especially generous.

On 9 May 1980, she was found guilty of acting as an accessory to murder and sentenced to ten years' imprisonment.

The court was not kind to Peter Okrent either. He was sentenced to life imprisonment.

11

POOR NATALIE

The fight in front of the Cézanne cinema was more
entertaining than most. In the first place, the combatants
were both pretty young women and, second, neither
appeared to be wearing underwear. As they rolled on
the pavement, hooked hands locked in each other's hair,
there was a spatter of applause from the mainly male
audience.

Regrettably, the spectacle did not last long. The
younger of the two women, monstrously pregnant,
banged the head of her opponent against the cement
with such violence that she became dazed and ceased to
struggle. Leaping to her feet, the victor began kicking
her helpless enemy savagely in the breasts and belly.

The pregnant girl's companion, dirty, long-haired and
with a pitiful attempt at a beard, continued to watch
with a dreamy, smiling expression and made no move to
intervene.

Others of the onlookers, perhaps fearing a summons
as a witness in a murder case, laid hands on the raging
woman and dragged her off her victim.

An ambulance was called; the injured woman was
lifted into it and driven away to the hospital.

A police patrol car arrived and the officers began questioning the spectators.

No one knew anything. When the girl who had carried
out the assault was asked for her name and address, she
replied that it was none of the police's business. Her

companion did not reply at all, gazing benignly on the officers with unfocused eyes.

Eventually, two or three persons were found, all women, who said that the pregnant woman had been involved in the fight, but by this time the girl and her companion had gone.

The officers shrugged and went back to their beat. The participants had obviously all been what the French call marginals, persons living on the fringes of society, unemployed and unemployable, squatting in abandoned buildings and engaging in a little prostitution and theft to finance whatever drugs they were addicted to. The quarrel had probably been over the male companion. Both women had wanted him and had been unwilling to share.

Marginals or not, the matter was legally assault and battery and on Tuesday, 22 June 1982, a bored detective from the department of criminal investigations of the Aix-en-Provence police went around to the hospital to take a statement from the victim. The fight had taken place at approximately eight-thirty of the preceding evening and the victim would, presumably, be capable of making a statement by now.

But not, as the detective expected, willing. The woman, who was not seriously injured, identified herself, rather reluctantly, as Hélène Thomi, aged thirty-four, divorced and living on public assistance. She had never seen her assailant before in her life, she said, and she had no idea why she had attacked her. She did not want to prefer charges.

The detective took all this down without comment, although he did not believe a word of it, and returned to headquarters.

Before closing the case, he ran the name through the records section computer and was rewarded with the information that the woman had been charged on four occasions with contributing to the delinquency of minors.

Mrs Thomi's interest in adolescent boys was, it seemed, not altogether motherly. None of the cases had come to trial, for lack of evidence. The victims had suffered little injury and were unwilling to testify.

None of this was very unusual. Aix-en-Provence, a charming, gracious city of some one hundred and twenty thousand inhabitants in the South of France, is a university town, and marginals tend to congregate around universities. If you are dirty, promiscuous, idle and wear your hair long, you can always claim to be a student.

Or an artist. Or a writer.

The detective, therefore, closed the file with the remark that this was some sort of squabble among members of the marginal society and that, as no charges had been preferred, no further action needed to be taken. It then being nearly five-thirty in the afternoon, he had a beer in the police canteen and went home.

As might be expected for the place and time of year, the weather was clear, sunny and becoming remarkably warm. The summer solstice was two days away and it would get dark only by nine o'clock.

Three hours later, almost twenty-four hours to the minute after the fight in front of the Cézanne cinema, a Mrs Beatrice Lalland, who was not a marginal but a hard-working and respectable cleaning woman, looked out of the window of the Brasseur Furniture Company and saw that something was burning on the other side of the car park in front of the building.

Mrs Lalland could not see what it was because there was a heavy screen of bushes and small trees surrounding the car park and the fire was on the other side of them, but she assumed that it was a group of adolescent vandals engaged in destroying someone's property.

Being a woman with, perhaps, more courage than common sense, she shouldered the mop which she had been applying to the floor of the closed furniture store and marched stoutly out to intervene.

Intervention was no longer possible. Upon pushing

671

her way through the bushes, Mrs Lalland saw with
amazement and horror that what was burning was a
woman. Her hair and clothing had already burned away
and the flames were rising from the seared flesh itself.

Mrs Lalland possessed solid nerves, but, when the
police arrived in response to her near-hysterical telephone call, they found her sitting in a Louis XIV chair
in the store, shaking over her entire body and weeping
like a child. Her mop lay at the edge of the screen of
trees where she had dropped it.

The first police unit to arrive had, of course, been a
patrol car, but it was quickly followed by half a dozen
cars and vans from the department of criminal investigations and a contingent of uniformed officers, who
formed a cordon around the scene of what was soon
determined to be a particularly vicious murder.

The fire had, by now, died down and there were only
a few trails of smoke rising from the blackened flesh, so
Dr Gerard Dunoyer, the department's squat, dark and
beetle-browed medical expert, was able to begin his
examination of the corpse immediately.

The cause of death, the doctor reported, had apparently been strangulation, for there was a woman's
partially melted plastic belt still drawn tightly about the
victim's neck. To the relief of all present, he was quite
positive that the woman had been dead for at least an
hour when she was set on fire at around nine that same
evening.

Otherwise, there was nothing that he could determine
at the scene. It was possible that something of interest
might turn up with the autopsy.

Inspector Jerome Credoux, the stocky, black-mous-
tached chief of the duty homicide squad, who had been
called away from his dinner table, asked if there were
any open wounds on the body. His assistant, Detective
Sergeant Pierre Paule, had found traces of blood on the
macadam paving eleven feet nine inches from the corpse.

The doctor replied that he could see no wounds and,

after having examined the traces of blood, remarked that they appeared to be mixed with some other secretions and so fresh that they almost had to be associated with the murder. He had certain suspicions, but he was unwilling to express an opinion until he had made tests.

'Make them,' said the inspector.

The doctor took samples of the blood and other substances and, while the specialists from the police laboratory began going over the area in search of potential clues, was driven back to headquarters to begin his tests.

He had not been there long when the inspector arrived. The specialists had found a plastic reserve cannister which contained petrol, but nothing else of significance and, although the investigations were continuing, he did not think they were going to find much more.

He had, therefore, left the sergeant in charge and come to find out what the doctor had determined with his tests.

The doctor said the tests had confirmed his suspicions. The blood and other secretions were from the womb of a woman giving birth.

'You mean somebody was having a baby while the murder was taking place?' said the inspector incredulously.

'Simultaneously or very near it,' said the doctor. 'Strange, isn't it?'

'Oh not at all,' said the inspector with exaggerated sarcasm. 'Kill one. Have a replacement immediately. Population balance. Anything else?'

'I can't say until I've received the corpse for the autopsy,' said the doctor a little stiffly.

'They'll be sending it to the morgue any time now,' said the inspector. 'I'm going back to my office. Let me know if anything significant turns up.'

Nothing significant turned up, either at the scene of the crime opposite the furniture store at 38 Avenue Brossolette or at the autopsy. All that the doctor could determine was that the woman had been rather badly beaten and scratched and that she had had treatment for her injuries.

'Meaning that they were not incurred at the time of the murder,' said the inspector.

'Seems a strange sequence to me,' remarked Sergeant Paule. 'The woman was beaten up. Then, some time later, she was strangled to death. Then, still later, she was set on fire. Were these things connected or not?'

He was a tall, loose-limbed, young man with a clean-shaven, open face and an earnest expression.

'What I want from you is answers, not questions,' said the inspector. 'I can think of enough questions myself. Get somebody from the identification section to go over to the morgue and try to get prints off the corpse. I wouldn't be surprised if she turns out to have a record.'

'What makes you think that?' asked the sergeant, who felt that the best way to learn the criminal investigation business was to ask questions.

'She was probably a prostitute,' said the inspector. 'Dunoyer says she was in her middle-thirties and would have been attractive when she was alive.'

The inspector's theory turned out to be incorrect. Although the identification specialists were able to recover identifiable fingerprints, the police had no record of them. Hélène Thomi had been charged, but the charges had been dropped and she had not been fingerprinted.

'Well, try the hospitals and doctors' offices then,' said the inspector. 'According to Dunoyer, she was treated for her injuries shortly before death. See if he can say exactly when and get a precise list of the injuries. Whoever treated her should be able to recognize them.'

Four hours later, the sergeant had a positive identification. The duty emergency hospital's records of Mrs Hélène Thomi's injuries, for which she had been admitted on the day before her murder, corresponded to the injuries established by the autopsy.

As the hospital records listed the cause of the injuries as assault, a police investigation had been obligatory and the sergeant was soon able to locate the detective who had taken Mrs Thomi's statement and obtain his report on the case.

Although this was not very useful as Mrs Thomi had provided no description of her assailant, it did contain one valuable piece of information: the number of the patrol car which had been called to the scene.

The officers were summoned, and they told the inspector what they knew of the matter – which was not much. The fight had been over by the time they arrived. Some of the spectators had said that the pregnant woman at the scene had been involved, but they had not actually seen her fighting. She and her companion had been marginal types who looked as if they had been rolling around in the street anyway.

The young man, late teens or early twenties, they thought, had been high on something, heroin probably.

'Very significant,' said the inspector. 'The victim has a fight with a pregnant woman that sends her to the hospital and twenty-four hours later she is murdered while somebody gives birth next to her. It would be one of the great coincidences of criminal investigation history if those two events were not connected.'

'Seems likely they would be,' agreed the sergeant, 'but I can't see that it helps us much if they are. If the woman was having a baby, she couldn't very well have strangled Mrs Thomi.'

'But she could have been a witness,' said the inspector.

'Maybe not,' said the sergeant. 'Maybe she was just pregnant and passing by and she came upon the burning corpse and it gave her such a shock that she went into labour.'

'Damn it, Pierre,' said the inspector mildly. 'That's an all too logical explanation. We may have to go at this from a different angle.'

'I can't think of any,' said the sergeant.

'I can,' said the inspector. 'What about motive? People kill people for a reason. It may not be a good reason or even one that makes much sense, but for the murderer, it's a reason. Now, why would anybody want to murder Mrs Thomi, maybe beat her up beforehand, and burn her body?'

The sergeant thought it over.

'No reason in the world,' he said finally. 'She wasn't a prostitute, so it wasn't her pimp or some business rival. She was on public assistance, so she didn't have any money. According to the records when she was charged, she preferred adolescent boys, but she would sleep with anything that looked like a human being, so it could hardly be an affair of the heart. Whoever killed her must have been completely mad, or he mistook her for someone else.'

'Possible, of course,' said the inspector, 'but, on the basis of the estimated time of death and the time when she was released from the hospital, the murderer would almost have had to meet her at the door when she came out, and that means he knew she was in the hospital. Check with the nurse and see if she had any visitors.'

The sergeant checked. Mrs Thomi had had a visitor, a young woman in the last stages of pregnancy.

'I thought it was her sister,' said the nurse. 'She was very affectionate toward the patient and there was a sort of family resemblance.'

'The pregnant woman again,' said the inspector. 'We've got to find that pregnant woman. There can't be any further doubt that she was mixed up in the murder in some way or other.'

'She's not pregnant now,' said the sergeant. 'She presumably had the baby at the scene of the crime.'

'Then she would have gone to see a doctor, at least,' said the inspector. 'Run a check of the city's physicians and maternity clinics and see who was admitted that evening. I'll see what I can do about tracing any sisters of Mrs Thomi.'

★

Hélène Thomi having been on public assistance, the inspector encountered little difficulty in obtaining information concerning her background as the social welfare authorities maintained records on their clients.

However, Hélène had been an only child. A native of Marseille, eighty miles to the south-west, she had been married once to a handicapped war veteran, by whom she had had a daughter named Marie-Ange, who was her closest living relative.

The social welfare office had no information in Hélène's file concerning the whereabouts of her daughter. The Thomis had divorced when Marie-Ange was three months old and the child had been raised by a paternal aunt. According to the records, she would have turned eighteen on 15 June that year.

The inspector, suspecting that he was now on to a valid lead, personally made the trip to Marseille to talk to the paternal aunt, who said that she was not at all surprised to learn that the police were interested in Marie-Ange and that the juvenile department of the social welfare service undoubtedly knew more about her than she did.

Marie-Ange, she said, had been precocious in every respect. She had been sexually promiscuous from the age of ten and probably before, both with boys of her own age and with adult men. She had been involved with drugs for nearly as long, but the aunt thought that she was not seriously addicted. She had been drunk as often as she could obtain enough alcohol in any form for the purpose. She had scarcely attended school at all, had no profession, had never held a job and lived in hippie communes or in the buildings occupied by squatters.

This unflattering description of Marie-Ange would later be confirmed by the social workers in the juvenile department who said, however, that they felt that Marie-Ange was basically a good person and that they expected eventually to make a useful member of society out of her.

677

The inspector did not see fit to comment on this project. What interested him was the information he had received from the aunt regarding Marie-Ange's relationship to her mother.

The girl, said the aunt, was morbidly fascinated with Hélène and convinced that she was a great sorceress. She thought that her mother was sitting in Aix-en-Provence continually casting spells to destroy her, and she was terrified of being bewitched.

Although she hated her bitterly for having abandoned her when she was three months old, she also seemed to love her and yearn for her love. At intervals, she would go to Aix-en-Provence and follow Hélène about in the streets for days on end.

Sometimes, she would be so overcome by her emotions that she would rush forward to kiss her mother and then fall upon her with fingernails and fists in a sort of panic-stricken effort to destroy that which she loved, hated and feared.

The aunt knew all about this as the juvenile department was invariably called in and social workers would come around to reproach her for failing to provide the loving care and nest warmth which they felt Marie-Ange needed.

As the aunt's control of the situation approximated that of a hog on roller skates, she was very bitter and indignant over these reproaches and did not consider herself to have any responsibility whatsoever for her ward.

She did not, she said, even know if Marie-Ange was in Marseille and, what was more, she did not care.

Marie-Ange was not in Marseille. When the inspector returned to Aix-en-Provence, the sergeant was waiting with the information that he had located the pregnant woman in the maternity ward of the same hospital where Hélène Thomi had been treated for her injuries.

'And you won't believe this,' he said, 'but her last name is the same as the victim's!'

The inspector believed it. He was not even surprised.

'I trust you've got her under surveillance,' he said. 'I think the woman killed her mother.'

The sergeant had not thought it necessary. Marie-Ange had given birth to a seven-pound daughter, tentatively named Natalie Thomi as she had no idea of the identity of the father, at nine-thirty in the evening of 21 June, and he thought it unlikely that she would attempt to flee with a new-born infant in her arms. In any case, he had not believed her to be a suspect in the murder nor did he believe her to be one now.

The inspector immediately corrected the situation by stationing a detective outside the door of Marie-Ange's room. This proved to be a wise precaution for, in a sense, the sergeant was right.

No more maternally inclined than her mother, Marie-Ange would not attempt to flee with the baby, but without it. The escape attempt was foiled by the detective and, as soon as the hospital would let him, the inspector began interrogating his unlikely suspect.

The interrogation was, by then, more of a formality than anything else as the inspector already knew the details of the crime and had two further suspects in custody.

The first of these was Marie-Ange's companion on the day of the fight in front of the Cézanne cinema. His name was Robert Boucher. He was twenty years old, unemployed, unwashed, uneducated and heavily addicted to heroin or anything else that would produce a high. Although he lived in abandoned buildings and earned his living by begging, he described himself as a surrealist artist.

Robert had been arrested when he came to visit Marie-Ange at the maternity ward and had proved very cooperative, immediately confessing to his part in the murder and naming the other participants. Although not particularly public-spirited, he had little interest in what happened to him or anyone else and found answering questions less tedious than continued interrogation.

The third suspect, fifteen-year-old François Lebeau, was equally cooperative and told essentially the same story as Boucher. Marie-Ange had asked him to help kill her mother and, as she was a friend who had introduced him to the joys of sex some two years earlier, he did not see how he could refuse her.

Even Marie-Ange cooperated with the police, saying that she had not only murdered her mother, but she felt she had performed a useful public service. The woman had been a great sorceress and heaven only knew how many people she had harmed with her spells.

She had, she said, become concerned over her mother's nefarious activities during the first part of June as she noted the approach of her eighteenth birthday, and she had resolved to put an end to them.

She and Robert had been squatting peacefully in Marseille with various friends and having a good time, but she could feel the baleful influence of her mother reaching down from Aix-en-Provence and she knew that she was seeking to destroy her.

She had, therefore, come with Robert to Aix-en-Provence on 15 June and celebrated her birthday by getting drunk and following her mother about in the streets.

She had not actually spoken to her until that afternoon in front of the Cézanne cinema when, unable to control her emotions, she rushed forward, kissed her on the cheek and sank her fingernails into her throat.

It had been Marie-Ange's intention to kill Hélène on the spot, but the spectators interfered and the murder had to be postponed.

She then sat down with Robert to think of a plan, but Robert being under the influence of something or other almost permanently, he found it difficult to think at all. The plan had, therefore, she stated with some pride, been entirely her own.

She would find out which hospital Hélène had been taken to and visit her, proclaiming repentance and a desire for reconciliation. She would propose to meet her mother when she was discharged and accompany her home. On the way there, they would kill her.

Robert found the plan brilliant and was all in favour of it, but pointed out that neither he nor Marie-Ange was in very good physical condition and he thought it doubtful they would be able to carry out the murder unassisted.

There was no denying the logic of this objection and Marie-Ange, casting about for a more sturdy helper, remembered François Lebeau, who was living, she thought, in Aix-en-Provence and should be in better physical shape than Robert, as she had only initiated him into the free life some two years earlier.

François was quickly located and, when told the plan, simply said, 'I'm with you.'

These preparations having been made, Marie-Ange set off for the hospital, where she assured her mother that she was a changed person and would love and care for her in the future. She would be waiting with friends to escort her home when she was discharged that evening.

Inexplicably, Hélène Thomi accepted this offer and, when she found Marie-Ange, Robert and François waiting for her outside the hospital that evening, she unsuspectingly went off with them, possibly reassured by the presence of two young boys, in view of her preferences.

Arriving at the screen of bushes around the car park, Marie-Ange gave the pre-arranged signal and the three adolescents fell over the victim, knocking her to the ground. Then Marie-Ange and Robert attempted to strangle her manually while François held her feet.

This was somewhat effective and, after a very considerable effort, Hélène lost consciousness.

Robert and François began congratulating their friend on her successful matricide, but Marie-Ange, having heard somewhere that sorceresses were extremely difficult to kill, pressed her ear to her mother's breast and heard the sound of her beating heart.

Crying out that the job was not yet done, she removed Hélène's belt, wrapped it around her throat and, handing one end to Robert, instructed him to pull with all his might while she did the same with the other end.

This proved successful and, after a time, no further sounds of a heartbeat could be heard.

Even then, Marie-Ange was not satisfied. A sorceress, she said, had to be burned or she was not really dead. She proposed that they burn her.

Robert and Francois had, however, become nervous. Talking about a murder was one thing. Finding yourself with a corpse was another. If there were no stirrings of contrition in their drug-ravaged minds, there was the beginning of fear of what consequences this act might have for them personally.

They voted against the burning, pointing out that they had nothing with which to set the corpse on fire anyway. Instead, they suggested that they all go off and have a good meal in a restaurant to celebrate a great deed well done.

Marie-Ange reluctantly agreed. François had recently received an allocation from the welfare office to further his education, although he was not actually enrolled in any school, and the funds necessary for the dinner were at hand.

They were also adequate to cover a good deal of wine, which so cheered the spirits of Robert and François that they agreed after dinner to go and burn up the corpse.

They stole a reserve cannister from a car and siphoned off a gallon or two of petrol with a rubber tube which Robert carried around for such purposes.

Returning to the scene of the crime, they doused the body liberally and set it on fire, but, as they were about to leave, Marie-Ange, understandably stimulated by the sight of her mother's corpse in flames, went into labour and barely missed giving birth on the spot.

The faithful Robert and François carried her off to the hospital where they had picked up her mother earlier that evening, and she had finished having her baby there.

The defence at the trial made a great deal of the youth and innocence of the defendants, all now suitably washed and sober. These children, cried the attorneys, were not criminals. They were victims of an unfair society. If sent to prison, their young lives could be ruined. If released and given counselling, they could be saved to become useful members of society.

These appeals might have been more effective had the prosecution not pointed out that all three defendants, even Marie-Ange, had had good, comfortable, middle-class homes and the opportunity to proceed as far in their schooling as they wished or were able. They had voluntarily chosen a life of drugs, promiscuous sex, idleness and, finally, murder. The fact that Marie-Ange had sincerely believed her mother to be a sorceress was no excuse for murdering her.

The jury also thought not, but they did accept that there had been certain extenuating circumstances. Marie-Ange was given the modest sentence of twenty years' imprisonment. Robert received fifteen and François, despite his youth, twelve. All should be out in less than ten years.

Is murdering and burning up your mother deviate behaviour?

Few would describe it as normal.

12

KEEPING IT IN THE FAMILY

Bad Soden is not a place where anyone would expect to find great numbers of deviates.

Or non-deviates either, for that matter.

A community of barely eight thousand permanent residents on the outskirts of the West German city of Frankfurt am Main, it owes its existence to the mineral springs found there and the beauty of the surrounding landscape.

People in need of rest and a cure in allegedly healing waters come to Bad Soden, but in modest numbers, for it is not one of the great spas and has no casino.

The visitors sometimes find Bad Soden a little too restful.

For the local residents, it can be more exciting.

On 22 October 1976, the excitement in Bad Soden began with the discovery of a corpse.

Thirty-eight-year-old Erwin Dreyser, strolling along the banks of a drainage ditch bordering his farm on the outskirts of the village, spotted the body at a little before two in the afternoon and, even though he could not see the features, immediately recognized that it was a stranger. Dreyser had been born and raised in Bad Soden and he knew every person there by sight, even floating face down in the water.

The discovery puzzled the farmer greatly. Having dug the ditch himself, he knew that the water in it was no more than three feet deep in any place and all that anyone who had fallen in needed to do to escape drowning was to stand up. Granted that the banks were rather steep and high, they would present no serious obstacle to an adult.

There was, however, no time to ponder the mystery. Here was a fat man lying in his drainage ditch, and the thing to do was get him out if he had not yet drowned.

Dreyser, therefore, plunged courageously down the bank and into the water, where he managed to turn the man over on his back and drag him over to the edge.

As he had expected, it was a stranger, a man in his late forties whom he had never seen before, but he realized with consternation that he was not only dead, but had been dead for some time. The body was not stiff, but it was cold as ice and there was no sign of respiration.

Dreyser left the body where it was and hurried home to telephone the town constable. He was not a big man himself and the corpse was very large and heavy. It would have been impossible for him to get it up the bank alone.

It was impossible with the aid of the constable as well. Only after a second farmer had been summoned could the body be dragged up the steep bank and laid out on level ground.

'Must be a visitor,' said the constable in dismay. 'Something like this is bad for Bad Soden. How could the damn fool manage to drown himself in a drainage ditch?'

'Must have been drunk out of his mind,' said Dreyser. 'I've said for years they ought to have more entertainment here. The visitors sit around watching television and drink themselves unconscious. That's no way to run a spa.'

Like most European villages, local politics were fiercely contested and Dreyser belonged to the party currently out of power.

'Don't blame the village council,' retorted the constable. 'They can't make a night club out of the place.'

He had been appointed by the party in power.

'Can't do anything else either,' said Dreyser sourly and went off in the direction of his house.

The constable, who did not want to leave the corpse alone for fear that a passing stray dog might eat part of it, immediately deputized the second farmer and ordered him to remain with the body until he could summon an ambulance to take it to the local undertaker. Bad Soden has no morgue.

Nor any ambulance. The village being within sight of the Frankfurt city limits, it makes use of the larger city's facilities for the few emergencies that occur.

The ambulance, therefore, came out from Frankfurt, but the body was taken to the police morgue in Frankfurt and not to the local undertaker, as the Bad Soden coroner refused to issue a death certificate.

'We not only don't know how he managed to drown like that,' he said. 'We don't even know who he is.'

'His name's Jan Fryderyk Fischer and he comes from Duisburg,' said the constable. 'His identity card was in his pocket. He was fifty-one years old.'

'And not registered at any of the hotels here,' said the coroner. 'So what was he doing in Bad Soden?'

The constable could not reply, and that same afternoon Detective Sergeant Max Higler came out from the Frankfurt department of criminal investigations, talked to the constable and a number of other persons and then went through the residents' registry in the mayor's office.

There were four Fischers listed. The name is common in Germany. The sergeant noted their addresses and set out to call upon them.

He got the right Fischer on his third call. Forty-two-year-old Daniel Fischer, who lived less than a hundred yards from the drainage ditch where the body had been found, said that he had a fifty-one-year-old brother named Jan Fryderyk who lived in Duisburg, but he assumed that he was still there.

The sergeant took him in to the morgue in Frankfurt,

where he made an official identification of the corpse. Jan Fryderyk was not, it seemed, in Duisburg.

Daniel wept copiously and said that his poor brother had, no doubt, been coming to visit him and fallen into the ditch. He was, he said, almost continuously drunk, which would explain how he came to drown in three feet of water.

Which was, according to the autopsy, how he had died: by drowning and while unbelievably drunk.

'The level of alcohol in the blood was the highest I have ever seen,' said Dr Ludwig Becker, the tall, balding police medical expert who had performed the autopsy. 'If he hadn't drowned, he would have stood a good chance of dying of alcohol poisoning.'

He was sitting in the office of Inspector Walter Grumann, Sergeant Higler's immediate superior, absently polishing his horn-rimmed glasses and reporting his findings. The official autopsy report was in the process of being typed up.

'Liver like a sponge, I suppose?' said the inspector. A dark, intense, hyper-active little man who was often described as dynamic, he was not very interested in a drunk drowning in a drainage ditch. What he preferred was a really spectacular murder case which was good for the career.

'As a matter of fact, no,' said the doctor. 'No indications at all of chronic alcoholism. He was in exceptionally good physical shape for a man of his age and weight.'

'Then why was his blood full of alcohol?' asked the sergeant, who had been listening to the report from his desk in the corner. 'Are you saying that he fell in a ditch and drowned the very first time he got drunk?'

'Of course not,' said the doctor. 'He could have been drunk a good many times before it did discernible damage to the organs. All I'm saying is that he wasn't an alcoholic.'

'How much would you say he drank before he

drowned?' asked the inspector, becoming a little more interested.

'The equivalent of an entire bottle of whisky, brandy, vodka or any other distilled spirits,' said the doctor. 'I didn't run stomach-content analysis. Should I?'

The inspector hesitated. 'Go ahead,' he said finally. 'And, Max, take a run back out to Bad Soden and at least find out where he did his drinking. It must have been in Bad Soden itself because he wouldn't have been able to go very far afterwards.'

The doctor went back to the morgue and the sergeant set off cheerfully for Bad Soden. He was a big man, blond, loose-limbed and slightly clumsy like a St Bernard puppy, and he preferred the outdoors to the office. Frankfurt was its usual grimy, noisy, polluted self, but, in Bad Soden, the air would be clear and crisp and the mixed forests around the little town would be a glory of red and gold autumn leaves.

There being a limited number of places in Bad Soden where alcohol was available, it did not take the sergeant long to determine that Fischer had not done his drinking in any of them. It was not a time of year when there were many visitors and a stranger, particularly one of Fischer's size, stood out.

No one, it seemed, had even seen him on the day on which he had drowned, Tuesday, 19 October, according to the autopsy, and it was a mystery as to how he had got out to the edge of town. No car had been found so he had, apparently, been on foot.

Meaning, the sergeant reasoned, that he had arrived in Bad Soden by train or by bus and, if so, perhaps he had taken a taxi.

There were only four taxis in Bad Soden and three of these had had no large, plump, male, non-resident fare on 19 October.

The fourth had not either, but only because he had refused him. Thirty-four-year-old Oscar Beisel told the sergeant that he had been summoned to the house of

Daniel Fischer in Koenigsberg Strasse on the afternoon of 19 October. Daniel and his thirty-eight-year-old wife, Marian, had been outside with a large, plump stranger between them. They had asked Beisel to drive the man to the hospital in Witzenhausen.

Beisel had not liked the look of the proposed fare at all. The man's head was lolling forward on his chest and he appeared to be unconscious. The Fischers were having a hard time holding him up. Beisel had recommended that they call an ambulance and gone back to his stand.

This testimony made the case so serious that the sergeant took Beisel back to police headquarters in Frankfurt so that he could make a formal statement there.

'In short,' said Inspector Grumann, now much more intrigued, 'the brother made a deliberate false statement to you. Suspicious, very, very suspicious.'

'That's what I thought,' said the sergeant. 'But why? Even if Daniel Fischer tossed his brother into the ditch when he was unconscious drunk so that he drowned, we couldn't prove it. Why didn't he simply say that Jan Fryderyk had been to visit him and left full of booze to the eyes? The coroner would almost surely have issued a death certificate naming accidental drowning as the cause. The ditch has steep banks and the autopsy did show that he was drunk as a coot.'

The inspector thought it over.

'He didn't want an investigation,' he said finally. 'And he was too stupid to realize that there would have to be one anyway. There must be something in his relationship to his brother which would make it obvious that he would have had a motive for murdering him.'

'Can't imagine what it would be,' said the sergeant. 'Duisburg is close to two hundred miles from here and Jan Fryderyk wasn't a frequent visitor, because nobody in Bad Soden knew him by sight.'

'You don't need to imagine,' said the inspector,

'because you are going to find out or, at least, I hope you are. As of this moment, the death of Jan Fryderyk Fischer is classed as suspected homicide and you are in charge of the investigation. You can start by finding out what the relationship between the brothers was.'

'Openly?' said the sergeant. 'Can I bring Fischer in for questioning?'

'Not if you plan to continue working in criminal investigations,' said the inspector. 'Fischer is to suspect nothing. We don't want him covering his tracks any more than he's already covered them. You're to be discreet, very, very discreet.'

The sergeant did not think that it would be possible to be very, very discreet in Bad Soden and, in any case, no one there had known the victim. He therefore drove up to Duisburg, which is in the Ruhr district some one hundred and eighty miles to the north.

Jan Fryderyk's identity card had listed him as married and his wife's maiden name as Antonie Boell. She was six years older than her husband and, when the sergeant finally located her, it turned out that he was not her husband any more. She had, she said, filed for divorce the preceding year and it had become final in May of 1976.

'Why?' said the sergeant. 'You were married for a long time?'

He knew that the couple had a fifteen-year-old daughter named Esther.

'Twenty-seven years,' said the former Mrs Fischer tersely. 'I don't want to talk about it.'

'Mrs Fischer . . .' began the sergeant.

'Boell,' said Mrs Fischer.

'Mrs Boell,' said the sergeant patiently. 'I am engaged in investigating a suspected homicide. We have reason to believe that your husband may have been murdered. Withholding information in connection with the investigation of a felony is an offence punishable by law and, if you refuse to cooperate, I shall have to take you back to Frankfurt to be questioned and, possibly, charged.'

'What do you want to know?' said Mrs Boell.

'Nothing about your relationship to your former husband,' said the sergeant. 'Only about his relationship to his brother in Bad Soden, Daniel Fischer.'

Mrs Boell reflected.

'The two things are connected,' she said finally. 'I can't tell you about one without the other.'

'Then, Mrs Boell,' said the sergeant, 'I am afraid you are going to have to reveal all.'

'Well, I suppose you'd find it out anyway,' said Mrs Boell. 'It's in the records of the divorce proceedings. I just wanted to spare Esther.'

'Your daughter?' said the sergeant, beginning to feel that he understood the situation. 'Your husband was . . .?'

'Not with Esther,' said Mrs Boell indignantly. 'Although I don't doubt that the swine was capable of it. With his niece.'

'Daniel's daughter?' said the sergeant. 'How old is she?'

'Twenty now,' said Mrs Boell, 'but this has been going for a long time. Since the little bitch was nine, I understand.'

'Your husband was having sex relations with his nine-year-old-niece for the past eleven years and you only divorce him now?' said the sergeant wonderingly.

German housewives do not, as a rule, call police officers idiots, but Antonie Boell looked the word at him.

'Not Jan Fryderyk,' she hissed. 'Daniel. Her own father. Jan Fryderyk only got in on the act last year. He and Daniel were estranged. They'd hardly seen each other in twenty years. Then that hussy came round telling Jan Fryderyk that her own father was abusing her and could he help. You bet he could help. He brought her up here to Duisburg and installed her in

691

our house. Of course, she was in bed with him almost before the door closed behind her. Insatiable little tart!'

The sergeant had found what he had been sent to find. An overwhelming motive for murder.

'I'm afraid I'm going to have to ask you to step down to police headquarters here to make a statement, Mrs Boell,' said the sergeant. 'This is a little more complicated than I thought it was.'

The case was, indeed, more complicated than anyone would have had reason to expect and, although Antonie Boell did not know all of the details, she knew enough to make a highly interesting statement.

The situation was not, however, as bad as it had originally appeared. There had been no actual incest. Mechthild Kiel was not Daniel Fischer's daughter, but the daughter of his wife, Marian, whose maiden name had been Kiel. The identity of the real father was not known.

According to the statement by Mrs Boell, her husband had brought Mechthild home with him on the afternoon of 7 June 1975 and told her that the girl had appealed to him for help as her stepfather was forcing her to have sex relations with him.

'She did not look like she needed much forcing,' said Mrs Boell grimly, 'but she was Jan Fryderyk's niece by marriage at least so I didn't throw her out of the house.

'It was a mistake. Within a day, I realized that Jan Fryderyk had a different idea of help than I did, but before it came to anything, Daniel showed up here in Duisburg and there was an awful row, which ended in his taking Mechthild back to Bad Soden with him.

'I thought that was the end of it, but no, a week later, Jan Fryderyk went down to Bad Soden and brought her back up here.

'He was crazy about her and she was completely shameless. If I hadn't been there, I think they'd have done it in front of Esther.

'There were some terrible scenes, but, again, before anything was actually settled, Daniel came back with a

692

regular commando. There were three or four of them and they practically carried Mechthild off by force. Jan Fryderyk said they were armed.

'Even after that, he wouldn't give up and he went running down to Bad Soden and brought her back, I don't know how.

'I'd had enough and I told him that it was either Mechthild or me.

'He said, "All right. It's Mechthild." And they left together.'

'I filed for divorce, and the only time I've seen him since was in court. Esther is with me, of course.'

Esther Fischer was with her mother in more senses than one and confirmed in a separate statement to a woman officer of the juvenile section everything that Antonie had said, adding certain details which the outraged wife had either been spared or which she had been unwilling to repeat.

As for the sergeant, having collected the statements on the affair and checked the records of the divorce court, he went back to Frankfurt in happy anticipation of startling his chief out of his executive-type chair.

If the inspector was startled, he managed to conceal it masterfully.

'About what I expected,' he said. 'The trouble is, we can't ask for an indictment on the basis of a motive and nothing else. Maybe it really was accidental. Maybe Jan Fryderyk got roaring drunk to drown his sorrows and drowned himself along with them. We can't prove it wasn't that.'

'You want me to drop it then?' said the sergeant hopefully. He did not care very much for the case.

'Not at all,' said the inspector. 'Where's your sense of duty? Fischer was murdered. It's up to you to collect the evidence to bring the murderer to justice.'

The sergeant went glumly off to do so, idly wondering a little how difficult it would be to get himself hired at some other city's department of criminal investigations.

The only comforting aspect to the whole affair was that the inspector had now given him a free hand to act as he saw fit.

He promptly made use of this freedom of action by taking into custody both Daniel Fischer and his wife and subjecting them to hard interrogation. As far as he was concerned, there was no point in continued discretion.

While this was going on, he sought out Mechthild Kiel, who had now, it seemed, run away and was living with a male non-relative. He asked her to make a statement.

She really was a remarkably attractive girl and, like Mrs Boell, she said she did not want to talk about it.

The sergeant then recited his piece about withholding information in connection with the investigation of a felony, but, unlike Mrs Boell, Mechthild said he would first have to prove she had any such information, and she still didn't want to talk about it.

This matter being settled, the sergeant went back to headquarters, where he learned that Daniel was still insisting he knew nothing about his brother's death and denying his relationship to his stepdaughter had ever been anything other than paternal. However, Marian had given up and was telling everything she knew, which, it seemed, was really everything.

She was, she said, aware that her husband had been having sexual relations with her daughter from about the age of nine, but the only complaint Mechthild had ever made was, in recent years, that Daniel was getting a bit old and sluggish. He had not forced her and she could have put a stop to the business any time she wanted.

She did not know why Mechthild had run off to her uncle, but she thought she had probably simply wanted a little change. She had never, to her knowledge, had intimate relations with anyone outside the family and seemed much attached to her older relatives. Or even older persons to whom she was not related. The man with whom Mechthild was now living was forty-six.

In any case, said Mrs Fischer, there had been a terrible tug-of-war between the two brothers over the girl which lasted for months and, when Jan Fryderyk came down to Bad Soden on 19 October, Daniel decided to put an end to it and him too.

He had apparently planned this in advance, for he told her two days earlier to buy a large bottle of brandy with the highest alcohol content she could find. When Jan Fryderyk turned up and began whining about Mechthild, Daniel pointed a shotgun at him and ordered him to drink the whole bottle of brandy neat.

Jan Fryderyk refused and Daniel produced a whip to beat him into submission.

This was not necessary as the sight of the whip proved sufficiently convincing, and Jan Fryderyk drank the entire bottle.

He then became semi-conscious and Daniel, apparently getting cold feet, told Marian to call a taxi and they would send him to the hospital.

The taxi, however, refused to accept him and Daniel led him off and, she supposed, pushed him into the ditch. She had not actually seen him do so.

Confronted with his wife's confession, Daniel Fischer added his own and, for good measure, incriminated two others: Johannes Kiel, his thirty-four-year-old brother-in-law, and a cousin, twenty-six-year-old Erich Becker.

The two had accompanied him on the commando raid to Duisburg, and Kiel, at least, had been present at the time of the murder. As he was her brother, Mrs Fischer had thought it better not to mention this.

All of these statements and confessions having been duly recorded and neatly typed up, indictments were handed out all round and, three months later, on 21 January 1978, a court found the defendants guilty of homicide and acting as an accessory to homicide, and sentenced Daniel to life imprisonment, Johannes Kiel to twenty years, Marian Fischer to six years and Erich

Becker to nothing as he appeared to have had no knowledge of the crime.

It can, of course, be argued that neither Daniel nor Jan Fryderyk was guilty of deviate behaviour.

After all, neither was related to Mechthild by blood and, if she was a trifle young at the beginning of the affair, well, the Dutch parliament is at this moment pondering the lowering of the age of consent to twelve, so why not nine? On that basis, their conduct was normal.

But what about Mechthild's behaviour?

13

NEVER TRUST ANYONE OVER SEVENTY

Not so very far to the north and a little to the west of
Bad Soden, where Mechthild Kiel wrought havoc within
the Fischer family, lies the German Westerwald which,
although perhaps not internationally famous, is regarded
with affection by many Germans.

An ancient mountain chain, now worn down to low
wooded hills, steep stone outcroppings and swampy
valleys, it enjoys the romantic appeal of Sherwood Forest
as bands of revolting peasants once made their headquarters there.

The Westerwald is a favoured site for campers in
summer, but few choose to live there permanently. The
climate is severe, with heavy snowfalls in winter and
extreme humidity all year round.

On the Easter weekend beginning 5 April 1980, the
Westerwald was as humid as ever, but, as the campers
expected nothing else, they came anyway. The sun was
shining and it was warm by German standards, which
are spartan generally but exaggerated in the country's
several million campers.

Already by Friday evening the camping site at Heimborn-Ehrlich on the Nister river was so filled with cara-
vans and camping cars that there was not room left for
so much as a pup tent. Groups of adults drank beer,
played cards and generally enjoyed themselves. The playground swarmed with children.

Saturday was no different. More beer was drunk, more
cards were played, sausages were consumed, people went

for walks, the children romped and shrieked in the playground, located a hundred and fifty yards from the campsite to spare the ears of the adult campers.

On Sunday, thirteen-year-old Beate Lohmann disappeared.

Exactly when was not possible to determine. A pretty, almost alarmingly well-developed girl who looked considerably older than she was, she had had lunch with her parents, Dora and Gerd Mechtel, outside their caravan and then gone off down the road in the direction of the playground. Beate might look eighteen, but she was still a little girl and she liked to play with the other children.

Beate's last name was not the same as that of her parents because Gerd was not her father. Mrs Mechtel had been previously married and divorced.

Gerd was, however, as attached to Beate as Daniel Fischer had been to Mechthild, although in a much different way, and, when she failed to appear for dinner at six-thirty, he went off to look for her.

Beate was not at the playground and he was unable to find any children there who had seen her at all that afternoon. Alarmed and concerned, he hurried back to the caravan to tell his wife, who immediately joined him in the search.

There is much solidarity among Germans, particularly among campers, and it was not long before the entire camp was searching for Beate.

They did not find her, but they did receive some frightening reports from other children. Four of them said they had seen Beate either getting into a green car or already in a green car. Unfortunately, they were all young children and they were not sure of the make of car. Three said it was an Opel. One said it was a Renault.

At the moment, the make of the car was not as important as the fact that Beate had been in it at all.

Being a little girl in West Germany today is a very high-risk condition indeed. More than twenty years of

698

lenient treatment of criminals in general and sex criminals in particular has left the country swarming with convicted rapists, child molesters and even murderers. A little girl or even a little boy stands in need of survival training.

And Beate had had it. Her parents had drummed into her ears from the moment that she could understand the language that she was never, never, never, under any circumstances, to go with a stranger, no matter who he said he was or even if he was wearing a uniform; she was never to get into a car unless her mother or father were in it and she was even not to put too much faith in her own family members. Over fifty per cent of sex offences against children are committed by relatives of the victim.

The Mechtels could not, therefore, believe that Beate had got into the green car of her own will, and no sooner had they heard the children's reports than they hastened to telephone the police.

The nearest police station was in Altkirchen, which is a community of under five thousand inhabitants and has a police force of corresponding size.

The entire force came out to the campsite, but they could not find Beate either. Even more conscious of the dangers to children in a modern, progressive society than were the Mechtels, they wasted no more time and called in the department of criminal investigations from the city of Koblenz, the largest community in the area, with a population of over a hundred and twenty thousand.

The Koblenz police took the matter as seriously as the officers from Altenkirchen and, by Monday, the entire area was filled with police, off-duty firemen, units of the German army and volunteers.

They were not really looking for Beate any more. They were looking for her body, but they did not find that either.

The search continued for a week and was then called off. Helicopters had criss-crossed the forest and failed to sight anything. Trained tracking dogs had sniffed articles of Beate's clothing and failed to pick up any trail. The searchers had combed every patch of brush thick enough to hide a body and skin-divers had gone over the bottoms of the ponds and lakes. Beate was not there. Alive or dead, she was no longer in the area.

The Nister river had, of course, always been considered a possibility, but it was relatively fast-flowing, which made it hard to say how far downstream a body might have passed in the length of time before the full-scale search began. Both banks had, however, been scoured for a distance of two miles downstream from the camp, but without result.

'He probably didn't want to chance disposing of the body near the camp,' said Inspector Karl Schoenherr of the criminal investigations department of the Koblenz police. 'He drove straight out of the district once he had her in the car. The only hope is that he may simply be holding her somewhere.'

A very experienced officer within five years of retirement, the inspector, stocky, hard-bodied and with iron-grey hair and a drooping moustache, had been assigned overall direction of the case as he was something of a specialist in offences against children.

'She could be better off dead,' said his assistant, Detective Sergeant Paul Feldner.

A tall, painfully thin man with a long, dark face, he was inclined to pessimism and had often found good reason for the attitude in the past.

'He wouldn't be holding her for ransom. The Mechtels don't have that kind of money. And she's too old for him to ever release her. She could identify him.'

'We'll release her,' said the inspector, but, privately he was not optimistic.

'Could have been a white-slaver,' continued the sergeant gloomily. 'The North Africans are taking them younger all the time. She'd even be a little too old for some of them, but she was pretty and . . .'

'Oh knock it off, Paul,' said the inspector mildly. 'If you want to indulge in groundless speculation, at least speculate about something cheerful. Did you ever hear of a white slaver kidnapping a child from a campsite where there were hundreds of people around at the time?'

'Four little kids saw it,' said the sergeant. 'Nobody else. He's probably torturing her to death right now, dragging it out as long as possible to get his kicks. You remember the Pfortzer case? What that fellow did . . .?'

'Get out,' said the inspector. 'Go and investigate something. I don't care what.'

He did not like remembering the Pfortzer case. The girl in that had been even younger and it had happened over five years earlier, but neither he nor the sergeant would ever forget it.

That was the trouble with working so long together as a team, he thought. You were always reminding each other of things that it was better to forget.

As the case neared the end of the second week with still no trace of the missing girl, even the inspector was inclined to doubt that either Beate or her body would ever be recovered. As the murderer had transport, the body could be anywhere in Germany. It was not a large country, but there was still plenty of room to hide a child's corpse in it.

As it turned out, however, Beate had not left the area in a car, but by water. Nearly twenty miles downstream from the camp site at Heimborn-Ehrlich there is a dam across the Nister and, as there is some traffic on the stream, there are locks.

Locks require a lock keeper, and on the morning of 20 October Arnold Kraemer came out of his neat little lock keeper's cottage and found Beate Lohmann floating at the top of the dam.

Kraemer did not immediately realize that it was Beate as she was inside a gunny sack which had been tied at the mouth with cord. However, whatever was in the

701

sack, it had no business floating around behind the dam, and Kraemer got a boat-hook and towed it over to the bank.

By the time he had done this, he had come to the conclusion that he would not try to get it out of the water. Beate had been in the sack for exactly two weeks and the odour of rotting flesh was quite noticeable.

Even so, it did not occur to Kraemer that the contents might be an adolescent girl. He had heard of Beate's disappearance, for it had been in all of the newspapers and on the radio and television newscasts, but he simply failed to connect the information to this stinking sack. Instead, he thought someone had butchered a hog and thrown the offal into the river.

As a result, Kraemer nearly passed the sack through the lock to let it go on down the river and, had he done so, it is possible that no one would ever have known what happened to Beate Lohmann, with the exception of two persons who were not likely to reveal their knowledge.

Attempting to get the sack into the lock, Kraemer found that it was remarkably heavy, too heavy to be simply the unwanted parts of a hog and, holding his nose with one hand, he cut the cord closing the mouth of the sack with his pocket knife.

The sight revealed left him utterly mystified.

Beate had been put into the sack doubled up with her feet nearly touching her shoulders. It was, therefore, her naked buttocks which lay framed in the open mouth of the sack and it was several minutes before Kraemer, who had never seen anyone from such an angle in his life, could work out what they were.

Even when he did, the thought of the missing Beate Lohmann did not cross his mind and his near-incoherent call to the police merely stated that there was a dead woman in a sack in the river.

Beate Lohmann did, of course, occur to the police. Inspector Schoenherr, Sergeant Feldner and a sleek,

702

plump, gold-rimmed bespectacled medical expert named Martin Eisenhauer arrived at the scene in under an hour.

The body was still in the river, but Kraemer had attached it with a line to the boat hook, which he had driven into the mud so that it would not float away again. He himself was in his cottage drinking neat brandy. A shy, mild-mannered man, his discovery had largely unnerved him.

It came close to unnerving such hardened characters as the inspector and the sergeant, but the doctor was not troubled at all. Corpses were his business and this was one, even if it was in poor shape.

'Would be in worse shape yet,' he said almost cheerfully, 'if it wasn't for the water being so cold. She won't smell much once we get her out of the sack.'

The inspector did not, however, want to take the girl out of the sack.

'This is no place,' he said. 'Who knows what clues might be lost here in the mud? We'll take her in to the morgue, sack and all.'

The sergeant was very much in favour of this solution. He did not want to take the girl out of the sack either, and it was obvious that there was no one to do it except himself and the inspector.

Somewhat over the doctor's objections, as regulations called for an examination of the corpse as found at the scene, the sack was pulled on to the bank and the sergeant went off to telephone for an ambulance.

In the meantime, the inspector took a statement from Arnold Kraemer and decided not to carry out any investigation at the scene. The body had obviously floated down the river to the dam, and there would be nothing for an investigation to uncover.

As the ambulance had to come out from Koblenz, there was a wait of some forty minutes. The inspector walked unhappily up and down the bank of the river, while the sergeant sat smoking and staring glumly through the windscreen of the police car and the doctor poked about in the sack.

The victim being in an advantageous position for a gynaecological examination, he soon called out to the inspector that the girl had been raped and that she had previously been a virgin.

The inspector did not reply or cease his pacing. He had expected nothing else and he did not feel like making conversation. Although he was a specialist in such cases, he hated murders of children. He had fathered two daughters himself and, although they were now grown women with children of their own, he still remembered them as little girls.

Despite the inspector's caution over removing the body from the sack, no clues were found in or on it. The police laboratory reported that it was an ordinary gunny sack, such as was used for storing potatoes and other things, and that it was untraceable.

Beate's clothing was also in the sack and on her, with the exception of her panties, which had been ripped off, but there was nothing about them to indicate the identity of the murderer.

The autopsy report was more informative. Beate had been hit on the back of the head with what had probably been a large stone. It had fractured her skull and undoubtedly dazed her, but it was not the cause of death.

The cause of death was drowning. Beate had been rendered helpless by the blow to the head, raped, put into the sack alive and perhaps conscious and thrown into the river to drown.

'About as brutal a procedure as I've encountered,' said the inspector grimly. 'How did the identification go off?'

The sergeant had had the unpleasant duty of bringing the Mechtels to the morgue for the official identification of their daughter.

'She looked good,' said the sergeant. 'Eisenhauer did a fine job cleaning up the face. Mrs Mechtel fainted.'

'Small wonder,' said the inspector. 'Well, let's get on

with it. I've asked the records section to give us a print-out on known sex offenders who attack adolescent females, and you can start a detail sorting and checking immediately. Almost surely somebody on the books. The thing was too brutal and deliberate to be a first offence.'

'If he's from this area at all,' said the sergeant. 'What about the kids who saw her get into the car? Do you think we can get anything more out of them?'

'We'll try,' said the inspector. 'I'm going to show them pictures of cars and see if we can get an identification of the make at least.'

The investigation therefore set off in two different directions simultaneously and, gratifyingly, both produced results.

The children who had seen Beate either getting into or already in the car were able to agree on a picture of a 1976 model Opel, and the little boy who had originally suggested a Renault was even able to come up with two letters of the licence plate.

Assuming that he was not mistaken, the car had been local, for German licence plate numbers indicate the city in which the car is registered and the letters were those used for Altenkirchen.

A six-year-old girl, the only one of the four witnesses who had seen Beate getting into the car, said that she thought she had been pulled in and that she had been trying to get away. It had been the driver who was pulling, but there was also another man in the back seat.

On the basis of this information, the investigators began a search of the records of the vehicle registration office in Altenkirchen.

In the meantime, the search of the police records for known sex offenders with a history of attacks on adolescent girls had resulted in a startlingly large number of potential suspects for such a sparsely populated district.

Having excluded the homosexuals who attacked only

boys, the impotent not capable of penetration and those with fixations on older or younger age groups, the sergeant still had eleven names on his list. All of these men had long records of sex offences against young girls, and each required individual attention.

Some could be eliminated immediately. Two were actually in jail. One was seventy-three years old. Another was in the hospital. Four had checkable alibis for the afternoon of the day in question.

In the end, three remained, but only one drove a green Opel and came from Altenkirchen. His name was Otto Fuchshammer; he was twenty-four years old, and six years previously he had raped and murdered a twelve-year-old girl, for which he had been given the maximum sentence possible under German juvenile law: ten years.

As usual, Fuchshammer had served less than half of his sentence, had been given some psychiatric counselling and released as a rehabilitated member-in-good-standing of society.

The Altenkirchen police suspected that he had raped at least two girls since then, but, as no charges had been preferred, he remained officially rehabilitated.

The only problem with Fuchshammer as a suspect was that his green Opel was not a 1976 model, but a nearly new 1980 model.

'Could the children have all made the same mistake in the model?' mused the inspector. 'They're young of course, but . . .'

'Not that young,' said the sergeant. 'There's a lot of difference in the appearance of the 1976 and 1980 models. It may have been Fuchshammer, but it wasn't the car he's driving now.'

'We'll try a line-up of green Opels and then we'll try a line-up with Fuchshammer,' said the inspector. 'Fortunately, the parents are cooperating.'

'And so are the kids,' said the sergeant, 'but what do you think a good defence counsel is going to do with an identification by four pre-school kids, even if it is all four of them?'

The inspector sighed. 'Tear it to pieces, of course,' he said. 'Do you have any better suggestion?'

The sergeant had no other suggestion at all and the line-ups took place. They were far from satisfactory to the investigators.

To begin with, all four of the little witnesses picked the 1976 model Opel which was not Fuchshammer's car.

Worse yet, none of the children picked Fuchshammer as the driver of the car. Two, however, said that he had been the man in the back seat!

'We're going to have to release him,' said the inspector in dismay. 'We're going to be accused of holding him purely on the basis of his past record.'

This was, as a matter of fact, exactly what Otto Fuchshammer had been saying ever since he was arrested, and the newspapers were beginning to agree.

'Do you think he really was the man in the back seat?' said the sergeant. 'The girl was raped by only one man, according to Eisenhauer, and, from what we know of Fuchshammer, he doesn't seem the type to let someone else do his raping for him.'

'He could be the man in the back seat and still be the rapist,' pointed out the inspector. 'There's no evidence that the driver was the rapist.'

'Maybe the driver has no previous record,' suggested the sergeant, 'and maybe . . .'

'. . . he drives a 1976 green Opel,' concluded the inspector. 'You may have it, Paul.'

But Paul did not. The vehicle registry records in Altenkirchen had produced a number of green 1976 model Opels, but none of the owners appeared to have any connection to Otto Fuchshammer.

Fuchshammer was released with not very sincere apologies from the police, and the inspector went back to poring over the files covering what had already been done in the case.

'There's one 1976 green Opel here that isn't checked off as investigated,' he called to the sergeant, who was typing up a report on another case at his desk in the corner.

'Belongs to the seventy-three-year-old man,' said the sergeant. 'He was eliminated because of his age. Couldn't have run the girl down, let alone rape her.'

'Ah, but don't forget there was another man in the car,' said the inspector, becoming slightly excited. 'I think we may have something here. What's the fellow's name – Maerzhaeuser – may have been the driver and the man in the back seat did the raping and murdering. Has Maerzhaeuser got a long record?'

'Long as your arm,' said the sergeant. 'Just a minute and I'll get you the file.'

Seventy-three-year-old Josef Maerzhaeuser did, indeed, have a criminal record nearly as long as the inspector's arm, but it was a rather monotonous one for, with the exception of a few convictions for theft, all of his offences were rape or attempted rape, mostly but not exclusively of adolescent girls.

'If the man were a little younger . . .' remarked the inspector. 'What does he look like? Is he in good shape?'

'He's a wreck,' said the sergeant. 'Looks ten years older than he is. If he's capable of rape, I'm capable of swimming the Atlantic.'

'You may regret that remark when you're doing the breast-stroke off the Azores,' said the inspector. 'I still say that he's a major suspect, if not as the actual murderer, then as aiding and abetting. There's too much against him. A life-long record of sex crimes against adolescents. A 1976 green Opel. A local man who knows the area. Bring him in. If he's half as feeble as you say he is, we shouldn't have much trouble interrogating the truth out of him.'

Unfortunately for the inspector's plans, Josef Maerzhaeuser was not feeble in the least. It was true that he was scrawny, mostly bald and badly wrinkled, but he was as tough as leather, and all the inspector could get out of him were threats of a suit for false arrest and demands for legal counsel.

The inspector was not impressed. He had heard such threats before. As legal counsel was required by law, he provided it, but then took into custody Maerzhaeuser's sixty-six-year-old wife, Maria, and their eighteen-year-old son, Peter, an apprentice house painter. Maria and Josef were not living together. Peter and Josef were.

'Well,' said the inspector rather smugly, 'now we have a driver of a 1976 green Opel and a man for the back seat. Let us see if our four young witnesses can identify them.'

Three of the young witnesses could! The fourth was not so sure.

'Probably worthless in court,' observed the sergeant, 'but I'm convinced. Peter must be following in his father's footsteps. The old man took him out for his trial rape.'

Maria Maerzhaeuser disagreed. 'Nonsense!' she snapped. 'If anybody raped the girl, it was Josef. He's been doing it all his life. Peter's only eighteen. He can have all the adolescent girls he wants without raping them.'

There was some basis to this argument. Peter Maerzhaeuser was a reasonably attractive young man and the adolescent girls of the eighties were thoroughly liberated. There were many younger than Beate Lohmann who would not have died virgins.

None the less, it was Peter who was charged. The inspector still did not believe that a man of seventy-three, even with Josef Maerzhaeuser's vast experience, was capable of the savage and violent rape of a strong, healthy teenager.

His son insisted that he was. Weeping copiously, he led the police to the point on the banks of the Nister where, he said, the crime had taken place, not only in his presence, as he later admitted, but with his assistance.

He had not wanted to rape anybody. Nor had he expected that there would be any such activity when his father took him for a drive on Easter Sunday.

It had all happened very suddenly. They had been passing the girl, who was walking along the road in the direction of the playground, when his father abruptly stopped the car and dragged the girl into the front seat.

Beate fought and struggled, and his father ordered him to hold her still. He had done so because a good son owed obedience to his father and, anyway, he was afraid that the old man would beat him up.

When they arrived at the spot where the crime took place, Beate managed to get away from him, jumped out of the car and ran.

His father ran after her and, catching up a stone, threw it so accurately or so luckily that he hit her in the back of the head, knocking her to the ground.

The girl was dazed but not unconscious, and Josef ripped away her underwear and raped her on the spot while his son watched, horrified, or so he said.

The rape completed, Josef ordered him to get a gunny sack from the trunk of the car and, together, they pulled it over the half-conscious girl and tied the mouth with cord.

They then simply carried the sack to the river and tossed it in.

Josef Maerzhaeuser denied bitterly everything in his son's statement. The boy was lying because he was jealous of his success with women. He was probably a homosexual, which was why nobody wanted to have anything to do with him. As for Maria, she was jealous for the same reason. She was an old woman and she resented his love affairs with young girls.

Josef could not, however, name any of the young girls with whom he had had love affairs – out of a desire to protect their reputations, he said. The jury not only did not believe this, but hardly anything else he had to say.

On 3 July 1981, Josef Maerzhaeuser was found guilty

of rape and murder and sentenced to life imprisonment. As he was now seventy-four-years-old, it was, presumably, a short sentence.

Peter Maerzhaeuser did not come out of the affair very well either. Being a juvenile, the maximum that he could receive was ten years, and that was what he got for aiding and abetting rape and murder.

14

AN ALL-ROUND MAN

The corpse was a horrifying sight. It lay face down between the rows of ripening corn, and the blood from the lacerated scalp had filled the plastic sack fastened with cord around the neck. Protected from the air, the blood had not congealed or lost its colour, so that the head looked like a plump red child's balloon.

Yves Belfontaine, a resident of Saint-Seine-en-Bache, rather more given to exercise than the average Frenchman, turned pale and narrowly escaped losing his lunch.

It would have been a pity, for the lunch had been a good one and, following it, Belfontaine, who was in comfortable circumstances and did not hold a job, had decided to take a walk. It was not exactly that he had a weight problem, but it was still always well to keep things within bounds.

He had not expected to see many other strollers in the country lanes outside the little town. It was a Friday, 3 September 1982, and nearly everyone would be at work. Saint-Seine-en-Bache, being rural and agricultural, did not have as high a rate of unemployment as some other parts of France.

Now, Belfontaine wished that there were more people about. He had averted his eyes immediately he realized what he was seeing, but he had no doubt the man was dead. That hideous red balloon where his head should have been was guarantee enough for that.

Backing out of the cornfield, Belfontaine hurried along the paths between the fields until he caught sight of a farmer working in the distance and began waving his arms, jumping up and down and shouting at the top of his lungs.

The farmer, at first inclined to run from an apparent madman, fortunately recognized Belfontaine and came to investigate.

Half an hour later, Captain Denis Serrault of the Dijon Gendarmerie, was made aware that another homicide had taken place in the so-called Triangle of Death.

The title was an invention of the press, who used it to describe what was thought to be a series of rapes and murders, most of which had taken place within an area bounded by the communities of Besançon, Dole and Lons-le-Saunier. All had taken place within the past three years. None had been solved.

The captain, a brisk, businesslike olive-skinned man with fine features and large slightly slanted dark eyes, was not pleased to learn that someone had been murdered, but he was relieved the anticipated murder had now finally taken place and the gendarmerie would have another chance to identify the murderer.

According to the theory, the victim of this new Triangle of Death crime would be a young blonde woman and she would have been raped. With few exceptions, all previous victims had answered to this description and the killer was believed to be a sex psychopath with a fixation.

To the captain's dismay, this latest victim did not match the pattern at all. He was young and he had been raped, but he was not a blonde woman. He was a dark-haired soldier, six feet four inches tall and muscled like a cart-horse.

'An unusual sex object for a rapist,' remarked Dr Charles Bressaud, the medical expert attached to the criminal investigations section of the Dijon Gendarmerie, 'but apparently a stimulating one. He achieved orgasm inside the anus. Cause of death was probably head wounds. I can't say for certain until I remove the sack

713

and I don't want to do that until I have the body in the morgue.'

'Right,' said the captain. 'Can you give me an estimate on the time of death? I want to know if we should set up road-blocks.'

'No need,' said the doctor. 'He's been dead since yesterday afternoon at least.'

'Keep an eye on things here, Jerome,' said the captain. 'I'm going back to the office. Let me know immediately if the laboratory people find anything.'

'Jerome' was Sergeant Jerome Poiron, the captain's silent, hulking, slightly sinister assistant officer-in-charge. 'The laboratory people' were the specialists and technicians attached to the gendarmerie laboratory who were now on their way to the scene and who would go over the area by the square centimetre in the hopes of finding some clue to the murderer's identity.

The captain was anxious to get back to his office as he wanted to institute a check by the records section of known homicidal homosexuals capable of raping six-foot-four soldiers. He did not think there would be many.

There were none.

'You must remember, however, that the case near Troyes the other day involved a homosexual rape too,' said the chief of the records section. 'He raped the wife first and then the husband. Granted, the victim was no six-foot-four athlete, but he was definitely male.'

'You think then that it could be the same man?' said the captain. 'The psychologists said he only raped the man because he was stimulated by the rape of the woman. She was young and blonde and so was the husband.'

The records chief shrugged. 'No idea,' he said. 'I only keep track of them. You and the brain mechanics will have to work out who they are and why they do it.'

The captain did not find this very helpful and went back to his office slightly out of sorts. It was all very well to say that it was up to him to work out the identity of the killer, but how was he to do that, if there were never any clues?

Actually, there were some clues, including a reasonably accurate description of the man who was probably the killer by the young couple he had raped.

According to them, he was a serious, respectable-looking man in his late twenties or early thirties. He had a pleasant manner, wore his hair short and stylishly cut, dressed well and neatly and drove a maroon Volkswagen Rabbit.

He had picked up the husband and wife, both blond and long-haired and neither twenty years old, as they were hitch-hiking outside the city of Troyes, which, like Dijon, is in the east of France, but somewhat more to the north.

The couple thought him a square, some kind of a businessman or civil servant.

He turned out to be businesslike enough and even reasonably civil, but far from square in his attitudes.

Turning into the first forest road leading off the main highway, he drove in far enough for privacy, produced a gun and ordered the couple to strip.

They were indignant, but had done so. The man looked dangerous now and, it being 28 August, the weather was not unsuited for nudity. As they admitted to the gendarmes, they had not been too upset at the prospect of sex with the man. He was clean and presentable, and they were a modern, liberated couple.

The man then attached the husband to a tree with cord which he took from the trunk of the car and raped the wife, laying her across the front seat of the car and standing in the open door.

The process did not take very long and the couple assumed that they would now be released.

To their surprise and consternation, the man attached the wife to the tree and, holding the gun to the back of the husband's head, bent him over the hood of the car and raped him anally.

This did not take very long either and, when it was finished, the psychopath took the husband to the tree and tied him next to his wife.

He then looked at them speculatively, weighing the gun in his hand, and the couple had the terrifying impression that he was trying to decide whether to kill them or not.

Apparently deciding against it, he finally got into the car and drove away.

The badly shaken couple had not been tied too securely and were soon able to free themselves. Getting back into their clothes, they resumed their hitch-hiking, but in the direction of Troyes, where they reported their experience to the police.

This being rape and threat of homicide within the Triangle of Death area, the report was immediately passed on to Captain Serrault, who had been in charge of the investigations since 12 September 1979. He was not at all happy about it.

The affair, the captain now reflected, sitting at his desk with the great mound of files representing the various cases nearly covering it, was beginning to have an unfortunate effect on his career. The press was becoming increasingly critical of the lack of progress in solving the murders and his superiors, sensitive to the political implications, were beginning to put a great deal of pressure on him. If the investigation were to be taken out of his hands, he could expect to retire with the rank of captain, if that.

This latest crime could be crucial, for it was basically different from those preceding it. It would tend to support the captain's private theory, which he had not revealed even to the sergeant, that what they were dealing with was not a single series sex criminal, but two or more such sex psychopaths operating in the same area and at the same time.

The captain suspected this theory would not be popular with his chiefs. It gave the impression that the country was swarming with homicidal sex maniacs. But it would explain why the gendarmerie efforts had, so far, been fruitless. The indications were unclear and the clues were contradictory because the crimes had not been committed in all cases by the same man.

Sighing, the captain opened the file of the case which had begun the series and which had been, in his opinion, the worst crime of all.

It had taken place on 12 September 1979, almost exactly three years earlier, in an open forest on the outskirts of the town of Dole, less than twenty miles to the south-east of Dijon.

On the afternoon of that day, twenty-three-year-old Yvonne Crosby had gone for a walk with her six-year-old daughter Lydia. Both were blonde, with long, straight hair.

They had never returned, and those who had gone to seek them eventually found mother and child naked, dead and disfigured. Yvonne had been raped.

Both victims had been stabbed repeatedly and beaten around the head with some heavy object, thought to be a hammer or the back of a small hatchet.

There was not the slightest clue to the identity of the murderer other than his semen in the body of the young mother and the obvious fact that he was a seriously deranged compulsive sex psychopath.

Such meager indications were not enough and, although Captain Serrault's men interrogated practically every soul living in Dole, a community of some thirty thousand inhabitants, no witnesses were ever found.

Murders such as those of Yvonne and Lydia Crosby are nearly always series crimes as the forces which drove the murderer to kill once will cause him to kill again. The classic response is to wait reluctantly for the next murder or rape in the hope that this time there will clues or witnesses.

The tactic had not worked in the Crosby murders. From 12 September 1979 to 1 May 1982, there had not been a single comparable crime in the entire east of France where it could not be shown that the perpetrator was not the murderer of Yvonne and Lydia Crosby.

The captain had done his best and he had failed, but there was no reason for criticism. Many criminal cases lack the information to make a solution possible. Gendarmes are not expected to work miracles.

May first of 1982 had really signalled the beginning of the captain's sorrows.

On that date, three months before the soldier's death, a twenty-five-year-old blonde woman of Eastern European extraction named Kaija Elena Koivvoja had been found dead near the town of Lons-le-Saunier, one of the points of what would later become the Triangle of Death. As there were certain parallels to the murder of Yvonne Crosby, the case was assigned to Captain Serrault.

The captain was convinced that it had been the sex psychopath for whom he had been waiting ever since September of 1979. The victim had been stabbed, stripped, raped and beaten about the head with something heavy and hard. The semen recovered from the corpse was that of a man with the same blood group as in the Crosby case.

Unfortunately, there was another parallel. There were no clues and no witnesses.

Or, at least, there had been none so far. The case was by no means closed and the investigation was continuing on 2 September when the young soldier had been raped and murdered in the cornfield.

It was not, however, the only investigation, for there had been a fourth murder, on 23 August.

It had taken place near the city of Besançon, forty miles to the east of Dijon and another of the points of the Triangle of Death.

The victim was a pretty woman with long, straight, blonde hair. She was twenty-three years old and her name was Andrea Kowe.

Like the other victims in the presumed series, Miss Kowe had been stripped, raped, stabbed and beaten about the head with a hard object. The blood group of the rapist corresponded to that determined in the other cases.

Blood group, of course, meant nothing. There were literally millions of persons with the same group. It was not really an indication.

Nor were there any others. The killer was either remarkably clever, remarkably cautious or remarkably lucky.

The captain was, perhaps, clever, but he was neither cautious nor, it seemed, lucky. He had barely started the investigation into the Kowe murder when the rape of the husband and wife took place.

More personnel had had to be assigned to that and, now the Crosby case had been reactivated on the basis of the more recent crimes, the captain found himself with four investigations going on simultaneously.

It was, perhaps, gratifying to be entrusted with so much responsibility, but it was also a dangerously exposed position for a civil servant and he felt himself far too vulnerable.

Now, it seemed, a fifth investigation was to be added and the captain was wondering just how many parallels there would be to the other cases. On the basis of what he now knew, there did not appear to be many.

The specialists from the gendarmerie laboratory reported with the monotonous regularity which had characterized their previous reports that they had found nothing at the scene which might be useful in identifying the murderer.

The victim had been identified. He was nineteen-year-old Christophe Breton, who had been performing his compulsory military service at Besançon. He was last seen setting out to hitch-hike back to his base from a visit home. Although hitch-hiking was known to be dangerous, Breton had not thought that he had much to fear. On the contrary, his size made it difficult for him to get rides.

But, unfortunately, not difficult enough. According to the indications at the scene and the findings of the autopsy, Breton had been brought to the cornfield in a car, marched into the corn, presumably at gunpoint with his hands tied behind his back, and had been raped anally where the body lay. His skull had been fractured with what was thought to be the butt of a pistol before the plastic sack was drawn over his head and tied around the neck. Breton had actually drowned in his own blood, although the autopsy showed that the head injuries were so serious they would have resulted in death in time as well.

The victim was not a blonde female. The cause of death did not include stabbing. There was little to tie the crime to the Triangle of Death murders other than the location.

There was much to tie it to what the captain now thought was the second series of rapes and murders overlapping in time and space the Triangle of Death cases.

On 15 August, a nineteen-year-old German hitch-hiker named Karl Bulcke had been found dead at the edge of a small forest near the town of Rochefort-Montagne. He had been raped anally and executed with a single twenty-two calibre bullet fired into the nape of the neck at point-blank range.

With the exception of the anal rape, the case was not remarkable. In August, France was full of hitch-hikers, foreign and domestic, and equally full of perverts waiting to pick them up. When these participants met, the case often became of interest to the homicide squad.

The matter probably would not have come to Captain

Serrault's attention at all, had it not been for the fact that there was a second, almost identical crime on 19 August which had taken place in the Triangle near Lons-le-Saunier. Rochefort-Montagne is close to four hundred miles to the south-west.

The victim in this case was French, a sixteen-year-old boy named Christian Klein. He too had been hitch-hiking. He too had been raped. He too had been shot in the neck with a twenty-two calibre weapon.

The double rape of the husband and wife had not yet taken place, and what Captain Serrault was looking for were cases involving the rape and murder of young blonde women. Therefore, it had not been included in the Triangle of Death file and the investigation was left to the gendarmerie station at Clermont-Ferrand, which was handling the Bulcke murder.

The soldier's murder appeared to fit these two murders better than any of the captain's cases. He was about to transfer it to the Clermont-Ferrand investigators when he was handed one of the lucky breaks that sometimes occur in a criminal investigation.

On the afternoon of 4 September, two days after the soldier's murder, a gendarmerie patrol car was stationed at the edge of State Highway E2 running from Dijon to Dole. The officers in it were watching for stolen vehicles for which they had a list of licence numbers.

Presently, a car bearing one of the listed licence numbers passed and the gendarmes set out in hot pursuit.

The chase was short. No sooner had the officers switched on the siren and set in motion the flashing revolving lights on the roof of the patrol car than the stolen vehicle slowed and pulled over to the side of the road.

The gendarmes approached cautiously. The penalties for murdering a police officer were not very severe in socialist France and other officers had approached other stolen cars to be met with a hail of bullets.

As it turned out, the driver was armed, but he was in such a state of abject terror, his teeth literally chattering and his entire body shaking violently, that he would have been in greater danger of shooting himself than anyone else.

In what was, perhaps, a record time for a confession, he gibbered at the astounded gendarmes that he was the notorious Hitch-hiker Murderer.

The title was another invention of the press and referred to the murderer of Karl Bulcke, Christian Klein and, more recently, Christophe Breton.

The delighted gendarmes drew their pistols, ordered him of out of the car, searched him, confiscated a twenty-two calibre long-rifle pistol, handcuffed the blubbering killer and brought him to gendarmerie headquarters in Dijon. There he was rushed to the department of criminal investigations, cautioned on his rights and interviewed personally by Captain Serrault.

Purely on the basis of appearance, twenty-one-year-old Pascal Bertrand was not a very satisfactory suspect. He was thin, frail, pimpled, wore glasses and was so painfully timid that he answered the captain's questions in a near-inaudible whisper.

In other respects, he was more suitable. He knew exactly where the bodies of Karl Bulcke and Christian Klein had been found. He knew exactly what he had done to them before he had murdered them. He did not know their names, but, as he shyly pointed out, that had not been necessary for his purposes. Many of the details that he described had not been released to the press and were known only to the police and the murderer.

Finally, there was physical evidence as well. The gun found in Bertrand's possession had been taken to the gendarmerie ballistics section for test firing and the slugs from the heads of the victims compared with the test bullets. They matched perfectly.

Without doubt, the captain had solved the murders of Karl Bulcke and Christian Klein for the Clermont-

Ferrand gendarmes, but, from his own point of view, he had solved the wrong cases.

Pascal Bertrand denied vigorously having had anything to do with the murders of Christophe Breton, Yvonne and Lydia Crosby, Kaija Koivvoja or Andrea Kowe and, as the penalty for seven murders was no more severe than the penalty for two, there was no reason why he should not be telling the truth.

The captain believed him, although he did not want to, but the press did not and splashed headlines everywhere to the effect that the Triangle of Death Killer had at last been trapped.

Captain Serrault knew better, and on 23 September, only nineteen days after the arrest of Pascal Bertrand, he was proved right.

Twenty-year-old Leon Guichard, another soldier serving his compulsory military service, was hitch-hiking home to spend a long weekend when he was picked up by a man driving a maroon Volkswagen Rabbit. The man was in his early thirties, reasonably good-looking, neatly dressed and conventional in his manner.

He drove Guichard to a forest near the town of Venarey-les-Laumes, put a pistol to his head and raped him anally.

Guichard wisely offered no resistance, which undoubtedly saved his life and made it possible for him to provide Captain Serrault with another detailed description of the Triangle of Death Killer as well as the licence-plate number of the car.

This latter proved valueless. The car had been reported stolen a month earlier in Bayonne, which is in the extreme south-west corner of the country and about as far from Dijon as it is possible to get and remain in France.

The knowledge was, however, disconcerting. The killer did not confine his activities to the Triangle of Death. He might strike anywhere and, indeed, Venarey-les-Laumes was not inside the Triangle itself, but thirty miles to the north-east of Dijon.

It was, none the less, definitely the killer or, at least, the killer of Christophe Breton and the rapist of the young married couple, for there was physical evidence connecting the crimes.

In all three cases, the victims had been bound with thick white cord, and the gendarmerie laboratory was able to establish that these cords were identical and cut from a single length.

This was an important conclusion, for the captain now knew that he was dealing with one man in all three cases and, the witnesses in two of these cases having survived, they could, perhaps, recognize a picture of their aggressor. The gendarmerie psychologists were unanimous in the opinion that the killer would have a police record.

Guichard, therefore, spent several days poring over the police mug books of known sex offenders, not only for the region, but for all of France.

The married couple had already done this and failed, but they had only seen pictures of sex offenders from the region. It had not been known at that time that the killer was moving about the country.

Things went better with this new approach and Guichard was able to identify one of the pictures as being that of the man who had raped him. The picture was then included among a few dozen others and the married couple also picked it out as being that of their attacker.

The Dijon gendarmes now not only knew the identity of the Triangle of Death Killer, but they knew a good deal about him as well.

His name was Daniel Baron. He was thirty-two years old. He came from Perreux, a town three hundred miles to the south of Dijon. He was dangerous.

Baron had apparently always been dangerous. Although he completed an apprenticeship as a cook, he had never worked at any place for longer than three months. Unstable, bisexual and unpredictable, he was believed to have committed a number of aggressions and sex offences for which he had not been charged.

Baron enlisted in the French Foreign Legion for five years, but proved to be no more suited to military life than to cooking. After three years he deserted and returned to France where, on 15 June 1974, he kidnapped a fifteen-year-old boy at a village fair near the town of Limoges and entertained himself with him sexually for three days.

At the end of that time the boy escaped and was able to identify Baron, who was arrested in Hermies, a village in the north of France, on 17 July.

Following a closed trial and testimony by state-appointed psychologists to the effect that Baron was extremely dangerous and could not be allowed to mingle with the public, he was sentenced to ten years' imprisonment and taken to the prison in Einsisheim, on the eastern border of the country.

Theoretically, Baron should have remained in prison until 1985, but, as is common in many places today, the prison authorities had the power to alter the findings of a court and they granted Baron leave from the prison on 13 March 1982.

Baron promptly disappeared and was arrested only two months later in the Drome region, where he then remained – at the prison in Valence.

Despite this escape attempt, Baron was still judged to be a potentially useful member of society by the penal authorities, who released him altogether on 11 August 1982.

Looking at this record, a number of things became obvious to Captain Serrault. To begin with, Baron could not be responsible for the murders of Yvonne and Lydia Crosby, for he had been in jail at the time. Ominously, however, he had been a fugitive from justice at the time of the Kaija Elena Koivvoja murder, and the rest of the crimes believed to be connected with the so-called Triangle of Death had all taken place after his release.

Baron was, without doubt, the right man, and only one important question remained.

Where was he?

He could be anywhere in France, but, on 27 September, he was actually in a small, pleasant town, with the somewhat unpleasant-sounding name of Berck, on the Channel coast not very far to the south of Calais.

He was still driving the stolen Volkswagen Rabbit and he parked it in front of a café frequented by students from a nearby lycée.

Entering the café, he introduced himself as Michel Beauvois, a director of the second national television chain. He was, he said, looking for adolescents to take part in a television programme for the sum of two hundred and fifty francs a day.

As Baron was well-dressed, clean and perfectly respectable in appearance, none of the students had the slightest doubt concerning the validity of his proposition and he was swamped with so many candidates that he literally could not make up his mind. The only fair way to settle the matter, he announced, was to draw straws.

This was done, and to a handsome youth who had apparently offended the gods in some way fell the fatal choice.

Rejoicing greatly, he went and climbed into Baron's car. He was within minutes of rape and, perhaps, death when he was saved by a fifteen-year-old girl named Hélène whose greatest ambition was to appear in television. Flinging herself upon the killer, she pleaded pitifully to be allowed to come along too.

Baron was bisexual. 'Well, if you insist,' he conceded generously.

Hélène, in raptures, went off to tell her father where she was going so that he would not be searching for her. Baron was fully in agreement as he did not want anyone searching for her either.

When Hélène returned, however, it was with her father, who was not so impressed with working for television and who thought he would like a look at this television director.

A large, athletic man, he asked to see Baron's papers. Baron replied easily that he had left them in the hotel. 'What hotel?' said the father.

Baron could not name one.

The nineteen-year-old boy in the car had been listening and now left the vehicle hurriedly. Baron got in and drove away.

But not before the suspicious father had had time to note down the licence-plate number, which he immediately telephoned to the Berck police.

It was a very wanted number anywhere in France and, within minutes, road-blocks were going up throughout the district.

Baron was not intercepted at any of them, but late that afternoon the car was spotted parked in front of a café and he was taken into custody as he came out.

Notified of the arrest, Captain Serrault and Sergeant Poiron hurried to Berck, where, after seven and a half hours of interrogation, Daniel Baron broke down and provided the gendarmes with a detailed account of his activities since leaving prison on 11 August.

He had been busy. He had stolen a car immediately, carried out a hold-up, stolen another car, raped and murdered Andrea Kowe, raped the husband and wife, swindled half a dozen hotels and restaurants, committed a number of thefts from department stores, raped and murdered Christophe Breton and raped Leon Guichard. He might, he pointed out, have overlooked a few things. A great deal had been crowded into a short space of time.

Daniel Baron was eventually tried, found guilty of many things and sentenced to life imprisonment. So too was Pascal Bertrand. The murderer of Yvonne and Lydia Crosby is still at large.

15

YOUTH! LIBERTY! PROGRESS!

Not so very long ago and not so very far away, there once lived a modern West German family named Hommerich.

There was Papa Hommerich, who was a successful executive and who could afford a large car and several mistresses (some part-time only).

There was Mama Hommerich, who was blonde and pretty and athletic and very vivacious and who taught aerobic dancing at the high school in Attendorn, which was where all of the Hommerichs originally lived.

There were the three little Hommerichs, of whom Thorsten, the youngest, was the best loved and the most pampered.

The Hommerichs were all very modern, very progressive and very happy. They owned a fine home, two cars and an enormous colour television. A video recorder was not beyond their reach.

Alas! One day in 1978, Hannelore Hommerich found out about the several mistresses and promptly filed for divorce and a generous amount of maintenance.

Papa Hommerich had no choice but to pay. Mama had the evidence and bringing up three children was obviously going to cost something.

On the other hand, so was maintaining several mistresses, to say nothing of the Mercedes. Papa did not, therefore, pay any more than he had to and, as he was a shrewd businessman, he managed to keep the total outlay somewhat under the average combined wages for three semi-skilled workers on union scale.

Mama and the three little Hommerichs, who were by now not so little, Thorsten having been fifteen at the time of the divorce, were reduced to economies. There was only one Mercedes left for the entire family and little hope of a video recorder.

Mama responded gallantly, taking on more aerobic dancing classes, and no one actually went hungry or naked (except by choice and then only in the house). It was possible for the two oldest young Hommerichs to complete their schooling and take up their rightful places in the production chain society.

For this purpose, they had to leave Attendorn, for there were few links in the production chain in that modest community of under twenty-five thousand inhabitants, located forty miles to the south-east of the great industrial complex of the Ruhr.

They left. They did not return. Until the funeral, for which they remained only briefly. They have no place in this story and that is the last that will be heard of them.

Not so Papa Hommerich, who was in the police detention cells at the time of the funeral, desperately trying to remember where he might have been on the afternoon and evening of 20 October 1983 and who would swear to it.

Thorsten was not in the detention cells nor in Attendorn either, but at his apartment in the village of Lenhausen some eleven miles distant from Attendorn. Now twenty years old and a fine, upstanding figure of a youth, he was known to his intimates as 'Wuschl', a German ephithet applied to persons with particularly abundant red hair.

Thorsten, or Wuschl, had an astonishing number of intimates because he was very successful both financially and socially.

A boy who kept an eye on the trend, he had begun by hating his father either when he found out about the mistresses or, perhaps, when he learned that the

729

maintenance would not extend to his having his own car *and* video recorder.

This was socially correct in Germany in the seventies and eighties. Up-to-date young people were supposed to hate at least one parent and, if possible, both – an idea which originated in the United States, where a number of journalists had made some money out of it and passed on to other ventures.

However, as in Arabia, where the dogs bark and the caravan passes, in America the writers bark and the trend passes.

In Germany the trend does not pass. Failing to understand the commercial nature of trend promotion, young Germans often tend to regard an American effort to turn a quick buck as a bona-fide wave of the future.

Throughout the eighties, young Germans were busily hating their parents when, with the exception of the usual percentage of freaks, the most recent generation in the United States would have found the idea so old-fashioned as to cause death by humiliation.

However, as it is hard work and inconvenient hating both parents, many young Germans settle for hating one and love the other dearly. This was the case with Wuschl, who loudly cursed his father in public places and proclaimed his love for his mother when he was drunk, which was not often as it is dangerous to drink when you are on hard drugs.

Wuschl was, of course, on hashish, but mostly cocaine. He was, after all, a normal youth and he had been assured by the press that narcotics were no worse than alcohol or tobacco or even coffee. They were, in fact, better because they were modern and up-to-the-minute.

Unfortunately, it is difficult to concentrate on your studies when you are in orbit on coke, and Wuschl had not done well at school. In fact, he had done so badly that he had had to leave altogether.

This was not as tragic as it seemed, for Wuschl had

inherited his father's business acumen and it was already obvious that he would never have to hold a job. Cocaine is not cheap, but Wuschl could afford it easily, and the rent on the apartment in Lenhausen and a video recorder to boot.

Actually, that was about all there was in the apartment: a television set, the video recorder and two mattresses, one of which was reserved for guests. Wuschl often entertained.

The spartan furnishings did not, however, make the cost of living any cheaper and, short of actually working, there was only one means of obtaining such an income in Attendorn.

And Wuschl mastered it! By the age of twenty, the talented youth had made himself king of the drug traffic in Attendorn! It was an accomplishment of which no modern youth need feel ashamed.

At regular intervals, Wuschl made business trips to the great drug centre of Amsterdam in nearby Holland, where he was able to purchase a wide selection of narcotics at wholesale prices for resale at substantial mark-ups in his sales district.

Applying the time-honoured principles of promoting the product through advertising and free samples, he steadily expanded the demand and, at the time of his mother's funeral, was carrying well over a hundred satisfied customers on his books. None were adult. Some were still in elementary school.

A typical, modern success story to confound the pessimists who claim that the spirit of enterprise is dead in Europe.

And yet, for all his success, Wuschl did not forget his mother. He was often in his old room in the house at Hellepaedchen 32, playing his old hard-rock favourites on the record player, smoking a few joints and providing that warm sense of continuing family so necessary to a mother whose children are grown and children no more.

His friends came with him. Although all of his

customers were, by necessity, his friends, three were more intimate than the others and, if Wuschl was D'Artagnan, Heiko Vogel, Andreas Waschek and Sabine Ahrens were the Three Musketeers, although some jealous tongues also compared them to the Four Horsemen of the Apocalypse.

Actually, of the four, Wuschl was probably the only one who would have had the strength to climb on to a horse. Close to six feet tall and solidly built, he had not yet been so weakened by narcotics that he could not beat up a recalcitrant customer, and he looked the picture of wholesome, slightly dirty, health.

The other three did not look unhealthy either, although they were rather frail. The two boys were barely eighteen and Sabine had just passed her fifteenth birthday, so none of them had lived long enough for the narcotics to affect their physical appearance.

Which was, unfortunately, not really all that impressive. Heiko, who was theoretically undergoing an apprenticeship as a metal former, was nearly as tall as Wuschl, but skinny, and his narrow face was a sort of dirty-lemon colour beneath a modified dark-blond Comanche haircut. The red plush jacket which he habitually wore did not flatter him.

Andreas was also dark-blond, but wore his hair long over a low, badly wrinkled forehead in a fringe, through which he peered with dark, sunken, sorrowful eyes. As the rest of his face was covered with acne, he was anxious to grow a beard, but had, so far, not succeeded in doing so. When he worked, he was a motor mechanic. He did not work often.

Sabine was more attractive. Being an adolescent girl, she looked like one. Straw-blonde straight hair stretching to below her shoulders. A little, pouting, red mouth. Round, pink cheeks, plump with baby fat. For her age, she was astoundingly well-built and dressed to show it.

Sabine was another of the many victims of society. She had become addicted to a startling array of drugs by the age of twelve, so her parents had put her into an institution where she was supposed to undergo withdrawal and, presumably, cure.

Sabine was not in agreement with this and, tying her bed-sheets together, shinned down two storeys to the street and freedom.

After supporting herself and her habit by cut-rate prostitution (she lacked Wuschl's business sense) for some months, she had encountered the gallant Drug King. He scooped her up from the gutter, more or less literally, and carried her off to the apartment in Lenhausen, where she had remained ever since. Her parents knew that she was there, but they had given up and abandoned her.

It might seem that in Attendorn all of the ingredients for happiness were present. Papa Hommerich was busy with his Mercedes and his mistresses. Mama Hommerich was joyfully contorting her fifty-four-year-old but lovely body in healthful and lucrative aerobic dances. Young Wuschl had successfully launched himself into the world of business and was enjoying the loving admiration of his little circle of friends. Even the drug addicts were happy, assured of a reliable source of supply. Who could ask more?

Many of the young people of Attendorn, it seemed. There were, they complained, few opportunities for entertainment for young persons in the little town and, perhaps, there was some truth to what they said.

Less than a mile and a half from the city was the mighty Schnellenberg Castle, a picturesque thirteenth-century ruin with a chapel where couples from all over the country came to be married, but few of the Attendorn youth were interested in castles or in getting married either.

Otherwise, there was only the town square, which, except for two park benches and a bus stop, was as bare as a billiard table. Fronting on this expanse of neatly swept concrete were the recreational facilities: a solitary

733

cinema, a stall selling French fries, an arcade with half a dozen pinball machines and a discothèque where cola cost four marks a bottle.

Drugs were actually cheaper. Although a joint cost twelve marks, the effect was more than three times as strong. Like any good businessman, Wuschl prided himself on quality. Cocaine was, of course, more expensive at three hundred marks a gram, but, if you wanted the best, you had to expect to pay for it.

The Attendorn youth seemed at least partially justified in their complaints and, as some organs of the press later pointed out, it was small wonder if they took to narcotics. They had been promised paradise as their right and all they had received was second-run films, pinball machines and soggy French fries.

Nor was it only the younger generation that was suffering. Hannelore Hommerich too was unhappy.

'Be reasonable, Thorsten,' she nagged. 'There's no future in the drug business. Sooner or later, the police are going to catch you and then you'll be in trouble. Why don't you take a course in accounting? You should learn a profession.'

'Mama,' said Thorsten patiently. 'I've told you repeatedly. I make in a week what an accountant earns in a year. And as for the police, there's one sergeant nearly due for retirement on narcotics and that's the whole squad for the Olpe district.'

Olpe was the district capital three miles to the south.

'I don't care,' said Hannelore stubbornly. 'I want you to get out of the drug business. If you don't stop it, I'll go to the police myself.'

This was a very foolish thing for Hannelore Hommerich to say and it clearly demonstrated that she had no understanding of modern young people and their problems. The dreaded generation gap had reared whatever passes for a head in a gap.

'I'll take it up with the board,' said Thorsten, and he did.

The Three Musketeers listened as attentively as anyone under the influence of narcotics can listen.

'As I have already told you many times,' said Wuschl, 'we are, unfortunately. going to have to waste Mama. If I don't stop dealing, she's going to blow the whistle on us.'

'We?' said Heiko. 'It's your mother.'

'All right. Me then,' said Wuschl, accepting responsibility with the courage of the born leader. 'You can still suggest something.'

'Get the first one straight in through the heart,' recommended Sabine. 'Then she won't squeak so much.'

'No cutting,' said Heiko. 'I can't stand the sight of blood.'

'Make it look like suicide,' said Andreas. 'You could throw her off the balcony.'

'Nobody commits suicide jumping off a first-floor balcony,' said Wuschl.

'An accident then,' said Heiko. 'She was drunk and she fell off the balcony.'

'Onto the lawn and sprained her ankle,' scoffed Wuschl. 'You're all worse than useless. I'll have to think of something myself.'

And, on the late afternoon of 20 October 1983, he did.

The four good friends were sitting in Wuschl's old room in his mother's house listening to rock records and rolling joints.

Hannelore Hommerich was in the kitchen baking cookies for her son and his friends.

She had just taken them out of the oven and gone into the living room when Wuschl got purposefully to his feet, went to the kitchen, came out immediately and went into the bathroom.

'Mama?' he called. 'Come here a minute. There's some kind of an animal in the bathtub.'

In Wuschl's old room down the hall, the Three

Musketeers exchanged thrilled glances. They did not think there was an animal in the bathtub.

Neither did Hannelore, but her son was calling her and she went.

'See?' said Wuschl, pointing into the tub.

Hannelore bent over the tub and her son plunged the ten-inch serrated blade of the family bread knife, which he had concealed inside his shirt, into her back with all his force.

The knife was sharp and, unlike most bread knives, had a sharp point. As the autopsy would later show, the blade penetrated for a depth of nearly eight inches, slicing into the pancreas, perforating the left lung and severing a number of important blood vessels.

For Hannelore, this was excruciatingly painful and she screamed terrifyingly, the shrill, throat-tearing scream of the human female in fear of death.

In Wuschl's room down the hall, the Three Musketeers moved instinctively closer together and Heiko turned up the volume of the record player, already operating at an ear-splitting level.

In the bathroom, Hannelore had swung about to face the son who was murdering her and was fighting for her life.

And as she fought, she pleaded. 'No, Torry!' calling him by his little boy's name. 'Don't do it! You'll go to prison, Torry. Don't hurt me! I'm your mother!'

But Torry was ten years gone and this was Wuschl, the successful businessman with an investment to protect. He jerked the knife out of her back and he stabbed and slashed at her stomach, her belly and her breasts, the same breasts from which he had once fed.

Hannelore continued to plead and to fight. 'No, Torry! Oh God! It hurts so! Stop, Torry! You're killing me!'

She was in superb physical condition as a result of the aerobic dancing and this was unfortunate for it took her a long time to die.

Precisely how long was never ascertained for none of

the participants was able to say with certainty when Wuschl had called his mother into the bathroom. It was, however, a little after nine-thirty when he appeared in the doorway of the bedroom, covered from head to foot with blood.

'Get these clothes off me,' he ordered.

The sounds from the bathroom had ceased. Under the violence of the blows, the bread knife had snapped in half and Wuschl had been forced to finish the job with the handleless blade gripped in his fingers, a dangerous operation as he could have cut himself painfully.

He had not, however, and his friends quickly stripped off his blood-soaked clothing and packed it into plastic grocery sacks.

Wuschl washed and got into fresh clothing and Sabine came to hold him tight and kiss him for close to half an hour. As she later said, he was in need of comfort at such a moment for the murder had upset him terribly and he kept saying, 'How awful! She made such a noise! And she took such a time about it.'

Heiko and Andreas were less concerned with Wuschl's emotions and more concerned with their own skins. Their drug-damaged minds were not always able to distinguish between imagination and reality and they had not grasped that Wuschl was really going to murder his mother until he was doing so.

Now, they not only realized that the murder had taken place, but that they were accessories to it. As they knew nothing about the German legal system, they believed they could be punished and it made them nervous.

'We'll have to make it look like somebody broke in and killed her,' said Heiko. 'Can you make it look like that, Wuschl?'

Wuschl could. Returning to the bathroom, he dragged his mother's still-warm corpse over the edge of the tub, pulled up her house-coat and ripped away her panties, getting his hands bloody again in the process.

He then picked up the handle of the knife from the

floor, pulled the blade out of Hannelore's rib-cage and returned to the room where the friends were waiting.

'We'll have to get rid of the knife and clothes,' he said. 'Maybe we can throw them in the Lenne.'

The Lenne river, a not very large steam, runs through Attendorn.

'Not here,' said Andreas. 'We'll throw the knife in the river at Lennestadt. It's deep under the bridge there.'

'And we can burn the clothes in the old quarry on the Lennestadt road,' added Heiko. Both he and Andreas were more mentally alert than they had been for years.

In Andreas' car, they drove silently to Lennestadt. The rays of the rising moon glinted briefly on the blade of the knife as it arced downward to the black waters beneath the bridge. Although the near-full moon was yellow, the reflection seemed strangely red.

It was approaching midnight when the pile of sticks soaked with petrol from the car's reserve cannister flared brightly beneath the bloody clothing in the old quarry, the garish light throwing grotesque, monstrous shadows along the vertical stone walls.

The young people were excited, exhilarated even. It was like the films or television. A tight little group of the best of friends united against the world. In a dull universe, something had finally happened in Attendorn.

But then the moon went in behind a cloud and the fire died down and it was dark and cold in the old quarry. The rising wind whistling through the crevices of the rock walls sounded almost like the voice of a woman, pleading, beseeching, 'Don't do it, Torry! You'll go to jail!'

Naturally, no mother wanted her boy to go to jail and Wuschl was determined to respect his mother's last wish. Getting back into the car, the four friends drove to Attendorn, where Wuschl got out in front of the police station while the others continued on to the apartment in Lenhausen.

At exactly seven minutes past midnight, according

738

to the police blotter, Thorsten Hommerich entered the charge room of the Attendorn police station and advanced to the desk.

The duty officer looked up from the magazine he was reading. 'Yes?' he said.

'My name is Thorsten Hommerich,' said Wuschl. 'I have just come from my mother's house at Hellepaedchen 32. It looks to me as if she's been murdered.'

The report caused the desk sergeant to drop his magazine and knock over the little tub of pencils and other equipment on the desk.

It was thirty-four years since there had been a homicide in Attendorn. Not a single member of the force at that time was still on active duty.

For an instant, the thought crossed the sergeant's mind that the caller must be drunk, but Thorsten did not look drunk. He was, as a matter of fact, cleaner, neater and more suitably dressed than he had been for years. Drugs did not occur to the sergeant. Like the other members of the police, he did not think that there was a drug problem in Attendorn.

Wuschl was waiting patiently and politely and the sergeant summoned his two duty constables, who were playing cards in the squad room, and told them to accompany Thorsten to the address and report back immediately on what they found.

A short time later, he received an almost hysterical report over the radio telephone. An ambulance was needed. The coroner was needed. The homicide squad was needed. This was murder, bloody murder!

The ambulance was sent and the coroner was pulled out of bed, but the homicide squad was not alerted because there was no homicide squad. With the last homicide thirty-four years back, one was scarcely needed.

The homicide squad, therefore, came up from Olpe and consisted initially of Inspector Ludwig Kranzer, Detective Sergeant Peter Berg and a medical expert named Alfred Dingermann. All had, of course, been in bed at the time that the call was received.

Arriving at the scene, the investigators found present an ambulance and crew, the Attendorn coroner and very nearly the entire Attendorn police force. Thorsten was not present. He had asked to be excused and gone back to Lenhausen. He was tired and he found the death of his mother very upsetting, he said.

The police found it, if anything, more so. Although the Olpe homicide unit had greater experience in such matters as they were responsible for the entire district, it was their first encounter with such a savage and apparently sexually motivated murder as this.

The sergeant and half a dozen members of the Attendorn police had gone through the house and found that money and jewellery were lying about exposed and had not been touched. Dr Dingermann, who had been examining the corpse in the meantime, reported that sex did not appear to have been the motive either.

'A rather clumsy attempt to fake a sex crime,' said the doctor, who was short, plump, blond and often struck women as cuddly. 'The indications are that she was already dead when she was draped over the edge of the bathtub and her clothing torn away. There's no trace of semen in or on the sex organs and no apparent attempt at penetration. She's been dead for three or four hours. Multiple stab wounds and fatal haemorrhaging. Remarkably good physical condition for her age. She must be in her fifties. Any idea who she was?'

The Attendorn police had a formal identification by the victim's son and, in any case, Hannelore's face was not marked and there were a number of pictures of her in the house, including one in her personal identity card.

Identification of the victim was, therefore, no problem, but identification of the murderer was.

As the first suspect in the murder of a married person is automatically the spouse, Inspector Kranzer, a comparatively young man with stylish sideburns and a near-classic profile, began by taking into custody Papa Hommerich, who, although no longer married to the victim, might have harboured ill feeling against her.

Papa Hommerich swore that he did not, but he was not arrested until the twenty-fourth, the day of his ex-wife's funeral and, by that time he was not completely certain where he had been or what he had been doing with whom on the afternoon and evening of the twentieth. Papa was still living the full life with more mistresses than ever, and his schedule was complex.

Eventually, however, he was able to recall his activities on the day in question and to provide enough evidence of the accuracy of his statements that he was released, although not removed entirely from the suspect list.

As a matter of fact, he was the only person on the list at the moment. No one suspected Wuschl because no one knew of any possible motive for the young man to murder his mother.

The outline of a motive only began to appear when Wuschl was, more or less routinely, included in the background studies of all persons close to the victim.

The investigators were intrigued by the fact that Wuschl appeared to enjoy an extremely affluent lifestyle (with the exception of household furnishings), but had no visible source of income.

Having had a look at Miss Ahrens, Sergeant Berg, a pleasant-appearing soul with a round, bland, pink-and-white face, came to the conclusion that Wuschl's income derived from the leasing of Miss Ahrens' anatomy, but the Attendorn police said no. There were teenage prostitutes in Attendorn, but Sabine was not one of them.

'Fascinating,' said the inspector. 'Well, the money's got to come from somewhere. Find out where.'

The sergeant found out and, actually, when he applied himself to it, it was not very hard. Wuschl was the sole dealer for the area and the traffic through the apartment in Lenhausen was roughly equivalent to that of a medium-size department store. It was noticeable.

And the customers were vulnerable. A few days in detention and they began to experience withdrawal symptoms, at which time they were willing and eager to tell the investigators anything they knew or even things they did not know in return for being allowed access to their favoured narcotic.

'This enterprising youth has the drug business sewn up for the whole area,' said the sergeant. 'He killed his mother because she was going to squeal on him or because she wanted a cut.'

'I don't believe it,' said the inspector. 'A fine young man like that? Good God! This isn't Berlin or Munich.'

The final statement was correct. It was not Berlin or Munich, but the fine young man had, indeed, killed his mother and, when the inspector talked to the police officers who had been in contact with him on the night of the crime, he too became convinced.

Wuschl, it seemed, had been cool, much, much too cool. Whatever excitement he had felt at the time of the murder had been comforted away by his friends and he had reported his mother's death with all the emotion of a spectator at a turtle race. The Attendorn officers had been so excited themselves that they had not been impressed by Wuschl's casual manner at the time, but they remembered it later.

Taken into custody, Wuschl, at first, stoutly denied all knowledge of his mother's death, but the Three Musketeers' principle of All for One and One for All did not bear up well in this case and D'Artagnan was roundly denounced by his companions, who strove heroically to load all of the blame on to him while whitewashing themselves.

Saddened by this lack of solidarity, Wuschl too broke down and filled in whatever details his friends had left out.

Some might fear that these sensitive, if somewhat misguided, young persons could have their lives ruined through harsh prison sentences, but only those who did not understand the German legal system.

Although, with the exception of Sabine, the participants were legally adults with all of the rights and privileges of such, in one respect and one respect only, they were children. Under the German juvenile code, the maximum sentence any of them could receive was ten years' imprisonment, and that was what they did receive on 16 November 1984.

It is very unusual that a juvenile receiving a ten-year sentence actually serves more than four years of it.

Who was the deviate? The dynamic, enterprising Wuschl?

How so? The man was in business. There was a lot of money involved. Was he to give it up because Mummy said so? After all, she wanted him to acquire a profession, and what could be more modern and progressive than pushing?

The Three Musketeers?

Hardly. They were really only spectators, or rather auditors, as they were to everything else in their lives.

Well, who then?

What about Hannelore Hommerich?

Germany is a democracy. She must have helped elect to office those who enact laws making it possible to kill your mother and suffer no more than minor inconvenience for it.

That should be deviate behaviour enough for our purposes.

16

A HAIRY TALE

From Lichtenau to Kassel is only about thirty-five miles. Both communities lie in the West German state of Hessen. Kassel is, however, a city of over two hundred thousand inhabitants and Lichtenau is a tiny village which barely appears on the map.

On 29 May 1981, a nineteen-year-old girl with a fine mane of long blonde hair set out to hitch-hike from Lichtenau to Kassel. She never made it.

Hessen is roughly in the centre of West Germany and not all May mornings are pleasant, but this one was. The sun shone golden yellow. Trees, bushes, grass, flowers, all were in leaf or in bloom and by ten o'clock the temperature was touching eighty degrees Fahrenheit.

Heike Freiheit left the home of her uncle in Lichtenau in high spirits. A pretty, good-natured girl, she did not have a great many problems. Her last name means freedom in German and she was worthy of it.

Heike's father had died in 1978 and, as her mother had left the family a good deal earlier, she had moved in with her father's brother, who kept a rather absent eye on her. He did not feel himself adequate to coping with a nineteen-year-old totally liberated female, but then, there are few who would.

In any case, Heike came and went more or less as she saw fit and it was, therefore, over a month before her uncle began to wonder what had happened to her. She was not an aggressively liberated girl and she usually let him know where she was, if not what she was doing.

This time, apparently not. The uncle did not know what to do. He had no idea of where she was planning to stay in Kassel, who she knew there or why she had wanted to go there in the first place. After a great deal of hesitation, he telephoned the Kassel police long-distance and asked if they could look for Heike.

The Kassel police replied that they would be happy to do so. One entire department of the police was devoted solely to looking for missing persons and, at the moment, there were around six hundred active cases, most of them young girls.

This did not sound very promising and it was not. The Kassel police did look for Heike, but they never found any trace of her at all, at all.

For a good reason, of course. Heike never made it to Kassel.

Now, the town of Padborg is a long way north of both Kassel and Lichtenau, such a long way, in fact, that it is not even in Germany, but just over the border in Denmark.

On 25 September 1981, six months after Heike Freiheit had set out for Kassel, the Padborg police made a descent upon a none-too-attractive apartment house located at 18 Jernbanegade, where they carried out a rather desultory search of an attic apartment occupied by twenty-nine-year-old Luigi Richard Longhi.

The police thought that Mr Longhi had stolen something, but, if he had, they did not find it and withdrew hurriedly as the apartment did not smell very good.

Even though they had found nothing in the small, untidy apartment where the ceiling sloped down to low partitions beneath the eaves, the police still regarded Longhi with a certain amount of suspicion. He was not only a foreigner, but a confusing sort of one.

Born in Switzerland, an occurrence which did not, however, confer Swiss nationality upon him, Longhi was of Italian descent and was legally a national of Italy.

From what the police knew about him, he had lived almost everywhere but Italy.

In 1977, he had been expelled from Switzerland for unknown reasons and lived for a time in Germany, where he held a number of unskilled jobs in the town of Neustadt an der Weinstrasse, which means merely New City on the Wine Road.

In 1979, he had come to Denmark, where he found a job in a saw mill at the town of Holbi. A year later he moved to Padborg, where he was currently employed as a filling-station attendant.

Why the police found Longhi suspicious was never explained. He had no police record in either Germany or Denmark and, if he had one in Switzerland, the Swiss were not prepared to discuss it. Possibly, it was simply because he was an obvious southern European and there are few from the sunny Mediterranean who live without extremely pressing reasons in such a frozen and freezing place as the Danish-German border.

In any case, they did not search his apartment nearly as thoroughly as they should have. All that they could find wrong with Luigi Richard Longhi was that he stank, which is not a chargeable offence in Denmark.

The other occupants of the apartment house were inclined to wish that it was. For months they had been complaining to the owner that the building stank abominably, but, as he did not live there himself, he regarded the complaints as typical tenant carping, possibly initiated in the hope of obtaining a reduction in the rent.

'I don't smell anything,' he said, standing in the front hall and holding his breath. 'It's your imagination.'

Water coming through the roof could not, however, be imagination and quite a bit having come through during that winter of 1981–82, the landlord engaged a roofing firm to come as soon as the weather permitted and effect repairs.

The roofing company workers arrived on Monday, 29 March 1982 and began tearing off the tiles of the old roof. The landlord would later complain that this was not necessary, but, fortunately, he did not know what was going on until a good part of the roof was already off.

One of the people actually pulling off those old tiles was a young Dane named Sven Jorgensen. He was an unskilled labourer, as no particular skill is needed for pulling off old tiles.

Good lungs were, however, and Jorgensen soon found himself nearly asphyxiated by the most vile stench he had ever encountered in his life, even though he was working out in the open air.

Because of the manner in which tiles are laid, it was necessary for Jorgensen to begin at the peak of the roof and work downward toward the eaves, and the closer he came to them, the worse the smell.

Removing a row of tiles a scant three feet from the edge of the roof, Jorgensen found himself gazing down into the space behind the partitions forming the walls of Luigi Richard Longhi's attic apartment.

It was a sunny day and he could see clearly between the slats which supported the tiles. There was something lying in the space, something long, strangely formed . . .

Jorgensen held his breath, put his head down, looked closer, gave a yell of horror and fell off the roof.

What he had seen was a sort of surrealist sculpture, a weirdly formed mass of a whitish-grey substance with a white powder covering everything, and projecting from this strange cocoon one skeletal hand and forearm and a grinning, nearly fleshless skull topped grotesquely by a great mane of long blonde hair.

Sven Jorgensen had accomplished what the Kassel police could not. He had found Heike Freiheit.

As he had never met her previously, he did not, of course, recognize her, but, even had he been her mother, he would have had difficulty in doing that.

'It would be even worse,' said Dr Olaf Sorensen, 'if she hadn't been sprinkled with lime.'

747

The doctor, tall, lean, black-haired and slightly awkward-looking, had just completed the on-the-spot examination of the body and crawled gratefully back out of the hole which the inspector and sergeant had made in the partition.

They, like the doctor, had come down from Abenra, twenty-five miles to the north, which, although a community of scarcely more than twenty thousand inhabitants, was the administrative centre for all of South Jutland.

Being sturdily built and lucky, Sven Jorgensen had not broken anything in his fall from the roof. He had run straight to the Padborg police, who investigated and promptly summoned the homicide squad in Abenra.

But not before taking into custody Luigi Richard Longhi at his place of work. They had not questioned him or even informed him why he was being arrested, and he was now sitting in the detention cell normally reserved for drunks at the Padborg police station.

As he had neither protested nor asked any questions, it seemed probable that he had a good idea of the reasons for his arrest.

And, indeed, he had. Confronted with the fact that the corpse of a girl had been found behind the partition of his apartment, he immediately admitted that he had put her there. The police had not needed to make a hole in the partition. One of the panels was removable.

Longhi said that he had put the girl there because she was dead and he had not known what else to do with her.

He had tried to cause as little trouble as possible and, when the other tenants of the building began complaining about the smell, he bought some containers of plastic foam and what he thought was a bag of cement. With this, he proposed to completely envelope the corpse and make it, more or less, a part of the building.

The plan had not worked out very well. The supposed cement turned out to be lime and the plastic foam was not adequate to entirely cover the body. He spread the lime over it anyway and withdrew. It had been, he said, very unpleasant working in the small space under the eaves with the corpse which was, by this time, more than half rotten.

'I'm sure,' said Inspector Karl Andersen, who was large, blond and looked the way that most people think Danes should look, 'but who was she and why did you do it?'

Like everyone else, the inspector assumed that the victim was Danish, but Longhi said, no, she was German or, at least, she had spoken German like a German.

Otherwise, he knew little about her. Her first name was Heike and he had met her in a small café near the railway station on the evening of 30 May 1981. She said that she was looking for a place to spend the night and he suggested his apartment. She accepted.

Up to this point, Longhi was cooperative and even appeared to be prepared to confess to the murder of the girl, but on the subject of what had actually happened at the apartment, he was much more reticent, saying merely that there had been an unfortunate misunderstanding.

The inspector thought that the misunderstanding had probably been of a sexual nature. Longhi would logically have assumed that, if the girl accepted an invitation to spend the night at his apartment, she was prepared to spend it with him in bed. It was possible that Heike had had different ideas.

Living so close to the border, the inspector had had some experience with liberated West German girls and he was aware that some, at least, would regard the exchange of sex for lodging as a violation of the principles of equality of the sexes. Sexual contacts were only permissible by mutual agreement, not subject to compensation and, ideally, in connection with a meaningful relationship.

Such a sophisticated philosophy might have been

difficult to explain to a sexually aroused filling-station attendant.

What happened then, the inspector surmised, was that Longhi had taken or attempted to take by force what he could not obtain by consent, and he had ended up strangling the girl.

According to the autopsy, that was exactly what he had done. Heike had been strangled with a thin cord, which was still around the place where her neck had been.

She had also been bound and gagged at the time, for the bonds and the gag were found in the plastic foam covering a part of the body.

Whether she had been raped or not could no longer be ascertained. Nothing remained of Heike's sex organs at all.

Nor much of the rest of her, with the exception of the long blonde hair. Dr Sorensen was able, however, to make a fairly accurate estimate of her height, weight and general build, and to determine that she had while yet a child broken one of the bones in her left foot and that this had been put right by a doctor.

The information from the autopsy, the date of the disappearance, the presumed nationality and the name of Heike were, perhaps, enough to effect an identification and the details were sent off to the West German authorities with an account of the circumstances of the crime and a request for any information that could be obtained concerning Luigi Richard Longhi during his sojourn in West Germany.

To the inspector's surprise, the response was quick.

Within less than a week, an answer was received from the national identification centre in Wiesbaden to the effect that the victim was possibly Heike Freiheit, reported missing in the Kassel area around the end of May 1981 and that, if Longhi had done anything illegal in Neustadt an der Weinstrasse, the police had not known of it. A search of the records of unsolved cases of missing or murdered females in the region for the period in question was being undertaken.

The inspector's case was, therefore, largely complete. There was a tentative identification of the victim, which would later be confirmed from Heike's medical records – she had broken a bone in her foot as a child – and there was an excellent suspect in the form of Luigi Richard Longhi, behind the partition of whose apartment the body had been found.

'He hasn't actually confessed to the murder,' said Sergeant of Detectives Baldur Kracken, the inspector's second in command of the Abenra homicide squad, who did not like to see his chief looking quite so smug.

'He will,' said the inspector confidently. 'What choice does he have? The body was behind the partition of his room and he admits he put it there.'

'But he only says that there was an unfortunate misunderstanding,' said the sergeant. 'I wonder what he'll testify in court and what the defence will make out of it.'

Although the sergeant had a very Scandinavian name, he was relatively short, with the brown hair, brown eyes and olive complexion of southern Europe.

The inspector looked slightly uneasy. There was something in what the sergeant said. Going to court with no clear idea of what the accused was going to testify was risky.

'You suggest?' he said.

'He was kicked out of Switzerland,' said the sergeant. 'He must have done something. This being a homicide case, the Swiss should cooperate and, if we know what he did there, it may throw light on what happened here. There's no evidence that it was a sex crime. We don't really have a motive.'

'True, true,' mused the inspector. 'I don't know about the Swiss. From what I've heard, they don't need a reason to throw you out of the country. Still, we can try.'

Before trying the Swiss, however, the inspector called in a psychologist to carry out an examination of Longhi, now formally indicted on an undefined homicide charge and bound over for trial. The psychologist was to attempt to get more information from Longhi concerning his motives for the murder than the police had succeeded in doing so far.

The psychologist spent a few weeks at this task, but was unable to penetrate Longhi's reserve.

'It's not that he's uncooperative,' he reported. 'It's that he's ashamed. There's something about women's hair that's connected with his mother and he won't or can't talk about it. He says he's going to plead guilty at the trial so that he won't have to explain anything.'

'So he says,' said the sergeant sceptically.

'You have a suspicious nature, Baldur,' said the inspector. 'Well, I suppose it's the Swiss.'

Contrary to expectations, there was no problem with the Swiss police nor, it seemed, had they been so brusque in their treatment of Longhi as had been believed.

The fact was, Longhi had not been too desirable a citizen by any country's standards. Born to a somewhat carefree mother, he landed in an orphanage at the age of two, where he remained until the age of nine. Then his mother decided to resume her responsibilities and took him to live with her.

Longhi stayed with his mother until the age of seventeen, at which time he was arrested on a curious charge. He had, according to police and court records, waited for a young female hairdresser to come out from work, threatened her with a knife and, having taken her to her own room, washed her hair against her will.

Longhi had done nothing else to the girl and the police were, for a time, at a loss as to what the charge should be. It had not occurred to the law-makers to provide an appropriate punishment for forced hair washes.

In the end, he was charged with threats with a deadly weapon and put on two years' probation. He had been more frank with the Swiss psychologists than with the one in Abenra and they came to the conclusion that he was not dangerous, in spite of the knife.

Longhi, it seemed, not having lived with his mother from the age of two to nine, did not regard her in an entirely filial manner. Although there was no suggestion of an incestuous relationship, he developed the habit of masturbating into her wig, which was long and blonde and to which he applied liberal amounts of shampoo for the purpose. She was, of course, neither wearing it nor present at the time.

Unfortunately, this comparatively harmless perversion soon turned into a less harmless one. Longhi could no longer obtain sexual satisfaction with his mother's wig. He required the hair of a living woman, and it had to be long and blonde.

There was also another difference. Longhi did not now masturbate directly into the hair, but achieved orgasm through simply applying shampoo and washing it.

The act put him into such a state that he was able to arrive at a climax three and more times in succession, the intervals between ejaculations becoming, understandably, increasingly longer so that the process took up the best part of an evening.

As Longhi showed no tendency to sadism or violence and as he was literally incapable of raping his victims in the conventional manner, the psychologists recommended treatment and probation rather than a prison sentence.

Longhi did not, however, respond to treatment. Less than a year later, he abducted a young physical therapist and subjected her to no less than six hours of continuous hair washing, an experience which left both exhausted.

This time the matter was more serious. Longhi had, once again, threatened the victim with a knife. Worse, he had also bound and gagged her and he had placed a noose around her neck, although he had not drawn it tight.

Despite this second offence and a less favourable opinion by the psychologists, Longhi was still allowed his freedom, but under closer surveillance.

This did not prevent him from washing several more young ladies' hair and, in 1977, the Swiss finally became impatient and put him out of the country. The reasons for his expulsion were not given, presumably because it would have made it difficult to find a country that would accept him.

From that date up to the time of his arrest in Padborg, Longhi had had no police record of any kind, either in Germany or in Denmark.

The inspector did not think that this meant he had given up washing girls' hair. He thought that he had simply become more clever about it.

'Giving up washing women's hair would be for him the equivalent of giving up sex altogether,' he said. 'There's nothing in the record that says he had to do it against their will. He probably just started paying them.'

'Undoubtedly,' agreed the sergeant, 'but, if so, why did he murder Heike Freiheit? A disagreement over the price? He said there was a misunderstanding.'

'There's only one person who can answer that,' said the inspector, 'and I think that once he realizes that we know all about his sex problems, he will.'

Luigi Richard Longhi would. He did not like being a pervert and he had no intention of evading responsibility for what he had done, but he had been reluctant to discuss his motives or his actions in the attic apartment as they appeared bizarre even to him.

He was, he said, cursed with a strange sickness. There was no way in the world that he could obtain sexual satisfaction other than through washing the long blonde hair of a girl. He had tried everything and nothing worked.

The girl did not have to resist. The process worked equally well if she was consenting, and he had managed well with prostitutes while he was in Germany.

On other occasions, he had picked up young girls and had simply asked them to let him wash their hair. Many had not objected.

One such pick-up had, however, turned out badly when the girl wanted intercourse and became abusive when she discovered that he was incapable of it. She threatened to go to the police and say that he had raped her and, as she was only fourteen years old, he became frightened and left Germany to come to Denmark.

The situation in Denmark was worse. Holbi was very small and there were no prostitutes at all. He had, therefore, moved to Padborg, where there were a few, but, by mischance, it turned out that none of them were blonde except one, and she wore her hair short.

He was badly frustrated sexually when he encountered Heike in the café, and he asked her almost point-blank whether she would mind him giving her a shampoo.

Heike, who was a good-natured girl and far from prudish, undoubtedly believed that she would end up with more than a hair wash and, as Longhi was not physically unattractive by the undemanding standards of modern youth, she agreed.

He had not even felt it necessary to tie and gag her at first, but, after the fourth hair wash, Heike became restless and he tied her up and gagged her as he was afraid that she would make enough noise to alarm the other tenants.

'The fourth?' said the inspector.

'Well, yes,' said Longhi modestly looking down at the floor. It had been a long time, he added apologetically.

'Continue,' said the inspector.

Heike became, said Longhi, not frightened, but angry and, as her feet were not tied, she began to stamp violently on the floor.

In order to stop her, he drew tight the noose that he had put around her neck and the next thing he knew, she was dead. It had been as simple as that.

'You continued to wash her hair after she was dead?' asked the inspector.

Longhi shook his head sadly. 'No,' he said, 'It has to be a live girl for me.'

On 11 February 1983, a jury in the nearby town of Sonderborg listened to Luigi Richard Longhi's account of the crime, heard his admission that he had previously shampooed the hair of twelve other more or less consenting maidens, making Heike the unlucky thirteenth, and tried to decide what was to be done with him.

It was obvious that he had not killed with premeditation or even with intent. Heike's death actually put an end to the only use that he had for her.

It was also obvious that he regretted very bitterly his act.

However, that did not alter the fact that he was potentially dangerous and could most certainly be expected to resume his hair-washing activities once the sexual pressure became too strong for him to resist.

In the end, the court found him guilty of unpremeditated murder and sentenced him to life, but not in prison. Sent to a closed institution for sex psychopaths, he was to benefit from a review of his case if it was believed that he had responded to treatment.

17

ARTISTS AND MODELS

Not all dogs in West Germany are named Waldi, but a great many are, and on the evening of 30 June 1978 a dachshund with a slightly dubious pedigree who bore this name was taking his associate for a walk in the fields near the village of Kirkel-Altstadt.

The walk was progressing a little too slowly for Waldi's taste. The associate, who preferred to think of himself as master, was forty-one years old and rather given to the pleasures of the table. He was not, therefore, as enthusiastic about running into all the ditches, snuffling through all the thickets and racing wildly down the field paths as was Waldi.

Even so, both Karl Bauer and his dog looked forward to their late-afternoon walks and this was a particularly fine one.

The summer solstice was only a week past and, at eight o'clock, it was still broad daylight. The weather was excellent and the entire countryside was in leaf and bloom. Although the great highway leading from the city of Saarbruecken on the German-French border to the town of Neunkirchen was not far away, the sound of the endless stream of vehicles passing over it did not reach this far and the tree-lined fields were quiet, fragrant and peaceful.

Except, of course, for the barking of stupid, far too exuberant dogs.

'Shut up, Waldi!' yelled Bauer, pounding with his walking stick on the ground. 'Shut up this minute!'

But Waldi would not shut up, which did not surprise Bauer very much. The little dachshund had many virtues, but obedience was not among them.

What did surprise Bauer was that the dog was standing still and barking. Barks were usually brought on by wild chases after real or imaginary rabbits, but now Waldi was standing rigidly alert and barking at what looked like a partially burned log.

As Bauer drew nearer, he saw the explanation for Waldi's concern. The log was apparently still burning, for thin trails of smoke were rising from it.

Conscious of the danger of fire in a wooded area such as this, Bauer hurried forward to stamp out the sparks.

The log moved!

And spoke! Or tried to speak. The sounds that rasped from the throat were barely human, a low, weak, keening sound, crying out a suffering beyond expression.

Rooted to the spot, Bauer stood staring down at a sight that burned itself so indelibly into his brain that he would never forget it, although he would have given anything in the world to be able to.

What lay there on the scorched grass was the body of a woman. There was no question of that, for her clothing had been burned entirely away. Whether she had been old or young, beautiful or ugly, blonde or brunette was impossible to say, for her hair had vanished and her skin was no more than a blackened crust, cracking and bursting in places to display the angry red, blood-oozing flesh beneath.

It seemed impossible that any human being could be burned in such a manner and remain alive.

This human was not only alive but conscious and, as Bauer later admitted, his first instinct was to kill her. The sight of such suffering was too much to bear. Death would be a release.

Bauer was, however, no killer and, like many Germans of his generation, he was public-spirited and he had faith in the authorities. It was up to them to do something.

At a pace of which he would not have believed himself capable, Bauer ran headlong in the direction of the village and a telephone.

Kirkel-Altstadt is too small to have much in the way of emergency services, but Saarbruecken is a scant seven miles away and it has a population of close to a quarter of a million.

Bauer did not, therefore, seek help in Kirkel-Altstadt, but telephoned directly the Saarbruecken emergency service, stammering out such a graphic and horrifying description of what he had found that a rescue helicopter took off immediately. Eight minutes later it set down at the point where Bauer was standing waving his cane with his handkerchief tied to the end of it.

He had not managed to make it all the way back to the woman and he was so out of breath from running that he could only point in the right direction. As his family doctor would later say, he only escaped by a whisker becoming a victim himself.

The stretcher-bearers from the helicopter set off on a run and, within minutes, the hideously burned woman, still conscious as the paramedic had not dared to give her an injection, was on her way to a hospital that specialized in the treatment of massive burns.

This hospital, one of the finest in Germany, was equipped with the most modern technology known to medical science. Miracles had taken place there, but there would be no miracle this time.

At ten-thirty in the evening of 1 July 1978, Carmen Cojaniz, who had been born Carmen Aeschlimann, drew her last agonized breath. She had retained consciousness up to the very end, although she was drowsy from the massive injections of pain-killers which she had received.

Carmen had fought to remain conscious because she too was public-spirited and she was afraid that what had happened to her could happen to another woman unless the madman responsible was rendered harmless.

Who this madman was, she could not say, for she

759

had never seen him before in her life until that Friday afternoon when she was waiting to cross the street at a traffic light on the corner of Eschberger Way in Saarbruecken.

The man, who was driving a grey Opel Ascona with a Saarbruecken licence plate, passed her, returned and passed her again three or four times.

Carmen was not unduly alarmed. She was used to such interest. An outstandingly beautiful woman with a magnificent figure, she was her husband's favourite model and her perfectly formed breasts appeared in nearly every picture he had ever painted since their meeting on the Spanish Costa Brava in 1966.

Carmen was Swiss and came from the city of Basel. Norbert Cojaniz was a professional artist and came from Duesseldorf. Both were on holiday and both fell head-over-heels in love at first sight. They married a month later.

And lived happily ever after, for twelve years at least. Norbert was successful with his painting, due, he swore, largely to the beauty of his subject, and Carmen was happy in her role of wife and model. They did not yet have any children for fear of the effect that it might have on Carmen's figure.

Carmen did not immediately tell the doctors about Norbert. She was anxious to provide a description of the man who had burned her before she died. It was utterly vital that he be caught for, otherwise, perhaps one day another woman or girl would be standing beside the street waiting to cross and the Opel Ascona would pull in to the kerb and the man would point the dangerous-looking pistol and order, 'Get in!'

And then it would be too late. The man would drive out towards Neunkirchen and force the girl to strip herself totally naked, and then he would kiss her.

Karl Bauer was mistaken. Carmen's clothing had not been burned away. She was naked when she was set on fire.

But not raped. The only intimacy was that single kiss. The man then drove to the field path near Kirkel-Altstadt, where he took a nylon rope from the trunk of the Opel and bound her hand and foot.

Carrying her some twenty or thirty feet from the car, he laid her on the grass and returned to the car to fetch a standard reserve cannister of petrol such as many motorists carried for emergencies.

Nearly insane with fear, Carmen felt him pour the cold petrol over her from head to foot, and then there was an unbearable short wait while he returned once again to the car.

She dared not think what he had gone for, but it was, of course, matches. She saw the deadly little flame spring up as he struck the match and then there was the sudden whoosh of burning petrol, black smoke before her eyes, an unbelievable sensation of heat and agony beyond description.

How long the agony went on or whether the man had stayed to gloat over her sufferings, she could not say. It was about six o'clock in the afternoon when she was forced into the car and she supposed that it was around six-thirty when she was set on fire. After that, she no longer had any clear concept of time or her surroundings. There was only the pain, the terrible, all-encompassing pain. Even now, despite the injections, she could feel it. It would never leave her.

The man, said Carmen Cojaniz, her cooked lips cracking from the movement in forming words, was young, not yet thirty. He had dark hair and brown eyes and comparatively regular features. He was five feet eight or nine inches tall and muscular. There was a black mole or birthmark the size of a small coin beneath his left ear at the point of the jaw. There was a larger, similar birthmark on the back of his left hand. He was clean-shaven and had a short, conventional haircut. His fingernails were rimmed with black as if he had washed his hands carefully but had not been able to get all of the dirt out from under the nails. He was wearing grey summer trousers with a broad belt, the buckle of which was of yellow metal like brass and in the shape of a lion's head. He had on a short-sleeved, pale-green sports shirt, open at the neck, and moccasin-type brown shoes. He smelled of shaving lotion, but she did not know what kind.

Having done all that she could to bring to justice the man who had murdered her, Carmen asked to see Norbert as she thought she was going to die very soon.

It was not as soon as she expected, but, when she was finally released from her suffering, it was with Norbert holding her blackened, mutilated hands while the tears streamed down his cheeks in an agony nearly as unbearable as hers.

The love story was over.

And so too was the detective story. Even before his victim was dead, one of the most cruel and inexcusable murderers in the annals of the German police had been taken into custody and was pouring out a self-pitying justification for a crime that could never be justified.

Carmen's description of what had taken place and her descriptions of the murderer, his clothing and his car were taken down on a tape recorder and the latter part of the statement was heard personally by Inspector Morris Belder and Detective Sergeant Leopold Freimann, both of the Saarbruecken police homicide squad.

Although it did not occur to Karl Bauer to summon the police, the pilot of the emergency helicopter had immediately realized that the burning was a criminal act and contacted police headquarters over the helicopter's radio while the craft was still in the air.

The pilot expressed the opinion that the victim's injuries would prove to be fatal and the homicide squad was, therefore, called away at the double, racing through the streets with the siren of the police car wide open, to the hospital in the hope of obtaining a statement from the victim before she died.

In this they were more successful than they expected. Carmen's description of the murderer was so precise the police artist would be able to prepare such an accurate drawing that even persons who did not know him could recognize him from it instantly.

The homicide squad officers brought with them a police medical expert. He was, however, unable to do anything at the hospital and could only report that death had been the result of massive burns covering the entire body when he performed the obligatory autopsy the following day.

Inspector Belder, a hatchet-faced man with a lean, hard body and very short-cut sandy-red hair, had been able to do more.

He had rushed the description of the killer to police headquarters, stood over the artist while he prepared the drawing, ran it personally through the duplicating machine and arranged for the drawing and a description of man and car to be distributed immediately to all police units in the area. As Saarbruecken is on the French border, he also alerted the customs and border police, and for a time the crossing point was closed.

Not possessing the ability to be in more than one place at one time, he had not done all of this personally, but had assigned what he could not manage to Sergeant Freimann, who was short, plump, had slightly protruding front teeth and was capable of moving a great deal faster than anyone would have suspected to look at him.

As a result of all this activity, the entire area was swarming with police throughout the night, every grey Opel Ascona was stopped and checked, and twenty-seven-year-old Hans Joachim Lauer was arrested as he was driving into Saarbruecken at a quarter to eight the next morning.

Lauer, a car mechanic, was on his way to work and

763

expressed great astonishment at his arrest. He had never, he protested, had any trouble with the police in his life.

This was quite true, but there was, none the less, a file on him at police headquarters as he had attempted suicide no less than four times, always apparently, with sincere intent, but, unfortunately, never with success.

He was also telling the truth when he said that he had never heard of Carmen Cojaniz and had no idea who she was.

He was less truthful when he said that he had not burned her alive.

Lauer matched the description given by Carmen Cojaniz to the last detail and, although he was not wearing them that day, the clothes that she had described were found in the wardrobe in the bedroom of the house which he occupied in the village of Bergweiler, not far to the north of Saarbruecken. His car was a grey Opel Ascona and it carried a Saarbruecken licence plate.

An identification by the victim was, of course, out of the question, although she was still alive at the time of Lauer's arrest. Even had she been able to stand the psychological shock of confronting her torturer, her eyes had been seared by the fire and she was blind.

The identification was not, however, necessary. The police were convinced that Lauer was their man and those who had seen the victim would probably have killed him and faced a murder charge rather than let him go free.

There was no need for such drastic measures either, for Lauer had not been very clever in his crime. At the time of his arrest, Carmen Cojaniz's clothing was still in the boot of his car.

Confronted with this irrefutable evidence, Lauer broke down and blamed the murder on his wife!

Her bullying, he said, and her threats of divorce fomented such a hatred of women in him that he had, accidentally and without intending any harm, set fire to a woman he picked up off the street because of her lovely breasts.

According to Lauer, his wife, Erika, who was the same age as himself, was very cruel to him. An employee in a Saarbruecken bank, she habitually drove the family car to work and he had to take the bus. The only reason that he had had the car that morning was that she did not work on Saturday and he did.

The inspector, who had seen Carmen not long after she was admitted to the hospital and was now having a little trouble keeping his hands off the suspect, asked grimly if it was not true that he had also had the car the evening before.

Lauer said, yes, but that it had been an exception.

Another of Mrs Lauer's cruelties which made her responsible for the death of Carmen Cojaniz was that she allowed her husband only very modest pocket money.

Informed of Hans Joachim's accusations, Mrs Lauer replied that they had an eight-year-old daughter to support, and after the money had been taken out for Hans Joachim's hobbies, a modest amount of pocket money was all that was left.

These hobbies, it seemed, were the basis of all of the Lauer family's domestic discord. A fanatic devotee of leisure-time avocations, he was a hobbyist to end all hobbyists and, incredibly, his greatest obsession was exactly that which Carmen's husband practised professionally. It was painting.

And, precisely like Cojaniz, Lauer's favourite and, indeed, only model had been his wife.

For over five years, Erika Lauer had patiently posed in her pretty pink skin during practically every minute that her husband was not working or asleep, while he struggled happily but incompetently to transfer her likeness to canvas.

She then decided that she had had enough. Posing naked seven evenings a week and all day Sunday was not her idea of marriage.

Lauer wept and complained. He did not drink away his money like other men. He did not chase women like other men. He did not smoke. All he wanted was to paint and his wife would not let him.

Erika countered with other suggestions. For two months she dragged him to a dancing school, where he learned to dance passably well.

But he did not want to dance. He wanted to paint.

Erika tried bowling. Once a week, they went bowling together. Hans Joachim became reasonably competent.

But he took no pleasure in his strikes and spares. What Hans Joachim wanted was to paint.

In desperation, Erika cleaned out the family savings account and bought him a ham radio outfit. Her reasoning was that, if she could get him interested in something other than painting, no matter what, it might dilute his enthusiasm for hobbies in general.

The result was a disaster. Hans Joachim became wildly enthusiastic about ham radio, but it did not cut down on his painting. Now, he painted in the evenings and stayed up most of the night with the ham radio. His wife and his daughter could scarcely speak to him he was so busy.

By that fateful Friday of 30 June, Erika Lauer had not yet actually filed for divorce, but she was giving the matter some very serious thought. She had finally come to the conclusion that nothing would separate Hans Joachim from his beloved hobbies.

She was quite right. When the presiding judge asked Lauer what he planned to do while in prison, he answered immediately and unhesitatingly, 'I'm going to paint.'

He was not going to paint Erika. Sick with horror at what her husband had done, she hired a lawyer the day following his confession and indictment and was granted a divorce in record time, the court failing to agree with Lauer's contention that the murder was her fault.

As for Hans Joachim Lauer, he confessed to the crime

766

and, when he found that he could not blame his wife for it, altered his statement to claim that the whole affair had been accidental and, therefore, no murder at all.

He had, he told the court, had no intention in the world of picking up any woman, let alone harming one, when he went off to work that Friday morning, but then he saw Carmen waiting to cross the street and he was so overwhelmed by the beauty of her breasts that he felt an irresistible impulse to paint her.

'You must understand me,' he told the judge earnestly. 'I am a painter and the creative urge . . .'

'I understand the creative urge perfectly,' responded the judge. 'What I do not understand is what happened afterward.'

That had all been an accident, protested Lauer. He just happened to have the pistol in the glove compartment of the car. It was only by chance that there was a nylon rope in the boot. It was sheer hazard that there was a box of matches in his pocket.

'You have testified that you are a non-smoker, Mr Lauer,' said the judge. 'Why would you carry matches in your pockets?'

Actually, the matches had not been in Lauer's pocket. Carmen Cojaniz had testified that he deliberately returned to the car to get them.

Lauer was unable to reply.

Erika Lauer was then called as a witness for the prosecution. Looking straight through her former husband, who smiled and waved, she testified that she had driven the car on Thursday, the day before the murder, and that there had been no pistol in the glove compartment and no nylon rope in the boot. To the best of her knowledge, there never had been either the one or the other in the car or in the house.

The police had been unable to trace where Lauer bought the pistol, a Belgian Fabrique National 7.65, but a hardware shop assistant identified Lauer as the man who had bought a coil of nylon rope two days before the murder.

Lauer's response was that he had been given the pistol as a birthday present, although he could not remember from whom. The rope, he said, he had never seen before he opened the boot. The hardware shop employee was mistaken.

Whatever his other failings, Hans Joachim Lauer was certainly not a man to give up easily, but his persistence did him, perhaps, more harm than good. The court took his efforts to reduce his responsibility badly and, on 16 March 1979, sentenced him to life imprisonment, the maximum sentence possible under German law.

There was probably nothing that Lauer could have done to avoid the maximum sentence. The jury had heard the tape recordings of Carmen's pitiful broken voice recounting the unpredictable horror that had overtaken her on a sunny summer afternoon and they had seen the pictures of her hideously tortured body.

As one of the jurors later told a reporter, 'There was no discussion on the verdict. The only question was how we could be sure that he would never be released.'

It was a question that went unanswered. No one serves a life sentence in Germany today and Hans Joachim Lauer will not either.

In the meantime, he is getting in a great deal of painting practice.

18

ALWAYS PREPARED

At ten minutes past eleven in the evening of 19 September 1982, thirty-two-year-old Jean Levallois reported for work at the entrance of the Carte Blanche club. It was a Sunday, but Levallois worked on Sundays. The club was open seven days a week and twelve hours a day from 11 p.m. to 11 a.m.

Open was, perhaps, not exactly the right term. The Carte Blanche was a very private club and admission was by membership card only.

Nor was the obtaining of a membership card such an easy matter. Unlike some of the other 'private' clubs in the Le Carré entertainment district of Liège, the Belgian city on the Meuse river, the Carte Blanche was a serious establishment where many of the owners and managers of the other night-spots came to relax from their labours. Annette Rosen, the thirty-nine-year-old manageress, was well known for running a superior place.

And also for her caution. Liège is a city of over a quarter of a million inhabitants and Le Carré is a tough district. Things happen to people there, unpleasant things.

Annette knew all about those things. She had been working in Le Carré most of her life, first as a waitress and then, beginning in 1979, just at the time that she was getting a divorce from her husband, as manager of the Carte Blanche.

Like most people who have worked hard to achieve their success, Annette was extremely conscientious and almost painfully punctual. The club opened on the dot of eleven and it closed on the dot of eleven.

And, because of this, Jean Levallois, a very large young man with a crew-cut who served not only as bartender but also as bouncer if the occasion arose, was amazed when she failed to respond to his knock at ten minutes past the hour. He had worked for Annette for over two years and this was the very first time that she had not been at the club when he arrived.

Or had she not heard him?

It was possible. If she was far at the back behind the bar, she might not have noticed a light rap on the door. After all, there was the vestibule in between the outside door and the actual entrance to the club rooms.

Levallois knocked again, harder. It did not occur to him that Annette might be sick. From what he knew of her, she would have dragged herself to work with two broken legs.

There was still no response, but, to his sudden alarm, the door seemed to move slightly under his knuckles.

Levallois pushed it. It swung open! The door was not locked!

Obviously, something catastrophic had taken place. It was unthinkable that the door should not be locked. It was Annette's first act upon arriving and her last when leaving. Whether she was inside or out, the door was always locked. The door was not broken nor was the lock. It had been opened with a key, and only Annette had a key.

Tense with apprehension, the bartender pushed wide the door and entered.

The vestibule was small, a passage some eight feet wide and ten feet long with the outside entrance at one end and a flight of three steps leading up to swing doors with glass port-holes at the other. It was floored with large squares of alternating black and white tiles and lit by sconces on both walls.

The lights were on and, lying on the black-and-white

tiles was the body of Annette Rosen. She was totally naked and she lay on her back with arms and legs spread wide. Against the white skin of her body, the bruises stood out, blue-black, like some strange, abstract design. From chin to shoulders, her throat was purple-black and swollen and, above it, her normally attractive features were distorted in the hideous grimace of the victim of strangulation, the eyes wide and staring and an unbelievable length of tongue protruding from the open mouth.

For an instant, Levallois stood paralysed, the great muscles of his thick shoulders swelling in anger. Annette had been a good woman and a good boss. It would have been a pleasure to get his hands on whoever had done this.

But, of course, he or they had long since gone and there was no way of even knowing who it had been.

Levallois relaxed, stepped carefully round the corpse, pushed through the doors to the club proper and headed for the telephone behind the bar.

He did not stop to examine the body for signs of life. Its appearance alone was enough to convince anyone that there would be none.

'A little over twelve hours,' said Dr Guillaume Sondrier, the tall, slender, balding medical expert attached to the department of criminal investigations of the Liège police.

'About the time the club would have closed this morning,' commented Inspector Victor Lejeune, chief of the homicide unit on duty that morning. 'Obviously, one of the customers.'

'The last,' said his assistant, Detective Sergeant Pierre-Louis Trefle. He was a very handsome man, dark-haired and dark-eyed with a fine, carefully-trimmed moustache.

The inspector also had a moustache, but it was neither fine nor carefully-trimmed and hung in a heavy black curve over the corners of his mouth so that he looked like a villain in a Victorian tragedy.

'Looks like a sex motive,' he observed. 'But was it

771

really? It's a strange place and a strange choice of victim for a sex psychopath.'

The doctor pressed his index finger and thumb on either side of his thin, prominent nose. 'I'm not certain,' he said. 'There appears to be no trace of semen in the vagina and, although she's bruised everywhere else, there are none of the typical bruise marks on the insides of the thighs which we could expect if she had resisted rape.'

'She did resist,' said the inspector. 'Otherwise, why all the bruises?'

'But she seems to have undressed herself,' said the sergeant. 'You see how the clothes are all lying here in a little heap? They'd have been scattered if he'd pulled them off her.'

'Seems likely,' agreed the inspector. 'What's that over there against the wall?'

The sergeant bent down to look. 'It's a tube of something,' he said. 'I can't see what it says on it unless I touch it.'

'Don't do that,' said the inspector. 'We'll wait until the lab crew gets here. There could be prints.'

There were, however, no fingerprints on what turned out to be a tube of vaseline. Too much of the contents had been smeared over the outside and it was less than half full.

'Strange,' said the inspector. 'A tube of vaseline? It must have belonged to her. I don't know what use a sex criminal could have for a tube of vaseline.'

Although an experienced investigator, the inspector was oddly naïve in some respects, but he was soon enlightened by the results of the autopsy.

'The vaseline served as a lubricant for anal intercourse,' said Dr Sondrier, who had come over to the inspector's office to discuss his findings. 'Her rectum was smeared with it and there is a high concentration of acid phosphotase in the lower bowel. It's not proof of intercourse, but it's recognized as a product of the break-down of semen.'

'Didn't occur to me that she'd have been raped like that,' said the inspector uncomfortably, rubbing his prominent chin, blue-black with a twenty-four-hour growth of beard. He had hardly had time to eat and sleep since the murder, let alone shave. 'Was there enough interval between the murder and the autopsy for the semen to break down?'

'Just about,' said the doctor. 'It was twelve hours before the body was discovered and then there was quite a delay before the laboratory people released the body for transfer to the morgue. Did they find anything useful?'

'Well, the tube of vaseline,' said the inspector. 'I don't know how useful it is. You can buy the stuff anywhere. The cash register was cleaned out. Levallois says there would have been around nine thousand francs in change in it.'

'He's not a suspect?' said the doctor.

The inspector shook his head. 'We checked his where-abouts at the time of the murder. His girl friend picked him up at the club at around ten-thirty and they went off to have lunch with another couple. He's clear, and all of the other employees are women.'

'Looks like you'll have an interesting time of it,' commented the doctor, getting to his feet. 'Well, good luck.'

'We'll need it,' said the inspector gloomily.

He was, as a matter of fact, not very optimistic concerning the chances of an early solution to the murder, or even any solution at all. Annette Rosen had probably not known her murderer and there would have been no previous contacts between them to trace. There had been no murder weapon other than the killer's hands and fingerprints were a waste of time. The only object that could be connected with the crime, the tube of vaseline, bore none. Of the hundreds of others recovered, there was no way of knowing which, if any, belonged to the murderer. The place was a night-club. It was normal that there would be fingerprints everywhere.

'What intrigues me,' said Sergeant Trefle, 'is why she undressed. The lab people agree. She took her clothes off herself.'

'She undressed because the fellow threatened her,' said the inspector impatiently. 'Why else?'

'No doubt,' said the sergeant, 'but what I mean is, why did she meekly undress herself and then put up a terrific fight? If she was going to resist, why didn't she resist while she had her clothes on?'

'Hmmm, I see what you're getting at,' said the inspector, hunting through his pockets and producing a very small, very black cigar, which he tucked into the corner of his mouth but did not light. 'Well, maybe it was because she thought she could save her life by submitting to rape and it was only when she realized what he had in mind that she started fighting.'

The sergeant looked slightly disappointed. He thought that he had, perhaps, hit upon something significant, but the inspector had easily explained away the mystery.

'I suppose you're right,' he said. 'Have you decided on a line of investigation yet?'

'Yes indeed,' said the inspector. 'Take as many people as you need and find out who was in the Carte Blanche on the night preceding the murder. It's a private club, so there's a membership list somewhere. Establish the whereabouts of every member for the time of the murder. One of them killed Annette Rosen.'

The sergeant was a little dismayed at this simple, apparently foolproof plan with which the inspector proposed to solve the case. He had expected something more complicated and difficult.

He did not realize that, privately, the inspector thought it would end up more difficult too. God knew how many current and former members of the Carte Blanche club there were or how easy it was to lay hands on a card if there was some good reason for getting one, such as raping and robbing the manageress.

Before hearing the results of the autopsy, the inspector had been inclined to think that the sexual aspects of the case were little more than a diversion to throw off the investigators. The prime motive would have been robbery.

Even after learning of the anal rape, he would still have thought so, but for one thing: the tube of vaseline. The murderer had come prepared. He had had the intention of raping Annette Rosen before he even entered the Carte Blanche.

This conclusion altered the direction of the investigation. What the sergeant was now instructed to search for were customers of the Carte Blanche who were known perverts. Anal intercourse might not be a very unusual sexual deviation, but anal rape was.

For a day or two, the sergeant made little progress. The district was not one in which a great deal of cooperation with the police could be expected. However, as the news of the murder became more widely known, matters speeded up and there were even volunteers coming in with bits of information which they thought might be useful. Annette had been popular and everyone in Le Carré had known her.

Even so, it was nearly the end of September before forty-one-year-old Maurice Labeau and thirty-six-year-old Paul Estry came to police headquarters and said that they had information which might have a bearing on the Annette Rosen murder.

Both men were managers of night-spots in Le Carré and both were members of the Carte Blanche club. They had been in the club on the morning of the murder and it seemed nearly certain that they had been the last people, aside from the murderer, to have seen Annette alive.

In their statements, Labeau and Estry said that they

had gone to the Carte Blanche at approximately eight o'clock on that morning after closing their own establishments. It was something that they did nearly every morning after finishing work.

The statement did not surprise the inspector. He was aware that night-club managers and owners often spend their free time in other night-clubs, just as restaurant owners and cooks often go to eat in other restaurants.

Normally, Labeau and Estry would have gone to the Carte Blanche alone, but, on that particular morning, they had had with them a customer from Labeau's establishment who had still not wanted to go home at eight in the morning. He had begged so piteously to be taken along that they introduced him into the Carte Blanche.

'Did he apply for a membership card?' said the inspector.

It was an important point. If the visitor had applied for membership, his name and address would be on the club membership list.

The man had not, it appeared, applied for membership, but came in simply as a guest of Labeau and Estry, both of whom Annette knew well.

They were, in fact, old personal friends and it was obvious the two men were now worried that their introduction of the stranger into the club was the direct cause of Annette's death.

'It was a stupid thing to do,' said Labeau. 'We didn't know the type from Adam. He was just a customer and he wasn't even a regular. I never saw him before in my life.'

'And he was still in the Carte Blanche when you left?' said the inspector.

'I thought he wasn't,' said Labeau. 'We were talking with Annette and Jean and, the next thing we knew, the guy was gone. I thought he'd left.'

'So did I,' said Estry. 'There were only the three of us in the place and then he wasn't there any more so I reckoned he must have left.'

'And you reckon now he didn't,' said the inspector. 'All right. What did he look like and what do you know about him?'

Neither Labeau nor Estry knew anything about the man. He was a customer who drank white wine and cognac, a potent mixture, but he had not, it seemed, drunk very much cognac.

On the description, they did better. The man was young, under thirty, clean-cut and good-looking. He was very big, six feet four inches tall or more and well-built. He was dressed in jeans and a checked shirt and he had the look of a working man about him. There was a large, crooked scar approximately two inches long on his left cheek. His eyes were brown and so was his short, not stylishly cut hair.

Labeau and Estry spent the remainder of the day with the police artist, who eventually produced a drawing which both described as a good likeness of the suspect, and that same evening the sergeant's men moved into Le Carré armed with copies of the picture. Unless Labeau and Estry had murdered Annette themselves, the man represented in the drawing was the murderer.

Labeau and Estry had, of course, immediately been investigated. The old ploy of coming to the police to report a murder you have committed yourself is still tried now and then.

It was not possible to clear them completely. After leaving the Carte Blanche, they had gone to still another bar where they were well known, and a number of witnesses had seen them. However, as the exact time of the murder and the exact time of their arrival at the other bar were not known, it was at least physically possible for one or the other of them to have committed the crime. It could not have been both. Annette had been raped by only one man.

Despite this possibility, neither man was ever considered a serious suspect. Estry had a police record of one conviction, but it was for receiving stolen goods and not for a morals offence.

Although now armed with a drawing and description of a highly promising suspect, there was still no immediate progress, for the sergeant's detectives had a great many places to canvass. It was only on 3 October that they were able to pick up the trail.

On that date, the owner of a bar called Le Crocodile tentatively identified the drawing as being that of a man who had come rushing into his bar at a few minutes before noon on Sunday 19 September.

The man, a stranger who had never been in the bar before, appeared excited and out of breath. He went straight to the bathroom, where he washed his hands very thoroughly, coming out to ask the bar-owner for more soap. He then spent about an hour and a half in the bar, drinking beer and becoming involved in conversation with one of the regulars.

A team from the police laboratory promptly descended on the bar, took apart the plumbing of the lavatory and were eventually able to report traces of vaseline in the trap. It was, of course, no proof, but it was an indication.

In the meantime, the regular customer from Le Crocodile who had had a conversation with the stranger was located and brought to police headquarters, where he too described the drawing as being a good likeness of the suspect.

He had not learned the man's name or where he came from, but he had asked him about the scar and the man had said that it was the result of an automobile accident in Vottem when he was seventeen.

As it was not known how old the man was now, the year in which the accident had taken place could not be determined and, as there was no way of knowing whether the accident had even been reported to the police, an identification from traffic accident records was not feasible.

The mention of Vottem was, however, important. It

was one of the working-class suburbs to the north of the city and, although there was no evidence that the suspect lived there or even had lived there at the time of the accident, it provided another link in the chain, if there was a chain at all.

The sergeant and his detectives moved out of Le Carré and into Vottem and, almost immediately, they began to receive positive identifications of the artist's drawing.

By 7 October, the man's name and address were known. He was twenty-six-year-old Francesco Cuestra-Ortega, a Spanish citizen born in Malaga, who had come to Belgium at the age of ten with his parents and been there ever since.

Cuestra-Ortega, a house painter, had been unemployed for the past fourteen months. He was married and the father of a three-month-old daughter, who had been baptised just one week after the Annette Rosen murder. Had it not been for his police record, he might have seemed an improbable suspect.

According to the records, however, he had already been convicted twice of morals offences, once in 1978 and again earlier in 1982.

The cases were identical. The Spaniard had simply jumped on women from behind in the open street and attempted to rape them, hauling up their skirts and stripping down their panties for the purpose.

The women had, of course, screamed and fought, and people in the vicinity had come to their rescue, in both cases restraining Cuestra-Ortega until the police arrived.

As neither victim had been raped or had suffered any injury other than to her dignity, the would-be rapist had been given a stern lecture by the judge and sent off about his business.

'The man's bisexual,' said the inspector. 'The victims thought he was trying to rape them vaginally, but he wasn't. He was going to attack them in the same manner that he attacked Annette Rosen.'

'He's certainly mixed up sexually in some way,' said

the sergeant. 'Ninety per cent of the identifications of the drawing were from homosexual bars and night-spots. On the other hand, he's been married for three years and he's the father of a child.'

'Well, whatever he is, he's a murderer,' said the inspector. 'Bring him in and we'll see what we can do about getting a confession out of him.'

Not much, it turned out. Taken into custody and charged with the murder of Annette Rosen, Cuestra-Ortega stubbornly denied all connection with the crime. He had, he said, not gone out in months. He was a family man and a father. His place was in the home.

If he thought that his wife would support this statement and provide him with an alibi, he was mistaken.

Twenty-two-year-old Josephine Cuestra-Ortega had been married for a scant three years, but already the magic had gone out of her marriage.

'He's been out all night three and four nights a week ever since we got married,' she said coldly. 'As I remember it, he was out that Saturday night and Sunday morning too.'

She then went off to talk to an attorney about a divorce.

The attorney assured her that it would be a simple matter if her husband were to be indicted for homicide and, as that was precisely what happened, Mrs Cuestra-Ortega had no difficulty in dissolving her marriage.

Although her husband still refused to confess, he was indicted on charges of rape and murder on the basis of physical evidence and the testimony of witnesses.

Both Maurice Labeau and Paul Estry were successful in picking Cuestra-Ortega out of a line-up as the man who had accompanied them to the Carte Blanche club on the morning of the murder. Both testified they had not seen him leave the club and only assumed that he had gone because he was not in the room.

'Instead of leaving the club, he went and hid in the men's room until Labeau and Estry left,' said the inspector. 'He'd already made up his mind to rape Annette Rosen and all he had to do was wait until the others were gone.'

'He couldn't have gone there with that intention,' argued the sergeant. 'There's no evidence that he ever saw the victim before in his life. The manager could have been a male, heavyweight wrestling champion.'

'It wouldn't have made any difference,' said the inspector. 'He was armed with that old Bulldog revolver we found in his apartment and he was bisexual. The wrestler would have got the same treatment as Annette Rosen, although he wouldn't have been able to strangle him to death, perhaps. The man was always prepared.'

'Yes, I suppose you could say he was,' said the sergeant.

At the time of his arrest, Francesco Cuestra-Ortega had been carrying on him a tube of vaseline of the same brand as the one found at the scene of the crime, and a small stock of similar tubes was recovered from his home.

Confronted with the testimony of the two night-club managers, Cuestra-Ortega changed his story slightly. He admitted that he had been in the Carte Blanche club on that morning, but said that he had left almost immediately.

Labeau and Estry had been there when he left and it was, undoubtedly, they who had murdered Annette.

The police, he charged, knew this, but they were trying to pin the crime on him because of his past record and because he was a foreigner. Labeau and Estry were both Belgians.

This was a popular and stylish defence. Defendants everywhere have long since learned that accusations of police brutality are nearly as effective as claims of racial discrimination in arousing the sympathy of courts and media.

But not always. On 6 January 1984, a jury found Francesco Cuestra-Ortega guilty of rape and murder with no extenuating circumstances. He was sentenced to life imprisonment.

He will probably not serve it. The Belgian taxpayers already carry a heavy enough load without paying for the lifetime support of Spanish citizens.

On some fine morning not too far in the future, Francesco Cuestra-Ortega may, perhaps, be quietly escorted to the border and shoved across with an earnest recommendation not to set foot in Belgium again.

19

GETTING TO KNOW THE NEIGHBOURS

Despite the confused though purposeful sexual aspirations of Francesco Cuestra-Ortega and his handy tubes of vaseline, Latins, in general, are not as sex-obsessed as is widely believed in the northern latitudes. Many southern Europeans live in economically depressed areas and they tend to give more thought to getting something to eat than to sexual frolics.

This is, of course, not true for such prosperous places as Turin, the centre of the Italian car industry in which many of the city's more than a million inhabitants are employed.

However, even though prosperous and able to devote more thought and energy to the procreative pleasures, many of the residents of Turin still appear to prefer the wholesome, church and government sanctioned and approved variety.

This spiritual and administrative approval was fully shared by Mrs Teresa Ambruzzi, coming round on the morning of Sunday, 25 November 1979, to visit her daughter and her son-in-law of just over a month.

Mrs Ambruzzi not only approved of the marriage; she approved of her son-in-law. Twenty-seven-year-old Paolo Nardin was not rich, but he was handsome, hardworking and gainfully employed.

Equally important, Margherita unquestionably loved him. Privately, Mrs Ambruzzi had been becoming a trifle concerned. Margherita was, after all, twenty-three and, although this was not Sicily, where she would have been practically an old woman, still . . .

Teresa Ambruzzi was, therefore, very happy as she climbed the stairs to the little apartment at 53 via Pascolo in the Turin suburb of Barta at approximately eleven o'clock that morning.

She would not remain in that state for long.

The fact that there was no immediate response to her knock did not alarm her. Margherita had told her earlier in the week that she and Paolo were entertaining another young married couple on Saturday evening, and she supposed they had got to bed late.

Mrs Ambruzzi knocked harder.

There was still no response.

Mrs Ambruzzi hammered on the door panels with her fists and cried out her daughter's name in piercing tones.

A sleep-drugged voice from the apartment next door protested, 'In the name of Christ, madam!'

Bewildered, Mrs Ambruzzi automatically tried the door handle.

The door was not locked!

Mrs Ambruzzi's emotions, which had gone from happiness to disappointment to bewilderment, abruptly changed to terror. There are few communities of over a million where people in their right minds go to bed with the door unlocked, and Turin was not one of them.

Her heart beginning to beat painfully hard, Mrs Ambruzzi pushed open the door and entered.

For an instant, she felt a sensation of relief. She had half expected to find her daughter and son-in-law trussed like turkeys and the apartment ransacked. There were, after all, the wedding presents.

However, the tiny entrance hall and the living room opening off it were in order and she could even see her own wedding gift, a fine silver coffee and tea service which had nearly bankrupted her, standing on the sideboard. There was no sign of Margherita and Paolo.

The feeling of foreboding returned tenfold. It would

have been far better had they actually been tied up in the living room. The combination of the appearance of normality in the apartment and the apparent absence of the occupants lent itself to the most frightful conjectures.

But not as frightful as reality. Crossing the living room on tip-toe as if she feared to awake someone or something, Teresa Abruzzi pushed open the door to the bedroom.

And crumpled to the floor as her knees gave way beneath her. The terrible premonitions which she had been experiencing since finding the door to the apartment unlocked were appallingly exceeded, and the shock struck her with all the force of a hammer blow.

After that, Teresa Abruzzi had only a vague concept of time. She was not certain how long she lay in a faint in the doorway of her daughter's bedroom, but, according to the hospital records, her telephone call for the ambulance was received at precisely eleven-thirty-seven.

Mrs Abruzzi had called the ambulance rather than the police because she was a mother and she could not accept that her beloved daughter was really dead, although she must have known it subconsciously, if nothing else.

The ambulance crew knew it almost as soon as they entered the bedroom, but they carried out a check for respiration and heartbeat on both corpses anyway.

There was none, of course, and both the bodies were cold and stiff with rigor mortis. The ambulance crew withdrew, leaving them undisturbed, and devoted their efforts to calming Mrs Abruzzi while they awaited the arrival of the police.

They were not long in coming, but the first unit to arrive was only a patrol car and the officers could do no more than confirm the report by the ambulance crew that a double homicide had taken place at 53 via Pascolo in Barta.

The duty homicide squad was, however, already on the way and, at a little after twelve, Inspector Luciano

Cavallo, Detective Sergeant Mario Brisetti and Dr Roberto Andreotti entered the bedroom of the little apartment.

The sight which met their eyes did not have the impact on the seasoned criminal investigators that it had had on Mrs Abruzzi, but, even though it was by no means the most gruesome murder scene they had ever encountered, it was exceptionally sickening simply by reason of the youth and beauty of the victims.

Paolo and Margherita Nardin had been unusually attractive young people and, even in death, they still were. Whatever expressions their faces had worn at the time of death, horror, fear, agony, they were now relaxed and peaceful.

Paolo lay on his back on the floor beside the bed, his right arm stretched out in the direction of Margherita as if he was still striving to reach her even in death.

He was fully dressed, but his clothing was disarranged as if he had been engaged in a scuffle. The front of his pale blue shirt was covered with an irregular dark-brown stain of dried blood and a thin trickle had run from each corner of his mouth. His eyes were closed.

On the bed, his wife lay totally naked in the classic position of the rape victim, her legs bent at the knee and tipped backward on either side. There were black bruise marks on her thighs and arms, but only a little blood had run from the narrow slit, scarcely half an inch long, between her breasts. It did not look like a serious wound.

'Switchblade,' said Dr Andreotti, tight-lipped. 'Touched the heart or a major blood-vessel. The bleeding was all internal.'

He was a tall man with an olive complexion, plump and well-groomed. His seemingly emotionless black eyes looked out of professional gold-rimmed glasses. The eyes were deceptive. The doctor was, in fact, almost too compassionate for the type of work he did, which did not, however, mean that he was not good at it.

'Time of death, around midnight last night,' he

continued. 'Cause, a single knife-wound in the chest in both cases. In all probability, the same knife. It was a switchblade, because a stiletto would have been double-edged and anything else would have left a wider cut.'

'She was raped, I suppose?' said the inspector, a short, dark, wiry man with a very heavy beard and black hair on the backs of his hands.

The doctor carried out an examination of the dead girl's genitals.

'Positive,' he said. 'She resisted so fiercely that he damaged her sex organs in effecting penetration, but he achieved his objective. There are definite traces of semen in the vagina.'

'Sex psychopath,' observed the sergeant. Like many northern Italians, he was blond, blue-eyed and looked as if he would be more at home in a German beer hall than an Italian police station. 'Should I get the records section started on pulling the known-sex-offender files?'

'Yes,' said the inspector, 'but first, let's see if we can arrive at a picture of what happened here. There may be some factors that the computer can make use of in establishing a profile.'

This was important because the profile was often the only means that the police had of identifying potential suspects in deviate sex crimes. Unlike crimes committed for other motives, there was often no previous contact between murderer and victim to be traced.

Later, the specialists from the police laboratory would attempt the same thing, but Inspector Cavallo preferred to make his own reconstruction independently.

'Midnight,' he mused. 'They were probably getting ready to go to bed. She was already undressed, because there are her clothes folded over the chair. He was still dressed. See if there's any sign of a forced entry, Mario.'

The inspector did not know that Mrs Abruzzi had found the door to the apartment unlocked. He had taken one look at her, judged her to be in no condition to

787

make a statement and ordered the ambulance to take her to the hospital. The statement could be taken later.

The sergeant returned to report that there was no sign of a forced entry on the apartment door.

'All right,' pursued the inspector. 'He simply knocked at the door and the husband answered. How did they all end up in here?'

'He must have forced him into the bedroom with the knife,' said the sergeant, 'but I don't see how he could have raped and stabbed the wife without the husband jumping him. Both of them seem to have put up a fight.'

'And, considering the resistance the wife put up, she wouldn't have simply remained quietly in the bed while he was killing her husband,' said the doctor. 'At the least, she'd have screamed her head off.'

'Maybe the husband couldn't take any action because the killer had the knife at his wife's throat,' said the inspector.

'Then, how could she put up such resistance?' said the doctor. 'She wasn't coerced under threat of the knife and she was a young, strong woman. He'd have needed both hands to subdue her.'

There was a short silence during which could be heard the sound of the siren of the police van bringing the specialists and technicians to the scene.

'Then the only explanation is that they weren't both present when she was killed,' said the inspector finally. 'He was out of the apartment for some reason and the rapist came in and raped the wife. She resisted. He stabbed her. At that moment, the husband returned. There was a fight and he killed the husband too.'

'That means it was somebody who knew them,' said the sergeant. 'He'd have to be able to observe when the husband left and he'd have to know that there was a young woman alone in the apartment.'

'Sounds logical,' said the inspector. 'And, if that's what it was, it'll make our job easier.'

He was, of course, speaking comparatively. Obviously, the job was not going to be easy. The killer might have known who the victims were and something about them, but that did not necessarily mean that he had had any traceable contact to them. He had probably been in the apartment for no more than twenty minutes or half a hour, and he would have touched scarcely anything. Even if he had, any fingerprints recovered would be of value only if he had a police record. The murder weapon he had apparently taken with him.

But, according to the laboratory technicians, he had left something else behind. A white imitation-leather jacket with the word AMERICA printed across the back in scarlet letters which had been found lying on the floor near the bed.

'It didn't belong to Nardin,' said the chief technician, reporting to the inspector. 'It's two sizes too large.'

It was past four in the afternoon and, by now, the investigators knew the names of the victims and everything else that there was to know about them.

It was not much. Paolo and Margherita had been very average in every respect except physical appearance. Children of middle-class families, both had completed their secondary school education and Paolo held an adequate job in a storage and warehousing firm. They had been engaged for two years before marrying and they had not lived together during that time.

Natives of Turin and, indeed, Barta, they had had many friends, but the young couple with whom they spent the last evening of their lives had been located and were now engaged in making a tearful statement to Sergeant Brisetti. It was not believed that it would be of much value to the investigation.

Surprisingly, it was, for it solved one of the major mysteries in the case: why had Paolo Nardin left the apartment after the guests had departed?

Paolo, said the couple, had gone out to look for his motorbike. They had left at approximately midnight and

789

Paolo politely accompanied them down to the courtyard in front of the house, where he immediately noticed that his motorbike, which had been parked in front of the house when they arrived at around eight, was missing.

He assumed that it had been stolen and was very upset, but they reassured him, saying that it was probably just some kid from the neighbourhood who had pinched it for a ride and would abandon it when the petrol ran out.

Paolo appeared relieved, but said that he was going off to look for it immediately. There had not been much petrol in the tank and it should have run out by now.

The last they saw of him, he was setting off down the via Pascolo.

'And upstairs the door to the apartment was, of course, unlocked,' said the sergeant, 'because he hadn't expected to go anywhere. He was just coming back up.'

'Incredible!' muttered the inspector. 'Was the whole thing simply bad luck? The murderer just happened to hit on what was probably the only unlocked door in the whole building?'

'And behind that door, the prettiest young woman in the neighbourhood,' added the sergeant. 'I don't see how it could be chance.'

'Nor I,' said the inspector. 'He knew who was in that apartment and he knew that Nardin would go out and leave his wife alone because he arranged it. It was he who took away the motorbike. Get out a notice to all uniform units that we're looking for a motorbike. You should be able to get the licence number and description from the vehicle registry.'

'Right,' said the sergeant. 'We're also canvassing in the neighbourhood for anyone seen wearing a white imitation-leather jacket with the word AMERICA printed on it. How late do you want them to continue?'

'Until they get something,' said the inspector grimly. 'I'll be here at the station until they do.'

All that the inspector was going to learn that night

790

was that the findings of the autopsies carried out by Dr Andreotti confirmed precisely what he had said at the scene. Margherita had been raped and stabbed through the heart. Paolo had been stabbed through the heart and the left lung. The interval between the two deaths was so short that it was not possible to say which had died first. The weapon had been a switchblade.

'Keep working on the jacket and the bike,' said the inspector. 'I want results. The boy is too dangerous to leave running around loose.'

No trace of Paolo Nardin's stolen motorbike was found, but the following afternoon the sergeant came in with two potential witnesses in connection with the white jacket.

Both married women, aged respectively thirty-one and thirty-two, they requested that their identities not be revealed, not, it developed, out of modesty, but fear. The party concerned was insanely violent, they said, and, if word of their testimony were to get back to his ears, they would have to flee Turin, if not Italy.

On the afternoon of Saturday, 24 November, said the women, whose statements were made separately but agreed in every detail, they had been visiting a Mrs Maria de Ronzo, a twenty-nine-year-old housewife and the mother of two children aged seven and five.

They were old friends of Mrs de Ronzo, whom they had known prior to her marriage. They were not friends of her husband, forty-year-old Arturo de Ronzo, for whom they used the term 'monster'.

And, if their story was true, he certainly was. While they were chatting with Maria, a modest and respectable woman, her husband suddenly appeared in the doorway of the room and brusquely ordered her to come with him.

Maria reluctantly and fearfully obeyed and her husband took her to a table in the next room, bent her over it and, turning up her skirts, subjected her to what struck the visitors as extremely brutal intercourse. As de

Ronzo had not bothered to close the door, they had an unobstructed view of the proceedings.

De Ronzo then went off somewhere and Maria returned to continue the chat. The visitors did not, however, feel entirely at their ease and left after a short time.

Mr de Ronzo, said the witnesses, was wearing a white imitation-leather jacket with the inscription AMERICA in scarlet letters across the back.

'The de Ronzos live at 56 via Pascolo,' said the sergeant. 'It's directly across from the Nardin apartment building and they're one floor higher.'

'Well, I suppose that does it,' said the inspector. 'Unless the ladies are simply trying to settle a personal grudge against de Ronzo. Keep him under permanent surveillance and see what else you can learn about him in the neighbourhood. Does he have a record?'

De Ronzo did not, but, according to what the sergeant learned in the neighbourhood, he should have had. He was regarded as a sort of sex fiend by almost every woman who knew him and several reported that he had made unsuccessful attempts to rape them or their children. De Ronzo had apparently never heard of the generation gap and was prepared to rape victims of any age.

'And, if any more proof is needed,' said the sergeant, 'there are dozens of statements that he habitually wears a white imitation-leather jacket with the word AMERICA on it in red and he's not wearing it now.'

'Bring him in,' said the inspector shortly.

De Ronzo, a short but extremely muscular man with a scraggly beard, was taken into custody and charged with the murders of Margherita and Paolo Nardin.

He denied all knowledge of the crimes and, when confronted with the white imitation-leather jacket with the word AMERICA on the back, said that it did not belong to him, he had never seen it and he had never owned such a jacket.

When the statements of his neighbours were read to

him, he accused them of trying to get him into trouble. Everyone in the neighbourhood hated him, he said, because he was poor.

De Ronzo was, as a matter of fact, no poorer than some, but he was right about everyone hating him. Quarrelsome and violent, he was a feared bar-room fighter and even his own wife testified against him, saying that she had wanted to get a divorce for a long time, but had been afraid that her husband would kill her if she even mentioned it.

De Ronzo, she said, was obsessed with sex and had subjected her to every form of perversion that the human body could withstand. She was also certain that he had raped women in the neighbourhood who had not dared to report it to the police, for he had bragged to her about it. She knew nothing about the Nardin murders, but she did not doubt her husband capable of them and she did not know where he had been on the evening in question.

The inspector did, and when Paolo Nardin's motorbike was found hidden in de Ronzo's garage and a switchblade still bearing bloodstains was recovered from a sewer-opening behind his house, de Ronzo was forced to agree.

It was true that he had murdered the Nardins but it was not his fault. It was partly the fault of the Nardins themselves and partly the fault of the television programmes.

The announcer on one of the programmes that evening was altogether too sexy and she put him into a state.

Then, the Nardins were not careful about drawing their curtains when they undressed for bed and he had had the opportunity to observe Margherita on several occasions nude or partly nude. She was a very pretty woman and the television announcer made him think of her.

Looking across the street, he was able to see that the Nardins were entertaining, and he hit upon the idea of luring Nardin away from the apartment by hiding his motorbike.

He thought that Nardin would go looking for it the moment he noticed it was gone, and he was right.

In the meantime, while Nardin was escorting the guests downstairs and going to look for his motorbike, Margherita went to the bedroom and undressed completely before climbing into bed to wait for Paolo.

He watched this from his own window and, the moment Paolo was out of sight, ran across the street and up the stairs to the Nardin apartment.

The door had not been locked and Margherita, hearing him enter, called out, 'Paolo? Hurry. I'm waiting for you.'

He went into the bedroom and took off his jacket as he thought it would interfere with what he had in mind.

Margherita, who did not know him as she and Paolo had only moved into the apartment a month earlier, was so amazed and indignant that she was not able to stammer out anything more than, 'Who are you? What are you doing here?' before he was upon her and had his hand over her mouth so that she could not scream.

Realizing then what he intended, she fought like a tigress and managed to scratch him slightly on the neck. Unable to keep his hand over her mouth and force her legs apart with the other, he lost patience, pulled out his switchblade and stabbed her.

She then, said de Ronzo with some satisfaction, lay still and there was no further problem.

Unfortunately, just as he was finishing his business, Nardin returned and flung himself upon him. There was a terrific battle, but he was stronger and more experienced in fighting and he soon gained the upper hand, pinning Nardin to the floor and driving the switchblade into his chest.

He was certain, now the police knew what had happened, they would agree that the murders had not been his fault. If Margherita had not made such a fuss and had held still for a minute, he would not have had to kill her. And, if Nardin had not attacked him, he would not have killed him either. It had been, basically, a case of legitimate self-defence.

The police did not agree. Nor did the court. On 5 September 1980, an indignant Arturo de Ronzo was found guilty of one count of rape with violence and two counts of murder with no extenuating circumstances.

To the relief of everyone in Barta, but, particularly, Mrs de Ronzo, he was sentenced to two terms of life imprisonment not to run concurrently.

20

THE ZOMBIES ARE COMING!

She had been a gentle woman and she looked it even in death.

Not unattractive either, despite her eighty-two years. Unlike many older women, she had not made the mistake of having her hair cut too short and it lay in thick, soft folds on the pillow beside her head, not snow-white, not grey, an in-between colour like mother-of-pearl but without the iridescence.

The cheeks were a little sunken of course. She had taken out her false teeth before going to bed and they lay in a tumbler of blue cleansing solution on the night table. Beside them were her gold-rimmed glasses, her handkerchief, her little tin of throat lozenges, all the modest equipment of an old woman settling down for the night in her own bed.

If the face above the mouth was peaceful, the rest was shocking. There was a livid bite mark on the chin and other bite marks on the breasts and thighs, obscenely exposed by the flannel nightgown bunched up around the neck. The imprints of the teeth could be plainly seen, human teeth.

'Miserable pervert!' said Inspector Walter Becker. 'Isn't there anything they'll stop at?'

His assistant did not reply. Sergeant of Detectives Max Grossmann was familiar with his chief's outbursts and knew that the question was rhetorical. Although in his forties and with close to twenty years of criminal investigation work behind him, the inspector never failed to be outraged and angered by murders of children or women of any age.

Fortunately, there were not all that many such murders in Weiden. The population of the city was only a little over fifty thousand and it lay well off the beaten track, not far from the Czech border in southern Germany. There was barely enough work to justify the nucleus homicide squad formed by the inspector and sergeant.

And, as a rule, the homicides required little or no investigation. Mostly they were domestic affairs with husband or wife rushing to the police station in an agony of contrition and guilt, crying out, 'I have killed Agnes!' or Ilse or Juergen or Gunter or whatever the case might be. Not real murders, the inspector called them, and, as a matter of fact, they were seldom so charged. In nearly all cases, the prosecutor would settle for manslaughter.

This was different. Mrs Martha Preiss had not been killed by her husband, because he had been dead for many years. She had been killed by some kind of a deviate or psychopath and he or, less likely, she was obviously not going to come in tearful repentance to confess to the crime.

'Well?' said the inspector impatiently. He had been waiting for nearly ten minutes while the Weiden coroner, an elderly, white-haired man, carried out a very deliberate examination of the corpse.

'She's been dead for about twelve hours,' said the coroner, startled into a rush of words. 'Strangulation. Manual. It didn't take much. She was very old and a little pressure on the arteries carrying blood to the brain . . . She didn't suffer much.'

'And the bites?' snarled the inspector. 'They didn't hurt?'

'Made after death, I think,' murmured the doctor. 'Otherwise, she would have thrashed around in the bed more.'

'Any suggestions as to the motive?' asked the sergeant.

'It wasn't sex in the normal sense,' said the doctor. 'There's no indication of attempted penetration. There are some spots here on the sheets and on her body too which I think may be semen. He probably masturbated over the corpse.'

'It's something,' said the inspector. 'Eliminates the possibility of a female suspect, at least.'

'And, I'm afraid, that's about all,' said the coroner apologetically. 'The laboratory technicians may find something or . . .?'

'Laboratory technicians!' snorted the inspector. He had little confidence in the four members of the Weiden police laboratory, who were, none the less, highly trained and competent. 'All right, Max. Tell them to come on over and you stay here to keep an eye on them. I'm going to take a statement from Mrs Tauchmann.'

It was fifty-one-year-old Rosa Tauchmann who had discovered her mother's body when she came to visit her on that Saturday morning of 3 March 1984. She immediately called the police and waited at the apartment at 11 Geiers Way until they arrived.

The inspector promptly sent her home in a patrol car, after having checked her identity and noted her address. She was obviously very badly shaken and there was no point in having her waiting at the scene until the doctor had finished with his preliminary examination of the corpse and the inspector had time to take her statement.

He had not thought that her statement would be of much value to the investigation and it was not. She had simply dropped in to see her mother, as she often did, and found her murdered. She searched for a pulse or any other sign of life and, finding none, called the police rather than a doctor or the ambulance.

'Would your mother have let a stranger into the apartment?' said the inspector.

'Never,' said Mrs Tauchmann. 'She read the newspapers and she watched television. She knew how safe an old person is today!'

798

'The door was locked when you arrived?' said the inspector. 'Do you have a key?'

'The door was locked,' said Mrs Tauchmann. 'I let myself in when she didn't answer the doorbell. I thought she was probably still in bed and didn't feel like getting up.'

'A silly question, perhaps, but I have to ask it,' said the inspector. 'Did she have enemies?'

'Very silly,' said Mrs Tauchmann. 'At eighty-two? Of course she had no enemies. Besides, even I could see it was some kind of a sex pervert.'

'There is such a thing as a faked sex crime,' said the inspector.

This one had not been faked. The spots on the sheets and on Mrs Preiss's body were semen and the bites were deep wounds and not token attempts to throw off the investigation.

The laboratory technicians had obtained excellent casts of the bite wounds. The marks of the teeth were so plain that they were confident of being able to identify a suspect by his teeth, should a suspect turn up.

So far, none had and, as the laboratory men had found nothing else at the scene and the search of the police records had turned up no previous cases of an offender biting the victim, the inspector was at something of a loss.

He had personally examined the door to the apartment and come to the conclusion that there was no way that the murderer could have entered other than with a key or through being let in by Mrs Preiss herself. He could, however, have gone out locking the door behind him as it was a Yale-type lock which snapped shut automatically when the door was closed. The only fingerprints on it were those of the victim.

He had had Sergeant Grossmann run a discreet check on Mrs Preiss's financial circumstances and the identity of her heirs.

Mrs Tauchmann was her sole heir, but she would

scarcely receive enough to cover the funeral expenses. Aside from her pension, Mrs Preiss had not possessed very much.

The case was, therefore, just what it seemed: a random murder by a psychopath whose only motive for the crime was the malfunctioning of his own mind. The sole mystery was why Mrs Preiss had let him into her apartment.

The inspector thought that, if that question could be answered, so too, perhaps, could be the other, more vital question of the identity of the psychopath.

It was highly unlikely that a woman of Mrs Preiss's age would have let a stranger into the apartment, particularly when she was already in her nightdress and either in bed or preparing to go there, simply because she found him attractive.

She had let him into the apartment because she knew him or had some compelling reason to believe that it was safe to do so.

If she knew him, however, that meant that someone within her circle of friends, relatives and acquaintances was a dangerous psychopath, and the inspector had been unable to find anyone among her contacts who had a record of mental illness.

This apparent contradiction troubled the inspector, a heavy-shouldered man with a broad forehead, a pronounced jaw and a black moustache like a broad bar across his upper lip, and it made him bad-tempered so that he growled at the other members of his family.

'Why do you watch such stupid junk?' he demanded of his fourteen-year-old son, who was watching with interest the forcible extraction of a pair of eyeballs in a video classic entitled *A Zombie Hung on the Bellrope*.

'What should I watch?' replied the young man. 'We don't have Little Red Ridinghood on the video.'

The inspector suppressed an impulse to kick his own flesh and blood and was about to pass on when he suddenly halted.

'Anybody get bitten in these things?' he barked.

It had just occurred to him the reason Mrs Preiss had let a stranger into her apartment might be that he had appeared so young she thought him harmless. At fourteen, the inspector's son was young enough to look like a boy, but strong enough to strangle an old woman.

Not, of course, that he suspected his own son in the crime, but all over the city other teenagers were watching horror films on television and in the movies, and there had been cases of attempts to translate into reality what they had seen. Less than three months earlier, a twelve-year-old girl had been gang-raped by her brother and four of his friends, who said that they had got the idea from a video film.

His question startled his son, who was not afraid of his father but, like many adolescents, sometimes feared for his sanity.

'Well, sure, yeah, Dad,' he said soothingly. 'People get bitten all the time. Vampires just about always bite the girls and zombies ... This film here, for example ...'

'Let's see it,' said the inspector. 'Let's see where the zombie bites the girl. Is it always a girl? Not an old woman?'

His offspring gave a guffaw. 'Who'd want to bite an old woman?' he chortled, and then, seeing the expression on his father's face, hurriedly ran the video cassette back to the last biting episode.

The inspector gave his son no reason to alter his opinion, watching the biting of the largely naked young actress in silence and then inquiring if there were any more such incidents in the film.

There were, and the inspector watched all of them as silently and as attentively. Zombies, it seemed, did little other than bite astoundingly well-built and mostly blonde young girls after tearing off their clothing.

The showing over, he absently thanked his son and departed, leaving the boy deeply concerned over the question of who would pay for his schooling once his father had been locked up in some institution for the incurably insane.

He would have been even more concerned had he known that the inspector himself was entertaining some doubts on the subject of his own sanity. For no logical reason, he became obsessed with the idea that Martha Preiss had been murdered by a zombie.

Not a real zombie, of course. The inspector did not believe that real zombies existed. But there were young, impressionable people who saw far too many horror and sex films, and one of them could have got the idea that he was a zombie and acted accordingly.

He tried to explain it to the sergeant, cautiously.

'Uh . . . that is, Max . . . what I mean is . . . uh, what do you think about zombies?' he asked diffidently when he and the sergeant were closeted in his private office with the door closed.

The sergeant, blond, blue-eyed and looking even younger than he was, stared at him for a moment without replying, his forehead slightly wrinkled.

'You're thinking of the Preiss case,' he exclaimed triumphantly, his face clearing.

The inspector admitted that he was.

'And horror films,' said the sergeant shrewdly. 'It's possible. The screens are full of it. It could be that somebody not entirely normal . . .'

'. . . was tipped over the edge,' finished the inspector. 'That's exactly what I've been thinking. The trouble is . . .'

'. . . it could be anybody,' said the sergeant, finishing the inspector's sentence in his turn.

'Well, no,' said the inspector. 'It would have to be either somebody she knew or somebody so young she didn't consider him dangerous.'

'So a limited number of suspects,' said the sergeant. 'If your theory is correct, we could solve it.'

The general opinion in the department of criminal

investigations had been that the murder would not be solved.

'The trouble, as I was saying,' said the inspector, 'is that we have no way of knowing who among the potential suspects might have gone over the edge. He may have no record of mental illness at all.'

'But he would be a horror-film fan,' said the sergeant. 'We could check how keen a potential suspect was on horror films. It would almost surely be video. The really rough stuff doesn't come on television or in the cinema.'

'The whole idea is fantastic,' said the inspector, 'but . . .'

'I'll start working up a list of every male she would have known well enough to let into the apartment,' said the sergeant. 'We already had one when we checked for mental cases among her contacts.'

'Don't forget the kids,' said the inspector. 'A woman that old and frail, a ten-year-old could have done it.'

Somewhat to everyone's relief, Mrs Preiss had known no ten-year-olds, not even casually, nor had she known any adolescents other than one boy who sometimes delivered groceries. He was quickly cleared. The autopsy had shown that Mrs Preiss died between eleven and midnight on 2 March, and the boy had a verifiable alibi for that time.

In the end, the list turned out to be shorter than had been expected. Mrs Preiss had had few friends. Like many older people, her friends were for the most part dead or in nursing homes and she had had little opportunity or inclination to make new ones. Outside the members of her family, a few delivery and service people and some of the other tenants in the same apartment building, she had known no one well enough to admit them into her apartment when she was in her nightgown.

'It must be one of the neighbours,' said the sergeant. 'We can place almost all of her relatives at the time of the crime and, anyway, they'd have had to come all the way across town to do it. I just can't see that. If they were nutty enough to do such a thing at all, they'd have picked somebody more convenient.'

'The delivery or public utilities people?' said the inspector. 'There was a mad meter-reader in Berlin a couple of years ago. Killed three or four old persons for their savings. They let him in because he had official identification as a meter-reader.'

'But he came round during the day surely,' said the sergeant. 'A man wanting to read the meter at eleven o'clock at night would rouse suspicion in anybody, and Mrs Preiss was known to be cautious.'

'All right,' said the inspector. 'The neighbours. How many are there?'

'Twenty-three, male,' said the sergeant. 'We've eliminated four who were demonstrably out of the building that evening, and two others are so old that they can't be considered valid suspects.'

'You're sure of that?' said the inspector.

'They haven't any teeth,' said the sergeant. 'Those bites weren't made with a set of dentures.'

'Hmmm, yes,' said the inspector. 'I wonder if we could take teeth prints of the other seventeen and . . .?'

'I asked the examining judge,' said the sergeant. 'He said only if they accepted voluntarily.'

'Then see how many will,' said the inspector. 'At the worst, we'll cut down the suspect list a little.'

The operation cut down the suspect list a great deal. Only seven of the tenants of the building where Martha Preiss had been murdered refused to permit casts of their teeth to be taken. The others were all cleared as their teeth did not match the bites on the victim's body.

'Excellent!' said the inspector, rubbing his hands together. 'We're closing in on him. Concentrate on those seven. If the theory is correct, he's among them.'

'If the theory's correct,' said the sergeant. 'As a matter of fact, we're already concentrating on one. He owns a video player and he's supposed to have the biggest collection of hard-core sex and violence films in Weiden.'

'Which would really be saying something,' said the inspector. 'What's his name and what is he?'

'He's nothing,' said the sergeant. 'That is, he's not studying and he's not working either. Nineteen years old. His name's Gerhard Beissel and he lives with his parents on the floor below Mrs Preiss's apartment.'

'Well, why don't you bring him in then?' said the inspector.

'We've got nothing against him,' said the sergeant. 'It's not illegal to collect porno and horror films.'

'It's illegal to murder old ladies,' said the inspector. 'Bring him in anyway.'

A man with old-fashioned ideas, he had never adjusted to the socialist principle of granting priority to the rights of the accused over those of the victims and the public.

The sergeant reluctantly took Gerhard Beissel into custody. He knew very well what would happen because it had happened before. The parents would get a lawyer who would arrange Beissel's release within a matter of hours, and the inspector would get another chewing-out by the examining judge who was ultimately responsible for the case.

And that was precisely what happened, but, before the lawyer was able to pry his client out of the inspector's clutches, there was a new development.

A young couple living on the same floor as Beissel came in voluntarily to the police station with information that they had apparently been withholding on the murder.

The couple, Peter and Karin Huber, both in their late twenties, said that they had heard of the arrest of Gerhard Beissel and that he was a friend of theirs. They did not believe him guilty and had come to tell the police of their mistake.

'Well?' said the inspector, scowling ferociously. He was quite certain that the Hubers were now going to provide Beissel with an alibi for the evening in question and he felt equally certain that it was false. However, even if it was, it would force him to release Beissel immediately.

To his surprise, the Hubers offered no such alibi, but began to hem and haw around and finally said that they thought someone else might have done it.

'Why?' demanded the inspector in a voice that sounded as if his vocal cords were made of brass.

'Well,' said Huber, 'the day after the murder, I mentioned it to Anton and he said, "So who cares? Another old bat out of the way." That was pretty callous.'

'Yes, indeed,' said the inspector, puzzled but gradually becoming interested. 'Is that all? Who is Anton?'

Anton, it seemed, was Anton Bleimeier, a journeyman baker who lived in the same building.

'We checked him out,' said the sergeant in response to the inspector's inquiring look. 'One of the seven who wouldn't let us take a bite cast, but nothing else. Not known to be a porno fan.'

'Not porno,' said Peter Huber. 'Horror. He's nuts about horror. Zombies in particular.'

'How do you know?' said the inspector. 'Is he a friend of yours too?'

Huber said, not exactly, but that Bleimeier often came to watch horror films on their video set. He did not own one of his own.

'He was with us on the evening of the murder,' he said, finally getting round to what he had come to the police to report. 'We watched *A Zombie Hung on the Bellrope*. He was like he was out of his mind with excitement. When the film was over, he jumped up and started hopping around the room on one leg, yelling, "I'm a little zombie too! I'll get all of you!" He scared Karin, so I told him he'd better leave – and he did. It was just about eleven o'clock.'

'Get some official witnesses and have this statement

806

sworn to and on tape,' said the inspector to Sergeant Grossmann. 'What does this zombie look like? Have I seen him?'

The inspector had not, but, even if he had, he would scarcely have taken Anton Bleimeier for even an imitation zombie. Thirty-two years old and considerably overweight, he had a clean-shaven, vacuous sort of face and a pear-shaped head with dark hair cut high over his ears and parted on one side. He was more flabby than muscular and he did not look dangerous.

Brought to police headquarters and accused of the murder, he protested his innocence at the top of his lungs and refused to answer any questions until he was represented by an attorney.

The attorney was produced, but the inspector, now convinced that he finally had the right man, possibly because he had seen parts of the film in question himself, demanded and received a court order to take a cast of Bleimeier's teeth with or without his approval.

It was without, and for good reason. The cast fitted the bite-mark casts taken from Martha Preiss's body perfectly. The case was solved. The murderer was a zombie.

Or, at least, an ex-zombie. Following his indictment for the murder of Martha Preiss, Bleimeier decided that he was not a zombie and never had been one.

Instead, he said he was an unfortunate, underprivileged person who had never had any breaks in his life and this had so warped his character that he had, more or less accidentally, killed Mrs Preiss, whom he knew only casually as a neighbour.

After the viewing of *A Zombie Hung on the Bellrope* he had been in a terrible state of excitement and he went to ring Mrs Preiss's doorbell simply because he knew that she was a woman living alone.

When she opened the door on the chain lock and saw that it was a neighbour, she let him in.

He rushed straight at her, dragged her into the

bedroom, strangled her on the bed and bit her in several places. It was, he said, what zombies did.

'If I am not mistaken,' said the inspector gravely, 'zombies generally rape their victims as well. Is that what you had in mind?'

He was trying to establish a motive that would make sense to a jury.

Oh no, said Bleimeier. He had had no such thing in mind. As a matter of fact, he couldn't rape anybody. He had never had contact with a woman in his life.

Rather incredibly, this was true, according to the psychiatrists who later examined him. At the age of thirty-two, in a society permissive enough to make Sodom and Gomorrah look like a Sunday school picnic, Anton Bleimeier was an intact virgin.

And, said the psychiatrists, likely to remain one. A latent homosexual, he was so confused sexually that he was probably incapable of intercourse with either sex, even if he remained at liberty.

Which he did not, although there was a good deal to his claim of being mistreated by society. He had been abandoned by his parents at the age of three, had grown up in an institution for homeless children, had never had any contact to a woman and had never had a friend of either sex. The court decided that they could not permit zombies to mingle freely with the public and, on 5 November 1984, sentenced him to life imprisonment.

Unfortunately, two of the judges at the trial had dozed off, an indication, perhaps, of the lack of interest which even a zombie can arouse in modern society, and the defence, noting this, moved for a mistrial.

A new date was set, but it did not help and, on 8 March 1985, the judges having managed to stay awake, another jury came to an identical conclusion and an identical sentence was handed down.